WHO OWNS BRITAIN

WHO OWNS BRITAIN

KEVIN CAHILL

CANONGATE

First published in Great Britain in 2001 by
Canongate Books, 14 High Street,
Edinburgh EH1 1TE

10 9 8 7 6 5 4 3 2 1

© Kevin Cahill, 2001

Kevin Cahill has asserted his right under the
Copyright, Designs and Patents Act, 1988
to be identified as the author of this work

Author's note: Since the completion of research on this book, Lord Camoys has registered his ownership of Stonor Park in the Land Registry. The Land Registry has amended its charge for a basic search to £4.

Maps created by Drawing Attention/Rhona and Robert Burns

British Library Cataloguing-in-Publication Data
A CIP catalogue record for this book
is available from the British Library

ISBN 0 86241 912 3

Designed and typeset by Palimpsest Book Production Limited,
Polmont, Stirlingshire
Printed and bound by Bath Press

www.canongate.net

To
Ros, Kay, Jane and Stella

Contents

List of tables ix
List of maps xi
Acknowledgments xii

PART I
BRITAIN'S GREATEST SECRET – THE OWNERSHIP OF ITS LAND

Preface: Who Does Own Britain – A Typical 'Great' Landowner 3
1 Why Land Matters 6
2 A Brief History of Landownership in Britain 20
3 The story of the 1872 Return of Owners of Land 29
4 Royal Land: The landed possessions of the Queen and her court 58
5 The Crown Estate 72
6 The Duchy of Cornwall 84
7 The Duchy of Lancaster 93
8 The House of Lords 102
9 The Plantagenet Inheritance: A tale of great survival 121
10 The Big Institutional Landowners 137
11 Land in London 148
12 The Church of England 163
13 Scotland 176
14 Ireland: Land, prosperity and nation building 186
15 England and the Inner Empire 199
16 Conclusion 206

PART II
THE COUNTIES OF GREAT BRITAIN AND IRELAND

England 222
Scotland 266
Wales 304
Northern Ireland 318
Republic of Ireland 326

PART III
THE LAND LISTS

1872:

1 – Top 100 landowners in the UK & Ireland ranked by
(a) acreage, and (b) land value ... 359

2 – Top 50 landowners in (a) England, (b) Wales, (c) Scotland,
(d) Northern Ireland and (e) the Republic of Ireland ranked by acreage ... 367

3 – Top 50 aristocratic landowners in the UK & Ireland ranked
by acreage ... 377

2001:

4 – Top 100 landowners in the UK & Republic of Ireland ranked
by (a) acreage, and (b) land value ... 379

5 – Top 100 landowners in the UK & Republic of Ireland ranked by wealth ... 387

6 – Top 100 aristocratic landowners in the UK & Republic of Ireland ranked
by acreage ... 391

Appendix 1 – A Note on Comparative Values ... 395
Appendix 2 – How Land is Owned in the UK and Ireland ... 397
Appendix 3 – The Inheritance of the Throne 1066–2001 ... 399

Notes ... 401

Bibliography ... 414

Index ... 421

List of Tables

Table 1/1 The basic land use structure of the UK and Ireland	9
Table 1/2 Land in the UK and Ireland and who lives where	11
Table 1/3 The ownership of land in the UK and Ireland	13
Table 1/3B Number of people owning land worth over £1 million	13
Table 1/4 The big acreages and their distribution and ownership	15
Table 1/5 Tenure of agricultural landholdings in the UK 1997–1999	15
Table 1/6 Breakdown of agricultural landholdings in the UK 1997–1999	17
Table 1/7 Top 20 Landowners in the UK (2001)	18
Table 1/7B An alternative breakdown of landownership	18
Table 3/1 Land Owned by Top Ten Dukes, 1872	40
Table 3/2 John Bateman's breakdown of landownership by class, 1872	45
Table 4/1 Value of the Queen's landholdings	61
Table 5/1 Growth of the Crown Estate from the late 1800s to 1938	73
Table 5/2 Significant Acquisitions in the Crown Estate in the Twentieth Century	75
Table 5/3 Crown Estate Acreage and Revenues 2000, before expenses	79
Table 8/1 Prevalence of Aristocracy in the *Sunday Times* Rich List, 1998 (pre reform) and 2000 (post reform).	106
Table 8/2 The Landowning Dukes	107
Table 9/1 The Plantagent Survivors	131
Table 9/2 The Wealth of the Plantagenet Dukes	136
Table 10/1 Leading UK landowners c.1962	139
Table 10/2 Top 20 institutional landowners in the UK	147
Table 11/1 Last-known record of 'tenants for life' of the Eyre Estate in St John's Wood	156
Table 11/2 London Landowners 1890 and 2001 (ranked by acreage)	158
Table 11/3 London Landowners 2001 (ranked by value of holding)	162
Table 12/1 Summary of the landholdings of the Church of England in England 1872	163
Table 12/2 The parish glebe: the secret acres of the Church of England	164

Table 12/3 The Church of England's missing acres — 165

Table 13/1 Land in Britain held in estates of over 1000 acres, 1872 — 177
Table 13/2 Land in Scotland held in estates of over 1000 acres, 1970–99 — 177
Table 13/3 John McEwan's breakdown of landownership in Scotland — 178
Table 13/4 Andy Wightman's breakdown of landownership in Scotland — 180

Table 14/1 The overall change from estates to farms in Ireland 1872–1998 — 192
Table 14/2 Home ownership in the Republic of Ireland 1998 — 193

Table 15/1 The top 10 English landowners in 1872 and their acres within the inner 'first' empire — 200
Table 15/2 The top 10 landowners living in Ireland in 1872 and their landholdings in England — 203
Table 15/3 Top 10 Welsh landowners in 1872 and their landholdings in England — 203
Table 15/4 Top 10 Scottish landowners in 1872 and their landholdings in England — 204
Table 15/5 Percentage of each country owned by top 10 landowners in 1872 — 204

List of Maps

i)	Great Britain and Ireland 1872 & 2001 – some basic figures	7
ii)	Principal London Landowners	159
iii)	The counties of England & Wales, 1872	224
iv)	The counties of England & Wales, 2001	225
v)	The counties of Scotland, 1872	268
vi)	The counties of Scotland, 2001	269
vii)	The counties of Ireland, 1872 & 2001	319, 328

Acknowledgments

The making of this book, for making, not writing, is the only way to describe the project, has taken about 13 years. It began when Dr Philip Beresford, editor and author of the *Sunday Times* annual Rich List, hauled me back from attempting to present an opera in Moscow in 1988 to help him research the first Rich List. He assigned me to actors, actresses, jockeys and the aristocracy. It was in pursuit of the wealth of the latter, mostly in the form of land, that I discovered the gap in the Land Registry, and the total absence of any accurate information at all as to who actually owned our four countries. Eventually, with the help of Philip and Ealing Public Library, a copy of Bateman was found. But not the 1872 Returns, the existence of which was denied by the Royal Agricultural Society and the Country Landowners Association, and to whom no thanks are due for either the discovery of the Returns in the Devon & Exeter Institution, or the use of the Returns in this book.

It is thanks to Philip, therefore, and his wife Della Bradshaw, a journalist with the *Financial Times*, that I owe the inspiration for this book. I am forever indebted to Glen Hughes and Michael Plumb for persuading me to carry on when I lost both track and plot. Richard Norton-Taylor the *Guardian* journalist and playwright, lent both books, time and encouragement. His colleagues on the *Guardian*, Paul Brown and David Pallister, have been a source of support and inspiration throughout. Andy Wightman, author of *Who Owns Scotland*, and the man who picked up the torch of truth on landowning after the chronicler John McEwen had laid it down, introduced me to the ever patient Jamie Byng, the Publisher at Canongate Books, and provided guidance and support throughout the project. The journalists Mark Watts, Peter Sawyer and Yvonne Ridley, all stood by their man as the real nature of the task emerged and, horror of horrors, deadlines were missed. Chris Blackhurst, recently deputy editor of the *Daily Express*, took a supportive interest as did Rachel Oldroyd, Gaynor Pengelly and Rodrick Gilchrist, the Rich Report team at the *Mail on Sunday*, and also Martin Tompkinson. Graham Smith of Westcountry Television gave the issue its first airing, and the general public their first sight of the Returns in over 130 years, in 1999. Tom Rubython, now the editor of *Eurobusiness* magazine, gave me both work and encouragement through the years, and above all the chance to examine landed and Royal wealth in Europe for the Richest 400 Europeans, published by *Eurobusiness* in 2000. Chris Butt, the Publisher and Editor of *BusinessAge* magazine has given encouragement and support in the closing stages of the book.

In Ireland I owe James Connolly SC and Garrett Wren CA an unlimited debt of gratitude, for friendship over decades, for books, for advice, and above all for wisdom, on a subject that remains sensitive even in the Republic. I also owe a debt of gratitude to the Hon. Richard Burke, former Vice President of the European Commission, to Eileen Murphy, Barry Flood, Jerry Doyle and Denis McSweeney for their support and encouragement. To Michael Addo, Dean of Exeter University Law School and his brother

Kwame, I am indebted for encouragement, and to Donald Hay and his family for introducing me to the Devon & Exeter Institution, and for other advice, a huge thanks. A word of thanks and a remembrance too for the late Tony Bambridge, Deputy Editor of the *Sunday Times*, for giving me a shot at the offshore wealth of the landed rich, and a slot on Insight.

Gloria Knight and John were there to encourage as was Patrick Martin, our man (almost) in Switzerland. The Osman family were constantly supportive. To Gerald James and his family I owe a debt for both support and for an insight into the inhumanity of the inner establishment when its secrets are uncovered. Gerald has paid a high price, but justice will prevail, in the end.

Tony Browne, my old editor at the New University of Ulster student magazine *Satyr*, burst pretentious bubbles when they appeared, and shouted encouragement from a big rock in a far place. May he always be the big man on the big rock, making legends and poems, which are in terrible short supply nowadays, good ones anyway.

Landownership remains a sensitive subject. There are a number of people, especially one who saw diamonds where others saw clay, who cannot be named, but who know they are thanked profoundly for their help, support and information.

Kay Cahill did extensive work on the London chapter and Stella Cahill compiled statistics on the larger landowners from the Returns, supported by Al Martin and Edward Cox. Ian Sheldon created the web sites assisted by Jane Cahill. Dr Ros Cahill helped, fed and encouraged the author right from the beginning.

Most writers thank their editors. In the case of Donald Reid at Canongate something a great deal more than mere thanks are owed. The book as it now exists is hugely due to his inspiration and guidance, especially the second half. He had the patience of Job throughout, and I think I can truly say that without Donald Reid this book would not exist.

Two people I have never met acted as a source of inspiration throughout. The first was the Scottish chronicler, the late John McEwen, and the other is Professor David Cannadine, author of *The Decline and Fall of the British Aristocracy*, a book that shows, truly, how history should be written.

To Jeff Wilcox at Jordan's in Bristol for invaluable support and to Bureau Van Dijk and its two absolutely indispensable databases of European, UK and Irish companies Amadeus and Fame, without which parts of this project would have been impossible. Also thanks to Ayesha at the Press Office of the Inland Revenue Valuation Office. The Valuation Office half yearly Property Market Report, giving land values throughout the United Kingdom across a huge range of items, was an absolutely invaluable reference work. To Joey Joseph, Akiva Kahan, Barbara Gold and Stephen Needham at Joseph Kahan Associates a sincere thanks is owed for continuous support to their penurious client. Also to Richard Johnson, Solicitor.

This book ends with an Index compiled by Ann Hall in record time, on a record scale. Faced with a short deadline and a colossal number of items; names alone come to over 2,500, Ann Hall worked day and night to complete the Index which completes the book, and did so on time. For that the author is hugely grateful.

Finally, to Microsoft for three things without which the overall project would never have been finished. The first is *Windows*, which gave computing power to the people, the second is the *Access* database system, which contains the seven huge databases upon which this book was built, and finally *Word*, the greatest tool since printing itself.

This book is a journalist's work, not that of a scholar or an academic. It was written because there was a story, a truly great story, to tell, one that falls well within Lord Thompson's paraphrased rules for news. 'News is what someone didn't want printed. All else is advertising.' It is no more than a sketch map for those who would seek to fill the gap in the historic record, and complete the economic and social history of our countries. The mistakes, and they are bound to be many, are all my own, as are the opinions expressed.

Kevin Cahill
Exeter
August 2001

Website – for amendments and corrections

The figures in this book, especially those from Government sources, are in constant need of update. Revisions and updates may be found on the website *who-owns-britain.com*. Anyone who feels their acres have been overstated or understated is welcome to correct the figures on this website. Information on landowners not named in the book is also welcome.

PART I
Britain's Greatest Secret – The Ownership of its Land

Preface

Who Does Own Britain? – A Typical 'Great' Landowner

HIDDEN DEEP IN the history of the United Kingdom is a great and secret book. It was published in four volumes and runs to over 2000 pages. Within its pages are the names and addresses of those who owned, at the time of the book's compilation, the most valuable treasure of this country, its land. The book is now more than 120 years old, yet its pages are the only way to trace the present ownership of as much as one third of the acreage of England and Wales. In this sense, the book is more important and more valuable than the Land Registry of England and Wales, which costs more than £200 million a year to run and which cannot provide any indication of who owns vast swathes of the land in the two countries.[1]

And this is very easy to illustrate. Five miles north of Henley-on-Thames in the rich, if densely populated, countryside of Oxfordshire, is a true treasure, Stonor Park, the home of Lord and Lady Camoys. The estate and house have their origins in the last decade of the twelfth century and are steeped in history. Martyrs hid here and the Catholic faith in England owes much of its survival to the fidelity with which the Stonor family protected its priests from persecution over the centuries. The house is lined with family portraits and out in the grounds is a replica stone circle, recreated on the site of the prehistoric original. The present head of this ancient family is Ralph Thomas Campion George Sherman Stonor, the 7th Baron Camoys, who, until recently forced to retire due to ill health, had been the Queen's Lord Chamberlain for three years. As such he was head of the Queen's household, her right hand man and in effect Chairman of The UK Royals, plc. And no man better qualified for the job! An aristocrat married to the daughter of a major Suffolk landowner, Sir W.S. Hyde Parker Bt, Camoys attended Eton, the landowners' school, and is a former managing director of large chunks of Barclays bank, Barclays BZW – chunks that have turned out to be an expensive failure for the bank.[2]

At Stonor Park the public may now stroll through its long history on most Sundays, bank holidays and other days by arrangement, for a small charge.[3] However, should any member of the public become curious about who actually owns Stonor House or its lands, and approach the Land Registry to find out, they will encounter a curious response. For the standard fee, currently £7.20 payable in advance, the enquirer will be told by the Land Registry on a small piece of headed notepaper, that

> *With reference to your recent application for office copies (form 109) of the above property* [Stonor Park], *I am afraid that your application cannot proceed as the property is not registered.*

The secrets of who owns Stonor and the extent of the estate are contained within its own walls, in its own records. They are not available to the public. Calls to the house are politely deflected. However, if the curious enquirer knew that something called *The Return of Owners of Land* (also known as the Second, or 'New' Domesday) existed, and that a copy was probably in his or her own local reference library, admittedly perhaps locked up in the 'cage', as the confidential areas in most local libraries are known, then he or she could go and find out who owned Stonor and the exact extent of its land, down to the last perch. Or the last perch in 1872, at any rate.

For *The Return of Owners of Land, in England, Scotland, Ireland and Wales*, commissioned by Parliament as a result of a debate in the House of Lords on the 19 February 1872, and published in four volumes between 1874 and 1876, is our lost book, a social, historical and present treasure that the academic and social historians of the UK have mostly ignored for 120 years. In that book the enquirer would have found that the 3rd Lord Camoys of Stonor Park in Henley-on-Thames owned 4500 acres in Oxfordshire, worth in rental value £5000, the modern equivalent of £350,000 pa.[4]

Name of Owner	Address of Owner	Extent of Lands A.	R.	P.*	Gross Estimated Rental £	s.
Camoys, Lord	Stonor Park, Henley-on-Thames	3,510	2	—	4582	4

*A = Acres, R = Roods, P = Perches

In 1872 the 3rd Lord Camoys also owned 900 acres in Buckinghamshire worth £1000 (modern equivalent £70,000), 300 acres in Staffordshire worth £1321 (£92,470), 810 acres in Leicestershire worth £1268 (£88,760) and 230 acres in Warwickshire worth £240 (£16,800). Gross annual rental was an assessed figure, similar to the way houses are assessed for Council Tax in the modern era. At that time, most taxable incomes came from rents, and income tax at the time was 4d in the pound of 240 pence, about the equivalent of 1.6p nowadays. Valuations were based on rentals, which were not always paid,[5] but on the basis that they were, Lord Camoys was drawing the modern equivalent of £618,030 a year from his lands and paying £9800 in tax on that income.

The same information is unavailable today. While the Ministry of Agriculture pays out hundreds of millions of pounds in agricultural grants each year, it refuses to identify the recipients of these public funds.[6] The public in turn cannot check who owns agricultural land because up to 50% of it is unregistered and the rest is registered in ways that make searches difficult or impossibly expensive. Since 1925, the law has required any land transaction in England and Wales to be registered at the Land Registry. But the 1925 law was introduced on a rolling basis, starting in London where some titles were already registered under an earlier Order in Council, and finally arriving in fourteen districts across four counties in 1990, 65 years later. A significant number of the large estates described in the 1872 Return made no transactions in that period, or if they did, sold off land, leaving the core of the estate 'untransacted' and thus unregistered. Many of these large estates are, in any case, in trust, with the current heirs merely tenants for life. A good example of this is the £1 billion St John's Wood estate in London, the property of the Eyre family. The entry in the last *Burke's Landed Gentry* (1965 edition) describes Mary Francis Elisabeth Eyre as the joint life tenant of St John's Wood with her sister, Alethea Fanny. Both were deceased by 1965 but the subsequent tenancies had not been notified to the *BLG*. When the tenants die they are simply replaced by their heirs, but the trust and its unregistered land simply carry on, untaxed by death duties.

However, in the interval between 1925 and 2000 about 99% of all domestic dwellings, homes and flats have been sold or inherited, according to the Land Registry, meaning that the main assets of the majority of people in the country are registered in the Land Registry. Those properties do not attract any state subsidies and no longer receive a tax break by way of mortgage tax relief. The owners of most of them pay a tax assessed on the value of their residence called the Council Tax. Yet any unregistered landowner can check on almost any ordinary householder, with ease and for the Land Registry fee, £7.20.

In the 1870s, had an enquirer been driven further by curiosity, he or she could have gone to the Parish Records at Henley and seen the tithe maps,[7] which would have shown the precise dimensions and location of the Stonor estate. Today, all that is available is that little note from the Land Registry, saying that they can tell you nothing. The tithe records are either destroyed, as they have been in many counties, or locked up in all but inaccessible archives. Lord Camoys is thus ensured a level of financial privacy not available to most of the rest of us. We cannot know what mortgage there is on Stonor Park, a fact easily determined on any dwelling listed in the Land Registry. We cannot know if Lord Camoys is likely to be enjoying a tax break by the fact that the estate is in a trust. And we cannot find out, as he can about most of us, exactly how much land he still owns, or how much of the 1872 estate exists and attracts agricultural grants.

All these advantages were deliberately conferred on the already privileged by a manipulation of the law which created the modern Land Registry, an act of deception which was made operational even as the 1872 Return was being air-brushed out of the historic and administrative record of the UK, to the extent that is hardly known about by anybody, including those in positions of power and influence today. Much more than a simple cover-up, it is an on-going conspiracy even in an age when such a term is frequently and wilfully over-used. A special interest group, the landowners, a group inextricably bound up with the Conservative Party that has been the dominant political influence in Parliament for most of the past 120 years, saw to it that information, such as that disclosed in the Return, would never again be available to the public. It is perhaps the most astonishing case of calculated civic deceit ever performed on a whole country.

This book is about that conspiracy and its consequences.

Chapter One

Why Land Matters

OUR COUNTRY, THE United Kingdom, is 60 million acres in size. Some 59 million of us live on those 60 million acres. The area taken up by the homes of these 59 million people takes up less than 10% of the land, a maximum of 6 million acres, but more probably just 4.4 million acres. It is impossible to settle on a more accurate figure as the statistics for most of the UK are estimates, drawn from samples (see Table 1/1, p.9), while the government of Northern Ireland has no figure at all available for its residential acreage. The scale of discrepancy can clearly be seen in Table 1/1, where 2.6 million acres of England alone are unaccounted for, and where there is a further 1.2 million-acre gap between the total the UK government thinks is farmed, and the amount the EU thinks we farm. Despite the discrepancies this still leaves a great deal of the country 'uncovered' by bricks and mortar, 55.6 million acres at least. Of this between 12 million and 14.5 million acres are mountain, forest, moorland, water, roadways and industrial land. Which leaves some 40 million acres of often beautiful, sometimes productive countryside. This is owned by just 189,000 families.[1]

Among the landholdings of these 189,000 families, there are 4778 estates over 741 acres in size in England alone, each averaging 1290 acres and valued at the end of 1999 at just under £4 million each.[2] This is more than one quarter (27%) of the entire agricultural estate, and makes this group of owners worth a total of £1.8 billion. This figure is not much different from the figure to be found in the 1872 *Return of Owners of Land* for this size of estate (there were a total of 5408 estates of over 1000 acres). The range in size of these large estates from which this average figure of 1290 acres derives is worth examining to ensure perspective is not lost. At one end are the Buccleuch Estates, spread across both England and Scotland, and ultimately owned by the Duke of Buccleuch, which are currently reckoned to be about 270,700 acres. At the other end, in the 700 to 900-acre range, are estates like Stonor, introduced in the preface.

The vast majority of these large estates are held by just three classes of people: aristocrats, who would, until November 1999, have sat in the House of Lords, baronets, and finally the residual landed gentry, a group once defined by their appearance in *Burke's Landed Gentry*.[3] Between them these three groups packed Parliament through three centuries and provided the captains of the militia, the officers of the Army, Navy and later the Air Force, the bishops and clergy of the church and the judges for the courts, at the same time keeping every one else out of those critical elements of the power structure. Even within the second official category of large estate, those between 247 and 741 acres in size, the average land holding is worth, exclusive of mortgages, over £1 million. In all, estates over 247 acres in size account for around 28 million acres of Britain, or 58% of the total land owned.

But are such figures important? Why do we need, or want, to know who owns the country we live in? Does it really matter who owns which parts of Britain? The answer is that it matters a lot more than we realise, and certainly a lot more than the tiny minority of those who own most of the land would like us to realise. If anything, the fact that the really rich and powerful do not seem to want us to know who owns the

Great Britain and Ireland 1872 and 2001 – some basic figures

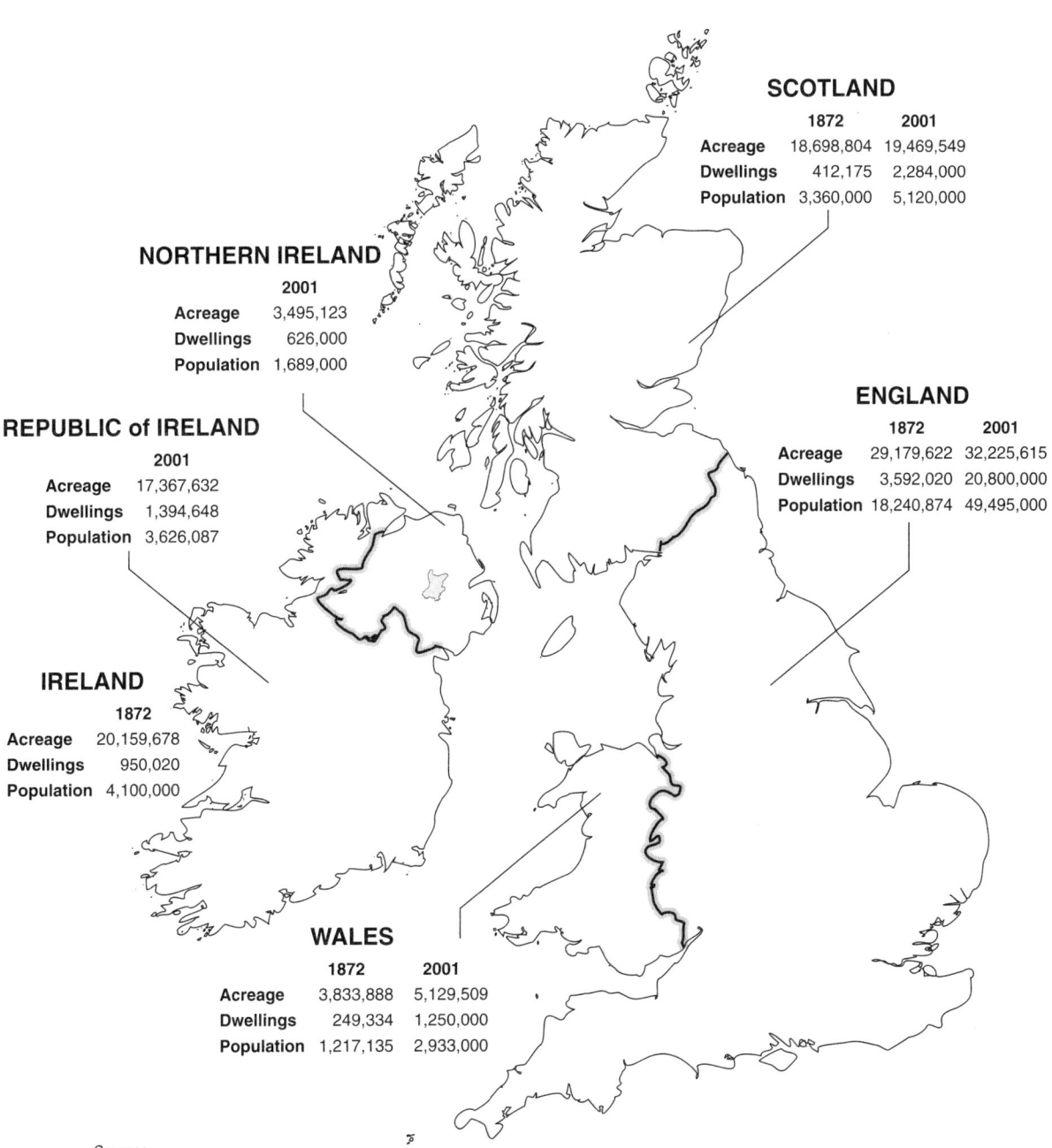

SCOTLAND

	1872	2001
Acreage	18,698,804	19,469,549
Dwellings	412,175	2,284,000
Population	3,360,000	5,120,000

NORTHERN IRELAND

	2001
Acreage	3,495,123
Dwellings	626,000
Population	1,689,000

REPUBLIC of IRELAND

	2001
Acreage	17,367,632
Dwellings	1,394,648
Population	3,626,087

ENGLAND

	1872	2001
Acreage	29,179,622	32,225,615
Dwellings	3,592,020	20,800,000
Population	18,240,874	49,495,000

IRELAND

	1872
Acreage	20,159,678
Dwellings	950,020
Population	4,100,000

WALES

	1872	2001
Acreage	3,833,888	5,129,509
Dwellings	249,334	1,250,000
Population	1,217,135	2,933,000

Sources:
1872 All figures are from the Returns of Owners of Land for each country.
2001 Acreage: *Whittaker's Concise Almanack 2001* from latest Government Statistics (MAFF/DETR).
Dwellings: Royal Chartered Institute of Housing 2001.
Population: *Whittaker's Concise Almanack 2001.*

WHY LAND MATTERS

country is encouragement enough to try and find out what they are hiding from us.

One obvious and instinctive link many people have to the land they inhabit is patriotism, an often incoherent, often emotional bond, but hugely real for all that. Loyalty to one's land and community has frequently been used by governments and monarchs to motivate people to take up arms and to die for their country. Yet the vast majority of Britons who died in the two World Wars of the twentieth century owned not a square yard of their country's soil. Indeed, many ordinary soldiers fought in both World Wars in the hope that one day their heirs would become owners of the land they had fought to keep free. After World War Two those who survived the conflict voted in a Labour government to do just that – share out the land between all the people of the country, and not just the privileged few. In 1945 redistribution of land was a manifesto commitment of the party, similar in many respects to Lloyd George's promise to those returning from World War One to make Britain a fit country for heroes to live in. They were betrayed, as they so often have been, by the inner elite who have maintained their influence at the heart of government no matter the agenda of the party elected at the ballot box. Today that inner elite still owns the country, both by operating the inner levers of power, often at board level in banks and financial institutions,[4] and by trading on the identification most of us make with the place of our birth and upbringing, be they fields and streams or urban streets.

Land also matters to those who own it, though for different reasons. The reasons aren't often heard from the lips of landowners today, not at least in public, which makes the words of the 15th Earl of Derby in the nineteenth century all the more illuminating. One of the greatest landowners of his age, and the man who demanded that *The Return of Owners of Land* should be created, Derby explained in 1881 why people want to own land:

> The object which men aim at when they become possessed of land in the British Isles may, I think, be enumerated as follows. One, political influence; two, social importance, founded on territorial possession, the most visible and unmistakable form of wealth; three, power exercised over tenantry; the pleasure of managing, directing and improving the estate itself; four, residential enjoyment, including what is called sport; five, the money return – the rent.[5]

And he should have known. Derby owned 68,942 acres in five counties, making him the 20th largest landowner in England and the 7th richest man in the United Kingdom with an annual income of £163,273 (about £16 million today). The current heir to the estate, the 19th Earl, owns about 30,000 of the acres attributed to the estate in 1872. Like Stonor, the current Earl of Derby's home at Knowsley on Merseyside is not recorded in the Land Registry. Like Camoys, he is a merchant banker, formerly with Flemings Private Asset Management, and like Camoys he went to Eton. And again like Camoys, he is married to the daughter of a major landowner in Essex, Baron Braybrooke. His father-in-law is an Old Etonian. The *Sunday Times* Rich List in 2000 ranked the 19th Earl the 747th richest man in England with a fortune of £40 million. This, as we shall later see, is a singular underestimate of the value of the 30,000-acre estate.

The 15th Earl's honesty is unusual, but, especially to modern ears, brutal. We, the landowners, he says, hold the land because it gives us power, status and sport, enables us to dominate the peasantry and finally, gives us money. In a sense this book is an exploration of Derby's five central points, and of his great mistake, at least from the landowners' point of view, the publication of *The Return of Owners of Land*.

TABLE 1/1
THE BASIC LAND USE STRUCTURE OF THE UK AND IRELAND
All in acres (except holdings)

	Total Acres	Agricultural	No. of agricultural holdings	Residential	Roads	Waste	Water	Unaccounted
England	32,224,963	22,791,277	144,777	3,544,745	451,149	2,577,997	187,305	2,672,510
Wales	5,129,405	3,650,845	27,937	512,940	71,811	410,352	32,123	451,334
Scotland	19,469,155	12,832,530	32,888	1,946,915	272,568	1,557,532	418,101	2,441,509
N. Ireland	3,495,053	2,641,211	32,118	349,000	48,930	79,604	157,652	18,656
Total for UK	**60,318,577**	**41,915,863**	**237,000**	**6,031,857**	**844,000**	**4,825,486**	**795,183**	**5,584,009**
	(40,647,289)*							
Rep. of Ireland	17,367,632	10,688,279*	153,400	1,736,763	243,146	1,389,410	471,040	2,838,994

Notes:
Tables 1/1 to 1/4 are compiled from figures provided by various Government departments. In the case of waste and commons the figure is taken from the table supplied by the DETR for the Open Access Bill but is based on 1990 figures, the latest available. It is by no means accurate. The Return of Owners of Land in 1872 had only 1,197,676 acres of waste and commons for England and 326,972 acres for Wales, figures that were unlikely to be in error by 50% or to have risen by 50% between 1872 and 1990. Conversely the figure provided by the DETR for roads is almost certainly far too low. The reason the figure for unaccounted acres is so large is that there are wide variations in the way different UK Government departments actually compile statistics, using different definitions and different breakdowns of the UK.

* Both these figures are taken from EU Agricultural statistics for 1999.

In his book *Who Owns Scotland*, Andy Wightman argues that 'the ownership and use of land is one of the most fundamental issues in any society.' While Wightman's book did much to post landownership on the political agenda in Scotland, it is clear that in general, in Britain, land is not a fundamental issue, nor has it been part of the political agenda for most of the twentieth century. Why? One of the reasons is that in the late nineteenth century the Return threatened to highlight the issue of landownership. Once aware of this, the Return was buried by the landowners it had exposed. Admittedly, the landowners were threatened by more than exposure in the Return. They were disturbed by land agitation in Ireland. The actual extent of landlessness among the English population in 1876 was not hugely different from that in Ireland. The potential for a revolution in landownership in England existed, but it simply never happened.

In what is now the Republic of Ireland, land was redistributed to a landless peasantry, beginning in the late 1800s and finally ending only a few years ago.[6] This proved so effective that by 1921 and independence, large landowners as a class in most of that country had largely been eliminated. There is reason to believe that this redistribution of land is one of the essential underpinnings of the Irish economic miracle of the 1990s, when this comparatively tiny state of less than 4 million people drove their GDP above that of the UK. The Republic does not require its citizens to pay a council tax, or water rates, and provides a far higher level of old age benefits than almost any other European state. Despite the huge and very British style of intense urbanisation around the capital Dublin, the community of the Irish Republic remains a largely rural one, but with most farms now adjusted to the post-European integration reality of having one quarter of their income arise from subsidy, one quarter from farming and fully half from other activities. What has never been analysed is the 'credit accelerator' based on landownership, which has drawn money and investment into the actual Irish economy, as opposed to the economy created in Ireland by foreign investment.

Understanding the way credit was generated for Irish families, through the possession of land on a widely distributed basis, is central to understanding why the British economy stalled, not in the last fifty years of the last century, but possibly as far back as the late 1800s, when economic decline first set in. And there is another lesson for Britain hidden in the Irish economy. As real wealth has spread, and the value of land and its potential as collateral has risen, so too has the pace and nature of house building in the Irish economy. It is a central argument of this book that in the post-industrial economy the single most important factor is home ownership. This is a perception endorsed by the Chinese government, whose Premier Zhu Rongji told his country in his first prime ministerial press conference in 1998 that he would turn his country into a 'nation of homeowners'.[7] No matter how far a leap this may have been from Chairman Mao's 'Iron Pot and a bowl of rice', it is the necessary means of moving China into the front rank of economic superpowers, while also guaranteeing the entire world economy the same level of growth in the twenty-first century that the United States gave the world throughout the twentieth century.

For the UK the lesson of the importance of homeownership cannot be underestimated, yet it is, especially by the Treasury, which remains locked into essentially neo-classical industrial models of the economy, models that cannot produce real growth, only a more genteel level of decline, aligned with truly appalling levels of pay and job security in a so-called service economy. And it is from its small neighbour, which is building more than twice as many houses a year per head of the population as the UK, that the UK will learn its most critical lesson in the creation of a viable economy for its people. Too often in

TABLE 1/2
LAND IN THE UK AND IRELAND AND WHO LIVES WHERE

	Total Acreage	Agricultural acreage	No. of agricultural holdings	Agric. holdings owned	Agric. holdings rented	Acres per person	Acres per person in agricultural/rural areas
England	32,224,963	22,791,277	144,777	111,594	33,183	57.9
Wales	5,129,405	3,650,845	27,937	23,100	4,837	62.0
Scotland	19,469,155	12,832,530	32,888	22,673	10,175	217.6
N. Ireland	3,495,053	2,641,211	32,118	—	—	42.0
Rep. of Ireland	17,367,632	10,688,279	153,400	—	—	—

Notes:
The figures for Northern Ireland and the Republic of Ireland for agricultural tenure (cols 4 & 5) are not available from Government or other sources.
This set of figures uses the MAFF figures for agricultural workers, including farm directors and owners, to obtain the number of acres per person in rural areas.

	Residential acreage	No. of dwellings	Dwellings owned	Dwellings rented	Persons per acre in residential/urban areas
England	3,544,745	20,800,000	14,144,000	6,656,000	13.5
Wales	512,942	1,250,000	812,500	437,500	5.4
Scotland	1,946,915	2,284,000	1,484,600	799,400	2.5
N. Ireland	349,000	626,000	406,900	219,100	4.7
Rep. of Ireland	1,736,763	1,394,648	1,115,722	278,926	1.9

Note:
As in the rest of this book, there is an assumption that dwellers in rural villages and towns are included in the overall figures for residential dwellings based on the fact that there is no breakdown between dwellings in rural and urban areas.

the past and too often in the existing UK Treasury model the people serve the economy, rather than the other way around. A great deal of the 'Irish miracle' relates to relaxed planning consents in rural areas, just as a great deal of the economic log jam in the UK relates to over restrictive planning restrictions in rural and semi-urban areas.

The Irish experience reveals just why the inefficiency of land registration is of such profound importance. For hidden behind the current pattern of landownership in Britain is the fact that the 59 million people who live on just 4.4 million residential acres in this country are subject to a land tax called the Council Tax, averaging £550 per household, which totals £10.4 billion a year. The 189,000 families who live on 40 million acres, pay £103 million in Council Tax on their actual homes, but not their acres, and receive a direct subsidy from the Ministry of Agriculture of £2.3 billion,[8] plus other subsidies from the EU and other bodies which probably brings the total closer to £4 billion or more. Each residential home coughs up an average of £550 in tax a year. Each landowning home gets an average handout of £12,169 per year.

These numbers are important and have very clear political implications. They speak of critical imbalances at the very heart of the UK economy, and they point towards a vast and persistent economic injustice. While Council Tax (along with its predecessors the Community Charge and the rates), are cast as revenue to pay for local services, they merely supplement budget grants paid directly to local authorities by central government. It is clear that these grants could be a lot larger, and Council Tax a lot lower, if central government was not paying out such large sums to millionaire landowners. The Irish pay no council tax, yet still benefit from local services. Were the subsidy to be ended, land and transactions in land taxed, and the avoidance of tax by placing land in offshore trusts plugged, the calculations would be very different. Somewhere between £12 billion and £17 billion would be raised, more than sufficient to cover the £10.4 billion currently raised by the Council Tax. Nor should a serious revision of the payment of land subsidies affect farmers – on the contrary, the system might well be more efficient if it ensured that subsidies were paid where required to help agricultural output, rather than to the landed aristocracy.

The Home of Democracy

The 59 million people who are the 'democracy' in the United Kingdom live in a grand total of 24 million dwellings.[9] Those 24 million dwellings, scattered across the main island and in Northern Ireland, sit on a maximum of six million acres, but more likely, just 4.4 million acres, or 7.5% of the total acreage.[10] The land these dwellings rest on is slightly confusingly described as 'urban' acreage by the DETR, but as it includes the land covered by *all* domestic dwellings, including gardens, whether located in urban or rural areas, it is perhaps better described as 'residential' acreage.

Of the 24 million dwellings in the UK, 16% of the housing stock is owned by local authorities, 11% of homes are owned by private landlords while housing associations own just 5%. The remainder, 65%, are privately owned.[11] (For more on how land is owned in the UK and Ireland, see Appendix 2, p. 397.) Although these are all government figures based on samples rather than an actual head count, it means 19 million privately owned homes or dwellings, including those owned by private landlords, sit on about 3.5 million acres, or about 5.8% of the land of the country. The overall average figure for the number of people living in each domestic dwelling in the UK is 2.4 people. On this basis 45.6 million people, men, women and children, live in privately owned homes in which a member of the family has a stake. Which means that the total stake of this group

TABLE 1/3
THE OWNERSHIP OF LAND IN THE UK AND IRELAND

	Agricultural acreage	Agric. holdings owned	Average acreage	Average value	Residential acreage	No. of owners	Average Acreage (inc. Rented)	Average Value
England	22,791,277	111,594	204 acres	£612,000	3,544,745	14,144,000	0.17	£100,000
Wales	3,650,845	23,100	158	£395,000	512,940	812,500	0.41	£60,000
Scotland	12,832,530	22,673	566	£1,132,000	1,946,915	1,484,000	0.82	£85,000
N.Ireland	2,641,211	32,118	82	£287,000	349,000	406,900	0.25	£70,000
Rep. of Ireland	10,688,279	153,400	70	£350,000	1,736,763	1,115,722	1.24	£95,000

Notes:
The average value of an acre of agricultural land is calculated from figures published in the UK Inland Revenue Property Market Report published by the Valuation Office in Autumn 1999. These are: England (£3000); Wales (£2500); Scotland (£2000); N. Ireland (£3500) and the Rep. of Ireland (£5000). The average value of a dwelling is taken from the same source and is the 'typical' figure for a post-1960 semi-detached house in a suburban area. The land occupied by residential building is based on estimates of urban land under bricks and mortar. The Irish and Scottish figures clearly include a big component of garden or small acreage and need further study.

TABLE 1/3B
NUMBER OF PEOPLE OWNING LAND WORTH OVER £1 MILLION

England	26,164
Wales	3761
Scotland	8765
N. Ireland	1596
Total UK	**40,286**
Rep. of Ireland	4141

Notes:
Calculations based on average value of an acre of agricultural land from figures published in the UK Inland Revenue Property Market Report published by the Valuation Office in Autumn 1999.

of people, about 77% of the population, in the land of the country is 5.8% of the land area or about 3.5 million acres. The average size of an residential plot is 0.18 of an acre and on that basis the average residential space available to members of each average dwelling is 0.07 of an acre, about 340 square yards. The average density of persons on a residential acre is twelve or thirteen, allowing for rounding up. Among the small group of major landowners, on the other hand, the population density transforms into acres per person, with an average figure of well over 88 acres per person for the UK as a whole.

There is one further relevant figure, that for the current value for an average private home, which is £100,000.[12] The overall value of the privately owned residential housing stock is £19,000 billion. At the end of 1999 just over 10.9 million privately owned homes carried a mortgage of some kind.[13] This is in huge contrast to the situation in the countryside, where just 189,000 families own 40 million acres (see Table 1/2), valued at £120 billion.

The financial implications of this for the homeowner are considerable. At the very heart of the housing market is the availability of development land. A building site now constitutes between half to two-thirds of the cost of a new house or dwelling.[14] As such it is the main driver across the country in the price a house, especially a new house, will fetch. However, the market for development land in the UK is rigged. In the words of Stuart Beevor, Managing Director of Legal & General Property and Chairman of the Property Investment Forum, a major property market player, speaking at the *Financial Times* property conference in London on 7 July 1998, 'The market is very imperfect. It proceeds on word of mouth and trade secrets.'[15]

What lies behind this statement is the existence of so much unregistered land. As indicated previously, more than 30% and maybe as much as half of the actual acreage of England and Wales is not recorded in the Land Registry for those two countries. Yet it is the unregistered portion of the Land Registry which is the main source of development land. It certainly does not come from the crowded 4.4 million acres on which most of us live.

The *Sunday Times* in 1999[16] noted that large landowners, the main owners of unregistered land, had sold options on about 25,000 acres of land to property developers aiming to build the three to four million new homes that the government believes the country will need by 2016.[17] According to the Inland Revenue the average value of an acre of development land across the UK in Autumn 1999 was £404,000.[18] This is taken from a low of £226,624 for an acre in the North East of England, to a high of £704,154 for an acre in the South East of England. London, naturally, is in a category of its own, with an acre costing £1,529,714 in inner London and £1,048,137 in outer London. Even then inner London does not include central London, where land values disappear off the scale.

The *Sunday Times* report was based on a study by Fred Willings, Michael Foster and Alex Latham at Credit Lyonnais Securities Europe, a London-based financial institution. They examined the land bank, the store of developable land held by builders, looked at the records of eighteen quoted housebuilders and derived their figures from the scale of land bank acquisition by the main quoted housebuilding companies. These builders account for about half the industry's output. The value of the 25,000 acres optioned by the builders is a minimum of £10 billion, more if the figure is adjusted for the fact that most of that building will be in the South East, which could raise the figure to as much as £17 billion. Given that these represent only half the industry output, the figures should be doubled to calculate the value for the entire sector.

What matters in relation to the tax-paying home owner is that this new housing land is mostly coming out of subsidised rural estates, very often from land held in special offshore trusts and companies, and effectively untaxed. The land is priced as it is because

TABLE 1/4
THE BIG ACREAGES AND THEIR DISTRIBUTION AND OWNERSHIP

	Size of holding	Number of holdings	Total acreage of holdings	Average size of holding	Average value
England	Over 741 acres	4778	6,165,077	1290	£3,970,914
England	Over 247 acres	21,216	8,489,218	400	£1,200,000
Wales	Over 741 acres	430	544,799	1266	£3,167,440
Wales	Over 247 acres	3331	1,253,343	376	£940,000
Scotland	Over 741 acres	2765	8,433,525	3050	£6,100,199
Scotland	Over 247 acres	6513	2,657,189	407	£815,964
N.Ireland	Over 741 acres	91	103,428	1136	£3,978,010
N.Ireland	Over 247 acres	1505	533,386	354	£1,240,432
Rep. of Ireland	Over 247 acres	4141	–	–	£1,235,000

Notes:
As with Table 1/3, the average value of an acre of agricultural land is calculated from figures published in the UK Inland Revenue Property Market Report published by the Valuation Office in Autumn 1999.

TABLE 1/5
TENURE OF AGRICULTURAL LANDHOLDINGS IN THE UK 1997–1999

1997

	Owned or mainly owned	Rented or mainly rented
UK	157,367 (25,916,280 acres)	48,195 (13,357,578 acres)
England	111,594 (14,838,429 acres)	33,183 (7,952,387 acres)
Wales	23,100 (2,816,789 acres)	4837 (833,982 acres)
Scotland	22,673 (8,261,062 acres)	10,175 (4,571,201 acres)

1998

	Owned or mainly owned	Rented or mainly rented
UK	158,560 (26,196,400 acres)	47,365 (12,994,069 acres)
England	112,303 (14,909,045 acres)	32,724 (7,793,595 acres)
Wales	23,271 (2,835,277 acres)	4632 (804,656 acres)
Scotland	22,985 (8,452,077 acres)	10,009 (4,395,817 acres)

1999

	Owned or mainly owned	Rented or mainly rented
UK	Not available	Not available
England	115,148 (14,127,448 acres)	32,072 (6,770,540 acres or 755,631 acres*)
Wales	23,661 (2,803,596 acres)	4357 (661,980 acres)
Scotland	Not available	Not available

* MAFF estimate of land owned by tenants who rent more than 50% of their holdings.

Notes:
No details are available for tenure arrangements in Northern Ireland as large-scale letting by landowners is not common, a characteristic that Northern Ireland shares with the Irish Republic, where less than 3% of farms are rented.

Tables 1/5 and 1/6 deliberately kept 'recent' in order to ensure that there are a set of reliable figures publicly available when the effects of the Foot and Mouth epidemic of spring 2001become available. What the above figures actually demonstrate is the general stability of the farming infrastructure year on year. They also give a very clear and specific picture of how the bulk of the country is owned.

The figures are produced by the Ministry of Agriculture Fisheries and Food, now the Department of the Environment, Food, Rural Affairs and Agriculture (DEFRA) and taken from the series known as 'The June Census' available from the statistics section of the MAFF website.

WHY LAND MATTERS

it is perceived as scarce when not only is it not scarce but it is kept from dereliction by huge public subsidy. It is perceived as scarce because neither the government, nor anyone else, has made any attempt to create a complete Land Registry, and therefore the nature of this land and its ownership in particular, is unknown. The high price of a site restricts the amount of space available for each home and determines whether a garden, however small, the dream of so many young families, can be provided. It also limits the amount of money which can be spent on materials for actual housebuilding.

And all this when the day-to-day workings of government, politics and the media fight tooth and nail to win the confidence and support of a democracy which is widely regarded as tax-averse, well-educated and healthily cynical. It is increasingly clear that the question the democracy should be asking a lot more forcibly is, 'Who Does Own Britain?'

The Largest Landowners
Who are the large landowners? And is their presence really of relevance within the landownership debate? This is a question that has not been answered properly for 125 years. One widely held assumption, for example, is that the Church of England is a major landowner. In fact the Church of England is now a minor player in the big league with at least four private individuals owning more land than the Church. However, a book deservedly still in print serves as well as anything else to demonstrate the nature of ignorance about the identity of the large landowners. In 1962 Anthony Sampson's seminal work *The Anatomy of Britain* noted that Britain, one of the most urbanised countries in the world, 'continues to take its values and habits from the land'.[19] But he found himself stymied when it came to trying to give some idea of who owned that land. He names just three landowners, the Crown with 292,000 acres, the Forestry Commission with 2,475,000 acres and the Church with 220,000 acres. 'The size of the big private estates is not published', he notes, going on to indicate four of the largest estates from the fourth edition of John Bateman's *Great Landowners of Great Britain and Ireland* 1883, those of the dukes of Sutherland, Buccleuch and Richmond, and the Earl of Breadalbane. He describes the bulk of the land in Northern Ireland and Scotland, 25 million acres in all, as 'virtually uninhabitable'. And there he stops, having accounted for less than 5% of the ownership of the UK and writing off over a third of it as uninhabitable. Such was the scale of ignorance 38 years ago, and it is little changed now.

Today, the largest single landowner in the UK is the Forestry Commission, which has lands in Scotland, England, Wales and Northern Ireland, and which produces some of the most indigestible and obscure accounts of any public body in the kingdom. It has about 2.4 million acres in ownership and is dealt with in Chapter 10 of this book. After the Forestry Commission comes the Ministry of Defence with around 750,000 acres. Next is the National Trust with around 550,000 acres, and it is followed by the insurance companies, with about 500,000 acres. The utilities, principally electricity, water and the railways, own about 500,000 acres. The Crown Estate, a very special case dealt with in Chapter Five, has just under 400,000 acres. The National Trust for Scotland has 176,827 acres. The Duchy of Cornwall, with 141,000 acres, is now bigger than the Church of England, which is down to a mere 135,000 acres. The largest farmer in the UK is the Co-op with 90,000 acres of farmland.

These, however, are all institutional owners. Of the private owners of great estates, the Duke of Buccleuch owns 270,700 acres in Scotland and in England. The next largest landowner is the Blair Trust, holding the lands of the Dukedom of Atholl, 148,000 acres. The Duke of Westminster has a grand total of about 140,000 acres, with 95,000 acres

TABLE 1/6

BREAKDOWN OF AGRICULTURAL LANDHOLDINGS IN THE UK 1997–1999

UK	1997	1998	1999
Total agricultural holdings	237,720 (41,915,019 acres)	237,856 (41,830,407 acres)	239,583 (41,774,090 acres)
Holdings over 741 acres	4666 (4,364,855 acres)	4622 (4,328,648 acres)	4706 (4,399,227 acres)
Holdings over 1235 acres	1428 (2,058,854 acres)	1459 (2,102,282 acres)	1492 (2,147,664 acres)
Holdings over 1729 acres	1970 (8,822,787 acres)	1971 (8,836,194 acres)	1969 (8,830,849 acres)

England	1997	1998	1999
Total agricultural holdings	144,777 (22,790,816 acres)	145,093 (22,702,641 acres)	147,220 (22,611,332 acres)
Over 741 acres	3161	3101	3167
Over 1235 acres	897	897	927
Over 1729 acres	738	742	731

Wales	1997	1998	1999
Total agricultural holdings	27,937 (3,650,771 acres)	27,907 (3,639,931 acres)	28,018 (3,689,039 acres)
Over 741 acres	303	304	324
Over 1235 acres	67	75	77
Over 1729 acres	60	59	62

Scotland	1997	1998	1999
Total agricultural holdings	32,888 (12,832,271 acres)	33,039 (12,847,895 acres)	33,213 (12,822,280 acres)
Over 741 acres	1131	1148	1150
Over 1235 acres	471	475	476
Over 1729 acres	1163	1162	1167

Northern Ireland	1997	1998	1999
Total agricultural holdings	32,118 (2,641,158 acres)	31,817 (2,639,937 acres)	31,132 (2,651,439 acres)
Over 741 acres	71	69	65
Over 1235 acres	11	12	12
Over 1729 acres	9	8	9

in Scotland, 20,000 in Lancashire, 15,000 in Cheshire, a further 10,000 scattered around the UK and with a golden clutch of 300 acres in London's Mayfair and Belgravia.

London, in fact, highlights disparities of wealth which even landownership tables such as the one published here cannot communicate fully. The most valuable real estate on earth is in three places, London, Manhattan and Shanghai, and it is probable that London has more ultra-high value real estate than either of the other two cities. London remains dominated, especially in its most expensive areas, by the aristocracy. The Duke of Westminster and his family own 100 acres of Mayfair and 200 acres of Belgravia, its even more expensive neighbour. The Earl Cadogan has a billion-pound estate in Belgravia, beside the Duke. The Lords Portman and the Howard de Walden family each own 100-plus acres in the West End. In the west of London the Hon Charlotte Morrison-Townshend still owns many hundreds of millions of pounds worth of the old Holland estate. In the north of the city the Eyre family still control more than a billion pounds worth of St John's Wood, and in St James in the centre, the Sutton Estates are worth more than £100 million.

TABLE 1/7
TOP LANDOWNERS IN THE UK (2001)[20]

1	The Forestry Commission	2,400,000 acres
2	The Ministry of Defence	750,000 acres
3	The National Trust E & W	550,000 acres
4	The Pension funds	500,000 acres
5	The utilities: water, electricity, railways	500,000 acres
6	The Crown Estate	384,000 acres
7	The Duke of Buccleuch	277,000 acres
8	The National Trust for Scotland	176,000 acres
9	The Duke of Atholl's trusts	148,000 acres
10	The Duchy of Cornwall	141,000 acres
11	The Duke of Westminster	140,000 acres
12	The Church of England	135,000 acres
13	The Invercauld and Torlisk Trusts	120,000 acres
14	Alcan Highland Estates	116,000 acres
15	The Duke of Northumberland's estates	110,000 acres
16	The Earl of Seafield	101,000 acres
17	The Portland Estates	95,000 acres
18	South Uist Estates	92,000 acres
19	The RSPB	90,000 acres
20	Co-op farms	90,000 acres

This is one ordering of the top landowners in the UK, but there is another, which perhaps better illustrates the huge concentration of ownership that lies concealed behind simplistic but useful lists like the above.

TABLE 1/7B

1	The top 40,000 millionaire agricultural landowners in the UK	28,180,212 acres
2	The 16,800,000 million private homeowners in the UK	2,800,000 acres
3	Forestry Commission	2,400,000 acres
4	The Ministry of Defence	750,000 acres
5	The lands controlled and owned by the Royal family (Crown Estate, Duchies of Cornwall and Lancs, and private)	677,000 acres

To put this in perspective, history has yielded the home owners of the UK just a little more land than it has allowed for the growing of trees, and one tenth of the land deemed needed for the support of just 40,000 families in agriculture.

Perhaps the most interesting large landowner of all, the Queen and her immediate family of just eight people, believe that to be comfortable they have to have, for their use in one way or another, a quarter of the land needed to house 45 million people in the private sector.

The Royal family emerge as, effectively, the fifth largest landowner in the UK. They achieve this position by combining four entities, the Crown Estate, of which the Queen is the effective freeholder[21] until she ceases to be sovereign, the Duchy of Lancaster, the Duchy of Cornwall and finally the Queen's own personal land at Sandringham and Balmoral. The revenues from the Crown Estate, which are rapidly rising, are taken by the government as a fee for running the estate and in return the Queen is given a fixed but guaranteed payment, known as the Civil List, to enable her to carry out her Royal duties. A Tory grandee, Tessa Keswick, tried to persuade John Major to run the privatisation of the Crown Estate as a policy for the 1997 election but he refused. The Queen has subsequently hired as her press officer a former Tory press officer who was involved in developing the privatisation policy for the Crown Estate. At the same time the next government in the UK will almost certainly look to the Crown Estate, which, if broken up and sold slowly in stages, could realise as much as £8 billion to £10 billion. One of the biggest controversies in the UK in the next few years will be the issue of how much the Queen and her family will receive from the sale of the Crown Estate.

In addition to the Crown Estate, there are the anomalies of the Duchies of Lancaster and Cornwall. Lancaster, a total curiosity, has over 47,000 acres of onshore land, which the Queen does not control, but whose income she receives in total and tax free. This too is ripe for privatisation and again the issue of how much the Royals get will cause great controversy. The Duchy of Cornwall is better stitched into legislation and the constitution than either the Crown Estate or the Duchy of Lancaster. Statute laws going back to the fourteenth century confirm that it is the patrimony of the Prince of Wales and that the revenues of the Duchy, which are not subject to tax until after the Prince has received them, are exclusively his. But while claiming that the Prince has no power to sell off the Duchy lands, it equally appears that no constraints exist to stop the Duchy buying up the West Country. It has more than doubled in size since 1872 and continues to acquire land, including 20,000 new acres in 1999, at a rapid rate. Finally there are the Queen's own lands, Balmoral, Delnadamph and Sandringham, which total 70,000 acres in all.

No author or commentator has ever looked at the issue of the real agglomeration of lands in the de facto ownership or control of the Royals, their persistent growth and their relevance to a country where the average private homeowning family has just 0.18 of an acre on which to pitch their bricks and mortar. Nor indeed has the cross linkage, not merely between the immediate royal courtiers, but between the Grosvenor Estate, the Church Commissioners and other institutional property giants, at directorial level, ever been scrutinised, especially in terms of the defective Land Registry, the disappearance of *The Return of Owners of Land* and the extraordinary tax breaks enjoyed by landowners. It is no coincidence that the irregular tax break the Royals enjoyed for fifty-five years between the mid 1930s and 1993 was paralleled by a series of tax breaks that have extended a benefit intended for farmers, the non-payment of rates, to landowners. Nor was it a coincidence that the Royals' tax break was curtailed in the wake of public outcry over the wealth of the Queen revealed by the Rich Lists of the early 1990s.

Chapter Two

A Brief History of Landownership in Britain

IN AN AGE which depends to such an extent on the media as its primary source of information, very little thought is given to the limitations of the media, least of all by the media itself. For a very obvious start, the media is all about now. Not only is history forgotten, but so too is yesterday as issues pass from the public gaze after no more than a few days' attention. The problem this poses for a topic like landownership is considerable. The subject combines three of the most intractable issues in the make-up of the UK: the land and the wealth it represents; the kind of power structures that landed wealth has generated and crafted to maintain control of the UK, right into the present day; and the law of the UK, which has a significant bias towards land and landowners. These are not matters which can be unravelled simply or tackled in easy sound bites as a here-today-gone-tomorrow news story. For just as it is difficult to understand the basics of landownership in the UK without knowing the physical dimensions of the country, as laid out in the previous chapter, so an understanding of the deeper anomalies of the inherited structure requires at least a brief outline of how our essentially unreformed system of landownership came into being.

For our purposes, since it settled both the principles upon which landownership would rest and established the primal justification for later land grabs, the start date for modern English (and, later, British) history is 1066, the year the Normans annexed England.

The First Great Land Grab – The Norman Conquest

Although the history books tell it in rather more sober terms, the bare facts of the Norman Conquest are that in 1066 a wanted criminal and his gang of villains arrived in England and overran the place. The next act of William the Bastard, as he was known in France, was to claim the place as his own. This is the common action of great robbers, who, as has been remarked upon by Professor Mancur Olson, 'Do set themselves up as kings and as governments to steal by taxation what they had earlier stolen by the sword.'[1]

William's next act is described in the elegant words of De Juvenel, the French historian:

> We have often seen them in the imagination – the greedy horde embarking at St Valery-sur-Somme and then, arrived at London, having the country carved up amongst themselves by a victorious bandit chief, seated on his throne of stone.[2]

Having usurped the administration of the country, William had next to regularise and institutionalise the revenues. In his great work *The City of God*, St Augustine in 432 described this process with amazing prescience:

> And if these ragamuffins grow but up to be able enough to keep forts, build habitations, possess cities and conquer adjoining nations, then their government is no longer called thievish, but graced with the eminent name of kingdom.[3]

William's method of legitimising his crime was the traditional one. He replaced the existing land records with one of his own, which became known as Domesday Book, a document much romanced in modern times. In fact the Domesday book is little more than a swag list, which was little regarded as a legal instrument at the time, since it consisted mostly of William's donation to himself and his brigands of the lands they had 'acquired' as victors after Hastings.[4] In France historians wrote that William was lucky to be beyond the reach of French law, which had him in mind for the long drop for various awful crimes, including rape, murder, pillage, arson and treason.

Over the centuries, however, his swag list has gradually been turned into a sacred manuscript of English history, alongside Magna Carta. It is romanced by some historians and by a largely ignorant media as the foundation stone of good administration and government in Britain. Yet according to most scholars, the Domesday Book of 1086 is no more than 5% accurate as to the legitimate owners of land in England in that year.[5] The local people in eleventh century England did not co-operate with William's monks and soldiers, who in their turn understood neither the language nor record keeping systems of the natives. It was not a primitive land registry, nor did it ever become one.

> Domesday Book was an inestimable boon to a learned posterity, but a vast administrative mistake. Devised as the Domesday survey obviously was, to augment the King's already swollen revenue, we cannot guess to what practical purposes its findings could have been put had he survived . . . The fruit of a personal whim of the king . . . within a generation Domesday Book itself had become a historical monument, respected but unused.[6]

Magna Carta, on the other hand, has come to be regarded as one of the most profound documents ever written. Its 63 articles have become the source of many of the modern concepts of human rights, and it finally returned in its modern form to its ancient home, when the UK adopted the European Convention on Human Rights as statute law on 2 October 2000. Yet the Magna Carta is also an extraordinary example of the power of land in English history. The barons, led by Roger of Wendover, who faced King John at Runnymede on 15 June 1215, made the King seal the rights he had granted them in the form of a land conveyancing grant, not trusting any other form of legal document available at the time.[7]

But William would have been proud indeed to see his Domesday, compiled in secret by foreign monks, guarded as they did it mostly by foreign soldiers, turned into something precious. And he, grand criminal that he was, would have instantly figured that fraud was afoot, that this romancing of his swag list had an ulterior motive. Indeed it does. It serves to divert the attention of the British public from the fact that the modern equivalent of a Domesday, one which would let them know who owns their country, does not exist. In terms of the day-to-day practice of power in Britain, it enables the heirs to those who benefited most from the three great land grabs of British history to keep their retained wealth hidden. In the twentieth century the original Domesday has been republished at least ten times in various major editions – many of them elaborately produced, 'commemorative' editons. The second, or real Domesday, the 1872 *Return of Owners of Land*, has not been republished once.

It only took William's monks and soldiers two years to write up most of England, using quill pens, between 1085 and 1087. Yet from 1086 to 1872, Great Britain proceeded without a centralised land registry, though this is not to say that there were no records of landownership. Far from it – each of the 13,000 or so manors that constituted the basic building block of the English (later the British) administrative system had their own records. The monasteries kept land records. The counties kept records. The Exchequer kept records. Over time the Church of England, through the parishes, created the most complete system of all, the parish tithe maps, which showed who owned every scrap of land in each parish and which formed the basis for church taxation in the country until 1929. It was the parishes, and the tithe maps, which enabled the 1872 survey to be conducted, and to be so substantially accurate, because each submission was sent back to the originating parish to be checked by the parish clerk.

According to Sidney Madge, an authority on the later Cromwellian land grab,[8] the broad distribution of land ownership before and after William changed little. He estimates that in 1065 the Crown owned 20.5% of England, the Church 28.8% and the barons 50.7%. By 1086 of course there was a different Crown and a different set of barons, and indeed a new set of monks as well, the latter two in various stages of usurping the native Anglo Saxons.

Out of a total of just under 33 million acres in England, William, in the same manner as the Queen today, had both a personal estate and a Crown Estate, which together came to about 6.5 million acres (19.7%). The church owned 9.7 million acres (29.4%) and the barons owned 16.6 million acres (50.3%). What was crucial however, and remains crucial, is that William managed to impose the idea that *all* lands, including, to an extent, monastic lands, were ultimately held with the king's consent. This strange principle lives on in the manner in which heirless estates still revert to the Crown in England and Wales, through the office of Bona Vacantia.

The idea that the king or emperor owned all the lands within his control was not totally novel. It was the principle in use during the Roman occupation of Britain in the first four centuries of the Christian era, but had fallen into disuse after they left. Until very recently it also persisted in Scotland as part of the feudal system whereby God was regarded as the superior landowner and devolved his ownership to the monarch who then devolved it to their 'tenants'. The feudal structure was abolished by the Scottish Parliament in 1999.[9]

The Second Great Land Grab – Henry VIII Dissolves The Monasteries

Between 1086 and 1550, Crown lands diminished somewhat, the monasteries increased a little and with the conquest of Ireland in 1172, the Crown, Church and the barons all increased the overall size of their estates by about 50%. In 1533 Henry VIII, King of England, France and Ireland, who ruled in England from 1509 to 1547, broke with Rome over his divorce from Catherine of Aragon and created himself Supreme Governor of the Church of England. Having done this, he then had to find some way to persuade the country to drop Catholicism, with the Pope at its head, and accept the new Church, with him at its head. As with all monarchs, especially those of the Tudor period, he used two weapons, violence and bribery.

For the man who butchered two of his queens on Tower Hill, the violence came easily. The bribery less so. However, lying before him following the change of Church allegiance were the lands of the Catholic Church and its monasteries. By dissolving the monasteries Henry at one stroke removed a major source of opposition to his rule and at the same time freed up around 10 million acres of England alone to distribute to those of his followers and barons willing to accept the new Church and impose it in their local districts. In William's land grab 500 years before there had been no significant alteration in the scale of landholding by the king, the Church or the barons. Henry VIII not only altered the balance of power hugely but also revolutionised the way it was wielded in England and Ireland by redistributing the ownership of land within a group of about 1500 families. Unlike the situation pertaining when the barons forced King John to sign Magna Carta in 1215, Henry VIII scattered the new barons and landowners he had created throughout the kingdom, interspersing them amongst the existing barons. In addition, with the incomes which came from the old Church lands the new barons had huge wealth at their disposal. From this point on there would only be two sources of real power in the country, the king and the peers. Even though it did possess a significant amount of land confiscated from its Catholic predecessor, after Henry, the Church was on the sidelines.

The obedience this combination of bribery and the fear of violence established was the key to Henry's power. In the words of D'Auvergne, 'The meekness of the haughty lords at the court of Henry VIII would have revolted a Franciscan nun.'[10]

D'Auvergne goes on to illustrate his point:

> The Duke of Norfolk, from whom I believe the present holder of the title is descended, acquiesced in the murder of his niece Katharine Howard, with unnecessary haste. 'He had learned,' he told the King, 'that his ungracious mother-in-law, his unhappy brother and wife, and his lewd sister of Bridgewater, were in the Tower, which from his long experience of his majesties justice, was not done but for false and traitorous proceedings.' Percy, Earl of Northumberland was beside himself with terror when he found his son had incurred Henry's ire by a flirtation with the Queen's maid-of-honour, Anne Boleyn. Those noble persons crouched like whipped curs before the Tudor sovereigns. Their servility was richly regarded, as we know, by the spoils of the Church.

The meek – at court – did indeed inherit the earth in Henry's England.

Other aspects of the picture in the kingdom had also changed since the Norman Conquest. Cities and towns had expanded hugely, and living within them were merchants, burgers, tradespeople and workers, all far freer than the peasantry in the countryside. This was where population growth was fastest and where the first signs of a franchise were born. After the Crown and the barons, this would become the third and ultimately triumphant force that would replace absolute monarchy with a constitutional monarchy, would make the House of Commons supreme and today stands on the verge of removing completely from the legislature the last vestiges of the hereditary peers, many going back to the time of Henry VIII and some even to the Bastard's conquest. But this will happen without the same 'commonfolk' knowing who owns much of the land of the country and with many of those throwbacks who do own it still in control of the bulk of the acreage. The last reform has not begun.

The Third Great Land Grab – Cromwell and his Republic

Three things distinguish England from most of the countries of the continent. It has not been invaded since 1066. It settled the major features of its power structures in one civil war, over 350 years ago. And finally, it did unto much of the globe what the Bastard had done to it, which was to occupy it.

The British Empire was the last great global land grab, possibly the last great land grab possible. The beginnings of Empire lay as far back as the conquest of Ireland in 1172, but really got under way in the time of Elizabeth I, Henry VIII's daughter. In this way the insatiable greed for land of the Norman/British aristocracy was in part satisfied, leaving Elizabeth's reign relatively untroubled by the kinds of local problems sovereigns in other countries faced, mostly from their own powerful landed aristocratic subjects. She consolidated her father's rule – with only two brief reigns in between, the two key Tudor monarchs reigned for a total of 94 years (1509 to 1603), a long run in that period.

By 1642, however, the balances within the country had changed. The House of Commons had acquired a degree of power, even if it was almost entirely filled with either the aristocracy or the landed gentry. In 1642 Charles I tried to arrest five Members of Parliament by arriving at the doors of Parliament and marching in with his guards. Civil war broke out, ending with the beheading of Charles in 1649.

A Commonwealth was instituted in 1648, incorporating a republic, and one of its first acts was to abolish the monarchy and also the House of Peers. Within a year the Commonwealth was so short of cash to pay the army that it started to sell off the Church Estate, the Crown Estate and the Royalist estates that it had sequestered. But first of all, the lawyers had to find 'precedent'. Broadly, the Commonwealth Parliament,

> . . . adopted a policy of selling land that . . . had a variety of forms few of which had novel features. In relation to the lands seized from Bishops, deans and chapters, the precedent was Henry VIII. The seizure and sale of the Royalist estates was based on the Irish confiscation act of 1640, and in relation to the confiscation of Crown lands, Parliament was following the example of William the Conqueror[11]

By 1659 the Commonwealth had obtained over £10 million, maybe as much as £1.4 billion in modern terms, from the sale of Church lands alone. The final total for Crown land sold was around £2 million (£280 million today). This latter figure includes rents sold on very short leases, and indicates that a total of around two million acres were involved.

The point to note about the Cromwellian land grab is that it came about as a result of civil war. In the Civil War, the bulk of the army commanders and politicians on both sides came broadly from the same classes of people, mostly aristocrats and large landowners. The war split both the country and its dominant class, the landowners, in about equal measure. The long term losers were the Irish landowners. They fled and Cromwell granted their lands to the rougher of his soldiery. The Restoration in England, however, saw many losing Royalists regain their estates. The other substantial losers were the Church of England and the Crown Estate. The Church of England never fully recovered as a landowner, and the Crown Estates not until the twentieth century.

Following the Restoration of 1660 there was an attempt to recover the Crown lands. However, in the words of Madge, 'The Crown lands so recovered proved to be but a shadow of their ancient bulk.'[12] Most of the Crown Estate seized by Cromwell was sold or lost through fraud. A significant number of former Royalist estates, such as that of the Aclands in Devon, were bought back by their former owners, and in general the status quo of government returned, by which the King reigned and the landowning barons, be they restored Royalists or tolerated Cromwellians, ruled. Having said that, it was not until the agricultural depression of the 1890s and World War One and the loss of many heirs to landed estates, that the Royal family and the Crown Estate and with it the duchies of Cornwall and Lancaster start to rebuild the lost portfolios. What is relevant here, however, is that this process of rebuilding was done behind a veil of secrecy, in which the estates in question were given exemption from registering in the skeleton Land Registry that was begun in 1925. In the 1872 Return there were no admitted exceptions to the registrations process at all.

What the Tudor and Cromwellian period, together with the Restoration of 1660, did was to settle the broad nature and ownership of the entire acreage of three of the four kingdoms, England, Wales and Scotland (Ireland went its own way from the 1880s with the Land Purchase Acts), through into the present time. Another crucial aspect of the picture came with the enclosures. Between the end of the seventeenth century and the end of the nineteenth century the industrial revolution, the conversion of the British economy from a mainly agricultural one, to a manufacturing one, occurred. This 'revolution' was paralleled by the enclosures, the legal device used to include common land into landed estates, and to exclude the peasantry who had lived off the common land from an economic existence. The peasantry were driven into the cities and towns and became the urban proletariat, leaving the rural areas of the country much as we find them today, which is more or less empty of people. But to maintain the momentum of enclosure on the one hand, and the labour supply to the factories on the other, needed legislative backing. This was easy to obtain.

The landed aristocracy controlled the House of Commons by ensuring that the majority of MPs came from rural areas and rotten boroughs, with the urban and metropolitan areas having no recognition proportionate to the numbers of people living in those areas, in the House of Commons. John Bateman in his *Great Landowners of Great Britain and Ireland*[13] identifies more than 600 landowners, almost the entire capacity of the House of Commons, who sat as MPs at one time or another. Out of a House of Lords of about 580 in number, 500 were significant landowners and were either the father, brother or cousin, of the landowners sitting as MPs. It is a truism of conventional British history that the landowners were the dominant force in British politics right up to World War Two. The composition of successive British governments, particularly Conservative administrations, shows this.[14]

In 1880, out of 14 in Gladstone's Cabinet, nine were major landowners. By 1895 Salisbury, a major landowner himself, had no less than 14 significant landowners in a Cabinet of 19. Half of Asquith's Cabinet in 1908, 10 out of 20 members, were major landowners. After World War One, in the land fit for heroes, Lloyd George had six major landowners in a Cabinet of 22. At the end of World War Two, just before the Labour election victory, Churchill had six major landowners in a Cabinet of 16. Attlee had one landowner amongst his cabinet of 22; Harold Wilson in 1964 also had just one in his 23-member cabinet. Margaret Thatcher gave them another lease of life, with five significant landowners in her first 22-member Cabinet. It should come as no surprise that scions of large landowning families, Lord O'Hagan in Devon, the Marquess of Duoro, son of the Duke of Wellington, in Hampshire, and Giles Chichester, descendant of the owners of most of north Devon, have in recent years been members of the European Parliament in the Conservative interest.

The results are the distribution of land that we have today, with, for example, less than 30,000 people living in 1.35 million of Devon's 1.5 million acres, while the urban mass, all 1 million of them, live on less than 130,000 acres.[15] What we have here, then, is a confluence of two enormously important economic factors. The first is the shifting of the population into towns, into the colonies or into graves. This focused the most active form of economic development, manufacturing, into areas of marginal Parliamentary representation with a consequent lack of capacity to influence the law. It left the law in the hands of those who controlled the bulk of the land. This law, some of it still on the statute book, overwhelmingly existed for the purpose of controlling the urban population in the towns; law and order by Parliament for the purpose of handling a crime wave that had been created by Parliament via the enclosures in the first place – most of the crime in London and the provinces in the late 1700s and early 1800s was committed by evicted peasantry. But the second effect was of equal importance. It emptied the countryside and defined the scale of the rural population at much the same levels at which it now exists. And by so doing it created a vast surplus acreage, should agriculture ever become uneconomic.

The Power of Land

What this very brief outline of the history of landownership in Britain has set out is three great land thefts, all accomplished by force, with the last of them, under Cromwell, relying explicitly on the precedent of the first as justification for its own depredations. In each case, the law, or rather legislation, was used corruptly to legitimise the changes made. But one consistent characteristic of the entire period, subsequent to 1086, but even more marked between 1660 and 1874, is the fragmentary and incomplete nature of the records retained, even by the Crown, for land transactions. A full survey of exactly what the Cromwellians had snatched and sold was not in fact compiled until Madge did it in 1938, almost 300 years after the event, and until 1872 there was no clear picture of who owned the land -- even among the landowners themselves. As David Cannadine points out in his magisterial work *The Decline and Fall of the British Aristiocracy*:

> Even as individuals many of them [the aristocracy] did not know how rich they were, how much land they owned, how many titles they possessed or who all their ancestors were.[16]

But beginning with the publication of the first part of *The Return of Owners of Land* in 1874 they soon found out. And they did not like it at all. So the Return was forced off the historic record and into oblivion.

The overt reason for this was obvious. Disclosure meant access, especially for governments in search of things to tax. But the covert reasons were perhaps even more pertinent. One of the most central concepts of maintaining power is by sustaining a creed or belief. According to De Juvenal, an otherwise democratically unattractive historian but the only author of stature ever to tackle power as a generic subject, populations will serve power if they believe in the concept or myth propagated by power. One of the most seductive of myths sustained in this country is that of England with its 'green and pleasant lands', an ideal rendered majestically lyrical and graphic by Blake in his poem (and revered hymn) 'Jerusalem'. A populace which believes such a powerful vision is committed to the maintenance of it, and are persuaded to support those who consider themselves the guardians of the green and pleasant land, in other words those who own it.

The core concept that the land has an enduring presence in the depths of the psyche of individuals throughout the world, not just in Britain, has been explored extensively in literature and psychology. But there are few countries in the world where the ruling elite who own the land have been so successful in selling the concept of a 'joint interest' between landowners and the landless, and using that common interest in the myth of England the golden to persuade the landless both to support the quest for Empire and to continue to support the landed and their associates in power for most of the twentieth century. Time may yet show that the only truly revolutionary act of the first Blair government was the ejection of the hereditaries from the House of Lords, and with it that chamber's inbuilt Tory majority. This act was utterly profound, as it broke the umbilical cord between the landed and the heart of power at Westminster, a cord that had survived even the creation of a universal franchise in the country.

Perhaps the best example of the ability of large landowners to cling to power, as well as their tenacity in adversity, is the survival of the Plantagenet inheritance in both England and Scotland. The Plantagenets ruled England, Wales, Ireland and occasionally Scotland, or parts of it, from around 1154 to 1485. In terms of ruling families their incumbency is nothing particularly remarkable in British history, just 331 years. They were, however, supposed to have departed the scene 516 years ago. Yet when Blair evicted the hereditaries from the House of Lords in 1999, he threw out no less than 49 Plantagenet heirs, 20 of whom appeared in the *Sunday Times* Rich List for 2000 and nine of whom appear amongst the top 30 landowners in the country, with five in the top ten of individual landowners. What confounds modern economists and historians is how a supposedly 'extinct' royal line continues to thrive and prosper right into the twenty-first century.

However, there is another level to the challenge posed by Blair to the hegemony of the landowners. With his majorities in the House of Commons of 178 and 165 seats respectively following the 1997 and 2001 general elections, the 'socialist' Labour government has put clear electoral water between it and the main opposition party, the landowners' Tory party. It is possible that to close the gap the Conservative party will be forced to abandon its historic roots and reinvent itself as some kind of urban-oriented body, because that is where the votes are. To do so they may have to face the fact that rates are unnecessary and that they can only be abolished if subsidies are shifted to where they belong in the national interest, to the farmers who feed us, and away from the landowners who batten on the farmers' backs. The landowners, the last bastion of privilege financially supported from the public purse, have to be exposed by any future government to the rigors of the market that Margaret Thatcher endorsed so strongly, and made to survive without tax breaks and without subsidies. Windfall gains on development land should be made subject to windfall taxes, and no land in the United Kingdom should be without an identifiable owner, or if a foreign resident, without an accessible local legal representative. The community and not privileged parts of it should be the vision that every political party seeks to represent and govern.

An additional factor in the political equation with regard to land is the Countryside Alliance, a well-heeled, well-financed lobby group which seeks to represent rural groups, and which has recently staged a number of well-attended rallies in London. Despite turnouts of over a quarter of a million to the rallies, the Alliance has had little influence at the ballot box. It is doubtful, with constituencies like Romsey lost to the Tories, that the Countryside Alliance can affect more than a few marginal constituencies. It also suffers from a 'split voice', seeking on the one hand to be the voice of hard-pressed farmers, for which there is public sympathy, and on the other hand to be the voice of the hunting lobby, for which there is no social sympathy, and little general sympathy, from the general UK public. The membership of the Countryside Alliance draws very strongly upon the Country Landowners Association, the real redoubt of the landowners, and is clearly seeking to create a public relations smoke screen over subsidies, an issue which the Alliance is reluctant to address.

The Lingering Bonds

What the history of landownership in Britain proves, and modern political economics demonstrates, is the inseparable bond between land and power. In the past, from the days of powerful kings such as William I and Henry VIII to the landowning majority in Parliament long into the twentieth century, the link was fairly obvious. However, it is by no means clear that modern politics has divorced itself from the land, despite the ejection of the hereditairies from the Lords. The inner tendency of liberal democratic politics, seen in every one of the modern liberal democracies, is towards Tammany Hall machine politics, with the best paid organisations winning the vote and thus power. The media has been wholly degraded from its function of protecting democracy by a process of beggaring the investigative function everywhere, in TV and in print. That the fortunes of 5000 landowning families have been revived by a surge in demand for development land, something which has not been investigated by the media, is a hugely significant development.

Understandably unwilling to see their power dissipated, the members of the inner landowning elite have engaged in a three-decade long programme of social dumbing down of their own members, with perhaps Eton being the best example. At that school the infamous drawl has all but vanished and been replaced either by Estuarial English, or at best received pronunciation, in order to merge, chameleon-like, with the general populace. With their background thus blurred, little history of the source of their fortunes in land available, and no way to establish it accurately in the Land Registry, they can thus blend into emerging political and power structures. Politics is so much easier, as Margaret Thatcher discovered, if your husband (or father) is a millionaire.

Much has been made in the previous chapter about the two classes of citizen created by the Land Registry; those who have to register their land, mainly the urban majority, and those who do not, mainly the rural landowners. But there is another compelling constitutional reason for insisting that all land is registered. Acres of territory, like shares in a company, are valuable and are a commodity. Shares in even the smallest company have to be registered at Companies House. Surely then should all land, not just some land, be registered at the Land Registry? In this new mercantile era, the Stock Exchange and the multinationals whose shares are traded there, seem to be the epitome of power. However, they remain subject to Parliament. Neither the Stock Exchange, the multinationals nor the banks can exercise power as effectively or as arbitrarily as they would like while Parliament is around. Nor can they create their own tax breaks if they do not control Parliament. Hence the competition between even apparently powerful institutions to control Parliament by placing their favoured party in that cockpit of control and power.

For so long as its laws have to be obeyed, Parliament remains the real source of power in the country. Which is why the laws, manipulated and massaged by the landowning interest down the centuries, require ruthless financial and constitutional examination, especially if we are to prevent a new hegemony of institutions replacing that of the landowners.

Chapter Three

The Story of the 1872 Return of Owners of Land

IN 1876 EVERY citizen of Great Britain could go to his or her local county hall, Parish office or library and find the names and addresses of the owners of 95% of the land area of England, Ireland, Scotland and Wales. Universal male suffrage was not to begin arriving until the next decade and women were still 52 years from gaining the vote, yet an almost politically powerless populace did have critical information, freely available, that even now is of radical importance in making informed political and economic decisions. In the years since 1876, as the population has become fully franchised and technology has increased the spread of information as never before, so the need for – and indeed expectation of – access to important information in order to make informed decisions has grown. Yet in the last 125 years access to information about the ownership of land has retreated rather than advanced.

In the second half of the nineteenth century, despite the progress of the industrial revolution and the growth of Empire, Great Britain was still largely an agricultural economy. Certainly the three smaller countries, Scotland, Wales and Ireland, were predominantly agricultural and rural, though they were affected to the same degree as England by urban or neo-urban agglomerations, accentuated by huge metropolitan conurbations. When *The Return of Owners of Land* was launched in 1872, the House of Lords was almost entirely composed of landowners, the House of Commons was about 70% representative of the landowning interest in one form or another and about 5% of the population had the vote. Nonetheless, there were reformers about. Richard Cobden was elected MP for Stockport in 1841, later representing Rochdale having lost his seat following his opposition to the Crimean War. With John Bright he formed the Anti Corn Law Association. He forecast the rise to world power status of the USA and developed the core argument that the huge incomes of the aristocratic landowners were essentially 'unearned'. John Bright MP, born in Rochdale, was the son of a Quaker cotton miller. Rated the foremost orator of his day and a reformer by nature, he led a life-long assault on the political position of the large and aristocratic landowners. An MP for Durham and then Manchester, in addition to his prominence in the Anti-Corn Law Association he was opposed to factory legislation, trade unions and social reform, although he was generally supportive of the 1867 Reform Act which enfranchised urban artisans but left the rest of the male population, labourers in factories and on farms, without the vote. He became President of the Board of Trade under Gladstone.

The careers of both Cobden and Bright are inextricably linked to their opposition to the Corn laws of 1815 and 1828, legislation highly relevant today in the context of the European Common Agricultural Policy. In essence the Corn laws imposed huge duties on imported corn in order to prop up the price of corn grown in Britain. This, according to Cobden, Bright and the reformers, distorted trade and imposed huge burdens on ordinary people trying to buy bread. It also gave huge subsidies to the landowners. The Corn laws were reduced substantially in 1846 in the face of the Irish famine which they helped to aggravate.[1] In fact, the most vocal of the proponents for land reform were those campaigning for change in Ireland, principally Charles Stewart Parnell and the land leaguers. Their main arguments were actually ventilated in the House of Commons, where they received support from Cobden (although he had died by the time the Return was ordered), and on some issues, from Bright. The English reformers such as Bright, however, were reluctant to take things as far as the Irish members, who were hell-bent on the confiscation of estates, elimination of landlords as a class, and then escape from the Union.

The Creation of the 1872 Return

Against the background of calls for reform, the census of 1861 was probably the single most important event in the lead up to the creation of the 1872 Return. According to the census, 30,000 people, many of them women, had set themselves down as landowners. This led John Bright to observe that the country was owned by a very small number of people and that the number was growing smaller as the great estates swallowed up smaller ones. His principal opponent in the matter was the 15th Earl of Derby, a landed aristocrat of considerable intelligence and huge influence, as well as vast wealth. Over the years he countered Bright's arguments arising from the census, arguing that the number of landowners was much greater than the census showed, based on the premise that the high proportion of women landowners immediately indicated that the number was unreliable.

Between 1836 and 1876 there had been about eight different acts dealing with land issues, all debated in one or other house of Parliament. The consequences of the 1862 Land Registration Act, which sought to set up a Land Registry, are illuminating in relation to what became of the Second Domesday. After the 1862 Act was passed a Land Registrar was appointed, Mr Robert Hallett QC, at a salary equivalent to £175,000 a year. According to the Land Registry's own history 'the intimate history of the ensuing years is hidden in the mists of history or buried in now undiscoverable files'.[2] By 1875 it emerged that over the previous thirteen years a grand total of 650 first registrations had been recorded, a rate of 50 a year. Apart from the general reluctance by landowners to register at all, the fact that Hallett was taking quite literally years to register a title (records show one title taking two years seven months to register, with a year or more being the average) didn't help.

In 1875 another attempt to set up a Land Registry was made under a new act, but it had a fateful start, coinciding with the controversy over the 1872 Return. According to the Land Registry history, 'the Act proved an even more dismal failure than its predecessor.' In fact it was the intended Land Registry which felt the real brunt of the reaction to the Return. In the first three-and-a-half years of the new act's operation, only 28 first registrations of title were made. By 1888 there were 3125 titles registered, out of a minimum total pool of about 5 million titles across Great Britain.[3] The pace of registration by the last years of the nineteenth century was around 500 to 700 a year, mostly in London.

With landowners voting with their feet against the Land Registry and even the most minimal form of disclosure, the newly enfranchised were voting in the first municipal MPs, men without a landed background and the forerunners of the Labour Party, to insert a wedge into the landowners' vice-like grip of Parliament. The lack of party whipping meant that MPs were far more effective then than now. Bright helped to bring down the pro-Crimean War Palmerston government on a single motion against the Conspiracy Bill in 1865, when Bright described Palmerston's arrangements for the overseas Diplomatic Service as a 'gigantic system of outdoor relief for the aristocracy'.

The second event which precipitated the Return was a relatively minor recommendation made by F.P. Fellows, an eminent Victorian statistician, during a lecture to the Statistical Section of the British Association for the Advancement of Science in August 1871.[4] Fellows suggested an inventory, or Domesday, of government assets be drawn up, and in passing mentioned that a similar list of the nation's landed property might be a good thing too. Aware that the 1861 census had given Bright a valuable set of statistics to support his cause, the Earl of Derby took up with alacrity Fellows' proposal for a Domesday Book. According to Professor David Spring,

> The 1861 census summed up for Derby the inadequacy of landed statistics in current use. That return, he rightly argued, was highly misleading, being a return only of those landowners who had chosen to designate themselves as landowners, most of them having chosen some other designation; that half of them were women was proof enough of something being wrong. In case of the 30,000 landowners Derby guessed that ten times that figure was closer to, although still well below, the true one. He also guessed that the Radical case for landed estates 'constantly tending to become fewer in number and bigger in size' was far from proved.[5]

Bright had argued that 'Fewer than 150 men own half the land of England'.[6] As it turned out, Derby and Bright, each in his own way, was half way to the truth. There were indeed more than 30,000 landowners, as Derby argued, but that vast amounts of the country overall were owned by very few people was amply proven.[7]

It is worth noting that while there was a general uncertainty about the validity of the available statistics, both sides were profoundly better informed than anyone at all is now, in 2001, about who owns Britain. Another difference is that today very few politicians of any party, with the exception of Labour in Scotland, have addressed the issue of landownership. Yet back in the early 1870s ignorance was the issue, even to the landowners.

To facilitate a New Domesday, which he felt sure would bear out his beliefs and trump the land reformers, Bright in particular, Derby was able to pull strings within the government. His father, after all, had been Prime Minister from 1866 to 1868. The only time the issue was debated in the Houses of Parliament was on 19 February 1872, in the House of Lords. The principal exchanges between the key landowners perfectly catch the tone of a place and age that has long since vanished, as well as the paternalistic tone and attitude of the more enlightened element of the aristocracy.

A report of the House of Lords debate is contained in the introduction to the English and Welsh Return, and is summarised here (landholdings and value calculated in the 1872 Return have been inserted where appropriate):

The Earl of Derby (68,942 acres, £163,273) asked the Lord Privy Seal, Viscount Halifax, whether it was the intention of Her Majesty's Government to take any steps for ascertaining accurately the number of proprietors of land and houses in the United Kingdom, with the quantity of land owned by each proprietor. He should not trouble the House at any length, because he understood that the suggestion that he had ventured to put into his question was acquiesced in, and would be acted upon by the Government. They all knew that out-of-doors there was from time to time a great outcry raised about what was called the monopoly of land, and, in support of that cry, the wildest and most reckless exaggerations and mis-statements of fact were uttered as to the number of persons who were actual owners of the soil. It had been said again and again that, according to the Census of 1861, there were in the United Kingdom not more than 30,000 landowners; and though it had been repeatedly shown that this estimate arose from a misreading of the figures contained in the Census returns, the statement was continually reproduced, just as though its accuracy had never been disputed. The real state of the case was at present a matter of conjecture, but he believed for his own part, that 300,000 would be nearer the truth, than the estimate which fixed the landowners of the United Kingdom at a tenth of that number. He entirely disbelieved the truth of the popular notion that small estates were undergoing a gradual process of absorption in the larger ones. It was true that the class of peasant proprietor formerly to be found in the rural districts was tending to disappear – for the very good reason that such proprietors could, as a general rule, obtain from 40 to 50 years purchase for their holdings, and thereby vastly increase their incomes. In the place of that class, however, there was rapidly growing up a new class of small owners, who, dwelling in or near towns or railway stations, were able to buy small freeholds. He believed this new class would fully replace, and perhaps more than replace, the diminution in the other class to which he had referred. He apprehended that through the agency of the Local Government Board it would be easy to obtain statistical information, which would be conclusive in regard to this matter.

He suggested that these returns ought to include the name of every owner and the extent of his property in acres. He did not wish to have included in the Returns the exact dimensions of very minute holdings; that could be met by giving the aggregate extent of the holdings not exceeding an acre each, the number of separate owners being stated, but not the extent of each holding.

The Duke of Richmond (286,411 acres, £79,683) thought this was a subject the importance of which could scarcely be overrated, and trusted that Her Majesty's Government would be able to furnish the return asked for by his noble friend. This, he thought, might easily be done through the agency of the Local Government Board. A vast amount of ignorance existed in regard to the question, and it was surely time that such ignorance was dispelled by means of documents possessing all the weight of Parliamentary Returns, and whose accuracy could not be disputed. There ought to be no alarm raised by such a Return as was asked for, because the rental need not be inserted in it, although even that was given in Scotland. In order to show the great errors into which the public might be led, he would mention a fact brought under his notice by the noble Marquess [Salisbury] sitting near him. According to the Census of 1861, the number of landed proprietors in Hertfordshire was only 245. The noble Marquess, however, doubted the accuracy of this statement, and after taking the trouble to investigate the matter for himself, he found that the number of landed proprietors in the county of Hertford at that time according to the rate book was 8833.

Viscount Halifax (10,142 acres, £12,169) said that his attention had been called, as had that of his noble friend opposite [Derby], to the extraordinary statements made in certain newspapers, and at some public meetings, respecting the wonderfully small number of landed proprietors in this country. The fact was that very few persons were returned in the Census under the designation of 'owners of land'. He had looked over pages of the Census returns. The owners of land appeared under various designations – gentlemen, merchants, shopkeepers, farmers etc. Very few were returned as 'landowners'.

For statistical purposes, he thought that we ought to know the number of owners of land in the United Kingdom, and there would be no difficulty in obtaining this information. He held in his hand the valuation list of a parish, giving the name of every owner, a description of the land, the estimated area and the estimated rental. Such returns existed for every parish in England, and from them a return for all England might be compiled. He quite agreed with his noble friend, that it might not be desirable to give the rental, although he might remark that this was done in Scotland. He had in his hand the valuation roll of the county of Edinburgh, which contained the rental of every owner in that county. He believed that in Scotland no objection had ever been taken to publishing the amount of the rental. The Government considered it most desirable that the return should be prepared, and what he proposed to do was to give a nominal list of every owner of land to the extent of one acre or upwards in every county of England, together with the quantity of land each owner had in the county. In regard to the owners of less than one acre, he thought it would be sufficient to state their numbers in each county without specifying their names. The same process would be gone through in Scotland and Ireland.

The Marquess of Salisbury (20,202 acres, £33,413) urged that the 999 year leaseholds ought to be included in the returns.

Viscount Halifax said that there would be great difficulty in ascertaining the precise tenure under which property was held. He quite agreed with the noble Marquess that returns of property held for 999 years, and of land under similar tenures, would appear as owners – and he thought it might be done. The valuation lists, however, to which he had referred, only gave information as to the ownership of land and the quantity owned. In his opinion the best plan would be to treat as owner the person immediately above the occupying tenant.

The Earl of Feversham (39,312 acres £34,328) suggested that the Returns should give a description of the land, stating whether it was in cultivation, woodland or moor.

> Viscount Halifax remarked that the Government could not undertake to state the description of the land. An attempt to do this would lead to inextricable confusion.

It sounds very much like five turkeys voting for Christmas, five turkeys holding between them 425,000 acres and with an income between them that is the equivalent of £22 million a year today. They got it. Yet these were not quite turkeys, but the red blooded, steel-clawed aristocracy of England, who, with their ancestors, had occupied one quarter of the planet and made themselves and their Queen the landlord thereof. Once 'Christmas' arrived they soon abolished the festival, with undue haste.

Derby and his colleagues had influence. Viscount Halifax, for example, was Lord Privy Seal and a member of the Cabinet. The debate of February 1872 lasted a little over 40 minutes. It was enough to set the ball rolling. A little over two years later, on 22 July 1875, John Lambert, the Secretary of the Local Government Board, presented the completed Return for England and Wales to Parliament.

The Compilation of the Return

The reason that Halifax was so confident that the Return could be compiled was that all the statements and information to be contained in the Return, with the exception of the addresses of the owners, were derived from the valuation lists, made out for the purposes of rating, in every parish. There were around 15,000 parishes in the four countries, containing around 5,000,000 separate assessments. However, despite the scale of effort involved, so well structured was the parish system that the Return was completed in a little over two years.

In addition to the report on the House of Lords debate which had preceded the order for the Return, the English and Welsh Return also included an introduction by John Lambert, the Secretary to the Local Government Board in 1875. According to this introduction, the Return was intended to show three things:

1. The number and names of owners of one acre and upwards, whether built upon or not, in each county, with the estimated acreage and annual gross estimated rental of the property belonging to each owner.
2. The number of owners of land, whether built upon or not, of less than one acre, with the estimated aggregate acreage and the aggregate gross estimated rental of the lands of such owners.
3. The estimated extent of commons and waste lands in each county.[8]

The Accuracy of the Return

Lambert indicated that, in theory, all that needed to be done to compile the Return, 'would be simply a consolidation for each county of the information contained in the valuation lists and rate books for the parishes in the county'. In other words, a record of all the acreage actually existed throughout the country – it was only a matter of pulling it all together. However,

> The first examination of the returns disclosed nearly 250,000 defects, and these have since had to be cleared up, as far as possible by correspondence and other means of inquiry. In many instances the clerks were unable to

furnish the additional particulars required, and in those cases amounting to several thousands, applications were addressed to the overseers of the separate parishes in order to obtain from them the necessary information.

Theory and reality were very different things, even in the apparently well-regulated administration of parish life in Victorian England. Lambert laments 'that the parish lists were defective, especially as regards the names of owners, and notwithstanding all the pains which have been taken, it is to be feared that many inaccuracies will be found in some of the detail of the return.'

The reason for this was simple enough. As real ownership of most of the land was concentrated in very few hands, a vast amount of sub letting, via tenancies, leases and other forms of tenure, were inevitable if the land was to be worked at all. This is what happened and in many of the parishes the name entered was that of the person paying the rates, frequently the tenant or lease holder, rather than the actual owner.

In fact, in a charmless example of the invidious hand of real power, the law actually did not require the disclosure of the real owner's names, and the clerks making up the Return could not resort to legal compulsion to get those names. Lambert's comment was that, 'Neither the valuation lists nor the rates would be invalidated if the owners were omitted altogether.' Ironically, the one place which did compel disclosure of owner's names under the 1867 Finance Act was the metropolis, the one place that was not included in the Return.

One of the earliest problems the compilers faced was how to determine who owned land subject to a long-term lease. In line with the terms of the debate in the Lords, leaseholders with 999 year leases were deemed owners. Eventually it was decided that leases of over 99 years, or with a right of perpetual renewal, 'should be considered as owners'. Lambert did note that '. . . it is not easy, with the various tenures of property in this country, to lay down a precise rule as to what constitutes ownership.'

Amongst the other defects identified by Lambert were the periodic appearance of corporate acres under the name of the individual acting as trustee or guardian. This may account for the absence in the subsequent Return of much of the Duchy of Lancaster acreage. Then there was another delightful problem, that of people with the same name. Lambert describes the problem thus:

> With reference to some of the Welsh counties, where there are large numbers of owners of the same Christian and surnames e.g. the county of Cardigan, where the name David Davies occurs above 53 times, and John Jones above 70 times, will show the labour involved in this branch of the inquiry, and it may be added that, independently of other inquiries, upwards of 300,000 separate applications had to be sent to the clerks in order to clear up questions in reference to duplicate entries.

Calculating the Rental Income

Lambert also refers to the problem of figures looking distorted where small acreages represent large rentals. In the Return in general the rental for agricultural land per acre was between £1 and £2 per annum, yet:

Sir William Neville Abdy Bt, of Albyns, Stapleford Abbots, Romford (Essex):

County	Acres	Rental Value
Essex	2903	£3990
Berks	170	£220
Surrey	48	£5500
Total	**3121**	**£9710**

A mere 1.5% of Abdy's acres provides more than 50% of his income. The clue, as Lambert points out, is 'the value of coal worked below its surface'.

A more interesting sample, assembled from the Return by John Bateman in *Great Landowners of Great Britain and Ireland*,[9] is that of the Marquess of Anglesey, who lived at Beaudesert Park, Lichfield, Staffordshire. His acres yielded him an annual income of £110,598, the modern equivalent of £7,735,000.

The Marquess of Anglesey:

County	Acres	Rental value
Stafford	17,441	£91,304
Anglesea	9620	£9784
Derby	1559	£8696
Dorset	1117	£814
Total	**29,737**	**£110,598**

His Stafford acres, all based in the then thriving potteries, where clay mining provided income alongside the industrial and tenement rents, were yielding more than six times his agricultural acres in Dorset. A similar situation arose on his Derby acreage, which benefited from the coalfields there.

Because the basis for both rent and valuation has changed so much, it is worth going back to Lambert for an explanation as to how the figures were calculated. 'Gross estimated rentals,' he indicates, were calculated with some care by the parish clerks, 'because it is the basis on which the rateable value is determined.' He then goes on to explain how the system worked:

> It must, however, always be borne in mind that the amount of the gross esimated rental as shown in the Parish Returns and consequently in this Return, is not the amount of the rent payable to the person under whose name as owner it appears, but the amount of the entire rents which the occupying tenant of the whole property would be presumed to pay to their immediate leasors.

He notes that in the case of agricultural land, which constituted the bulk of the acreage covered in the Returns, 'The item "gross estimated rental" is intended to show the rent at which the property might reasonably be expected to be let from year to year, the tenant undertaking to pay all usual tenant's rates and taxes and tithe commutation.' Lambert notes that 'the value contained in this column will probably be found not to differ widely from the actual rental of the owner.'

It is important to note that property which was not rated, for whatever reason, was not included in the Return. Neither, of course, was it shown in the Parish Returns. Coal mines were rated, whereas lead, iron and other mines were not. Woodland, unless it contained saleable underwood, was not recorded.

Waste and Common Land

The third item on the stated aims of the Returns was to determine 'The estimated extent of commons and waste lands in each county.' This was quite a controvertial matter, particularly because of the links between common land and the infamous enclosures of the previous two centuries.

The term 'enclosure' in the history of English landownership refers to the appropriation of waste or common land. While this is often thought to involve land which had no defined owner, in fact common land was commonly 'owned' by a principal landowner or noble, but the terms of that ownership was that it was land held in trust for the use of the common people. The enclosures, according to Mingay[10] proceeded in three ways. First there was the creation of closes (closed land), taken out of common fields by their owners – by 1750 this had led to the loss of up to half the common fields of many English villages. Secondly, there was enclosure by proprietors, owners who acted together, usually small farmers or squires, leading to the enclosure of whole parishes. Finally there were enclosures by Acts of Parliament. Mingay, quoting John Chapman in the *Agricultural History Review*,[11] says that the Parliamentary acts had enclosed 8.4 million acres of England and Wales by the mid nineteenth century. The outcome of those three forms of enclosure are disclosed in the Return in the shape of the huge estates they revealed.

However, despite the enclosures, some common and some waste land still existed in the United Kingdom in 1872.

It is possible that one of the more covert purposes of the Return may have been to see how much more land was available for appropriation by the landowners, in both commons and waste. As it turned out there was quite a lot, some 1,524,648 acres. Lambert's comment was:

> There is great uncertainty as to the lands under this heading [Commons & Waste]. If they yield no profit they are not rated, and are not included in the valuation lists, and it is only where a parish map or survey has shown the extent of those lands that the clerk to the guardians or the parish officers could be expected to state the area accurately. In other cases an estimate, more or less conjectural, of the actual extent is all the information which could be obtained.

In general, however, almost none of the criticism later levelled at the accuracy of the Return was not anticipated and articulated by Lambert. The shortcomings could have been remedied had more time been available to the compilers, and indeed many of the errors were remedied by John Bateman in his four editions of *Great Landowners of Great Britain and Ireland*. More important, the basic information was in such discrete chunks – the parishes – that a survey of virtually 100% coverage was possible, if the additional time and effort had been invested. The post-completion criticisms of the Return were inherent in the project before it was undertaken, and were well known to the bureaucrats. Further, the undertaking of the Return, ordered as it was by the overwhelming authority of the government and the opposition in tandem, is a stirring example of how the limitations of bureaucracy can be beaten. Had those opposed to it been able to create a secret cabal in Whitehall, or make their secret application to the men of power, they would have been able to stop the project. The potential defects were manifestly there and could have been made to look crippling. The only thing that could deal with the bureaucratic objections was the project itself.

The point to make, since the criticisms persist in academia and are used in landowning circles, is that the overwhelming purpose of *The Return of Owners of Land* was achieved. From both a statistical and pragmatic point of view the Return is valid and safe to use as a working tool for determining of the ownership of most of the land of England, Scotland, Ireland and Wales in 1872. The Returns are much safer than the original or 'mythologised' Domesday, which was neither a contemporary record of land ownership, nor was it more than 5% or 10% accurate. It only covered part of England. The Return is safer, in addition, than the present land registry system across all four countries, which has a huge gap in the English and Welsh version, is not universally accessible and cannot provide, at less than utterly prohibitive cost, the comprehensive information provided in the 1872 Return. Further, the errors in the 1872 Return were detailed by its compilers in such a way that anyone sufficiently interested could have easily rectified them at local level. In addition, there was a local record which does not now exist, to consult. Indeed, the whole catastrophe of centralisation, and its hidden effect, and the beneficiaries of that effect, are laid bare by the Return and what happened to it. Once upon a time every person in England, Wales, Scotland and Ireland, was within walking distance of a free list of those landowners who most affected their lives, at the local parish office. In the last 120 years the parishes have not been abolished, but their land-owning records have. In the meantime, all formal tax on land has also been abolished, and the specific taxes which have been substituted have placed the larger burden of taxes on the smallest landowners, domestic homeowners, while removing it altogether on the largest landowners. In addition, the larger landowners, whose identity cannot be established, are in receipt of subsidy to the tune of £4 billion annually.

The Publication of the Return

The Return of Owners of Land was published in a number of separate parts. The completion of each country's return was first announced during Parliamentary proceedings; at a later stage each was published in book format by the Stationery Office. First past the post was Scotland, where the Inland Revenue had charge of the production of the Return. Angus Fletcher, Comptroller-General of the Inland Revenue, delivered the Scottish version in two parts, one for the areas outside boroughs of more than 20,000 inhabitants, the other for the boroughs themselves. The price of the 211-page work was two shillings and thruppence (about £8.75 today).

The next part of the Return to appear was that for England and Wales, in two massive volumes, delivered on 25 July 1875 by John Lambert, Secretary of the Local Government Board. Volume One contained returns from Bedford to Norfolk, and was priced at ten shillings and six pence (about £35 today). The second volume covered Northampton to York, and included all of Wales, again at ten shillings and six pence. Both volumes were published in book form later that year. The last volume, that for the whole island of Ireland, was printed in Dublin and delivered on 20 April 1876 by B. Banks, Secretary to the Local Government Board, Ireland. It was divided up by the four ancient provinces of Ireland, and cost three shillings and six pence.

The reaction to and interest in the Return was immediate. John Bateman, the country squire whose *Great Landowners of Great Britain and Ireland* did most to keep the survey alive, noted:

> Not only have Mr Frederick Purdy and others analysed it, Mr Lyulph Stanley abused it, Mr John Bright moved its digestion in the House and the *Spectator* and other London journals scathingly criticised it, but the immense herd of country newspapers have actually reproduced it, as far as their own neighbourhoods are concerned, in their columns, much, probably, to the satisfaction of the bulk of their readers, to whom twenty-six shillings ... is prohibitory.

At national level three main approaches emerged to the Return, in particular the English volumes of 1875, all more or less consistent with the politics of the key newspapers of the day. Professor Spring spells them out as follows:

> *The Times*, Tory in its politics, declared with evident satisfaction that 'the legend of 30,000 landowners has been found to be as mythical as that of St Ursula and her company of 10,000 virgins.' *The Daily News*, Liberal in its politics, complained that the aggregate figure of English and Welsh landowners was useless, that 'persons who have theories or prejudices or interests concerning what is commonly called the land question, are not thinking of fragments of land of less than an acre.'[12]
>
> The *Spectator*, also Liberal, and the most illuminating perhaps of the great weeklies, took the discussion furthest. The point of its first article was that 'neither Mr Bright nor Lord Derby is wholly in the wrong. On the one hand nearly a million of persons [972,836] in England and Wales outside London own a freehold, be it only a house, or a garden, or a patch of building.' On the other hand, by dint of some hasty researches in the Returns, the *Spectator* estimated that landowners, 'in the political sense – in the sense in which the word has always been present to Mr Bright's mind' – numbered only 43,000. These were owners of 100 acres or more – that is they were persons of some political influence. Moreover, the *Spectator* argued, 'this 43,000 is in practice influenced by a much smaller number, the great territorialists, who claim the right, usually conceded to them, to lead opinion in country districts.'

Some weeks later the *Spectator* described precisely who those 'territorialists' were, publishing what it called 'the true Libro d'Oro of England, a nominal roll of every man in England and Wales who possesses 5000 acres in any one county and therefore belongs to the Territorial Aristocracy.' These comprised 710 persons, titled and untitled, the 'Seven Hundred'. According to the *Spectator*,

... the total result is a most extraordinary one, and one that would justify any club which interests itself in the repeal of the Land Laws, in expending a few hundreds [pounds] in a short but thoroughly complete analysis of 'Domesday Book'. Whatever else is certain about the position of English landlords, this one fact is certain. Seven hundred and ten individuals own more than a fourth of the soil of England and Wales, exclusive of lakes, roads, rivers, London, waste spaces and Crown property, and within a fraction of a fourth of the entire geographical area of the country. And those 710 own also, immediately or in reversion, one seventh of the entire rental of the kingdom, a proportion which, if London could be included, would be very greatly increased ... Mr Bright was undoubtedly wrong in believing that Englishmen have been divorced from the soil ... but was as undoubtedly right in believing that a most limited number of gentlemen ... wield still an enormous territorial and political influence. They own a fourth of the Kingdom – more probably, than the same class in any country in Europe, unless it be Hungary or Bohemia.

There was a substantial reaction in Scotland in 1874 when the Scottish Return was published. The *Highlander*, an Inverness paper with a radical proprietor, John Murdoch, began a campaign that led eventually to the creation of the Highland Land Reform Association by Professor Blackie, amongst others, in 1883.[13] In Ireland, the publication of the Return was greeted with predictable outrage by the Land League and by many others, though it added little to what was already known, merely consolidating it in one, easily read, place.

However, clearly evident from the moment they were published was that the Return was enormously important both politically and economically. The biggest landowners in the four countries were all aristocrats, they were all essentially British, not Scottish, Irish or Welsh, and they were almost all interrelated. Not only did they belong to the very top of the socio-economic scale, almost every one of the top 100 landowners were also members of the House of Lords at a time when the upper house had considerable powers. The most influential politicians in the House of Lords at the time were almost certainly the Dukes, whose holdings made engaging reading.

TABLE 3/1

		1872 landholding (acres)	Income value	2001 equivalent income value	2001 landholding acres
1	Duke of Sutherland	1,358,545	£141,667	£9,916,690	12,000
2	Duke of Buccleuch	460,108	£217,163	£15,201,410	270,700
3	Duke of Fife	249,220	£72,563	£5,079,410	1600
4	Duke of Richmond	286,411	£79,683	£5,577,810	12,000
5	Duke of Devonshire	198,572	£180,750	£12,652,500	73,000
6	Duke of Argyll	175,114	£50,842	£3,558,940	60,800
7	Duke of Atholl	201,604	£42,030	£2,942,100	148,000 with trustees
8	Duke of Northumberland	186,397	£176,048	£12,348,560	132,200
9	Duke of Montrose	103,447	£24,872	£1,741,040	8800
10	Duke of Hamilton	157,386	£73,636	£5,154,520	12,600 with trustees

All top ten dukes owned over 100,000 acres each. And for those who might claim that much of the acreage was Scottish moorland, it is worth perusing the value of the rentals expressed in present-day value in the right hand column. There is one major omission here. The then Marquess of Westminster, only later a duke, is shown in the Return with only 19,749 acres, none of them in London (which wasn't included in the Return). Bateman's *Great Landowners of Great Britain and Ireland* notes that if Westminster's London acres and rentals had been shown, he would probably top the list in money terms. The Marquess's income was believed to be over £300,000 a year, worth about £21 million today.

Bateman's book listed all landowners with more than 3000 acres and an income of £3000 a year, the modern equivalent of £210,000. By the time he had done his final counting, for the fourth (1883) edition of his book, he had been persuaded to include the Return for both Ireland and Scotland. However, a vital point for future scholars was the number of people he included in his first list in 1876, which was 1500. This was based mainly on the English volumes, but included Wales, more or less. While this would have left out many entrants from *Burke's Landed Gentry*,[14] it bore a remarkable resemblance to the 1400 tenants-in-chief appointed by William in the 1086 Domesday.[15] It argues that the relationship between power and landownership had changed little in the interval, with the two great subsequent land grabs, those of Henry VIII and Cromwell, merely redistributing the spoils to people at about the same level of society as that at which William had chosen to do so more than 500 years earlier – in other words some to trusted lieutenants, most of them aristocrats, and more to men who had emerged as military commanders, some from humble backgrounds, most from the equivalent of the squirearchy. If the manors (and then the parishes) were the bedrock of both administration and taxation in post-conquest England, then they largely remained the same in Victorian England. In summary, there were different dukes and different earls, but the same distribution of large acreages at the top.

Interpreting the Return — the role of John Bateman

With the publication of the Return, the lines of the debate had been drawn. As Professor Spring notes, Lord Derby and those on his side of the debate, while inevitably continuing to defend the value and reality of large estates, kept remarkably silent about the small number of large owners and the size of their estates. The way they chose to interpret the Return is succinctly put by Bateman:

> A lie of this kind [that there were only 30,000 landowners in Great Britain] was the original cause of the compilation of the much-abused 'Return of Landowners 1873' – viz, that in the census tables of [1861][16] some 30,000 persons only were entered under the head of 'Landowners'. Which so-called fact was much gloated over by those who would fain apply Mr Bright's 'blazing principles' to our existing land system. This lie vanished with the publication of the Government return of 1873, in the year 1876; the landowners being found to come to something like a million.

The lie did not so much vanish as be replaced by another one. And the propaganda of the landowners, as exemplified by Bateman, not only won the day against any immediate reform, at least in England, Wales and Scotland, but set the course for the burial of the Return.

Bright and his Radicals simply did not possess enough power to cause anything to happen in England or Scotland. Nor was their radicalism real in any meaningful modern sense. The die in Ireland had already been cast, as John Bateman observed in his characteristically un-politically correct way: 'In half that distracted kingdom [Ireland] the peasantry are now virtually owners of the soil – paid for though it may have been, and in many cases was, with Saxon cash, the fruit of Saxon toil and industry.'

To this he added a remark that was quite prescient, given that most of the big Irish estates were on the way out. 'Or do they [the Irish landowners] consider that Irish proprietorship is so utterly illusory under the present regime that to correct [the Return] is a work of supererogation?' He made this remark having had only two of the Irish landowners bother to correct their acreage. This compared with the hundreds of English, Welsh and Scottish landowners who had been in touch with him over errors as small as incorrect initials.

In the context of all subsequent debate on the Return, Bateman's role was vital. The four volumes of the 1872 Return listed the owners of more than one acre, in alphabetic order, within each county of the four countries, a total of 116 counties. The total number of names and addresses printed was 269,547 for England and Wales, 19,225 for Scotland and 32,614 for Ireland. The names and addresses of owners of less than an acre were not printed, but came to 671,667 in England, 31,622 in Wales, 113,005 in Scotland and 36,144 in Ireland. What John Bateman did in *The Great Landowners of Great Britain and Ireland* was to consolidate and correct the landholdings of those landholders with more than £3000 in annual income, and more than 3000 acres. In the case of England and Wales, this produced about 1500 entries for Bateman's first edition, called the *Acreocracy of England*, published in 1876.[17] Over the next five years he amended and corrected his summary further, eventually producing a book of 2500 entries, including those holding just 2000 acres and with an income of £2000 a year. His entries also contained details of parliamentary, military and government service as well as schools, universities and clubs.

There are few books in the last 120 years which have addressed the issue of land in the UK, in whatever form, which have not referred to Bateman and regarded it as a summary of the 1872 Return.[18] Few, if any, however, have taken the time to look at this very unusual man. For Bateman's role in the wider debate about landownership is a bit of a contradiction – he was a landowner, and very much from that class, yet he seemed so confident of the system of landownership, and so engrossed in his statistical analysis of it, that he didn't notice the threat to the landowning class wider knowledge would bring. Others, however, did. In his introduction to the Leicester University Press reprint of the 4th edition of Bateman in 1970, Professor David Spring notes that *The Times* in its obituary in 1910 failed to mention that Bateman was the author of the four editions of the summary of the Return. Professor Spring gives no indication of Bateman's background, other than to say that he came from an established Staffordshire family.

In fact the family originally came from Westmoreland and were descended from Robert Branthwayt, keeper of the Tower of London in the time of James I and VI. Branthwayt's estates at Carlinghill came to one John Bateman, the Lord of the Manor of Tolson, also in Westmoreland, when he married the granddaughter of Robert

Branthwayt. The Carlinghill estates were sold off and Bateman's son, also John, bought the Knypersley Hall estate in Staffordshire. John Bateman became High Sheriff of Staffordshire in 1830 and he was succeeded by James Bateman, the author John Bateman's father, in 1858. Once again a new estate appears, that of Biddulph Grange near Congleton in Cheshire, as Tolson and the Westmoreland connection ended.

James Bateman was an unusual country squire, firstly in owning two large estates, secondly in the range of his education and activities. He was an Oxford MA, a Fellow of the Royal Society and a Deputy Lieutenant of Staffordshire. His one published work was *Orchidacae of Mexico and Guatamala*, a rare early book on orchids in those two countries. He married Maria-Sybella Egerton Warburton, daughter of a landed cleric with 7562 acres at Northwich in Cheshire. They had four children: Katherine married the son of Charles Granby Burke, Master of the Common Pleas in Ireland; Rowland took holy orders and was rector of Fawley in Bucks; Robert lived in various places in Wiltshire, Somerset and Shropshire, and married a daughter of the Dean of Lichfield, who was himself a member of the Howard family, relatives of the Duke of Norfolk and one of the largest landowning families of all in Britain. John Bateman, the author, born in 1839, was educated at Trinity College Cambridge and married the Hon Jessie Caroline-Bootle-Wilbraham, sister of the 2nd Lord Skelmersdale, in 1865. Skelmersdale later became the Earl of Lathom, a title now extinct. The Barony of Skelmersdale, however, still continues, and the 7th Lord Skelmersdale, a minister in the Lords throughout the Thatcher years, has maintained the family interest in horticulture as a director of Broadleigh Nurseries in Somerset.

It was through this connection that John Bateman was connected directly to the Imperial palace, where his brother-in-law was a lord-in-waiting, later a Captain of the Yeoman of the Guard and finally Lord Chamberlain to Queen Victoria, from 1885 to 1892 and again from 1895 to 1898. He owned 7213 acres in Lancashire. Skelmersdale's wife was the only daughter of the 4th Earl of Clarendon, who owned 2298 acres at Ware in Herts. Her brother, the 5th Earl of Clarendon, having been lord-in-waiting to the Queen when her husband was Lord Chamberlain, in turn became the Lord Chamberlain to Victoria's son Edward VII from 1901 to 1905. In Imperial Britain the Lord Chamberlain was probably the second most influential person in the Empire, after the Prime Minister. Which, given that the palace was not generally approving of 'writin' people', may explain why John Bateman's obituary in *The Times* overlooked his publishing career and why his only other publication was a series of eight articles in the local paper *The Essex County Standard* in 1882, on a trip he made from Essex to South America, entitled 'From the Colne to the Plate'.

Bateman came into his inheritance in 1897 when his father died. By that time John Bateman had moved south, first to Bromley and finally to Brightlingsea Hall on the banks of the river Colne in Essex. At Brightlingsea he had 1413 acres, with a further 2997 acres in County Mayo in Ireland. The two together, with an income of £3045, earned him an entry in his own book. Prior to his move south, Bateman served as Deputy Lieutenant of Staffordshire, and later served as a magistrate (Justice of the Peace) on the Essex bench. He was also an original member of the Essex County Council and a member of the Brightlingsea Urban District Council. He was chairman of the Harwich Division of the Conservative and Unionist Association, and chairman of the Lexden and Winstree branch of the same body. Professor Spring notes that Bateman was 'an agricultural improver, an experimenter in forestry and tobacco growing who had firm ideas about proper ensilage. He was kindly to his dependants, to Nonconformists no less than to Anglicans.'[19] Bateman's only daughter, Agnes Mary, who married Captain Robert Maxwell D'Arcy Hildyard of Colborn Hall in Yorkshire, was divorced in 1906, something quite rare at the time and of considerable potential scandal because of her father and mother's palace connections. There is no mention of grandchildren.

Another generally overlooked connection was that John Bateman's wife's aunt was the wife of the three-times Prime Minister, the 14th Earl of Derby, and the mother of the 15th Earl of Derby, the man who launched the Return. Bateman had a home in London at 1 Whitehall Gardens, very close to parliament, the palace and government.

Professor Spring speculates on why, given his close associations with the landowning classes ostensibly threatened by wider promulgation of the Return, Bateman compiled the books and why he contributed to George Brodrick's *English Land and English Landlords*, a later book which did much to undermine and destroy the Return? He concludes that Bateman probably loved doing it, even to the extent of believing his book to be a labour of love. There was no doubt that Bateman believed in landowning. To him it was the God-given order of things, 'the Lord in his castle, the peasant at the gate'. He could not conceive of a society ordered on a different basis. It is likely that Bateman regarded Brodrick's book as one as steadfastly rooted as his own in the idea of landownership by an elite as the foundation stone of society. Throughout his commentary, reproduced at various points in this book, it is clear that, while he may have been clever and articulate, Bateman was seriously and stridently dogmatic. But what confuses the modern enquirer such as Professor Spring is that Bateman's dogmatism was practical, inherited, and fully reflective of the attitudes and beliefs of the strata of society in which he moved and lived.

In addition to his interpretation of the 1872 Return, Bateman proved a valuable commentator in a number of other ways. Firstly, he was able to summarise landownership in England and Wales as never before. Reproduced here is a table (3/2) compiled, in fact, for George Brodrick's book. Two additional columns have been added to Bateman's original, one to give the average holding of the class identified by Bateman, the other to give the approximate percentage of England and Wales held by that class. A row has also been added below cottagers, to show the population as a whole, and the percentage of the population which was represented in the sample. Nothing better shows the real feudal mind of both Bateman and the rest of the landowners at the time than the fact that all his tables and statistics, with the exception of the Returns themselves, omit the non-landowning population, which was most of the population. Only landowners counted in the political equation; lacklands were of no consideration. Paradoxically, the numbers such as those in the Return and in Bateman's book would only excite the masses, as well as people like Gladstone, who aspired to lead the masses.

It is worth noting that nothing even approximating to this table could be constructed today. There is simply no way of establishing to the level of detail shown below, which is after all only down as far as six social classes, who owns the land of the United Kingdom now.

TABLE 3/2

No. of Owners	Class	Extent in acres	% acres	Average holding (acres)	% of pop
400	Peers & peeresses	5,728,979	16.5%	14,322	0.002
1288	Great landowners	8,497,699	24.6%	6597	0.006
2529	Squires	4,319,271	12.5%	1797	0.012
9585	Greater Yeomen	4,782,627	13.8%	499	0.049
24,412	Lesser Yeomen	4,144,272	12.0%	169	0.125
217,049	Small Proprietors	3,931,806	11.3%	18	1.1
703,289	Cottagers	151,148	0.4%	0.2	3.6
958,552	**Total**				4.9
18,499,457	Remainder of pop	Nil	nil		95.1
14,459	The Crown, barracks, prisons, lighthouses, etc.	165,427			
	Religious, education, philanthropic	947,655			
	Commercial & Misc.	330,436			
	Waste (& Commons)	1,524,624			
Total		**34,523,974**			

Interestingly, one of the significant items to emerge in the Returns and shown in Bateman's table was the very large volume of waste and common land then existing in England and Wales. Delineated and identified waste and common land came to 1,524,648 acres, or 4.4% of the acreage of the two countries. That was actually a larger area than was occupied by dwelling places – urbanised – at the time. Those waste and common lands have apparently expanded in the past 128 years to 2,988,349 acres, without any very clear explanation of why this has happened.

Bateman's take on the subject, however, sheds some light on the landowners' attitude to waste and commons land.

> But on what principles can one reconcile figures like the following – Kent – waste, five thousand odd acres, Surrey – forty thousand? Kent is more than twice the size of Surrey, and as a fact contains, though perhaps in smaller proportion to its area, quite as much 'heath', 'common' and 'chart' as Surrey. We must guess that in the rate-books of Kent those wastes swell the estates of the Lords of the Manor.

While Bateman shows us some of the minor problems connected with waste and common land, that does not end the matter. When the Return for England and Wales was finally completed, there was a discrepancy of almost 3 million acres. This is about 7.4% of the land area of the two countries. Looking at Table 1 (see Chapter One) we find something that should, in theory, be impossible. Lands unaccounted for in England and Wales come to 3,123,844 acres, a little more than the lands unaccounted for in the 1872 Return. In other words, 128 years of British history have produced almost the same level of error in land statistics as the men with the quill pens and the cloth tithe maps produced all those years ago.

Making a Living on the Land in 1876

Another of Bateman's insights into landownership in the nineteenth century was his entertaining illustration of an imaginary landowner.

He states: 'For the benefit of the guileless fundholders who have not as yet dabbled in land, I will give them what I consider a fair specimen of what a "landed income" of £5000 a year means when analysed.' The accounts for his typical £5000-a-year squire, John Steadyman of Wearywork Hall, Cidershire, were as follows:

	Acres	Gross annual value	Equivalent value 2001
	3500	£5000	£350,000
Deduct for value in the rate books put upon Mansion, grounds, fish ponds etc.		220	£15,400
Deduct also the value put upon cottages lived in by old workmen and pensioners of late Mr Steadyman		30	£2100
[Total deductions]		250	£17,500
Leaving a clear rent roll of		**£4750**	**£332,500**

Now deduct as under.

His late father's two maiden sisters, Jane and Esther Steadyman, who each have a rent charge of £180 per annum. (N.B. Both these old ladies seem immortal)	360	£25,500
His mother, Lady Louisa Steadyman, a rent charge of	700	£49,000
His sisters, Louisa, Marian and Eva (all plain) each £150	450	£31,500
His brother, Wildbore Steadyman, who was paid off and emigrated, but almost annual comes down on the good-natured head of the family for say	50	£3500
Mortgage on Sloppyside Farm and Hungry Hill (started when his father contested the county) interest	650	£45,500
Do. on Wearywork End (started when his one pretty sister married Sir Shortt Shortt, Bart, and was paid off) interest	150	£10,500
His estate agent, Mr Harrable, salary	150	£10,500
Keep a horse for do., £35; house for do., £45	80	£5600
Average of lawyer's bill (settlements, conveyances, etc.)	60	£4200
Average cost of farm repairs, etc.	350	£24,500
Draining tiles furnished gratis to the tenants	40	£2800
Repairs to the family mansion	70	£4900
Voluntary church rate, school at Wearywork, do. at Wearywork End, pension and purely local charities (N.B. - If Mr Steadyman is a Roman Catholic, which I do not think he is, a private chaplin, chapel, school, etc. would increase this to at least £225 (£15,750))	175	£12,250
Subscription to county (Liberal or Tory) registration fund	10	£700
Do. to the Cidershire Foxhounds (£25) & Boggymore Harriers (£5)	30	£2100
Do. to Diocesan -? (everything now-a-days is Diocesan, we shall soon be taking pills from Diocsean dispensaries)	25	£1750
Other county subscriptions – hospitals, flower shows, races, etc.	35	£2450
Returned 15% of rents in 'hard Times averaging perhaps one year in five (would that we could say so now in 1882)	150	£10,500
Loss on occasional bankrupt tenants (Mr Harrable dislikes distraint), average	30	£2100

	Acres	Gross annual value	Equivalent value 2001
Arrears of rent, say annually £300 loss of interest at 5%		15	£1050
Income tax at 4p in the £ on rents paid and unpaid		83	£5810
Insurance on all buildings		55	£3850
Total		£3718	£260,260
Leaving our worthy squire the magnificent annual sum of		£1032	£72,240

Bateman had no successor, and as with the Return, there is no modern equivalent to his amusing and probably averagely accurate account of an average squire's yearly finances. But we do have a glimpse of the radically changed circumstances of landowners in East Anglia, especially when compared with the right hand column added to the Bateman description.

Today, a 3000 acre estate in East Anglia, minus a home farm of 200 acres, will rent the remaining 2800 acres for between £200 and £300 an acre.[20] This will yield about £840,000 before expenses. This is nearly three times the equivalent rental at the time of the Return, and in a sector that claims to be impoverished and ill used. Admittedly, Bateman's tax of 1.6%, is now two taxes, PAYE and NI, averaging 30%, and Corporation Tax, averaging about 20–25%, but very few companies, or farms, pay the full tax, on the full income, which will have innumerable expenses deducted from it.

Bateman and Ireland

Bateman is eloquent about Ireland, viciously eloquent. If we look at his entry in the Returns, we can see why.

Bateman, John, of Brightlingsea, Colchester

	Acres	Income value	2001 eqivalent
Co. Mayo	2997	£135	£9450
Essex	1413	£2910	£203,700

His 3000 Irish acres were yielding him all but nothing at all, whereas, his Essex acres were returning an annual rental of over £2 each (£140 equivalent), twice the overall national average in the Return as a whole. His overall view of the place is that 'Ireland is Nature's buffer and umbrella to break the wild violence of the storms so oft and so unkindly sent us from New York, and the gutter to carry off the superfluous rain. England thereby benefits.'

He suggests that Ireland's main problem is 'the want of bright sunshine' and that the best solution to the Irish problem is to cultivate cattle. This, however, was a secondary cause of the famine, in that while there were sufficient cattle in the country to feed the population, they were exported by John Bateman and his peers.

It is worth remembering that Bateman was making his remarks just 25 years after one out of every two of the Irish population had either died in the potato famine or emigrated. Many of Bateman's tenants, who lived in one of the worst affected areas, would have been the sole survivors of whole families wiped out by starvation or emigration. Yet Bateman's attack on his Irish tenants is little short of racist:

> [T]he Irish coasts swarm with fish which they seldom even try to catch. Any capitalist who introduces a new manufacture or handicraft is sure to suffer in purse, even if he escapes a bullet in the head.

Nor is it shy of perpetuating stereotypes, particularly those Bateman and his predecessors had created by economic and political oppression.

> Why, again, may I ask, is it that an Irishman will only dig a pratie out of his own easily dug, friable peat soil? He does not care for the same job on the stiffer lands of New York, Ohio, or Illinois. No; he severely sticks to town life and its joy, the whiskey shop; he hardly ever enters the country parts of Yankee land. No; the industrious Irish peasant, as I know him best in County Mayo, loves to work ten minutes, then to rest on his long handled spade for another twenty, then perhaps he does a furious spurt of labour for a quarter of an hour, which deserves to be rewarded, as it generally is, by well earned rest against the nearest cabin wall, and a pipe of tobacco as a soother, and so on ad lib. Irish soil for the Irish! – hurrah, t'would demean a bold peasant to delve in stiff clays, such as the East Saxon hirelings of our East Saxon agricultural prophet Mechi, delve and moil in, from six till six, or something like seven hours more work than the most industrious Galway or Mayo man ever did in a day.

The ultimate refutation of Bateman may have taken over one hundred years to come about, but it has arrived. Irish acres are now one third more valuable than English acres, and Irish economic growth is now four times higher than economic growth in England.[21] The Irish now work mostly for themselves, not for absentee owners who starved the country of capital while milking it of rents.

Killing the Return
One of the most intriguing mysteries of the recent history of landownership in Britain is the removal of *The Return of Owners of Land* from the historic record. It was one of the greatest single achievements of Victorian statistical inquiry, and yet it lies buried and forgotten at a time when its supposed successor, the current Land Registry, is unable to disclose the owners of huge tracts of England and Wales, owners whose ancestors and whose acres were fully revealed in the Returns. The removal and suppression of the Returns can fairly be said to have changed both the economic and legal history of the United Kingdom, to the serious constitutional and fiscal health of the majority of the citizens of the country.

By 1880, the Return was, to all intents and purposes, a dead issue. There were three main reasons for this. The first was the unwelcome media attention the Return brought to the landowners in the countryside. Bateman noted that 'the immense herd of country newspapers have actually reproduced it as far as their own neighbourhoods are concerned', and very few local landowners liked it. It is a phenomenon paralleled today whereby the titled rich like everyone to know who they are and what they are through the pages of *Debrett's*, but are rather less than amused when someone puts a figure, as the *Sunday Times* Rich List does, to their fortunes. So too the landed of the 1870s when a number was put on their acres and the value of those acres. The initial hostility was local, personal, and widespread. This was buttressed by Parliamentary criticism of the detailed inaccuracies, especially by the Earl of Derby's relative in the Commons, Lyulph Stanley. Finally, there was the reaction of the Palace, which then had enormous influence over both government and society and which played a neatly discreet hand in demolishing the most important statistical work of its era.

It is also worth noting the role played, or rather not played, by Bright. Having started the controversy in Parliament, Bright failed to follow it through, by way of instituting either a Land Commission, or by any other measure. Bright was never the radical that history, and particularly the history of this issue, makes him appear. When he might have been following through on the combined revelations of the Return and Bateman, he opted instead to became Chancellor of the Duchy of Lancaster in Gladstone's second ministry in 1881, and to oppose his Prime Minister on the issue of Home Rule for Ireland, over which he resigned in 1882. Cobden, his fellow rebel, had died in 1865.

Bright's resignation over Home Rule was based on his objection to giving the reins of government to Irish nationalists who, he declared, 'had made a mockery of Parliamentary government'. But by reacting to the political aspect of the Irish issue, he helped to obscure the land agitation underpinning the Irish question. From the landowners' point of view, Ireland had become not only ungovernable but unprofitable too. Many of them could see the Irish land purchase acts coming, as rents went unpaid and estates teetered on the edge of bankruptcy, and many of them feared a similar reaction in England, certainly in Scotland and Wales. John Bateman's faith in the system, and the divine right of landowners to exist forever as they existed in Victorian Britain, was not shared by the wiser and more prescient of his fellow landowners. The widespread publication of the details of the Return in the countryside had deeply unsettled the battalions of the landed gentry, the opponents of change and reform such as an expansion of the franchise. This was the class which effectively controlled Parliament. For the Lords the issue was as simple as Bateman's faith in the divine right of landowners to own. If it took three and a half years to get 28 titles registered in the Land Registry, it was going to take an age or two either to have the Return institutionalised or rendered into law if the Lords had anything to do with it. In fact an age or two was optimistic; it simply never happened.

A single book encapsulated and summed up the earlier attacks on the Return by Lyulph Stanley and the *Spectator*, and at the same time reflected the attitude within the Palace. The book *English Land and English Landlords* was published in 1881 by Cassel, Petter, Galpin and Co for the Cobden Club. Its author was the Hon George Brodrick, described in the 1916 edition of *Who Was Who*, as 'an active and earnest member of the liberal Unionist party from 1886'. Professor David Spring describes him as a Radical, although on what basis other than Brodrick's own claim is unclear. In actual fact he was the second son of the 7th Viscount Middleton, part beneficiary of an estate that ran to 3100 acres in Surrey and 6475 acres in Cork, together worth then £10,725 (£750,750 today). He lived at 11 Pall Mall in London and was the Warden of Merton College Oxford from 1881 until his death in 1903. He never married and unsuccessfully fought elections under the Liberal banner at Woodstock and in Monmouthshire. With the exception of his attack on the Return his publications were of excruciating turgidity and obscurity: *Ecclesiastical Judgements of the Privy Council*, produced jointly with the Dean of Ripon, was one; *Memorials of Merton* another. One indication of why this obscure Victorian worthy might have suddenly broken cover to write outside his normal subjects is his school, Eton. Another is his Palace connections: his father was Dean of Exeter and chaplain to Queen Victoria. His father first married a daughter of the Earl of Cardigan and secondly Brodrick's mother, a cousin. George Brodrick's nephew was Secretary of State for War from 1900 to 1903. All in all an arch establishment family.

Although *English Land and English Landlords* was published only five years after the publication of the last of the Returns, Brodrick does not mention them until page 157 of the 500-page book. He then disposes of the Return in just 15 pages, reprinting tables and comments specially prepared for him by John Bateman, while studiously ignoring their meaning.

With regard to the 1861 Census, which Bright had used to criticise the landowning system, and which eventually drove Derby to ask for the compilation of the Return, Brodrick is dismissive:

> In the Occupation Returns of the Census for 1861, only 30,766 persons described themselves as land-proprietors, and those figures were most persistently quoted as official evidence on the subject, in the face of the patent fact that about half the whole number were females.

In other words, they couldn't really be landowners at all. Which leads him to comment,

> At all events, the mere existence of so palpable a flaw in the return utterly destroyed its purpose of statistical argument.

So it's hardly a shock that he is unconvinced by the actual Return:

> The appearance of the 'New Domesday Book' as it was called, was the first step towards a thorough investigation of this question, which it ought to have finally set at rest. It purported to show that England and Wales, exclusive of the metropolis, were divided in 1874–5, among 972,836 proprietors in all, owning 33,013,514 acres, with a 'gross estimated rental' of £99,352,301. Of these proprietors, however, no less than 703,289, owning 151,171 acres, with a gross estimated rental of £29,127,679 were returned as possessors of less than one acre each . . . This Return, prepared by the Local Government Board, was represented as no more than 'proximately accurate' and a very cursory inspection sufficed to disclose errors of detail so numerous and important as to cast suspicion even upon its proximate accuracy . . . Further analysis of its contents has amply confirmed this suspicion, and although the New Domesday Book contains a mine of precious materials for an exhaustive treatise on the distribution of landed property in England and Wales, the actual figures given in it cannot be accepted, without large corrections, as the basis of any sound conclusion on the subject.

It is unlikely today that anyone would pay the slightest attention to the ramblings of an over-educated dullard such as Brodrick. Unfortunately, the dullard with the Palace connections sang with the establishment's most influential voice, from its most influential choir stall and everyone, but especially academia, joined the chorus.

So what had he so summarily dismissed? Only the first centralised, public record of land ownership to appear in any part of the United Kingdom in 790 years. His critique of the overall errors was made at a time when reputable scholars knew the scale of inaccuracy in the original Domesday, and when it was clear that they now had a replacement, but one which was largely accurate, or at least as accurate as the source documents and structures were. Not only that, John Bateman had proved conclusively that the Returns were easily correctible and Brodrick had included Bateman's corrected records in his treatise.

Brodrick points out that because the Returns 'do not include any property except that assessed to rates', they are effectively invalid. The actual terms of reference for the Returns excluded unrated land. Brodrick then criticises the Returns for not including waste and common lands, both of which are, as he notes, ignored in the rate books. He then describes the waste and commons columns as 'very rough and untrustworthy', ignoring the fact that, according to the terms of reference of the Returns, they did not need to be there at all. It is impossible to believe that Brodrick was not aware that the main errors in the Return were the result of inaccuracies and bad record keeping in the parishes. The source of the errors had been widely discussed for six years, a far greater length of time than it would have taken to rectify the actual errors in the Parish chancelleries – what the Victorians had was a manageable structure, with no element of it too great for a parish clerk or two to correct over a period no greater than it took to create the Return, a maximum of say four years. Most parishes were no more than 4000 acres in extent, and where they were larger seldom had more than one or two landowners.

Another of Brodrick's criticism's however, that of the 'unaccounted acres', sheds an interesting light on the additional probable scale of large landholdings in the country. According to Brodrick, the whole acreage of England and Wales was 37,319,221 acres, but only 33,013,514 acres plus 1,524,648 acres of waste actually appear in the Return. This left 2,781,063 acres unaccounted for. As we have seen, this is only slightly less than the 3,123,844 acres currently unaccounted for in the various Government statistics available in the year 2000. The Return did at least put a name to the owners of most of the rest of the island, and did not, unlike the present Land Registry, leave half the country blank as to ownership. Brodrick suggests that the missing acres 'must belong to great landowners, the real extent of whose estates is therefore very much understated, by virtue of this omission alone.'

He attacks the Returns because they did not include London, despite the fact that creators of the Return took the eminently sensible view that London would make the publication of the Return unmanageable, and would impede a rapid result. Brodrick complained that by leaving out London the total values for gross annual rental were misleading, but the London GAR was widely known anyhow, and what was of great value in the Return was the identification of the main rate payers outside London.

One of the most persistent criticisms of the Return, voiced by Brodrick as well as others, was double counting. It is fundamentally a spurious argument, in that the Returns were county based and the approach adopted did not allow for any form of grouping of estates by owner, such as Bateman made in his book. The very structure of land records in the parishes precluded the kind of consolidation that Brodrick argues for. Yet,

> The consequence of this slovenly and haphazard registration is that, instead of being a perfect record of 'owners' the New Domesday is, at best, an imperfect record of estates, many of which, as we have seen, belong to public bodies, and many others of which are mere fragments of great properties owned by a single individual.

To prove how invidious all this was, Brodrick produces figures for the Dukes, of whom the 28 then alive owned a mere 158 separate estates covering 3,991,811 acres. The Duke of Buccleuch, he notes, counts as fourteen landowners because he has fourteen separate estates in England and Scotland. But to have produced the result that Brodrick wanted, the bounds of administrative reality would have had to be changed.

To conclude his tirade against the Return Brodrick casts an eye far back in history, to the first Domesday of 1086:

> It is extremely difficult to compare the distribution of ownership disclosed by these returns with that recorded in the original Domesday book. This marvellous survey included neither the Welsh counties nor the Northern counties of Northumberland, Cumberland, Westmoreland and Durham, the collective area of which is about one fifth of all England and Wales; nor is it possible to identify with certainty those who can properly be called landowners among the various classes of landholders therein enumerated. According to the analysis of Sir Henry Ellis, which is adopted by the compilers of the New Domesday Book, the whole number of genuine freeholders, registered under various titles, amounted to 54,813, including 1000 presbyteri [clergy].

Brodrick then increases the number of landholders by adding 7968 burgesses and 108,407 villeins [slaves] to the 53,000 lay freeholders, enabling him to argue, based on the comparative populations of 2 million in 1086 and 19.4 million in 1876, that 'in the time of William the Conqueror the soil of England was divided among a larger body of landowners than it is at present.'

This is disputable in the extreme. Legally there were no freeholders in England in the period of the first Domesday. Everyone was a tenant of the king. What Brodrick calls freeholders were sub under-tenants at best. To quote Thomas Hinde in his very accessible introduction to the reproduction of the Domesday Book of 1985 sponsored by the English Tourist Board:

> Of the Land described in Domesday's 35 counties the King and his family held about 17 per cent, the Bishops and abbots about 26 per cent and the 190-odd lay tenants in chief held about 54 percent.[22]

The implication that Brodrick makes that in England in 1086 there were freeholders in the modern sense of people who owned land without obligations to superiors, is totally wrong. Furthermore, the first Domesday did not cover Wales and much of northern England. The second Domesday covered all of the four countries, in all a total of 116 counties as opposed to just 35. It was at least 90% accurate as to the ownership of estates within counties, and was, as Bateman showed, eminently correctible. With regard to Brodrick's population comparison, as Hinde points out, over 200,000 of the 2 million population of William's England were slaves:

> The great majority of the Domesday peasantry, the villagers (villans), the smallholders (bordars) and the cottagers (cottars) were personally unfree. They had to render labour service to their Lord, and they were tied to their manor, but they had a stake in its resources.

Ellis, Brodrick's authority, was totally wrong in describing landholders as lay freeholders. They were at best sub tenants, as the concept of independent freehold, the legal tenure of most of those identified in the second Domesday, only arose generally in England many hundreds of years after Domesday (probably as a consequence of the one really important medieval document, Magna Carta).

It is important not to underestimate the influence in Victorian England of Brodrick's position as the son of an aristocrat, a Viscount, who was also a clergyman and a chaplain to the very Imperial Queen Victoria, and his status as Warden of an Oxford College. It meant that his arguments were never properly challenged, but were allowed to prevail throughout the academic world in particular, whenever the issue of examining the Returns on a proper basis came up. His detailed criticisms are, therefore, less important than what amounted to a trumpet blast from the top of Victorian society, endorsed by Oxford University, however indirectly.

The echoes of that 'blast' have travelled down through the years. Haldane's attempt at a land registry in 1897 failed. The Land Registration Act of 1925 was never debated in Parliament or outside it, leading to a land registry that, in 2001, is deficient of 2 million titles, covering up to half of England and Wales, and with no current prospect of that deficit ever being remedied. Further, both the land registries of England and Wales, and those of Scotland, Northern Ireland and the Irish Republic, are so constructed as to preclude the computerised creation of a domesday to equal that of 1876. By manipulating the detail, the forces of reaction have deprived government of a vital tool of administration and taxation, and the public of information on who is receiving a state handout of £4 billion a year. Government, at the end of the day, is far too important to be left to politicians who fail to watch those who fiddle the books while the public pays.

There was one time when the legacy of the Return might have prevailed. This was in 1909, when the Liberal Prime Minister Herbert Asquith's Chancellor of the Exchequer, David Lloyd George, produced the Finance Act, or budget, for that year. Lloyd George proposed a series of land and land related taxes, principally a capital appreciation tax, intended to claw back for the government any capital appreciation in land values attributable to public expenditure on roads and similar services. This was called 'increment value duty' and owed much to the theories of Henry George.[23] In order to collect the tax, the Board of the Inland Revenue was ordered to ascertain the site value of all land in the UK as on April 1909 and to use this as a 'base line' for the determination of changes in value. The 1909 budget, the famous 'People's Budget', was defeated in the House of Lords, an unprecedented event. Asquith twice went to the country in 1910 and assembled a sufficient majority in the Commons to get the Finance Act through. Opposition in the House of Lords, almost entirely from the large landowners, was focused on the tax itself, but implicit was their opposition to the potential new Domesday. The cost of opposition was to prove fatal for the power of the Lords, which was seriously curbed in the Parliament Act the following year.[24] The Parliament Act removed the power of the peers to interfere with money bills and limited their powers to delaying bills for strictly limited periods of time.

To accomplish the task of assessing and collecting the 'increment value duty' the Revenue set up the Valuation Office and by 1914 there were 118 valuation districts in England and Wales. The work of valuing every site in England, Wales and Scotland was more or less complete by 1915. In short, the Inland Revenue, by 1915, had both maps and books, identifying every site and its owner, in the UK. The books were divided into two series. One was called the Domesday Books and contained details of all payments, rents and so on, made as a result of landownership to the Inland Revenue. The second series, the Field Books, were more akin to the 1872 record, containing the names of owners, the area covered by the property, and other related details. Unlike the 1872 Domesday however, the Field Books, some of which are still extant and available in the Public Records Office, are indexed, not by name or address, but by valuation district, then by area and finally by assessment number. To find those particulars, the plans have to be obtained. Some original plans survive in Valuation Offices and at the Public Records Office, but many have been lost, in a way very similar to how the tithe maps were lost, by carelessness over time. In fact the return was never fully completed, partly due to the start of World War One, and like the Return of 1872, lies collecting dust in the public records office. The increment value duty was abolished in the 1920 Finance Act, during Lloyd George's premiership, and it is from that point that the Valuation Office maps, Domesday Books and Field Books began to be lost. No central compilation or registry, similar to the 1872 Return, was ever created. Worse than that, the records, unworkable in terms of creating a successor Domesday to that of 1872 as they were, are so incomplete, so dispersed and so damaged, that nothing could even now be created to resemble the Second Domesday. It is a truly stranded historic masterpiece, without visibility and without a successor.

The Legacy of the 1872 Return
The simple facts are revealing. By April 1876 most parishes had received a copy of their own county record from *The Return of Owners of Land*. Certainly all county halls had a copy of the full record of landowners, as did all public libraries, while anyone could check that the record was accurate by looking at the tithe maps held by the parishes. The local newspapers of the period carried extensive excerpts from the Returns when they appeared and the national papers identified the larger landowners.

Compare this with today. In 2001, the same information is scattered in four land registries, those for England and Wales, Scotland, Northern Ireland and for the Republic of Ireland. Access to the four land registries is on a one-at-a-time basis. In the case of the most economically important of those four land registries, that of England and Wales, between 30% and 50% of the acreage of the two countries is unregistered. The accuracy of the registries is in parallel with the volume of unregistered land. No such hole existed in the 1872 Return. The Return did not cover London and some unrated areas, but this gap only amounted to about 5% of the four countries. Even then, most large metropolitan areas, including London, had embryo land or deed registries, and of course there were always the tithe maps in the metropolitan parishes to fall back on. Generally speaking, the 1872 Returns covered about 95% of Great Britain and Ireland, they were about 90% to 95% accurate, and access to them was both universal and free. The cost of privately owning the entire survey was the modern equivalent of about £70. The cost of the complete set from the four land registries today would be about £150 million pounds, if it were available, which it is not.

In 1872 only 972,836 people out of a population of 36,000,000 owned any land at all. Only 269,547 people, 0.7% of the population, owned more than one acre, and despite the Reform acts of 1832 and 1867 only about 5% of the population were enfranchised.[25] The democratic and political deficit implied by this has profound implications. Even as the population at large acquired a small measure of power over those who ran their country, between 1876 and 1925 they simultaneously lost the capacity to find out the connection between those who owned the land of the country, those who were running the country and those who were benefiting from the way the country was run. Having been provided with the most important document in the economic history of the two islands for 1000 years, the people are then served with 125 years of silence as the document is buried and its logical consequence, a proper land registry, is thwarted. It shows as never before the hidden and corrupt hand of power at work in the UK.

Yet no one noticed, apparently. Who should have noticed?

The academic population should have noticed, especially political and economic historians. The growing Labour movement should have noticed. Finally, the media should have noticed. But the watchdogs were asleep at their posts, or looking the other way, bribed or bamboozled by the overweening and all-pervasive networks of the landowning interest.

It is interesting in this context to note that among a population where about 77% have a stake in a significant financial asset, a home, and about one eighth of the population, six million people, own shares in companies on the Stock Exchange, the one newspaper which provides serious information on these matters, the *Financial Times*, had a paid-for circulation within the UK in August 2000 of 186,000.[26] The paper which provides the least enlightenment in terms of these two economic assets, the *Sun*, has a circulation of about 2.2 million. The FT is not cheap at 85p, but the *Financial Times* assumes that its overwhelming purpose is to inform. For the *FT* entertainment comes in specifically defined places and pages, but for the rest of the print media, the battle against the inroads of television has been reduced to an attempt to entertain rather than to inform, and that includes even such august papers as the *Guardian*. A culture is promoted in which information is seen as having no value unless it entertains. Facts have almost become a futility, partly because they cost so much to obtain.

However, hard information, and hard news, creates and informs a context in which people can make more of their lives and their assets. Yet with the huge increase in the tools and, especially, the delivery systems, for information, there has been a vast decline in the volume and availability of truly relevant information. Four good television channels are replaced by 400 bad ones, in order to satisfy a bogus concept of choice. Yet no organ of the print media, and no television station, has apparently ever spotted the connection between homeowners and the land registry, and run a series to show how the defective registry impacts on the major asset of the majority of the population. As with all the vested interests behind the sale of consumables and commodities, the media dare not cast the light of disclosure upon their benefactors.

Fully 20% of all the print media's revenues come from those at the selling end of the property system. It does not encourage a critical mentality in relation to land.

For the fact is that, compared to 1872, a different form of repression has hold of the British population. It is now worked by more indirect means than the direct feudal control of Bateman's time. But it is a legacy of that feudal control, and exists because the broad population of Britain has never, through political liberation, been able to achieve the economic liberation that follows the end of a rentier economy. A mere 189,000 people own 88% of the land. They get a £4 billion a year in subsidy to own it. They pay no tax on that asset. The rest of us pay tax for our land, however small the plot. In a strange way Bateman did have an inkling of how things should really have worked. He wanted a million 'small proprietors' in England each owning 20 acres, which would have amended land ownership enormously. But he wanted this because he saw it as buttressing the system of narrow control and rentier domination of which he was a beneficiary and a defender. The bottom line is that the more people who are participants, as proprietors and owners, in even a capitalist economy, the better it works.

In his book *The Decline and Fall of the British Aristocracy*, David Cannadine catches the higher tone of the ultimate level of British political society as it looked into the abyss of the universal franchise and mass democracy in the late 1800s. He quotes Lord Dufferin, with 18,238 acres and income the equivalent of £1.4 million, writing to the Duke of Argyll, with 175,114 acres and an income the equivalent of £2.2 million, in April 1881:

> The tendency of the extreme section of the Liberal party is to buy the support of the masses by distributing among them the property of their own political opponents, and it is towards a social rather than a political revolution that we are tending.

In practice, England, Scotland and Wales got neither a political nor a social revolution, much less an economic one. Cannadine quotes Gladstone, the great Liberal Prime Minister: 'When it comes to a battle between the "masses" and the "classes" it was the "masses" who were ultimately going to win.' Except they didn't. What this book shows, against the background of a country without a proper constitution, currently separating into its four constituent parts, is that the landowners and their descendants hung on to the jewel in the crown, the land, and have kept the rest of the population, as in 1872, corralled in the same relatively small portion of the landscape, the urban redoubt.

According to government statistics,[27] about 3.4 million acres, or about 7.5% of England and Wales, is under residential occupation – in other words, taken up by the homes we live in. Approximately 19.2 million people have homes in England, out of a population of 47.8 million, sited on this 3.4 million acres, giving each urban dweller about 0.17 of an acre. This still leaves about 26.9 million acres, most of it in the hands of as few as 135,000 people. Apart from the light this throws on the imbalance between a very small and privileged group in the population, and the population in general, it also shows that, though there has been an increase in the number of people in the population who own some land, however small, there has actually been a shift towards the land-owning group as a whole. In fact what seems to have happened is that 77% of the population own some land, but 0.125% now own as much as 89.9% of the non public land of England alone. (Note that the latter percentage would be reduced if various corporate ownerships are established.) Taking the figure for small proprietors in Bateman's table on p.45, the 217,049 owners of between 1 and 100 acres, who between them owned 3.9 million acres, we can see that today 19.2 million people actually own less in total than this group, which has been significantly reduced in size since then, mainly due to farm mergers.[28] In considering what happened it is important to look at populations, as well as land ownership. The total population of England in 1871 was 18.2 million, of Wales 1.2 million. The two current figures, from the Government projections for 2001, are England 49.8 million and Wales 3.1 million.[29] The population has gone up a little over two and a half times, but the volume of land occupied by the bulk of the population has gone up by slightly less (2.3%), from about 3.3% urbanised in 1871, to about 7.5% now. In spreading thus, the homeowning population has obtained little by way of extra land, yet it has lost vital information and has taken on the burden of paying all such land taxes as are being paid, the actual landowners paying virtually none and being heavily subsidised as well. Which lends great urgency to restoring some semblance of the information that was available in 1876.

Chapter Four

Royal Land
The landed possessions of the Queen and her court

AS THE TWENTY-FIRST century gets under way the UK finds itself with a monarchy perfectly designed for the close of the nineteenth century. The institution of monarchy that we recognise today was largely fashioned by Victoria and her advisors. Like most powerful figures through history the Queen Empress based her strength on an acute awareness of her weakness. The British monarchy had been altered profoundly by the events of the mid-seventeenth century. Following the Civil War, Charles II was 'elected' to return as monarch by Parliament in 1660. Even more significantly, in 1688 William of Orange had been 'elected' by the British peers as a replacement for Charles' heir, James II. This power to change, or at least sanction, the head of state has never again been invoked, but it lurks in the unwritten constitution of the country.

Victoria believed that her position as monarch was at the mercy of the peers, the direct descendants and ruling representatives of the hirers and firers of 1660 and 1688 and who, in extremis, could exercise that power again. In the nineteenth century the aristocracy was the ruling class of the country and the Empire. They ruled from their landed estates in Britain, their home and their redoubt in the event of disaster. Victoria merely reigned over them, with their consent. It was clear that the existence of the monarchy depended, not on the popular will, but on the support of the peers, and of the government, composed largely of those peers and their relatives. This was especially evident following the death of Prince Albert, Victoria's husband. She all but disappeared from public view and subsequently lost a great deal of public support. In a normal democracy Victoria would have been out at the next election.

Victoria's defence was to break her financial dependence on Parliament by making the monarch independently wealthy. She would then be able to set about making the monarch as powerful as the peers, if not more so, and consequently pre-eminent among them. By comparison with most of the upper peerage, Victoria was singularly short in both land and money. In the ranks of the landed recorded in the 1872 Return she came somewhere around number 299 with her 25,000 acres.[1] Forty-four of her peers had over 100,000 acres each and one of them, the Duke of Sutherland, had over 1,000,000 acres.[2] In terms of wealth she probably never had much more than the modern equivalent of £50 million,[3] at a time when most of her non-Royal Dukes would be worth the equivalent of £250 million and one of them, Westminster, probably had the equivalent of £2 billion.

Philip Hall, whose book on Royal finances did much to concentrate the mind of government and Queen on the issue of over 50 years of unpaid tax, estimates that in 1871 Victoria had around £509,000 of her own money, the modern equivalent of £35 million. A great deal of this had come from savings on the Civil List that Victoria had transferred to her private funds. What Hall makes clear is that Victoria deliberately set out to accumulate a private fortune for the Royal Family, a project in which she was singularly successful. In relation to land, however, she was less so. She was handicapped in the early part of her reign by earlier acts of Parliament that in effect prevented the sovereign from owning land. The Crown Estate would have absorbed anything she might have bought in her own name. For this reason most of Victoria's land acquisitions were made in the name of either the Prince Consort or her children. By 1862 an act of Parliament had been passed to bring the land ownership bar to an end,[4] but the project of making the Royal Family the country's largest landowners, begun in her lifetime, has had surprising results a hundred years later.

Victoria's great-great-granddaughter Queen Elizabeth II, together with her son Prince Charles, are together the second largest private landowner in Britain. They are also the largest institutional landowners in Europe, in terms of their legal entitlement to three huge Crown assets, the Crown Estates, the Duchy of Lancaster and the Duchy of Cornwall. Perhaps most significantly of all both the Queen's private lands, and those she has a claim on as Queen, such as the Crown Estate, have more than doubled in size, on the landward side at least, in the course of the twentieth century, the Windsors' mostly tax-free century.

The seeds sown by Victoria in seeking to break free of the shackles imposed on British monarchs since the Glorious Revolution in 1688 have grown into seriously big plants. If the aristocratic fathers of British freedom from the barons at Runnymede in 1215 through to the signatories to the Bill of Rights in 1688 were trying to design a powerless, nominal monarchy, then they have failed. The richest family in Britain may lack formal or coercive powers, but they more than make up for this in influence, which, practically speaking, is how power functions in a democracy in the intervals between elections.

However, the Victorian plant hasn't blossomed without some very thorny complications. At the start of the twenty-first century the monarchy is no longer in competition with the hereditary peerage. The kings and queens of England have won the race against their ancient foes, the barons, in every sense. The barons are almost gone from their last hold on power, the House of Lords, while the monarchy remains in place. The Windsor family have possession, in one form or another, of more acres than anyone in the country and they are wealthy to an extreme. But the triumph of Victoria's secret plan has also left them marooned in a society where the aristocracy have been marginalised, where a home-owning electorate are generally satisfied with their simple domestic freeholds and where performance on the job counts for far more than inherited wealth. Indeed, excessive wealth, like all excesses, is looked at askance by an overwhelmingly middle class electorate. The middle class like nothing more, in the end, than that everything should fall within the narrow bands in which they live. Excess is tolerated within narrow limits. In that scale of things the Windsors have a very large, country-wide problem.

The Queen's Wealth

It is perfectly clear that the Queen is one of the richest individuals in the country, a status not unconnected with her landholdings. For the first five years of its life the *Sunday Times* Rich List placed the Queen at the head of Britain's rich, largely on the basis of the value of the Crown Estate and the Royal art collection. In the first Rich List in 1989 she was valued at £5.2 billion. The following year her calculated wealth had risen to £6.7 billion. In 1991 this had risen to £7 billion, where it remained in 1992, dropping to £5 billion in 1993 and 1994. During these years the Palace became well practised at brushing off all attempts by the *Sunday Times* researchers to get any factual hold on the Royal fortune or how it is structured. They had not bothered to make any formal refutation of the very high figures quoted in the early days of the *Sunday Times* list. Journalists phoning the Palace when the list was published were simply told that the figure was absurd, that Her Majesty did not own Buckingham Palace or the Crown jewels and that her private wealth was her own affair.

In 1994 Andrew Neil, that strange mixture of conventionalist and radical, who had encouraged the *Sunday Times* higher valuations of the Queen's wealth, left the paper. This followed demands from the Malaysian Prime Minister, Dr Mahathir, to his proprietor, the Australian-born Papal Knight Rupert Murdoch, that he be sacked. This itself followed a bribery allegation against Dr M, as he is known, which had appeared in the paper. Seeing how one autocrat could get his way with the *Sunday Times*, the Palace followed suit. Palace associates within and without the paper plagued Dr Philip Beresford, compiler of the *Sunday Times* Rich List since its inception, and his editor to lower the figure and by implication remove the Queen from pole position. Other friends of the Palace whispered in the ear of Rupert Murdoch, by then an American citizen, and his cronies that the 'silly' valuation was bringing the paper into disrepute. Murdoch took due note of the 16% plus rise in circulation on the Sunday the paper published the list and ignored the pleas. But within the paper the pressure from the Palace told and eventually, in 1995, her wealth was recalculated to £450 million. Philip Beresford rationalised the apparent decline in the Queen's fortune in 1995 by attempting to separate her personal wealth from her wealth as Sovereign. This is a perfectly reasonable thing to do. Tom Rubython, the editor of *Business Age*, a monthly business magazine, had gone even further in 1992 by lowering the Queen to a notional £100 million in that magazine's list of the richest women in Britain. Rubython argued that this is all she would be worth if she was stripped of the Crown Estate and made to pay back taxes to 1932.[5]

For Rubython, the revaluation on the basis of back tax was a cheeky way of producing a list different from the *Sunday Times*, but for the Palace it raised an ominous topic. Tax and the royals were not synonymous. Unknown to the public, and in parallel with the manner in which the Land Registry has been rendered ineffective, the Palace had struck a secret deal excusing the monarch from paying any tax at all on anything since the mid 1930s. In 1993 the Queen agreed to pay tax on her private income, as her predecessors had done up to the secret deal with the Baldwin government, but this was a minimal concession which headed off the real criticism, which was the continuous deceit practised by the Palace and by its cronies in Parliament when the issue of taxation was raised.

The *Sunday Times* 2000 list put the Queen 106th in the rankings, worth a mere £275 million, while acknowledging that if the Royal art collection and Crown Estate were included she would be worth £13 billion. It is a significant grey area, dominated by a rather desirable collection of real estate known as The Crown Estate. Nowhere in the brochure on Royal finances issued by Buckingham Palace in 1993 and 1995,[6] and not currently updated, is there specific mention of it, other than an explanation that the Civil List is provided by Parliament in exchange for the surrender by the Sovereign of the 'hereditary revenues'. What the brochure fails to mention is the source of these hereditary revenues. In fact they come from the income on the 24 million acres that constitute the Crown Estate. Admittedly 23.6 million of those acres lie underwater, between the low tide mark and the twelve-mile territorial limit, but they are real acres currently producing £26.1 million in revenues[7] from various licences granted for mining, dredging and so on. No watery wastelands these. In fact they produce significantly more revenue than the agricultural acres of the Crown Estate, which yielded only £17.7 million in revenues in 2000.[8] Indeed, as time goes by the marine revenues, which include valuable mineral rights, are likely to become very much more valuable, with income from the seabed in the next century is likely to be up to three times current receipts, according to some experts.

Greater detail on the extent and value of the Crown Estate is given in Chapter 5. In general, however, it means that as an institutional landowner the Queen owns the freehold on the Crown Estate of 24.3 million acres, in addition to the revenues from the Duchy of Lancaster, with 66,000 acres (see Chapter 7). Her son has lifetime possession of the Duchy of Cornwall with its 141,000 acres (see Chapter 6), with the estate passing on to his heirs in perpetuity. Based on the examination of the landed estates made in this and subsequent chapters, the Queen is worth, in landed assets, as follows:

TABLE 4/1

Estate	Basis for calculation of value	Estimated value
Balmoral	Current Scottish land values	£50 million
Sandringham	Current English land values	£100 million
Crown Estate	50% of current book value of £3.5 billion	£1.25 billion
	or 10 times current revenues	£1.3 billion
Duchy of Lancaster	15 times current revenues	£88.5 million
Total		**£1.5 billion**

The Queen's Personal Land Holdings

Amongst her peers in the aristocracy, of which she was the titular head, Queen Victoria cut a pretty minuscule figure with regard to her land holdings and personal wealth. At a time when 44 peers each owned more than 100,000 acres, she owned just 27,441 acres: 25,350 at Balmoral and 1,963 in Hampshire, mostly on the Isle of Wight. Her son Bertie, later Edward VII, owned 14,889 acres, 6810 near Balmoral and 8079 near Sandringham in Norfolk. Together, they owned just over 42,000 acres, with, in the background, the Duchy of Cornwall at 74,000 acres and the Crown Estate of 200,000 landbased acres. Over the course of the next 120 years this private estate has swollen to over 75,000 acres, mostly by acquisition. Prince Charles's estate, the Duchy of Cornwall, has doubled in size since 1872, from roughly 74,113 acres, to 141,000 acres. Meanwhile, the bulk of the Prince's fellow aristocrats were losing some, occasionally all, of their acres. Of course the aristocracy did not have that singular advantage enjoyed by the Windsors of paying no tax. It is clearly easier to build up a large landed estate if you are paying no taxes and no inheritance tax either. (In future the monarch will pay inheritance tax on her personal estate, though not on bequests left by her as Queen to her successor as sovereign.[9]) This is another perk of the monarchy not much talked about, despite its pivotal role in elevating the Windsors to the very top rank of the rich in the UK.

Balmoral (49,470 acres)

Queen Victoria made her first land purchase, in her husband's name, in Scotland in February 1848 by taking on a lease at Balmoral from the estate of Sir Robert Gordon, who had died the previous year. The lease had 27 years to run and the owner was the Earl of Fife, who at that time owned over 249,000 acres, 135,829 of which were in Aberdeen around Balmoral. (The current Duke of Fife is down to just 1600 acres at Elsick in Kincardine.[10] The promotion from Earl of Fife to Duke of Fife came following his great-uncle's marriage to Princess Louise, the daughter of the then Prince of Wales, in 1889. The elevation occurred in 1900 and is the only (and probably last) non-Royal dukedom to be created since 1874.)

In 1852 Queen Victoria bought out the lease, again in her husband's name, and became the owner of 25,350 acres of Aberdeen, albeit with a minuscule gross annual valuation of only £2392. She then purchased the 6810 acres of neighbouring Birkhall for her son and heir. In addition she took on a long lease at Abergeldie, next door to Balmoral.

According to Ralph Whitlock, the chronicler of Royal farming, Victoria first became interested in having an estate in Scotland following a visit she made to Taymouth Castle in 1842. There she was the guest of the Marquess of Breadalbane, the proprietor of 438,358 acres of Perth and Argyll. In subsequent years Victoria and Albert sailed the Western Isles in the Royal Yacht and despite being put off by the incessant rain, decided to buy in 1847. This was a period when the romanticism of Sir Walter Scott and his largely fictional account of Scottish history was being put to good use to deflect the persistent claims of Scottish nationalists for an independent state. English indulgence of Scottish romanticism was simply another way to protect the union. Victoria's purchase of a Scottish estate had as much to do with issues of state as it had to do with any interest, real or imagined, that Victoria might have had in Balmoral itself. But by having a home in Scotland she did signal quite clearly that Scotland was a decisive part of the union. And in the years that followed she spent enough time there to ensure that this point was fully emphasised, north and south of the border. Following the death of Albert from typhoid in 1860 Victoria took to spending at least a quarter of the year, usually August, September and October, at Balmoral. As had been envisaged, this had a huge influence on the inner politics of the UK at that period. Scotland was still controlled and owned to an extent now almost unimaginable by the heirs of the peers, many of whom had been bribed into signing away the Scottish parliament in 1707. They now found that they had the Queen Empress on hand to lend both glamour and effect to their position as the de facto governors of the Scottish province. They made the maximum use of this, with a whole sub court and sub government system growing up around the Queen's sojourn at Balmoral.

The Scottish peers made the most of the opportunity to draw themselves even closer than they were before to the British crown, culminating in the marriage in 1923 of a daughter of the Earl of Strathmore and Kinghorn, Lady Elizabeth Bowes Lyons, to Prince Albert, Duke of York, a grandson of Victoria and later King George VI. It was an accident of fact that Victoria personally loved Balmoral, but that affection for her Scottish acreage probably set back Scottish home rule by at least 120 years. In practice her love for Balmoral was the love of the Queen Empress of the greatest and most powerful empire the world had ever known. All those with an interest in that power, especially where it buttressed their insecure position, surrounded that embrace with their loyalty and behind that loyalty with their interests. Their interest was land and its possession, in quantities so great as to defy the imagination, and in most cases in defiance of any meaningful economic utility either. It is no accident that the son of the Marquess who had first excited Victoria's interest in Scottish acres became a lord-in-waiting to the Queen in the 1880s. Later chapters will look in detail at who owned what in Scotland in recent history, but it is worth very briefly noting the titanic scale of aristocratic land ownership in Scotland when Victoria bought her 'little patch' there.

At the top of the tree dwelt the Duke of Sutherland, the owner of 1,358,545 acres. This is the equivalent of two average-sized English counties. It did not make him the richest duke in Victoria's reign – that honour fell to the Marquess, later Duke, of Westminster. But it made Sutherland powerful and a force to be reckoned with. And to ensure that his voice was heard he sat in the British Parliament as MP for Sutherland. In Sutherland he owned 1,176,454 acres in a county which totalled 1,299,194 acres. This left the other 432 landowners in Sutherland sharing just 122,000 acres between them while the population of 24,000 were almost entirely tenants of the Duke. The other nine Scottish-British behemoths of landownership in Scotland at the time (with details of their school, where known), were: the Duke of Buccleuch (Eton), 460,108 acres; the Earl of Breadalbane, 438,358 acres; Lady Matheson, 424,560 acres; Sir Charles Ross (Eton), 356,500 acres; the Earl of Seafield (Eton), 305,930 acres; the Earl of Fife (Eton), 249,220 acres; Sir Alexander Matheson, 220,663 acres; the Duke of Atholl (Eton), 210,640 acres; Lord Lovat, 181,791 acres. Here is a situation where one person, Sutherland, owned the equivalent of two English counties and the next nine individual Scottish landowners between them owned the equivalent of four English counties.

With the exception of the Mathesons, one of whom, Lady Matheson, was the widow of an MP, and a few other landowners, all the Scottish peers sat in the British House of Lords, and prior to succeeding to their titles usually sat as MPs in the House of Commons. Before that most of them had been to school in England, at Eton. They were, in fact, British rather than Scottish and their real role in Scotland was as the representatives of the Imperial power in the south. In terms of offering succour to their oppressive position there can have been few more important events since the union in 1707 than the arrival in Scotland of the Queen Empress.

Whether the establishment of a separate parliament for Scotland in Edinburgh in 1999 will prove as significant time is yet to tell. For the time being the Queen remains in possession of her Scottish acres, which she extended by 10% in 1977 by taking on the Delnadamph estate of 6700 acres from the trustees of Lady Louisa Stockdale.[11] As might be expected, this addition is not a working farm but yet another grouse moor. Adjacent to Balmoral are the remnants of the Gordon family holding that Balmoral once formed part of and which is now leased for shooting by Balmoral. This gives the Royal Family sway over another 10,200 acres of Scottish soil. Prince Charles has spoken of handing over Balmoral to the Scottish people when he becomes Sovereign. For the time being, however, while the property remains his mother's private possession, he cannot do this.

In his book on Royal farming Ralph Whitlock[12] identifies only 380 acres of Balmoral as actual arable farm, the rest being deer forest, mountain and moorland. According to Whitlock the Queen and Prince Philip take a personal interest in the farms and receive a monthly report on progress. The gardens of the estate have been open to the public since 1931 and the public does have wide access to walk, climb and birdwatch across the estate. The deer herd has been maintained at around 2500 for over 30 years, mostly by culling about 450 stags and hinds annually, generally by stalking.

According to Whitlock the Queen is 'an expert and experienced shot'. This is not an aspect of the Queen's life that the Palace is too keen to advertise to the public that is, apparently, overwhelmingly against blood sports in any form. This is perhaps one of the few areas in which there is real conflict between public perception as cultivated by the Palace, and the private inclinations of the human being who is Elizabeth II. While the public were predominantly working class, and while there was still a significant rural population, there was a degree of sympathy between peasant and peer, including the Queen. The poor pursued rabbits while the monarch might pursue deer. The disappearance of the rural peasantry and the conversion of most of the British working class into at least pseudo middle class owner-proprietors has changed that relationship almost totally. The population want a popular monarchy and the huntin', shootin', fishin' landowners are not a popular class, partly because of their occupation, partly because of their attitude and partly because of the sharp disparity in wealth between the population and this group. This is a problem that the Palace is even now trying to wrestle with, not overlooking the fact that Prince Charles rides to hounds.

Sandringham (20,100 acres)

Nine years after completing the purchase of Balmoral Victoria and Albert decided that the Prince of Wales, Albert Edward (Bertie), who had just started his university career at Cambridge, should have a country seat to learn and practise the habits of a country gentleman. A suitable location had not been found when Albert died suddenly in December 1861. The following year Sandringham in Norfolk was put on the market by Charles Spencer Cowper. The initial purchase was of an estate of 8079 acres, complete with a fair number of dwellings and farm buildings. However, not long after his marriage to Princess Alexandra of Denmark, Bertie began a huge reconstruction of virtually everything that was on the estate, finishing in 1870. Given his reputation as a worldly wise prince and sometime dilettante Bertie was a surprisingly keen farmer, following in his father's footsteps by installing pedigree herds of animals and birds on the Sandringham farms. He was, over a number of years, President of the Royal Agricultural Society, a duty that he took seriously. According to Whitlock, 'The office was no sinecure. He [Bertie] often attended Council meetings and took part in discussions.'[13] Victoria took no interest in Sandringham and only visited twice during the remainder of her life.

For the rest of the family, however, Sandringham was special. After Edward VII's death in 1910, Queen Alexandra lived there until her death in 1925. Edward's successor, George V, lived in York House on the estate until his mother died. George V himself died at Sandringham in January 1936. He was succeeded by Edward VIII, the only one of his six children not born at Sandringham. Edward abdicated the throne in December 1936 and was succeeded by his brother George VI who had been born at Sandringham and who lived there. Never expecting to be King, George had taken to almost personal management of the Sandringham estate, making all sorts of improvements, including draining and recovering 1400 acres from the sea. During World War Two the Royal Family, in what was probably their finest hour, spent most of the time with the population of the capital, London, enduring with them the terrors of the Nazi bombing offensive. They rarely visited Sandringham, although the estate was intensively farmed to assist with wartime food supplies. When the war ended there were over 1600 cattle grazing at Sandringham. A measure of George VI's interest in the two estates of Sandringham and Balmoral, which he had to purchase from Edward as part of the abdication settlement,[14] is that given in Sir John Wheeler-Bennet's biography of the king, quoted by Whitlock:

> He was essentially a country gentleman, taking a meticulous concern in the day-to-day details of his estates, the welfare of his tenants and the upkeep of his properties. Indeed he wore himself out with his care for detail. No addition could be made to a cottage at either Sandringham or Balmoral, no new tenant taken on, no employee discharged, no tree cut down, without the King's approval, the decision being submitted to him personally, even if he was in London. In this correspondence he replied invariably in his own hand.[15]

Which, in its own, quite accidental way, explains why any concept of personal freedom and any practice of monarchy are in such absolute conflict. Those who cannot paint a window frame without their landlord's permission are suffering some considerable curtailment of that freedom enjoyed by their fellow citizens who are freeholders.

George VI died at Sandringham in February 1952 and was succeeded by his daughter Elizabeth. She inherited, free of the inheritance tax that was both crippling and destroying what remained of the great landed estate of the previous century which had not been smart enough to place their acres in trust, her father's estate. At Sandringham this consisted of about 20,100 acres, including the villages of Wolferton, West Newton, Appleton, Flitcham, Anmer and Shernbourne. Whitlock lists the way the estate was organised:

> 3,200 acres are farmed by the estate. 11,890 acres are let to tenant farmers. 450 acres are let to smallholders. 117 acres are devoted to fruit. 243 acres are devoted to the thoroughbred stud. 1950 acres are woodland. 470 acres are parkland around Sandringham House. 1,780 are devoted to the Sandringham Country Park.[16]

Whitlock's book was published in 1980 and seems extraordinarily dated just over 20 years later. It is a measure of the death of deference amongst the population generally and the young in particular, that this is so. But neither Sandringham nor Balmoral have proved to be a bad investment. At the time of purchase in 1862, land in Norfolk was selling at £20 to £30 or so per acre. In 2000 prices that would be about £1400, whereas good acres in Norfolk now sell for anything between £3000 and £5000 per acre. This would give Sandringham alone a value of around £100,000,000 and Balmoral perhaps half that, given the value now attached to Scottish sporting estates.

Sandringham, especially the stud, have remained highly popular with Queen Elizabeth and her family throughout her reign and she and Prince Philip still take a close interest in how the estate is run. Much of it is open to the public at various times of the year and the Park is enormously popular in East Anglia, attracting thousands of visitors each year.

The Windsors' Other Estates

Princess Anne runs a thoroughly modern 'big farm' of 1263 acres at Gatcombe in Gloucestershire. She is, however, primarily a horsewoman and spends a great deal of her time on her royal duties and her charities. Prince Charles has his own spread of 1100 acres at Highgrove in Gloucestershire, where he operates primarily as a horticulturist, though his detailed and personal interest in the workings of the Duchy of Cornwall should not be overlooked. When he becomes king, he will be entrusted with Sandringham and Balmoral. What will happen to the Crown Estate and the two duchies remains to be seen.

The Inner Royal Household

Queen Victoria's little experiment in Scottish landownership at once buttressed a local aristocracy which was essentially British rather than Scottish, and at the same time enabled that aristocracy to persist with landholdings that were simply medieval, if not feudal in their origin and their operation. Over a century later, the landowning aristocracy, the heirs of the British Scottish behemoths of the last century, still surround the monarchy and have almost certainly trapped it in outmoded ritual and, even more damagingly, outmoded ways of thinking and operating. A look at the non-managerial structure of the Palace reveals the closet influences on the Queen that have moulded her often inadequate responses to the modern world. The Palace and its spokespeople often try to dismiss the inherited structure as some kind of outmoded – which it is – or non-functioning – which it is not – structure. It is the real network of royal aristocrats who are the Queen's closest confidantes and friends and whose appointments, save where hereditary, display the personal favour of Elizabeth II.

The Lord Chamberlain
The Lord Chamberlain is head of the Queen's household and is probably her closest professional advisor. He normally has care of all the personal finances of the Sovereign. He is appointed by the Queen, not by the Government. In 1998 the 7th Baron (Lord) Camoys (land unregistered; last stated at 4000 acres in 1872) replaced the 13th Earl of Airlie (land in 1995 37,300 acres in Scotland[17]) as Lord Chamberlain and head of the Queen's household. One old Etonian replaced another, and one banker replaced another too – Airlie was chairman of Schroeders merchant bank, chairman of Ashddown Investments and a director of J. Henry Schroder Wagg & Co Ltd, while Balliol-educated Camoys was a managing director of Barclays Merchant Bank, chief executive of Barclays de Zote Wedd (BZW) and a director of Barclays. In 2000 Camoys, the first Catholic to hold the post since the Reformation, retired early, partly due to ill health, and has been replaced by the Rt. Hon. Lord Luce, the former Tory MP for Shoreham, Richard Luce. Educated at Wellington College and the son of a Foreign Office mandarin, Sir William Luce KCMG, Lord Luce has a background in industry, the army and as a district officer in Kenya in the last days of Empire. Educated at Cambridge University, he was until 1996 the Vice Chancellor of the private Buckingham University, having left the Commons in 1992. He held middle ranking ministerial posts throughout the Thatcher government, mainly in the Foreign Office, finishing up as Minister for the Arts, a post without Cabinet rank. Luce's wife is the daughter of a baronet, the late Sir Godfrey Nicholson, former Tory MP for Farnham in Surrey. Her mother was a daughter of the 27th Earl of Crawford and Balcarres, a Scottish landowning family still holding land in Fife. Her cousin, the 29th Earl of Crawford and 12th Earl of Balcarres, an old Etonian and the ex-Tory MP, Robert Lindsay, is the Lord Chamberlain and head of household to the Queen Mother. Unlike his predecessor, Luce continues to have a seat in the House of Lords as a life peer. His sister-in-law is the Liberal Democrat peeress, Baroness Nicholson, the former Tory MP Emma Nicholson.

Both Airlie and Camoys had ancestors who served in the Palace. The 3rd Lord Camoys was a lord-in-waiting to Queen Victoria on four separate occasions and his grandson, the 4th Lord Camoys, continued the tradition by becoming lord-in-waiting to Queen Victoria in 1886 and from 1892 to 1895. The Earl of Airlie's father was lord-in-waiting to King George V from 1926 to 1929 and was also Lord Chamberlain to the Queen Mother from 1937 to 1965, a stint which gave his son, who had a distinguished career in World War II, plenty of time to learn the ropes. And in both cases there was employment for both husband and wife. Airlie's wife, Virginia Fortune, is first lady of the bedchamber, the third highest appointment in the Queen's private set up. Camoy's wife is an extra lady-in-waiting to the Duke and Duchess of Gloucester. She is also the daughter of the late Sir William Stephen Hyde Parker Bt., and her brother, Sir Richard, has his seat at Melford Hall at Long Melford in Suffolk. Here the land is unregistered but was last shown at 3482 acres in 1872.

The Lord Steward
This is the number two job in the Palace structure and it is currently held by Matthew Ridley, the 4th Viscount and brother of the late Nicholas Ridley (latterly Lord Ridley), Margaret Thatcher's favourite minister. In terms of the current Palace stereotype Matthew Ridley is all but the institutional clone of Camoys, having gone to Eton and then Balliol College, Oxford, the latter described by Anthony Sampson in *The Anatomy of Britain*[18] as a college which seems to have students from nowhere else but Eton. Ridley is the proprietor of numerous unregistered acres. They were last declared to the public in 1872 and came to 10,152. Ridley's sister-in-law, Lady Elisabeth Lumley, is married to an old Etonian, Lord Grimthorpe (4000 acres), and just happens to be lady of the bedchamber to the Queen Mother. Ridley's father-in-law, the 11th Earl of Scarborough, also an old Etonian, was Lord Chamberlain to the Queen at the beginning of her reign in 1952, and owned around 21,698 acres in Yorkshire. He was succeeded by his son the 12th Earl of Scarborough (the acreage is now said to be down to 5000). The 12th Earl was also Grand Master of the Freemasons in England and his mother-in-law, the Countess of Dalhousie was, in her time, also lady of the bedchamber to the Queen Mother.

Master of the Horse
Savile William Francis Crossley, the 3rd Baron Somerleyton, is the current Master of the Horse, holding what until the end of the last century was one of the most prestigious of all posts at the Palace. He went to Eton and has 3492 unregistered acres at Somerleyton Hall in Norfolk, beginning his career in the Royal household as a lord-in-waiting to the Queen in 1978. Like Ridley and several others, he did a stint in the Coldstream Guards, though not as a professional soldier having retired as a captain. He held the post of Deputy Lord Lieutenant for Suffolk from 1964.

Mistress of the Robes
This is presently the Duchess of Grafton, wife of an old Etonian, the Duke of Grafton. He is of Royal descent, his ancestor being the illegitimate son of Charles II by Barbara Villiers, Duchess of Cleveland. The Duchess of Grafton, Ann Fortune, is mistress of Euston Hall in Norfolk, set in an unregistered estate that was 25,773 acres in 1872 and shows every sign of still being at least half that size. She is the daughter of Captain (Evan Cadogan) Eric Smith and sent her two sons to Eton. One, the heir to the dukedom, has married a daughter of the 12th Marquess of Lothian, who was educated at the Benedictine foundation of Ampleforth (regarded by many as the Catholic equivalent of Eton). The Duchess's youngest daughter married a son of the same 12th Marquess. Her eldest daughter married Edward Gerald Patrick St George, a widower. The diarist Nigel Dempster noted that Maurice 'Mo' Dalitz, a Mafia godfather according to the FBI, attended the wedding. Edward St George's brother was the raffish Charles St George, a racehorse owner and friend of Henry Cecil, the Queen's trainer. Edward St George is a baron in the nobility of Malta. Most of the St George offspring, like their father, went to Eton.

The Ladies of the Bedchamber
The first lady of the bedchamber is the Countess of Airlie, née Virginia Fortune Ryan, an American by birth. She is married to the old Etonian Earl of Airlie, recently retired as Lord Chamberlain. She is the daughter of Barry Fortune Ryan, an American billionaire who financed one half of the British secret intelligence service between the two World Wars. This was the Z organisation, run by an old Etonian called Claude, later Sir Claude,

Dancey. When World War Two broke out Dancey's organisation was merged with M16, the official British secret service run by Sir Stuart Menzies, another old Etonian. Virginia Fortune Ryan's husband, the Earl of Airlie, was Allied High Commissioner in Austria in 1947/48 and his brother Sir Angus Ogilvy, an old Etonian, is married to the Queen's first cousin, Princess Alexandra. The Queen is the titular boss of all Britain's secret services and old Etonians in the services, especially M16, have always paid loyalty to her above and beyond that which they owe to the Government of the day.

The second lady of the bedchamber is The Lady Farnham, Diana Marion, née Gunnis. She married the 12th Baron Farnham, a landowner in Northern Ireland who is also an old Etonian with a small estate in Cavan that once stretched to 25,000 acres. A former banker, having chaired Brown Shipley, a city merchant bank, between 1984 and 1991, he was also Pro Grand Master of the United Lodge of Freemasons of England. The 12th Baron died in 2001.

Extra Lady of the Bedchamber
The Marchioness of Abergavenny, Mary Patricia Harrison, married the 5th Marquess of Abergavenny in 1938. He is, like all the others, an old Etonian and a banker – with Lloyds. He rose to be a lieutenant colonel in the Life Guards, the senior regiment in the household brigade, during World War Two. Their son, the late Earl of Lewes, was a page of honour to the Queen from 1962 to 1964 but died in 1965. There is no record of Palace service in recent times, but Abergavenny is Senior Steward of the National Hunt Committee and he was the Queen's representative at Ascot for ten years between 1982 and 1992. His ancestor had 25,800 acres in 1872 and the land at his seat in Kent is unregistered.

Women of the Bedchamber
The Hon. Mary Morrison is the daughter of the old Etonian Lord Margadale. Her three brothers, including the late Sir Peter Morrison MP, were all educated at Eton and are, through a variety of marriages, their own and their siblings', related to a fair swathe of the aristocracy, including the Duke of Devonshire, Viscount Trenchard, Viscount Long, Earl Beauchamp and the Earl Dudley. The obvious link to the monarchy is Mary Morrison's elder brother James, who was Chairman of Tattersall's Committee of the Turf Club. The Morrisons are of Scottish origins and their wealth is intimately bound up with whisky on Islay. Her father was a Deputy Lieutenant of both Wiltshire, where the family home is, and of Argyll, where the whisky estate is located. The acreage in 1872 came to 75,873 and the land at Fonthill in Wiltshire is not registered.

Lady Susan Hussey is the wife of the former Chairman of the Governors of the BBC, Marmaduke, now Lord, Hussey. He did not go to Eton, but to its famous, if downmarket rival Rugby. She used the title 'Lady' prior to her husband's ennoblement as the daughter of the 12th Earl Waldegrave, an old Etonian, as is the current holder of the title, her brother James. Her other brother, William, also an old Etonian, was a Cabinet minister in the Major administration and found himself described as a 'sophist' by Sir Richard Scott during the inquiry into arms for Iraq. The Waldegrave lands in 1872 ran to 15,000 acres.

Lady Dugdale is the mistress of Tickwood Hall at Much Wenlock in Shropshire and is married to Sir John Dugdale Bt., an old Etonian and the Lord Lieutenant of Shropshire since 1975.

Lady Richenda Elton is the second wife of the 2nd Lord Elton, an Old Etonian and a 'working peer' in the Lords. He has been a Tory whip, junior minister and chairman of various Parliamentary committees.

Extra Women of the Bedchamber

The Hon. Mrs van der Woude is the daughter of the old Etonian 2nd Viscount Rothermere and the aunt of the present press baron, the 4th Viscount Rothermere, also an old Etonian. She is the widow of the 3rd Earl of Cromer, an old Etonian, and mother of the present Earl Cromer, an old Etonian and international company director with the Inchcape group. The Earldom of Cromer is one of the four Baring family titles in the House of Lords – the Barings family has been the key merchant bank to the Palace for two or three generations.

Jean Francis Woodroffe is a daughter of Captain Angus Valdimar Hambro, scion of the banking family, old Etonian and Tory MP. Her first husband was Captain the Hon. Vicary Paul Gibbs, son of Baron Aldenham, old Etonians both. Aldenham was chairman of the merchant bank Anthony Gibbs and Co. Captain Gibbs was killed in action in 1944 serving with the Grenadier Guards. The present Baron Aldenham, an old Etonian, lives at the family estate in Elstree, Hertfordshire, which was recorded in 1872 at 3405 acres. In 1945 Mrs Gibbs was appointed a lady-in-waiting to Princess Elizabeth, the future Queen. In 1946 she married Rev. the Hon. A.C.V. Elphinstone, son of the old Etonian 16th Lord Elphinstone. When the 17th Lord Elphinstone died, his nephew, the old Etonian son of Jean Francis Gibbs, succeeded him. Both of her sisters-in-law are attached to the Palace, the Hon. Jean Constance Wills as extra lady-in-waiting to Princess Margaret and the Hon. Margaret Rhodes as an extra lady-in-waiting to the Queen Mother. Neither of those appointments are unusual, given that the 16th Lord Elphinstone was married to Lady Mary Frances Bowes Lyons, the Queen Mother's sister. In 1980 Jean Francis Elphinstone married Lieutenant Colonel J.W.R. Woodroffe, a relative of the Earls of Ducie, who died in 1990.

Mrs Michael Wall is the cousin of one of the Queen's oldest friends, the 9th Duke of Buccleuch, the old Etonian owner of about 277,000 acres of Scotland and various English counties. She worked at the Palace as assistant press secretary to the Queen from 1958 to 1981. Her mother was the daughter of the 7th Duke of Buccleuch and her father was a Royal Navy Admiral. Her husband is Commander Michael E. St Q. Wall, RN.

Lady Abel Smith comes from a family of rich London landowners headed by the Earl Cadogan. She married Major Sir Anthony Frederick Mark Palmer, an old Etonian, in 1939. He was killed in action in 1941 and the title is now held by his son, an old Etonian landowner in Gloucestershire. She married Brigadier Sir Alexander Abel Smith, an old Etonian and a cousin of the Duke of Somerset, in 1953. He died in 1980.

The late Lady Rose Baring was a daughter of the old Etonian 7th Earl of Antrim and widow of Francis Anthony Baring, old Etonian son of old Etonian Lord Revelstoke. Francis Anthony Baring was killed in action in 1940. Her two sons, Nicholas and Peter, both old Etonians, were the senior directors at Barings when it went under in 1995, following unauthorised dealings in the Far East by a minor trader called Nick Leeson. Not one hint of what happened to the Palace's investments with or in Barings have leaked out, but holdings there were. Lady Rose Baring died in 1993.

The Greatest Landowners in Europe

From the analysis above it can be seen that the Queen has surrounded herself with a very particular kind of person, with a very specific icon, Eton, in the background, almost without exception. Those closest to and most likely to have real influence with the Queen are almost all hereditary aristocrats and landowners. But it is not a broadly based selection and reflects only a tiny part of the aristocracy itself, with about half of fairly recent creation (post-1850) and overwhelmingly connected to a very small group of banks.

It goes without saying that these courtiers will have used their broader influence to assist the progress of Victoria's project to make the Royal Family pre-eminent in wealth and in land. That broad influence, though now waning, amounted, via the Eton link, to a capacity to cow the Tory party and to bend it slowly, but successfully, to the Royal will. Beyond that, it gave the Queen access to the inner world of London banking, and allied with it, a hidden connection to the inner world of intelligence, which, contrary to the impression given by spy writers, was, in the post-war world, mostly about economics.

In respect of the influence of this relatively small coterie around the Queen, the analysis of the late Mancur Olson, an economic philosopher who at the time of his death in 1998, aged 66, was rapidly acquiring guru status in the United States. It it is his work on how small groups in society gang together to create monopolies, and who then cause serious decline in a whole country, that will probably be his enduring monument. He stated:

> In any given case of market combination or of special interest lobbying, then, the problem is that a tiny minority, both in terms of voting power and wealth, rips off the rest of the society in ways that reduce the efficiency and dynamism of the society.[19]

The particular coalition which crowds the Palace, the Crown Estate and the two duchies, with its secret lobbyists and advocates, is the same group that stand to benefit the most from perpetuating the black hole at the heart of the land registry. These are people distinguished from the rest of the population by owning the vast bulk of the land on which the population at large depends for homes and, to a lesser extent, food. They conform exactly to Olson's description of why Britain started to fall behind in the economic growth leagues as long ago as the end of the nineteenth century:

> Thus the problem of societies losing their efficiency and dynamism through collusion and organisations for collective action is mainly a problem of tiny minorities exploiting society at large.[20]

In Britain at the end of the nineteenth century a group of people, probably numbering no more than 3000 in total, had monopoly control of the four most critical elements of the state: the Palace, Parliament, land and finally, via land, the banks. To look at landowners in Britain in the 1890s is to look straight at the dark heart of an economic decline that is not yet over.[21] In the words of Professor John Scott, writing of a marginally extended group of the descendants of these same people, at a later date in time, 'This small but extremely wealthy social class depends on the operations of the monopoly sector of the economy for its various privileges.'[22]

The state of landownership in Britain today is symptomatic of the continuing exploitation of the four monopolies by the descendants of the people who lost the country the economic success it had achieved through the expansion of Empire and the creation of the industrial revolution. For those who pay tax on their tiny stake in the land of our country, it is the last great battle: to inform ourselves properly as to who owns the country and having so done to end the monopoly of that tiny group on this vital asset.

Olson's explanation of how these tiny groups get away with it bears directly on the royal lands in Britain:

> If the victims of distributional coalitions had even a faint idea of what was really going on, they could easily put a stop to it. They lose only because of their rational ignorance and the shortcomings of the ideologies they accordingly rely on. [23]

He also points out in the same article, that 'Typical citizens are rationally ignorant about public affairs.' Rational ignorance is another name for the ignorance generated by believing that if you read a modern newspaper you are an informed person.[24]

For most of this century there was an absolute alliance between the Palace, the landowners and the average UK press baron, such as Harmsworth, Rothermere, Northcliffe and Thompson. Where the alliance wasn't explicit, as with Thomson, it was rendered so by his subscribing to the general political ethos, which protected the Palace and the landowners. Robert Maxwell, the thief who ran the *Mirror* for a period, was outside the magic circle, but never let his papers really get at the real facts of Royal tax dodging and Royal land aggrandisement. As is indicated earlier in the chapter, the spell broke with Rupert Murdoch's *Sunday Times* and its Rich Lists that began appearing in 1989.

Until those lists appeared, and until Philip Hall's book on Royal wealth appeared at the end of 1992, the public was ignorant of most of the facts relating to Royal finances. The media had gone along with the deceit perpetratated by the Palace and by successive governments about Royal taxes, finances, and land. The full extent of the Royals' massive institutional landholdings are outlined in the following three chapters.

Chapter Five

The Crown Estate

THE FIRST ATTEMPT to make all the land of England subject to ownership by one figurehead was carried out during the Roman occupation in the first four centuries of the Christian era. While the occupation lasted, all land belonged to the emperor in Rome and was distributed only to what amounted to sub tenants; a good way to ensure loyalty in disloyal times. But during the interval of 600 years between the ending of the Roman occupation and the arrival of William the Bastard, a system not unlike that which has emerged in the last two hundred years became prevalent.

Sidney Madge, well versed in the authorities of his time, describes the pattern in general terms:

> The victorious leader of an invading tribe, disposing of the spoils of war, divided the conquered territory [England] into three portions, one of which, the royal lands, he retained for his own needs; the second he shared among the armed followers who composed the 'host' and the 'hundred', a share ever after to be known as the private lands; and the third portion he reserved, under the name of the public lands for the constitutional needs of the newly established community.[1]

This scheme covered most of England up to 1066, but was then usurped by William, who reimposed the Roman concept of one freeholder only, namely the king. From the private lands of the defeated Anglo Saxons he hijacked vast tracts for his own private use, as royal land, and granted his followers most of the rest of the private lands. Rights on the common lands, now described as *terra regis*, the public lands described by Madge, were distributed by the king through the manors, which became the key instrument in the actual administration of what was essentially an agricultural and rural kingdom.

Much later the ultimate issue of the ownership of the common lands was decided in favour of the peerage, by the peerage. This was done through the various Enclosure acts in the seventeenth, eighteenth and nineteenth centuries, demonstrating the irreversible nature of the change in both power and ownership in Britain which stood revealed in the 1873–6 survey. The enclosures were particularly invidious in that the aristocracy took from a weak monarchy rights which were really those of the common people, but at a time when the common people had neither representation nor power, the monarchy was too debilitated to defend these rights.

Following the abolition of the monarchy in 1648 and the merging of crown and private royal lands under Cromwell it is not clear how much of either were recovered by Charles II, though it is accepted that they were 'a fraction of their former size.'[2] Some royal lands were restored to the royal family, who promptly began to sell off bits to finance their various extravagances – so much so that an act was passed in the middle of the reign of Queen Anne to prevent the monarch from selling off any more crown land without the consent of Parliament. All these actions, however, made it fairly clear that the Crown Estates were treated as the personal lands of the monarch.

At his accession to the throne in 1760 George III made a deal whereby he accepted a stipend of £1.2 million from Parliament, known as the Civil List, surrendering in return the revenues from the Crown Estate.[3] At the time the deal was highly advantageous to the king as the Crown Estate was in a pretty shambolic state. The exact nature of the crown lands was unclear, as was their extent, and the income was very low, down to £6000 a year in the eighteenth century,[4] the equivalent of £600,000 or so now. This state of affairs was due almost entirely to corruption on the part of Parliament and the king, as both used the Crown Estate and its revenues to bribe and buy political influence and enrich favourites.

At the beginning of Victoria's reign in 1841 the Crown Estate amounted to around 106,000 acres. Towards the end of her reign, in 1890, the estate had crept past the 220,000 acre mark and was producing the modern equivalent of £35 million in income, the key part of that income coming from the residential estate. The seabed was contributing nothing and was effectively worthless.

One of the principal reasons for the Crown Estate doubling in these years come about from the general clean-up of Government that had begun around 1829 and which reached its apotheosis in the Trevelyan reforms of the Civil Service starting in 1872. By 1890, the agricultural estate was producing about £4.5 million in modern terms, compared with £17.7 million now. More interestingly, the Crown Estate woodlands and waste were producing a little over £115,000, about £8 million in modern money. Nowadays forestry produces less than £3 million. This is partly due to the fact that in 1923 about 120,000 acres of woodland were transferred from the Crown Estate to the Forestry Commission. In theory this transfer should have cut the Crown Estate in size by about 60%. But if it did, by 1928 the Estate's managers had organised a remarkable recovery as the overall Estate had actually increased in size by 20,000 acres compared with 1890. The woodland acreage was itself down by only 27,000 acres. Admittedly this was a period when the deaths of the heirs to so many landed estates in World War One led to a rise in sales of country estates, and the Crown Estate seems to have had little trouble in picking up acreage.

TABLE 5/1

GROWTH OF THE CROWN ESTATE FROM THE LATE 1800s TO 1938

Acreage

	1890	1928	1937
Agricultural	69,617	108,000	138,000
Woodland & Waste	115,293	88,300*	88,000
Total Acreage	206,720	226,000	261,500

Revenues (£)

	1890	1928	1937
Agricultural	82,081	120,241	147,387
House Property	252,188	1,237,909	1,413,572
Mines and Quarries	30,656	95,349	137,540
Fee farm rents, etc.	43,891	20,244	17,027
Total	**£529,862**	**£1,595,843**	**£1,866,389**
Current value	**£37,000,000**	**£63,000,000**	**£65,000,000**

* In 1923 the Forest of Dean and New Forest (120,000 acres) was transferred to Forestry Commission.

The Crown Estate in the Twentieth Century

Even compared to Victoria's achievements, the greatest growth spurt in the Crown Estate, however, happened in the twentieth century. This century has seen a historic 'interregnum' marked by the ending of part of the land-owning peerage's absolute grip on both Houses of Parliament, and by the rise of universal adult suffrage. Yet it would seem that the electorate has been as uninformed about the expansion of the royals' landed estates as they were about the affair leading to the abdication of Edward VIII and of the royal exemption from tax. The period has been characterised by a failure to move the role of head of state along with the democratic tide of the times. The monarchy remains in place, apparently powerless, but with awesome influence behind the scenes. One of the ways that influence was used ruthlessly was to corrupt essentially the only means the population has to know what is going on, the media. The media, controlled by press barons almost universally tied to the royal or neo-royal circle, censored most of the facts about the reality of monarchy in the UK for most of the twentieth century. They certainly did not encourage reporters to investigate the abdication, the tax exemption, and far more invidiously, the unending expansion of royal lands in both duchies (Lancaster and Cornwall) and in the Crown Estate.

Today the Crown Estate has a total of 202,131 acres of rural land in England and Wales. (This excludes the Welsh acreage described in the Crown Estate accounts as miscellaneous and amounting to 63,000 acres.) Out of that massive acreage 175,321 acres were bought in the twentieth century. Put another way, less than 14% of the present estate was part of the Crown Estate in the nineteenth century. In Scotland the Crown Estate owns 93,049 acres, of which 78,575 acres have been bought since 1937. Less than 2% of the holding is nineteenth-century Crown Estate.

Unless Parliament calls a halt to what amounts to state purchases for a private endowment, the Crown Estate and the Duchy of Cornwall, which are already the largest related land holdings in the country and which between them constitute the largest two agricultural conglomerates in the UK, will achieve neo-monopolistic status in the real estate market. All further expansion by either corporation needs to be halted immediately, and the whole situation made the subject of a special commission. The alternative is to accept the fact that, in law, the Queen and her family are the largest landowners in the UK, and are going to become even bigger landowners, as a result of state patronage and state tolerance. The *Sunday Times* can now legitimately put the Queen back at or near the top of its annual Rich lists.

TABLE 5/2

SIGNIFICANT ACQUISITIONS IN THE CROWN ESTATE IN THE TWENTIETH CENTURY[5]

	County	Name of Estate	Acreage	Year Of Purchase
	ENGLAND			
1	Bedfordshire	Chicksands	282	1936
2	Berkshire	Windsor	3930	20th Century
3	Cambs	Holmewood	5088	1947
4	Cheshire	Delamere	184	Ancient
5	Cumbria	Aldingham	985	Ancient
		Manor Of Muchland And Torver	330 + 2110	Ancient
6	Devon	North Wyke	618	1981
7	Dorset	Bryanston	5878	1950, 1992, 1999
8	Yorks East Riding	Derwent	2700	1947/48, 1992
		Gardham	1083	1950
		Garton On The Wolds	2027	1981
		Sunk Island	12,363	1913, 1947, 1981
		Swine	4974	1859, 1871, 1962, 1999
9	Essex	Stapleford Abbots	3721	Part In 1996
10	Gloucestershire	Clearwell	1235	1907, 1912
		Hagloe	720	1853, 1902
11	Herefordshire	Gorhamury	3421	1931
		Putteridge	3501	1932
12	Kent	Bedgebury	7	1919
		Neats Court	741	1850, 1900
		Romney Marsh	9275	1958, 1992
13	Leicestershire	Gopsall	8080	1932
14	Lincolnshire	Billingsborough	14,031	1855 To 1999
		Ewerby	8570	1948, 1992, 1995, 1997
		Friskney	3096	1989, 1992
		Louth	5351	1989
		Whaplode	6798	Part Enclosure
		Wingland	11,562	1972, 1996, 1998
15	Norfolk	Croxton	8834	1930 And 1992
		King's Lynn	5177	1964, 1992, 1999
16	North Yorks	Boroughbridge	3224	1860, 1876
17	Nottingham	Bingham	8572	1926, 1938, 1992, 1997
		Laxton	1861	1981
18	Oxford	Wychwood	1251	Undated
19	Somerset	Dunster	9937	1950
		Taunton	9944	1944, 1952
20	Staffs And Shropshire	Patshull	3853	1959
21	Surrey	Oxshott	1625	1800s
22	Sussex	Poynings	1	1700s
23	Wiltshire	Devizes	10,342	1858, 1962, 1964
		Savernake	10,152	1950
	WALES			
24	Monmouthshire	Tintern	484	1901, 1996
25	Powys	Bronydd Mawyr	567	1983

	County	Name of Estate	Acreage	Year Of Purchase
26	Cardiganshire	Aberystwyth	91	1985, 1987
		Plynlimon	2970	Undated

SCOTLAND

	County	Name of Estate	Acreage	Year Of Purchase
27	Stirling	Stirling	447	Ancient, 1972
28	Dumfries & Galloway	Applegirth	17,399	1993
29	Moray	Fochabers	11,775	1937, 1990
		Glenlivet	45,895	1937, 1985
30	Highland	Caithness	1534	Ancient, 1909
31	Midlothian	Whitehill	3506	1969

WINDSOR ESTATE

		Name of Estate	Acreage	Year Of Purchase
		Windsor Park Etc	14,002	Ancient, 1930s

MISCELLANEOUS 63,587 acres (Described in the annual reports as Commons and Wasteland, revenues from sporting rights, fishing, sales of timber. Acreage in individual counties, which are all in Wales, is not identified.)

Note:
Lands described as Ancient are pre-1900 and in many cases pre-1649. The accounts apply no date.

Who Owns the Crown Estate?

The Palace brochures on Royal Finance of 1993 and 1995 may not make explicit reference to the Crown Estate, but the legal implication of their explanation of the arrangement by which the Civil List is granted by Parliament is that the surrender of the Crown Estate revenues (note, revenues) is voluntary:

> This system was changed in 1760 on George III's accession when it was decided that the whole of the cost of the Civil List should be provided by Parliament in return for the surrender of the hereditary revenues by the King for the duration of the reign. This arrangement, whereby at the beginning of each reign the Sovereign agrees to continue the surrender of the hereditary revenues in return for the receipt of the annual Civil List, has continued to this day.[6]

This 'voluntary surrender' is confirmed in the Act of Succession passed by Parliament at the time of each coronation. So, quite clearly, the next, or indeed any future sovereign, does not have to surrender the Crown Estate revenues, a fact obliquely referred to by Prince Charles on at least one occasion in public. The Crown Estate itself lays out the legal position quite clearly in the front page of its accounts:

> The Crown Estate is not the property of the Government. Nor is it the Sovereign's private estate. It is part of the hereditary possessions of the Sovereign 'in right of the crown'.[7]

In other words, the Queen as Mrs Windsor does not own the Crown Estate, but Mrs Windsor as the Queen does own the Crown Estate. Practically speaking she can't sell it off. Neither can the government. There is a legal logjam, arising out of a historic muddle. But the muddle can be resolved if both parties agree that it should.

In the context of the ownership of the Crown Estate, it is enlightening to look at the legal position of the Duchy of Lancaster and its 66,000 acres. Here is what the Palace has to say:

> The history of the landed estate known as the Duchy of Lancaster goes back to the 13th century. Since 1399 this estate passed to each reigning monarch, with the Duchy revenues providing a source of income separate from other Crown inheritances. This separate identity was preserved when in 1760 George III surrendered the revenue from the Crown Estates to the Government in exchange for the Civil List, but retained the Duchy of Lancaster revenues. The Sovereign has no access to the capital of the Duchy.[8]

The Duchy provided the Queen with a tax-free sum of £5.9 million in 2000.

The Queen owns the revenues from the Duchy of Lancaster, but not the freeholds. She does not own the revenues from the Crown Estate having voluntarily leased them to the Government at her Coronation in 1953, but she clearly believes that she does own the freehold.

Privatising the Crown Estate

The issue of the nature of the tenure of the Crown Estate is not simply theoretic. The European Convention of Human Rights, recently incorporated into UK law, prohibits confiscation of any property without compensation, for any citizen whose government has signed up to the convention. The original convention was largely the brainchild of Sir Winston Churchill, who no doubt had his historical eye on the charter drawn up by the barons at Runnymede in 1215. On this basis any attempt by the Government to dispose of either the Crown Estate or the Duchy of Lancaster would have to lead to compensation for the Queen. A common form of compensation today is one based on some kind of compounding of the annual revenues.[9] A conservative figure would be ten years, which would mean offering the Queen £59 million for the Duchy of Lancaster and £1.3 billion for the Crown Estate. In practice, both figures ill reflect the capital values of the property portfolios held by the Crown Estate and the Duchy of Lancaster. Given that the last Tory government was touting the idea of privatising the Crown Estate, the question of how the Queen would be compensated is a very real one. The Tories neither mentioned nor addressed this particular aspect of the policy. Now the question has become a real one for Gordon Brown, the current Chancellor of the Exchequer, who has actually published a list of state assets which are potential candidates for privatisation.[10]

The Palace are enormously reluctant to clarify the position of the Crown Estate and the Duchy, precisely because any sell-off would involve a huge, probably tax-free sum in compensation to the Queen. Their sensitivity arose not because of the threat of socialist nationalisation under a Labour government, but because of the potentially disastrous confluence of antipathy to the Royal family with the tidal wave of antipathy to the Tory government in the mid 1990s. Some argued that so insensitive had the Tories become that they could not see that the Crown Estate settlement, if it had come about, might have actually scuppered the monarchy, whose purchase on public support was even then in serious decline.

With its 24.5 million acres, the revenue-based value of the institutional crown lands is at least £1.6 billion.[11] The monarchy knows that the public is not going to buy a state handout on that scale to anyone, not even the Queen, whatever level of personal respect she still commands. The alternative is for the Queen to relinquish the claim graciously and donate the proceeds to the nation. This is unlikely to happen for two reasons.

Neither the Queen nor most of her immediate entourage are absolutely confident that the monarchy will continue much beyond Charles, maybe his sons. Combined with this is the fact that the Windsors have shown a very real interest in and parsimony with money – witness Edward VIII's haggling over how much he would take with him when he abdicated.[12] It is rumoured that some of the courtiers are playing to both the uncertainty and the parsimony abroad in the family by suggesting that when the handout comes it should be taken whatever the risks, with a propaganda offensive to soften up the public in advance. Oddly, there is a better chance of the propaganda working, and achieving a degree of public acceptance, under a Labour government than there ever was under the 1992–7 Tory government.

In discussions that took place between various Treasury officials during Ken Clarke's period as Chancellor of the Exchequer, the issue of exactly how to compensate the Queen in the event of the privatisation of the Crown Estate, in effect to buy her out, was raised. The official most directly involved in those discussions was Ken Clarke's special political advisor, the Hon. Tessa Keswick. She is the daughter of the late 14th Lord Lovat, a much-decorated soldier, who went to the Catholic Eton, Ampleforth. During her childhood Lord Lovat was one of the largest hereditary landowners in Scotland, owning 76,000 acres.[13] This was a fall on the Lovat lands in 1876, when they ran to 181,719 acres. Tessa, or more correctly Teresa, Fraser first married Lord Reay, scion of the banking family of Reay, and an old Etonian who was also a Government minister in the Lords in the early 1980s. They were divorced in 1978 and she went on to marry Henry Keswick, an old Etonian banker and heir to part of the huge Hong Kong based Jardine Matheson empire. The Keswick family own over 22,000 acres in Scotland. Henry Keswick is a director of Robert Fleming Holdings Ltd, the number two banking advisor to the Palace. Her brother-in-law, Simon, is a member of the Queen's Bodyguard in Scotland, an old Etonian who is married to a sister of the Earl of Dalhousie, who owns 43,800 acres in Scotland.[14] The point of this little litany is to show that the moving force in the drive to privatise the Crown Estate was not exactly a disinterested outsider. She shared a common background with the Earl of Airlie, the then Lord Chamberlain, and she married into a family directly connected with the Palace. Nothing in her activities – she is a distinctly right wing Tory – gives any hint that she would embark on a course of action likely to offend the Palace. Quite the contrary. For much of the period that she was 'taking soundings' in the Treasury, a Scottish landowner and old Etonian, the 8th Earl of Mansfield, was the First Crown Estate Commissioner. Proprietor of 37,000 Scottish acres and owner of Scone Palace, Mansfield comes with all the arrogance that Eton can inculcate. He refused to be interviewed on the issue of the 'informal' talks that had taken place about the privatisation plan that Keswick was pushing. His bluster when approached[15] made it impossible to know whether he was denying that talks had taken place, or denying that anything official was happening. He departed the role of First Crown Estate Commissioner in 1995, the same year that Tessa Keswick took off from the Treasury to head the Centre for Policy Studies, where she proceeded to publish a paper advocating the privatisation of the Crown Estate, although this did not include any hint as to how the Queen's interest was to be bought out.[16] She tried to have the privatisation of the Crown Estate included in the Tory election manifesto of 1997, but failed.

The Value of the Crown Estate

The largest physical part of the Crown Estate is the seabed from the low water mark to the twelve mile limit for all of the UK, including Northern Ireland. This amounts to about

23.8 million acres. The second largest part of the estate is the foreshore, for about half the UK. This is the real estate between the high and low tide mark and comes to something like 320,000 acres. Together with the seabed it is called the marine estate and they produced £26.1 million in 1999/2000.

The third part of the Crown Estate is the urban estate, which includes some of the most desirable freeholds in London. The total acreage of this is small at 512 acres, but the revenues are not. The figure for 1999/2000 was £127.1 million.

The fourth part of the Crown Estate is the rural estate. Covering about 198,000 acres, this produced £17.7 million net in 1999/2000. All the above figures are before expenses. In addition there is the Scottish estate of over 90,000 acres, which with the rural estate, and the Windsor estate of 14,000 acres, brings the Crown Estate's agricultural holdings to 293,000 acres. It is the largest single landholder in the agricultural sector in the UK. (Excludes Miscl 63,000 acres and some other small holdings)

TABLE 5/3

CROWN ESTATE ACREAGE AND REVENUES 2000, BEFORE EXPENSES

	Acreage	Revenues
Urban	512	£127,000,000
Agricultural	359,600	£31,000,000
Foreshore	320,000	£14,000,000
Seabed	23,300,000	£12,000,000
Totals	**23,970,714**	**£184,00,000**

Over and above the question of its earning potential is the issue of what the Crown Estate is worth. *Business Age* magazine, then in Dutch ownership, suggested in its 1995 Rich List that the valuation of the Crown Estate property quoted in the annual report at £2.2 billion was too conservative by far.[17] The magazine had done a trawl of London estate agents and others, most of whom suggested that the valuation was indeed on the low side. This is very easy to prove.

The Crown Estate is, on the surface, one of the truly great property success stories of the last decade. Revenues, exclusive of costs and expenses, have grown from £32.4 million in 1988 to £187.9 million in the latest accounts (1999/2000). This is a growth record better than that of any other property company in the UK, and does not disguise the fact that the estate is capable of significant development in a number of areas.

The price-earnings ratio, the formula that describes the relationship between the price paid for a share and the pre-tax earnings, in the property sector of the London Stock Exchange, was 32.5 in August 1997, coming down to 20.2 by October 2000. Using this as a guide to what the Crown Estate might be worth, and the revenue surplus as the equivalent of profit, we get a figure of £4.2 billion for 1997 or £2.6 billion for 2000. But the Crown Estate isn't like most of the property companies quoted on the Stock Exchange. For a start it has no debt. Secondly it has a lot of cash. Thirdly, its metropolitan assets are in quite the classiest part of London, on the edge of Regent's Park, no normal urban acreage.

Property companies in this category, like Ashquay Gp (p/e 41.6), Grantchester Holdings

(40.4) and Benchmark (50.3) are all trading at price-earnings ratios in excess of 40, in some cases 50. Using Benchmark trading at 50 in 2000, the Crown Estate is worth £6.6 billion. But this, according to some analysts, still undervalues the Estate, because it takes no account of the growing and potential value of the river beds, salmon fishing, and rights of way on the foreshore, not to mention the huge potential for non oil, gas and coal exploration on the seabed. If stone aggregates from the seabed in a bad year can yield £26 million, what can proper exploitation in a good year yield? Up to ten times that amount, according to exploration analysts.[18]

The very conservative book valuation placed on the assets of the estate by the Commissioners has travelled from £1.69 billion in 1988, through a high point of £2.4 billion in the boom of 1988, down to £1.7 billion in the bust of 1993 and back up to £3.6 billion for 1999/2000. It is here that the potential of the estate can be seen. The top five UK property companies, British Land, Slough Estates, Grosvenor Estates, Land Securities and Rugby Estates, have a relationship of 6% between net profit and asset value in their books. The Crown Estate is actually well below that, at only 3.9%. In addition, none of the major UK property companies have a special income similar to the £26 million that the Crown Estate derives from the seabed. With that stripped out the actual revenue-to-asset figure falls significantly, to 3%. This is not the accounting trick that it might appear.

The Crown Estate has placed a value of £188 million on the marine estate, which, in Stock Exchange terms is a price-earnings ratio of 7.2. The minimum valuation should be ten times current income, which is £26 million, giving a very conservative £260 million, which in turn is just one third of current Stock Exchange property-to-income valuations. The estate itself admits that the sea bed income is poor, while analysts say that it has significant development potential, which is of course what investors pay for in the Stock Exchange.

And the concluding argument for the government is even simpler. It manages and controls an asset worth at least £4 billion–£6 billion on the Stock Market, maybe twice that. Out of its revenues of £187 million the asset currently produces a net income for the government of £132 million. £4 billion placed on deposit would earn at least 6.5%, maybe 7%. That is a sum of £260 million at the lower figure. At the higher figure of 7%, and the higher valuation of £6 billion, the net income for government would be £420 million, more than three times what it gets now. And that is not the end of it for government. On the basis of replaced government borrowings the government would save the same sum, doubling the value of the cash it would raise by selling the estate. And of course the government would receive tax on the privatised estates profits, which at a minimum of 20% on £300 million, would be upwards of £60 million.

The Crown Estate had £50 million in the bank in cash and £132.5 million in gilt edged securities (Government stock) in the 1999/2000 accounts. Those two assets generated income of £13 million a return of 7.1%. By taking this sum out of the turnover of £187 million, we find, very roughly, that assets valued at £3.4 billion generated income of £174 million, before expenses of around £35 million, to yield a gross surplus of around £139 million. This is a 4% yield and it needs to be taken in context with a 9.7% increase in the value of the underlying property assets. Further, the income stream is likely to do an extraordinary jump over the next ten years, when 25 long leases in London's Regent Street, currently yielding only £500,000, fall in and the Crown Estate regains control of the buildings. Those buildings are currently valued at £130 million, which is very low for one of the world's top shopping streets. The total area of Crown Estate property in

Regent St is about 3.2 million square feet, in an area where shopping space is renting for between £30 and £40 a square foot. Fully let, the estate is looking at gross revenues of over £100 million from one street alone, before refurbishment costs. For any Chancellor thinking of a flotation, these kinds of prospects need to be considered because they add up to a debt-free property company with serious cash in the bank and prospective net revenues of about £300 million, something that would place the estate into the price-earning brackets of the late 1990s, around 40 (with a Stock Market capitalisation of £12 billion) or 50 (capitalisation of £15 billion).

There is only one way to value the Crown Estate, just as there is only one way to sell it. That is piecemeal and that is the advice now being given to the government internally. Any 'global sell off', however accomplished, would overvalue some assets, probably the London properties, and undervalue others, such as the seabed. But a series of flotations would have the desired effect of ridding the government of a corporation which has no direct relevance or bearing on the work of government. It would also prevent the kind of monstrous give aways such as British Rail that occurred with such frequency during the last years of the Tory government and which cost the taxpayer at least £6 billion.[19]

A piecemeal open sale would also prevent the cherry picking of certain assets of the estate, such as its Scottish landholdings, by existing Scottish landowners, which might happen if the sales were on a private basis. It would certainly balance the books in relation to a century and a half of overpayments by the state to the Crown between 1760 and 1910, and help to compensate for the unpaid tax between 1932 and 1993.

All that would be left to settle would be how many of the shares were given to the Queen. Palace negotiators have already been there with the sharpest of claims, backed by the sharpest of brains. A Palace source says that the opening position was that the Queen owns the estate and it is up to the government to suggest what proportion should be allocated to her in a sell off. The position of the government is unknown but 10%, or around £660 million, is what is being considered, according to some sources.

But for any Chancellor thinking of a flotation, he also has to think of this: that the next Sovereign might just refuse, as he has hinted, to 'volunteer' this little gem to the government, and by doing so could block any flotation, since he is now protected by the Human Rights bill. And there is no way around this. The negotiations with the Palace on this matter are going to be exceedingly interesting in the next year or two.

The Crown Estate Commission

In the words of the present First Crown Estate Commissioner, Sir Denys Henderson, the Crown Estate has changed from 'a traditional landed estate to one of the UK's top performing property owners.'[20] And Sir Denys, despite only being two and a half years in the job at the time, had been quite critical to the changed ethos at the Crown Estate.[21] A Scottish solicitor by training, with a degree from Aberdeen University, he was from 1987 to 1995 the chairman of ICI, the UK's largest industrial group. He is also the non-executive chairman of the Rank Organisation and the Dalgety Group.

He is, unashamedly, an industrialist, and a very modern manager. A greater contrast with his predecessor, the Earl of Mansfield, other than the Scottish background, it would be hard to find. Appointed by the Tory government, he would appear to have buried all talk of a privatisation of the Estate.

The day-to-day running of the estate is in the hands of a high ranking former civil servant from the Department of the Environment, Professor Christopher Howes. He took over what is the chief executive's job in 1989 and has put in place many of the reforms and administrative changes which have been so successfully represented by Sir Denys Henderson. Though there was never any visible tension between Howes and Mansfield, there was a sharp contrast in their approaches. Howes was a highly successful partner in a surveying practice in Norwich before he joined the Department of the Environment. A visiting professor of architecture at the Bartlett School of Architecture in University College London, he is a very modern manager.

Both Sir Denys and Professor Howes are members of the Prince of Wales Trust but neither went to an English public school. In fact only three of the eight Crown Commissioners, the board of the Estate, went to public school in England. The first is Lord de Ramsey a peer who went to Oundle school and is the chairman of the Environment Agency, the successor to the National River Authority. The predominant flavour of the entire board of commissioners is of modern professional people. The Comissioner for the Urban Estate is Sir John James, a trustee of the Grosvenor Estate where he was once the chief agent. He is a former director of the Sun Alliance Insurance company, which has historic links with the Grosvenor Estate. He has also been a director of a number of banks, including the Royal Bank of Scotland. Like De Ramsey, he went to a first rank English public school, Sherbourne. The fourth commissioner is John Norris. Like James, he went to a public school, Brentwood, and like James he does not appear to have gone on to university, but runs his own farm in Essex where he is the Lord Lieutenant, the Queen's representative. He has been on the executive committee of the Country Landowners Association since 1973 and was its president from 1985 to 1987. The Deputy Chief Executive and a commissioner since 1995 is D.E.G. Griffiths, a former senior civil servant in the Ministry of Defence and at the Treasury.

The seventh commissioner is another farmer, Ian Grant, a Scot like the top two men. He went to a Scottish public school, Strathallan, and then to agricultural college. He has been president of both the National Farmers Union in Scotland and of the Confederation of British Industry in Scotland. The last of the Commissioners, Helen Chapman, is a partner in the surveying and auctioneering firm of Jones Lang Wooton and is a director of Legal and General, the insurance company.

Quite visibly this is a board of professionals, headed by two very professional managers. It is also a board of considerable experience in the property field, which makes complete sense. Five of the eight have honours of some kind, mostly CBEs, and of course all were advised for appointment to the Queen by the Conservative government 1979–1997. As a result there is a strong flavour of 'small c' conservatism about all of the commissioners. Indeed, three of the eight have close links to the Prince of Wales or the Duchy of Cornwall, Sir John James being the keeper of the records for that institution. Nonetheless, what is absolutely striking is the transparency and completeness of the annual report. It is a model document from the very model of a modern board of management.

The Future of the Crown Estate

The openness of the Crown Estate accounts has clearly brought no jeopardy to the safety of the Crown or the State, as the more old fashioned courtiers once thought. But it has presented the Government with an open and shut case for ending the anomaly whereby an estate whose freehold belongs to another party, and over which it does not have final control or ownership, can go on expanding for ever thanks to abnormal financial privileges.

The low real rate of return on the non financial assets of the Estate is something that a breakup and disposal could help to rectify. On top of which, the Government could begin the long overdue experiment of placing overlarge estates on the market, in small pieces, to try and achieve some kind of better economic return from land in the country.

Chapter Six

The Duchy of Cornwall

THE DUCHY OF Cornwall is a landed estate stretching across 22 English counties, mostly in the southwest of the country. It now runs to more than 255,000 acres, more than twice its size in 1872. Common estimates of the size of the Duchy at 141,000 land-based acres overlooks its ownership of most of the Cornish foreshore of 230 miles, which gives it an additional 100,000 acres or more and of 14,000 acres of estuarial riverbeds in Cornwall and in Devon. The ownership of the Duchy is not in doubt. It belongs to Prince Charles as Duke of Cornwall until he becomes king. At this point it will revert to his son William, who automatically succeeds his father to the dukedom. In the event that Charles and his sons were killed the estate would revert to the Crown, and would be administered by trustees. In the absence of a male heir to the throne, as was the case when the present Queen was a child, her father George VI appointed trustees to administer the estate, making it quite clear that the Duchy land belongs, ultimately, to the sovereign personally. For the purposes of any disposal the government or Parliament remain trapped by the European Convention of Human Rights, which prohibits confiscation without compensation of any form of property.

The Duke cannot, by law, sell the estate, or any part of it other than for minor adjustments in local areas.[1] The Duchy is governed by a series of acts of Parliament, several dating back to the last century. This, in fact, is one of the arguments proposed by the Duchy for its beneficent ownership, but the issue of an ever growing, never diminishing estate, is an important one. It makes the estate, together with the rest of the Queen's lands, a huge encumbrance to a progressive monarchy at the start of the third millennium. It also represents counter democratic and constitutional activity that is at odds with the original concept of the relationship between monarch and Parliament in recent history. The inevitable growth of the Duchy represents an approach to monarchy that was consistent with the Imperial aims of Victoria's courtiers who sought to make the British monarch as pre-eminent in wealth as it was in honours and glory. And it has also helped to achieve another purpose, which was to make the monarchy independent of Parliament.[2]

Charles Windsor, the 24th Duke of Cornwall, has not made his money. He has inherited it, though he has made significant gains on that inheritance, albeit on the back of a series of tax dodges. This is hardly the picture the Prince wants to paint of himself, especially to the general public. It may not even be the picture he wants to paint of himself, to himself. For this genial, kindly and totally professional man is as trapped as the Queen by the wealth-encrusted project in which the Victorians enfolded the monarchy.

The History of the Duchy
Following the Norman Conquest in 1066 Cornwall, the westernmost of the English counties, was created an earldom. The lands, first granted to Count Brian of Brittany, were then granted to Count Robert of Mortain, who by 1086 had 277 manors assigned to him. This represented most of Cornwall, with the exception of 18 royal and 44 monastic estates. This was an unusual distribution and it is not clear just how many of these manors were actually within Robert's control. Between the Conquest and the fourteenth century

the earldom was held by a variety of people, including Richard, the second son of King John. On the death of John of Eltham in 1336 the earldom and lands passed to the Crown through the process known as escheat, whereby the Crown took possession for itself of any estate where there were no heirs. It was a valuable if turbulent prize. At the time the county was the source of a significant proportion of the world's tin output. But the miners were a rebellious and independent people, whose lives appear to have been brutish and short, fixed that way by the poisonous tin they mined.

On 16 March 1337 Edward III, under the shadow of his mother Isabelle, daughter of Philip IV of France, and her lover, and with the murder of his father ten years before still on his conscience, summoned a Parliament. There England's first dukedom was formally created by royal proclamation, with the lands and revenues of the Duchy of Cornwall conferred on his son, Edward of Woodstock, the 'Black' Prince of Wales.

Historians are not agreed on the king's motives, but the heir to the throne was now the pre-eminent peer in England after the king. The charter of creation contains two key provisions that still operate and are reflected in the various acts of Parliament which now govern the functioning of the Duchy. The first of these reverts the title and the lands to the Crown when there is no male heir. The second is that the Crown must surrender the title and lands to the male heir when he reaches his majority. Over time a bar on the sell-off of the estate evolved, although this is something which has often been ignored through the Duchy's history. In a curious remark in an article in the book published to celebrate the 650th anniversary of the creation of the Duchy in 1987, the Duchy librarian Graham Haslam wrote that

> At its creation and subsequently, it has continued as one of the largest private landed estates in England. The Crown Estates, Church Commissioners and British Rail are much larger, but they are institutions rather than individuals.

The crucial word here is 'England'. In Britain as a whole it is not the largest private estate in the land. In Scotland the Duke of Buccleuch has more than double the acreage of the Duchy, at 270,700 acres, while the Earl of Seafield has 101,000 acres. There is also an English duke, Westminster, with a far larger landed estate across both England and Scotland. In the UK alone Westminster has about 129,300 acres, 55,000 of which are in England. Abroad he has as many as 400,000 acres.

Haslam is undoubtedly correct in terms of the ancient, pre-1660 Duchy, but it is inaccurate to say it 'continued' that way. The whole of the Duchy was confiscated by the Cromwellian Parliament in 1648 and sold off. By the time of the Return of Owners of Land in 1872 it had recovered only 74,113 of those acres, across seven counties.[3]

Edward, 23rd Duke of Cornwall

By the early 1900s the overall estate, especially the urban acres in London's Kennington, were in a dreadful state of decay, as were much of the Scilly Isles. Prince Edward, the eldest son of George V and heir to the throne, was both an earnest and profligate man. He needed all the cash he could get and his main source of income was the Duchy of Cornwall.

Not that the Duchy was much of a farming proposition at the time. Most of the income, as Bateman had observed in 1876, came from mining. In 1910, the year before Edward was invested as Prince of Wales, the mining income was £20,208, about £1 million today. It is interesting to note that the government was also paying the Duchy over £16,000 a year in lieu of tin coinage at the same time, so Edward was drawing close to the equivalent of £2 million a year from the non-farming side of the Duchy. Despite Haslam's attempt to paint Edward as a caring landlord, even he is pressed to put a good gloss on the fact that Edward did not make his home in the Duchy or any of its properties, choosing instead to live at Fort Belvedere in Kent. In fact he visited the Duchy only five times between 1919 and his abdication in 1936.

Edward initiated a number of purchases for the Duchy, mostly of farms around Dartmoor in Devon. In 1927 Edward persuaded the Duchy to buy a farm in Nottingham. Following this he purchased a cattle ranch in western Canada. In doing so he was treading in the footsteps of the wealthiest man in England, Bendor, the 2nd Duke of Westminster. Fearing a new European war Bendor had made huge purchases in western Canada, buying up much of what was, and much of what was later to become, Vancouver. How much Bendor was influenced by another aristocrat, the Earl of Iveagh, the Guinness magnate, who had been investing in western Canada since around the time of World War One, is not known. But a whole group of British aristocrats had followed Iveagh and Westminster, some buying in Canada, some investing in Switzerland, not just because of the threat of war, but perhaps more importantly because of the threat of taxation. Tax was less of an issue with Edward, who had managed to avoid most taxes. But by the middle of the 1930s the Prince of Wales was seriously distracted by his affair with Mrs Wallis Simpson, and with the fact that he would at some time become king. He mixed seriously with the 'appeasement' set and it is still not clear to what extent Prime Minister Stanley Baldwin's opposition to Edward's marriage to Wallis Simpson was based on the Prince's deep ambivalence towards the new German Reich.

In 1932 Edward had appointed Sir Walter Moncton as the Attorney General of the Duchy, a London-based job that was seen as part of the Prince's household and had little or nothing to do with the land or people of Cornwall, who, like the rest of England, remained ignorant of their Duke's affair with Mrs Simpson, and who were totally ignorant of what actually went on in London amongst the royal set. The Duchy's secretary, Sir Clive Burn, Sir Walter and another member of the Duchy Council, Sir Edward Peacock, were critical advisors during the actual abdication itself. Sir Walter Moncton acted as the go between with Stanley Baldwin, while Sir Edward Peacock stayed with the king throughout the crisis.[4]

Moncton's career is an interesting one. When war broke out he was appointed Director General of the Press and Censorship bureau, a post for which he was perhaps ideally suited following his success in censoring the story of the Duke of Cornwall's affair with Wallis Simpson from the British press, and from the British public, through influence with the proprietors.[5] Following this he was sent to Cairo as propaganda supremo in the Middle East theatre of war. His various biographical entries list this latter appointment as lasting from 1941 to 1942, with no subsequent listing until 1945, when he was briefly Solicitor General. There is an assumption that Moncton was deeply involved in some of the war's darkest operations, and that he was the one who organised the despatch of (Sir) Anthony Blunt, the Soviet double agent, to Germany in 1945 to recover correspondence which would have compromised the Duke of Windsor, as Edward was known after the abdication. Moncton was elected an MP for Bristol in 1951 and eventually became the Secretary of State for Defence and was created Viscount in 1957. By 1960 he was the President of the British Bankers Association, although he had never formally been a banker. Sir Edward Peacock went on to head Barings bank and remained an advisor to both King George VI and to the Queen until his death at the age of 89.

What is clear is that Edward used Duchy appointments to create his own inner circle of advisors, who seamlessly took over when he became king. What it also shows is the integrated nature of the inner establishment, which thrives whatever happens to the country, and which retains secret and undeclared influence long after the electorate have cast their vote.[6]

Following his abdication, Edward went abroad, first to Austria, then France. At the beginning of the war he was called up and commissioned a major general in the reserves. Based in Paris he was ordered by the British government to return to England in 1940, ahead of the invading Germans. He ignored the order, motored south through France and then to Spain, where he continued to ignore his orders.

Churchill asked the Duke of Westminster, Bendor, to intervene and persuade the wayward officer back to his duty. This Bendor tried to do by offering Edward the Westminster family home, the palatial Eaton Hall, as his residence for the duration of the war. When the Palace refused to allow the Duchess of Windsor to call herself Her Royal Highness, Edward refused his orders yet again, declined even Eaton Hall, and by way of yet another compromise went instead to become Governor of the Bahamas. There he consorted with the Nazi agent Wenner Gren and became a dabbler in currencies, a crime under wartime regulations in Britain and her colonies. At the same time some of those from the circles in which he had moved before the war were in touch with people in Hitler's entourage in Germany, something possibly condoned by the British Government. Amongst these who were pro appeasement were many of the great landowners, Buccleuch, Westminster, Londonderry, the Duke of Bedford, Lord Rothermere, Lord Arnold, Lord Halifax and Lord Rushcliffe. During 1940–1 a plot was hatched to replace Churchill with an appeasement Prime Minister, probably Halifax. In addition, George VI would be forced to abdicate and would be replaced by Edward. The date of the coup was fixed for 11 May 1941. The night before Hitler's deputy flew to England to be in place when the new government was announced. Hess parachuted onto the lands of the Duke of Hamilton, mistaking him, so it is said officially, for the pro-German Duke of Buccleuch. The full details will never be known for sure as all the records relating to Hess have been destroyed, to ensure that the public never find out what was really going on between the 23rd Duke of Cornwall and Hitler's government.[7]

The Duchy under George VI

When Edward abdicated there was no male heir to the throne and therefore no Prince of Wales. Instead, the Duchy reverted to the Crown, in the person of King George VI. George succeeded to the throne soon after taxation ended for the monarch. On top of that, he had been left the equivalent of over £20 million by his father (George V), who had left nothing to Edward on the grounds that Edward should have been able to save from his income from the Duchy and would have ample funds from the Civil List.[8] In other words the abdication put on the throne a very wealthy man who had no tax obligations and now had the additional untaxed revenues of the Duchy of Cornwall to add to his late father's beneficence.

Unlike his brother, the new king had some interest in his Cornish estates. Haslam notes that 'King George VI and Queen Elizabeth introduced an active management. The king personally attended Council meetings. After the abdication in December 1936 the new king and queen toured the Duchy estates in Devon and Cornwall the following year.' In 1941 he purchased the Newton Park Estate near Bath, adding 4797 acres to the Duchy. This was followed by the 2127-acre Pawton Estate in Cornwall, later added to further with the Pencalenick Estate in 1952 (918 acres) and the Arrallas estate of 2500 acres.

In 1951 the Duchy bought the 2900-acre Duloe Estate from the Church Commissioners. By the time George V1 died in 1952 the Duchy had expanded by over 14,000 acres. A great deal of this expansion occurred under a new restriction imposed by the post-war Labour Government that all Duchy profits should be handed to the Treasury while there was no Duke or a Duke was in his minority. What profits were left each year after this bout of buying are not easy to establish, but they were clearly minimal.[9] George and his advisors, especially the financial ones, had driven the usual coach and horses through the tax arrangements and had cocked a snook at the profit rule by making sure there were little or none. Nor did the situation change under the regime imposed by the Queen and Prince Philip. In 1959 the Duchy bought the 1247-acre Daglinworth Estate in Gloucestershire. And there is the huge Prudential purchase referred to later.

Charles, Duke of Cornwall

In 1952 Prince Charles, aged four, became the Duke of Cornwall on his mother's accession to the throne. In 1969, at his 21st birthday, he was invested with the title of Prince of Wales and inherited the Duchy. The Duchy he inherited was roughly composed as follows:

Devon	72,397	acres
Cornwall	21,292	acres
Somerset	7752	acres
Wiltshire	3768	acres
Isles of Scilly	3980	acres
Dorset	3600	acres
Avon	8916	acres
Lincolnshire	1936	acres
Gloucestershire	1863	acres
Cambridgeshire	1185	acres

The remaining holdings are all below 1000 acres. There is a very valuable estate of 40 acres in London around the Oval cricket ground at Kennington.

The total, which excluded the foreshore and esturial acreage, came to about 128,000 acres.[10]

The Duchy, strictly speaking, has no great house. Until recently, the successive dukes' princely title came first and they lived in London, or Kent as did Edward VIII. But Prince Charles, a committed environmentalist, has made a modest change in this respect by making his home at the 1100 acre Highgrove estate, the site of the Duchy's home farm, which was previously at Stoke Climsland in Cornwall. At Highgrove he has created one of the largest organic farms in the country, as well as one of the most attractive gardens in England. And Highgrove's influence spreads into the surrounding areas where local designers use Highgrove wool to make fashionable and expensive knitwear.

The valuation placed on this huge estate, however, is curious. In the three years from 1994 to 1997 the valuation moves very little, from £58.3 million in 1994, to £61.5 million in 1995 to £64.3 million in 1997.[11] Based on recent London freehold sales the minimum value of the Kennington acres alone, according to one London estate agent, is £400 million.[12] As with the Crown Estate accounts, there is a significant underestimate of the market value of the land involved.

Applying the same Stock Exchange valuation as was applied to the Crown Estate in the previous chapter, the price-earning ratio of 32.5 (1997) on the Duchy's net surplus of £6.8 million for 1997 indicates a potential value of £221 million. And, while the figure of 32.5 is very high (in 2000 the p/e for the Crown Estate was 20.2), it almost certainly undervalues the Duchy. The Duchy has, in addition to its acres, an investment portfolio worth £44.9 million in 1997. This is a sharp rise from £33 million in 1995 and displays a greater appreciation of assets on the Stock Exchange compared with land. Indeed the appreciation of the investment portfolio, from a cost at purchase of £5.2 million, is fairly staggering. It gives the Duchy considerable freedom and latitude when it comes to raising extra money for the Prince, when for example he was struck by the less than minor problems of making his divorce settlement with the late Princess Diana.[13] The apparently poor growth in the value of the land should be viewed with scepticism, however. It is highly likely that the land in the Duchy is worth at least three times its book valuation and that it has put on considerable growth in the last few years, in a similar way to the Crown Estate. Unlike the Crown Estate the Duchy actually has debt in the form of loan stock paying a very princely rate of 10.48%, a good deal better than most bank deposits and not redeemable until 2014. It would be interesting to know who the holders of the loan stock are, which, although unsecured, is a blue chip investment indeed.

In addition to these investments, the Duchy doesn't believe in encountering cash crises. It carried £4.3 million in the bank in 1995 and £7.7 million in the bank in 1997. The 1999/2000 accounts for the Duchy show that total income was £15 million, with £2.3 million of that coming from the share portfolio and from cash deposits. Operating costs rose from £6.8 million to £7 million, leaving a net surplus of £6.9 million, up £6.4 million in the previous year. Investments in repairs, maintenance, etc. were just over £3 million, the average over the last ten years. However, to lend strength to the critique of an estate which claims that it cannot sell off any major assets, but which has no legal limit on its expansion, the Duchy in 1999–2000 spent £49 million buying most of the rural portfolio of the Prudential Insurance company. This added over 20,000 acres to the estate, after the 7000-acre Scottish element of the Prudential portfolio had been sold off because the Duchy cannot hold land in Scotland.

Turning to the rural acres, one way of assessing their value is to look at rents. However, all the rental income of the Duchy is grouped together with only woodlands broken out. The estate, which includes Kennington, brought in £12 million before expenses in 1997, an average of £93 per acre, with the woodlands bringing in £980,000 and showing a loss of £570,000. The biggest piece of the rural estate is in Devon, with just under 73,000 acres, comprising most of the Dartmoor National Park, but including much other land as well. There are about 20 working farms on the moor but they are not the most profitable and Duchy revenue is boosted by income from the lease on Dartmoor prison, which includes a 1600-acre farm, and from the Ministry of Defence, which trains heavily on the moor. The Duchy's position on the military lease is defensive. The 24,000 acres rented to the MoD are used as an artillery range and are the subject of considerable opposition from local groups, including the National Park Authority, the Countryside Commission and the Dartmoor Preservation Society, the latter now over 100 years old. But the Duchy cites 'the national interest' and continues to permit the army to train there. The moor also attracts a vast number of visitors, most of them local. This growth in internal tourism has done much to enhance the value of what might be called the more minor of the Duchy's activities, the renting of food and refreshment booths, vehicles and sites around the moor. The Duchy also owns a certain amount of the town of Okehampton.

In Cornwall itself the Duchy is neither the largest landowner nor the most influential.

With a holding of around 21,000 acres it is larger than the County farm establishment of 14,000 acres and is much smaller than the estate of the Viscount Falmouth, with an estimated 42,000 acres, and much the same size as the residue of the Rashleigh estate at Menabilly, which is reputed still to be over 20,000 acres. Then there are both the Fortescue estates of 10,000 acres and the Molesworth estate of 20,000 acres (9000 in Devon). The Cornish estate of the Duchy is now valuable, thanks in large part to internal tourism, in a similar way to Devon. The Duchy estate is concentrated around some very desirable and fashionable resorts, Padstow and Newquay in the north of the county and Looe in the south. Land appreciation here will seriously outweigh that of the farmland and old mine workings all around Liskeard and towards Launceston. It it is worth noting here that the Duchy is fortunate to hold land all round towns in the west country, and in Taunton, one of the fastest growing urban areas in the country. Both Taunton and Bath, where the same situation applies, are also popular commuter dormitories for the better off.

Thirty miles beyond Cornwall is Lyonness or the Scilly Isles. This tiny group of islands, about 3900 acres in all, is almost entirely owned by the Duchy with the exception of the island of Tresco, which is on a long lease to the Dorrien Smith family, who originally leased the whole of the Scillies in the nineteenth century. The Scillies, which are almost sub tropical, have always been a popular internal tourist resort for people in Devon and Cornwall, but have become even more popular in the last twenty years, with up to 100,000 people visiting the islands annually. Despite this the islands can boast tranquillity, fresh air, and miles of unpopulated strand even at the busiest times of the year. The Duchy exercises significant control and is not infrequently at variance with its tenants in the form of the Island Council. However, the two rub along and the Duchy does make a significant effort to try and maintain the singular features of the islands, while at the same time trying to provide employment for the native Scillies population.

At the time of writing the Duchy pays no capital gains and no corporation tax. Since 1993, as part of the general and undisclosed settlement made between the Queen and the government in relation to tax, Prince Charles has paid normal tax rates. Prior to that, between 1981 and 1993, he made a voluntary donation of 25% of his income from the Duchy, having previously paid 50% of his income.[14] The excuse in 1981 was that because he had married he could not afford to pay the same tax as everyone else. The dodge here was breathtakingly bold. Had the rest of us insisted on the same privilege, that of halving our tax on marriage, it is unlikely the Chancellor would have been so accommodating. And despite the 1993 settlement, the Prince continues to enjoy a privilege of enormous value. His private company, the Duchy of Cornwall, pays no tax and it is highly profitable. Had the Duchy paid tax like any other company it would probably have seen around £2.4 million lopped off its 1997 surplus of £6.8 million. It would also have seen a further tax bill of around £2 million on the sale of estates. In practice Prince Charles received £5.9 million on which he would have paid about £1.9 million in tax, depending how his expenses are treated. What the arrangement permits, however, is a very favourable environment for the Duchy to expand its estate or investments, both of which it did in 1997. (Between 1988 and 1997 the Duchy sold £6.9 million worth of land and in 1997 bought estate worth £3.3 million.) This peculiar form of accounting for sales over a nine-year period and purchases in a single year, makes it very difficult to follow the precise pattern of growth in the Duchy recently with the exception of the Prudential purchase. It is also noticeable that the entire investment portfolio is in quoted stocks and there is nothing from this huge tax-free pool invested in small or venture capital style companies.

Not, one would imagine, what the ultra conservative banker, Earl Cairns, the Receiver General or Finance Director of the Duchy, would be recommending.

The Duchy Council
In relation to the Duchy Prince Charles is by far the most engaged royal for over two centuries and his personal influence is benign and beneficial within its very conventional limits. But the Duchy remains an anachronism, if an extraordinarily valuable one. And it is partly trapped within the Etonian circle that separates the Palace from the ordinary people of the country.

This is reflected in the chief executive, Robert 'Bertie' Ross. He is an old Etonian, and joins three other old Etonians on the ten-man council of the Duchy. The Council is entirely male and has never had a woman at its elegant table. Ross, who comes from Scotland, is a small landowner himself and retains a farm in Scotland. After Eton he went to the Royal Agricultural College at Cirencester. He took over from a Cornishman, Jimmy James, who is given much of the credit for the modernisation of the Duchy. Now Sir Jimmy, James has a public school background (Sherbourne), and is a distant relative of the Courtneys, the family of the Earls of Devon who still retain about 3400 acres around Powderham Castle near Exeter. In addition he is a Crown Commissioner on the Crown Estate, and also a director of the Woolwich, William's and Glyn's bank and the Royal Bank of Scotland. He started out as the executive trustee of the Grosvenor Estate which runs to 130,000 acres in the UK.

The senior member of the Council is the Earl Peel, educated at the Catholic Eton, Ampleforth and the Royal Agricultural College, Cirencester and a landowner from Yorkshire. Known as the Lord Warden of the Stannaries, he is divorced and re-married to Mrs Charlotte Hambro, a daughter of the late Lord Soames. He is also president of the Gun Trade association.

The second ranking voice on the Council is that of Earl Cairns, an old Etonian banker of distinctly downbeat views. He was Chairman of BAT, the tobacco giant, Chairman of the Commonwealth Development Corporation, a financing outfit, and former managing director of SG Warburg, the City merchant bank. Next on the list of Council member is Michael Galsworth, educated at Radley public school and with a long track record as a director of companies, including English China Clay, the largest employer in Cornwall. He is chairman of the Trewithen Estate company at Grampound in Cornwall. Councillor John Pugsley, the next most senior Council member, does not post a CV. Perhaps the key professional member of the Council, familiar from the overview of the Crown Estate, is Professor Christopher Howes, the Chief Executive of the Crown Estate and Second Crown Commissioner.

Also on the Council is the Earl of Shelbourne, an old Etonian and the son of the Scottish landowner the Marquess of Lansdowne. Shelbourne himself lives at the family estate in Wiltshire. Alongside him is Nicholas Hood CBE, chairman of Wessex Water and of a number of other companies. He was educated at Clifton College, a public school. The last member of the Council is Prince Charles' private secretary, Stephen Lamport.

The legal background to the Duchy makes it clear that it belongs to the Crown, but by a less complicated legal lineage than that of the Crown Estate. What is invidious about the position of the Duchy is its compromising of the original principle of English constitutional law, that the Monarch should be dependant on Parliament for finance. That and its de facto tax-free status, as well as its capacity to grow eternally, yet never sell off any significant portion of its lands. The time has clearly come to privatise part of the acreage back to the Royal family, and make the Duchy a purely private concern that pays Capital Gains Tax and Corporation Tax in the ordinary way. Because it has been enabled to grow to its present size by courtesy of tax breaks and special privileges, a once-and-for-all tax payment to the state would be in order, with an absolute limit of perhaps 2500 acres imposed on its post-privatised size.

Chapter Seven

The Duchy of Lancaster

THE DUCHY OF Lancaster is a very large landed estate, mostly based in the north of England with some land in London. The Queen, who is also Duke of Lancaster receives the revenues from this estate tax free, but the freeholder, as this chapter will show, is not clearly known. The estate was created in 1351.

The Duchy of Lancaster now runs to almost 47,220 land-based acres, but taken with its estuarial waters and riverbeds of 125,000 acres, it actually comprises close on 172,000 acres. To these can be added £66 million in Stock Exchange investments and £5 million in cash. Predictably, the Duchy pays no tax on anything. The money it pays to the Queen, £5.7 million in the most recent accounts, is tax-free. The Queen may pay some tax on that income, after her expenses are deducted, but no details are available.[1]

In this way the Duchy is the residue and epitome of all the tax dodges associated with the Crown and its unreformed hold on land in the United Kingdom. It is a little tax haven, but one that still, like all the best tax havens, milks its residents for their taxable revenue and then retains it, tax free, for the monarchy. It is also one of the best examples of formal administrative deceit, deceit aimed solely at maintaining the rational ignorance of the public and at concealing the irrational privileges of the Royal family.

And like everything else connected with Royalty and land, its affairs and management are obscured by the unreformed accretions of historical privilege and anachronisms. It is run by a Cabinet minister on behalf of the Sovereign. He or she is answerable to Parliament for the affairs of the Duchy. As such he or she is one of the very few members of the Cabinet to have to take an interest in the state of the drains in a small number of let farms in the northeast of England. In practice, the Chancellorship is a gift of the Prime Minister and is retained to disguise what would otherwise be a post occupied by a minister without portfolio. The Duchy is actually run, like the Duchy of Cornwall, by a council, which is even more entrenched within the inner stockade of royalty than its counterpart in the southwest.

According to the Duchy handbook 1999[2] the Duchy belongs to 'the Sovereign of the day and has done so for some six hundred years'. This is not an accurate statement as it conceals the fact that the Commonwealth confiscated the Duchy in 1648 and sold it off. In fact the handbook later refers to the fact that Parliament put the 'Duchy up for sale' which is a rather curious way of avoiding the actual fact, which is that it was sold off.

Had it railed against the Cromwellian seizure, or even referred to it, the Duchy would be questioning the particular form that legislative sovereignty has now assumed in the UK, a form that reflects a running compromise between monarch and state. Under the present arrangements the monarch retains outmoded privileges and lots of tax-free income in return for obeying a Parliament that has come to contain all the ancient powers held by the monarchs of old. Central to that bargain is that no one in authority should query the supreme sovereignty of Parliament. The catch about the Cromwellian seizure of the Duchy lands is that it was done by Parliament. And it was within the power of Parliament to do so again, if the current concept of parliamentary sovereignty is accepted. It is

Parliament, with these peculiar and seldom-invoked absolute powers, which keeps the monarch on her throne and the people at bay.

If Parliament became what it should actually be, which is an instrument of the people in plebiscite with only such powers as those given to it by the people, and it was stripped of its secret, monarchical powers, then the current royal arrangements would be seen for what they are, expensive anachronisms which exist only to benefit the Windsors financially. And that might be the point at which 1648 is re-enacted and the privileges cancelled. Ironically, the monarch now has protection from a Cromwellian type confiscation in the form of the European Convention of Human Rights Act, now part of the domestic legislation of the UK, which guarantees that unravelling the capital asset privileges of the Windsors is going to be an expensive operation. For the people of Britain, at least.

The History of the Duchy

The history of the estate dates to 1265 when Henry III granted his youngest son, Edmund Plantagenet, the lands of Simon de Montfort, Earl of Leicester, together with the lands of Robert Ferrers, Earl of Derby, following the king's victory in the Barons' War, in which these two were leading figures. Two years later, in 1267, Edmund was made Earl of Lancaster and in 1284 received from his mother, Queen Eleanor, the manor of the Savoy. Edmund's son Thomas inherited five earldoms, including Lancashire, and the lands that went with them, but in opposing Edward II he lost his life on the headsman's block at the gates of his own castle in Pontefract. His brother Henry received the estates and titles back and Henry's grandson, Henry Grosmount, was created Duke of Lancaster by Edward III on 6 March 1351. But far more important, Edward made Lancashire a Palatine county for the duration of Henry's lifetime. This gave the new duke the rights of a sovereign within the county, allowing him to appoint courts, have vassels and behave in every way as a king would, though within the territorial limits of Lancashire. Henry died without a male heir and the dukedom and lands reverted to the king, who split them between Henry's two daughters, Maude and Blanche. Maude died without heirs while Blanche married the king's son, John of Gaunt, having had her sister's portion of the estates given to her. In 1362 John of Gaunt was created the 2nd Duke of Lancaster. By 1377 he had obtained Palatine rights for his lifetime and in 1390 he obtained them for his heirs forever. The Duchy as a Palatinate had been instituted and it had also been incorporated into the monarchy as 'private' land, separate from the Crown lands. John of Gaunt died in 1399, the year in which his son Henry Bolingbroke returned from banishment and took the crown from his cousin Richard II. His first act on obtaining the crown was to declare that Lancaster was his and his male heirs' forever, held separate from Crown lands. Much of the broad history of these events is theatrically recounted in Shakespeare's great cycle of historic plays but there is little reference to the immense wealth of this possession, which would remain in contention throughout the turbulent history of England's monarchy over the next 600 years.[3]

In 1461 Edward IV, who was not a blood descendant of John of Gaunt, amended the title by act of Parliament so that it became 'held forever to us and our heirs, Kings of England, separate from all our other royal possessions'. This, together with the Charter of Henry VII in 1485 is the defining charter under which the Duchy is deemed 'incorporated' and under which it purports to operate.

It is interesting to note that when Philip Hall was looking at the Duchy in the course of his research into royal finances in 1990 he was offered a copy of the official history of the Duchy written by Sir Robert Somerville, the former keeper of the Duchy records.

Researching this book, the present author was offered the same volume. Neither Hall nor myself were told of the second volume of the history, privately printed in 1970 and available only inside the Duchy office. Hall found out about the second volume when he noticed it in Sir Robert's *Who's Who* entry.[4]

What this second volume of Somerville's history shows, according to Hall, is that the claim advanced in the Duchy literature, and more importantly, to the House of Commons during various select committee investigations and debates on the Civil List, that the Queen's ownership of the Duchy is valid based on the acts of 1351 and 1461 is a 'dead letter'. Hall shows, as does Somerville in the unpublished second volume, that the Charters did not talk of the king owning the Duchy assets as private property, since the concept in relation to the sovereign was unknown at the time, but of owning them as the Duke of Lancaster. It is as Duke of Lancaster that the Queen bases her claim to the Duchy. Hall contends that this being so, the Duchy and its income should be given up to Parliament, in the same way as the Crown Estate. Interestingly, Hall also notes that Ken Clarke, who was Chancellor of the Duchy in the 1980s, totally confused himself over the ownership of the Duchy. Clarke, following the line spun to the Select Committees, thought that the Duchy belonged to the Queen, but expressed himself 'puzzled' as to why, if that was the case, the Duchy was run by a cabinet minister and presented its accounts to Parliament. But Clarke took it no further and did nothing to address the confusion he had discovered.

The Duchy changed hands several time during the War of the Roses, a civil war within the Plantagenet family (see Chapter 9) which ended in 1485. Throughout the fifteenth and sixteenth centuries the Duchy was a powerful institution, but the Dukedom was held by the Crown, and both Henry VII and Henry VIII, as well as his daughter Elizabeth I, were Dukes of Lancaster, as is the Queen today.

According to the Duchy pamphlet the Stuart kings at the beginning of the seventeenth century sold off large parts of the estate to raise money. When the first Stuart king, James I, took the throne in 1601 the royal revenues were in a hugely depleted state and badly managed. The Commonwealth later solved the problem in its own unique way, by beheading the king in 1649 and selling all the royal estates, Crown and Duchy alike. Following the accession of the House of Orange to the English throne in 1688, Parliament, or to be more accurate the great landowners and peers, got panicky and started to circumscribe the monarchy once more. By 1702 Parliament had to pass a specific act to halt sales of Crown and Royal land by Queen Anne.[5] When it came to George III's turn to improve his finances by swapping the Crown Estate revenues for the Civil List in 1760, the once all-powerful Duchy of Lancaster was down to producing just sixteen pounds, eighteen shillings and four pence a year. This was on the basis of accounts that were six years out of date. In company with the Duchy of Cornwall, the Duchy of Lancaster was excluded from the settlement between George III and Parliament.

Various reforms were imposed on the Duchy throughout the eighteenth century. At the beginning of Victoria's reign in 1838 the Duchy treasurer, who was and is the Keeper of the Privy Purse, in short the Queen's treasurer, was paying about £5000 (the equivalent of about £500,000 today) into the queen's coffers. By the end of the century that sum had risen to £60,000, the equivalent of £4.2 million today. Unlike the Crown Estate or the Duchy of Cornwall, however, the Duchy of Lancaster has hardly improved its revenues to the monarch in over 100 years, despite its tax privileges.

The efforts made to improve the affairs of the Duchy during Victoria's reign were yet another part of the long-term project of creating a monarchy that would outshine its peers in both wealth and lands. Indeed it was in the middle of Victoria's reign that the blanket ban on the sale of land was lifted. In 1855 the Duchy of Lancaster Lands Act permitted the disposal of parts of the estate that were no longer deemed of value. The biggest disposal was of foreshore, which would have included much of the Liverpool docks.

The Lands of the Duchy of Lancaster

Today the land-based estate runs to 47,220 acres, mostly situated in Lancashire and Yorkshire. The foreshore holding covers the area between the centre point of the River Mersey and Barrow-in-Furness and runs to around 125,000 acres. The most valuable single possession of the Duchy is the remains of the manor of Savoy in London, an area of about 2.7 acres. This is an area between the Strand and the Embankment, but excluding the Savoy Hotel. It is mostly let as shops and offices and has the Duchy office situated at its centre. The Savoy parcel alone is probably worth one third of the entire valuation of the rest of the estate.

The various landed elements of the Duchy of Lancaster are known as Surveys, with two elements designated estates.

The Lancashire Survey

The second largest of the surveys is Lancashire. It comprises 11,830 acres situated between Preston and Lancaster and between the Fylde coast and the Lancashire/Yorkshire county boundary. The survey is divided into five agricultural estates, with farm sizes ranging from 17 acres to 1000 acres. Only one of the estates, Myerscough, is an ancient Duchy inheritance. The rest, Wryeside, Whitewell, Salwick and Winmarleigh, were bought in by the Duchy at various times, mostly during the nineteenth century – in fact the Lancashire survey increased in agricultural acreage by more than 300% during this period. Had the Duchy been following the pattern of Victoria's dukes more closely they would have been investing in towns like Barrow in Furness and Eastbourne, or in industry. Instead, the Duchy administrators swapped revenues and capital from foreshore ownership and invested in landed estates, a fluctuating asset at the best of times, but something that inextricably spoke of power and wealth in the age in which they lived.

Lancaster Castle is a Duchy possession and is let to Lancashire County Council, who use it as a prison, court and for some ceremonial occasions. The castle is open to the public.

The Yorkshire Survey

This is the biggest landholding of the Duchy, running to 17,270 acres. The largest part, situated between Pickering and Scarborough, is a mixture of farmland and woodland. A good deal of land was added to this part of the estate in the period after World War Two. The Duchy owns 7200 acres of Goathland Moor, a popular local rambling area. Revenues here derive from a mixture of sources, including 21 farms and shops and businesses in Harrogate and Knaresborough. A local open space of 250 acres known as The Stray belongs to the Duchy. The castle at Knaresborough is a Duchy property, currently leased to Harrogate Borough Council.

The Crewe Survey

This is a relatively small parcel of land, about 4910 acres in all. It is also very scattered, with small areas outside Derbyshire in Cheshire, Leicestershire and Shropshire. According to the Duchy literature there are 27 farms, mainly dairy and arable. The estate at Crewe itself, a key industrial town in the North Midlands, was bought in 1936 and produces important business rentals.

Perhaps more importantly within this survey, the Duchy owns a considerable amount of the mineral rights in the high peak district, an area of great natural beauty and also part of the National Parks system. Attempts to open quarries and to start mining operations have led to considerable controversy but most of the time the Duchy, which is managed as a de facto Government department, has got its way.

The South Survey
In some senses this is the ancient heart of the Duchy, and contains one of its oldest possessions, the Higham Ferrers Estate in Northamptonshire. This was seized from Robert Ferrers, the Earl of Derby, in 1266, following the Barons' Wars. The estate is now very small, consisting of just 1220 acres. It is made up of five farms, some grazing land and a golf course. As a small footnote to history there is still both an Earl Ferrers and an Earl of Derby. The former holds the title of Earl Ferrers following a revival of the Earldom in 1711, in favour of a relative of the Earl of Northampton. The Derby earldom was created in 1485 and is the second oldest earldom in the kingdom.

In 1946 the Duchy augmented a small farm it had possessed at Olney since 1558, with about 1000 acres at Strixton. Also included as part of the South Survey are some cottages and ground rents at Cockfosters and Hadley Wood near London, which derive from the Duchy's onetime ownership of Enfield Chase. Apart from this ancient estate, the South Survey owns 3900 acres of common land at Ogmore in South Wales. The South Survey now has 5680 acres in its remit.

The Needwood Estate
This is the one part of the Duchy that may perhaps justify the claim to be 'ancient possessions'. It consists of 7530 acres of what was once Needwood Forest in Staffordshire. The forest and lands were attached to a landholding, rather like a large manor, known as the Honour of Tutbury, which was granted by Henry III to his son Edmund, the first Earl of Lancaster, in 1266. About 1200 acres of the forest remain standing.

The remainder of the estate is let in the shape of 31 farms. The most valuable part of this holding are the gypsum works at Tutbury, which are owned and leased out by the Duchy.

The Urban Estate
The urban estate consists mostly of 2.7 acres of London around the Strand. It includes the freehold of offices such as Stanley Gibbons the stamp auctioneer, Charing Cross Station and the Charing Cross Hotel. The Queen's chapel of the Savoy and the Duchy offices are situated here.

Valuing the Estate
According to the Duchy accounts up to the year 2000:

> Many of the Duchy's property assets have been in the ownership of the inheritance since the 13th and 14th centuries. No cost amounts for estates have been included in these accounts.

This statement, like so many others connected with the royal lands, is seriously inaccurate. As we have just seen, the Duchy bought three-quarters of the Lancashire survey in the nineteenth century. The same goes for much of the rest of the acreage. The statement implies that because the estate is so old it can not realistically be valued. This is a deceit. There was no holding of the Duchy that could not be valued by a professional valuer from one of the big auctioning and estate agencies, in the way that the Crown Estate is valued. That at least would have moved the story along a bit. But by avoiding a sensible modern practice on valuation, the Duchy was able to produce a set of accounts that failed to disclose any value for the principal real estate assets. This was what might have been called administrative dishonesty. It was certainly political dishonesty, since it hid from Parliament the true value of an asset over which Parliament has jurisdiction.

However, all this has been changed by the current Government. Working from the 1997 accounts, the present author estimated that the land assets of the Duchy concealed by the claim of 'ancient possessions' were worth about £150 million. The only assets actually valued in the 1997 accounts were the cash in the bank of £2.2 million and stocks and shares worth £35 million. Because so much of the true value of the Duchy was concealed, the Council of the Duchy were able to get away with a terrible return on their assets, which was about 14.2% if the disclosed assets were used as the basis of the calculation, or a miserable 2.7% if the true value were shown. Interestingly, the accounts for 2000 disclose a value of £195.8 million for the Duchy assets.

Revenue from the Duchy

Two contiguous statements appear in the accounts of the Duchy for 1997:

> The net revenues of the Duchy are the property of the Sovereign in Right of Her Duchy of Lancaster. Capital may not be distributed.

Back in 1855 the Duchy obtained the right to devolve from the prohibition on the sale of Royal Lands enacted in the Bill of 1702. It used that right to sell off a great deal of the Duchy estate in the nineteenth century and acquire farmland. In 1988 a new act removed the residual constraints on the Duchy in terms of sales. This seems to have propelled the estate into a bout of disposals; none of them clearly identified. By comparing the Duchy brochure of 1996 and the accounts for the following year what we see is a decrease in the acreage of about 1800 acres from the Yorkshire Survey and 700 acres from the Crewe and South surveys. Sticking to an estimate of £2000 an acre for farmland this should come to £5 million. In fact the sale of those 2500 acres brought in £9.2 million. This is not matched by a purchase of estates but is combined with £4.5 million received from the sale of investments and ploughed back into the purchase of a further £14.8 million in stocks and bonds. The evidence is that the Duchy is seriously switching away from land and into the Stock Exchange. Unlike the Duchy of Cornwall, the merit here is hard to establish, as the cost of investments is not stated, merely their value, which was £44 million in 1997, up £12 million on 1996.

The total income of the Duchy in 1997 from its property portfolio, after expenses, was £4.1 million. The income from investments was £1.8 million, or almost half the level of revenue coming from the property side. The approximate capital assets behind the two income streams were £150 million of property producing £4.1 million and £32 million in stocks and securities producing £1.8 million. This would be a good reason for switching from real estate to the Stock Exchange, especially where the Queen is concerned since she benefits only from the income from the Duchy. But if the switch proceeds, as it may very well do, then she could look forward to an enormous boost in her income, from about £5 million to anything around £10 million.

As with the Duchy of Cornwall, the Duchy of Lancaster pays no capital gains tax and no corporation tax. If the Duchy had paid corporation tax and capital gains tax at the standard rate of 40% in 1997 (which they would not have done as hardly any corporation pays the full level) the Duchy would probably have had to shell out at least £3 million to £4 million to the Exchequer.

In 1997 the Duchy paid £5.7 million to the Queen, up from £5.3 million in 1996. This sum of money is tax-free and is used by the Queen to pay various expenses not included in the Civil List. In 1990 those payments were regarded as a gift and therefore (at that time) tax-free. Even now the sums look more than considerable. The Duke of Gloucester received £119,500, the Duke of Kent received £161,500 and Princess Alexandra received £154,000. According to the Palace press office, this no longer pertains and all such payments are treated as taxable income.

All governments have to deal with the estates of those who die without heirs. In the UK, where no heir can be found there is a system of bona vacantia, whereby such estates revert to the Crown on William the Bastard's principle that if no one else owned it, it belonged to the king. With the exception of the duchies of Cornwall and Lancashire, bona vacantia estates are administered by the official solicitor, who maintains a fund for those who may appear many years later to claim an inheritance, and hands the rest over to the Treasury. In the Duchy of Lancaster territory, the income from Bona Vacantia came to £1,282,459 in 1997. £141,649 of this went in administration, £280,000 to the Duchy administration, with £852,233 going into a charitable fund. This system of placing the income from heirless estates into a charitable fund was adopted by the Duchy of Cornwall in 1971-2, but not until 1983 by the Duchy of Lancaster. And for years it was less than wholehearted in its transfers, placing only quarter of the income in the charity and apparently continuing to give the Queen about £1 million a year, according to Philip Hall.[6]

Who Governs the Duchy?

The very first statement in the annual accounts 1997 says:

> The Duchy is a body incorporated by charter in 1461 which is both an owner of property and the medium through which the remainder of certain Palatinate rights and responsibilities are exercised in Greater Manchester, Lancashire and Merseyside. Its origins lie in the grant of lands to Edmund, 1st Earl of Lancaster in 1265; and in the elevation of Lancaster to a county Palatine in 1351.[7]

The Queen, as has been set out, owns the income. But who owns the Duchy? The answer is no one. It owns itself. It is a body corporate that operates as a trust for the revenues that go to the Queen. This is reinforced by a note in the accounts, which says that 'The Duchy manages the land and investments in its ownership'.

The nominal boss of the Duchy is the Queen who appoints a Chancellor to run it on her behalf. In practice, the Prime Minister appoints the Chancellor of the Duchy of Lancaster as one of his Cabinet team, who in practice sees the Duchy as one of the least of his burdens. The actual running of the Duchy is done by two people, the Clerk of the Council and Keeper of the Records and the Chief Clerk. These two report to a council whose key member is the Keeper of the Privy Purse, the Queen's treasurer.

The council is advised by an Attorney General, a Receiver General and a Vice Chancellor. There are usually four other members of the council.

At present, 2001, the Chancellor of the Duchy is Lord MacDonald of Tradeston.

The Clerk of the Council and Keeper of the Records is Michael Kershaw Ridley CVO, who was educated at Stowe public school and who previously worked for the Grosvenor Estates and was a Commissioner of the Inland Revenue. His Chief Clerk is Colonel Nicholas Davies, a product of King's College, Taunton and the Royal Military Academy Sandhurst, and a former commander of the Royal Regiment of Artillery. The Attorney General is Richard McCombe QC, who was educated at Sedberg School and is a sometime member of the bars of Singapore and the Cayman Islands. He was the junior counsel to the Director of Fair Trading 1982 to 1987. The Receiver General is Michael Peat CVO. He is a former member of the accountancy practice of KPMG and has both an MA from Oxford and an MBA from the international management school at Fontainebleu.

The Vice Chancellor of the County Palatine is the Hon. Sir Jonathan Frederick Parker, a judge of the Chancellery (civil) division of the High Court. He was educated at Winchester public school and Cambridge and is a former Attorney General of the Duchy.

The senior member of the Council is Sir Michael Bunbury, the 13th baronet, and an old Etonian stockbroker who was also a Chairman of one of the Flemings financial trusts. The second most senior member of the Council is Professor Christopher Howes, the Chief Executive of the Crown Estate and a member of the Council of the Duchy of Cornwall.

The third lay member of the Council is probably the most important in financial terms. He is John Richard Sclater, educated at Charterhouse public school, Cambridge, Yale and Harvard. His list of banking and corporate appointments fills two inches of *Who's Who*, but, as with at least one councillor on each of the other two Royal estates, he is a trustee of the Grosvenor Estate and is a director of the holding company. He is also a director of Holker Estates, connected with the Leicester earldom. Briefly, he is or was a director of Guinness Peat, Yamaichi International, Union Discount Co, and several other financial institutions.

Until 1996 the final member of the Council was Sir Simon Towneley, the Lord Lieutenant of Lancashire, educated at Stowe School, who retired from both posts that year. He was replaced by Lord Shuttleworth (see below).

The Duchy has managed to hang onto a string of privileges associated with either its less-than accurately stated history, or with its status as the relic of Palatine government in Lancashire. The Duchy supports with a pittance of £2000 a minister in the Cabinet. The Duchy appoints something like 4300 magistrates in Lancashire, Merseyside and Greater Manchester. The entire system behind the appointments is redolent of ancient privilege and cumbersome practice, adding a layer of special bureaucracy to the justice system. In the rest of England and Wales the Lord Chancellor appoints magistrates. In the Duchy the Chancellor of the Duchy makes the appointments, based on lists submitted by the senior magistrate in the area, who just happens to be the Lord Lieutenant, or Queens's representative. There are three Lord Lieutenants involved, one each for Lancashire, Greater Manchester and Merseyside.

The present Lord Lieutenants (2001) are as follows:

Lancashire
The 5th Lord Shuttleworth, Charles Geoffrey Nicholas Kay-Shuttleworth, is an old Etonian, born in 1948 and a landowner in Lancashire. He was a deputy chairman of Abbey National between 1996 and 1999 and is a chartered surveyor. He joined the Council of the Duchy in 1998. His wife Mary was the High Sheriff of Lancashire in 1999.

Merseyside
Alan William Waterworth is a product of Uppingham School, with a degree from Trinity College Cambridge. He served in the local regiment as a lieutenant during national service. He is a former general Commissioner of the Inland Revenue. His predecessor was Sir Simon Towneley.

Greater Manchester
Despite the military title, Colonel John Bradford Timmins OBE TD, is the only non public school boy in the whole line up. He was educated at Dudley Grammar school then Wolverhampton Technical College with, finally, a Masters degree from Birmingham University. Like Waterworth his military service was at the time of national service and the rank came later, when he was made an honorary Colonel in the Territorial Army. He is Chairman of Warburton Properties and headed the local builders' federation for a number of years.

The Duchy of Lancaster is a landed estate, mostly constructed during the nineteenth century, that is in the process of transforming itself into an investment trust. Its existence and the privileges it exercises are based on enormously dubious legal grounds. Its tax privileges are illogical and its performance as a proprietor is very poor, with the bulk of its assets undisclosed in its balance sheet for most of the last century. The Queen claims to own the revenues. The Duchy owns the assets, which it alleges cannot be distributed. Parliament, however, has responsibility for the Duchy and clearly is the custodian of the trustees, who are the Council of the Duchy.

All three royally connected estates have directors in common, and the directors of each of the three estates have formal links with the Grosvenor Estate. All but one of the directors, or councillors, are men and all were educated at public schools, with old Etonians common to each of the Councils. None of the three estates has had its legal structure made subject to independent legal investigation and all have various tax advantages conferred on them that non royal corporations do not have available to them. Compared with most property companies the performance of the property element of the estates, especially the two which are only just beginning to value their assets, is very poor.

The current Government has made a start to modernising this anachronism with a proper valuation of assets in its accounts. However, the basic task of examining the legal structure behind the Duchy is yet to be done. As has been seen with the Crown Estate in particular, and royal lands in general, it is a subject which needs to be addressed.

Chapter Eight

The House of Lords

AT THE TIME of the first phase of reforms of the House of Lords in November 1999 no other democracy in the world could claim as a governing institution a place in which more than 60% of its members sat by an accident of birth. Nor could any other country in the world point to one of its houses of Parliament and say that its members owned more than one third of the country and that at least 60% of them were millionaires, with a few billionaires among those. Apart from the land, money and titles, in many ways the House of Lords represented the UK sociologically better than most institutions. It was at once wildly idiosyncratic and a delightful, collegiate place in which to work. And work it did, if at the pace of another, more leisurely age. It maintained a humane atmosphere of eccentricity and functionality in which the elderly amongst its members, and some were very elderly indeed, retained a function in the world and a degree of respect that has been lost in much of the country beyond its walls.

Yet it was very much an aristocratic institution, despite the fact that the bulk of the hereditary aristocracy did not attend. Every so often the iciness of unremitting arrogance that created the place and underlaid its well-mannered surface could be felt. One life peer recalled the way he and a group in the House were once approached by the late Viscount Willie Whitelaw, Margaret Thatcher's former Deputy Prime Minister and a rare modern hereditary peer.

> There were four of us, I think, standing outside the Library. Willie padded up and addressed the person he wished to speak to, straight across the conversation and across the faces of the group. No one would do that in normal company. Yet he is an aristocrat with, it is to be assumed, perfect manners.[1]

The same Willie Whitelaw, a landowner from Cumbria, was the man who almost defeated the IRA in Northern Ireland in 1974. He is a good example of both the best and worst of the old House of Lords. Charming, discreet and worldly wise, the one person who could prevail against the wilder ideas of Margaret Thatcher when she was Prime Minister, he nonetheless possessed an iron fist within his velvet glove. He was utter geniality and bonhomie until you crossed him; if you did he would then cross you out and pass on without compunction.

Unlike the Commons, the Lords has communal areas which all its members use together – in the Commons members can chose any one of 16 bars or tea rooms. The total membership of the Lords was twice that of the Commons yet somehow it never had the impression of being crowded. One of its more charming customs, going back to an age in which talented amateurism was the norm, is that no offices are provided for any peers unless they are government ministers or shadow ministers. Ordinary working peers, whose number included hereditaries like Lord Wise of King's Lynn and Lord Blythe, would work on their correspondence or make telephone calls from one of the small tables in the alcoves which line the corridors, or in the library. Once established, they might qualify for a locker. On the day Margaret Thatcher's elevation to the peerage was announced, a member of her staff made a call to Black Rod, the general manager of the Lords, currently General Sir Edward Jones, demanding two car parking spaces and an office. No one quite knows how the General replied but car parking in the most desirable lot in London, the space in front of the Lords and beneath the statue of King Alfred, is granted on the basis of seniority. At that stage she was the newest woman on the block, without even a day's seniority. A single desk in a room with other peers generally requires a ten-year stint as a working peer, and even then is not guaranteed. Curiously, Margaret Thatcher has rarely been seen in the Lords since she became Baroness Thatcher of Kestaven. In this administrative 'democracy', a Duke ranks with the humblest baron, and ten years as Prime Minister entitles you to nothing.

But the House of Lords did have and still does have influence, a level of influence that is a very serious and weighty power indeed in a democracy where arbitrary force and arbitrary decision making are more or less things of the past. It numbered (and still does, post-reform) some of the very richest people in the United Kingdom amongst its members. Indeed, the *Sunday Times* richest man in Britain in its 1998 Rich List, David Sainsbury, became a member of the House of Lords earlier that same year. At number two in that list (and number one in the 2001 list), the Duke of Westminster is the richest aristocrat in Britain. His wealth, probably in excess of £10 billion, is based entirely on landholdings. The top 30 names in the 1998 list included representatives of four other aristocratic families, of whom one, the Earl Cadogan, was in the list solely because of his landholdings. Included amongst the hereditaries in the House of Lords, almost without exception, were all of the top 300 individual landowners in Britain, most of whom attended Eton, thus cementing in blood and social amity the links between the Lords, the Palace and 'that school', pre reform.[2] The Lords had and still has the capacity to revise and amend all non-financial legislation emanating from the Commons. The latest proposals from the government are to restore the power of the Lords to look at some financial matters.

The History of the House of Lords

The origins of the House of Lords are as obscure as those of parliament itself. Most commentators seem agreed that the first Parliament in the modern sense was that summoned by Simon de Montfort in 1264 after the Battle of Lewes, and met in 1265. In the words of Goldwin Smith, writing in his *Constitutional and Legal History of England*, 'The tale [of the early history of Parliament] is complex. The plot is often obscure. That which at first seems simple is often shown to be an enigma.' A number of scholars describe Parliament as 'having been created by nobody,' and that 'at every stage in its early growth Parliament's functions determined its composition and organisation.'[3] What does seem clear is that Parliament as we know it grew out of 'additions', often involuntary, to the King's Council in the period between 1265 and 1350. The 'additions' mostly consisted of knights and burgesses – representatives of town and county who were not peers or great landowners. They were often invited by either the king or by the barons to bolster either side in the ebb and flow of the tide of power. But in the Easter Parliament of 1341 the prelates, together the custodian of vast acreages encompassing one third of the country, and landed magnates, who held all of the rest of the country not held by the king, were ordered to meet separately in the White Chamber in the oldest section of the Palace of Westminster. The knights and burgesses met elsewhere and it is from this event that the foundation of the House of Lords is normally dated.

By the end of the Middle Ages the House of Lords as a fixed element of Parliament, with two archbishops, 19 bishops, 30 or 40 abbots and about 40 hereditary temporal peers, was an established fact. And, given its composition it is easy to see why Henry VIII wanted to replace the Pope's men, the Catholic prelates and abbots, with his own appointees. The abbots he simply eliminated, though why he did not insert all the bishops to replace them is not clear. The Commons, as it evolved, was anything but 'common' and was simply that part of the state wherein the knights of the shires, who were the big county landowners, and the merchants and burgers of the towns and corporations, were represented. The general population of the UK were excluded from power, and power was dispensed by those who owned, but did not populate, the country. This is important because most of the laws, customs and legislation of the United Kingdom, and most specifically its absurd unwritten constitution, were created by landowners, for the benefit of landowners. The country is not ready to face the present, never mind the future, until this straitjacket imposed from the past is thrown off.

But what was true in the middle ages was still true when the 1872 Return appeared. In the words of Professor Cannadine in *The Decline and Fall of the British Aristocracy*:

> As late as the 1870s British patricians were still the most wealthy, the most powerful and the most glamorous people in the country, corporately – and understandably – conscious of themselves as God's elect.[4]

'All too frequently,' he adds later,

> the contemporary cult of the country house depicts the old land-owning classes as elegant, exquisite patrons of the arts, living lives of tasteful ease in beautiful surroundings. Of course, there is some truth in this. But as a representation of the totality of patrician existence, it misleads and distorts, by failing to recognise them for what they really were: a tough, tenacious and resourceful elite, who loved money, loved power and loved the good life.[5]

By excluding the hereditary peerage from the House of Lords, the Blair government took a first, vital, and far reaching step towards dragging the UK into the third millennium and disposing of some of the baggage of history. The nature of the event was hugely obscured by the tabloid press, who trivialised it, and the heavy duty media, whose sense of the institutional history and mechanics of the UK is little better than that of the tabloids, who misread it. Had any part of the media stated that what Blair was actually doing was disconnecting the 785 wealthiest families in the UK, who between them owned perhaps a one third of the land of the country, from the inner levers of power, and putting those people on a par with the rest of the democracy for the first time in 800 years, perhaps the country might have understood what was happening. But no one did, and the taste of final defeat amongst the expelees inhibited all except the Marquess of Burford, who didn't even have a right to sit in the Lords, from fighting the eviction. Burford, son of the Duke of St Albans, occupied the Woolsack briefly in the final session before the reforms took effect, howling treason, but no one was listening.

The Composition of the Lords

The official composition of the House of Lords immediately prior to the House of Lords Act of 1999 was, based on precedence, as follows: four peers of the Blood Royal, in other words Prince Charles and the dukes of Gloucester, Kent and York, but excluding Prince Edward. The Queen's husband, Prince Philip, sat as the Duke of Edinburgh; two archbishops, of York and Canterbury; 25 dukes, 34 marquesses, 174 earls and countesses, 104 viscounts, 24 bishops, 931 barons and baronesses, of which 512 were life peers whose number is constantly changing. The total membership was 1297. By October 2000 the roll call was down to two dukes, two archbishops, one marquess, 28 earls and countesses, 17 viscounts, 24 bishops, 513 barons/lords, 110 baronesses and just one lady. Of this number 567 hold life peerages and the total number of people entitled to vote in the Lords is 698, of which 90 are elected hereditary members who will presumably depart in the next stage of reform.[6] Pre reform the total number of peers entitled to be summoned to the Lords as members of Parliament was 1297.[7]

In addition there were the following minor idiosyncrasies in the composition of the Lords.

Two dukedoms, those of Albany & Clarence and of Cumberland & Teviotdale, are 'deprived', their holders having taken up arms against the king in World War One. The Queen, on the advice of the Privy Council, can restore the titles if she is petitioned by either of the descendants who are, respectively, Prince Hubertus Saxe-Coburg and Gotha and Prince Ernst August, the Prince of Hanover. Now, of course, they will never be able to sit in the Lords. In fact there are only two dukedoms left in the House of Lords. The first is that of Norfolk, who retained his seat as the hereditary Earl Marshal of England. For the time being the Duke of Montrose also sits, having been elected by the departing hereditaries to represent them until the Blair reforms are complete and all the hereditaries leave. Twelve peerages, of which the best known is Tony Wedgwood Benn's title of Viscount Stansgate, had been disclaimed for life. Sixteen titles were either dormant or abeyant, meaning that the title was not extinct but there is no immediate heir, or there were potentially contending candidates. Around 84 peers, including the Duke of Manchester who was in jail in America, and Lord Brocket who was in jail in England, were on leave of absence from the Lords, pre reform. Post reform only three are on leave of absence. Over the years many of the hereditaries, perhaps 50%, simply failed to turn up regularly or at all.

Pre reform the political composition of the Lords was as follows. Conservative 473, Labour 169, Liberal Democrat 67 and Cross Bench 322. This accounts for 985 of the members, the remaining 266 members (minus two minors) either failing to declare their position or failing to attend. The post-reform house of Lords has 698 members, with 233 Conservatives, 200 Labour, 123 Cross Bench, 63 Liberal Democrat, 30 others and three on leave of absence.[8] In 1876, after the *Returns of Owners of Land* appeared, there were only 431 hereditary members of the House of Lords, including seven peeresses. There were other aristocrats with titles who could not sit in the House at that time because they held Irish peerages. Many of those, such as the Duke of Abercorn, were subsequently granted British titles (normally of lesser status, for example the Duke of Abercorn became the Marquesss of Abercorn) to allow them to sit in the Upper House. There were 46 of these promotions/demotions in the Lords between 1872 and 1999, though, just to confuse the issue, they are socially referred to by their higher, or Irish, title. The Scottish peerage, much of it created to 'buy' the Union in 1707, sat in the Lords under their actual titles, for the most part.

Life peerages were first conferred on appeal court judges in 1876, but came into wider use from 1958 when the practice of giving politicians in retirement hereditary peerages was dropped. Traditionally, former Prime Ministers were usually offered earldoms or at least viscountcies – Harold Macmillian, for example, became the Earl of Stockton. However, Edward Heath insisted on staying in the Commons with a knighthood until 2001, with no sign of his being inclined to accept a peerage, while Harold Wilson and James Callaghan adopted simple baron's titles, as did Margaret Thatcher after an unseemly row about being made a countess. She did get her way to an extent as her husband Dennis received a baronetcy, making him Sir Dennis, which is hereditary and which will pass to their son Mark.

Max Weber adopts a methodology for examining any social group according to three categories.[9] The first is according to the wealth of the group. The second is according to the social status of the group. The third is according to the power of the group. Applying this to the House of Lords the following was evident.

In terms of wealth the pre reform House of Lords represented the single most concentrated group of the wealthy in the United Kingdom. One hundred and one members of the House of Lords appeared in the *Sunday Times* Rich List in 1998, and despite the ejection of the hereditaries, there were still over 40 members of the House of Lords in the 2000 list. There would have been many more hereditaries in the 1998 list if there were a reliable method of estimating the extent of lands owned by aristocrats. More than 80% of the hereditary members of the House of Lords were estimated to be millionaires and ten of the dukes and seven of the marquesses make the post reform *Sunday Times* list.

Humans have always shown a tendency to operate social hierarchies and to equate titles with some form of superiority or status. Many people, such as gossip columnists and the tabloid press, make a good living out of telling tales of the dubious doings of those deemed socially important because they have a title. This plays to the apparently ineradicable human desire to see those we think superior take a tumble. Aristocratic titles in particular have provided the staple of the British media for several centuries, beginning with fly sheet diaries such as Farringdon's in the eighteenth century. In this kind of society and in terms of social standing a duke is quite clearly socially superior to a plain mister, if in no other way than by simple possession of the title. Practically speaking, most dukes also have that other attribute which draws forth deference, which is bags of cash.

TABLE 8/1

PREVALENCE OF ARISTOCRACY IN THE *SUNDAY TIMES* RICH LIST,
1998 (PRE REFORM) AND 2000 (POST REFORM)

Rank	Number in House of Lords		Number Amongst 1000 Richest 1998	Number Amongst 1000 Richest 2000	% of each rank in list 1998	% of each rank in list 2000
Royals/Bishops	30	(26 clergy/4 Royals)	1*	1*	–	–
Duke	25		10	10	40%	40%
Marquess	34		9	7	25%	20.5%
Earl and Countess	17		22	19	12.6%	10.9%
Viscount	10		9	7	8.6%	6.7%
Baron/Baroness	93	(512 life peers)	32	25	7.63%	5.9%
Total hereditary	78		83	69	10.8%	8.7%
Total	1295	(2 minors excluded)				

* The Queen does not have and did not have a vote in the House of Lords, but she does have a 'seat' there, the throne, and is included here for that reason.

The Dukes and their Land

In the 1870s, when the dukes were at the peak of their power, Bateman's *Great Landowners of Great Britain and Ireland* listed 28 landowning dukes, together with one French duke, D'Maule, one Italian duchess, Sforza, as well as the Duchess of Northumberland, who held ducal rank. They owned a total of approximately 4.1 million acres. Of the 25 modern dukes, three own no land and the remaining 22 own, between them, over one million acres, around one and a half English counties. No less than 40% of the dukes appeared in the *Sunday Times* Rich List for 2000. Amongst the aristocracy the dukes offer a useful snapshot of how wealth, combined with high status, conferred power, but in a unique way in the UK. Aristocrats of lower ranks still holding great tracts of the country are documented in other chapters and in Part II of the book. Below, however, a survey of the dukes looks at their land holdings, both in 1872 and today. Where intermediate estimates of landownership are known, such as those established by John MacEwan in 1977[10] and Andy Wightman in 1996,[11] these are also cited.

TABLE 8/2
THE LANDOWNING DUKES

Landowner	Total acreage 1872	Total acreage 2001	Total value 2001 (land only)
Duke of Sutherland	1,358,545	12,000	£72,000,000
Duke of Buccleuch & Queensbury	460,108	270,700	£282,000,000
Duke of Richmond and Gordon	286,411	12,000	£260,000,000
Duke of Atholl	201,640	148,000	£430,000,000
Duke of Devonshire	198,572	73,000	£435,000,000
Duke of Northumberland	186,397	132,200	£800,000,000
Duke of Portland	183,199	(Ext)	(Ext)
Duke of Argyll	175,114	60,800	£12,500,000
Duke of Hamilton and Brandon	157,368	12,000	£3,000,000
Duke of Cleveland	104,194	(Ext)	(Ext)
Duke of Montrose	103,447	8800	£1,000,000
Duke of Bedford	86,335	23,020	£340,000,000
Duke of Abercorn	78,662	15,000	£95,000,000
Duke of Leinster	73,100	Nil	Nil
Duke of Rutland	70,137	26,000	£150,000,000
Duke of Roxburghe	60,418	65,600	£150,000,000
Duke of Beaufort	51,085	52,000	£310,000,000
Duke of Norfolk	49,866	46,000	£210,000,000
Duke of Newcastle	35,547	(Ext)	(Ext)
Duke of Manchester	27,312	Nil	Nil
Duke of Grafton	25,773	11,000	£91,000,000
Duke of Somerset	25,387	2000	£6,000,000
Duke of Leeds	24,237	(Ext)	(Ext)
Duke of Marlborough	23,511	11,500	£91,000,000
Duke of Westminster	19,749	129,300	£11,500,000,000
Duke of Wellington	19,116	31,700	£50,000,000
Duke of Buckingham & Chandos	10,482	(Ext)	(Ext)
Duke of St Albans	8998	4000	£12,000,000

Notes:
The biggest variations in value with the modern acreages occur when a percentage, usually 1%, is added to take account of potential development. Almost without exception, all the land identified is in trust and is not the personal landholding of the peer, although the peer and his heirs are both the temporary beneficiaries of the trusts and the ultimate beneficiaries if the trusts are wound up.

1. The 6th Duke of Sutherland
1872   1,358,545 acres
2001   12,000 acres

The largest individual landowner in the United Kingdom in 1872 was the Duke of Sutherland. At that time the lands of both the dukedom and those of the Countess of Sutherland, a separate title with a separate seat in the Lords, were united. At the time most of the acreage was in the county of Sutherland in Scotland and they brought an income equivalent to £6,375,015 today.

The present duke, the 6th, John Sutherland Egerton, born in 1915, lives mostly in Newmarket, and has 12,000 acres in Suffolk and in the Scottish Borders. He has retained valuable paintings and is estimated to be worth about £160 million by the *Sunday Times*.

His first wife, a daughter of the Duke of Northumberland, died in 1978. He married again, but has no children and his heir is his nephew, John Marjoriebanks Askew. The Duke and his nephew were both educated at Eton.

1a. The 24th Countess of Sutherland
(Shown here because of the direct link with the Sutherland dukedom, whose lands she largely inherited.)

1872   0 acres. See Duke of Sutherland, above.
1977   158,000 acres
1996   83,239 acres

Elisabeth Millicent Sutherland, or Mrs Janson as she appears in some of the Scottish land records, held the second oldest title in the pre reform House of Lords, after that of her fellow Scot, Margaret of Mar, Countess of Mar. The Sutherland title was created in 1235, that of her compatriot in 1114. The Countess of Sutherland is also the heiress to what is left of the original ducal lands, something that happens from time to time. Born in 1921, she succeeded to the title as the only daughter of Lord Alistair St Clair Sutherland-Leveson-Gower MC, the second son of the 4th Duke of Sutherland. In 1946 she married a former officer in the Welsh Guards, Charles Noel Janson. The estate is currently run from the estate office in Golspie by her son Alistair, Lord Strathnaver and Master of Sutherland, who was educated at Eton.

2. The 9th Duke of Buccleuch and 11th Duke of Queensberry
1872   460,108 acres
1977   277,000 acres
2001   270,700 acres

This is the biggest single landholding in the United Kingdom after those of the Royal family. It is also one of the least reduced, in acreage terms, from 1872. In that year the income from the estate was estimated at the equivalent of £9,772,335. The present duke, who holds both dukedoms as well as being the Marquess of Dumfriesshire, the Earl of Dumfriesshire, the Earl of Drumlanrig, the Earl of Buccleuch, the Earl of Doncaster, the Earl of Dalkeith, Viscount Nith, Thorwold & Ross, Lord Douglas of Kinmont, Middlebie

& Dornoch, Lord Scott of Buccleuch, Lord Scott of Whitchester & Eskdaill, and Baron Scott of Tyndale, was educated at Eton and served in the Royal Navy during World War Two. Born in 1923, Walter Francis John Montague Douglas Scott is a close personal friend of the Queen and, despite a hunting accident which left him wheelchair bound, is one of the most active peers in Scotland. In the early *Sunday Times* Rich Lists he was valued at £300 million, but has recently persuaded Dr Beresford to put him in at a more modest £40 million. His argument is that the estate is actually owned by a company in which he has just a handful of shares. Both statements are true, but they are only half, or rather a fraction, of the picture. The bulk of the shares in the Buccleuch Estate company are held in trust by an Edinburgh solicitor. The duke refuses to say who they are held in trust for, or whether the beneficiaries or trusts are domiciled in the UK.

In the meantime he acts as the owner of three great houses, Bowhill in Selkirk, Boughton House at Kettring and Drumlanrig Castle in Dumfriesshire. He, or perhaps more accurately his trusts, own a number of old masters which together are worth two or three times the figure for his wealth given in the *Sunday Times*.

His heir is Richard Walter John Montague Douglas Scott, the Earl of Dalkeith, who, like his father, was educated at Eton and Christ Church College Oxford. Richard is married to Lady Elisabeth Kerr, the youngest daughter of the 12th Marquess of Lothian. He was a page of honour to the Queen Mother in the 1960s.

3. The Duke of Richmond & Gordon
1872 286,411 acres
2001 12,000 acres

Charles Henry Gordon Lennox is the 10th Duke of Richmond and the 5th Duke of Gordon. Like the Duke of Dorset in Max Beerbohm's novel *Zulika Dobson*, he is also a duke in France. He is a descendent of King Charles II by his mistress Louise de Keroualle, who later became the Duchess of Portsmouth and then the Duchess of Aubigny in France courtesy of Louis XIV. In 1872 his ancestor was Secretary of State for Scotland and indeed, the entire Gordon Lennox family history is full of public and palace appointments. Today, the family estate no longer has Scottish acres attached: 159,000 acres in Banff were sold after World War Two to meet death duties and the income equivalent to £3.5 million in today's terms that accrued to the dukedom in 1872 is long gone.

However, the *Sunday Times* rated the present Duke at £45 million in 1990. (This had dropped to £30 million by 2000.) Most of this was attributed to an estate of about 12,000 acres, the residue of the Sussex acreage of 17,000 in 1872. It is believed that the remaining 12,000 acres, much of which consists of prime development sites connected with car racing and industrial and domestic building, and is probably worth as much as £260 million, is in trust. The duke was educated at Eton and has been Lord Lieutenant of Sussex for five years. He has been intimately linked with the General Synod for most of his life, and is a Chartered Accountant by profession.

4. The 3rd Duke of Fife
1872   249,000 acres
2001   1500 acres

The Fife dukedom was the last non-royal dukedom created. It was a personal promotion made in 1900 for the husband of King Edward VII's daughter Princess Louise, who married the Earl of Fife in 1889. He was at the time the fourth largest landowner in Scotland and was receiving an income the equivalent of £3.2 million today. The present duke's acreage is very hard to establish. He succeeded to the title through his aunt HH Princess Maud, daughter of the 1st Duke of Fife. There is no record of what happened to the Fife acreage, but the 1st Duke had started to sell it off as early as 1889, the year of his marriage to royalty. Along with another relative of Victoria, the Duke of Abercorn, he joined Cecil Rhodes in the British South Africa Company. Trailed by controversy, the company nonetheless prospered and so did the two dukes. Whether their descendants still have shares in the successor company De Beers is not known. Both are prosperous and do not work for a living. The present Duke of Fife, James George Alexander Bannerman Carnegie, born in 1929, served in the Scots Guards during the communist insurgency in Malaysia. He was educated at Gordonstoun but sent his son and heir, the Earl of Southesk, to Eton.

5. The late 10th Duke of Atholl
1872   201,100 acres
1970   130,000 acres
2001   148,000 acres

George Ian Murray, the 10th Duke of Atholl, died in 1997. He left no direct heir and the title went to a distant cousin in South Africa, John Murray, who has neither a seat in the Lords nor the estate. The lands, which the 10th Duke had placed in trust many years ago are split between a charitable trust, the Blair Charitable Trust, which runs Blair Castle and its adjoining grounds, and a private trust which holds the bulk of the lands for Scottish relatives of the late Duke. A distinguished if slightly eccentric figure, the 10th Duke was educated at Eton and Christ Church, Oxford. The last man in the kingdom allowed to raise a private army – of just 80 men – 'wee Ian', as he was known, was chairman of the Westminster Press and then of the Royal National Life Boat Institution. He lived at the magnificent Victorian-style Blair Castle, which is open to the public.

6. The 11th Duke of Devonshire
1872   198,572 acres
2001   65,000 acres in the UK, with 8000 acres in the Republic of Ireland.

Andrew Cavendish, the 11th Duke of Devonshire, born in 1920, was a distinguished and decorated soldier in World War Two. He probably did more to restore the fortunes of the Cavendish family than any of his predecessors. Chatsworth, his main residence in Derbyshire, is the centre of a 'heritage' operation that employs several hundred people and which receives over 500,000 paying visitors every year. The building, now beautifully restored and open to the public, is surrounded by 55 square miles of Devonshire land, including whole villages and many farms. The total size of the remaining estate is set out in the Duchesses's book, *The Estate*, published by Macmillan in 1990.[12] She is Deborah Freeman-Mitford, one of the six daughters of the 2nd Baron Redesdale, three of whom became famous through marriage to people such as Sir Oswald Mosley and the Duke of Devonshire. She has been a key figure in the revival of the estate and is an authoress in her own right. Their son and heir is the Marquess of Hartingdon. Eton-educated he is the Senior Steward of the Jockey Club, the Queen's representative at Ascot and a noted figure in racing circles.

7. The 12th Duke of Northumberland
1872   186,397 acres
2001   130,200 acres

Lord Ralph George Algernon Percy, the 12th Duke, succeeded his brother, the 11th Duke, who died heirless at the age of 42 in 1995. The 12th Duke, born in 1956, was educated at Eton and Christ Church Oxford. Married to Jane Miller from Edinburgh, they have four children. The duchess is currently engaged in a £30 million restoration of the gardens around the family home at Alnwick Castle. The eldest son, educated at Eton like his father, is known as the Earl Percy. A Plantagenet by descent, the family own land in London, at Syon Park to the west of the city, and in Northumberland, all in trust so that no onerous death duties have been payable for most of this century. It is the biggest surviving estate in England from the Return of 1872. The *Sunday Times* values the family wealth, which includes many works of art, at about £250 million in its year 2000 Rich List.

(The Dukedom of Portland is now extinct. For the residual lands see Lady Ann Cavendish Bentinck, Nottinghamshire. p.251.)

8. The late 12th Duke of Argyll
1872   175,114 acres
1970   73,400 acres
2001   60,800 acres

Ian Campbell, who died suddenly in 2001, was the 12th Duke of Argyll. He was born in 1937 and succeeded to the title in 1973. Unusually, he went to school in Switzerland, attending Le Rosy, and from there went to McGill University in Canada. About one third of the 1872 lands survive and were placed in trust for the Dukedom by the 10th Duke. He married the only daughter of Sir Ivar Cloquhoun of Luss, a major landowner in 1872 who still owns 50,000 acres in Dumbarton. Sir Ivar's sister is the widow of the 8th Earl of Arran, another major land-owning family in the 1872 list (they had 29,964 acres in Ireland) but no longer in occupation of any land. The 12th Duke was the hereditary master of the Queen's household in Scotland and did a stint in the Argyll and Sutherland Highlanders before taking over the family estate at Inverary Castle. His son, now the 13th Duke, is Ian Torquil Campbell, who was known as the Marquess of Lorne while his father was alive.

9. The 15th Duke of Hamilton and 12th Duke of Brandon
1872   157,368 acres
1977   5200 acres
2001   12,000 acres

Angus Alan Douglas Douglas-Hamilton is the Premier peer in Scotland and the Hereditary keeper of the Palace of Holyroodhouse. Born in 1938 he was educated at Eton and at Balliol College, Oxford. Despite the diminution of his acres he maintains a range of aristocratic interests, including that of Prior in Scotland for the Order of St John of Jerusalem, and is a member of the Queen's Bodyguard in Scotland. An honorary air commodore in a unit of the Royal Auxiliary Air Force, he is currently separated from his second wife, Jillian, daughter of Sir Edward Hulton. The duke's first wife, a daughter of the late Sir Walter Scott Bt., a farmer in Berwickshire, died in 1994. They divorced in 1987. The duke's brother, the Rt. Hon. Lord James Douglas Hamilton, is the former Tory MP for Edinburgh West. His original title of Lord James Hamilton was a courtesy title, which meant that, unlike his brother, he could sit in the House of Commons if elected, but not the House of Lords. In 1994 he succeeded his uncle as the Earl of Selkirk, but renounced the title in order to stay in the House of Commons. He was made a life peer in Prime Minister John Major's resignation honours list in 1997 and now sits as a Member of the Scottish Parliament for Lothian as a Conservative.

10. The 8th Duke of Montrose
1872   103,447 acres
1977   8800 acres
2001   8800 acres

James Graham is the 12th Duke of Montrose. He was born in 1935 and is a brigadier in the Royal Company of Archers, the Queen Bodyguard for Scotland. Like many of the Scottish aristocracy he is a long-standing member of the Order of St John of Jerusalem. Unlike most of the other Scottish dukes he was educated at a Scottish school, Loretto, and is a past president of the Scottish National Union of Farmers. He is the Hereditary Sheriff of Dumbarton. His son, James, the Marquess of Graham, runs the estate which is the largest remaining estate in Stirlingshire. The title is an ancient one, going back to 1445 to when Patrick Graham was one of the Lords of the Regency during the minority of James II of Scotland, known as James of the Fiery Face. The first earl was killed at Flodden in 1513. The first marquess was Captain General of the Parliamentary forces until he changed sides, lost to the Parliamentary forces at Strachan and was hanged by order of the Scottish Parliament in 1650. The dukedom was created at the time of the Union in 1707.

11. The 13th Duke of Bedford
1872   86,335 acres
2001   23,020 acres

The present Duke of Bedford, born in 1917, is John Robert Russell, who more or less founded the modern stately home business. He did this at Woburn Abbey, one of the most popular tourist attractions north of London, starting in 1955. His motive was to pay off the huge death duty levied on the 12th Duke's estate, but having done that, the underlying value of the Bedford assets, which still include 20 acres around Covent Garden, asserted themselves and the duke went into tax exile in Monaco in 1974. He still lives there with his third wife, who is French. He was wounded while serving in the Coldstream Guards during World War Two. The management of the estate was handed to his very reluctant stockbroker heir, Henry Robin Russell, the Marquess of Tavistock. The marquess, born in 1940, was educated at Le Rosy, the Swiss school attended by many of the aristocratic rich and famous including the late Duke of Argyll. He has an MBA from Harvard. Married to a model and heiress, Henrietta Tiarks, he suffered a devastating stroke in 1988 but has since recovered. He was a director of a number of companies prior to his illness, including United Racecourse and TR Property Trust.

The Russells have produced some very eminent scientists and scholars, including the philosopher Bertrand Russell. The original estate and title were a gift from Henry VIII, made up of seized monastery land.

12. The 5th Duke of Abercorn
1872   78,662 acres
2001   15,000 acres (in trust)

James Hamilton, the 5th Duke of Hamilton, being an Irish Duke, sat in the House of Lords as the Marquess of Abercorn. Born in 1934, he was educated at Eton and the Royal Agricultural College, Cirencester. He also served as a lieutenant in the Grenadier Guards. Although Professor Cannadine records his ancestor selling off many of his acres in the 1880s, almost half appear to have survived at his palatial seat, Baron's Court in Northern Ireland. He is a former Unionist MP for Fermanagh, and his wife, Alexandra Anastasia, is a sister of the Duchess of Westminster, and both Duchesses are descendants of the Romanoffs, the pre revolutionary Russian royal house. The family have been very closely linked to royalty since the Victorian era, when the then Duke was a courtier in the inner circle at the Imperial palace. The Duke of Abercorn would also appear to be the Duke of Chatelberault in France, a title granted in 1548 and revived by the 1st Marquess in 1864, four years before he became a duke in the Irish peerage. Unfortunately, Napoleon III of France recreated the title around the same time (1864) and gave it to the then 12th Duke of Hamilton (see above). Perhaps it's a mark of nobless oblige to each other that neither duke mentions the duplicate dukedom in their *Debrett's* entries. The Royal connection continues, with the Abercorn heir, the Marquess of Hamilton, born in 1969, performing as a page of honour for Queen Elizabeth II between 1982 and 1984.

13. The 8th Duke of Leinster
1872   73,100
2001   Nil

Gerald Fitzgerald, born in 1914 and educated at Eton and the Royal Military College Sandhurst, is the Premier duke, marquess and earl of Ireland. Unfortunately, the Irish Republic does not recognise Irish titles and neither does the House of Lords, so he sat in Parliament as Viscount Leinster. A number of the Irish peers used the money they gained from the early land purchase arrangements in Ireland in the 1880s to establish an estate in England, but the duke's ancestors do not appear to have followed suit. His son and heir is Maurice Fitzgerald, the Marquess of Kildare, born in 1948 but unlike his father went to Millfield School. The duke's second son, Lord John Fitzgerald, also went to Millfield, but after that followed in his father's footsteps, went to Sandhurst and, like his father, served in the 5th Royal Eniskillen Dragoon Guards. Maurice's heir was killed in a car crash, and John is now the heir to the marquessate.

14. The 11th Duke of Rutland
1872   70,137 acres
2001   26,000 acres

David Charles Robert Manners, born in 1959, is one of those English dukes who has retained, if not all his family's acres, then some of the most important minerals which lie underneath them. Coal is still mined on the estate, though the duke's father tried to prevent it by threatening to lie in front of a bulldozer working the coal seam in 1977. Originally entered in the *Sunday Times* Rich List in 1990 at £45 million, the value of some of his paintings soared and the year 2000 list promoted the duke to the £80 million class. A year later this was downgraded to £50 million. His father was educated at Eton and served in the Grenadier Guards but the new duke, who succeeded to the title in 1999, does not disclose his education. He is a patron of eleven livings, making him one of the larger patrons of the parishes of the Church of England but he cannot officially 'present' the priests to their livings as he is a Roman Catholic. He has two seats, Haddon Hall in Derbyshire, and Belvoir Castle at Grantham in Lincolnshire. He is a Liveryman of the Gunmakers company in London and is married with three daughters and a son, the Marquess of Granby, born in 1999.

15. The 10th Duke of Roxburghe
1872   60,418 acres
2001   65,600 acres

Guy David Innes-Ker, the 10th Duke of Roxburghe, was born in 1954 and succeeded to the title at the age of 20 in 1974. He was educated at Eton, Magdalene College Cambridge and the Royal Military Academy Sandhurst from where he was commissioned into the Blues and Royals, an elite household cavalry regiment. In 1977 he married Lady Jane Grosvenor, the daughter of the 5th Duke of Westminster. He met her at one of the Grosvenor family estates in Fermanagh while he was serving with his regiment in Northern Ireland, and their 1977 wedding was the society event of that year. Her marriage to Roxburghe made her the daughter of a duke, the sister of a duke, the wife of a duke and finally the mother of a future duke. The marriage collapsed and they were divorced in 1990. He still lives in the family seat, Floors Castle, with his former duchess just down the road in a house set aside for her and their three children. He has remarried. The *Sunday Times* 2001 list valued the dukedom at £50 million and Roxburghe has been active recently in business in the area, including tourist ventures and hotels. His heir, the Marquess of Bowmont and Cessford, was born in 1981.

16. The 11th Duke of Beaufort
1872   51,085 acres
2001   52,000 acres

David Robert Somerset, the 11th Duke of Somerset, succeeded to the dukedom by a slightly complicated but not untypical route. The 10th Duke died without an heir, so the bloodlines had to be traced back via the 8th Duke. David Robert Somerset is the grandson of the 8th Duke's second son, and he inherited a 52,000-acre estate worth about £100 million, which was the value placed on his assets by the *Sunday Times* in its year 2000 list, with £20 million of that for an art collection which is not publicly catalogued. (The 2001 list has the duke down to £48 million.) He was born in 1928. His duchess, a sister of the present Marquess of Bath, died in 1995. His heir is Henry John Fitzroy, the Marquess of Worcester, born in 1952. Like his predecessor, the 11th Duke has maintained the hunt, although his daughter-in-law, the Marchioness of Worcester, is a prominent figure in the environmental lobby. The duke was educated at Eton, as was his son and heir. His big-money dealings in the art world ensure that he mixes with the very top end of the international jet set, including the Agnellis and the Aga Khan.

His predecessor, the 10th Duke, was Master of the Horse to the Queen as well as to her father, from 1936 to 1978. He founded the Badminton Horse Trials and was Master of Foxhounds of the Beaufort Hunt from 1924 until he died in 1985. This was the most exclusive hunt in England: even Royalty vied for an invitation to ride with the Beaufort and it was one of the most important inner circles of power during World War Two. Winston Churchill's Spymaster, Sir Stuart Menzies, lived at Bridges Court in Luckinton close to the Beaufort Estate and hunted with this exclusive group. But the Beaufort extended its reach to White's Club in London, Sir Stuart's other haunt, whose members were a vital source of support for both Churchill and Menzies at a personal level during the worst days of the conflict.

17. The 17th Duke of Norfolk
1872   49,866 acres
2001   46,000 acres (in unusually complex trusts)

Major General Miles Fitzalan Howard is the premier duke and premier earl of England. He is also the Earl Marshall and Hereditary Marshall of England. He is the only duke to have survived the Blair reforms with a permanent seat in the Lords, on the basis of the Earl Marshall title. In this latter role he would, as his kinsman the 16th Duke did before him, act as major domo at the coronation of the monarch. The Norfolk dukedom is the oldest surviving non-royal dukedom in the UK, going back as a dukedom to 1483, and the duke is the leading layman in the Roman Catholic church in England. In this capacity he took the names of the two final candidates for the Catholic archbishopric of Westminster to the Pope in Rome in 1999. Born in 1915, the present duke had a distinguished career in the army prior to succeeding to the title when his cousin died in 1975, serving in the Grenadier Guards and winning the Military Cross in World War Two. He later became director of Service Intelligence at the Ministry of Defence and retired as a major general. He was educated at Ampleforth and Christ Church, Oxford. After the army he had a further career in banking at Robert Fleming & Co, and as President of the Building Societies Association.

The dukedom is one of the most complex in the aristocracy, having been forfeited several times, along with the heads of the then holders of the title, for treason and various other alleged offences during the 1500s. But over the following 300 years the heirs fought back until Parliament restored both the title and honour of being the Earl Marshall. The 13th Duke became Master of Victoria's Horse restoring the family to royal as well as financial favour. The title, which incorporates a range of other titles, including that of Earl of Arundel and Surrey, takes almost six pages of *Debrett's Peerage* to describe. The landholdings of the Norfolk/Howard family have been carefully hidden in trusts since the 1872 Returns, possibly because of the Returns.

The family is clearly very well off but the complex descent of the dukedom, and the many other peerages involved have made it impossible for the *Sunday Times* to establish a value for it. The *Mail on Sunday* valued the assets of the ducal trusts at £125 million in 2000. The family seat is Arundel Castle and the duke has two other homes, in Yorkshire and Oxford.

18. The 12th Duke of Manchester
1872   27,312 acres
2001   Nil

Angus Charles Drogo Montague, the 12th Duke of Manchester, might best be called 'The unfortunate duke'. He recently served a 22-month jail sentence in the United States following a failed consortium bid to buy an ice hockey team in Florida. He had previously escaped conviction in another prosecution following a failed business deal, but not without severe criticism from the judge. Financial problems were not unknown in the family: both the 8th and 9th dukes went bankrupt, the former for the equivalent of £7 million in 1889, the year before he succeeded to the title. The 9th Duke was branded in the American press as 'England's poorest duke in pursuit of our richest heiress'. The heiress was Mary Golet, who, as Professor Cannadine records, refused Manchester and eventually married the Duke of Roxburghe.[13] The 9th Duke did find an heiress, Helen Zimmerman, but was declared bankrupt just before the wedding.

The present duke was educated at Gordonstoun and succeeded his brother to the title. He has been married three times. His career illustrates an interesting aspect of the House of Lords. Imprisonment means the loss of neither seat nor title. The various bankrupt dukes still left the family seat, Kimbolton Castle, and the estates largely intact, as they were in the hands of trustees. Had the hereditaries not been ejected from the Lords, the duke would have been able to resume his seat.

19. The 11th Duke of Grafton
1872   25,773 acres
2001   11,000 acres

Hugh Denis Charles FitzRoy, the 11th Duke of Grafton, is a descendant of King Charles II by his mistress Barbara Villiers, the Duchess of Cleveland. His home is Euston Hall at Thetford in Norfolk. According to Professor Cannadine, a good deal of the land around the Hall, and certainly the land in London around Euston Station, was sold in the 1920s or earlier.[14] Nonetheless, this patrician gentleman, one of the 24 Knights of the Garter and husband of Ann Fortune, the Mistress of the Robes to the Queen, has all the appearances of considerable wealth. Euston Hall is not open to the public. He is the patron of four livings, Chairman of the Architectural Heritage Fund and president or significant member of various other committees for the preservation of cathedrals, historic buildings and churches. He is also a member of the executive committee of the National Trust and of English Heritage.

Born in 1919, the duke was educated at Eton, Magdalene College Cambridge and was a Captain in the Grenadier Guards. He was ADC to the last Viceroy of India from 1943 until 1947. The *Sunday Times* rated him at £20 million in its Wealth Register,[15] although the pictures at Eton Hall are said to be worth much more than that. His heir is the Earl of Euston, born in 1947 and educated at Eton. He is a serious figure in City of London financial circles and was a page of honour to the Queen in the early 1960s.

20. The 19th Duke of Somerset
1872   25,387 acres
2001   2000 acres (in trust)

John Michael Edward Seymour is the 19th Duke of Somerset, a title that traces its ancestry back to Edward III and then to Queen Jane Seymour, Henry VIII's last wife. Like the other dukedoms linked to royal affairs prior to 1700, its history is punctuated by executions and imprisonments, but also recovery under Queen Victoria. The present duke, who was educated at Eton, is a chartered surveyor and a patron of two livings of the Church of England. His family seat is the beautiful manor of Maiden Bradley in Wiltshire (sold recently), which is surrounded by what is left of the family acreage. He lives at Totnes in Devon. He was a Deputy Lieutenant of Wiltshire in 1993. Born in 1952, he succeeded to the title in 1984. Maiden Bradley is not open to the public and the duke is probably the least visible of those of his rank involved in any form of public affairs. His heir is Lord Seymour, born in 1982.

21. The 11th Duke of Marlborough
1872   23,511 acres
2001   11,500 acres

John George Vanderbilt Henry Spencer-Churchill is the 11th Duke, having succeeded his father in 1972. Along with the dukedom he is also a Prince of the Holy Roman Empire and of Swabia in Germany. All the family assets are in trust, and the house, Blenheim, is open to the public. Born in 1926 he was educated at Eton and was a captain in the Life Guards. His parents were remote and he has confessed to great personal unhappiness as a child, something he seems to have passed on to his son, the tragic Marquess of Blandford, who has turned to drugs, as well as suffering a broken marriage that has graced page after page of the tabloid press. Three times married, the duke's second wife Tina was the former wife of one of the richest men of his time, the shipping magnate Aristotle Onassis. In turn Tina Onassis was the daughter of Stavros Livanos, himself a dollar billionaire. Tina, Duchess of Marlborough, died in 1974. The wayward streak in the family was perhaps exemplified by the greatest Englishman of the twentieth century, Sir Winston Churchill, the present duke's cousin. Feted for his wartime leadership, it is often forgotten that Churchill was frequently described as a rogue by his peers and his contemporaries. In his book *Aspects of Aristocracy*, Professor Cannadine devotes a whole chapter to the Churchillian warts, warts that made him perhaps the only warrior who could take on and defeat Hitler.

22. The 6th Duke of Westminster
1872   19,749 acres
2001   129,300 acres (UK) plus at least 400,000 more acres worldwide.

Gerald Grosvenor, the 6th Duke of Westminster born in 1951, is a very modern duke in some ways. His children have been educated at the local primary and secondary schools in Chester, and he has preserved a stable marriage, despite the disintegration of the marriages of many of his friends and family, including that of the Prince of Wales and those of the duke's two sisters. Not academically inclined at school, which was Harrow, he has nonetheless made a useful and rewarding career as an officer in the Territorial Army, achieving the rank of brigadier and commanding officer of the Queen's Own Yeomanry. But he is wealthy beyond the normal meaning of the word and in 1998 was ranked fourth in the *Sunday Times* Rich List at a value of £1.7 billion. By 2000 and following the discovery of an additional 200 acres of Belgravia which belong to the family, he was revalued at £3.75 billion. By 2001 he was the richest person in Britain, topping the Rich List at a value of £4.6 billion. However, the chronicler of the *Sunday Times* list, Dr Philip Beresford, admits that even this is too low following the price of £335 million achieved by the BP pension fund for 10 acres of Mayfair in April 2001. The duke has narrowed the range of his directorships to just a few directly connected with the family estate company, Grosvenor Estate Holdings, and an associated insurance company, Sun Alliance.

The duke's landholdings are unique in that his is the only dukedom to increase its acreage in a meaningful way since 1872, in his case by about eight times. The spread is world wide, with huge acreages in Canada and Australia and smaller holdings in Hong Kong and Hawaii. There was a huge acreage in Fermanagh in Ireland of 30,000 acres, but this was sold to the tenants after his mother died in 1987. The duke is also now the seventh largest private landowner in Scotland. The jewel in the crown is, however, quite small, being just 300 acres in London's Mayfair and Belgravia. The duke fought a strenuous rearguard action in the early 1990s to prevent the forced sale to his leaseholders of the freeholds of their properties, including a petition to the European Court of Human Rights under Article 26 of the European Convention on Human Rights which guarantees property owners the peaceful enjoyment of their property and protection against confiscation. He lost.

However, the Grosvenor Estate is rated a good landlord and the 2nd Duke made a gift of six acres of Pimlico for dwellings for working class people in the 1950s, a donation the present duke refused to amend when the Tory council in Westminster tried to sell off the properties in the 1980s. Six acres of Pimlico are probably worth £120 million. The assets of the dukedom are held in twelve trusts created with extraordinary foresight by the 2nd Duke, who virtually targeted the two-year-old son of his cousin and arranged for the assets, but not the dukedom, to by-pass the 3rd, 4th and 5th Dukes. And there is another respect in which Gerald Grosvenor is an unusual duke. His entry in *Debrett's* is shorter than that of some Labour life peers, despite there being some evidence that the family go back to a Norman invader, Hugh le Gros Veneur, who seized lands in the Cheshire area, where the Grosvenors have their family seat.

The estate traces its great wealth to the marriage in 1677 of Sir Tom Grosvenor and Mary Davies, the heiress to the Manor of Ebury, an area of marsh and bog that is now Mayfair and Victoria. Following the boom of the late 1700s and early 1800s this became the most valuable slice of London real estate. By 1874 the Marquess of Westminster was the richest man in the kingdom and was promoted to a dukedom by Queen Victoria, almost entirely because of his wealth.

23. The 8th Duke of Wellington
1872   19,116 acres
2001   31,700 acres (much of it in Belgium and Spain)

Arthur Valerian Wellesley, born in 1915, is another of the modern dukes to have made a career in the army. He rose to the rank of brigadier, having commanded the Household Cavalry from 1959 to 1960, and the 1st British Corps in Germany from 1962 to 1964. Educated at Eton and New College Oxford, he is a patron of four Church of England livings. Since leaving the army he has overseen the family estate, at Stratfield Saye in Hampshire, which is largely in trust, and has been President of the Rare Breeds Survival Trust and of the Atlantic Salmon Trust. He is also the bearer of many hereditary honours heaped on his illustrious ancestor, the Iron Duke, who defeated Napoleon at Waterloo. This includes being a Prince of Waterloo in the Netherlands, Duke of Vittoria and Marquess of Torres Vedras, Duke of Ciudad Rodrigo and a Grandee first class of Spain, as well as holding eight other British titles. His son, the Marquess of Duoro, born in 1945 and educated at Eton, was a competent Tory MEP from 1979 to 1989. He is married to a Guinness heiress, the Princess Antonia von Preusen, who is a cousin of the Queen.

24. The 14th Duke of St Albans
1872   8998 acres
2001   4000 acres

Murray de Vere Beauclerk, the 14th Duke of St Albans, was born in 1939 and succeeded to the dukedom in 1988. Educated at Tonbridge School, he qualified as a chartered accountant, and is a Liveryman of the Drapers Company, as is his son the Earl of Burford. He is descended from the natural son of Charles II by Nell Gwyn. A staunch royalist and traditionalist, he is Governor General of the Royal Stuart Society, and his son is a vice president of the same society. Never a great landed family, the present duke's father was a successful soldier in World War Two, but never took his seat in the House of Lords. The present duke took the Tory whip in the pre reform House of Lords.

25. The Duke of Edinburgh

A modern creation to honour the Queen's husband. He has no personal landholdings.

When Tony Blair has ejected all the hereditaries from the House of Lords, he will have achieved a *coup de main* few thought possible, given the history of failure by previous Labour governments to carry out manifesto promises to do so. But politics aside, what he has actually done is move the richest 700 or so families in the UK, who together own land equivalent to about four and a half English counties, and who are together worth a staggering £16 billion or more, into a political wilderness these families have not known for the better part of 800 years. The consequences are, to say the least, unpredictable, especially if the Prime Minister also begins to close down the agricultural subsidy which has propped these families up for much of the last 50 years. This chapter has concentrated on the very top end of the system – there were at least another 190 significant landowners amongst the hereditaries whose landholdings have remained legally hidden throughout the last century. Perhaps Prime Minister Blair has hit upon a key truth of power, that you cannot govern a country if those who actually own it are occupying the building next to the House of Commons.

Chapter Nine

The Plantagenet Inheritance
A tale of great survival

THERE IS A single family in Britain whose descendants, direct and indirect, have owned about ten percent of the landed wealth of both England, and to a lesser extent of its empire, for most of the last 840 years. They are, as a family group, still worth over £4 billion, and they still own over 700,000 acres of land in the UK, about the equivalent of an average English county. As a single related family group, they clung to power and wealth so tenaciously that when Tony Blair evicted the hereditaries from the House of Lords he threw out 42 of them (five await ejection in the final reform), and no less than 23 of them have appeared in the *Sunday Times* Rich List over the past 13 years. Not one of the ejected hereditaries bears the actual family name, and amongst the current general population it occurs just once for the whole of the United Kingdom, in Cheltenham.[1] Despite this, there is a web site[2] which has over 15,415 entries for this family, called Plantagenet, and it takes 617 web pages (many duplicated, admittedly) to display the family history – and even this only covers the years between AD924 and AD1470. The web site itself contains over 49 million other names, and over 1 million different surnames. But the name Plantagenet occurs only three times outside the core historical Plantagenet record, and this is in the early part of the last century when three women of that name died in America.

The overall purpose of this book is to reintroduce some concealed or forgotten facts and to give them a context. The main impediment to the book achieving its purpose is a prevailing attitude called 'convention'. The first obstructive convention is that of the educational system, which says that history is not real unless all the exciting bits are removed. The second convention, also embedded in the educational system, is that you learn history, you do not analyse it. The third convention, a combination of the previous two and of a covert political input, is that you will learn from history what you are told to learn, and ignore any lessons that your native curiosity might suggest are lurking in the highly edited version of what most histories suggest is history. There are few more 'edited' versions of history, and few more interesting and exciting, than that of the survival of the Plantagenets, into the year 2001, with most of their wealth intact.

And it is within the context of landownership in Britain, which is the main concern of this book, that the story of Plantagenet survival stands out. Set against a very destructive human society, that of England for the past thousand years, the Plantagenets have accumulated wealth, power and influence throughout that era, and have held onto that wealth right into the modern period. If we are to believe Shakespeare, even as only an indirect commentator on history rather than a chronicler of its facts, we have few records to match that of the Plantagenet family for bloodiness, violent warfare and internecine murder. So who were they?

The Plantagenet Kings
Originally the Plantagenets were Norman French, close henchmen from the vanguard of William the Bastard's robber gang. The name Plantagenet first surfaces formally with

Geoffrey, Count of Anjou (also known as 'Angevin' from the family name) and father of Henry II, the first Plantagenet king of England, crowned in 1154. Henry II's mother was Matilda, Empress of The Holy Roman Empire and the daughter of Henry I of England. Henry I, son of William the Bastard, succeeded to the throne when his elder brother William II (Rufus) was killed while hunting in the New Forest. Matilda's bloodline was important, as her mother, also Matilda, was a descendant of Edmund Ironsides, the last Saxon King of England through whom the legitimate succession to the throne ran. Marrying her was as close to legitimising the coup d'état of 1066 as the family of William ever came.[3]

Genealogists have subsequently produced, with what certitude it is hard to say, both an English Plantagenet, Edgar the Peaceful, who is supposed to have lived in Wessex around 944, and a French one, Samoens Plantagenet, allegedly living at Loiret in 904. It is thought that the name was actually a nickname derived from *planta genistae*, or yellow broom, which Geoffrey of Anjou always wore in his helmet, and it was not used by any of Henry's successors until Richard III, the last Plantagenet king, killed at Bosworth in 1485. The mystique of the Plantagenet name seems to have more to do with post hoc proselytising than history itself between 1154 and about 1460. The use of the name by subsequent historians was to give semantic cohesion to a line of 14 kings, who, together, might be described as a pretty wild bunch, much married, much murdered and much slain in combat. Some historians speak of violent and bloodstained times. They usually forget to point out that it was the Plantagenets themselves who made the times violent and bloodstained. Of the 14 Plantagenet kings, six died violently. The mayhem amongst their families was even worse. A total of about 25 near relatives of the kings died violently, many by beheading. The worst interfamilial slaughter was associated with Edward III, who reigned from 1327 to 1377, when almost all the senior males of his Plantagenet line or their descendants who lived to be adults died on the block or were murdered.

It was, then, a familiar story when Richard, Duke of York and Protector of England, was killed at the battle of Wakefield in 1460. This was a key battle in the Wars of the Roses, the civil war that tore the Plantagenets and England apart from 1450 to 1485. Richard, the great-great-grandson of Edward III, had married Cicely, daughter of Ralph Nevill, Earl of Westmorland, around 1440. Cicely carried the line of succession to the throne via her mother, the daughter of Roger Mortimer, Earl of March. March was directly descended from the marriage of Phillipa, daughter of Lionel, Duke of Clarence, eldest surviving son of Edward III after the death of Edward's eldest son the Black Prince. Richard of York had seven children including four boys, two of whom became king. His second son Edmond died with him at Wakefield. The eldest of the three remaining, Edward, came to the throne as Edward IV in 1461, dying in 1483. The third child, George, Duke of Clarence, also married a Nevill, Isabel, daughter and co-heiress of Richard Nevill, Earl of Westmorland. George was murdered on 31 May 1477, the year after his wife died. They had two children, Edward, Earl of Warwick and Margaret, Countess of Salisbury. Richard of York's fourth son, Richard, reigned as Richard III for 25 months and was killed at Bosworth Field, ending the direct Plantagenet succession and opening the way for the Tudors. Henry Tudor, a descendant of Edward III via his fourth son, John of Gaunt, was declared king on the battle field by Sir Oliver Stanley. He assumed the throne and started the Tudor line by marrying Princess Elizabeth Plantagenet, daughter and heiress of Edward IV in 1486. She was the mother of Henry VIII and the grandmother of Elizabeth I, making both of them part Plantagenet.

But while Edward of Warwick and Margaret of Salisbury were alive, there remained a potential alternative claimant to the throne from the Plantagenet line which they carried. Henry VII dealt with this by beheading Edward on 28 November 1499. The genealogical entry in *Burke's* for Edward says that he died unmarried. This implies that he had an heir or heirs, as the genealogical convention when there are no legitimate heirs is '*d.s.p.*' Henry VII's son, Henry VIII, dealt in the same way with Margaret of Salisbury, having her beheaded aged 72 at the Tower of London on 27 May 1541, two years after her eldest son, Henry Pole, Lord Montague, met the same fate. Officially, the deaths of Edward and Margaret ended the direct male and female Plantagenet lines, even though Margaret had other children besides her eldest son. However, the indirect bloodlines ran elsewhere.[4] And the effect of the Plantagenet connection was to create an inner aristocracy who thrived because of the deference paid to their Plantagenet blood by the rest of the landowning aristocracy, especially when they ran as well as owned the country.

Power after the Throne

The lengths to which the Tudor monarchs went to extirpate all possible *direct* Plantagenet claimants to the throne is clear, as is the manoeuvring amongst the Plantagenet descendants which usually ended with execution. So why take such terrible risks? The first answer was for the right to exercise the arbitrary power of the monarchy. The second was for the booty that went with it. The revenues of the realm, despite Parliament, were more or less the private property of the monarch, and were one vast trough for his or her relatives to dig into. Claimants normally had little trouble in finding adherents since the right to the spoils was pretty unrestricted in those days.

The big 'spoil' of course, was the subject of this book: land. Out of each twist and turn of the struggle to obtain the monarchy, someone lost their lands and someone gained those lands. Yet the circle within which that contest took place was small. None of the participant families vanished. They merely popped up, sometimes years later, and in most cases got their titles and their lands back, usually having paid a suitable 'fine' or bribe to both officials and monarch.

Between 1172 and the beginning of the reign of Elizabeth I in 1559 much of what might be called the spoils of high position were lands in nearby countries such as Scotland, Ireland and, more remotely, France. By the end of Elizabeth's reign in 1603, the possibility of the Americas, India and a wider empire and a wider source of booty were in prospect. The Imperial project was only disturbed, and then not very much, by the Civil War in 1642. From the restoration in 1660 onwards, the internal disposition of the ownership of England, Scotland, Wales and Ireland was fixed for 220 years, and in the case of the first two countries, was fixed for well over 300 years, until the present time. Incidences of assassination, murder and execution ended, in part because the contest for land had widened and its acquisition via the colonial administrations became much easier. It was no longer necessary to murder your neighbour in order to acquire land or to murder the monarch because the monarchy was now so restricted that it was not worth risking the executioner's axe to obtain it.

Fundamentally, the Plantagenets, while they reigned, were little better than their remote ancestor William I. While in control of the throne between 1160 and 1485, they retained a bandit instinct and an inclination for lawlessness on the grand scale which they deemed outside the law's remit, but within their rights. This included making war and committing judicial murder. But it is the concept of where they fitted in relation to the law, whether as creators of the law and thus beyond its remit, or as powerful rulers who were above the law when it came to defending their personal and family interests, that we need to look for clues to the mentality their successors displayed, and perhaps the clue to their survival as a family group. During the high noon of modern landowner power, the period from about 1700 to about 1890, the enclosures[5] occurred, the penal laws were imposed in Ireland, and through the game laws the life of a peasant in England was held to be equal with that of a wild rabbit. The net effect of these was to increase the power of the landowners, with the Plantagenet descendants chief among them, on an extraordinary scale. The enclosures launched a crime wave in England as starving peasants forced off the land sought food while the wealth of the landowners increased hugely from their newly added acres. The penal laws essentially criminalised the entire native Irish population, giving most of their land to British aristocrats, many of them Plantagenets. The game laws led to hangings and transportation for thousands of English men and women, who, having being driven off the land, were faced with a choice between crime and starvation. The Parliament that drove these two evils, enclosures and the penal laws, had no less than 60 Plantagenets in the Lords and between 25 and 30 Plantagenets in the Commons, at the same time.[6]

This was also a period when a subtle and little-remarked transformation was taking place at the very pinnacle of power in the UK. For the first time in six centuries, issues of succession within the ruling elite, along with many other issues within that group, were settled, for the most part, without resort to either personal or public violence. True, there were wars in Scotland and wars in Ireland, but in the heartland a truce amongst the inner elite prevailed that deepened into permanency over time. Influence grew to replace arbitrary fiat as the key mode of power's operation. The issue of competition within the power elite was settled by manoeuvre, not murder. The Empire increased and consolidated until the American colonies were lost, but India remained a thoroughly lootable prize. During this period the aristocracy was small and tightly knit, the House of Lords had no more than 400 or so members, and the most influential individuals in the country were the dukes. Of the 30 or so alive at any time, a third of them were of Plantagenet origin, and they were the important ones: Northumberland, Norfolk, Bedford, Atholl, Sutherland, Rutland, Beaufort, Somerset, Richmond, and Manchester. The bedrock of their influence was their ownership of vast and profitable acreages, which they had inherited and which they had augmented by using the law itself for criminal purposes. At the end of the day it was their capacity to hang onto wealth, even as the number of the wealthy outside the core aristocracy increased, which enabled them to sustain the positions created for them by the Plantagenets when they were in power and on the throne. That and the myth of their origin, which was easy enough to promote if you could afford the feasts, banquets and balls necessary to the social promotion of position.

The lesson that history seems to be showing here is a simple one. The ruling elite in Britain from about 1700 to 1900, heavily populated with Plantagenets, perhaps even dominated by them, having moved over time from physical violence to Parliamentary government, altered their mode of operation and used the law to achieve what they had previously achieved by the sword. Its effects were no less brutal upon the mass of the British population, who were hunted off the land of their ancestors in their millions, in order that the aristocracy could increase its millions. In fact the Plantagenet survivors achieved more by the cruel use of bad law than they had ever achieved by force of arms, acquiring at least 8 million acres in England alone via the enclosures.[7] By 1872 the 60 Plantagenet related families in the Lords owned a grand total of over 3.2 million acres. They were the single biggest related bloc in the upper chamber and the richest. To date, no historian has tried to look beneath the surface splits of party politics of the period, and to reconcile the voting patterns of big landowners in apparently opposing political factions in any bill related to land. The chances are that any such analysis would show that when it came to land, and the landowning interest, there were no political divisions. The enclosures went through virtually unopposed, as did the game laws and the early penal laws. The Plantagenet descendants voted almost unanimously for these measures and there was no party split on the issues. The Plantagenets remained as cruel in the eighteenth and nineteenth centuries as they had been in the fourteenth and fifteenth centuries, only they disguised it better. And if they didn't own the Crown any more, their titles, especially the high ones, and their wealth, gave them convincing influence with the Crown, whoever wore it. Indeed, the fact is that even the Hanovers, from whom the present royal family are descended, all carry Plantagenet blood (see Appendix 3). What is striking about this table of 40 people, covering a period that is now close to 1000 years long, is the extraordinary inner cohesion of the ruling family itself. Given that Henry 7th married a Plantagenet, and that he was partly a Plantagenet himself, and that it is their blood too that flows in present royal veins, by a quite discernible descent, the so-called Tudor and Hanoverian 'family lines' have the look of being simply superimposed. Perhaps the precise observation should be that, while one part of the Plantagenet family lost its right of succession to the throne itself, their cousins have hung onto it, and the present Royals should be treated as part of the Plantagenet 'survival'.

Recalling that murder, assassination and child mortality were rampant amongst the Plantagenets, it was statistically unlikely that after they ostensibly lost the Crown to Henry Tudor in 1485 they and their lands would survive for a further 387 years to 1872 and then onward for a total of 516 years, to 2001. But they have.

The Plantagenet Families

The descents could be indirect.[8] For instance, the current Northumberland dukedom, which dates only from 1766, actually goes back to the Barony of Percy, created in 1299. The older genealogies trace the Percy family back to 912 and to the village of Percy in Villedieu in France. The first Percy in England, William de Percy, arrived with William in 1066, and was granted large acreage in the north of England. His successors married into the royal family, and acquired an alliance with a descendant of Charlemange, the Holy Roman Emperor. By 1272 the head of the family was married to a daughter of one of the richest families in the land, the Warenne earls of Surrey, whose family name at that stage was Plantagenet, via a marriage with the ruling family, probably that of Isabel de Warenne to Hamelin Plantagenet in 1160. Isabel was a descendant of William of Warenne, created Earl of Surrey by William I and shown by the *Sunday Times* to have been the richest person ever to have lived in England, worth the equivalent of £57.6 billion today.[9] The Warenne family claimed descent from a harpist in France for which a record going back to 924 has been produced.[10] William died in 1088, a year after his king.

In 1299 Henry de Percy, the 9th feudal lord, was summoned to Parliament as a baron. This was a significant change in status, turning Henry Percy from a local magnate into a national figure and a councillor to the king. By 1308 he had bought the barony of Alnwick from the Bishop of Durham, and established the Percys as the Plantagenet lieutenants in the north. A successor of his, Henry, the 3rd Baron, married Lady Mary Plantagenet, great granddaughter of Henry III. The Plantagenet alliance was thus sealed and in 1377 he was granted the earldom of Northumberland. Between 1377 and the last murder in the tower in 1585, few of the earls escaped execution or imprisonment, the

6th Earl only escaping with his life by switching his affections for Anne Boleyn, Henry VIII's intended, to Lady Mary Talbot. The 6th Earl died of natural causes, but without heirs and his brother having been executed for treason, the titles were forfeited. The king, Edward VI, elevated the earldom to a dukedom and gave it to John Dudley, Earl of Warwick. Dudley subsequently lost both the title and his head when he fell foul of Queen Mary in 1553. In April 1557 the titles were restored to the Percy heir, Thomas. By 1670 the Northumberland dukedom had been taken over by the Crown, but was extinct, and the earldom was without male heir and suspended (in abeyance).

Then, in 1750 the 7th Duke of Somerset's additional titles, other than the dukedom, passed in 1750 from the 7th Duke to Sir Hugh Smithson, the husband of the duke's only daughter Elizabeth. The 7th Duke of Somerset happened to be the Earl of Northumberland. Smithson adopted the name Percy by act of Parliament in 1750, and had himself made Duke of Northumberland in 1766. The Dukedom of Somerset, properly stated in the modern *Debrett's* as in line of descent from Edward III, passed, in 1750, to the surviving heir of the 1st Duke by his first marriage. The dukedom had been created in 1547, over 200 years before and to get a new duke required a six generation chase through the male descendants of the 1st Duke. They were not entirely inconspicuous, having acquired a baronetage and been MPs for Devon for four generations, the 4th being the speaker of the House of Commons in the Long Parliament. The 6th Baronet, Edward, upon whom the title descended, was MP for Salisbury when he became the 8th Duke of Somerset. And with the dukedom came a seat in Parliament and 25,000 acres producing revenues equivalent to £2.6 million today. Nothing could more clearly demonstrate why keeping genealogies accurate and intact mattered in the past. Rates of death, execution and extinction were so frequent that even remote cousins could keep half an eye on a title and the lands that went with it. Within the nobility was 95% of the acreage of the country. Accident of birth entered you for that lottery and the ticket was a well-preserved genealogical tree, with proof.

Like the other Plantagenet lines, the Somerset dukedom had a rough passage at the time of the Tudors. The first duke, Sir Edward Seymour, was brother of Queen Jane Seymour, Henry VIII's third wife who died in childbirth. Seymour's nephew, Henry VIII's only male heir, Edward VI, was crowned king in 1547 but died, unmarried and heirless in 1553. Seymour was indicted for felony in 1551 and executed on Tower Hill. All his titles were abolished and his son reduced to a baronetage, though not for long. Seven years later the son was Baron Beauchamp and the Earl of Hereford. By 1605 he was ambassador to Brussels but there he marrried, in secret, Lady Katherine Grey, sister of Lady Jane Grey, who had been Queen for a few months in 1553, before being beheaded in 1554. Seymour was fined £15,000 for 'seducing a virgin of the blood royal' and both he and his wife were banged up in the Tower. She died in captivity in Suffolk. He paid £3000 of the fine, probably the equivalent of £1 million to £2 million nowadays. His grandson inherited the title in 1621. The grandson had already lost his first wife, Lady Arabella Stewart, whom he had married in secret and for which both of them had done time in the Tower. Bad luck continued in the Somerset line. The 5th Duke was shot dead at the door of an inn in Italy in 1678, his assailant, Horatio Bottio alleging that the Duke's friends had insulted his, Bottio's, wife. In 1923 the dukedom of Somerset was abeyant for two years, until the 16th Duke established his claim in the House of Lords in 1925. The present duke, a chartered surveyor, recently sold the ducal seat of Maiden Bradley in Wiltshire. His assets are valued at £10 million by the *Sunday Times*.

One of the more interesting entrants in the above list is the Duke of Norfolk. He is the only one of the Plantagenets to have obtained a hereditary seat in the reformed House of Lords on the basis of his hereditary title as Earl Marshal of England. The current Duke, Miles Francis Stapleton Fitzalan Howard, is the senior layman in the Catholic church in England and a former major general in the army. While in the services he was director of military intelligence and when he left the army he became a director of the merchant bank Robert Fleming and Co, the Palace's second bank, and was also President of the Building Societies Association. Educated at the Benedictine foundation of Ampleforth, he went to university at Christ Church Oxford, and then served as an officer in the Grenadier Guards, winning a Military Cross for bravery in World War Two. For a man with three homes, one in Yorkshire, one in Sussex and one in Oxfordshire, the *Sunday Times* rates him low in the wealth stakes, perhaps inaccurately. In 1872 the duke's predecessor had 49,866 acres and an income equivalent to £5.2 million a year. Cannadine mentions a sale of 20,000 acres in Yorkshire in 1920, but there is no further evidence of serious diminution of the estate, only a careful incorporation in perpetual trusts and transfer to his heir, the Earl of Arundel and Surrey, who lives at the family seat, Arundel Castle. The castle was restored at great expense in 1914. In respect to his conspicuously successful military career, the present duke, the 17th, far outclasses his predecessor in 1872. And the estate is still probably well in excess of 45,000 acres, if it could be identified. But it cannot. The duke's brothers have also distinguished themselves. His next youngest brother, Lord Michael Fitzalan Howard, was also a major general in the army, General Officer Commanding London District, and Marshal of the Diplomatic Corps after he retired. His daughter was a lady in waiting to the late Diana, Princess of Wales. His third brother, Lord Martin Fitzalan Howard, was High Sheriff of North Yorkshire and Deputy Lieutenant of the Riding. His fourth brother, Lord Mark, was a Chairman of the Association of Investment Trust Companies. All four were educated at Ampleforth and all four were officers in Guards regiments. The present duke has two sons and three daughters. He also has four sisters and a vast collection of blood cousins, including the offspring of the many daughters of the 16th and 15th dukes.

In short, the Howards, to give them their oldest family name, are a numerous clan. But that is only the half of it. The Norfolk, or Howard, family are Plantagenet descendants from the marriage of Thomas of Brotherton to Alice Halys. Thomas was the second son of Edward I by his second marriage, in 1299, to Margaret, daughter of Philip the Hardy, King of France. Thomas was created Earl of Norfolk by his father and made Earl Marshal of England. No less than 23 of the 1872 Plantagenet survivors and 15 of the current survivors arise from this particular line. In time past it was not a happy descent. This is a brief excerpt from some of the family history of the period.

Edmund of Woodstock, brother of Thomas of Brotherton, was beheaded in 1329. The 1st Duke of Norfolk was killed at Bosworth Field in 1485. His son was captured at Bosworth and spent three years in the Tower of London. The 3rd Duke spent seven years in the Tower. The 4th Duke was executed for treason in 1547. His father was executed for the same offence in 1572. The dukedom was then abolished and a brother of the 4th Duke spent six years in the Tower, from 1589 and died there in 1595. By 1660 all the titles, including the dukedom, were restored with precedence from 1483. Some 212 years later, in 1872, the Duke has almost 50,000 acres and an income equivalent to £5.2 million a year. Today, 341 years later, the family still has castles, 46,500 acres, innumerable titles and probably wealth in excess of £100 million.

But by taking a look at the details of the creations of the peerages themselves, we find something not often remarked upon amongst students of the peerage. Within the Norfolk family, or more properly the Howard family, there is a concentration of connections that is unique. The present duke, the 17th, actually holds the extinct title of Howard of Glossop, and another title with lands, that of Beaumont. Lord Beaumont had 5754 acres in Yorkshire in 1872. Howard of Glossop had a total of 17,911 acres in 1872, and was the then duke's deputy as Earl Marshal. There are six Howards, including Glossup, in Bateman, almost all relatives of the then duke. Excluding the duke they held over 50,000 acres between them. The present duke's son is the Earl of Arundel and Surrey. His titles were once accompanied by lands, some of which appear in the 1872 ducal holding, in Sussex (21,446 acres) and Surrey (3172 acres). But it is even more intriguing to look at who was made what at various times. For instance, in 1283 Roger de Mowbray, a Plantagenet-Howard, was summoned to Parliament and created a baron. Following one beheading and various other vicissitudes, a De Mowbray was first created Earl of Nottingham 1383 and Duke of Norfolk in 1397. That creation of the Norfolk dukedom passed along the line until the 2nd Duke lost it, with his head, for rebelling against Henry IV in 1405. The dukedom was restored in 1483 but the baronies, and with them the lands, of Mowbray and Seagrave, went into abeyance via a daughter. They stayed joined to the dukedom until 1777 when they again became abeyant until terminated in favour of Alfred Joseph Stourton in 1877, a descendant of the 6th Lord Mowbray and Sir Robert Howard. Stourton's son made an unsuccessful case for becoming Earl of Norfolk in 1906, and was also unsuccessful in usurping Baron de Ros as premier Baron of England. In 1872 the lands at Knaresborough in Yorkshire ran to 5097 acres and the rents were worth the equivalent today of £654,290. The present peer, Charles Edward Stourton, who was a working peer, is one of the transitional elected heriditaries, has a flat in London and another home in Scotland and is a director of many companies. Like many of his Howard cousins, he went to Ampleforth, Christ Church College Oxford and was a lieutenant in the Grenadier Guards. Elsewhere in the list there are a string of Plantagenet Howards who were or are peers from what might best be described as internal tribal promotions. First there is the duke himself, then there is his daughter, the 16th Lady Herries of Terreagles, a title held by the duke, but passed to his daughter in 1975, thereby creating another Howard family seat in the Lords. She was married to the late Sir Colin Cowdrey, the former cricketer.

In 1554 the eldest son of the 2nd Duke of Norfolk was created Earl of Effingham. In 1597 the second son of the 4th Duke of Norfolk was created Earl of Suffolk and Berkshire. In that same year the eldest son of the 4th Duke of Norfolk was created Baron Howard de Walden. The last holder of the Howard de Walden title was rated at £10 million by the *Sunday Times*, although he has split the London estate, worth up to £2 billion, amongst his four daughters, each of whom got a quarter of the total, and, up to his death, only retained a small country seat for himself. It is quite an achievement to have kept £2 billion in the family for almost 400 years. In 1640 the third son of the Earl of Norfolk was created Baron Stafford. In 1657 Cromwell made the great-great-grandson of the 4th Duke of Norfolk the Earl of Carlisle. So far that makes six Howards who had seats in the Lords. But the Howard cousins include the Baronies of Strange, Berkeley, Willoughby de Broke and many others.

In modern times the Howards continue to pick up peerages. Lord Howard of Penrith, a Howard, was ennobled in 1930 and Howard of Henderskelf, proprietor of Castle Howard, held a life peerage until his death in 1984. The other titles in the same line of descent, from Edmund of Woodstock, had equally rough patches. The earls of Devon, the Courtney family, started the practice of losing their heads in 1462, when the first earl lost his on the block. His brother died the same way in 1466. The estates were then confiscated and granted to Baron Stafford. But the curse of the Courtneys continued. Stafford was beheaded in 1469. The next earl joined Edward, the Earl of Warwick, and was killed at the Battle of Tewkesbury in 1472. Warwick lost his head in 1499. The 6th Earl married a daughter of Edward IV and spent the reign of Henry VII in the Tower. Released by Henry VIII be died before he could resume the earldom. His successor was created Marquess of Exeter in 1525 but was beheaded for attempting to make the Dean of Exeter King of England in 1539. His son was incarcerated in the Tower from the age of 12 in 1539 and not released until 1553 when he was created Earl of Devon. He was imprisoned again and upon release fled to Italy where he died unmarried at Padua in 1556. The Earl of Devon in 1872 had 53,075 acres and an income worth the modern equivalent of £3.1 million a year. The current Earl of Devon is reputed still to own, in trust, about 3400 of the Devon acres, and runs a thriving heritage and forestry business from the family seat at Powderham Castle near Exeter. The *Sunday Times* does not include him in its list.

The Plantagenets in 1872 and Today

The Table 9/1 lists the key members of the Plantagenet family, based on Bateman's list, but mainly for those who either continue to hold land, or who had seats in the House of Lords prior to the Blair reforms. The date alongside the title is the date of either the most recent creation of the title, or its revival. Without exception, the bearers of the title have Plantagenet links, even if they go back to lower or earlier forms of the title.[11] They were the royal family for about 329 of those 800 years and what the survivors represent in their land holdings is the accumulations of land, not by the monarchs of the Plantagenet line, but of the offspring of the family.

Table 9/1 displays an example of gilded survival of an extraordinary kind. At the entry point for the list in the year 1872 the Plantagenets constituted about 10.3% of the peerage. But unlike some continental countries, where titles proliferate and 2% to 3% of the population carry a title, the UK, or rather those controlling the peerage, from the Palace, had restricted actual peerages to about 0.0021% of the population.[12] In the UK peerages were defined and supported in law, and the holder of a title was entitled to sit in Parliament, in what was then known as The House of Peers. This made for an extraordinarily narrow statutory aristocracy, very narrow indeed if only the English peerage was counted: 431 peers in 1872 out of a total of 580 peers entitled to sit in the Lords. But Great Britain had a broader nobility, if untitled. In the words of *Burke's Landed Gentry* of Great Britain and Ireland for 1871, 'it must be remembered that "Nobility", a larger word than "Peerage", is not exclusively confined to titled families'. *Burke's* then described the nobility of Great Britain and Ireland as 'Peers and Baronets and landed Gentlemen entitled to hereditary arms'. This extended the concept of the aristocracy, but not by much, to about 0.011% of the population. And the key distinction was focused on one word, 'landed'. It was land that gave you wealth, status and power, Weber's three key characteristics of superiority.[13]

In the British peerage there are five ranks: the highest is that of duke, followed by marquess, earl/countess, then viscount and finally baron. In 1872 there were around 580 people holding these ranks. Next came the baronets, styled Sir, of which there were perhaps 1200 or so. Although hereditary, baronets could not sit in the Lords. As can by seen from the *Burke's* lineage, one sixth of the 1872 Plantagenets were baronets, with big estates. In the hierarchy these are followed by knights, also styled Sir, usually without large estates and with use of the title only for their lifetime. Finally, there were the untitled nobility, referred to by *Burke's* and known as the Landed Gentry, whose numbers came to about 3000 or so.

The 'nobility', as the 1872 Return showed, and as the county tables in Part II of this book demonstrate even more clearly, owned well over 95% of the country. This situation had evolved over the course of about 800 years and had been confined to a very small number of what might be called 'persistent families'. Amongst the most persistent were the Plantagenets.

In the 1872 Returns, the list of Plantagenet inheritors ran to ten dukes, four marquesses, twenty earls and one countess, five viscounts, nineteen barons and three baronesses. There were eleven baronets. Of these 71 people, 11 had no land at all. The remaining 61 had a grand total of 3.86 million acres between them. This is about 11% of England and Wales, or about 5.2% of the land area of all four countries. In theory, 60 of them were entitled to sit in the House of Lords. In fact 25 of them had sat, at one time or another as Members of the House of Commons as well. And 24 of them had been to Eton. By 1998, eleven of the peerages and five of the baronetcies had become extinct or abeyant. This still left 48 of the Plantagenet descendants with a seat in the 1998 House of Lords. Few availed themselves of this privilege or duty. The Duke of Beaufort's predecessor, who as far as is known had never attended the House of Lords, remained on the list of absent peers for about eight years after his death in 1984. Five of the baronies have become extinct, as has one of the baronesses, with one other in abeyance. And one countess, the Countess of Sutherland, has joined the ranks, her title being released from the dukedom in 1963. Three of the earldoms and one of the viscountcies have become extinct. This is a total of 11 departures over a period of 126 years. By way of comparison, between 1950 and 1995, a period of 45 years, 214 hereditary peerages, including two dukedoms, those of Leeds and Newcastle, became extinct or abeyant, out of a total of 964 hereditary peerages in 1950. This is a rate of attrition of slightly under five hereditary peerages a year vanishing from the rolls.

One of the most interesting aspects of the Plantagenet descent is the extent to which they used possession of land and of titles to springboard themselves into the House of Commons. Of the 60 Plantagenet descendants with the right to sit in the Lords in 1872, 25 sat or had sat as MPs, usually for the area in which their estate was situated. This pattern is endemic in the 1870s, with the landowners who controlled the Lords also controlling the Commons. Historians have done little to focus on this aspect of 'gross control' in the political situation, and on its meaning. Most histories focus on the political parties, the Whigs and the Tories, and finally the Liberals, forgetting that all three in 1872 came from the same extraordinarily narrow class, and none was prepared to do other than support that class in a crisis. Hence the near universal support for the various Irish land purchase acts in the late eighteen hundreds, which did no more than bail out the bankrupt Irish cousins of the British governing class. The three factions differed over many things, but not over enhancing families already well installed in the elite, and over preserving landed estates. The Howards are a good example of a family collecting peerages through the centuries, but it is worth noting that there were very few creations outside already established families. Implicitly, all the Plantagenet descendants were 'established'. But promotion into the peerage was almost always from a significant existing position. The Earl of Abingdon was made earl as the fourth son of the 6th Lord Crawford. The Marquess of Exeter was promoted from knight and Secretary of State. The Earl of Loudoun was promoted from knight but with two baronies, those of Botreux and Moleyns,

TABLE 9/1
THE PLANTAGENET SURVIVORS

	Name	Title	Date title created	Acreage 2001	Land value 2001	Acres 1872	Modern equivalent of 1872 value	School in 2001	School in 1872	University in 2001	University in 1872	Regiment in 2001	Regiment in 1872	Lords in 1996/1997 session	Political Position In 1872
1	Northumberland	Duke	1749	132,200	£260m	186,397	£12.3m	Eton	Eton	Oxford	Cambridge		G.Guards	XB/A	MP
2	Bedford	Duke	1506	23,020	£170m	86,335	£9.9m	Le Rosey		Harvard			SFG	N	MP
3	Sutherland	Duke	1833	12,000	£140m	1,358,545	£9.9m	Eton		Cambridge			RHG	N	MP
4	Beaufort	Duke	1461	52,000	£100m	51,085	£3.9m	Eton	Eton			C.Gds.	7th H	C/N	MP
5	Rutland	Duke	1264	26,000	£80m	70,137	£6.8m	Eton	Eton	Cambridge	Oxford	G.Gds		N	MP
6	Spencer	Earl	1765	13,000	£96m	27,185	£3.2m	Eton	Harrow	Oxford	Cambridge			XB/N	MP
7	Atholl	Duke	1604	148,000	£430m	201,640	£2.9m	Eton	Eton	Oxford			SG	N	
8	Jersey	Earl	1620	3000	£60m	19,389	£2.4m	Eton	Eton	Oxford	Oxford	RA		N	LIW
9	Braybrook	Lord	1788	7000	£52m	13,511	£1.2m	Eton	Eton	Cambridge	Cambridge			C/A	
10	St Germans	Earl	1784	4000	£11m	12,791	£1.2m	Eton	Eton				RN	C/N	
11	Somerset	Duke	1547	2000	£6m	25,387	£2.6m	Eton	Eton	FRICS	Oxford		XB/A	MP	
12	Bradford	Earl	1660	10,000	£10m	21,710	£2.9m	Harrow	Harrow	Cambridge	Cambridge			C/A	MOH & MP
13	Suffolk & Berkshire	Earl	1597	5000	£10m	11,098	£0.99m	Winchester	Harrow			RNVR		C/A	MP
14	Stafford	Baron	1640	6000	£10m	11,050	£1.5m	Ampleforth						C/A	MP
15	Howard de Walden (abnt)	Baron	1597	3100	£2000m				Eton	Cambridge		TA		N	
16	Sutherland	Countess	1235	83,239	£15m	149,999	£0.84m							N	
17	Gage	Viscount	1633	2000	£10m	12,352	£0.93m	Eton	Eton	Oxford	Oxford	CG		C/A	
18	Dudley	Earl	1359	2000	£5m	25,554	£8.6m	Eton	Eton	Oxford	Oxford	RH		C/A	
19	Norfolk	Duke	1483	46,000	£125m	49,866	£5.2m	Ampleforth		Oxford		Maj Gen		C/A	Earl M
20	Lansdowne	Marquess	1280	8000	£4m	142,916	£4.3m	Eton	Eton	Oxford	Oxford	S.Greys		N	Cabinet
21	Richmond	Duke	1675	12,000	£260m	286,411	£5.5m	Eton	Westminster		Oxford	KRRC	RHG	XB/N	Cabinet & MP
22	Carlisle	Earl	1657	10,000	£10m	78,540	£3.4m	Eton		FRICS		R.Bde		LD/A	

	Name	Title	Date title created	Acerage 2001	Land value 2001	Acres 1872	Modern equivalent of 1872 value	School in 2001	School in 1872	University in 2001	University in 1872	Regiment in 2001	Regiment in 1872	Lords in 1996/1997 session	Political Position In 1872
23	Scarsdale	Viscount	1761	6050	£6m	9929	£1.2m	Eton	Rugby		Oxford	SG		N	
24	Brownlow	Baron	1776	22000	£66m	58,335	£6.0m	Eton	Eton			GG		N	MP
25	Ferrers	Earl	1299	2000	£6m	8665	£0.88m	Winchester		Cambs	Cambs	CG		C/A	
26	Herries	Lady	1490	5050	£1.5m	18,895	£1.3m		Stonyhurst					N	
27	Loudoun	Countess	1601	4400	£1.25m	32,910	£2.7m							XB/N	
28	Petre	Baron	1603	15000	£95m	19,085	£1.5m	Eton		Oxford				XB/N	
29	Clifford of Chudleigh	Baron	1672	4000	£12m	7860	£0.63m	Downside	Stonyhurst		London University		CG	XB/A	
30	Waterford	Marquess	1665	10900	£30m	66,684	£2.2m	Eton	Eton			RHG	ILG	C/A	MP
31	Huntingdon	Earl	1461	600	£1.5m	13,523	£0.47m	Winchester		Cambs.	Oxford			XB/A	
32	Devon	Earl	1553	3400	£10m	53,075	£3.2m	Winchester	Westminster	RMA	Oxford		CG	N	Cabinet MP
33	Lovelace	Earl	1838			18,481	£1.5m	Pvt.	Eton		Cambridge			XB/A	
34	Vaux of H	Baron	1523			4323	£0.16m	Ampleforth		Oxford		DWR		C/A	
35	Falkland	Viscount	1617			3011	£0.31m	Wellington College				8H	YoG	LD/A	Colonial Governor
36	Teynham	Baron	1616					Eton					CG		C/A	
37	Cobham	Viscount	1718											Leave of Absence	
38	Tankerville (in USA)	Earl	1714			31,423	£2.3m	USA	Harrow	Oxford	Oxford		Capt HCGA	N	Lord Steward MP
39	Kinloss	Lady	1597											XB/A	
40	Dunmore (In Australia)	Earl	1686			78,620	£0.72m	Eton	Eton				SFG	N	Lord in Waiting
41	Berkeley	Baron	1421						Eton	Camb				L/A	
42	Exeter (In Canada)	Marquess	1571	4000	£4m	28,271	£3.4m	Eton	Eton	Camb			Capt HC OGA	XB/N	ADC to HM MP
43	Manchester	Duke	1620			27,312	£2.8m	Gordonstoun		RMA			GG	XB/N	MP

132 WHO OWNS BRITAIN

	Name	Title	Date title created	Acerage 2001	Land value 2001	Acres 1872	Modern equivalent of 1872 value	School in 2001	School in 1872	University in 2001	University in 1872	Regiment in 2001	Regiment in 1872	Lords in 1996/1997 session	Political Position In 1872
44	Hereford	Viscount	1550			2100	£0.15m	Eton						N	
45	Manners	Baron	1807					Eton	Oxford	Oxford		RAF		C/N	
46	Mowbray & Stourton	Baron	1283			5097	£0.65m	Ampleforth		Oxford	Oxford			C/A	
47	Berners	Baroness	1455											C/A	
48	Effingham	Earl	1554			5731	£0.55m	Lancing.	Harrrow			RN		XB/A	MP

Extinct since 1872

49	Ellesmere	Earl	Baroness
50	Brownlow	Earl	Baron
51	Berkeley	Earl	Baron
52	Edgerton	Baron	Baron

53	Burdett Coutts	
54	Howard of Glossop	
55	Dorchester	
56	Arundell of Wardour	

57	Canterbury	Viscount
58	Berwick	Baron
59	Howth	Earl
60	Hatherton	Baron

GUIDE TO TABLE 9/I

The total of direct Plantagenet descendants identified by *Burke's Peerage and Baronetage* (1896 and previous) as entitled to use the arms of the Plantagenets on their family arms included in Bateman's *Great Landowners of Great Britain and Ireland* was 71. The total number of Plantagenet families identified by *Burke's* was actually 72. A few of the Bateman entrants, including Burdett-Coutts and Berkeley, were shown as incorporated with other estates. There is an identifiable inclination by the Plantagenets to 'mind' estates until an heir can be found. The largest single family group identified by *Burke's* as Plantagenet descendants were the Howard clan with 23 entrants. Two major direct Plantagenet descendants not included in this category by *Burke's* were the Dukes of Beaufort and of Somerset. This is presumably because they are Plantagenets and do not quarter their shields. They are included above. This list does not include numerous indirect cousins and connections.

Table headings

Name The name of the title, not the family name
Title The title as currently known
Date title created Titles were upgraded over time, or restored from abeyance, or restored after executions etc. This is the date of the title as it is currently used.
Acerage in 2001 The estimated acreage still in the possession of this family
Land value in 2001 All are taken from Bateman's *Great Landowners*.
Acreage in 1872 All are taken from Bateman's *Great Landowners*.
Modern equivalent of rental income in 1872 See Appendix I for details of equivalent values used in this book.
School in 2001/1872 This column indicates the strength of the Etonian connection, but also the narrowness of school attended.
University in 2001/1872 Universities are named. FRICS is Fellow of the Royal Institute of Chartered Surveyors. RMA is Royal Military Academy, Sandhurst.
Regiment in 2001 CG = Coldstream Guards. GG = Grenadier Guards. RA = Royal Artillery. DL = Durham Light Infantry. RNVR = Royal Naval Volunteer Reserve. TA = Territorial Army. RH = Royal Hussars (10th). Maj Gen = Major General (Grenadier Guards). S.Greys = Scots Greys. KRRC = Kings Royal Rifle Corp. R.Bde = Rifle Brigade. SG = Scots Guards. 8H = Eight Hussars. RAF = Royal Air Force. RN = Royal Navy.
Regiment in 1872 G.Guards = Grenadier Guards. SFG = Scots Fusilier Guards. RHG = Royal Horse Guards. 7th H = 7th Hussars. SG= Scots Guards. RN = Royal Navy. CG = Coldstream Guards. ILG = 1st Life Guards. YoG = Yeoman of the Guard. Capt HCGA = Captain in the Honourable Company of the Gentlemen at Arms.
House of Lords in the 1996/1997 session Political affiliation: XB = Cross Bencher without a main party affiliation. C= Conservative whip. LD = Liberal Democrat. L = Labour. Where no party is indicated the peer did not declare a political affiliation. In the second part A = the peer attended at least once. N = the peer did not attend at all.
Political position 1872 LIW = Lord in Waiting to the Sovereign (now a whip). MOH = Master of the Horse. Earl M = Earl Marshall. Cabinet = Member of the Cabinet. ADC to HM = Aide de Camp to the Queen Empress. Of the 71 Plantagenets extant in 1872, no less than 25 had been or were MPs. A total of 60 of them in addition were entitled, upon succeeding to their title, to seats in the Lords. At any one time the 60 Plantagenet members of the Lords had 25 of their cousins in the Commons.

THE PLANTAGENETS 133

in the background. The Dukedom of Atholl was conferred on the 12th feudal lord, the Marquess of Townshend was an MP and the Sutherland dukedom was preceded by a barony created in 1620, not to mention the earldom/countess title that went back to 1235. Outsiders were not welcome, contrary to a constant impression given in recent literature, and they only became so in the late 1800s and the early 1990s, as Gladstone's 'masses' increased in number and influence while the 'classes' remained static.

The Plantagenet group also exhibit several other characteristics, which are of great importance if the Blair experiment in political egalitarianism is to be successful and not ambushed by historic forces still in possession of sufficient funds to launch new political parties. Of the 71 Plantagenets identified in the 1872 list, 23 went to Eton. Of the 55 Plantagenet survivors in 1998, no less than 31 went to Eton. In many cases, attendance at Eton, like the title, had become hereditary. Many of those same people then exhibited a very strong affinity for either Oxford or Cambridge and a short 'finishing school' stint in one of the Guards regiments. Of the 55 Plantagenet survivors in 2001, 48 went to one of the top five English public schools. One, the Marquess of Tavistock, heir to the Duke of Bedford, went to school in Switzerland, and one, the Earl of Lovelace, was educated privately. Old habits die hard, though, and 14 of the modern Plantagenets wound up in the military, compared with 15 in 1872. Interestingly, where the military connection is particularly strong is amongst the untitled nobility, the landed gentry. In a system of control, and a dispensation of power, that seldom extended beyond 1400 or 1500 well-connected families, along with a further 1500 closely related families, it was at this level, that of the local representative of the landed gentry, that running the military of Britain, as its officers, was most common. In this they fulfilled a very special function. Large and small landed estates were how the country was finally knit together, socially, politically and in terms of control. In the event of trouble, it was the peerage as Lords Lieutenant who would call out the militia, the baronetage and lesser nobility who would read the riot act, but it was the sons of the landed gentry who would lead the militia against the mob. And this revolving door between the landed gentry and the military, in which the heir did a short tour with a part of the armed forces, while his brothers probably made professional careers in it, lent enormous weight to the local control exercised by the ruling elite. This very small group owned 95% of the acreage of the country, totally controlled Parliament and, far more important, controlled, totally, the local administration of the country. They supplied the entire Lord Lieutenancy, more than 90% of Justices of the Peace, the entire magistracy, and when push came to shove, the entire officer corps of the militia. This is one, frequently misunderstood, reason why England in particular did not develop a highly centralised administration like many countries on the continent. It did not need to. The state went all the way down to all but the smallest landholdings through blood links between the families of the wider nobility, and the state was the law and the militia. Even the Church was an integrated part of the state, with the Anglican clergy no more than civil servants in a quasi state department of morals.

Nor can the links between land and wealth in the Plantagenet inheritance be ignored. In 1872 the largest individual landowner in the whole of the four countries of the then United Kingdom was the 6th Duke of Sutherland. He owned 1,358,545 acres of land, more than three times as much as the next largest landowner in the UK. He had an Olympian income to match, the modern equivalent of around £10 million a year. Two descendants of the duke, both big land owners in the modern age, held seats in the House of Lords until the Blair reforms. The current Duke of Sutherland appeared in the *Sunday Times* Rich List 2000 at number 118, worth no less than £150 million. His cousin the Countess of Sutherland appears in *Sunday Times* Wealth Register.[14]

But the duke is not the only Plantagenet descendant to appear in the *Sunday Times* Rich List, nor is he top of the pile. He is outranked in wealth, and hugely in lands, by the Duke of Northumberland, who is worth £250 million and still has 132,200 of the ancestral acres. Immediately below him is the Duke of Bedford, with a fortune of £175 million and an estimated acreage of 23,020. In all 20 Plantagenet descendants appear in the *Sunday Times* Rich List or in its rival the *Mail on Sunday* Rich Report (see table 9/2).

It is clear that the Plantagenets had hung onto their wealth and their titles, but what about power, and what about government, not of the country, but of the Empire which then encompassed one quarter of the surface of the planet and a third of its population in 1872? Sutherland was merely an MP, but the next Plantagenet in the landownership league, the Duke of Richmond, educated at Westminster and Oxford, was at various times a President of the Poor Law Board, President of the Board of Trade, Lord President of the Council and MP for West Sussex. The old Etonian Duke of Atholl, or Athole as his title was then known, was only 21 at the time and had done a stint in the Scots Guards, but did not subsequently occupy any office of state. The eleventh largest landowner in those days was the Duke of Northumberland, an old Etonian who served in the Grenadier Guards and then served as a Lord of the Admiralty, Vice President of the Board of Trade and finally as Lord Privy Seal. The Earl of Bradford, a Plantagenet, was Victoria's Master of the Horse, the 3rd most important post in the Palace after the Lord Chamberlain. The Earl of Tankerville, another Plantagenet, was the Lord Steward, the Palace number two. The Marquess of Exeter, a Plantagenet, was the Queen Empresse's Aide de Camp. The cousinhood stuck like limpets to the Palace.

Nearly 130 years on from 1872 it is interesting to see how the 10 Plantagenet dukes have fared. Despite possessing fortunes and lands that most ordinary people would find inconceivable, they have slipped from their pre-eminence, with the richest of the Plantagenet dukes now worth a mere £250 million and ranked at 134th in the *Sunday Times* list. In practice, Northumberland's land may well be worth more than Dr Beresford's cautious assessment, as some of it is in London. The modern Duke of Bedford, whose ancestor was the third richest man in England, is worth a mere £170 million and is only just in amongst the top 200 richest people in the UK. Not that the Duke of Bedford intends to have his family fortune any further damaged by the UK tax man. The entire fortune is in trust and he lives in tax exile in Monaco, with his grandson, Lord Howland, taking over from his son, the Marquess of Tavistock, in the running of the estate.

But of the ten, only one, Manchester, is not a millionaire. The poorest of the remainder, Somerset, is worth at least £10 million according to the *Sunday Times*. Where that puts you nowadays is at a lowly 1622nd in the wealth stakes in the modern UK. Where there is a real difference, however is in political power. The dukes in 1872 had seats in the Lords and seats in the Commons – eight of the ten Plantagenet Dukes had been or were MPs as well as Peers. Only one of the current top ten richest people in the UK has any political power and that is Lord Sainsbury, the labour peer who is the scion of an essentially Tory family. He is a junior minister in the Department of Trade and Industry. Compared with the sway the 1872 Plantagent dukes had in both the Palace and Parliament in relation to their wealth and land, the modern rich in the UK have nothing at all. Power and wealth are no longer synonymous, even in power's transmuted form of influence.

Table 9/2

THE WEALTH OF THE PLANTAGENET DUKES

Title	Rich list valuation (see notes)	Rank in 2001 Rich Lists	Rank in 1872 Return	Wealth in 1872 (Modern equivalent)
Northumberland	£250m (ST 2001)	134	6	£12.3m
Bedford	£170m (ST 2001)	193	3	£15.7m
Atholl (Lands)*	£143m (ST BoR 1990)	230	104	£2.9m
Sutherland	£140m (ST 2001)	233	9	£9.9m
Beaufort	£140m (MoS 2001)	227	56	£3.9m
Norfolk	£125m (MoS 2000)	226	29	£5.2m
Rutland	£80m (ST 2001)	418	16	£6.8m
Richmond & Gordon	£40m (ST 2001)	829	26	£5.5m
Somerset	£10m (STWR 1997)	1622	127	£2.6m
Manchester	Nil	Nil	112	£2.8m

* Lands in trust; not held by current duke.
Notes:
Sources for the Rich List valuations:
Beresford, Dr Philip *The Sunday Times Book of the Rich* (Weidenfeld & Nicholson, London 1990).
Sunday Times Rich Lists 1989–2001, edited and written by Dr Philip Beresford.
Sunday Times Wealth Register, 1997.
Mail on Sunday Rich Report 2000 and 2001, edited by Rachel Oldroyd and Rodney Gilchrist.

Perhaps now that the hereditaries, and with them most of the Plantagenets, have left the Lords and ceased to be the operators of history, they will become the proper subject of historians. They were and are a unique bunch, with, above all, a unique grip on survival at the very top of the social and financial heap.

Now that Tony Blair has evicted almost all of them from the House of Lords he needs to rectify a residual flaw in the law, which, if not created by the Plantagenet descendants, is one which benefits them hugely. This is the flawed Land Registry of England and Wales, which conceals from public gaze the residual landholdings of the residue of a violent past, and the beneficiaries of that violence. Nor should any modern government flinch from another step, that of dissolving the large land holdings, if that action is in the public interest. The Plantagenets and their associates once thought nothing of using the law to steal eight million acres of England and Wales that they did not already own. England should think nothing of dissolving that ill-gotten inheritance – after all the European Convention of Human Rights, opposed for 50 years by the Plantagenets and their associates in Parliament, gives them adequate protection by way of guaranteed compensation. It is a form of justice that their ancestors withheld from the British population between 1700 and 1890 or so.

Chapter Ten

The Big Institutional Landowners

'HISTORY, AS A reflection of nature in the raw, is unjust in its dealings. Civilisation, as a reflection of intelligence at work, is how that injustice is remedied.' Not a quote; just a half remembered phrase from somewhere but one that offers a degree of illumination to the landownership question. For the accumulation of huge tracts of lands by small numbers of individuals is clearly a form of communal injustice and but a very thinly disguised human version of the territorial instinct of animals. How thin was vividly illustrated by the Highland clearances in Scotland in the 1800s, the enclosures in England across two centuries, and the evictions of the starving during the Irish famine in 1845. Unusually, it also runs counter to what we know of primitive societies, both historically and in those which continue to exist, where land tends to be held communally. The instrument within civilisation that best reflects the effort to humanise the brutality of nature in the raw is the law, however inadequate and however incomplete.

On the continent the inherently primitive and unjust concept of excessive individual ownership of land is recognised in law and stringent limits are set upon the number of acres any person may own. In Denmark no individual can own more than two farms; and the second farm can be no more than 15km from where the owner lives. There is an upper limit of 185 acres on amalgamations.[1] In France there is a more complex, but nonetheless effective system, of controlling estate sizes through the locally based SAFER organisations. These are effectively co-operatives which intervene in land transactions and have the power to 'buy in' blocks of land coming up for sale, and to allocate acreage, especially to younger families starting out in the agricultural sector. In Holland a tenant has first right on a sale of land; there are extensive official financial supports in place for those wishing to buy and finally there is a government council through which all farmland sales are referred. In Germany, the Land Settlement Society has the power to intervene in transactions, including those involving farmers trying to increase their acreage. It is clear that most of these arrangements, some aimed directly at curbing foreign ownership of local land, contrary to the principles of EU law, are mostly about farmland. The orientation of the arrangements is local, even in Holland, and is virtually wholly local in France. This is an inherent reflection of the social use of land by humans, innately organised on a communal basis. This arises in part from the various revolutions on the continent, which often saw the huge estates of the aristocracy swept away; those that were not swept away by revolution were often swept away by war. In some parts of the former Eastern Bloc, especially Poland and East Germany, there has been a determined attempt by former junkers and aristocrats to regain their old lands, but with only limited success, financial compensation often being offered rather than disturb the private ownership that is emerging as the old communist collective farm system vanishes totally. Regrettably, many of the new governments in the former Eastern Bloc are being advised by officials from the most reactionary country in relation to landownership in Europe, the UK.

The UK, and particularly England, suffered neither revolution nor invasion for over 900 years. The pattern of aristocratic ownership that has underlain land ownership in

England since 1066 persists, albeit in a watered down version compared even with 1872. One reason that such a system has been able to survive is the lack of the kind of accessible, universal and usable information that was available in the 1872 Returns. It has enabled secrecy to flourish, and behind the cloak of secrecy it has enabled deals to be done that have anything but the public good as their objective. Further, it has stifled an informed debate and left would-be reforming administrations, especially those of post-war Labour governments, largely in the dark on this issue. It is quite clear that had the Returns been institutionalised either as a land registry or in, for example, a five-yearly survey, both government and people could have known on a regular basis where the large acreages were, and could at least have monitored what was happening to those very large acreages, allegedly owned or held in trust for the public. By confining the institutionalised version of the Returns to holdings of over an acre, it is very doubtful if an abstract of a modern Return would have much more than two million names; perhaps half that number. We know that the agricultural sector, which owns about 70% of the country, numbers less than 239,600 owners, which accounts for the bulk of owners over one acre. The big change from 1876 would be the number of suburban owners of around an acre – a figure not currently available.[2]

What the UK demonstrates is that huge tracts of land concentrated in a small number of hands leads to the creation of undemocratic fiscal and tax privileges. It also leads to an unbalanced political structure, where those who own big tracts of land live a life that is separate from that of their fellow citizens, whose democratic choices can be undone and indeed are undone, by the secret machinations of landowners. The country house weekend, so celebrated in glossy magazines, is often the home of those cocktail conspiracies which seek to curb, twist and undo, gently but egregiously, the work of democracy expressed through party manifestos and elections. Previous chapters have shown how the tower of privilege, the fortress of tax concession, is erected for the royals out of the mystique of their landholdings. These towers and fortresses have their walls cemented by the semantic dishonesty seen in all three duchies' publications and by the administrative dishonesty of the various duchy accounts. But all this is small beer indeed compared with the overall dishonesty of having lost the 1872 survey and at having been denied the benefits of its development into a real land registry, or more pertinently, into a scheme to monitor large landholdings. Had this happened, and had the principles of universality, openness, accessibility and completeness demonstrated by the Return been pursued, grand tales of larceny such as the following would not have been possible.

Between 1985 and 1997 up to one million acres, some of it immensely valuable development land, was transferred, often without a proper evaluation, often without any disclosure as to its scale, through the medium of privatisation. The table below gives the best estimate of the undeclared 'endowment' that went with the four main areas privatised, water, electricity, coal and rail.[3]

To understand how poor the disclosure by those bodies was, it is relevant to look at the experiences of a considerable authority on the state of modern Britain. In the first edition of his *Anatomy of Britain* in 1962, Anthony Sampson was totally frustrated in his attempt to look at land ownership. All he could say was that 'Today, the biggest landowner, by far, is the Forestry Commission, which owns 2.47 million acres . . . the other rich landowners are the Crown, 292,000 acres, and the church, 220,000 acres.' He adds that 'the size of the big private estates is not published.'

Had Anthony Sampson had access to the records of John McEwen,[4] he could have amended his estimates and shown that the Duke of Buccleuch and the Wills family owned 277,000 acres and 263,000 acres respectively, ranking them far higher than the Church as landowners. He would also have found that there were nine landowners in Scotland each of whom owned over 100,000 acres. But his book does give a valuable insight into how secretive everyone, including the state, was at that time, and to some extent still is. The probable ranking of landowners in 1962 was as follows.

TABLE 10/1

LEADING UK LANDOWNERS C.1962

1	Forestry Commission	2,470,000	acres
2	Ministry of Defence	1,100,000	acres
3	Local Authorities	993,652	acres
4	National Trust	400,000	acres (including covenants)
5	Crown Estate	370,000	acres (excluding 23.4 million acres of seabed)
6	National Coal Board	320,000	acres
7	The electricity utilities	300,000	acres (or possibly 500,000 acres)
8	Water utilities	300,000	acres (or 560,000 acres)
9	British Rail	250,000	acres
10	The Duke of Buccleuch	277,000	acres
11	The Wills family	263,000	acres

Note:
The figures are the author's estimates from the available sources but are believed to be broadly accurate. The two personal landholdings are provided, from McEwen, to give perspective to the list.

The third of Anthony Sampson's 'richest' landowners, the Church, at least in the sense of the Church Commissioners, does not even make it onto this list. And this list is by no means complete. It is at best a good estimate. Local authority holdings, and the utility holdings, may have been much larger than indicated and besides the MoD there were other government landholdings such as those in Royal Ordnance, the Ministry of Agriculture, and the Scottish and Northern Irish offices.

What Sampson, and the other commentators who used John Batemans's book, failed to do, was ask two questions. The first was why the Land Registry could not produce a list of large landowners. The second was why the Victorians, but no contemporary government, could produce the *Return of Owners of Land*.

The Big Institutions

The purpose of this book is to display the infrastructure of landownership in the UK insofar as that is possible, given the structural flaws in the Land Registry. It is outside the scope of this book to go into detail about every single landowning institution and for that reason only the two main institutional landowners are looked at in any detail. First, the Forestry Commission because it is the largest landowner in the modern UK, because it has been the least transparent and the most insensitive to its public responsibilities over the years, and remains so, despite significant changes in its structure and reporting since 1997. Secondly the Ministry of Defence, because it is the next largest institutional landowner, and because it raises crucial issues about the defence of the realm and the willingness of individuals located where training for that defence is done to accommodate the military

The Forestry Commission
In 1990 the Forestry Commission, the largest landed estate in the country, owned by the government on behalf of the public, had a holding of 2,816,013 acres.[5] By 1995 that had fallen to 2,690,271 acres and in the year 2000 the figure was 2,612,588 acres, a figure which reflected the moratorium on sales imposed by the incoming Labour government in 1997. Total sales in the period between 1990 and 1997 were over 203,425 acres, worth an estimated £101 million. This was public land sold to private interests. The Forestry Commission had, up to 1995, refused to identify the buyers of this land, contrary to the public administration convention that all details of transactions in public assets be fully disclosed. The refusal paralleled the last, and indeed present, government's unconstitutional refusal to publish the names of those benefiting from the £4 billion handout to the landowning community by the Ministry of Agriculture.

The Forestry Commission is the biggest single landowner in the United Kingdom despite the fact that it is a relatively new institution. It was created by act of Parliament in 1919, at the end of World War One. Its creation sprung from the recommendations of the Acland Committee, set up to examine Britain's timber needs during the middle years of the war then ravaging Europe. Originally devised by Prime Minister Herbert Asquith as part of the main post-war reconstruction committee in 1916, it started life as the Forestry sub committee of that body. Not unpredictable, its first concern was Britain's strategic situation in time of war. The conflict on the continent had shown the precarious position of the country's timber supply, with German U-boats sinking vast tonnage coming from both Canada and Russia, much of it carrying timber for trenches and other military operations. Even before war began, Britain was dependent on Russia for almost half of its timber supply and on Canada for much of the rest. Both supply lines were highly vulnerable, as the war at sea and then revolution in Russia proved. For a country that was once richly forested, Britain had become almost denuded of woodlands during the Elizabethan period and at the time of the Commonwealth seizure of all Crown and royalist land in 1648.[6] The ensuing needs of war plus the financing of the Commonwealth armies at home and abroad and the need of many of the Commonwealth officers to produce cash fast to pay for the purchase of royal lands, led to the sale and cutting down of much old forest. The expansion of Empire in the East and the occupation of vast tracts of forest land in Siam, Burma and what is now Malaysia, did not encourage any attempt to reforest the UK in the 1700s and 1800s. Thus, Britain went into World War One with a serious timber shortage, which became acute in 1917 when Russia fell to the Communist revolution.

The Acland committee reported in 1918 to Prime Minister Lloyd George, suggesting that there were between three million and five million acres of land that was little better than waste which could be used to 'grow first class coniferous timber of the same character imported'. The final goals for the Forestry Commission recommended by the committee were for 1,770,000 acres of conifers to be planted over a period of 80 years, with two thirds of that amount to be planted in the first 40 years. In fact, just 60 years later, the Forestry Commission had almost doubled that acreage under management. But the critical test came long before even the first of the Commission's plantings were available for cutting.

In September 1939 World War Two broke out. This event had been considered a near certainty by the inner elite of Britain's ruling class since the treaty of Versailles and the imposition of huge war reparations on Germany in 1919. The inner core of officials in MI6, and in the parallel private organisation Z, some of whom had been at Versailles in various capacities, had also considered war with Germany inevitable, and certainly so after Hitler came to power in 1933. Their views had gained sufficient strength within the political establishment that the first steps towards putting the Forestry Commission on a virtual war footing were taken in 1937. The Commission, which became responsible, either directly or indirectly, for all Britain's war time timber needs, divided Britain's woodlands into three categories: (a) woods which could be felled forthwith; (b) woods which would be felled if necessary; (c) woods which would be felled only as a matter of extreme urgency.

The first trees to fall were those that the Commission had first acquired at its formation in the transfer from what is now the Crown Estate. These were the Forest of Dean and the New Forest, the latter alone producing 12.5 million cubic feet of the overall 51 million cubic feet of timber the Commission produced during the war.

The original board of Commissioners, appointed on the 1 September 1919, is interesting, particularly from the perspective of the amount of land the Forestry Commission was to acquire. The chairman was Lord Lovat, proprietor of 181,791 acres in Inverness-shire. The second commissioner was the Rt. Hon. Sir Francis Dyke Acland Bt., MP, chairman of the committee which recommended the setting up of the Forestry Commission, and owner of 39,896 acres of Devon and Somerset. A good deal of his lands were also woodland. Among the other commissioners were Lord Clinton, a fellow Devon landowner, with a smaller holding of 34,776 acres at Beaford; L. Forestier-Walker, a relative of the Earl of Seafield, and an MP who still owned 305,930 acres in Scotland; and Sir John Stirling Maxwell, a Scottish landowner with 20,814 acres across several counties in Scotland. The remaining commissioners were either minor landowners or relatives of aristocrats. The makeup of the board of Commissioners changed little over the years and a look at the incumbents up to 1997, several appointed in order to secure compliance with the former Tory government's sell-off policy, is equally interesting.

The chairman (1997–2001) is Sir Peter Hutchinson Bt., CBE, an old Etonian Scot who gained a degree from Cambridge and was a lieutenant in the Scots Greys. He had a strong commercial career at the family firm of Glasgow insurance brokers. Following spells on the British Waterways Board, he was appointed as a trustee of the Edinburgh Botanical Gardens and to the board of Scottish Heritage. He was joined on the board of Forestry Commissioners by Sir Fiennes Michael Strang Steel, a fellow old Etonian and former major in the 17th/21st Lancers. He is also a Member of the Queen's Bodyguard for Scotland.

The remaining commissioners are an eclectic bunch, including two writers, Bridget Bloom and Robin Grove White. The latter is director of the Ecological Centre at Lancaster University. John Edmonds of the General and Municipal Workers Union is also a commissioner.

For a number of years under the Tory government of the 1990s, the Forestry Commission has been making significant disposals, as much as 200,000 acres between 1987 and 1997. Until 1995 the Commission refused to disclose the identity of those to whom they sold the properties, the price obtained, or any other details. The accounts were the most opaque of any public body at the time and were a measure of the institutional arrogance and landowner indolence at the heart of this huge enterprise. The Forestry Commission has three national committees, one each for England, Wales and Scotland. During the year

1996 to 1997 no meetings at all took place of these committees. John Edmonds from the GMB union was on all three committees and he seems to have thought that either the writer Bridget Bloom, who was chair of the English committee, or Sir Michael Strang Steel, the chairman of the Scottish committee or Harry Fetherstonhaugh, chair of the Welsh committee would convene the meetings. No one did.

The accounts of the Forestry Commission for 1996–7 are, like the meetings of the national committees, a deeply unsatisfactory document. If they were to be believed, the Commission did not own the forests and lands it controlled. In fact, the assets of the Forestry Commission were and are held in a subsidiary, Forest Enterprise Ltd. What looked like a reasonable administrative measure was used to deny further detailed information about a public asset. Forest Enterprise has extensive commercial transactions with both the Chairman of the Forestry Commission Scottish Committee, Sir Michael Strang Steel, and with another commissioner, Tom Bruce Jones, who bought over £5 million worth of timber from Forest Enterprises.

Richard Norton Taylor, the distinguished Guardian journalist and playwright, wrote in his seminal book *Whose Land is it Anyway?*, of the activities of the Commission in Wales:

> With little real consultation with local interests, it has drawn a line along Welsh hills, changed the nature of the landscape, restricting grazing area for livestock, and not even contributed to rural employment and the local economy. I shall never forget the disdain with which a local Forestry Commission representative was greeted by Welsh hill farmers one evening in a pub in Tregaron.[7]

Earlier, Norton Taylor remarked on how the Commission had treated its oldest possession, its founding acreage of the Forest of Dean, where 'the Commission has fenced and sold off land – which for hundreds of years had been open to the public – to private investors.'

That was in the early 1980s. In 1996 Andy Wightman, the chronicler of Scottish landownership in succession to John McEwen, wrote that

> Unlike most other European countries, which not only consider the ownership of forests to matter a great deal but collect and publish extensive data on the subject, the Forestry Commission collects minimal information on forest holdings and publishes nothing.[8]

The Forestry Commission is the main grant-making body in the forestry area. In 1996–7 it paid out £31.6 million to participants in the Private Woodland Owners Woodland Grant Scheme. Not one of the recipients of public funds is identified in the accounts, as they should be by constitutional convention. Wightman records that

> As recently as May 1994 the Forestry Commission responded to queries about grant payments by claiming that such matters were confidential. In response to a Parliamentary Question from Calum Macdonald MP in 1995 however, the Commission published for the first time a list of recipients for 1993.[9]

That year only £10.3 million was doled out. The sums have increased threefold and the transparency is as dark as ever.

Along with the annual accounts of the Commission for 1997 a small booklet containing some facts and figures on the Forestry Commission was published. Printed in an almost invisible shade of wartime orange the total amount of various types of conifers, broadleafs and coppice, etc. are given for areas no more specific than England, Scotland and Wales. Admittedly, there is a map in the Forest Enterprise accounts which offers a marginally improved guide to the location of the forests (Scotland is divided into north and south). Given the difference between the Forestry Commission's own accounts and those of Forest Enterprise it is clear that somewhere in the organisation someone is trying to be more informative. There has been a significant improvement in the level of information published by the Forestry Commission since the early days of the Labour Government in 1997, but much remains to be done to get the Commission up to the standard of the Crown Estate annual report. Labour has made only mid level changes to the Commissioners, who remain top heavy with landowning interests. Of the eleven commissioners, three remain representatives of the landowning aristocracy: Sir Peter Hutchinson, the chairman, Andrew Raven, owner of a 34,500 acre estate at Lochaber in Scotland, and Anthony Bosanquet, owner and manager of the 1200 acre Dingestow Estate in Monmouth. The executive commissioners on the other hand, David Bills and Dr Bob McIntosh, are forestry professionals, and the non executive commissioner for Wales is Gareth Wardell, a former Labour MP and chairman of the Welsh Assembly Standing Orders Commission. The distinguished academic, Dr Victoria Edwards, is the English Commissioner.

There is a further and important element of the Forest Enterprise accounts, which exhibits significant policy confusion, as well as accounting confusion, within the organisation. In the same faded orange as that used in the facts and figures brieflet, Forest Enterprises prints a table which indicates that in 1997 the total area managed by the company was 2,651,903 acres, 17,297 acres down on the previous year. The reason the figure is odd is because in the interval the company sold, to unnamed parties, public property amounting to 26,791 acres for a sum of £19.8 million. It can only be assumed that the company acquired some new land. In the actual accounts there is an entry for payments to acquire tangible fixed assets of £4.6 million. There is no elaboration on this item in the accounts, as there ought to be, since it is public money being paid out. By placing the assets of a government department in a trading company it is clear that there was an inclination on the part of the former Tory government to privatise the Forestry lands. This is compounded by the lack of any statement about the acquisition policy of the Commission, despite its statutory duty to expand its base where possible.

It is important to note that Forest Enterprise quotes only the total area *managed* by the Commission. It was impossible from either the accounts of the Forestry Commission or Forest Enterprise to find out exactly how many acres the Commission actually owns. This is important, as the privatisation of the Water authorities without proper disclosure of their land holdings proved.

Richard Norton Taylor, writing in 1982, noted the following:

> The Forestry Commission has a little over three million acres at its disposal, more than two thirds of which are under plantation. The rest is waiting planting or is made up of agricultural and grazing land, or rock. 757,000 acres are in England, about 402,000 acres in Wales and 1,980,000 acres in Scotland.[10]

This adds up to a total of 3,139,000 acres. In 1997 the Forestry Commission was managing 2,651,490 acres. The difference is 487,210 acres. In the four years from 1994 the Commission sold off about 25,000 acres a year.

In addition, the 1997 accounts of the Commission value the Forest Estate at £1.56 billion. On the possibly wrong assumption that the 2.65 million managed acres are the property of the Commission, then the average value of a Commission acre is £588. However, the sale in 1997 of 26,791 acres realised £19.1 million, an average value of £712 per acre. The only way in which the book value of the Forest Estate could match market value is if it actually owns a significantly smaller number of acres than it manages. Again, the accounts concealed rather than revealed information that the public has an absolute right to know.

And there is another issue of great public importance. The accounts quite properly disclose the deals done between the two commissioners Sir Michael Strang Steel and Tom Bruce Jones. But in the rather small world of forestry dealings, there is no indication of whether the Commission as a body was trading with companies to which it was also making grants. Both these items should have been shown in the accounts and the Auditor General, Sir John Bourn, who signed them, should have made sure they were.

In the three years since 1997, there have been some advances in both the information coming out of the Forestry Commission, and in its attempts to acknowledge its duties to the public in specific localities. There is a web site that helps those who want to make personal visits to some Forestry Commission sites. There are helpful brochures. But there is no evidence of either a coherent policy towards the forests themselves or towards the damage done by the Commission to the public's rights by fencing and sell offs. Neither has the Government resolved its policy conundrum over the forestry estate.

In his book *The National Wealth*,[11] Dominic Hobson raises a number of issues in relation to the Forestry Commission. First of all he observes that environmentalism has come to the rescue of the Forestry Commission, at least in the eyes of an increasingly 'green' population. The Commission's activities of planting trees, handing out grants for planting trees and finally supervising tree cutting, are seen as benign. But they are benign at an annual cost of about £50 million and without any clear objective. As a matter of ideology, the Tories told the Forestry Commission to sell off land to make good the annual cost of the estate, starting in 1981, but Hobson notes that in 1986 and again in 1994, the Tories shelved the issue of a full scale privatisation on the grounds that it would be too controversial. The government of the day kept in place a secretive, totally unimaginative and singularly ineffective board. The staff of the Commission have contributed widely to the academic and scientific literature on their subject. By contrast the Board of Commissioners had contributed almost nothing to the public debate, and have made no impact on government policy or public perceptions of forestry.

Any increase in forest cover in the UK would help the UK meet its greenhouse gas emission quotas and at the same time contribute to the balance of payments. Despite these hugely attractive policy goals, the Forestry Commission seems to have done nothing to encourage the government to consider those goals, and to formulate a policy to achieve them. The cost of expanding the forest estate by one million acres a year would be between £588 million and £750 million. This is infinitely less than the amount spent propping up the small tribe of rural landowners with handouts of £4 billion a year. It would be investment expenditure, not current expenditure like the agricultural subsidy. Over time there would be five rewards for the state. The first would be an increase in forestry related employment, the second a profit from the sale of wood and pulp, the third would be a reduction in the balance of payments deficit, the fourth would be an investment gain as land values rise, as they have always done. Finally there would be a significant reduction in the volume of greehouse gases being emitted by the UK. Nor does the sacred cow of privatisation have to be ignored. The goal of a 7 million-acre forestry estate, as Hobson notes was the goal in the 1960s, could easily be met by giving the management of the estate to a company floated on the Stock Exchange and tasked with meeting both environmental and fiscal objectives. And to add a cynical footnote, such a programme might also play its part in absorbing marginal agricultural land released by the ending of subsidies to landowners. There would be a form of historic justice in such an outcome. A great deal of Forestry Commission acreage originally arose from the purchase of bankrupt or near bankrupt aristocratic estates in the early part of the last century.

The Ministry of Defence
At the time of the 1872 Return, the War Department owned just 165,000 acres. Just before World War Two, the Ministry of Defence, then known as the War Office, had 252,000 acres in use. During the war it acquired something like 11.5 million acres of land, or 20% of the country.[12] Two years after the end of World War Two there was a review of the defence land requirement. This decided that 1,027,200 acres were needed. Even this is a very large amount of land, amounting to about one and one third average English counties. However, put in context, which is seldom what is done, it is not a lot of land, and generally, would impinge on only a relatively small number of people, According to Richard Norton Taylor, in 1982 there were still between 1.1 million and 1.5 million acres of common land in the UK. No one knows how much waste land there is, but 2,500,000 acres is one estimate.[13]

In this context it is worth reflecting that the urban population in England alone lives on a maximum of just 3.42 million acres, with 28.8 million acres in rural use. The area in rural use is subject to significant subsidies: without public subvention it would not be in use at all. In Wales there are large areas of moor and mountain, as there are in Scotland and in Northern Ireland. For the military to ask for 1.6% of the land area to rehearse the nation's defence does not seem unreasonable. As Lord Nugent said in his defence land review in 1971, 'The security of the State is paramount.' At that point the defence requirement was down to 1.1% of the land area, or about 662,000 acres. It has since fallen below even this figure, and the estimate given in the annual defence review for 1998 was just 562,000 acres which is about 0.8% of the land area of the country.

During the period of Cold War confrontation with the former Soviet Union, it was relatively easy to identify the nation's defence requirement, even if this was seldom done in a way that the public could understand. With the Soviet Union's disintegration and a Tory government struggling to cut the government budget, no coherent defence strategy to replace the unclear strategy of MAD (mutually assured destruction) emerged in the period between 1990 and 1997. Despite this a huge amount of the defence estate was sold off, willy nilly. Even the forces' married quarters were sold to an overseas buyer, The Nomura Corporation of Japan.[14] The government's 1998–2000 defence review has left the issue unclear and the House of Commons Select Committee on Defence was due to make an examination of defence land needs in Autumn 2001. The Committee may help to clarify the situation and produce a rational evaluation of just how much land the armed forces need. But by focusing the argument about land ownership on the apparently excessive amount of land owned by the Ministry of Defence, those with an interest in acquiring the 'excess' MoD land for themselves are in a position to deflect the argument from how the country is actually owned and how the land is used. The real argument is, in fact, whether we are prepared to allow the MoD to retain a certain amount of land for national defence, or have the land released to farming interests who can make the land profitable only with a huge subsidy from public funds. At the global level, the overall agricultural subsidy is actually more than 17% of the defence budget, £4 billion as against £23 billion.[15]

So what does the MoD currently own and why is the issue a controversial one? The problem with military use of land is that the military like to fire big guns, little guns, and race huge tanks around the place. In the air the RAF likes to fly very noisy jets close to the ground. Only the Navy can sneak off over the horizon or under the water, and stay away from the public for most of the time. But the issue as stated by Lord Nugent, should neither be abused or avoided. The defence of the country is the paramount issue. The military should not abuse that principle to retain land that they do not need. Neither, on the other hand, should desirable but luxury interests, such as 365 days a year silence on Dartmoor, stop essential training. All progress is compromise, but the one compromise that should not be made is with national defence.

The Ministry of Defence owns or leases the following major areas of land:

Dartmoor National Park
The park is largely owned by the Duchy of Cornwall, not by the National Parks Agency which actually owns very little land, merely overseeing certain rules applicable to areas designated as a National Park. On Dartmoor the MoD leases 34,000 acres, for both training and firing ranges. Parts of the park are an area of outstanding national beauty, and there are both ancient archaeological sites and Sites of Special Scientific Interest. There is a vociferous lobby which ultimately seeks to eject the MoD from the Park. So far, however, the Duchy of Cornwall has supported the MoD and the military continue to be able to use the area.

Northumberland National Park
The MoD leases 56,000 acres in the area of Otterburn which are used for training and live firing. The MoD now makes much less use of this area than it used to and local opposition has slowed down.

Peak District National Park
2500 acres of training and firing ranges.

Pembrokeshire National Park
30,000 acres plus a 5000-acre tank and artillery range at Castlemartin.

Salisbury Plain in Wiltshire
90,000 acres. Salisbury Plain contains hundreds of Sites of Special Scientific Interest and some of the most important historical and prehistoric sites in Europe, if not in the world.

Shoeburyness, Essex
30,000 acres of ranges and training area.

Stamford in Norfolk
17,000 acres of training area.

Aldershot, Hants.
Known as the Aldershot Complex, this occupies about 21,000 acres of land in one of the

most prized development areas outside London. It is also the home of the British army. Other MoD holdings are identified, where the MoD has provided details, with each of the counties in the county section. The Parliamentary Select Committee will be provided with a full list of MoD lands which will be publicly available via the web probably in late 2001.

TABLE 10/2

TOP 20 INSTITUTIONAL LANDOWNERS IN THE UK

(estimated acreage)

1	The Forestry Commission*1	2,400,000
2	The Ministry of Defence*2	750,000
3	The National Trust for England & Wales	550,000
4	The Pension funds	500,000
5	The utilities: water, electricity, railways	500,000
6	The Crown Estate	384,000
7	The County Farms*3	300,000
8	Scottish Dept of Agriculture	281,355
9	The RSPB	275,000
10	The National Trust for Scotland	176,000
11	The Dioceses of the Church of England*4	160,000
12	Scottish local authorities	152,771
13	The Duchy of Cornwall	141,000
14	The Church Commissioners	120,000
15	The Invercauld and Torlisk Trusts	120,000
16	Alcan Highland Estates	116,000
17	South Uist Estates	92,000
18	Co-operative Farms	90,000
19	The Duchy of Lancaster	66,000
20	English local authorities*5	65,000

*1 New figures in 2001.
*2 An accurate list is expected to be given to the House of Commons Select Committee on Defence in Autumn 2001.
*3 New figures in Autumn 2001.
*4 Based on 50% sample. Accurate figures may become available in 2002.
*5 Local authorities are excused land registration at the Land Registry and there are no accurate centralised figures available.

Chapter Eleven

Land in London

IN APRIL 2001, Ropemaker, the property arm of the BP-Amoco Pension fund, announced that it had sold 10 acres of Mayfair for £335 million.[1] This remarkable sale confirmed top spot for London in the league of the world's most expensive real estate, where previously it had been neck-and-neck with the Bund in Shanghai, both having seen off Manhattan. The sale was slightly embarrassing for the *Sunday Times*, which two days later published its 13th Rich List with the Duke of Westminster, owner of 129,300 acres across the UK, in pole position at a very conservative value of £4.4 billion. The duke, through his wholly owned but unlimited company, Grosvenor Estate Holdings, owns the freehold of a little over 100 acres of the 255 acres that make up Mayfair. A simple calculation based on the Ropemaker sale indicates that in Mayfair alone the duke is worth at least £3.35 billion.

On 18 February 2000, the *Evening Standard*'s Allan Gill penned a two-page story that showed how a house in Elgin Crescent in Notting Hill in West London had risen in value by 3773% over the course of just 25 years. Starting in 1974, with sales records provided by the prestigious estate agents John D Wood, the article showed how the price in that year, £71,000, had escalated to £2.5 million in 2000. The house has six bedrooms and runs to about 3000 square feet, but, sited in a quiet street, would hardly compare with the elegance of Mayfair, the crown jewel of the capital's real estate. With help from the *Economist*, Gill shows that inflation has risen between 1974 and 2000 by 570%, house prices generally by 893%, the *Financial Times* All Share Index by 2065%, and Elgin Crescent by 3773%.[2]

Just beyond Notting Hill to the west is Holland Park. Here too, house prices are showing interesting upward momentum. The former home of the Debenham family, Peacock House, which stands on about an acre of ground, had its lease fall in and came onto the market in 2000 for around £20 million. The vendors were the Ilchester (Holland) Estate, whose life tenant is the Hon. Mrs Charlotte Townshend, mistress of Melbury Estate and its 15,000 acres in Dorset. She is the only surviving daughter of the 9th Viscount Galway. Her mother, through whom her London and Dorset fortunes came, was the only daughter of the 7th Earl of Ilchester. Her will was probated in 1996 for over £40 million, excluding the land, which was in trust and already settled on Mrs Townshend.

Mrs Townshend's estate in London helps to illustrate two sub themes of this book. The first is the general gross underestimate of the real value of land, both generally and specifically in the books of companies, especially development land, and secondly, the capacity of the system to over-price land in specific areas, on the basis of a scarcity which does not necessarily exist.

To illustrate the 'book' under-valuation, it is worth taking a brief look at the Crown Estate lands in London. The open market value of all its land assets as stated in the annual accounts for 1998–9 was £ 2.7 billion. But the Crown Estate owns almost 13 million square feet (almost 300 acres) of commercial property in the City of London and Central London itself. This includes over one and a half million square feet of Regent

Street and New Oxford Street, still reckoned to be the world's premier shopping thoroughfare despite the gross tattiness of many of the premises. Taking an average value for central London shop, office and commercial holdings, as suggested by the London Commercial Research Agency, of £400 per square foot, the London commercial properties of the Crown Estate alone have a value of around £5 billion, more than all the 384,000 acres of the Estate as recorded in the books of the company in March 2000. The Crown Estate also owns 2217 residences in Central London, which at an average of just £500,000 each comes to £1.1 billion (although this is a conservative average – the Crown Estate has sold at least one of its residential properties in Regent's Park for over £20 million).

But the Crown Estate is not London's largest landowner and neither is it the owner of the most valuable land in London. This privilege falls to that most diffident of dukes, Gerald Grosvenor, the 6th Duke of Westminster.

In the 1890s the Grosvenor estates in London amounted to 475.6 acres, worth £423,786 in rentals, about £40 million nowadays. Regrettably, from the duke's point of view, his ancestors let some of the land on very long leases, such as the 999 year lease on the American Embassy in Grosvenor Square where the Americans paid a peppercorn rent of £1 a year, eventually paying £1 million for the lease in the mid 1900s, the equivalent of £20 million today.

If the Americans had to buy the lease now it would cost them at least £350 million. Not that they would get such a lease. Grosvenor Estates will not normally let for longer than 125 years, with regular upward revisions of the lease rentals, and will almost never sell freeholds where they can avoid it. With 350 years of occupation in Mayfair behind them, the Grosvenors think long-term indeed. During the negotiations to obtain the Embassy lease the then duke offered the Americans the freehold if they would return Grosvenor lands in Florida confiscated during the American War of Independence. The American government of the day declined to do so, which was a pity from the Grosvenors' point of view. That land is now known as Cape Canaveral, the launch site for most of America's space vehicles.

For many years it was thought that the Grosvenor Estate owned 200 acres of Mayfair, but just as the duke authorises a huge new strategic advance into property on both the continent of Europe and in the Far East, it has become clear that the estate is more complex than anyone had previously realised. For a start, the Mayfair plot is smaller than thought, though the freeholds do belong to the company. What the company does not own but what it manages for the Grosvenor family trusts, is 200 acres of the neighbouring Belgravia estate. This is relatively easy to value, as it is bounded by a 90 acre estate which was valued at open market value in 1998. This is the Cadogan estate, held in the books of the Cadogan Estate company at £970 million. But the Ropemaker sale throws a new light on the Cadogan valuation, suggesting that it is very conservative indeed. Based on the Ropemaker sale, the Grosvenor assets in London come to a total value of about £10 billion, £3.3 billion for Mayfair and about £6.6 billion for the Belgravia estate.

The Grosvenor Estate in London is notable both for its longevity – in London the Mayfair and Belgravia elements of the estate go back to 1677 – and its strategic importance at the heart of London. The Grosvenor lands in London are worth a fortune because the Grosvenors made them so, by focusing on the concept of value and quality – and sticking with those two concepts for over 300 years.

Gerald Cavendish Grosvenor, the 6th and current duke, traces his family no further back on a formal basis in *Debrett's* than 1622, when Sir Richard Grosvenor Kt, MP for

Cheshire, was created a baronet. But in the *Burke's Peerage* of 1896 the full family history is cited.

> This noble house traces its descent in the male line to a family which is stated to have flourished in Normandy for a century and a half before the Conquest of England [1066] and obtained its surname from having held the high and powerful office of *Le Grovenour*. The founder of the English Grosvenors Gilbert Le Grosvenour came over in the train of the conqueror.[3]

Burke's goes on to state that this Gilbert was the nephew of Hugh Lupus, who is described in Domesday as the Earl of Chester and a nephew of the Conqueror. In the late 1300s a row broke out between two Cheshire families, the Scropes and the Grosvenors, over their right to a particular coat of arms. This forced the two families to produce proof of their descent in court, which tends to suggest that most of the lineage of the family, now over 1100 years old, is fairly accurate. By the early 1400s the Grosvenors were Lords of Hulme in Cheshire and in 1509, when Henry VIII came to the throne, they were established at Eaton, which is where the main family residence still stands. It is difficult to know exactly how much land they held at this time, but they were staunch royalists and lost most of it during the English Civil War in the seventeenth century, getting it back at the restoration in 1660 and thereafter. Then came fortune. In 1677 Sir Tom Grosvenor married Mary Davies, heiress to part of a fortune originally accumulated by her great uncle Hugh Awdeley, a clerk at the Court of Wards who died in 1662, worth about £400,000, the modern equivalent of £8.8 billion.[4] At the heart of the legacy to Mary was what was left of the Manor of Ebury, itself a portion of the Domesday manor of Eia, totalling about 1090 acres and covering what is now Hyde Park, St James, Belgravia and parts of Westminster. The Manor of Eia belonged to the Abbey of Westminster until it was seized by Henry VIII at the dissolution of the monasteries in 1535. The value of the land escalated rapidly, as the following transactions show.

Transaction	Value	Equivalent value 2001
From Henry VIII in 1544, for 41 years rent of	£21 5s 8p	£11m
From Elizabeth I in 1567 for 31 years sold for	£450	£22m
From Sir Symon Clarke 1618 moity of the lease	£4760	£143m
Freehold sold to Sir Lionel Cranfield 1623	£1501	£33m
Hugh Awdeley buys freehold from Cranfield 1626	£9400	£208.6m

There are allegations of impropriety in the sale by Clark's trustees to Cranfield and this is not a reliable value. The price Awdeley paid is probably reasonable for the period.

Mary Davies was born in 1664, a year before her father died. In 1672, at the age of eight, she was sold as a bride for the 10-year-old son of Lord Berkeley, the Lord Lieutenant of Ireland, for £5000. Berkeley could not make up the bride price and Mary came on the market again in 1677, her mother having spent the £2000 Berkeley had raised and needing to repay it to him. There were many offers for the childish hand of Mary Davies, and her mother had little trouble settling for the 20-year-old Sir Thomas Grosvenor, who was twice as rich as Mary Davies at that time.

They were married in St Clements Dane's church in London on 10 October 1677, Mary being 12 years and 8 months old. She took up full married life at Eaton in 1680, aged 15. Sir Thomas died in 1700 leaving Mary at 35 with three sons and one daughter.

The entire estate was held in trust for the eldest son, Sir Richard, aged 11. The two key trustees were Tom and Francis Cholmondeley, landowning neighbours of the Grosvenors. For many years Mary Grosvenor had flirted with Catholicism and in 1701 she went on a visit to Paris, where she was taken ill. On the third day of her illness, having had an emetic, been bled and had opium pills twice, Edward Fenwick, the brother of her chaplain, announced that they had been married at the Hotel Castile where she was staying. Mary Grosvenor, who had already shown signs of mental instability, rushed home to England and soon found herself facing a demand from her 'husband' that he was entitled to 'his conjugal rights . . . and the lady's fortune, amounting he believes to £30,000 at least [the equivalent of £400 million today], and an interest in lands in Cheshire, Westminster and Chelsea etc.' The Cholmondleys then showed their metal. Over the course of four years they fought the fraudster Fenwick through half the courts of England, eventually securing wardship of both Dame Mary and her four children, who were brought up in the Cholmondeley home at Vale Royal in Cheshire. Mary Grosvenor died in 1730. Her sons continued the family tradition and were MPs for Chester, as was her grandson. In 1761 the then Sir Richard was created Baron Grosvenor. By 1784 he was an earl and in 1831 his descendant was elevated to Marquess. His son in turn was made a Duke by Queen Victoria in 1874 and was her Master of the Horse. By this time the Grosvenors were reckoned to be the richest family in the United Kingdom by a significant margin.[5]

They still are.

The Grosvenors do not just have landholdings in London. The present duke's father was a Unionist MP in Northern Ireland, and lived on the old Ely estate which once ran to 30,000 acres. That estate was sold to its tenants after the death of the 5th Duke's widow in 1987. But between the 2nd Duke, the extraordinary Bendor, who died in 1953, and the 6th Duke, the estate did not devolve to either the 3rd, 4th or 5th dukes, instead passing, in a series of convoluted trusts, directly to the 6th and present duke.

One of the great myths of the wealthy in England is Bendor's estate. His trustees paid £19 million on an estate valued for probate at about £20 million, with death duty charged at 98%. £20 million in 1953 is about £400 millon now, and is clearly nothing like the real value of the Grosvenor estate then or now, but rather represented Bendor's 'personality', the money he had saved or made during his life time. One of the most extravagant men of his time, he had two yachts for his pleasure, one of them a converted destroyer. But behind the extravagances there was a shrewd brain and an even shrewder advisor, his land agent George Ridley. Between them they created a second Grosvenor estate in Vancouver in Canada and around the Orange River in South Africa. Little is known about the Orange River part of the estate, but Vancouver is now the centrepiece of Grosvenor International, a part of Grosvenor Estate Holdings. GI itself now has offshoots in Australia, Hawaii, the United States, France, Germany, China (mostly Hong Kong), Singapore and Ireland.[6] There are innumerable newspaper cuttings at the time of Bendor's death on the night of 18 July 1953 and in the subsequent two or three years, almost all of which assume that it was the estate and not the duke who was taxed. The Inland Revenue had to open a special office to deal with Bendor's estate. The son of a family retainer from the Orange River colony told the author in 1998 that a number of trucks were kept filled with the more sensitive papers and moved from place to place ahead of the tax men, who never found them. Leslie Field estimates that Bendor had 156,000 acres in the estate in England, Scotland and Ireland, when he died.

On the assumption that certain portions of the international assets are, like Belgravia, held in Grosvenor family trusts, and managed but not owned by the companies, the very low asset valuation, particularly in relation to the Canadian assets, becomes explicable. It also suggests that the actual Grosvenor family are worth abroad at least as much as they are worth in England.

The Other Great London Estates
Soon after the 1872 Return of Owners of Land was published and after Bateman had made his extracts, John Lloyd of the Municipal Reform League began to survey and map the metropolitan estates in London in 1892, abandoning the project in 1915. Lloyd saw his work as a complement to the Return, which had not covered metropolitan acres. The map on p.159 is based on Lloyd's map of the period and shows that north of the river Thames there were 35 significant estates. Of those 35 about 20 were aristocratic estates – though four important aristocratic estates were missing from the map, those of the Duke of Norfolk around the Temple area and of the Sir Richard Sutton estates in St James and in Clerkenwell. Then there is the Stanhope estate of the earls of Stanhope, later merged with the estates of the earldom of Harrington. There were also significant holdings by the Rothschild family: Piccadilly was known as Rothschild Row and they owned the Gunnersbury estate, not shown on the map but running to over 9959 acres west of Holland Park, according to the Return, which picked it up in the Buckingham estates of the family, rather than in London itself. Of those aristocratic estates, 10 of some size or value still remain.

Numbers by the title refer to the areas identified on Lloyd's map.

14. The Grosvenor estate
This is clearly the great survivor, with almost all of its 100 acres of Mayfair and its 200 acres of Belgravia, less the Pimlico element of the estate around Victoria Street, intact. The total value of this estate is now in the region of £10 billion.

3. The Harley Portland estate, now the Howard de Walden estate
This is about 110 acres bounded by Marylebone High Street to the west, Marylebone Road to the north, Great Portland Street to the east and Wigmore Street to the south. It is owned by the family trusts of the four daughters of the late 9th Lord Howard de Walden who died in 1999 and is operated through a group of companies centred on Howard de Walden Estates Ltd and its subsidiaries. The title is not extinct but is in abeyance between the four daughters. The estate passed to the Howard de Waldens in 1828, when the 6th Lord married Lucy Cavendish Bentinck, daughter of the 4th Duke of Portland, a dukedom that is now extinct but whose treasures and lands belong to the Howard de Walden's cousin, Lady Ann Cavendish Bentinck, daughter of the 7th Duke (see p.251). The Howard de Waldens are a branch of the huge Howard family headed by the Duke of Norfolk and are descended from the eldest son of the 4th Duke by his second marriage.

In the 1890s this estate ran to 150.6 acres and was producing rentals of £145,143, the modern equivalent of about £14.5 million a year. The estate is valued in the books of the company at £57 million and produced an income in 1999 of £10.7 million.

The *Sunday Times* valued the estate at 30 times earnings, the standard p/e ratio for a first class property company. But property in the area is selling for around £600 a square foot and most of the freeholds belong to the estate. This would place a real value on the holding of about £2.8 billion. Even if 50% is knocked off for freeholds sold and long leases, it still amounts to £1.4 billion shared by the Hon. Mrs Czernin, wife of Count Czernin, the Hon. Mrs Blanch Buchan, the Hon. Mrs Jessica White and the Hon. Mrs Camilla Acloque, and their 18 children and grandchildren. A portion of the estate's income will also still be going to the three daughters and the grandchildren of the 8th Lord Howard de Walden who died in 1946.

13. The Portman Estate

This is another block of about 110 acres, adjacent to the Howard de Walden estate and bounded to the south by Oxford Street, to the west by Edgware Road, to the north by Crawford Street and to the east by Manchester Square. It is the oldest of the big estates still intact in London and was given to Lord Chief Justice Portman, an ancestor of the present Viscount Portman, by Henry VIII in 1533. The present Viscount Portman, the 10th, inherited the estate in 1999 on the death of his father. The title only goes back to 1873 and the lineage in *Debrett's* commences in 1799. However, *Burke's* of 1896 indicates that the family were from Somerset and flourished as early as the reign of Edward I (1239–1307). Henry VIII's Lord Chief Justice, the first of the family to be knighted, was from Orchard Portman in Somerset, but the 1st Viscount, elevated from the Barony of Orchard Portman given to him as MP for Dorset in 1823, later sat as the MP for Marylebone, in effect MP for the estate. The 1999 accounts for the Portman Settled Estates Ltd show a revenue of only £1 million. This fails to reflect anything like the real value of the estate where freehold land is selling for over £500 per square foot, placing a maximum value of £2.3 billion on the estate. If, again, this is knocked down by 50% to account for long leases and sold-off freeholds, the real estate is still worth about £1.1 billion.

In the 1890s the Portman estate ran to 226.8 acres producing a revenue the equivalent of about £21 million a year.

35. The Cadogan Estate

Charles Gerald John Cadogan, the 8th Earl, succeeded to the title in 1997 when his father died. He is the only aristocrat to send the accounts of his company, the Cadogan Group, voluntarily to Dr Philip Beresford of the *Sunday Times* Rich List. His entry in *Debrett's* is suitably restrained, going back only as far as the first Baron Cadogan created baron in 1716. *Burke's* is more eclectic, tracing the Cadogans to Elystan Glodrydd, Prince of Fferlys and founder of the 4th Royal Tribe of Wales. *Burke's* places no date on the prince but brings the Cadogans into documented history via the will of Thomas Cadwgn in 1511. In 1717 the then Baron Cadogan married Elizabeth, daughter and co-heir of Sir Hans Sloane, the eminent physician, and had the manor of Chelsea devolved to him as his wife's dowry. Sloane, after whom Sloane Street is named, bought the manor only in 1712.

The Cadogan Group produce an open market valuation for their 90 acres of Chelsea of £970 million based on very conservative assessments, now more than two years old. The Ropemaker sale has highlighted the conservative nature of these valuations and a doubling of the estimate would bring them more in line with post-Ropemaker values. The earl, a former merchant banker, had been running the estate on modern lines since 1974 under his courtesy title of Viscount Chelsea, which now passes to his son, Edward.

The Cadogan estate in the 1890s came to 211.4 acres and was producing rental income of about £180,499, about £18 million today.

21. The Bedford Estate
This estate is now down to about 20 acres in London, most of it in Bloomsbury. In the 1870s there were holdings north and south of the Euston Road down to New Oxford Street, with a further site including most of Covent Garden, totalling in all perhaps 130 acres. In 1914 the 11th Duke sold Covent Garden for £2 million, about £100 million now, and invested the lot in Tsarist bonds. According to Shirley Green in her book, *Who Owns London?*, those bonds have been gathering dust ever since in the Bedford archives.[7] The same duke also sold off the British Museum site and most of the rest of the Bloomsbury acres. Like the Portman estate the Bedford estate goes back to a grant by Henry VIII of monastery lands, to his soldier and courtier John Russell KG. The first grant, the Abbey of Tavistock, came the year after his barony in 1540, and the second, the monastery of Woburn which included Covent Garden, arrived in 1550. Land in Bloomsbury is currently selling for about £400 a square foot and this makes the Bedford holdings worth about £348 million, reduced to £170 million to reflect long leases and disposed freeholds.

In the 1880s the Bedford estate was 284.7 acres and was the second most profitable in London producing £339,458 in rentals, about £33 million a year today.

The Bailiwick of St James and Sir Richard Sutton, 9th Baronet (not on map).
Sir John Poulteney, who died in 1349, was the richest London merchant of his time and has been judged the 26th richest person ever to have lived in the UK.[8] When he died he owned 23 manors, and between 40,000 and 100,000 acres, but the most important acreage was that of the Bailiwick of St James on the edge of the manor of Ebury. A descendant of his, Sir William Poulteney, held most of the leases in the area at the beginning of the seventeenth century but it is described as part of the dowry of Queen Henrietta Maria, the daughter of Henry IV, King of France, who married the unfortunate Charles I in 1625.

After Charles was executed in 1649 the Queen surrendered the dowry to her son Charles II in 1668. She died in 1669 in France. Charles II did a deal with Poulteney, swapping leases held by Poulteney on 26 acres south of Piccadilly, for 999 year leases north of Piccadilly. Not long after George I came to the throne in 1714 an act of Parliament allowed the Poulteney family to buy the freeholds of St James, with most of the 26 acres becoming Green Park. Sir William's son, also Sir William, was eventually created Earl of Bath, a title now extinct and unconnected with the Marquessate of Bath in Wiltshire. As that line became extinct, the last countess of Bath, Henrietta Laura Poulteney, transferred the estate to her cousin Sir Richard Sutton Bt. in the late 1700s. The freeholds continue with the descendant of Sir Richard, also Sir Richard Sutton, the 9th Baronet, who lives in Dorset and has extensive lands in that county, Wiltshire and Buckinghamshire as well as London. The Sutton estate in London in the 1880s was much the same size as today, 21.3 acres (depending on how the Clerkenwell acres were owned) and produced income of £42,071, about £4.2 million today.

12. The Crown Estate
The Crown Estate is not identified at all on Lloyd's map. Instead, the entire London acreage of the Government and Crown, 5272 acres in all, is attributed to Her Majesty Queen Victoria. The Crown Estate's portion of this is not merely intact but has expanded significantly since 1870, mostly outside London, and now owns acreage in central London worth the same or a little more than the Grosvenor estate. The interesting issue (as raised in chapter 5) is government plans to begin a staged privatisation that pays off the Queen and removes Crown privileges from the company.

The Lost Fortunes
The following estates are shown on Lloyd's map but do not exist any more.

16. The estates of Henry Jermyn, Lord St Albans
This small parcel of about 15 acres was retained by the Jermyn family, descendants of Henry Jermyn, Lord St Albans, lover, chief retainer and, according to some sources, the second husband of Queen Henrietta Maria, Charles I's widow. The freeholds have been widely dispersed and sold.

17. The Berkeley estate
Until April 2001 most of this site belonged to the BP pension fund, Ropemaker. The Berkeley earldom and family were one of the most important and ubiquitous in English politics in the first four centuries after the Norman conquest. The earldom became extinct in 1942 but the Barony, created in 1421, is now held by Baroness Berkeley. When the estate was put on the market the Grosvenor estate bid against the eventual Saudi purchaser, Prince al Waleed Alsaud in 2001, and there was a hint that they also tried to buy from the residual Berkeley interests in the 1960s, but were outbid by BP and Ropemaker at the time.

18. The Albermarle estate
The family name of the earls of Albermarle is Kepple. The 1st Earl arrived with William of Orange in 1688 and was created an earl in 1696 for his part in installing William as King of England. Nothing of this small estate remains in the hands of the Albermarle family.

19. The Burlington Estate
Originally the London estate of the Boyle family, the first Earls of Burlington. The site passed to the Devonshire family when the 4th Duke married the Boyle heiress, Baroness Clifford, in the eighteenth century. Devonshire House, which was the family palace in London, was pulled down in 1925, although it is still commemorated by the Burlington Arcade. The freeholds, or some of them, may still belong to the Devonshire estates, but they have not been easy to trace.

Other Notable Central London Estates
The Duke of Norfolk owns four valuable acres in Central London. For further details on the duke's other landholdings see Sussex (p.259).

William Henry Leicester Stanhope, the 11th Earl Harrington, a major landowner in Limerick in the Republic of Ireland, has a small land holding in London. See Limerick (p.341) for further details.

Notable London Estates Outwith the Centre
2. The Eyre Estate in St John's Wood
In 1872 this was about 300 acres in size, one of the biggest estates in the London area. There are still about 190 acres in family hands. With land selling in St John's Wood for over £400 a square foot, this makes the eight Eyre 'tenants for life' of the estate worth a theoretical £3.3 billion, but halved for long leases and disposed freeholds to £1.1 billion.

Based on the original manor of St John, it was purchased in 1732 by Henry Samuel Eyre from Philip Dormer, the Earl of Chesterfield. The Eyres were the original knights of the shires and rural plutocrats. They entered the records as followers of Richard I, the

Lionheart, on his first crusade to the Holy Land in 1190-1. Known then as Le Heyr, by 1433 when they are recorded as 'gentlemen of Wiltshire adhering to Henry VI', the name had become Eyre. For the next few hundred years they are MPs for Wiltshire and mayors of Salisbury, but too far from the seat of power in London to make the peerage.

In the late 1600s the then MP for Salisbury, Robert Eyre, became Chancellor to the Prince of Wales and afterwards, when the Prince became George II, Lord Justice of the Common Pleas. He was knighted and made a Privy Counsellor. He was rich to start with, and it was his wealth that enabled his son to purchase the estate. He died without issue and settled the estate on his nephew Walpole Eyre, the godson of Prime Minster Sir Robert Walpole.

TABLE 11/1

LAST-KNOWN RECORD OF 'TENANTS FOR LIFE' OF THE EYRE ESTATE IN ST JOHN'S WOOD (Source: *Burke's Landed Gentry of Great Britain*, 1952)

Tenants for Life of Eyre Estate 1952	Offspring recorded in *Burke's*
Henry Samuel Robert Eyre DOB 16.5.1872 (Deceased)	Henry Samuel Robert DOB 29.6.1920
	Edwin Rufus Walpole DOB 26.4.1926
	Rosemary Irene Margaret DOB 17.6.1922
Edwin Rufus Walpole Eyre DOB 4.6.1884 (Dcd)	died without heirs
John Stephen Giles Eyre DOB 19.12. 1899 (Dcd)	Michael Robert Giles DOB 23.5.1927
	Sheila DOB 19.5.1935
Frederick Charles Eyre DOB 1.9.1901 (Dcd)	died without heirs
Commander Walpole John Eyre DOB 14.03.1906 (Dcd)	Charles George Samuel 6.6.1948
	Ruth Evlyn DOB 4.9.1938
Rosemary Irene Margaret Eyre DOB 17.6.1922	Marriage not shown at June 1952
Mrs Dorothy Sybil Wilkins DOB 9.9.1903 (Dcd)	Children not identified.
Mrs Florence Beatrix Lomas DOB 11.4.1885 (Dcd)	Hugh Eyre Lomas Born 1905 Died 1905
	Giles John Lomas DOB 15.1.1915
Margaret Florence Eyre DOB 17.7.1904	No details

1. The Maryon Wilson Estate

In 1935 the heir to the estate, Sir Spencer Pocklington Maryon Wilson, the 11th Baronet, born in 1859, appears in *Whittaker's Peerage and Baronetage* as Deputy Lieutenant of London and a director of Royal Insurance. His son Thomas was his heir. His country seat was Yattendon near Newbury and he had a town house in St James. By 1955 *Who's Who* shows that Sir Spencer has been succeeded by his nephew, Rev Canon Sir George Maryon Wilson, born in 1888 and Rector of St Leonard on Sea. He is also a Canon of Chichester Cathedral and served in the Grenadier Guards as a lieutenant in World War One. He was educated at Eton. He died in 1965 and was succeeded by his cousin Sir Hubert Guy Maryon. He was widowed in 1920 and married again in 1923, but had no children. Born in 1888 he was educated in Radley and lived at the Grange, Great Canfield, in Dunmow, Essex. He died in the late 1970s without an heir and his nearest relatives were the family of Baron Headley, a title that itself became extinct in 1994, although there are three surviving daughters of the 7th and last Baron. Of the estate itself there are no readily accessible modern records available.

Paul Raymond's Soho Estate
Only one really significant private estate of any note has been created in the twentieth century in London. This is the Soho estate of Paul Raymond. Born Geoffrey Quinn in Liverpool in the 1930s he started working life as a drummer in a band. He later became an impresario opening the famous Raymond Revue bar, a topless show, in Soho in 1958. Almost immediately he began buying freeholds in the area and now owns the freehold of more than half of Soho and adjacent areas, about 70 acres in all. He lives in a flat in St James, formerly occupied by the press magnate, Lord Beaverbrook, although the freehold is owned by the Duke of Westminster. Raymond never developed the social graces to go with the extraordinary empire he has created, mainly from the cash flow generated by both soft porn magazines and soft porn shows. Estranged from his son for years, he was divorced in 1974. His chosen successor in the business, his daughter Debbie, died in tragic circumstances in the 1990s. The heirs to the estate are her two daughters. His success has almost never been acknowledged, though his shrewdness is legendary among the inner London property dealers. In many ways he resembles the merchant owners of London in the fifteenth and sixteenth centuries, men like Poulteney who started the estate that is now part of the Grosvenor empire. As the effective Duke of Soho he has run a surprisingly clean 'manor' with little overt drug dealing or violence. Only the nature of the entertainment on offer has limited the value of real estate in the area. That is changing and a value of £10 million per acre is, if not yet established, certainly on its way.

The London List

The map is an important guide to the central London estates, both in 1890 and today. Nonetheless the comparison between Lloyd's map and the list that Professor Lindart was able to extract from the maps and rate records at the GLR Records office is illuminating. The Holland/Ilchester estate is clearly shown on the Lloyd map, and is big, probably more than 300 acres. But it had disappeared from the historic rating records available to Professor Lindert in 1983. The Eton College estate, most of which was sold off in the 1990s, but which was also around 200 acres, has also disappeared from the old rating list.

The Lloyd map, however, is particularly useful in identifying a number of still extant charities or trusts in and around Bloomsbury. These are the Foundling, Somers and Tonbridge charities. It will be interesting to see whether they, like the Church of England, have lost or retained their acreage. The Lloyd-Baker, New River and Penton Estates off Clerkenwell and Goswell Road, appear in the Lloyd Map but not in the ratings list; on the other hand, the Lloyd Map misses out critical landowners such as the Livery companies, the huge St Germans estate and the Northbrook (Barings) Estate. Neither list nor map shows the Order of St John of Jerusalem which has property in Clerkenwell.

There are four very valuable central London landowners not shown on the Lloyd map, but who retain estates in London and these have been added. They are

36 Sir Richard Sutton's estates, mainly St James Park but also Soho
37 The Duke of Norfolk at Arundel St off the Aldwych
38 The Marquess of Salisbury around Charing Cross
39 The Stanhope Estate in Kensington.

Using the maps created by John Lloyd of the Municipal Reform League, Professor Peter Lindert of the Agricultural History Center at the University of California at Davis drew up a list of the great London aristocratic and landed estates.[9] Lloyd's maps were housed in the Greater London Record Office in Clerkenwell when consulted by Professor Lindert in 1983. The list applied to the period between 1872 and 1890, but it gives us a very good starting point for our modern list.[10]

This list is based on that compiled by Lindert, with the four estates missing from the Lloyd map added. In addition, a number of the better known modern landowners have been included.

TABLE 11/2

LONDON LANDOWNERS 1890 AND 2001

(ranked by acreage)

	Name of owner	Associated Title	London acres 1890	London acres 2001	Rateable 1890 value in 1890	Current value of London acreage
1	Her Majesty Queen Victoria	Queen*	5272 (see Note A)	300	£1,019,896	£6,000,000,000
2	Local Government	None*	5103	0	£1,008,236	–
3	Railways	None*	2845	0	£1,008,236	–
4	Schools	None*	1719	0	£136,976	–
5	Church Institutions	None*	1617	0	£255,898	–
6	Canals and Docks	None*	1128	0	£372,219	–
7	St Germans	Earl#	1069	0	£24,498	–
8	Northbrook (Baring)	Lord#	854	0	£21,164	–
9	Livery Companies	None*	814	0	£99,200	–
10	Barron	Sir (Ext)	798	0	£15,390	–
11	Spencer Maryon Wilson	Sir (Ext)	754	200	£38,342	(£1,900,000,000 see Note B)
12	Other companies	None*	675	0	£90,552	–
13	Identity unknown	None*	638	0	£106,257	–
14	Oxbridge Colleges	None*	573	0	£25,767	–
15	Grosvenor	Duke of Westminster	476	300	£189,611	£10,000,000,000
16	Dartmouth	Earl#	420	0	£19,865	–
17	Charities	None*	416	0	£65,191	–
18	Eyre Trustees	None	324	190	£66,713	£1,900,000,000
19	Cator	None*	297	0	£5904	–
20	Russell	Duke of Bedford	249	20	£123,586	£374,000,000
21	Portman	Viscount	227	110	£80,352	£2,000,000,000
22	Cadogan	Earl	211	100	£51,337	£3,000,000,000
23	Mansfield	Earl#	207	0	£34,737	–
24	Gunter	None*	202	100	£57,144	£500,000,000
25	Charteris Trustees	None	193	0	£15,355	–
26	St Quentin	None	191	0	£77,969	–
27	Kensington	Lord#	172	0	£70,208	–
28	Evelyn	None	168	0	£11,860	–
29	Hospitals, asylums	None*	165	0	£79,173	–
30	de Beauvoir	None	159	0	£22,123	–
31	Leader	None	154	0	£4559	–

Principal London landowners c.1890

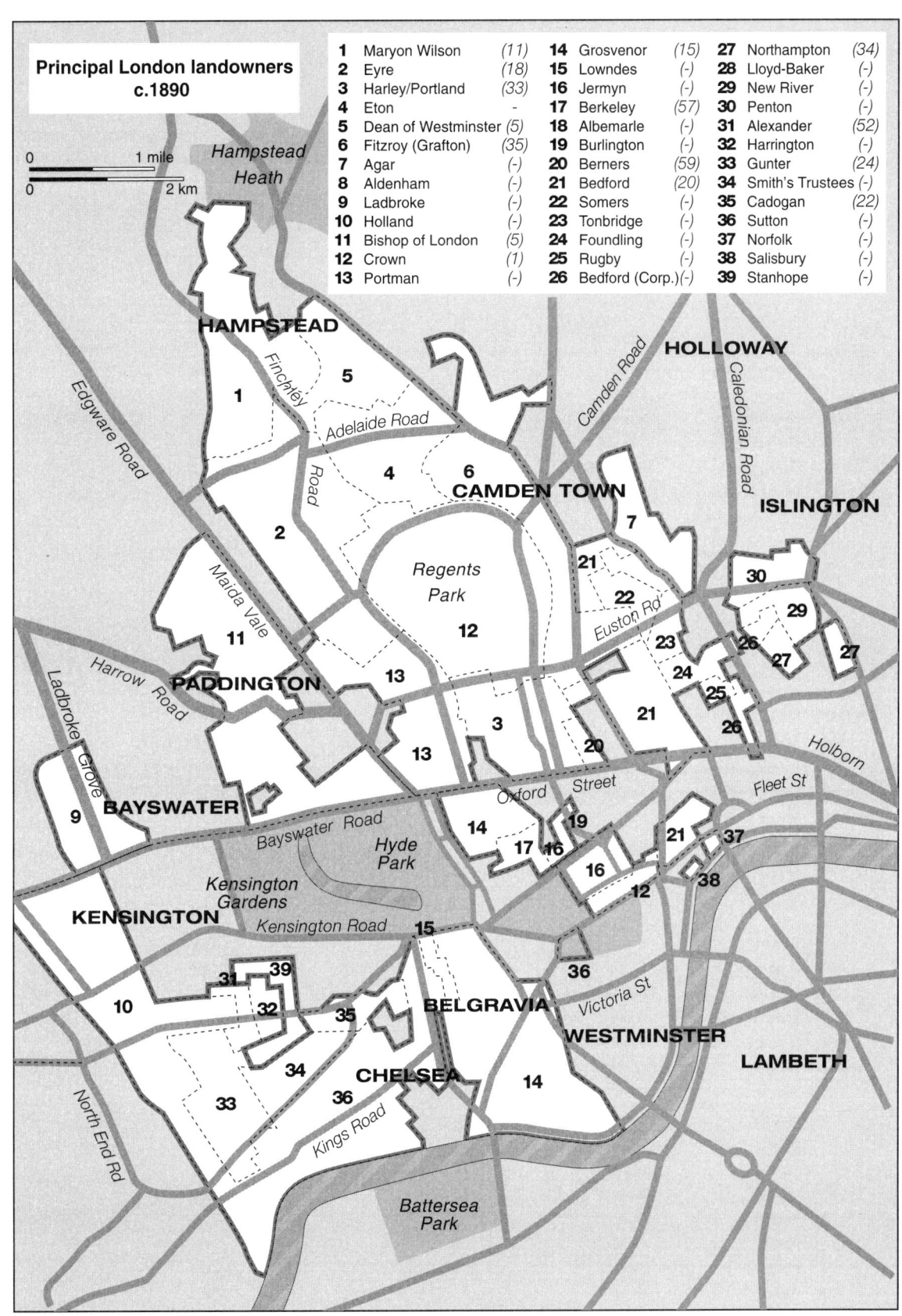

#	Owner		#	Owner		#	Owner	
1	Maryon Wilson	(11)	14	Grosvenor	(15)	27	Northampton	(34)
2	Eyre	(18)	15	Lowndes	(-)	28	Lloyd-Baker	(-)
3	Harley/Portland	(33)	16	Jermyn	(-)	29	New River	(-)
4	Eton	-	17	Berkeley	(57)	30	Penton	(-)
5	Dean of Westminster	(5)	18	Albemarle	(-)	31	Alexander	(52)
6	Fitzroy (Grafton)	(35)	19	Burlington	(-)	32	Harrington	(-)
7	Agar	(-)	20	Berners	(59)	33	Gunter	(24)
8	Aldenham	(-)	21	Bedford	(20)	34	Smith's Trustees	(-)
9	Ladbroke	(-)	22	Somers	(-)	35	Cadogan	(22)
10	Holland	(-)	23	Tonbridge	(-)	36	Sutton	(-)
11	Bishop of London	(5)	24	Foundling	(-)	37	Norfolk	(-)
12	Crown	(1)	25	Rugby	(-)	38	Salisbury	(-)
13	Portman	(-)	26	Bedford (Corp.)	(-)	39	Stanhope	(-)

Source:
Lloyd's map of 1890 after Theobold *(The London Rich)* with amendments.

	Name of owner	Associated Title	London acres 1890	London acres 2001	Rateable 1890 value in 1890	Current value of London acreage
32	Poynder	Sir (Ext)	151	0	£23,192	–
33	Portland-Howard de Walden (see Note C)	Duke (Ext 1977)	150	110	£23,000	£2,000,000,000
34	Northampton	Marquess	149	20	£24,569	£200,000,000
35	Camden (Fitzroy?)	Marquess#	148	0	£26,013	–
36	de Crespigny	Sir (Ext 1952)	141	0	£7826	–
37	Holland (Ilchester)	Earl (1872)	140	40	–	£400,000,000
38	Tufnell Trustees	None	125	0	£19,512	–
39	Angerstein	Esq	112	0	£7214	–
40	Petersham (Stanhope)	Viscount	112	29	–	£290,000,000
41	Stanhope	Earl (1872)	112	0	–	–
42	Duchy of Cornwall	Prince	99	40	£9513	£400,000,000
43	Jackson's trustees	None	94	0	£1,757	–
44	Thornhill	None	86	0	£14,224	–
45	Bourdett-Coutts	None*	86	0	£15,011	–
46	Paul Raymond	Mr		73		£1,095,000,000
47	Sanders	None	83	0	£5421	–
48	Neeld	None	79	0	£23,766	–
49	Angell	None	56	0	£5360	–
50	Phillimore	Lord#	54	0	£22,194	–
51	Blackburn Trustees	None	53	0	£5088	–
52	Alexander	None	52	0	£21,369	–
53	Batson trustees	None	50	0	£8248	–
54	Scotts trustees	None	43	0	£12,021	–
55	Simpson	None	31	0	£7261	–
56	Peterborough	None	30	0	£2167	–
57	Fitzhardinge (Berkeley)	Baroness#	29	0	£11,431	–
58	Yates	None	27	0	£1347	–
59	Berners	Barony#	23	0	£8204	–
60	Sutton	Sir (1872)	21	21	£7990	£630,000,000
61	Salisbury	Marquess	20	20	–	£200,000,000
62	Lettes trustees	None	19	0	£937	–
63	Jenkins	None	17	0	£6714	–
64	Alington	Lord (Ext 1940)	16	0	£2,603	–
65	Winterton	Earl#	16	0	£3318	–
66	Norfolk	Duke (1872)	16	0	–	–
67	Bacon	Sir	14	14	£5,248	£140,000,000
68	Aldridge	None	13	0	£4,010	–
69	Lucas	None	10	0	£1,730	–
70	Norfolk	Duke	10	10	–	£100,000,000
71	Phillips	None	9	0	£9916	–
72	Miscl	None	8	0	£26,224	–
73	Howe	Earl#	7	0	£2963	–

	Name of owner	Associated Title	London acres 1890	London acres 2001	Rateable 1890 value in 1890	Current value of London acreage
74	Tredegar	Lord (Ext 1962)	6	0	£479	–
75	Randall	None	6	0	£1023	–
76	Roberts-West	Esq	6	0	£49,097	–
77	Peyton	None	5	0	£1483	–
78	Rothwell	None	4	0	£745	–
79	Gotto	None*	4	0	£745	–
80	Neal	None	3	0	£619	–
81	Cochran Trustees	None	3	0	£1305	–
82	Pope's trustees	None	2	0	£103	–
83	Mark Pears & family	Mr	0	50	–	£750,000,000
84	Chris Lazari	Mr	0	45	–	£450,000,000
85	Benzion Freshwater	Mr	0	35	–	£350,000,000
86	Alsaud (see Note D)	Prince al Waleed	0	30	–	£335,000,000
87	Walduck	Mr	0	20	–	£200,000,000
88	Radnor	Earl	0	5	–	£50,000,000
89	Rothschild (see Note E)	Baron*	0	4	–	£80,000,000
90	Wates	Sir Christopher	0	3	–	£30,000,000
91	Moran	Mr Christopher	0	3	–	£30,000,000
92	Aberdeen	Marquess	0	1	–	£10,000,000

Notes:
* = indicates that the estate is believed to have survived in some form or other, but is not currently identifiable.
# = indicates that the title still exists, though there is no indication that the holder has any part of the estate nowadays.
Ext = the title is now extinct.
Note A – The Queen is assumed to represent the Crown Estate but also, incorrectly, land belonging to Government. The actual Crown Estate in London was nowhere near 5000 acres in size, and was somewhere between 150 acres and its current size (300 acres).
Note B – estimated value of residual estate.
Note C – The Howard de Walden estate is now 'divided' in terms of beneficiaries, between the four daughters of the late Lord Howard de Walden. They are the Hon Mrs Blanche Buchan, the Hon Mrs Mary Czernin, the Hon Mrs Camilla Acloque and the Hon Mrs Jessica White. Each is 'assigned' approximately 27.5 acres – the exact size of the estate is not known but is reckoned to be a maximum of 110 acres and a minimum of 100 acres. As land in the West End it is estimated to be worth around £20 million per acre.
Note D – purchaser of the Ropemaker estate in April 2001
Note E – Professor Lindert's list included an estate, identified only as Phillip's, of 9.956 acres in Paddington. A newspaper using Professor Lindert's figure subsequently made a serious error, replacing the decimal point with a comma, thereby creating London's largest estate by over 100%. The error was, however, useful in that it drew attention to what is also clearly an error in the Returns in relation to the Rothschilds. One of the other excluded estates is that of the Rothschild's, given as 9,956 acres of Middlesex at Gunnersbury Park in West London.

TABLE 11/3

LONDON LANDOWNERS 2001

(ranked by value of holding)

	Name of owner	Associated Title	London acres 2001	Current value of London acreage
1	Grosvenor	Duke of Westminster	300	£10,000,000,000
2	HM Queen (Crown Estate)	Queen	300	£6,000,000,000
3	Cadogan	Earl	100	£3,000,000,000
4	Portman	Viscount	110	£2,000,000,000
5	Portland-Howard de Walden	Duke (Ext 1977)	110	£2,000,000,000
6	Spencer Maryon Wilson	Sir (Ext)	200	(£1,900,000,000) est.
7	Eyre Trustees	None	190	£1,900,000,000
8	Paul Raymond	Mr	73	£1,095,000,000
9	Mark Pears & family	Mr	50	£750,000,000
10	Sutton	Sir (1872)	21	£630,000,000
11	Gunter*	None	100	£500,000,000
12	Chris Lazari	Mr	45	£450,000,000
13	Holland (Ilchester)	Earl (1872)	40	£400,000,000
14	Duchy of Cornwall	Prince	40	£400,000,000
15	Russell	Duke of Bedford	20	£374,000,000
16	Benzion Freshwater	Mr	35	£350,000,000
17	Alsaud	Prince al Waleed	30	£335,000,000
18	Petersham (Stanhope)	Viscount	29	£290,000,000
19	Northampton	Marquess	20	£200,000,000
20	Salisbury	Marquess	20	£200,000,000
21	Walduck	Mr	20	£200,000,000
22	Bacon	Sir	14	£140,000,000
23	Norfolk	Duke	10	£100,000,000
24	Rothschild	Baron	4	£80,000,000
25	Radnor	Earl	5	£50,000,000
26	Wates	Sir Christopher	3	£30,000,000
27	Moran	Mr Christopher	3	£30,000,000
28	Aberdeen	Marquess	1	£10,000,000

* The Gunter land is in the East End and is valued here at £5 million per acre, which may be too high but does reflect current values (2001).

Chapter Twelve

The Church of England

> 'We are here as a Church to represent Christ crucified and the compassion of Christ crucified before the world.'
> The Most Reverend Dr Michael Ramsey, 100th Archbishop of Canterbury and Primate of All England, 1961[1]

How Much Land Does the Church of England Own?

TABLE 12/1

SUMMARY OF THE LANDHOLDINGS OF THE CHURCH OF ENGLAND IN ENGLAND 1872

(Figures are taken from the 1872 Returns of Owners of Land.[2])

Landholdings less than 1000 acres in extent attributed to clergy (it is assumed that these are parish glebe & parsonage land) [see Note A]	1,256,000 acres
Landholdings between 1000 and 2500 acres attributed to clergy (given the size of these holdings, it is less likely they were glebelands, and some of these holdings may have been personal estates)	210,000 acres
Landholdings directly attributed to deaneries and bishoprics (unlike glebe and parsonage lands, recording of deaneries and bishoprics was erratic and possibly incomplete)	88,000 acres
Church (Ecclesiastical) Commissioners	144,000 acres
Total	**1,690,000 acres**
Known landowners who were clergymen (some of this acreage may have been Church land but was recorded separately) [see Note B]	440,000 acres
Grand total of land owned or controlled by the Church of England and its clergy in 1872	**2,130,000 acres**

Note A: All glebe and parish land was recorded in the *Returns of Owners of Land* against the name of the vicar of the parish. It was not centrally recorded and neither Bateman nor anyone else analysed the Returns to establish the exact facts about the Church of England's landholdings. Bateman in fact gives a figure for 'religious, educational and philanthropic' landholdings of 947,655 acres, 'calculated from entries at the foot of each county in the Returns.' In fact there is no entry for 'religious' in the Returns and it is not clear how he calculated this figure apart from by an uncharacteristically slovenly method (for him) of taking the greater and lesser yeoman class of landowners (between 100 and 1000 acres), of which about 10% were 'Reverends', and allowing that class 10% of the acreage, which comes to about 8.9 million acres. To this he seems to have added the Oxbridge colleges and other similar institutions.

Note B: There is an assumption that most of the 440,000 acres held by the titled and 'great' landowners who were clergymen and who were identified individually in Bateman went back to their families after the clergyman's death.

IN 1976 THE GLEBELANDS of the Church of England parishes were transferred to the dioceses by act of Parliament.3 No account of the quantity of land involved has ever been published, despite the act requiring a return of the landholdings to be made to the dioceses and ultimately to the Church Commissioners by 1978. Although the 1880 Ecclesiastical Lease acts and earlier acts, including that of 1571, allowed limited sales of glebe and parsonage, the land was essentially inalienable. The bulk of the landholdings identified above as glebeland and parsonage should have been in existence and should have been transferred to the dioceses when the 1976 act took effect in 1978.

By the above figures, the Church of England should currently be the second largest landowner in the UK after the Forestry Commission. Instead, and without any formal explanation, the Church probably has less than 250,000 acres. One and a half million acres of land are missing and unaccounted for. The dioceses of Winchester, for instance, asked a retired solicitor to compile a record of its parish glebe in 1978, to establish what it should have as a result of the 1976 act. He found 450.5 acres. Yet in 1872 the dioceses of Winchester held around 30,000 acres in Hampshire alone. One of the explanations offered by the Winchester authorities to the author was that there was no way to check what holdings the parishes should have had, because, as the land had never been sold, it was not recorded in the Land Registry. In actual fact this explanation, also offered later by the Church Commissioners, is contradictory. If the land had been sold, it *might* have been in the Land Registry and could have been located. But if it hadn't been sold, where was it? Rightly or wrongly, the defective Land Registry for England and Wales had contributed to the Church of England's inability to locate its own acreage.

TABLE 12/2

THE PARISH GLEBE: THE SECRET ACRES OF THE CHURCH OF ENGLAND

	County	No. of Parishes	Church of England Glebe Holdings 1872	Average per Parish	Deanery Holdings	Church Commissioners
			Acres	Acres	Acres	Acres
1	Bedford	136	21,896	161	214	699
2	Berks	193	18,142	94.2	998	1836
3	Bucks	225	21,847	97.1	734	941
4	Cambs	176	16,544	94.8	2649	4748
5	Cheshire	502	28,614	57.2	2976	516
6	Cornwall	217	27,617	127.2	694	2119
7	Cumbria	208	21,216	102	2017	3820
8	Derby	331	21,250	64.2	183	363
9	Devon	480	58,527	121.9	365	5390
10	Dorset	289	19,536	67.6	11	1030
11	Durham	269	37,660	140	9273	26,868
12	Essex	413	29,529	71	4721	1142
13	Glos	391	43,088	110.2	3667	3434
14	Hants	345	22,484	65.1	7724	2400
15	Hereford	262	30,811	117.6	1803	3390
16	Herts	141	12,249	89.0	1036	901
17	Hunts	107	13,803	129	1847	3559
18	Kent	419	31,425	75	7942	10,591
19	Lancs	453	27,904	61.6	195	235
20	Leics	334	39,078	117	52	1319
21	Lincs	752	99,264	132	6018	8774
22	Middlesex	53	1,749	33	794	1308
23	Mons	147	13,083	89	693	125
24	Norfolk	740	56,240	76	4761	3753
25	Northants	346	57,612	166	3725	4677
26	Northumbs	541	39,580	73	517	98

	County	No. of Parishes	Church of England Glebe Holdings 1872	Average per Parish	Deanery Holdings	Church Commissioners
27	Notts	275	21,551	78.3	1190	6700
28	Oxford	300	35,822	119.4	657	2263
29	Rutland	58	7349	126.7	166	507
30	Salop	254	25,005	98.4	197	–
31	Somerset	490	36,628	74.7	345	8464
32	Staffs	249	13,999	56.2	1229	3166
33	Suffolk	525	61,802	117.7	4181	214
34	Surrey	137	12,546	91.5	476	1101
35	Sussex	324	17,508	54	812	3640
36	Warwicks	259	29,253	112.9	673	37
37	Westmorland	109	15,757	144.5	2	–
38	Wilts	343	21,140	61.6	1918	6580
39	Worcs	242	19,301	79.75	1518	5213
40	Yorks ER	384	41,849	108.9	1549	667
41	Yorks NR	553	34,538	62.4	1910	8357
42	Yorks WR	689	64,592	93.7	775	3435
Total		13,661	1,269,388		83,207	144,000

The Church of England, like most of the institutions examined in this book connected with large landholdings, has used presentational deceit to conceal its landholdings over the years. The veil is only now being lifted but even then with little help from the people responsible for 90% of the Church's real estate, the diocesan boards of finance. In response to a written application by the present author for details of the current glebeland holdings to each of the 44 dioceses in England in November 2000, only two dioceses, Birmingham and Hereford, made available a copy of their annual financial records, which should show the extent of the acreage now held by way of a note to the balance sheet. This did not appear. A total of 24 dioceses had replied by the time of going to press, with only 19 actually disclosing, or able to disclose, acreage. They are listed below, along with the approximate acreage the 1872 Return indicates they should hold.

TABLE 12/3

THE CHURCH OF ENGLAND'S MISSING ACRES

Dioceses	Current acreage	Approximate church acreage in relevant county 1872
Birmingham	Not known	29,253 (Warwicks)
Blackburn	550	27,904 (Lancs)
Bristol	300	New diocese
Canterbury	210.8	31,425 (Kent)
Chichester	539	17,508 (Sussex)
Coventry	3700	29,253 (Warwicks)
Ely	5793	16,544 (Cambs)
Guildford	152.2	12,546 (Surrey)
Hereford	1534	30,811 (Hereford)

Dioceses	Current acreage	Approximate church acreage in relevant county 1872
Leicester	5000	39,078 (Leics)
Lichfield	2122	39,078 (Leicester)
Lincoln	15,266	99,264 (Lincs)
Liverpool	Not known	Not readily calculable
Peterborough	5016	57,612 (Northants)
Ripon & Leeds	800	46,000 (Yorks West Riding)
Salisbury	2064	21,140 (Wilts)
St Albans	3734	12,249 (Herts)
Truro	2520	30,000 (Cornwall)
Winchester	450.5	30,000 (Hants)
Refused to disclose		
Bradford	–	46,000 (Yorks West Riding)
Derby	–	21,250 (Derby)
Exeter	–	58,000 (Devon)
Sodor & Man	New dioceses	
Wakefield	–	41,849 (Yorks East Riding)

Note:
The dioceses do not coincide precisely with the counties in which they are headquartered. But the figures above give a guide to the scale of difference between what was recorded in 1872 and what is there now.

The glebe in 1872, minus the Church Commissioners' acreage, comes to a figure of 1,546,000 acres. Had this been retained, it would now be worth a minimum of £4.6 billion at an average agricultural value of £3000 per acre. In practice, a significant percentage of this land, even in 1872, was urban or semi urban, and was raising revenues far in excess of agricultural rents. If it is assumed that about 10% of the acreage was development land, currently worth about £444,000 an acre, the total package would now be worth in excess of £10 billion, more than double the total value of the Church Commissioners' assets. In conversation with the author an official at the Church Commissioners suggested that perhaps the glebe had been sold over the years, but even he admitted that to comply with the inalienable status of the land 'as capital' the proceeds of any sale would have had to be invested in a capital fund somewhere. No such fund appears to exist. The question therefore remains and remains highly pertinent. Where is the glebe land, and if it was disposed of, where is the capital fund that should have replaced it?

Church and State

What the vast landholdings of 1872 reflected was the nature and status of the Church of England as a crucial component of the power structure of the English, later British, state and empire. The Church of England is the 'established' church in England, which means that it is governed by statute and regulated by parliament. The head, or Governor, of the Church of England is the head of state of the United Kingdom. For centuries the Church of England obtained major financial benefits from the state, including an initial endowment of millions of acres of land in the sixteenth century.

When Henry VIII began the formal dissolution of the monasteries in 1536 his chancellor Cardinal Wolsey, the 38th richest Briton of the last ten centuries, according to the

Sunday Times historic rich list of April 2000,[4] had already closed more than 30 monasteries and seized their assets for the Crown with a 'scalp' for himself. His 'scalps' eventually made him a fortune worth the equivalent of £8.6 billion. His grounds for forcing dissolution were a lack of either religion or fear of the Lord. His deputy and successor as chancellor, Thomas Cromwell, keenly aware of the public antipathy to the monastic institutions, persuaded Henry VIII that there would be little or no public opposition to his seizing all the monasteries and church land. Henry needed little persuasion. He was broke. As Cromwell had predicted, the majority of monks and parish clergy took the oath of Supremacy and Succession and accepted Henry as head of the Church of England without demur. To ordinary lay folk the changes must have looked little more than cosmetic, with life and religion carrying on in the parish churches much as it always had, with much the same clergy as before. The landless laity's purchase on the means of salvation, confession and the sacraments, remained in place. Amongst the landed, there were now new owners, closely tied to the Crown as a result of their acquisitions of monastic land from Henry. Opposition had been eliminated, supporters had been gained and the king was once more solvent.

In relation to this book the importance of the Church of England is first of all historic. The Church played a significant role in the evolution of landownership and its distribution in the UK, even if its role as a major landowner has remained hidden for the better part of a century. For centuries the Church of England was the third arm of the state and its most efficient and original national tax gatherer. Over the centuries the Church played a major role as a prime organ of social control in a country that has specialised in state control, especially of a covert or subliminal kind, over the centuries. Anthony Sampson describes the Church of England as part of the ancient fabric of the country, noting that 'Throughout the eighteenth and nineteenth centuries, it remained closely identified with the aristocracy and with Conservatism.'[5]

The link between the three groups is, of course, land. The Church of England, with its network of parishes that were the very bedrock of administrative as well as religious life, provided a natural source of universal information for the ecclesiastical authorities who were based in London and totally subordinated to the Crown and to Parliament. Henry had not only made himself solvent by commencing the dissolution of the monasteries, he had drawn formally into the structure of the state a superior source of information down to parish level throughout the length and breadth of his realms. And he had made the population of the country beholden to the state for both their spiritual and temporal welfare. Like all state structures, the state church attracted corruption, in this case moral rather than financial. As an arm of the state its structure attracted those who, like modern landowners, liked to live off the state. It took very little time for the younger sons of the 3000 families who owned most of the land which didn't belong to the Crown, to 'adopt' the Church as a way of making a living.

For centuries the execution of civil authority throughout Britain but principally in England was based with the manors, the seat of the local landowner. The Lord of the Manor ran the local courts and looked after justice on a local basis. Most parishes, although village centred, were more or less contiguous in area with the local manor, and operated in tandem with the Lord of the Manor, who paid his tithes to the Church and often appointed the vicar.[6] The manors, in the form they came to assume after the conquest in 1066 in particular, are roughly similar in number to the number of parishes that exist in the country.

The institution of the parishes as both an extra arm of government, and as a form of balance to the Lords of the Manors, really got under way after Henry VIII had sold off monastic lands to the aristocracy and his supporters. However, because a good deal of parish work and a good many parishes, were run by the monasteries, Henry had to ensure that the religious arm of government went on functioning, in short, he had to keep the priests of his new church fed and clothed. His first answer was to grant or confirm some land, the glebe, to each parish. This the priest could let or till, thus guaranteeing some income. He also left a certain amount of land to central institutions of his new church such as Eton and the Oxbridge colleges. This was later confiscated and sold off by the Cromwellian Commonwealth, but, as with many Royalist Estates, a good deal of this was bought back and the glebeland in most parishes was restored. It did, however, lead to a significant anomaly in the 1872 Returns. To quote Bateman:

> [Those with the title Rev] total number is 3185, out of a total landed yeomanry of 33,998; in other words not far short of 10% . . . This of course means that the glebeland has not been entered, as the Local Government Board directed, as the property of 'The vicar of Blank' but in the vicar's name as 'Rev. J Smith'.[7]

In this way Bateman contributed to the creation of the illusion that the land holdings of the Church were the holdings of the Church Commissioners. It seems extraordinary that he, with his knowledge of the Returns and of local administration, failed to recognise that the Returns did constitute a more or less accurate account of the larger bloc of Church land, the glebe land. Obsessed as he was by class, we can partly see why he approached the matter the way he did.

In terms of class he paid no attention to classes below that of yeoman farmer. Thus, only clerics with a holding of over 100 acres make his extracts, leaving about 10,000 clerics, and their glebes, unaccounted for. History, and historians, instead of using the Returns themselves, got used to using Bateman's extracts, partly because they represented corrected entries for the larger owners, neatly gathered together on an alphabetic basis, and partly because Bateman was so much easier to use than the Returns, which had anyhow been questioned by the son of the Queen's chaplain and a senior Oxford don, George Brodrick, in *English Land and English Landlords* (see chapter 3).

The analysis of the Church of England's landholdings made for this book, the first in 128 years, investigates the holdings Bateman ignored, establishing an almost complete picture of those acres actually owned by the Church of England in 1872 and allowing us to pose the question of the missing lands in a way which has never been possible before.

A Great British Landowner

There is a commonly held perception of the Church of England as a great landowner, and although the totals shown in Table 12/1 have never before been compiled from the 1872 Return, it is clear that this perception is justified. The Church was the largest single landowner in Victorian England, with acreage in excess of that of the Duke of Sutherland with 1,358,545 acres, the largest individual landowner at that time. The Church was the largest landowner in 29 of the 42 counties of England. Taken together with the great landowners who were clerics, each of whom is identified in the county lists in Part II of this book and who together owned over 440,000 acres of land, it gave the Church of England a commanding reach in all land matters. In those counties where it was not the dominant owner, it was the second largest owner in six counties and the third largest owner in four counties. In only one county, Rutland, did it fall further, to fifth place. The glebe and parsonage lands owned by the parishes at the time of the Return were almost certainly largely unchanged up to at least 1914 and maybe much later. But by 1976 something like the reduction displayed in Table 12/3 above had occurred, though no one knows how or why.

Much of the confusion regarding glebelands has arisen from a misunderstanding about the structure of the Church of England, perpetrated by secular writers for over fifty years. All the modern authorities on landownership attribute only the Church Commissioners' landholdings as the Church of England landholdings. Anthony Sampson in *The Anatomy of Britain* estimated that the Church of England had about 223,000 acres.[8] Marion Shoard in *This Land is Our Land* states that 'by 1972 the Church of England had recovered its lost ground (since Henry VIII) sufficiently to be rated in a BBC survey as the tenth largest landowner in Britain. Thirteen years later the Church of England's farm and forest land covered 170,000 acres and attracted a market value of £173 million.'[9] In his book *Whose Land is it Anyway* Richard Norton Taylor wrote in 1982 that 'The Church of England is now the tenth single largest landowner, but although more than 90% of its 170,000 acres is farmland, it is also London's biggest private residential landowner.'[10] In the absence of a full analysis on the 1872 Return, the BBC figure had gone into 'echo mode' unchecked. In *The National Wealth* Dominic Hobson defines the 1997 Annual Report acreage of 130,000 as the church's full acreage.[11] Almost without exception writers have assumed that the Church Commissioners are the financial controllers of the Church of England, and the holders of all the Church's assets. In fact the Church Commissioners hold land that originated with either Queen Anne's Bounty, the royal charity which distributed the taxes levied on the church, known as tithes and first fruits, until the early 1700s, and which later became the Ecclesiastical Commissioners or land owned by the Ecclesiastical Commissioners. The Church of England is essentially a federal corporation of 44 dioceses, each of which holds, as its own property, the former acreages of the parishes, summarised in Table 12/2.

The rather lame reason given by the current Church establishment for never referring to the glebeland and parsonage as Church of England property is that until the 1976 act which transferred ownership of the glebeland from the parish to the dioceses the legal formula covering ownership had a parish clergyman as the tenant for life of land that was inalienably endowed in perpetuity to the parish he served.[12] In theory an incumbent could not legally sell off the land, although the 1571 and 1880 Ecclesiastical Leasing acts provided for sales in very limited situations. Clearly all sorts of things had happened to these parish acres – they had been leased, sub let, lost, stolen even, but the freehold in most cases should have been retained in some form, as required by law. In the absence of any willingness by the Church authorities to provide a centralised summary of their current land holdings, the assumption being made here is that the dioceses should have at least retained the legal right to the bulk of the freeholds of the old glebeland, even if some sales have taken place, and even if some are truly 'lost'. Certainly, there is no record, in academia or in the media, of any big sell off by the church anytime since 1872.[13]

Neither is there any public record of what volume of land was transferred from parish to dioceses between 1976 and 1978. It is all eerily reminiscent of the absence from the historic record of the *Returns of Owners of Land*.

In *The National Wealth*, Dominic Hobson identifies two further dilemmas facing the Church of England, both indirectly related to land.[14] The first is the problem of the

Church's heritage of great and important buildings, the 42 cathedrals. More than 30 times as many tourists visit the cathedrals as do worshippers. Perhaps the time has come to recognise the portent implicit in the Secretary of State for Culture, Media and Sport joining the board of the Church of England and to abandon the care of the cathedrals to the tourist authority? Secondly, Hobson makes much of huge losses made and later unmade in the property boom of the late 1980s by the Church Commissioners. These losses, partly in the form of cash paid out, and partly in the form of losses on revaluation, where values had declined from the time of purchase, came to about £400 million. The story is fairly fully set out in Terry Lovell's book *Number One Millbank*.[15] Not once, however, does the book mention glebeland. What it does do is point to the kind of administrative incompetence in British institutions that gives rise to catastrophic losses. But £400 million is peanuts compared with the assets that should have been there, had the glebe been retained.

Landholding and Church Mission

One of the most intriguing things to emerge from the parish by parish analysis of 1872 is how much of the glebe was clearly non agricultural but already in urban use of some kind. As with the Church Commissioners' holdings detailed later in the chapter, it is this inheritance which should provide the most valuable real estate for the dioceses. It is hard to imagine, for instance, that in 1872 the Rev R.S. Hopkinson at Hilderstone in Staffordshire, with one acre and 18 perches, raised £119, the modern equivalent of £8330, by letting it to a local farmer. Average annual rents for agricultural land in those days at £1–2 were the equivalent of between £70 and £140 per acre today. At Newborough parish in the same county, the Rev R.M. Hope was receiving the equivalent of £2345 per annum for his one acre and two roods. Over in Hampshire, known in those days as Southampton county, the Rev W.H. Maddock at Bonchurch was also receiving the equivalent of over £8000 a year for his one acre, two roods and 28 perches. On the other side of the coin, some incumbents had only the agricultural income of an acre or two to live on. The Rev Richard Hull at Shitlington in Bedfordshire received the modern equivalent of about £74 per annum for his one acre, one rood and nine perches. The Rev D.H. Murray, listed in Bedfordshire as a priest of that dioceses but living at Oxford (presumably he'd abandoned his parish, as did many clergy in that period), still received the equivalent of about £145 for his parish's two acres, one rood and eight perches.

Perhaps it was this institutionalised impoverishment of a whole sector of its own clergy which has made the Church of England so reluctant to reveal its landholdings in 1872 or at any other time. Or perhaps it is the fact that about one in five of the clergy lived in considerable comfort and between four and eight clergymen in most counties had salaries the equivalent of between £100,000 and £140,000 a year. The *Return of Owners of Land* gave anyone who cared to look an instant means of establishing the exact status of the Church as landowner and provided an exact guide to the inequitable distribution of parish acreage and income. The Returns were a detailed guide to wealth and poverty in the Church of England. They revealed how closely it was wedded to the very heart of the state, and just how distant it was as an institution from the bulk of the population. The population was landless. Land ownership in any form was confined to less than 5% of the population and ownership of more than one acre confined to just 1.3% of the population. England had only two meaningful classes, either economically or socially, and thus politically. These were the landowners and the landless, between whom existed a bond of financial dependence, and of tenancy dependence, the latter probably even more important than the former. The Church of England, through its clergy, whose background was almost uniformly landed, and through its immense landholdings, was at once both a key state agency and a monolithic and homogenous component of that tiny part of British society, the landowners, who controlled the state. The church also played a role in managing the state, with 26 bishops and archbishops sitting in Parliament. As the biggest landowner in the UK, especially in the nineteenth and early twentieth centuries, the church's second role was to support the institutions of landownership, which were wholly integral to the functioning of the owners of the state. Its two key roles, that of landowner and of state agent for religion, effectively crippled it in terms of its mission as defined by Archbishop Ramsey at the head of this chapter. Managing over two million acres inevitably absorbed a great deal of clerical energy.

Taking just one county as an example, in Devon in 1872 there were 11 clergymen with sufficient acreage to give them an income the equivalent of over £70,000 a year. Four clergymen in that county appear in Bateman's *Great Landowners of Great Britain and Ireland*. These were the Rev. Archdeacon Woolcombe with 6850 acres and an income the equivalent of £249,480 a year; the Rev. Thomas Bewes with 4711 acres and an income the equivalent of £380,940 a year; the Rev. Sir Henry Wrey had 7985 acres and was earning the equivalent of £648,830, while the Rev. the Earl of Buckingham had 5203 acres and the equivalent of £412,300 a year. At the other end of the scale, of Devon's 480 parishes, the priests in 78 had less than 10 acres on which to subsist. The priests in 107 parishes were subsisting on the equivalent of less than £3500 a year, with a number of those receiving less than £300 a year. Bishops in this period had a total average income that was the equivalent of about £1 million a year. For the poor clergy there were both Church and family sponsored handouts. Many of the clergy in any case came from wealthy landed families and could rely on an annual donation from that quarter. But like the undoubted sanctity of many individuals in the Church of England, the issue is institutional, not personal. At its heart the Church of England was a creature of the English state, rather than the spiritual instrument of a Galilean preacher. It emulated in every way the fiscal heart of that state, which demanded rents, not prayers. It often rated for promotion those who showed competence as landlords and landowners, rather than piety in the exercise of their priestly function. Among the bishops, who were in any case nominated for appointment to the Queen by the Prime Minister, the Church in its recommendations to the Prime Minister showed a preference for those who had been to public school.[16]

The Church should never have been caught in a position where its own officials were responsible for matters beyond their capability, and way beyond the Church's mission as defined by Michael Ramsey. But what any organisation can do, easily, is look at its mission and check, or get objective observers to check, its mission performance. For the Church of England two thing stand between it and its mission. The first is the scale of mammon in its belly; its financial assets including land. The second is the sustained institutional deceit used to conceal those landholdings over many years. Why was it necessary? And why continue with it now that it has been revealed?

The Role of the Church Commissioners

Based on their own relatively small landholding, the Church Commissioners of the Church of England are still in the top 20 of institutional landowners and rank 14th in the overall list of landowners with the Dioceses at number 11. This is about 120,000 acres of mostly agricultural land, a figure not far short of that of 1872, at 135,000 acres. In the annual accounts of 1996 the agricultural holdings are listed in full. In the 1999 accounts the list is reduced to just county or place names. In the interval about 9000 acres were sold. A spokesperson for the Church Commissioners claimed that the removal of acreage details was 'an advance towards openness'.[17]

In relation to the glebeland there is as much obscurity and confusion inside the church as outside. Of five senior clergymen spoken to by the author, four genuinely thought that the Church Commissioners were responsible for land owned by the dioceses. The fifth had no idea that the glebeland had been transferred to the dioceses in 1976. The actual position is not exactly clear in that the spokesperson for the Church Commissioners said that the Commissioners act in relation to the dioceses in the same way the Charity Commissioners act towards individual charities. They keep an eye on them and give advice. But the dioceses, like individual charities, remain autonomous. In its own minor right the Church Commissioners are a major player in commercial and urban property development, with inner circle links to the big London property players. For example, the Church of England owns a large residential estate near Hyde Park in central London, and the Octavia Hill estate in south London. In addition the church owns a small estate near Savile Row in London's Mayfair, one of the main Department of Trade and Industry buildings in Victoria and 30 buildings in the fashionable King's Road, in Chelsea. Most major property players, even if they have no exact knowledge of the diocesan acreage, do know that the dioceses have or should have, large landholdings. This adds weight to the Commissioners' position. But there is another factor involved. The Church has access to and retains a role alongside the higher echelons of government, Parliament, the City and the Palace. The list of Government officials who were Church Commissioners as recently as 1997, reads like something out of Gilbert and Sullivan. They included the First Lord of the Treasury (the Prime Minister), the Lord President of the Council (Leader of the House of Commons), the Speaker of the House of Commons, the Secretary of State for the Home Office, the Chancellor of the Exchequer, the Lord Chief Justice, The Master of the Rolls, the Attorney General, the Solicitor General, the Lord Mayor of London and the Lord Mayor of York. Since 1997 the Church Commissioners have received a new charter, and the total number of Commissioners has fallen from 54 to 33, with the Lord Chief Justice, the Master of the Rolls, the Attorney General, the Solicitor General and the Lord Mayors of York and London being replaced by the Secretary of State for Culture, Media and Sport.

The state makes no special contribution from taxpayers' funds to the state Church. As a religious charity, the Church does recover tax from gift covenants, but then so do all other charities. In 1999 the tax recovered by the Church Commissioners was worth £35 million. The clergy are charged income tax on their mostly meagre salaries. The majority of the people in the country no longer claim formal adherence to the official Church nor make any financial contribution to it. Those making covenanted donations number a little over 440,000. However, as Ysenda Maxtone Graham points out in her delightful book, *The Church Hesitant*, 'The modern English do not want to be monks, but they would hate the monks not to be there.'[18] In the same way, they do not want to belong to the Church of England, but they would hate it not to be there.

The Church itself makes no financial contribution to its titular head, the head of state, and she makes no significant financial contribution to the Church she heads. Hers is one of the richest families in the UK, and she heads a church which is the 14th largest landowner in the UK. Unlike the Pope, whose wealth is purely institutional, and equally at odds with the message of the founder of both churches, the wealth of the head of the Church of England is personal. The anomalies of land, history, the state and religious morality, all caught up in a single institution, are compelling.

The clergy of the Church of England are reliant for their salaries partly on the success of the Church Commissioners and diocesan boards as financiers, and partly on the offertory plate at Sunday service in an ever diminishing number of parish churches.[19] The mission of the Church Commissioners, in their own words, is to 'manage the investments entrusted to us to maximise our financial support for the ministry of the Church of England, particularly in areas of need and opportunity.'[20] In fact, without the money from the Church Commissioners, the Church of England as an institution would have to restructure completely.[21]

The Church Commissioners, and by implication the diocesan boards of finance, were freed of any moral obligations in relation to their land and other investments, by a High Court ruling in 1991. The judgment said that '[The Church Commissioners] must not use property held by them for investment purposes as a means of making moral statements at the expense of the charity of which they are trustees.'[22] In fact the Commissioners have a list of excluded investments, including armaments, tobacco, alcohol, newspapers and gambling, which ignore the High Court ruling. But what the very existence of the Church Commissioners, with their amoral charter from the High Court, does, is point towards the institutional flaw that has destroyed the Church of England as the repository of faith for the bulk of the country. From its birth, the Church has not been able to finance itself from its alleged adherents alone. It was created by a land gift from a king, Henry VIII, and his daughter Elizabeth I, during a major realignment of the power structure in both Europe and in England in the sixteenth century. It survived structurally for centuries by imposing a tax on believer and unbeliever alike and by being the largest single landowner in the country. Not only that, for centuries it supported laws that not only banned others from practising their faith, but excluded all except its own adherents from membership of Parliament, the law, and many government jobs. In relation to the story of landownership in the UK, the bitter grip held on Oxford and Cambridge by the Church of England until 1871, may have much to do with both the suppression of the Returns and the parallel suppression of information about the real nature of the Church's landholdings. Francois Bedarida, the French academic, notes the importance of this fact in his book *A Social History of England 1851–1990*, juxtaposing it with the religious bigotry which for eleven years from 1847 until 1858 kept Lionel de Rothschild out of the Parliament to which he had been elected. Bradlaugh, the radical campaigner, was kept out of Parliament from his election in 1880 until 1886, because he was an atheist and would not take the essentially Church of England oath of loyalty to Parliament and Crown required of every MP. Bedarida notes that 'Until 1871 it was impossible to teach at Oxford or Cambridge if one had not signed a declaration of loyalty to the Thirty Nine Articles, the basic beliefs of the Church of England.'[23]

While the country's hereditary head of state remains as the head of a church which no longer commands the active support of even 3% of the population, Parliament has maintained its right to control and regulate that church and its residual landholdings. Despite the eviction of the hereditaries from the House of Lords, 26 archbishops and bishops of the Church of England have retained their seats. Those seats are hereditary in relation to the Church. No other denomination has seats in Parliament, as of right. There is no sign of the bishops applying to have their seats abolished, despite the democratic divergence between their support base and their Parliamentary position. Yet the bishops are as specific and as real a representation of landowner power as were the hereditary aristocracy. Historically they represented 50,000 acres each, a slice of the country that most of the aristocracy did not own or represent while they were still in the upper house. What size of acreage they now represent is, as our returns from the modern dioceses show, unclear.

Four of the bishops are also members of the Privy Council. Only Prince Charles, that considerable landowner, in his perceptive observation that he wants to be defender of faiths, rather than defender of the faith, when he is king, has focused on the true function of the state to provide structures for all to practise their own faith, in freedom. Prince Charles has grasped the essential fact that the state must be the guardian of individual rights and therefore neutral between religions, and the right to profess any religion. Yet the fact that it is an issue at all indicates that the Church of England was all about land and power. Land and power explain both its origins and the anomaly of its continued links with the state and also its decline.

Landholdings and Survival

As has been suggested above, the Church of England exists in its present form only because it is one of the larger landowners in modern Britain, and not because it has a meaningful membership amongst the faithful, or because it has carried out its mission to the people. In the words of Leslie Paul, the church's failure is so enormous that it now treats the country's heartlands as mission fields, and not the thriving parishes they once were.[24] In fact the Church spends £27 million a year, partly on these 'internal' mission fields. But it survives this failure because it has enough revenues, a goodly portion from landholdings, to maintain an establishment of archbishops, bishops, priests and others, to minister to an ever decreasing band of the faithful, a band whose numbers have been in serious decline since a peak in 1851. In England as a whole, there are 1,325,000 people on the electoral roll of the Church of England, which represents 2.8% of the population at large. The number of communicants, those who take communion at least three times a year, is believed to be less than 1 million. The Church of England as a whole has over 13,000 parishes in 43 of the 44 dioceses, serviced by just over 11,000 paid clergy, including 110 bishops. The 44th dioceses is Europe, the subdivisions of which are congregations rather than parishes. There are 42 cathedrals and 16,000 churches, 12,000 of them listed buildings within the 44 dioceses.

To put it in crude terms, the market for religion remains. About 44% of the population of the UK, or 30 million people, still believe in a Christian God, and about the same number believe in a life hereafter.[25] Despite these figures, less than one million people regularly attend a Church of England service, with just over 440,000 of those making a regular donation by way of covenant.[26] And the market is willing to pay for religion. The Rev Dr Ian Paisley, the politician preacher from Northern Ireland, regularly raises hundreds of thousands, if not millions, of pounds for his church and its mission.[27] The Catholic Church in England has restored itself to parity of numbers and attendance with the Church of England, with almost no landholdings, present or historic, to support its clergy. The implication is that the vast landholdings of the Church of England did nothing to assist its mission and probably impeded that mission enormously.

Yet the importance of land to the Church in terms of income is easy to illustrate. The total income and expenditure of the Church of England for 1997, the last year full figures were available, was £705 million. In the 1996 accounts land was valued at £835.5 million. Shares held were valued at £1,778.7 million. The landed investment provided income of £51.5 million, a return of 6.1% net. Shares provided an income of £87.3 million, a return of 4.9%. For an institution that has to produce annual income, land was clearly outperforming shares. In fact with much of its land purchase costs lost in history, especially the glebe land, the gain on any sale will be 100%. Running costs will be low as there is no loan to service.

What is so important about the Church of England, however, is the model it offers for institutional survival, long after the institution in question has lost or almost lost its function. More than almost any other example we have, it shows how the possession of land can enable that which is essentially dead to live. The Church of England is full of men and women of goodwill and holiness. Regrettably that is not the point. Its mission was stated by Michael Ramsey in the only possible terms that can describe a Christian institution. In those terms it is a near total failure, that failure being exemplified by attendance at its services, and payment in support of its activities by the people of the nation it is named to serve.

Chapter Thirteen

Scotland

IN SCOTLAND THE knots tied into its history by its southern neighbour are unravelling fast. Ancient wrongs, most particularly the Act of Union of 1707, are now being righted, at least in part, with the creation in 1999 of the first Scottish Parliament in nearly 300 years. At the heart of the unsuccessful resistance to the return of the Scottish parliament were the landowners and their extended tribes of relations. And for obvious reasons. These are the 1200 or so families who still own more than half of Scotland. According to the new chronicler of Scotland's ownership, Andy Wightman, two thirds of the country's privately owned rural land, 10,804,824 million acres, and about 57% of the country as a whole, was owned by just 1252 families in 1999.[1] To give perspective to this figure it is worth noting that in 1872 in England, 4736 families owned 12.8 million acres, around 56.1% of that country. The grip of the great individual landowners which has slowly loosened in England over the last century or so is still tight in Scotland.

The ownership of Scotland's land is a representation of arrested history, with wider implications, particularly in its economic effects, which are fundamentally unknown. That this is the case should not come as a surprise, however. The Act of Union in 1707, which ended Scottish independence and incorporated Scotland into the British Empire, was bought with money and titles. Those who were paid the money and who were granted the titles were in many cases the ancestors of the 1252 families identified by Wightman. And they used their new association with England to great advantage. By 1750 the number of electors in Scotland was only 2662 for 33 seats in the Westminster Parliament and just 1250 people elected the 15 MPs to Westminster from the Scottish boroughs. The British Parliament in the 1700s and 1800s, in which landowners occupied the whole of the Upper House and 90% of the Commons, made it a hanging offence to kill a deer and transportation for life was the penalty for killing a rabbit under the game laws, which applied to Scotland as well as England, Wales & Ireland. These draconian laws hurt the most in areas with a dispersed peasant population, mostly Scotland, Wales and Ireland.

Even as Parliament allowed political reforms to take hold after 1832, land reform, even the kind of natural incremental change taking place south of the border, failed to happen in Scotland. In 1872 over 17.5 million acres or 92.8% of Scotland was owned by just 1758 families. As has been seen in previous chapters, in that same year the Duke of Sutherland owned 1,176,343 acres of a county whose total acreage was 1,299,194. The same duke's ancestors had swept half the population of the county into the grave ships and emigration, to make way for sheep during the Highland Clearances. Even Ireland, by 1872, was in a slightly more equitable situation than Scotland, with 3745 families owning 78% of the country, a statistic that was to change drastically within twenty years. But there was no land commission in Scotland, no opening of the economy by offering the land to the people. Scotland remained as economically undemocratic internally as it did externally in relation to its own sovereignty.

TABLE 13/1

LAND IN BRITAIN HELD IN ESTATES OF OVER 1000 ACRES, 1872

Country	Number of owners of estates over 1000 acres	Total acres owned	% of total land area owned	Total acres of country	Population
England	4736	12,825,643	56.1%	30,377,298	18,240,874
Wales	672	1,490,915	60.7%	4,160,860	1,217,135
Ireland	3745	15,802,737	78.4%	20,159,678	4,100,000
Scotland	1758	17,584,828	92.8%	18,946,694	3,360,000
Total	**10,911**	**47,704,123**	**66.14%**	**73,369,640**	**26,900,000**

Source: From Bateman and after Cannadine and Thompson.

Something Scotland has benefitted from in the last 120 years in contrast to England and Wales is the work of two great chroniclers, John McEwen and Andy Wightman, and as a result we have a much better idea of the state of Scotland in relation to landownership. A list similar to the one above could not be constructed now, except in the case of Scotland, thanks to the work of its contemporary chroniclers.

TABLE 13/2

LAND IN SCOTLAND HELD IN ESTATES OF OVER 1000 ACRES, 1970–99

	Number of owners of estates over 1000 acres	Total acres owned in 1000-acre plus estates	% of total land area owned in 1000-acre plus estates
Scotland (McEwen 1970)	1739	12,000,000	62.9%
Scotland (Wightman 1995)	1411	11,015,405	57.8%
Scotland (Wightman 1999)	1252	10,804,824	57% or 66% of all private rural land (16,207,230 acres)

The Scottish Chroniclers

In 1970, John McEwen's *Who Owns Scotland* was able to produce figures for the breakdown of the ownership of land in Scotland for the first time since 1876.

TABLE 13/3

JOHN MCEWAN'S BREAKDOWN OF
LANDOWNERSHIP IN SCOTLAND[2]

Private estates

Estates above 1000 acres	12,000,000 acres
Estates under 1000 acres	4,500,000 acres
Total	**16,500,000 acres**

State owned

Forestry Commission	1,895,000 acres
Dept of Agriculture	445,800 acres
British Railways	45,000 acres
National Coal Board	49,000 acres
Defence	48,900 acres
Total	2,500,000 acres
Grand total	**19,000,000 acres**

Now clearly McEwen lost some acreage along the way; neither the maps he used nor the then Scottish land registry, known as Sassines, were anything like complete enough to give him 100% accuracy. Andy Wightman has been able to advance the figures because of better records in the new Scottish land registry, and better general information, but still falling well short of 100% information as he indicates in his book.

When McEwen's *Who Owns Scotland* was published, many of McEwen's critics charged him with inaccuracy, including John Christie of Lochdochart, a senior member of the Royal Scottish Forestry Society. McEwan had been the only working forester ever to be president of the society, yet Christie wrote the following critique in its journal:

> It is sad that the family and friends of a very old man cannot dissuade him from exhibiting in print his envy of those more fortunate, hard working and thrifty than himself and his ignorance of an industry in which he claims to have worked for a lifetime . . . My main regret is that the early thinnings of privately owned and managed woods may have been pulped to produce the paper upon which this silly little booklet was published.

Twenty-five years on, Wightman found himself the victim of the following veiled warning in the Scottish Landowners Federation Bulletin of September 1995.

PUBLICATIONS ON WHO OWNS SCOTLAND

> From time to time members may receive request from authors for details of their landholdings. Before providing or confirming any information, members

should consider very carefully the use to which it may be likely to be put. Where owners do not wish to cooperate and are asked to confirm or alter inaccurate information provided by an author, they may wish to respond simply by stating that the information is inaccurate.

In practice, of the 258 owners contacted, only nine, representing less than 6% of the owners and 13% of the acreage, were unhelpful, according to Wightman. In a follow-up note he shows how landowners, many of whom had criticised and discredited John McEwen's work for its inaccuracies, were prone to wild inaccuracies themselves. For instance, the Brahan estate in Ross-shire was quoted in the Scottish Landowners Federation journal at 4000 acres by the estate's own forestry advisor, yet when Wightman approached the estate he was told the figure was inaccurate. When he was interviewed in *The Field*, Paul van Vlissigen, the owner of the Letterewe Estate in Wester Ross, was credited with owning 100,000 acres, a figure he agreed with *The Field* was correct. But when Wightman checked the maps and records the figure was 81,000 acres.

John McEwen had produced a vital set of facts, wholly in the public interest, that neither government nor academia had seen fit to produce. The government, in the general sense of those who had ruled Scotland since 1872, have a formal duty to the public interest to provide a land registry which is accurate, accessible, comprehensive and complete. This the government of Scotland, nor the Government of the UK, did not do and does not currently propose to do. Any inaccuracies in McEwen were minor compared with the bright shining default of successive governments. And no less negligent were the Scottish academic establishment, whose agricultural, economic, political, social science and history departments had no less a duty to their own specialisations, and to Scotland generally, to maintain the information in the returns and keep it updated.

The key figure in John McEwen's book is the total of families owning estates of more than 1000 acres. This he calculated to be 1739, down just 19 on 1872. It tells us clearly, that, though the acres had been trimmed, in some cases significantly, there had been almost no change at all in the way the land of Scotland was pre-dominantly owned, which was by a very small number of families. In practice, there had been some changes amongst the families, with great landowners like the Breadalbanes and the Lovats now almost departed from the scene. In some cases (less than 100 in total), the older families had been replaced by new owners from south of the border, and more interestingly still, from abroad.

But the pace of change was extraordinarily slow. The Scottish establishment, predominantly a land-owning, aristocratic elite, weathered wars and economic crashes, and 100 years after the Returns were published, were still in control of most privately owned Scottish land and remain so today. And to show that the claim to arrogance amongst the aristocracy is not dead, hear how they treated John McEwen.

In 1967 he had been given the opportunity to find out who the landowners were in Perthshire, his own county. The local Fabian society backed the project with a little money as did several people, all living in the county. As McEwen recounts it,

> We thought it would be a simple project to complete. It took us four years' gruelling work and even then we did not come near completing the task. Our pamphlet, 'The Acreocracy of Perthshire – Who owns our land?' (written by Alasdair Steven in conjunction with a small committee, published in 1971) tells how we were thwarted and obstructed in our researches.

In 1995 Andy Wightman began his revision of John McEwen's work, a monumental task, despite what McEwen had done. And he encountered the same massive arrogance and unwillingness to help in some corners of the land-owning elite. Allathan Estates, who act for the Marquess of Huntly, a large landowner in Aberdeenshire, 'kindly informed me that my information was "substantially incorrect in all respects. Beyond what is a matter of public record, we do not feel it serves any purpose to divulge precise details of property titles."' The Dunecht estate, another large holding in the county then in trusteeship for the late Viscount Cowdray, sent the following response: 'The plans you sent are inaccurate in several major respects, but I am not authorised to assist you with specific information.'

In Angus, where Wightman encountered a good deal of goodwill and assistance he received the following response from the Strathmore Estate, the family estate of the Queen Mother: 'The acreage is a good deal lower than that suggested by you and the boundaries are correspondingly inaccurate. But, unfortunately it is not our policy to make public a great deal of information about the estate and I regret that I am unable to help you further.'

Despite all this resistance, Andy Wightman published his magnificent *Who Owns Scotland* in 1996. Dedicated to John McEwen, the book was serialised in the *Glasgow Herald*, and opened up the debate on the ownership of land further than ever before. His work on individual counties, combined with data from the 1872 Returns and from John McEwen, can be found in the section on Scotland in Part II of this book. The summary of his figures is as follows:

TABLE 13/4

ANDY WIGHTMAN'S BREAKDOWN OF LANDOWNERSHIP IN SCOTLAND[3]

	acres	% of total land in Scotland
Total land area of Scotland	19,068,631	100%
Urban Scotland	585,627	3.07%
Publicly owned land:		
Secretary of State for Scotland – Forestry Commission	1,660,923	8.71%
Secretary of State for Scotland – Agriculture, Environment and Fisheries Dept.	281,355	1.48%
Local authorities	152,771	0.80%
Scottish Natural Heritage	84,488	0.44%
MoD	50,429	0.26%
British Coal	40,000	0.21%
Highland & Island Enterprises	5802	0.03%
Total publicly owned	**2,275,768**	**11.93%**
Non publicly owned	**16,792,863**	**88.07%**

Note: Wightman correctly classifies the Crown Estate lands of 94,000 acres as private land.

The Financial Implications of Scotland's Land Distribution

The original Returns of 1872 highlighted the relationship in Britain as a whole between the ownership of any land at all, however small, and the non-landowning population.

The total population in the four countries in 1872 was about 26.9 million. Out of that number just over one million owned some land, but only 232,000 owned more than an acre. In other words, 98% of the population of Britain owned virtually nothing at all, and less than 2% owned 98% of everything. The situation in Scotland was, however, markedly different from the other three countries at the upper end, where so very few owned so very much, and where the 'landless' at the bottom were even more relatively numerous than in the other three countries. Such statistics, however, explain very little. It is nearly impossible to prove the negative statement, that this grossly unbalanced distribution of landownership was economically detrimental. The United Nations, however, refuses aid to some South American countries with a less intense concentration of land ownership than Scotland, unless land reform programmes, including the redistribution of land, are undertaken. The UN position arises from a mainly economic perspective, based on years of studies, reports and analysis, some of which have been done by UN economists, others by the IMF and the World Bank. And it is possible to assert that where land was plentiful and access to ownership relatively easy, huge economic progress was made, at least in the nineteenth century. The outstanding example of this situation is of course America.

The next most important example of the economic consequences of land redistribution is Ireland, particularly the Irish Republic. (Denmark, with GDP almost one third higher than that of the UK, is also an interesting example of the long term effects of land redistribution. Danish land was redistributed to the peasantry as early as 1800.) Ireland's agricultural industry thrives, and the value of its acreage outstrips that of the United Kingdom by as much as 50%.[4] Its industrial economy, however, now outstrips that of the Asian Tigers before they lost their teeth. The catalyst that initiated this growth was undoubtedly European Union grants.[5] These were, in practice, a substitute for the capital that the Irish/British landlords had not put into what were potentially some of the most productive acres in the world. Out of the growth in the agricultural sector initiated by EU capital Ireland invested in education, education, and education. And that huge expansion in education met a rising tide of widely spread wealth in the countryside. This soon led to a much more internationalised outlook amongst that tiny country's politicians, an outlook that led to the recruitment of the long-term descendants of famine and later, emigrants from America, to put their dollars and companies into Ireland. It worked.

What the Irish example suggests to Scotland is the importance of righting an ancient wrong, the theft of land in the past and the uneconomic concentration of ownership that followed. The Irish land commission was able to achieve this and allow a more economically natural distribution of land to occur. John McEwen proposed the nationalisation of the major estates, but this was and is a non-starter. Replacing bad private landlords with an inevitably bad state bureaucracy is no solution to anything, social or economic. But the forced break-up of the big ownerships, by acts similar to those which limit landholding on the continent, is essential. The placing of at least 80% of Scotland's acres at the disposal of its people, through a land commission, would make the market work for the people, by 'discovering' the natural number of people within the economy who would want to operate the land in whatever form. In this way the Irish example is instructive. The Irish land commission started its life long before independence, in 1880, with the first Westminster-sanctioned land purchase acts. Independence did not come for 41 years, and the real economic advantages of independence did not arrive for another 65 years, with membership of the European Community. In this sense Scotland stands where Ireland did in relation to its land in 1880. The land of Scotland is still held in large, inequitable, economically limiting blocs. The ownership of that land is mostly tied to a single political interest, which is Tory. That interest opposed Scottish devolution, and still does, even if it pays lip service to the overwhelming wishes of the Scottish people as displayed in the devolution referendum of 1997. And they remain clearly and implacably opposed to full independence.

However, it is by no means clear just how an ancient wrong is righted, other than with a Land Commission, particularly where the wrong is hundreds of years old, and where the injured are long dead and their heirs are dispersed. In this respect England has a major historical difference with Scotland. The three great English land grabs by William I, Henry VIII and Cromwell more or less defined the nature of large scale land ownership in that country, right up to the present time. Historically in Scotland the clans held large tracts of land, held in de facto trust by the clan chief. Over time the clan lands were converted into the private possessions of the clan chiefs, many of whom became 'British' aristocrats, especially around the time of the Union. The heart of the Scottish land grab, was the conversion of clan or community land into private land, by the aristocracy. By the time of the major clearances the community of the clan had been reduced to tenants of landowners operating under the principles of land ownership originating in England, where the concept of 'common ownership' was being obliterated by the enclosures.

However, it is possible to offer pointers towards an answer. First of all there is a general legal principle that stolen goods must be returned to their rightful owner. This principle has been much extended in recent years, in the realm of international antiquities, the stolen gold and belongings of Holocaust victims, and in other areas. However, in the case of Scotland land was taken up to three hundred years ago or more, and is now owned by the relatively innocent descendants of the thieves, carpetbaggers or fraudsters, and more recently the buyers, of those acres. Some of these buyers will be familiar with the concept of a legal limit on the scale of ownership of land, as in many cases they looked to Scotland to avoid limits on ownership in their home countries, limits that are legal under the European Convention on Human Rights. The case is made even more complex by the forced designation of much of the Highlands as 'sporting estates'. This should be a movable item in relation to the break up of the estates. Some sporting estates are only such because the owners made them such, often by driving the inhabitants out and into the emigrant ships to America. This is a new era. Tourism is not only about rich foreigners coming to Scotland to shoot over land that might have other, more interesting, applications such as small-scale crofts/allotments, local community fishing schemes and so on. The real potential for land use remains indeterminate until land is available and planning applications can be made for its use. But as factories close or are automated, as offices close while their workers go home and work from their front rooms, the beginnings of the next age are apparent. Those beginnings imply, and some statistics already show that the overall population will decrease, that city dwellers increasingly want to live in the country or by the coast, and that it can all be done with the maximum benefit to both the environment and to the population. This makes it even more urgent that Scotland should review its extraordinary land-owning pattern, and redistribute the land through the market to the people.

But it wasn't only land that was stolen. It was rights. The right to walk, the right to graze and other common rights that were never in dispute until the rapacious landowners of the eighteenth century captured the 'King in the South' and all political power and extinguished them through the enclosures, acts of prescription, commons division, entail and game laws. However, the heirs to those rights are easy to find and are available to receive the restored rights. For they are us, the people. This is one injustice that should and could be reversed with the minimum of compensation. The benefits obtained through the criminal usurpation of the law for private purposes 200 or more years ago, have been sufficiently enjoyed by the heirs to the crime, for the restoration to be done forthwith.

For this is how a nation builds itself, through hard choices that will be opposed by those who opposed Scottish devolution because they now stand to lose the historic proceeds of the high crime of selling Scottish independence at the time of the Union. For over 290 years they have corralled the population of Scotland in towns and cities and often in the slums they owned, in order to maintain a level of ownership of land that beggars description, and defies economic logic. The time has come to make the market discover just what the real economic level of landownership in Scotland should be, and to give the people of the country the chance to experiment with a larger involvement in land ownership and land use. Certainly, the experiment worked wonders in Ireland, even if it did take over 100 years to do so. The only limit on the exercise should be the continental one of about 200 hectares per unit, and maybe 2000 hectares where the site really is fit only to shoot over. The level of compensation should be at market level, and there should be no barrier to re-entry by existing owners. Indeed, so many of the existing owners have interests in England, and so many of the aristocrats are British, not Scottish, that it would be no surprise to see many of them take their money and run, leaving Scotland to the Scots as they left Ireland to the Irish.

The Ownership of Land in Scotland

In Scotland the Crown Estate owns over 95,000 acres. In his book *How Scotland is Owned*, Robin Callander raises the issue of the lands of the Crown in Scotland and the role of the Crown.[6] His approach is astonishing, not in Scotland, where the concept he articulates is accepted, but in England where it has not been addressed in recent history. What Callander says is that the Crown is not a detached entity which provides the state with a sovereign to carry out certain functions, but actually represents 'the Community of the Realm'.

> Sovereignty in Scotland is founded in constitutional law on the sovereignty of the people and, as popularly expressed over the centuries, the Crown is the representative of the Community of the Realm.

From this principle, well understood in Scotland, it follows that items like the lands of the Crown Estate are not owned by either the Crown or the Government, but are held in trust for the people. Callander puts it thus:

> In Scotland's system of land tenure, under the Crown's sovereign rights, parts of the territory . . . are held inalienably in trust for the people of Scotland in the Crown's name.

This contrasts sharply with the disputed ownership of the Crown Estate in England, where the Queen has made her personal rights to the estate perfectly clear, and where Parliament has conceded that right in the Coronation Act at every Parliament. No question of the people here, but of the primeval land greed that drove ancient bandits and made the more successful into sovereigns.

Worse still, there is no record of the British Government ever having asserted either a 'people's right' or a 'community right' or an ownership in trust for the people, by the sovereign. These are all expressions that are absent from the constitutional literature in England. Indeed, it is the Scottish understanding of the Crown that rings most true on two counts. In the first count, the older one, sovereigns were elected by the chiefs of tribes, who themselves had been elected, quite often by the entire adult membership of the tribe. There was no hereditary principle. And, as reflected in the Scottish tradition, the sovereign represented the people, and drew his or her power from the people, not from God as the medieval system supposed. On the second count, it is perfectly clear that all power in modern states arises from the electorate. The rest is historic fiction. We the people are the power, as the constitution of the United States proclaims, reflecting both the Scottish as well as a more modern understanding of authority.

But despite this well-established principle Scotland persisted until devolution with a form of landownership that exists nowhere else in the modern world. This was feudal tenure, and the words mean what they say. All ownership in Scotland operates to a greater or lesser extent under the hierarchical principle of feudalism. Callander explains it:

> Feudal land ownership in Scotland is a hierarchical system within which all the rights of land ownership derive from the highest authority in Scotland. In legal theory this is God, but in practice it is the Crown who is taken as the ultimate owner of all of Scotland. The Crown is known as the Paramount Superior and all other owners are known as vassals of the Crown.

Very simply put, most Scottish land ownership had a structure of feudal superiors inserted into it, with the Crown at the top. Each of the superiors above the vassal, the actual de facto owner on the site, could insert additional conditions on ownership, such as retaining the ownership of mineral rights and holding onto a right to sell or build. Not unpredictably, this means that the apparent owner of a piece of land is in fact often sharing ownership and conditions of ownership with a pyramidical structure of additional owners and with a burden of conditions paralleled only in the leasehold structure in the south of England, but never to the extent it was in Scotland. There is in fact not a lot of difference between Scottish feudal rights and English leasing rights, save in the way that the Scottish feudal system has been promoted to cover most of Scotland, by those who own most of Scotland, the 1200-odd families who emerge in the Returns and then in McEwen and Wightman. There is a very instructive analysis in Callander of the way these 1200 families have waxed and waned over the last 800 years. No rebel he, as someone who has worked with the Prince of Wales, but even he has made the following remarks:

> The pattern of land ownership in a country is a telling measure of its system of land tenure and it is no coincidence that Scotland is both the only country in the world with a feudal system of land tenure and the country with the most concentrated pattern of large scale private estates.

In an even more telling paragraph, he develops his theme.

> The ownership of land in Scotland has always granted wide-ranging rights over that land and these rights have conferred economic, social and political advantages on the holders. However, within Scotland's system of feudal tenure, the distribution of those rights between land owners does not coincide with the

pattern of land holdings on a map. The owners of land do not own their land outright and their authority over their land has always been constrained not only by the general laws of the country, but also by the nature of their feudal title to their land.

He quotes a nineteenth-century authority on land ownership and management in Scotland, Sir John Sinclair, who stated that 'In no other country in Europe are the rights of proprietors so well defined and so well protected.'

And they still are, making their position exceptional amongst their fellow citizens, granting them rights that other citizens do not have, and sustaining a system so archaic that even the Vatican does not use it. The key reform of principle ought to be that ownership of land should neither directly nor indirectly, advantage one citizen above another, nor confer any rights not available to non-landholding citizens. The ownership of property should confer no rights, other than those contained in the European Convention of Human Rights, and should grant no rights to determine the behaviour, economic or personal, of any citizen, other than within the ordinary law.

And there is a very practical consequence. With the 1200 families almost certainly inserted in almost every single land title in Scotland, they held a hidden power to intimidate or coerce their feudal inferiors into doing what they wanted, economically and politically. And to some degree they still can, despite the secret ballot. Robin Callander's book helped persuade the new Scottish Parliament to carry out Labour's electoral commitment to law reform in relation to Scottish land. Originally, there was no guarantee that Labour would have a majority in the Scottish parliament, and with the Tories against, and the Liberal Democrats and the Scots Nationalists luke warm the prospects were not promising. In the event the coalition of Labour and the Lib Dems has abolished the worst of the abuses inherent in a system that should have ended in the sixteenth century or before.

Callander deliberately avoided the issue of land distribution, the heart of many UN aid programmes in the developing world. But this is the key economic issue. He perceptively argued that the issue of law reform and of land redistribution are best kept separate. But they cannot be separated in the long run and this is the great challenge facing a devolved Scotland: to right old wrongs, to redistribute land in an economic and equitable way, to the maximum advantage of the whole people of Scotland and not just to halt at the ending of the feudal abuses.

Scotland has had three great chroniclers to show the way; the late John McEwen, Andy Wightman and finally, Robin Callander. The rest of the United Kingdom has not been so lucky.

Chapter Fourteen

Ireland
Land, prosperity and nation building

'Forever henceforth, the owners of our soil must be Irish'
James Fintan Lalor, January 1847.[1]

IN 1845 THE native Irish peasantry owned less than half of one percent of the land of their country. Five years later, one quarter of the Irish peasantry were dead of famine and plague, and another quarter had fled the country, or were in the process of doing so. By 1997, 87% of the citizens of the Irish Republic, almost all of whom are descendants of famine survivors, owned 97% of the land, either as home owners or family farmers.

What a difference 150 years makes.

History is a long game, rarely understood in the short play. In 1847, James Fintan Lalor, a nationalist rebel smallholder from one of Ireland's then poorest counties, Laois, saw the long game of Irish history in an issue that has done more to shape the real nature of modern Ireland than any subsequent nationalist uprising. Lalor, who died in 1849 of bronchial pneumonia shortly after the failure of a minor insurrection, partly led by him, in which a rebel and a policeman died, sowed the seeds of his ideas in a series of letters and articles directed at the dominant political organisation of the time, the Young Ireland Movement. They had a profound effect, but it is only now that we can measure the effect of what he advocated.

The Landowning Republic of Ireland

The Republic of Ireland is an area of 17.4 million acres. Some 9.6 million acres of that is farmland, 1.1 million acres is woodland and 108,000 acres are covered by water. The rest is mountain, bog and urban land. The country has a population of 3.5 million people.[2] The indigenous population is homogeneous and owns the country in a unique way. Private home ownership in the Republic stands at 82.2% of all homes. There are 149,000 farms in the Republic, of which 97% are family owned, at an average size of 64 acres. The country is super stable both socially and politically, despite 30 years of guerrilla war just over its northern border. It has the lowest crime rate in Europe – hardly a surprise, given the level of personal property ownership. Property owners tend to go along with laws which protect their main asset, property. At the time Lalor wrote his words in 1847 the indigenous population owned virtually nothing, certainly less than one half percent of the country. Now they own it all. The basis of ownership is use: use of urban land for homes, use of rural land for farming. There is no gap between ownership and use. The owners are the users. Landlords are the missing element. The Irish Republic has no community charge or rates system. Water is free. Real unemployment in the Irish Republic is probably zero and there is a skill and labour shortage.[3]

Compare this with the UK, especially England and Wales. The land area of these two countries is 33 million acres. More than 99% of the population of 51.6 million people live in an area of between 2.4 million acres and 3.3 million acres (in the range 7.5% to 10% – more accurate figures being simply unavailable from any source, Government or private) of the two countries. Between 1990 and 2000 more than 500,000 of the 23 million homes in the UK were repossessed. Home ownership officially stands at 66.9% and has grown by only 1.1% since 1990. Half of that growth is accounted for by the sale of council homes to their occupants, yet a significant number of those sales have been a disaster for the purchasers, who have seen the value of their home fall, and in many cases become unsaleable. If the repossessions are extracted, the ten year record in home ownership growth is 0.5% or just above.

Of the remaining acres of England & Wales, about 26.3 million acres are farmed by 175,238 farming families or persons.[4] Of this number, a total of 9684 families or persons own holdings of under 2.2 acres. About one quarter of the farms, some 36,429, are rented, while two thirds, 138,809 in number, are owner-occupied. A pointer towards the scale of concentration in large, mostly inherited, estates, is easy to extract from the figures. For the whole of England and Wales there are only 6560 'farms' of over 450 acres, but each of those farms averages over 1200 acres. In addition, from figures recently available, the number of owners of farms of over 1729 acres has become available. According to MAFF there are 793 of these farms, each with an average size of 2670 acres. This figure changes dramatically if the overall number of holdings over 1729 acres for Britain as a whole is divided into the acreage. The average size of the 'farms' in this category rises to 4484 acres. The UK is the only country in Europe with either this scale of ownership, or with farms of this size. These large 'farms' cover a total of 8.8 million acres. What should be considered with this figure is the figure for rented farms, 47,365, covering a total of 12.9 million acres. Most of those rented farms are rented out by families who own most of the farms over 741 acres. Which means that over 28 million acres of the UK are probably owned by around 8100 families.

Taking England alone, where urban pressure is the greatest and the economics of basic farming are at their weakest, there are 4285 families who own farms larger than 741 acres. Those families own 6.2 million acres. If we assume that most of the rented land is rented by this group, then we can say that under 5000 families own over 13 million acres of England, about 40% of the surface area of the country. That acreage is worth about £39 billion[5] and if an allowance of 1% is made for development potential (at around £500,000 an acre) then those 5000 families are looking at gains of £65 billion. It also makes the average landowning family worth about £8 million each, and worth up to £21 million each if the development potential became real.

The group which can probably be considered the real farming community in England and Wales are the owners of farms that run from 2.2 acres to 440 acres. The total number is 119,010. They own between them just 10 million acres. The average acreage is 90 acres. It is not all that different from the 149,500 farming families who own the agricultural land of the Irish Republic.[6] But what England and Wales have, that the Republic does not have, is a final tier of just 5000 families who own over 40% of all agricultural land, and who derive the bulk of their revenues from renting the land. The scandal is that the UK farm subsidy does not go to support farming families, but to support rents paid to estate owners.

By separating farmers from landowners, it becomes possible to look at the real cost of supporting genuine farming in England and Wales. To give the 119,010 families whose farms run from 2.2 acres to 440 acres the same direct subsidy as that given to Irish farmers by the EU would cost around £1.3 billion as opposed to the £4 billion currently handed out by MAFF/DEFRA. To give each family a direct subsidy of £100 per acre would cost a little over £1 billion. By restoring real world economics to the owners of land, or what might be better described as the owners of huge capital assets, would involve a saving to the exchequer of up to £3 billion, and the beginnings of rationality in the land market.

In Wales and England in 1872, and little changed from 1847, 972,836 people owned something, however small, while 18.4 million people owned nothing at all. A mere 269,547 people owned everything over an acre. Currently, at least one third of rural England and Wales has an owner who rents it to the user. The same applies to urban or residential land, where approximately 35% is rented. The change from 'tenant' to owner in England and Wales in the period 1872–1998 is less than 30%. The notional land wealth of the average English individual is £1714. The average 'land' worth of the average Irish individual is £14,800.[7] The average family unit in England and Wales pays over £500 a year in community charge or rates, no matter the extent of acreage they own.

To calculate the change in levels of ownership in the UK over the interval since 1872 is very difficult, but a few facts from Devon may help to illustrate the level of stagnation in the UK between 1872 and today. In 1872, Devon had a population of 601,374 people, of whom 10,162 owned more than one acre of land, 21,647 owned less than an acre and 569,565 owned nothing at all. In Devon's countryside, which now occupies about 1.3 million acres of the county's total of 1.5 million acres, there are now 11,001 farms, against 10,162 in 1872. Assuming that general UK statistics apply and that one third of those farms are tenanted and two thirds are family owned, the change in the ownership of Devon's farmland has been at most 8% over a period of more than 126 years. In Ireland it has been an average of 833%.

Homeownership looks better until the figures are analysed. In 1872 there were a total of 105,200 'dwellings' in Devon. There are now 449,000. The population has risen by about 66%, and the number of houses by around 300%. Of the current Devon housing stock, about 65% is privately owned, with about 35% rented by public or private bodies. There are no statistics for home ownership in 1872, but assuming that the owners of land also owned a dwelling, which ought to be approximately correct for statistical purposes, there was an absolute maximum of just under 28% home ownership in 1872.

The nearest county to Devon in size in Ireland is Galway. In 1872 Galway, with 1.4 million acres, had a population of 228,615 people and 42,199 dwellings. But of that total only 1235 people owned anything at all, while 97% of the population owned neither home nor land. Unlike Devon, the population of Galway has fallen by 27% to 180,304 but the number of farms has risen by almost 1516% to 16,244 and the number of homes to 49,916. Of these homes, only 14,886 have a mortgage, and 24,450 are owned outright. Of 2852 homes rented from the council, 1771 are currently being bought by their owners. Only 9.8% of the homes of Galway are not owned by their occupants. The remaining 90.2% are owned by their occupants with a mere 40% having a mortgage.

Essentially these figures indicate that popular capitalism based on personal ownership of property for use, at least within the family, has risen by over 75% in urban Ireland, and by well in excess of 90% in rural Ireland. In England, on the other hand, rural capitalism has hardly advanced, with farm ownership static and still dominantly in the hands of the family descendants of the owners shown in the 1872 returns.

Urban home ownership in the UK has advanced, but much more slowly and to a much lesser extent than in Ireland, with the Thatcher/Major recessions giving a warning that meaningful growth in home ownership has stalled almost completely. In 1980 the number of owner-occupied homes in Great Britain as a whole was 11.6 million. Sixteen years later, in 1996, it was 16 million, an increase of 4.4 million. Two million of that increase is accounted for by the sale of council homes to their occupants. During those years the volume of rented accommodation offered by Housing Associations rose by 600,000 units, from 404,000 units in 1980, to 1,092,000 in 1996. The number of repossessions between 1990 and 1997 was 420,460 units.

What the figures really show is this. Between 1980 and 1990 there was a 10% rise in home ownership, from 11.6 million homes out of a total housing stock of 20.9 million to 16 million homes out of an increased stock of 23.9 million homes. The impetus for this rise was laid in the 1960s and 1970s, and weathered the first Thatcherite recession fairly well. Repossessions, at 6860 in 1982, peaked at 26,300 in 1986 and fell back to 15,800 by 1989. But in 1990 repossessions rose sharply to 43,890 and peaked at 75,540 in 1991. Between 1990 and 1996, however, the number of homeowners increased by just 1.1%, a total of less than one million homes, half of it accounted for by a transfer of council homes to their tenants. The rise in homeownership, based on newly built homes, was about half of one percent, over a period of seven years. This is serious stagnation.

For almost the entire period, 1990 to 1997, the Tory promise of a property-owning democracy has been a lie. Ireland is a reasonable guide to what is achievable by way of home ownership, and the UK has ground to a halt 12.4% short of it. The UK has done this with a level of loss built into the system that is costing as many as 25% of all new homeowners intolerable grief by way of repossession. Meanwhile, mortgage tax relief for homeowners, a total of 6,584,190 families, has been withdrawn and up to £4 billion a year has been transferred to about 100,000 property owners in the countryside each year. During this time in Ireland domestic rates have been abolished and mortgage tax relief retained. The country has achieved a very high degree of economic and social cohesion through a system of land ownership based on family ownership and the virtually indivisible relationship between use and ownership. The rewards of growing asset value are widely distributed throughout the population and are the foundation stone for future development, social stability and some kind of egalitarian economic justice other than through the tax system.

In the coming years the moribund situation in the UK may have quite drastic social consequences, especially in the rural areas, which will need massive support either from British taxpayers via the British Government or from European taxpayers via the EU.

The Extermination of the Irish Peasantry

In 1847, when James Lalor wrote his prophetic words, Ireland was about to be plunged into the final, genocidal two years of the great famine. Lalor pointed out to the leaders of the nationalist movement that the famine, already killing tens of thousands of peasants a week and soon to kill and exile more than two million of them, made repeal of the union with England, then the dominant cause of the nationalist movement, irrelevant. The land question 'dwarfs down into a petty parish question' the repeal of the Union, he stated. 'A new adjustment is now to be formed, a new social order to be arranged; a new people to be organised.'[8]

In 1845 the potato crop was struck by blight and destroyed. Between 1845 and 1849 and in the decade after those years, the population of Ireland was reduced by half, from between 8 million and 9 million people, to about 4 million. Between 1 million and 2 million people died from famine and famine-related diseases and 2 million emigrated. The official figures given at the time by the Government and never corrected officially, claimed that 21,770 people had died of famine. As Cecil Woodham Smith so clearly demonstrates in *The Great Hunger*, and as most economists have clearly shown since, the famine grew not out of the loss of the potato crop, the staple food of nine million peasants who owned not a blade of grass between them, but out of the way the land was owned. Food production and the export of food from Ireland grew substantially during the famine. The country was teeming with game and fish. But woe betide the peasant caught taking a rabbit to feed his starving family. Seven years' transportation was the penalty. Parliament, law and 100,000 British troops (many of them Irish) in Ireland backed the landlords.

At that time the 616 major landlords who owned 95% of the island rented it to the peasants. In a country of 20.1 million acres, between 8 million and 9 million people owned nothing at all. In most of the country this mass of people rented a marginal number of acres, not in return for a share of the sale of the crops or cattle, but for the right to sow and reap a crop of potatoes on which they lived. The landlord took the non potato crop. A great number of the Irish peasantry had never seen coinage and in most of rural Ireland in 1845 there were no shops, or even towns such as dotted the English countryside. Any improvements on a peasant's holding in Ireland were the property of the landlord. And all tenants were tenants 'at will', and could be evicted at any time.

The American populist economist Henry George, writing in 1879,[9] claimed that 'The potato blight might have come and gone without stinting a single human being of a full meal. For it was not, as English economists coldly said "the imprudence of Irish peasants" that induced them to make the potato the staple of their food . . . They lived on the potato because rack rents stripped everything else from them.'

George described the status of the Irish peasantry as that of 'an abject slave'. While British economists, British politicians and the servile British press laid the entire blame for the catastrophe on the 'imprudence' of the Irish peasantry, British officialdom during the famine knew the facts full well, and knew them directly from the Queen's representative in Ireland, the Viceroy, Lord Clarendon. He made an appeal to the Prime Minister, Lord John Russell, against the policies of men like Charles Trevelyan, the Treasury secretary, and Charles Wood, the Chancellor of the Exchequer:

> Surely this is a state of things to justify you asking the House of Commons for an advance [of aid money], for I don't think there is another legislature in Europe that would disregard such suffering as now exists in the west of Ireland, or coldly persist in a policy of extermination.[10]

If the concept of 'genocide' and 'extermination' seems extreme, it is worth noting the words of Nassau Senior, an economic advisor to the British Government in the third year of the great famine: 'I fear that the famine in Ireland will not kill more than a million people, and that would scarcely be enough to do much good.'[11]

The British Government chose to lie and to blame the victims. For them the lie had become a habit. The lesson here is simple. Governments, all governments, lie. They lie even to their own servants, agents and to themselves. They lie to conceal actions taken to achieve covert policies injurious to the general good of the public. To roll the same theme forward to today, if 500,000 repossessions occur, it is because the government, once aware of the problem, decided that they should occur. Compared with the famine the repossessions of the 1990s pale into insignificance. But, like the Irish famine deaths and Diaspora, the repossessions were unnecessary, particularly in a country with 800,000 or more empty homes.

The Landowners of the Famine

What is important, however, is that these attempts to destroy the peasantry, by landlords, by nature, and by government, failed. And out of that failure has grown the most stable, most democratic, and now the most prosperous small state in Europe. The owners of Ireland now, at least that part of the island which is known as the Irish Republic, are the direct descendants of those peasants who survived the famine.

The owners of the major acreage of England, Wales and Scotland are the direct descendants of the landlords who destroyed their peasantry and who so very nearly did the same to the Irish. In Ireland, however, the relationship between the landlords and the natives was different to that in the rest of the UK. The Irish landlords, who were not so much the owners of Ireland as 'an alien conqueror', according to the Earl of Devon's commission in 1843, have vanished almost without trace. The results are quite astonishing.

The Return of Owners of Land for Ireland, published in 1876, covers the whole of the island of Ireland and includes Ulster, part of which is now Northern Ireland. Unlike the returns for England, Scotland and Wales, the Irish return does not include population figures, in either the provincial summary — Ireland was reported by county within each of the four historic provinces of Ulster, Munster, Leinster and Connaught – or in the final, countrywide summary. One reason for this was the continuing sensitivity of the British Government to the evidence that its figures for the depredations of the famine in Ireland were false beyond absurdity. The second was that, once more, the landless state of the Irish population was being shown to the world.

The largest landowner in Ireland, when the returns appeared, turned out to be Richard Berridge of Clifden Castle in Galway. He owned 160,152 acres in his home county and 9965 acres in neighbouring Mayo. In Middlesex he owned 321 acres and in Kent 79 acres. The second largest landowner was the Marquess of Sligo, with 114,811 acres. During the famine the Marquess for a time supported his tenants, and paid for the costs of the Westport workhouse. By 1848 he had had no rent for three years, had been without servants or a carriage since the start of the famine and was faced with either ejecting his tenants or being ejected himself. He chose the latter course. His descendant, Jeremy Ulick Browne, the 11th Marquess, sat in the House of Lords as Baron Monteagle until the ejection of the hereditaries. Most of the Sligo lands were bought by the Irish Land Commission, but the Marquess maintains his seat at Westport House in Mayo. The third largest landowner, Lord Ventry, held 93,629 acres of Kerry. His descendant, Andrew Wesley Daubeney de Molyens lives in Perthshire and does not appear in Andy Wightman's list of Perthshire landowners. He has no English title and did not sit in the House of Lords.

The fourth largest landowner in Ireland in 1876 was the Earl of Kenmare, MP for Kerry, and Lord Chamberlain to the Queen Empress Victoria. He owned 91,080 acres in Kerry, 22,700 acres of Cork and 4826 acres of Limerick. This peerage is long extinct. The fifth largest landowner was Sir Roger Palmer, an old Etonian Lieutenant General who was also MP for Mayo. He owned land in three Irish counties, Mayo, Sligo and Dublin, amounting to over 93,000 acres and land in five English and Welsh counties amounting to over 4000 acres. The title no longer appears in *Debrett's*. The sixth largest landowner in Ireland was the Duke of Leinster, the premier peer and Duke of Ireland and representative of the Geraldines, a great Norman Irish family. He owned 71,977 acres in Kildare and 1123 in Meath. Not one of the Duke's tenants was evicted during the famine and the duke was active from the day the potato blight first appeared, to the very end, in organising relief committees, often with his own money. His descendant, Gerald Fitzgerald, the 8th Duke, sat in the Lords, until ejected, as a Viscount, was a major in the 5th Royal Inniskilling Dragoon Guards and lives in Oxfordshire. Next on the list was the Earl of Bantry, who owned 69,500 acres of Cork. The title is extinct. The eighth largest landowner in Ireland was the Earl of Lucan, an absentee landlord who owned 60,570 acres of Mayo and land in Dublin, Surrey, Middlesex and Cheshire. He was a General in the Army, commanded the cavalry in the Crimea and at the charge of the Light Brigade and did a stint with the Russian army against the Turks in 1829. The 7th Earl, now succeeded by his son the 8th Earl, went missing in 1974 following the murder of the family nanny and he is presumed dead. His son sat as Baron Bingham until the ejection of the hereditaries. His ancestor was one of the most hated famine landlords.

The ninth largest landowner was the Marquess of Clanricarde, who owned 56,826 acres of Galway and was the local MP. His contribution to the Irish peasantry in the first year of the famine, 1845, was to ask for a coercion bill in the Lords. His request was granted. This enabled the Lord Lieutenant of a county to declare what amounted to martial law. It wasn't the first ever coercion bill, but as Lord Brougham remarked 'it possessed a superior degree of severity'.[12] A nationalist MP, William Smith O'Brien, attacked the bill in the Commons: 'famine was menacing Ireland and what the Government sent was not food but soldiers.' The Clanricarde title is long extinct.

The tenth largest landlord in Ireland was the Earl of Leitrim, an absentee living in Mayfair who owned 56,852 acres in Leitrim and Donegal, two of the worst hit counties during the famine. The title became extinct in 1952.

The 50 largest landowners in Ireland in 1876, most of whom had held their lands since before the famine, had holdings in excess of 22,658 acres each. A total of 616 landlords owned more than 3000 acres each and in total the 616 owned about 80% of the island.

From Landlord to Tenant

TABLE 14/1

THE OVERALL CHANGE FROM ESTATES TO FARMS IN IRELAND 1872–1998

Province	Farms 2.2 acres to over 200 acres 1998	Farms over 1 acre 1872	% change
Leinster	42,338	10,040	397
Munster	55,783	7677	626
Connaught	48,861	2941	1516
Cavan	6673	716	831
Donegal	10194	1003	916
Monaghan	5199	637	716

Note:
The population of the Irish Republic at 3.5 million is 0.5 million people less than the figure for the estimated population in 1876 (4,050,062).

TABLE 14/2

HOME OWNERSHIP IN THE REPUBLIC OF IRELAND 1998

County	Total dwellings	Council Rented	Private Rented	Owner-occupied Mortgage	Unmortgaged
Province of Leinster					
Carlow	11,135	942	680	4380	4792
Dublin	310,076	43,141	36,579	152,099	71,202
Kildare	32,589	2117	1956	18,008	9387
Kilkenny	20,294	1547	1018	8014	9151
Laois	14,130	1182	595	5159	7021
Longford	8827	799	392	2936	4356
Louth	25,728	2746	1495	11,801	9085
Meath	28,596	1669	1182	14,105	10,450
Offaly	15,951	1225	708	6147	7371
Westmeath	17,477	918	1279	7488	7127
Wexford	28,099	2880	1567	9926	12,725
Wicklow	27,756	2762	1675	12,702	9793
Province of Munster					
Clare	26,188	1516	1460	9894	12,413
Cork	118,326	10,803	9777	46,829	47,346
Kerry	35,677	2926	2124	10,027	19,200
Limerick	46,174	4598	3423	18,881	17,374
Tipperary	38,036	3723	1771	13,738	17,441
Waterford	26,507	3114	1813	11,158	9648
Province of Connaught					
Galway	49,916	2852	4362	16,657	24,450
Leitrim	8,112	472	288	1899	5099
Mayo	32,457	1707	1532	9150	19,025
Roscommon	15,704	568	540	4826	9237
Sligo	16,253	1070	1160	5722	7720
Province of Ulster					
(Irish Republic only)					
Cavan	15,446	784	713	4406	8903
Donegal	35,757	2290	2588	9633	19,727
Monaghan	14,512	795	747	5122	7235
Ireland	**1,019,723**	**98,929**	**81,424**	**421,107**	**387,288**

Notes:
Figures provided by the Irish Government Statistics Office. Comparative figures for Northern Ireland are not available.
Total home ownership is 79.2% (1998) and is said to have risen to 81.7% in 2001. 52% of homes have a mortgage; 48% are mortgage free.
When Dublin and the three surrounding 'dormitory' counties are excluded, the percentage of overall home ownership rises to over 90% with only 38% having a mortgage while 62% have no mortgage.

During the famine records in Ireland fell into an extraordinary state of disrepair, some of it deliberate. The final tally for famine deaths at 21,770, a mere million or two short of the actual figure, is an example. What we do know fairly reliably is that about five million acres of land, one quarter of the whole country, changed hands in the years after the famine. This was mostly due to the bankruptcy of landed estates, many in the west and south of Ireland. Initially, this helped the native Irish not a whit. *The Times* noted on the passing of the Encumbered Estates Act that, 'In a few years more a Celtic Irishman will be as rare in Connemara as is the Red Indian on the shores of Manhattan.'[13]

The Encumbered Estates Act in 1849 was an attempt to sell off those estates which had become bankrupt during the famine, or were so indebted as to be unworkable, by removing the burden of debt for a new owner. It was hoped there would be an influx of British capitalists and highly skilled Scottish and English farmers to replace ineffective landlords. In all, between 1849, when the act was passed, and 1857, 3000 estates were sold. But as Professor Beckett remarks in his book *The Making of Modern Ireland 1603–1923*, 'There was no influx either of landlords or of capital. Of some 7200 purchasers only about 300 came from England or Scotland and they contributed less than £3,000,000 [£210,000,000 today] to the total purchase money of £20,000,000 [£1,400,000,000 today].'[14] Professor Beckett goes on to point out that these new investors were '. . . for the most part speculators'. Furthermore, 'Bad as the old landlords had been, the new tended to be worse, and their conduct helped to embitter the agrarian struggle.' By 1869 the Chief Secretary of Ireland was told officially that the tenantry were being treated even worse by the new landlords than they had been by the old. The act had simply attracted a pack of rapacious speculators who tried to strip further the already naked tenantry.

To get moderately reliable figures about land ownership in Ireland we have to move on from the last year of the great famine, 1850, to 1876, when the Return of Owners of land was produced for Ireland. This was an interesting year because in that year the first move was made by the British Government to take on board the lessons of the famine and to begin the beginnings of a redistribution of land.

In an act passed that year, and known as the Landlord and Tenant Act, the government provided £347,480, the modern equivalent of £25 million, so that 469 tenants could buy a total of 34,924 acres of land. The tenants themselves advanced the equivalent of £16 million in cash to make up the total purchase price, the equivalent of £41 million. The average price of an acre was the equivalent of £1173, whereas the average price of an Irish acre nowadays is £4000 or more. This first real step in the direction of tenant ownership was executed through the Commissioners of Public Works.

Between 1881 and 1889, the British exchequer advanced £7.3 million, the modern equivalent of £365 million, so that Irish tenants could buy out their landholdings. Compared with the sums put up by the purchasers under the Landlord and Tenant Act, the cash lodged by the buyers was relatively small, just £229,904, or £11.4 million in today's terms. The 1881–9 acts placed a total of 702,435 acres in the hands of native farmers, in 16,629 holdings averaging 42 acres each.

Between 1891 and 1896 the government put up £10.3 million, the modern equivalent of about £515 million, to help a further 33,142 tenants to buy out their landlords. The alternative way to look at this was that the British Government was merely buying out its own bankrupt aristocracy, and at a generous price too. The average price per acre in modern money in the second round was £442 per acre, less than twenty years before, but well above the going rate by 1896.

The big push, however, came in 1903, when a six-year programme saw 171,263 tenants join the ranks of owner occupiers. Over the next six years, the British Government put up £63.6 million, the modern equivalent of about £3.1 billion. The price per acre was about £504, again a better rate than that obtaining generally. By 1909, roughly half of Ireland, 8 million acres, had been sold to native farmers, and 221,034 families were set on the road to personal property ownership. Much of the 'money' put up by the exchequer after 1889 was in the form of land bonds, the earlier schemes having been financed in cash. Between 1909 and 1919 the exchequer authorised the equivalent of another £550 million and 2.2 million further acres were bought by tenants, bringing the total purchases to over 10 million acres, about two-thirds of all the arable land in the country. It is worth noting that the scheme of sale and purchase went on, right through World War One and the Easter Rebellion.

In 1922, the Irish Free State, the precursor of the Irish Republic declared in 1949, was created. Between 1923 and 1965 a further sum of £47.6 million was spent by the Irish Government in buying out 4.4 million acres of landlord-owned holdings and selling them on to the tenants. This sum is much more difficult to translate into modern terms, but £1.1 billion is a rough approximation.

In the year 2000 the Irish Government finally wound up the Land Commission. This almost forgotten body, initially set up in 1861 by the British Government as a rent fixing institution, closed its doors having seen through the single most comprehensive transfer of land, from landlord to peasant, in recorded history. Of the 17.3 million acres which comprise the land area of the Republic, of which 14 million acres was farmland, 97% was owned by landlords in 1881. In the space of about 60 years, from 1870 to 1930, 13 million acres of that farmland had been taken over and sold to owner occupiers. This transfer created about 413,000 tenant farmers and families, all living on their own farms.

The entire price of buying a nation for its people was between £5 billion and £7 billion, around two years of EU subsidy to modern British agriculture. The average price paid was the equivalent of around £330 an acre.

The other side of this coin is that a very small group of 'English' landlords, amazingly similar to the same small group now drawing most of Britain's EU agricultural subsidy, were bailed out to the tune of £5 billion from their bankrupt post-Elizabethan colonial possession.

The Landowners of Twenty-First Century Ireland

The average farm bought by those pioneer tenants was approximately 74 acres in extent. The average size of an Irish farm nowadays is 64.2 acres. The Irish Ministry of Agriculture modifies this statistic by pointing out that 48% of all Irish farms are under 44 acres. According to the Irish Government, the average income per family from a farm in Ireland in 1996 was £10,920. The survey of households on the other hand showed that the average gross household income for farm households was £18,582 per year, compared with the average industrial wage in Ireland of £15,000 a year. The average industrial wage in England is £22,000.

One notable feature of Irish farm income is the percentage that arises from EU funds. By 1997 about 47% of the family farm income of £18,582 came directly from EU funds. What is radically different about this application of EU funds, when compared to Britain, is that in Ireland it reaches an integrated, related part of the human factor in the economy. The number of small farms means that this income is widely distributed amongst the working rural population. It does not go, as it does in Britain, to reinforce the fortunes of those who are both the dominant and disproportionate owners of acres, and whose acreage confers no benefit on the population at large, with whom the landowners have few ties of blood or any other social relationships. And there is another, profound difference. In Ireland, as in many other EU countries, the EU payments go directly to the actual people who by their normal labour in the fields maintain the working, living countryside. In Britain the bulk of the EU payments go to those who rent out the countryside, and who earn their day to day bread and butter from that rent, not from tilling fields and herding cattle. And the long term purpose of that rental is to await the regular and usually predictable lottery bonanza which arises when yet another slice of aristocratic, rural Britain, is re-zoned for urban development.

It is interesting to see what has happened to the 413,000 peasant farmers who became owners of their own farms through the land acts up to about 1930. By 1975 their numbers were down to 228,000, a drop of almost half from the peak of 413,000. In 1998, the number had fallen to 149,500, a fall of almost three quarters from the original 413,000 figure and a drop of almost half again on the 1975 figure. This represents two factors. The original farms created by the schemes were far too small, and emigration, especially in the western counties, thinned out the population continuously between 1850 and 1990. Joining the EU in 1973 led to a further round of consolidation, buttressed by a whole range of targeted schemes which offered tax advantages and cash incentives to farmers to increase their holdings and to retire early. The average farm size is still clearly far too small at 64.2 acres, but further consolidation will impact severely on the social structure erected in Ireland over the past 150 years.

What the figures tell us is that farming is neither financially justifiable nor economically meaningful. With the Irish example of a quarter of family farm income coming from EU grants, and about half from non farming activity, the writing is on the wall and has been for some time. The main point in supporting farming is to secure a basic food supply for the population in the event of some unforeseen international disaster. The next purpose is to ensure that the social infrastructure of the countryside stays intact. But if farming, especially on small to medium sized farms, is not viable now, it will be a lot less so as the European Union expands eastwards, bringing within its remit the vast grain fields of Russia, the Ukraine and other former East Bloc states. A critical decision that should have been made years ago about the very meaning of farming in the older states of Europe, is now becoming more than urgent. And the urgency is greatest where the failure to reform land ownership has led to the urban population funding the rural population on a massive scale, out of all proportion to the numbers involved. This is particularly so in England, where the urban population are corralled onto a small amount of grossly overpriced land, by legislation, not supply and demand or any other rational economic factor.

The *Guardian* reported in Autumn 1998 that something like 25,000 farms in England and Wales were likely to go under in the farming recession of that year. This is just under 10% of the British total, and would have involved at least 3.7 million acres either reverting to landowners, or being made part of ranch-sized holdings such as have become commonplace in East Anglia. The British Government has no solution to this crisis, because it has no analysis of the land ownership structure underpinning Britain itself, especially that in the countryside. In Ireland, a structure has evolved that makes a degree of economic, social and national security sense, entirely because the state made sure that all those who wanted to own and run a farm could do so. In this way economically and socially absurd landholdings were bought out and the population got ready for the changes of the twentieth century. There is an urgent need in the UK for a new analysis, and for all land holdings over a certain size to be deprived of all subsidy, tax advantages and all artificial financial aid from government. This would force the owners to sell down and create a more rational market in land. Land held purely for letting needs to be made subject to some form of taxation that would at least force the owners onto parity with their penalised urban neighbours.

The readjustments are not just in the rural area, but in the relationships between rural and urban landowners. In the urban areas of Ireland 79.2% of homes are owned by the occupiers, with mortgages on 52% of those houses, a little over half the total. In other words, 48% of homes in the Irish Republic have no mortgage. This is the highest level of home ownership in Europe and probably in the world. By comparison, home ownership in the UK is about 65% of all homes and is in decline – 500,000 repossessions in the past ten years have lowered that figure from around 67% in 1990. More than 70% of all UK homes bear a mortgage.

Ireland, despite being caught in the slipstream of the UK's fiscal irresponsibility in the 1980s and early 1990s, managed to avoid the disaster of widespread repossession. This is at least partly due to the retention in Ireland of a degree of social responsibility by the lending institutions. It is also due to a rooted, though perhaps visceral is a better word, understanding by both the lending institutions and the government that the level of social irresponsibility tolerated in England would not be tolerated in Ireland. This understanding by the financial institutions owes much to Ireland's unique experience of genocide at the hands of landlords, but it also owes much to an Irish perception that the supreme measure of real social advance in any modern society is the level of personal property ownership achieved by the population, often expressed as a home, or a working farm. The same perception is evinced in many progressive European states, including most of the Nordic states and Switzerland.

Unlike the UK, urban and rural Ireland are umbilically connected by ties of blood – there are very few urban dwellers in Ireland without a cousin, more often many cousins, who are farmers in the hinterland. The word 'farmer' is used definitively. There are almost no landowners in Ireland in the sense in which landowners still exist in the UK. Those who own the land in Ireland occupy the land and till it. Their cousins man and work the shining new software and computer factories that dot but do not crowd, the landscape. Visits to the city are most often visits to the family, and vice versa.

The current ownership figures for rural Ireland are interesting, especially when compared with those for England and Wales. In the two UK countries about one third of the 175,238 farms are tenanted. This is in a rural area of 26.3 million acres. In Ireland, in a rural area of about 11 million acres, there are 149,500 farms.[15] More than 97% are owner-occupied and owner farmed. According to the Irish Department of Agriculture the actual ownership is almost always by a family. There are very few tenant farmers. Most of the great landowners of modern England and Scotland, and to a lesser extent Wales, are aristocratic families and their cousins. Moreover, many are the descendants of the landlords who owned and occupied Ireland during the famine and for half a century afterwards. Their wealth comes from the possession of land, not from farming and using that land. Their prosperity has not been an integral part of British economic success for over a century,[16] but has been a financial parasite and social burden upon it. The capacity of the aristocratic landowners to retain their lands and treasures has not arisen from any productive use they have made of the land, or even from renting it out, but has come from trickling the rural land they own onto the urban market.

In this way they have been able to maintain gross accumulations of lands in the teeth of every form of normal economic reality throughout modern history, including the penal tax regimes of the UK in the aftermath of World War Two. Morally, they have never paid the price for extinguishing the British peasantry from the lands of the United Kingdom.

The message from Ireland 150 years ago, but relevant now in a different way, is that no population is safe while the bulk of the land is held by a small number of landlords. They may no longer be able to kill large swathes of the population to protect their ownership, but they can continue to rob the population through sophisticated raids on the public purse, and they continue to be able to decimate the real users of rural land, tenant farmers.

The Republic of Ireland has, more or less, prepared itself for the post industrial world, in which employment in manufacturing or allied undertakings will dwindle away and in which whole industries will arise and vanish over the course of a decade or two. It has done this at root, by having a balanced distribution of land ownership based on use. The UK has failed to do this and is in danger of being unable to manage the future as the population, trapped in towns designed with manufacturing in mind, no longer function. All UK economics remain a derivative of the unreconstructed capitalism of the eighteenth and nineteenth centuries.

The country that paid the highest price for the ruthless application of landlord capitalism supported by the law, was Ireland. Trevelyan, the cabinet secretary and controller of Ireland for most of the famine years, put capitalist principles before everything and then used the law to enforce that form of capitalism, in the form of the landlords, in Ireland. Two million people died in just four years and two million fled the country. This was hardly an example of 'a steady increase of wealth and welfare for society as a whole'. To suggest that it was is to suggest that Irish peasants were not people, but some kind of sub humans, whose lives and deaths were too worthless to count. It is an enormous irony that real capitalism, achieved through the widest possible distribution of land amongst both the rural and urban population, has produced, one hundred and fifty years later, one of the stablest and most prosperous small states in Europe. And virtually the entirety of that state is owned by the survivors of the famine. But central to the current achievements of the Irish Republic was the removal of the landlords from the scene.

Chapter Fifteen

England and the Inner Empire

WHEN LABOUR WON the 1997 election, the UK was on the verge of losing Scotland from the Union. Tory MPs, characterised by ideological rigidities and attitudes inherited from the past, were unable to see that their very existence was the main stimulant to both opposition to London and support for Scottish independence. Had the Conservatives won the 1997 election, Scotland would almost certainly have moved decisively to the nationalist cause. Yet after four years of self government, the atmosphere in Edinburgh and Glasgow is notably brighter, economic growth is apparent, and the two cities resemble nothing so much as Dublin, the capital of the Celtic fringe. What Blair has proved is that the centre can still control the periphery, if the controls are relaxed. What the periphery is proving is that it can thrive with the dead paw of London off its back. What Blair has yet to prove is that this new 'lite' control can produce the economic growth that Ireland has, and that is clearly possible in both England and Wales. To move beyond his constitutional reshaping of the UK, Tony Blair has to find a path to growth. He has to find the bottlenecks within the system.

The biggest economic bottleneck in the UK is land, its regulation, cost and availability. The key institutional support for the status quo, for the subsidies, the offshore capital gains tax dodge, the planning rigidities, the defective land registry, was the House of Lords. In removing the hereditaries Tony Blair has removed both the majority of the present landowning elite, and the residue of the Imperial landowning class, from the House of Lords and thus from Parliament. Their ancestors invented Britain and the Empire, and owned most of the latter. Out of the top 500 landowners in the UK in 2001, 187 had seats in the House of Lords until 1999. Of the top 100 aristocrats in the modern day list of top landowners on p.391, 68 had seats in the House of Lords until 1999. Of the 68 only two survived the Blair cull: one duke, Norfolk, survived as a full member of the House of Lords because of his office as Earl Marshall of England; the Earl of Home, son of a former Prime Minister, was the other temporary survivor from an internal election which produced a list of 90 elected hereditary peers who will sit until the final removal of all hereditaries, expected to occur during Labour's second term in office. Amongst those ejected by Blair was the richest man in England, the 6th Duke of Westminster. The total acreage owned by the 66 ejected peers is about 3,012,000 acres, the equivalent of almost four and a half average English counties. The total wealth of the 66 ejected hereditaries is approximately £16 billion.

Blair's eviction, while cutting the umbilical cord of history, was also an act of immense power in relation to the weight of wealth he put out on the street, and the ownership of modern acreage that he literally put out to grass. Money can and does buy influence in modern politics, but this was an immense and extraordinary demonstration of the implicit power of the people, even if it was mediated through the defective unwritten British constitution and the party system in the House of Commons. In the United States that weight of wealth would have almost certainly conspired, within the party system, to prevent such an alteration in the nature of power itself. Those who would trifle with Tony Blair should consider carefully the way he has 'trifled' with history, saving the union on the one hand

and ending forever the Parliamentary power of the richest group of individuals in the country on the other hand. By removing the hereditaries Blair unplugged the power cable between a landowner-dominated British history and Britain's future. Most commentators, unaware of the financial and political ties that connected history to the landowning hereditaries, and the continued depth and breath of that connection to the present ruling elite, especially the Conservative element of it, failed to see the profundity of the action taken by Blair.

Many books have been written about the 'power' of the aristocracy, and the extent of their influence in the mid to late nineteenth century, at the apogee of Empire. Most accounts start 'ad hominem', and few get to the root of that power, which lay in the possession of land backed up by laws that gave absolute powers over life and death to those who owned land. How absolute that power was became clear during the Irish famine, when the landlords either put to death by deprivation, or starved to death, over a million people and did so with impunity. But the scale and detail of how English aristocrats owned Ireland before the famine has never been so clearly visible as it is in the four tables below.

To illustrate exactly how this ownership worked, a table of the top ten landowners for each country, England, Scotland, Wales and Ireland, has been constructed from John Bateman's *Great Landowners*.[1] What the table reveals is the extent to which acreage held in Scotland, Wales and Ireland makes up the estates of the great English landowners. This is not reciprocated by any such counter holdings in the English heartland by the resident magnates of Ireland, Scotland and Wales, with the exception perhaps of Buccleuch and Sutherland, those most English of Scottish dukes and even then their holdings were proportionately tiny. The argument within this book that the imperial conquest sprang from a prolonged expansion out of England in the centuries after the Norman invasion and settlement, is enormously reinforced by the pattern, as much as the extent, of landholdings amongst the English landowners. It also shows the true nature of the English hold on both the inner 'empire' of Ireland, Scotland and Wales and by implication, the land lust underpinning the greater world empire. It also suggests that it was the loss of the Irish acreage which began the final decline from the pinnacle of Empire in the 1870s so well chronicled by David Cannadine in his book *The Decline and Fall of the British Aristocracy*.[2] But the Irish acreage was 'lost' in a curious way, with the British taxpayer putting up the modern equivalent of between £5 billion and £7 billion, ostensibly to enable Irish peasants to buy out their plots, but all of it handed out to these magnates and their families.

TABLE 15/1

THE TOP 10 ENGLISH LANDOWNERS IN 1872 AND THEIR ACRES WITHIN THE INNER 'FIRST' EMPIRE

	Landowner	Total land holding (acres)	Irish acres	Irish acres as a % of holding	Non English acres as a % of holding
1	Duke of Richmond*	286,149	Nil	Nil	93.9%
2	Duke of Devonshire*	198,572	60,033	30.2%	30.2%
3	Duke of Northumberland*	186,397	Nil	Nil	0%
4	Duke of Portland*	183,199	Nil	Nil	64.5%
5	Marquess Conyngham*	166,710	156,793	94.1%	94.1%

	Landowner	Total land holding (acres)	Irish acres	Irish acres as a % of holding	Non English acres as a % of holding
6	Sir John Ramsden	150,048	Nil	Nil	91.9%
7	Marquess of Lansdowne*	142,916	119,049	83.3%	89.6%
8	Baroness W. D'Eresby*	132,220	Nil	Nil	81.3%
9	Earl Fitzwilliam*	115,743	91,748	79.2%	79.2%
10	Lord Leconfield*	109,935	43,834	39.8%	39.8%

* The descendant is still a major landowner in 2001.

At the top of the list in 1872 was the Duke of Richmond and Gordon, who, despite a very Scottish title was a very British duke, with service in the Royal Horse Guards, as MP for Sussex, and membership of the Cabinet as Lord President of the Council. He owned a total of 286,411 acres, most of it in Scotland. His income was the modern equivalent of £5.5 million. There is one holding in England, in Sussex, of 17,117, acres. This was and remains the ducal seat. There are no Irish holdings, but vast holdings in Scotland. His successors' holdings today are put at a mere 12,000 acres, entirely in Sussex around the original English holding. What is worth noting, however, is that the present Duke of Richmond, the 10th, is probably richer by far than his ancestor was in 1872. The present duke's estate in Sussex is worth a minimum of £36 million as agricultural land alone, but it also contains the famous Goodwood car racing circuit, and is the scene of extensive industrial and urban development.

Second in the list in 1872 was the Duke of Devonshire, with almost 100,000 acres less, but over £7 million in income more, than the Duke of Richmond. Devonshire, whose successor still holds 73,000 acres today, held 198,572 acres in 14 counties, with just over 60,000 acres in Ireland. The Duke in 1872 was also a Member of Parliament, sitting mostly for seats on or near his acres. His income was the modern equivalent of £12.6 million a year. He held no land in Scotland or Wales. His enormous landholdings in Ireland were decimated by the land purchase acts, but his descendant, the 11th Duke, retains Lismore Castle and 8000 acres in Waterford. The castle was offered for rent during the 1980s at over £2000 a week and the value of the castle and lands is well in excess of £20 million. The present duke's heir, the Marquess of Hartington, is part of the super-rich Irish horseracing set, which includes Michael Smurfit, Dermot Desmond and Sir Tony O'Reilly. The *Sunday Times* assessment of the Duke's wealth, at £270 million, is probably seriously understated. As Cannadine notes, the Duke made sales during the 1980s of about one twentieth of the art at Chatsworth, the family seat, for £30 million.

The third ranking landowner in England in 1872 was the Duke of Northumberland, a descendant of Henry VII through his Queen, Elizabeth Plantagenet. He does not conform to the overall pattern, having neither Scottish, Irish nor Welsh landholdings, and his successor today, the 12th Duke, who succeeded his brother in 1995, remains the owner of 132,000 acres and does have 9000 acres in Berwickshire in Scotland. This duke belongs to what might be best described as the inner core of the Imperial English, a group of people who have retained wealth they first started to obtain in the middle of the thirteenth century as the Royal family of Edward I.

The fourth ranking landowner in England in 1872, the Duke of Portland, had strong links to Scotland, with over 118,000 acres there, but no stated links with Ireland. The dukedom became extinct in 1990 with the death of the 9th Duke. The ducal assets had been passed by the 7th Duke, who died in 1977, to his daughter, Lady Anne Cavendish Bentinck, the 18th largest aristocratic landowner in the UK today.

The Marquess of Conyngham, the fifth largest landowner in England in 1872, is on the other hand a clear example of the Anglo-Irish links. His seat was at Bifrons, in the midst of his Kent estate, but the imperial landholdings were in Ireland, with 122,000 acres of Donegal and 27,613 acres of Clare. There was a small estate in Meath, dominated by Slane Castle. There are still around 3000 acres near the castle and the present heir to the current Marquess, the Earl of Mount Charles, is a minor public figure in Ireland. The current Marquess, the 7th, who has been married four times and divorced three times, lives in tax exile on the Isle of Man.

The sixth largest landowner in England in 1872, Sir John Ramsden, owned 138,000 acres in Inverness-shire from a seat at Byram in Yorkshire in England. He had no Irish acres. He was the fourth richest man in Great Britain in 1872, his Yorkshire acreage producing the modern equivalent of around £12.5 million a year. He was an MP for Taunton, Hythe, Yorkshire and Monmouth at various times and for a year was Under Secretary of State for War. His heir, the 9th Baronet, was educated at Eton like his forebearer and is a foreign office official.

The seventh largest landowner, the Marquess of Lansdowne, is another good example of how the last inner reconquest of the imperial drive, Ireland, was held by the inner core of the Imperial aristocracy. Lansdowne owned over 100,000 Irish acres in counties Kerry, Meath, Dublin and the then Queen's County (now called Laois) with a 9000 acre holding in Scotland. Like Richmond, Conyngham and Northumberland, he belongs to the inner core who trace their descent from the Plantagenets. And he governed his Irish and Scottish holdings from a seat in Wiltshire at Bowood House. The present Marquess, the 8th, lives at Meikleour in Perth surrounded by 4200 acres, while his son and heir runs Bowood House and its 4000 acres in Wiltshire.

The eight largest landowner in England in 1872 was Baroness Willoughby d'Eresby. For a baroness she seemed to have had a ducal holding, with its imperial extensions in Perth in Scotland, and in Denbigh in Wales. A brief examination shows that the Dukedom of Ancaster, which became extinct in 1779, was the origin of much of the D'Eresby land holdings, and that the estates passed with the barony right down to the present incumbent, Baroness Nancy Jane Marie Heathcote-Willoughby-Drummond, the 27th to hold the title first recorded in 1313. She is the Joint Hereditary Great Chamberlain of England, with her kinsman, the Marquess of Cholmondeley. She retains at least 15,000 acres in England and 63,200 acres in Perth in Scotland, making her one of the major survivors of the major landowners of a hundred years ago. It also makes her the tenth largest landowner in the UK today.

The bulk of the estates of the Earl Fitzwilliam, the ninth largest landowner in England in 1872, were in Ireland as they had been for several hundred years. His ancestor was Elizabeth I's Lord Deputy and Lord Justice in Ireland during her attempt to eliminate the Irish by expulsion and plantation. Fitzwilliam operated the estates from his massive house at Wentworth Woodhouse near Rotherham in Yorkshire. The title is now extinct, but the daughter of the last Earl, the 8th, Lady Juliet de Chair, is still living and is a landowner in Essex.

The tenth largest landowner in England in 1872 was Lord Leconfield, who had a little under half his landholdings in Ireland at the time. The Leconfield lands in England were originally possessions of the Percys, the Plantagenet dukes of Northumberland, which were passed to another branch of the family, with only 11,147 acres of the lands in the north surviving into the nineteenth century. But the theme of serious imperial English landholdings in Ireland, held from England, is here maintained. The present peer, the 7th Baron Leconfield who also holds the title Baron Egremont, lives at Petworth House in Sussex, now partly in the hands of the National Trust, and at Cockermouth Castle in Cumbria, still with a holding of 22,000 acres.

TABLE 15/2

THE TOP 10 LANDOWNERS LIVING IN IRELAND IN 1872 AND THEIR LANDHOLDINGS IN ENGLAND

	Landowner	Irish acres	English acres	English acres as % of total holding
1	Mr Richard Berridge	170,117	400	0.2%
2	Marquess of Downshire*	114,621	5287	4.6%
3	Earl of Kenmare	118,606	Nil	0%
4	Marquess of Sligo*	114,881	Nil	0%
5	Sir Richard Palmer	94,491	3329	3.3% (excluding Wales)
6	H.G. Murray Stewart	50,818	Nil	0%
7	Lord Ventry*	93,629	Nil	0%
8	Duke of Abercorn*	76,500	Nil	0%
9	Duke of Leinster	73,110	Nil	0%
10	Mr E. King Harman	72,913	Nil	0%

* The descendant is still a landowner in 2001.

TABLE 15/3

TOP 10 WELSH LANDOWNERS IN 1872 AND THEIR LANDHOLDINGS IN ENGLAND

	Landowner	Welsh acres	English acres	English acres as % of total holding
1	Sir W. Wynn Williams*	141,914	3856	2.6%
2	Earl of Cawdor*	51,538	Nil	0%
3	Earl of Powis*	33,573	26,986	44.56%
4	Lord Penrhyn	43,973	5575	11.25%
5	Earl of Lisburne	42,718	1	0.002%
6	Mr R. Price	41,264	Nil	0%
7	Lord Tredegar	38,957	200	0.5%
8	Mr D.A. Smith	34,482	Nil	0%
9	Mr C. Talbot	33,920	Nil	0%
10	Mr G. Powell	33,674	Nil	0%

* The descendant is still a landowner in 2001.

TABLE 15/4

TOP 10 SCOTTISH LANDOWNERS IN 1872 AND THEIR LANDHOLDINGS IN ENGLAND

	Landowner	Welsh acres	English acres	English acres as % of total holding
1	Duke of Sutherland*	1,326,453	32,092	2.3%
2	Duke of Buccleuch*	432,262	24,846	5.4%
3	Earl of Breadalbane	438,358	Nil	0%
4	Lady Matheson*	424,560	Nil	0%
5	Sir Charles Ross*	356,500	Nil	0%
6	Earl of Seafield*	305,930	Nil	0%
7	Earl of Fife*	249,220	Nil	0%
8	Duke of Atholl*	201,640	Nil	0%
9	Lord Lovat*	181,791	Nil	0%
10	Duke of Argyll*	175,114	Nil	0%

* The descendant is still a landowner in 2001.

TABLE 15/5

PERCENTAGE OF EACH COUNTRY OWNED BY TOP 10 LANDOWNERS IN 1872

1 England	1.8%
2 Scotland	21.9%
3 Wales	15.1%
4 Ireland	5.1%

Of the major landowners in Ireland during and immediately after the famine period, five were from amongst the top ten landowners in England. Critically, of the five, four – Conyngham, Lansdowne, Fitzwilliam and Leconfield – had Irish acres which constituted more than half of their estates. If these aristocrats were the core of the imperial complex, and they were suddenly to lose half their landholdings, the imperial psyche was likely to suffer a serious blow. The Return of 1872 were the last public record of what was about to happen. This was the collapse of the inner redoubt of the imperial enterprise, and it is possible to say that the imperial project suffered a mortal blow during the Irish famine. The imperial moral imperative, that of bringing Christian values to the natives, was shown for what it was, an absolute sham. The natives were dying in their droves, yet with food owned by the imperial representative available, they were dying in the full glare of publicity, and dying a day's travel from the imperial capital in London. Those who did not die fled, mostly to America, where they formed the praetorian guard of American anti-British imperialism, something that was to have a decisive effect during World War Two. The paymaster for that victory was America, but as Henry Hobhouse suggests, were it not for the physical legacy of the famine by way of the Irish lobby in American politics, and the psychological hatred that the race memory of the famine deaths had imbued in that lobby, Churchill might never have had to surrender the Empire as the price for American suppport.[3]

It is possible that we are indeed at a special point in time. The imperial myths provide no assistance to modern Britain as Tony Blair forces the country back into a pre imperial situation politically. The union at the heart of empire is over. England, the country that created the British Empire beginning with the conquest of its three nearest neighbours, and which has not been politically visible for hundreds of years, is about to reappear. Analysing and recovering the real facts of history may help England to forge a new destiny as a nation, led by its people, and not by that strange class of landowners, who lived even in their own country as occupying conquerors. This is where the famine comes in.

The lessons of the famine were too difficult for even the imperialists to face at the time, given the scale of death and destruction, but above all the inability of the imperial machinery to ameliorate it. The famine represented failure and failure is not something that is normally incorporated into a nation's working mythology, much less the mythology of an empire. The effects of the famine were all too visible and they went on for an inexplicably long period. By 1860 the population had fallen from between 8 or 9 million to just over 6 million. By 1871 it was down to 5.4 million, maybe much lower. Between 1960 and 1970 the population of Ireland bottomed out at around 2.7 million in the south and about 1.5 million in the north. This was 4.2 million people, half the pre-famine population. Nowhere in Europe, not in war-ravaged Russia or overrun Germany after World War Two, has such a sustained fall in population been seen. And it is the very reverse of the Jewish experience, insofar as it relates to the state of Israel, after the holocaust. The population of Israel has grown to fill the gap left by the holocaust in less than 50 years. In Ireland, though the overall population is back at around 5 million, there is no sign of births doing their normal thing and replenishing wartime deaths. Like the Irish, the Jews created a powerful political lobby in the United States, the new Empire in the west. And like the Irish they used that lobby to help create and protect the state of Israel, just as the Irish exiles lobbied for Irish independence after 1850.

No country has benefited so much from entry into Europe as Ireland, but then no country has put quite so much energy into the marriage with Europe as has 'young' Ireland. The honeymoon has been a long one, over a quarter of a century. In the meantime, Ireland's neighbour, England, has been going through the stormiest political 'disengagement' in its long history, as it tries to find for itself a post imperial role. And it is England in particular which must now stand on its own and try and recover an identity it lost centuries ago. And every soul in England should note that the leading Eurosceptics are also predominantly the representatives of the imperial core – the Tory aristocracy and its political hangers on. Not only are they misleading an England about to be reborn. There is no place for England in trying to occupy the position that Ireland had for so long, as the prime occupant of 'the dark edge of Europe'. The time has come for England to recover the leadership role that most of Europe expected it to occupy at the end of World War Two.

Chapter 16

Conclusion

IN THE HISTORIC time frame 126 years is but the blink of an eye. In relation to land reform in England, Wales and Scotland, it is a period in which the eye of history did not blink and in which all change became frozen in invisible aspic. Some great estates were broken up and some sold, as Cannadine shows.[1] But lacking a coherent Land Registry, Professor Cannadine was unable to add to his great work on the decline of the British aristocracy one final item. He could tell us who the sellers of land were but not, in many cases, who the buyers were, and who their current successors are. His book, in any case, was about the aristocracy and the landlords, not their victims. And there were victims, for the most part quite unwilling victims, at the heart of the aristocratic landowning enterprise. The victims have never before been highlighted, and they have almost certainly been kept concealed by the efforts of the landowners who could bear neither the source of those figures, *The Return of Owners of Land*, nor its content. The victims are the people of Britain.

Devon 1872

Population	604,374	
Owners of 1 acre or less	21,647	
Owners of more than 1 acre	10,162	
Owners of nothing at all	**569,565**	**94.2%**

Laois 1872

Population	79,771	
Owners of 1 acre or less	426	
Owners of more than 1 acre	623	
Owners of nothing at all	**78,722**	**98.6%**

Glamorgan 1872

Population	397,859	
Owners of 1 acre or less	6570	
Owners of more than 1 acre	1856	
Owners of nothing at all	**389,433**	**97.8%**

Aberdeenshire 1872

Population	244,603	
Owners of 1 acre or less	3620	
Owners of more than 1 acre	869	
Owners of nothing at all	**240,114**	**98.1%**

Here is the true reality of the United Kingdom in 1872, just over 126 years ago. The landless in each part of the Kingdom constituted the overwhelming bulk of the population. They were held in that position by the legislation of the time, and lurking behind the legislation, by the threat of eviction, and if not of eviction, by the threat of military force. It was, despite all the apologists for the situation and for the state of 'merrie England and its merrie peasants', a situation of constructive slavery.[2] In sociological terms it was the reduction of the population to farm animal status, and in relation to the state, it was the preservation of the population for use as cannon fodder. Stark statements, starker truths. But what's the point of raising the issue in 2001?

The answer is that in three of the four constituent elements of the UK in 1872, there has been no redistribution of land. What the homeowners have in 2001, about 6% of the land of the UK, is what the landowners have allowed them to have, at vast expense, and via legislation often enacted by the landowning interest. But does this matter? The example of the country which redistributed land, Ireland, shows that it can matter. Ireland is experiencing economic growth of 10.7% with a four year average of 9.95% growth. The UK is experiencing growth of about a third of this, at about 2.75% over four years.[3] In the hundred or so years after the 1872 Return Ireland stagnated and Britain declined. When Ireland joined the European Community, membership brought recognition of Ireland's neglected economic situation and an inflow of capital that has, despite being marginal in relation to Irish GDP, quite literally changed everything in Ireland. For a start, there is no council tax in the Republic. This is a measure which puts urban dwellers and rural dwellers on an equal footing. Urban dwellers in the UK, by far the largest segment of the population, continue to pay an average of £550 per dwelling per annum, while rural owners only pay council tax on their residence, not on their rolling acres, which are instead subsidised. Old age pensioners in the Irish Republic enjoy a multiplicity of benefits not available in the UK, including free television, free transport, free glasses and so on. Many of those benefits are available in continental countries too.

There are many causes for Britain's decline, though no consensus has ever emerged amongst historians or economists as to what it was or is. But one of the potential causes, the failure to redistribute land, has never even been argued, much less analysed. One reason for this is that land owning and farming have always been publicly identified in the United Kingdom as a single entity, which they are not. More than one third of the farms in England and Wales are rented from landowners.[4] In Northumberland, one of the areas worst hit by the present crisis in farm incomes, more than half of the county, 495,722 acres, is rented. Most of that rented land is owned by those who also own the other 432,954 acres of agricultural land in Northumberland. Rent paid to landowners is a major factor in the present crisis, yet most of the media have not commented on this. The impact is likely to be drastic and to have far-reaching economic significance in backing up the huge fortunes of the rural landowners. The National Farmers Union published a report in February 2000 which showed that 51% of tenant farmers were having difficulty in raising the rent currently, while 61% say that the rent burden means that they cannot see how they will continue in farming.[5] Translated into real numbers, this means that over 24,000 out of 48,000 tenant farmers are having difficulty paying the rent right now, and almost 30,000 out of 48,000 can see no way to continue in farming and to pay the rent. When a tenant leaves a farm, it reverts to the landowner, who either incorporates it into his or her home farm, or lets it again. Sales are uncommon. The limited evidence from the National Farmers Union is that few new tenants are being found and that the small pool of large landowners are increasing their acreage, increasing their opportunity for subsidy and increasing their opportunity for development sell offs. In acreage terms, what that means is this. With 25,918,370 million acres currently occupied by 157,367 individuals or families, the number of owners will stay more or less static, but their directly controlled acreage will increase by up to 7 million acres, and with it the share of the UK they own directly. (The book assumes that they are the owners of most of the let acreage, with the exception of the Forestry Commission, the MoD, Crown Estate, the Duchies of Cornwall and Lancaster, and the insurance and pension funds and other institutional owners.)

Indeed it is the confusion between farmers and landowners that has served to disguise the growing levels of subsidy which are supposed to keep farming afloat, while actually serving to subsidise the residual great estates of the last century and their current owners. Yet that is only the beginning of the distortion, and probably the cheapest part of it. This book has argued that, far from suffering a land shortage, the UK actually has a huge land surplus. If it is assumed that the bulk of surplus land in the UK is agricultural land and the rest either unusable or already under bricks, mortar and tarmacadam, then fewer than 157,000 families, 0.28% of the population, currently own 64% of the land area of the country. The collapse in tenant farming means that within a very few years the number of tenant farmers will be down to about 24,000 and the scale of ownership of the 157,000 land owners will have risen to 70% of the country. That tiny group will then be the recipients of between £2.3 billion and £4 billion in revenue support for their acres, while retaining 70% of the country's assets, subsidised and tax free. This is not a minor fact in the country's economic structure. The tenant farmers and the homeowners of today own a miniscule amount of the country and they pay the bulk of its taxes. But the most invidious part of it is that a portion of their tax payments go to those who own most of the country, and who do so tax free. Nothing could better illustrate the meaning of the application of real power than that it should protect and subsidise the powerful and wealthy few at the expense of the relatively poor individuals who constitute the majority of the population.

Power has a psychological value to individuals in that it assists them to act unaccountably and arbitrarily in relation to the lives of others. It puts them above the law to a degree and enables them to create laws which, in the modern world, protect the powerful.[6] A powerful group will attempt to retain for its individual members, the capacity to act unaccountably and arbitrarily too. For a wider grouping around the powerful core it is wealth, not power, that they seek and can expect to obtain through control of the state or government. Nothing better illustrates this than landownership in the UK. Absolute arbitrary power along with absolute wealth, historically associated with monarchy, now resides with the state or government. Groups seeking to exercise the ancient power of monarchs and to access the kind of patronage and wealth that flowed from the monarch, must, in the modern world, obtain control of the state or the government, but for what purpose? For some the exercise of power alone is clearly adequate satisfaction for the effort of acquiring it. But for much of the wider group supporting those driven by power alone, the rewards are purely financial. The object of power is wealth, and not vice versa.

To illustrate the core facts about wealth in the UK, the following table might assist.

UK Stock Exchange

Market capitalisation (value of all shares in UK companies at 31 Dec 2000)	£1,796,000,000,000
Number of individual shareholders (27% of UK population)	12,500,000
Average value of shareholding (excluding institutions)	£10,000

(Figures compiled by London Stock Exchange & Pro-Share 2000)

UK Housing

Market capitalisation (16.5 million private homes at an average value of £84,500)	£1,394,000,000,000
Number of individual stakeholders (2.2 persons per household)	36.2 million
Average value of each stakeholder's share in family home	£38,400

UK Land

Value of non domestic land in the UK (40,000,000 acres)	£120,000,000,000
Value of development land (1% or 400,000 acres)	£176,000,000,000
Number of owners/families	157,000
Average value of holding	£1,800,000

(All the above figures are gross and ignore debt and mortgages.)

The above outlines the real relationship between the three main categories of assets in the UK. The disparity between the average value of the average family or individual stake in shares or a house, and the average stake in the land, is truly enormous. But what really distinguishes the tiny group of land asset holders from the other two classes of asset holders is their relationship with power.

As with most countries, power in the UK has evolved over time from absolute forms of monarchical government. Unlike most countries, however, the UK has no written constitution and thus the government, the heir to the powers of the monarchy, retains a series of powers that are arbitrary and absolute. These powers are known as the Royal prerogative and allow the executive committee of the Privy Council, the cabinet in practice, to act without reference to Parliament. The most significant of these powers is the power to go to war but there are others. Anyone winning an election in the UK effects a democratic coup in what is essentially a lottery for the right, not to govern wisely or well, but to govern using these peculiar powers. The preservation of those powers outside the reach of Parliament and of democracy, was uniquely the work over centuries of the richest group in the UK, the landowners. However, what we can now see for the first time is what else they preserved for themselves and their heirs, which is subsidised wealth. In other words, the secondary effect of controlling power, the capacity to amass money for the wider group supporting the inner power elite. For it is out of the twisted inner mechanisms of Britain's laws and constitution, carefully crafted by the landowners and their political representatives, that the annual windfall of subsidies has evolved. Precisely because no one has ever had even the skeletal facts presented in this book, it has never been possible to tackle this abuse at the heart of the system. The Return of Owners of Land blew the cover on the landowners in 1872, but the cover was soon restored and we now live with the absurd consequences.

Elsewhere in this book the nature of power is discussed, but there can have been few more specific examples of the brutality of power in relation to land and its ownership than the period 1990 to 1997, when a total of over 500,000 families had their homes repossessed.[7] The probable cost of keeping all these people housed in the homes they had bought was a maximum of £5 billion over those seven years, about £700 million a year, and might have been as low as £2.4 billion. During that same period the 157,000 wealthiest families in the UK received up to £21 billion in subsidies.[8] The events of 1990 to 1997 also illustrate something even more critical about power in the UK. This is the relative helplessness of even very large numbers of people in a democracy. The numbers affected by the repossessions were, based on the average occupancy of a UK home, about 1.2 million people. Not only were they unable to stop the repossessions, they were unable to obtain any effective help from the government, nor able to obtain a voice in the media either, bound as it is to the property market and its operators. Yet the government handed out to the richest in the land, in any one year of the seven, enough money to halt all repossessions and more, over that whole seven year period.

In a mature and economically efficient democracy those with their feet on the first rung of the property ladder should have been the first to receive assistance when their toehold became vulnerable. The atoms of the modern economy are its households, not its factories. It is household consumption which drives the post industrial economy. Yet the government of the day stood by while a whole chunk of the economic future was destroyed by repossessions between 1990 and 1997.

The reason this happened is because at its heart power in the UK is unreconstructed. The civil service elite and their supporters in the upper reaches of the establishment, should have shown chancellors, Conservative and Labour alike, where the benefit to the national interest lay in accepting the repossessions and continuing the subsidies to the landowners. It is the Treasury which should have shown the chancellor of the day that the agricultural subsidy was simply a gravy train for the least productive part of the economy, the landowning substructure of agriculture. Between £800 million and £1.2 billion of the agricultural subsidy passes directly from tenant farmers to landowners as rent. The bulk of the remainder of the subsidy goes directly to landowners. In the post industrial globalised economy food production is a national security issue, not an economic one. While the world remains at peace food comes from the cheapest sources wherever they are. But the world may not always be at peace. Twice in the last century Britain almost lost a war because it was almost starved into submission. Never has the future security of the nation been so imperilled as it has in the last twenty years, due to the total muddle over the tax free status of the landowners and their huge subsidy, and the failure to balance the national economic interest towards home ownership and the national strategic interest in adequate food production.

Clearly, not every member of the landowning class identified in the MAFF statistics is actually a paid-up member of the inner power elite, or even a member of the Country Landowners Association, the 'club' of landowners. Nor indeed even a relative of either category. The statistics themselves tell us that only about 15,000 people or families own the kinds of acreage associated with landownership as opposed to farming, which gave them entry to the circles from which emanate the tax and subsidy privileges that we have identified. But there are two clear guides as to the size of the 'significant' group within the landowners. *Debrett's Baronetage and Peerage* contains the names of a little over 2000 heads of aristocratic families, but also lists about 50,000 relatives of the top 2000 families.[9] Many of the 50,000 relatives of the *Debrett's* aristocracy are in fact members of the CLA, which also has about 50,000 members. What *Debrett's* does is identify the wider circle of influence attached directly to the core landholders. While the hereditary House of Lords existed, the formal links inside this group were buttressed by family links to both the upper House of Parliament and to the monarchy, and were actually the social mainstay of government itself when Conservative governments ruled, up to 1997. But what made this group itself so durable, and its power so durable too, was its shared values at the very core of which lay landownership. They held themselves together by seldom articulating a basic truth, which was that they were prepared to do almost anything, so long as it left them and their landholdings intact. Nothing could better illustrate this than the story of the Plantagenets, told elsewhere in this book. Time has rendered the violence which created their landholdings invisible, but its consequences, the retention of unfair landholdings by a tiny group, is only possible, as we have shown, so long as the rights of others are violated.

There is social violence implicit in the continued exclusion of the general public from what was once their ancestors' birthright, the land taken by the aristocracy during the enclosures. There is serious social violence implicit in the dumping on the side of the street of 500,000 families while the privileged get subsidies and tax breaks. Because the passage of time has thankfully removed physical violence from most transactions in our society these acts of social violence go unremarked. And how could it be otherwise? A vast imbalance was created in British society by the landowner–landless division which has permeated the country's history. It took its most terrible form in the Irish famine, but almost certainly no less a toll of life in England, Scotland and Wales during the enclosures. Ireland was dramatic and is noted because it was sudden and overwhelming. The pain and suffering of the enclosure dispossessed in the UK was no less great, and they too were struck by famine, but more slowly and over a longer period of time. More sadly still, because it happened in their own country, where the victors, those who enclosed the land, were writing history, the dispossessed of the English enclosures hardly rate a footnote in that history. It should come as no surprise then to find that the descendants of the people who were able to inflict so much misery on their own people, should, even in a more civilised age, be able to line their pockets from the public purse, while retaining their ancestors' ill-gotten gains.

Which brings us to a core contradiction. There are few more charming and pleasant people in the world than those whose names are found in *Debrett's*, and who used to be found in the House of Lords. But the overt good manners are merely a mask, which perfectly matches in duplicity the unremitting propaganda about the fate of 'farmers' all over the UK. The manners exist so long as their divine right to power and its benefits, especially financial ones, continues. For power, especially in the semi democratic and semi liberal institutions that we now have, is now a matter of influence, rather that direct executive fiat. This is why time will demonstrate the critical nature of the Blair reform of the House of Lords. He decisively cut the permanent link between power and the landowners, a link that had lasted over 800 years and which had enabled the same tiny group of families to protect their core financial interests right up to the present day. The decisive nature of the Blair strike was much enhanced by the almost total decline of both the City of London as the controller of domestic wealth in the UK, and by the parallel decline in the influence of the elite families in banking, insurance and stockbroking boardrooms.

Nomura, a Japanese financial group, have bought the entire housing estate of the Ministry of Defence. A group that is 80% Irish owned has bid, unsuccessfully, for the defunct Millennium Dome. Each of these deals and hundreds more like them, would never have gone to foreign groups before 1990. The aristocratic representatives on the boards of the financial institutions would have seen to that. How extraordinary that influence was can be easily reconstructed by looking through the first few pages of the very latest edition of *Debrett's*.

Entry No.	
1	Baron Aberconway 88, Eton, Oxford, Royal Artillery, Landowner. *Formerly chairman of John Brown & Co, Sheepbridge Engineering, English China Clays. Director of Nat West Bank and Deputy Chairman Sun Alliance and Provincial Insurance Co.*
2	Duke of Abercorn 67, Eton, Royal Agricultural College, Cirencester, Grenadier Guards. Landowner *Formerly President of the Building Societies Association.*
3	Baron Aberdare 82, Winchester, Oxford Welsh Guards. Landowner *Formerly Chairman Albany Life Assurance Co, Metlife UK.*
4	Marquess of Aberdeen & Temair 81, Harrow, Scots Guards. *No significant directorships.*
5	Marquess of Abergavenny 87, Eton, Cambridge, Life Guards. Landowner. *Formerley director of Lloyds Bank and other companies.*
6	Baron Abinger 87. Eton, Cambridge, Royal Artillery. *No significant directorships.*
7	Baron Acton 60, St George's College, Oxford, Colonial civil servant. Landowner. *Formerly a director of Coutt's private bank.*
8	Baron Addington 38, Hewett Comprehensive Norwich, Aberdeen University. *No significant directorships.*
9	Viscount Addison 56, Kings School Bruton, Essex Inst of Agriculture. *No significant directorships.*
10	Marquess of Aylesbury 75, Eton. Royal Horse Guards. Landowner. *Member of the London Stock Exchange.*

This tiny sample, in which 6 out of the first 10 hereditary aristocrats listed in the latest *Debrett's* (2000) were former directors of the country's key financial institutions, is repeated throughout that extraordinary book, with the next 200 hereditary peers across the alphabet clocking up 29 key directorships. In the *Debrett's* of the 1960s and 70s, the number of aristocrats holding directorships in key financial institutions was more than double this number. There is a striking correlation between these directorships and large, predominanently English landholdings. For instance, the present Duke of Westminster was a director of Sun Alliance Insurance Co, a company his family had maintained financial links with over the centuries. He has more than 129,300 acres in the UK and Scotland. In the Palace, the last-but-two Lord Chamberlain was the Earl of Airlie, who was also chairman of merchant bank Schroeders, deputy chairman of General Accident and a director of many other financial organisations. His landholdings come to over 37,000 acres. The earl's successor was Lord Camoys, an English landowner and also a former managing director of Barclays Merchant Bank.

In their heyday, there was no need to find a dark smoky room in a pub somewhere in order to arrange a deal. Most of the landowners did not need to be introduced either, since those few who were not actually related to each other, had probably been to Eton together. It is almost impossible to catch exactly the fast fading atmosphere of this hegemony, and the huge support given it by the phalanx of cousins and public school boys – it was a singularly male dominated ethos – throughout the middle and higher reaches of management in most financial institutions right up to the end of the 1980s. But the underpinning value was that of land, land owned and land as collateral.

The international financier George Soros, who once worked in the City of London merchant bank Singer & Friedlander, remarked in his autobiography that he left the bank because there was no future there for anyone who did not bring money with him when he joined.[10] He might have suggested money and land, the possession of the latter characterising many of the bank's directors in the same period.

This seamless web of control of the country's finances through the city by the same families who dominated the upper house of Parliament and who were the abiding influence within the Conservative party gave the landowners such an intimate and enduring link to, and grip on, power. It was power which made their ancestors rich, as the *Sunday Times* Richest of the Rich lists in 2000 showed,[11] and it is power which has kept them rich right into the first year of the new millennium.

What happens if this truth becomes universally known? What happens if the government, and it doesn't matter which party it is, realises that the British public are soon going to want what the Irish public have, which is a council tax free area? What happens if government advisors stop pandering to the landowning lobby and advise the government that far from facing a shortage of land, the country faces a huge surplus of land, which is being financed at a cost and in a way that no wine lake ever was? Suppose that the government were to double the amount of land in England and Wales available for housing, from 3.3 million acres to 6.6 million acres. For a start, more than 30 million acres, 80% of the land area, would remain rural, and as economically inefficient as it is now.

The immediate economic effect would be a sharp fall in the value of building land, and a sharp fall in the value of the existing housing stock. For some this would mean negative equity, but for the 50% of homes on which there is no mortgage, the fall in value would be notional, and would be counterbalanced by the abandonment of the council tax. But those are merely the short-term advantages.

Taking it as read that the general economic value of paying a landowner £500,000 an acre for building land is zero to the community as a whole, it follows that reducing the cost of a house site by 75% has a potential value to the community as a whole. Firstly, it allows more of the investment in a house to go where it makes the most sense, into the infrastructure of a house. This would increase the utility value of a house. This is becoming vital, as more and more work moves out of conventional offices, and into family homes. It would also mean that housing could have more and better features, it could be larger, and it could have a bigger and better garden. But it would also stimulate economic activity in the occupations and trades required to erect houses, which have a very real employment value in a community.

Currently, there is huge pressure to erect housing in smaller and smaller areas and to have smaller and smaller houses, all built on the mass assembly principle. That pressure currently comes almost entirely from the increasing cost of the sites on which housing is erected. Which is illogical when you think how much surplus land there really is.

The landowners will argue that the situation in the countryside is the outcome, not of a conspiracy to clear the peasantry, but as a result of market forces and of market economics. The countryside has as many people as it does because that is all it can economically support, or not economically support, as we have shown. But we don't have to accept this man-made disaster. It can be changed, but it can only be changed when the information on the situation is accurate. The clearing banks have had 74 years to suggest that the government reform the Land Registry. Their real policy towards this move can be deduced from their silence on the matter. In fact the clearing banks have had another and also wholly disastrous effect on non metropolitan and provincial Britain. The branches of the clearers take in deposits in the high streets and towns of the United Kingdom. Those deposits are remitted nightly to London and placed on deposit in the international money markets. In the longer term those sums are used for the kind of ludicrous lending Barclay's were making in the 1980s, most of it metropolitan, much of it international, to speculators in fancy and often close to fraudulent future bonds and options as well as property. Where it was not invested was in non metropolitan Britain. Instead, when non metropolitan borrowers entered a branch of any clearing bank to request a loan, especially for new business ventures, what they would meet was a banking bureaucrat who, even if they did have entrepreneurial instincts, was severely limited by the structure erected over their heads by the head offices in London. The long-term effect has been profound. The factories and companies of the industrial age were not replaced and during the Thatcher era the industrial heartland was stripped of its factories by her government's industrial policy, and of its investment capital by the clearing banks and building societies.

There is a vast amount of economically inefficient and heavily subsidised land in the UK. The argument about what should be done about it has not even commenced because the ultimate destination of the subsidy, the landowners, has never been systematically identified.

To date the argument has been pre-empted by two groups of people. The first group and by far the most insidious and powerful, is the landowning lobby. The second group is the Greens in the narrow sense of the 'Save the Countryside' lobby and in the broader sense as the Countryside Alliance. When the personalities involved in this lobby are examined it is clear that it has the strongest possible links with the landowning group. Friends of the Earth, for example, is headed by an interesting character, Sir Jonathan Porritt Bt, son of the 1st Baron Porritt. Porritt's father was a court physician to the royal family from 1936 to 1967. Jonathan Porritt was brought up within the most intimate circle of palace courtiers and went to Eton. None of which disbars him from being a sincere environmentalist. However, his environmentalism comes coloured by his background and without any apparent reference to the real facts of how the countryside is owned and what that means or might mean. Further, he is a leading light in the attempt to persuade the public that there is a shortage of rural land when there is not, and that the rural environment is under mortal threat from the urban hordes when it all too clearly is not so threatened.

The environmentalists can be taken seriously when they join the march of democracy in its next phase and insist on a democratic Land Registry in which the rich landowner as well as the urban house dweller is identified. It seems strange that they campaign so hard for the countryside, but are unwilling that anyone should know who owns it. It also seems strange that the environmentalists do not always make clear who benefits from their fight. For if the environmental cause is effective, an extraordinary benefit will be conferred on a very small group of people, the landowners of the UK. They will have a new shield against the public use of the huge acreages, and they will have a new disguise for the continued public subsidy of the very rich, by the average urban homeowner. Porritt's lobby is in search of statutory protection for the new, hidden rights of the landowners and in part has obtained it in the form of the main policy of the post-2001 Ministry of Agriculture, known as the Environment, Food and Rural Affairs Ministry, whose mission according to *The Times* is to shift EU subsidies away from food production into land management.[12] As such the lobby are in direct line of descent from the landowners in the seventeenth and eighteenth century who used Parliament and law as an instrument of extermination in Ireland and as an instrument of mass dispossession in England, Scotland and Wales.

The greater goal of a better environment for all is a noble one. But not when those who claim to have that goal at heart are also operating against the public interest by disguising the actual, immediate beneficiaries of the state protection and the public subsidy they are demanding in support of their objectives.

But it is not just the environmentalists who are playing the landowners' tune. The heritage lobby invite us to spend our weekends, and our cash, in the countryside admiring the homes of the landowners, some vacant, most of them not. In a lie as cheeky as that of the environmentalists, though no less invidious, they are asking us to pay homage at the headquarters of those who kept our ancestors in a state where 96% of the population owned nothing at all.

The National Trust's approach to the country estates it owns is a desecration of the memory of thousands, hundreds of thousands and possibly millions, who perished in the legalised greed of the enclosures which made so many of those mansions possible. If this seems a harsh analogy, look no further than Ireland and the famine, where the landlords and the law, and not the failure of the potato crop, killed a million people and sent another million into exile. To the heritage lobby the surviving country houses are a thing of beauty and a joy forever. Never mind the pain endured to make them possible.

This narrative is not a plea for a return to some kind of peasant-occupied rural idyll, nor even less a call for the occupation of the countryside by unlimited urban housing. Rather it is a call to analyse the economic consequences of what the landed aristocracy did to one portion of the population and to ensure that those economic effects – a rigged and overpriced land market, a farming sector maintained in existence almost wholly by public subsidy, diverted ultimately into the pockets of large landowners, and a defective Land Registry to conceal the ownership of the UK – do not persist for any further length of time.

PART II
The Counties

The Counties of Great Britain and Ireland

The general purpose of the counties tables which appear on the following pages is to provide two things. The first is to give a general picture of population, home ownership and landownership in Britain and Ireland in both 1872 and today, in so far as that is possible. The second thing is to provide a workable first sketch of how landownership has evolved between 1872 and 2001, by restoring the 1872 Return to its rightful place as one of the most important statistical documents ever produced in this country.

The summaries contained in the counties tables are designed to allow a concise and easily comparable picture of landownership in each county. However, changes in local government, administration and the variable availability of figures across the constituent parts of the United Kingdom and Ireland mean that these records are never entirely consistent. Particular regional variations or characteristics are explained at the start of each country's section. In broad outline the counties listed here represent the counties (or their direct sucessors) which appeared in the 1872 Return.

Notes explaining the tables

For each county in England, Wales, Scotland, Northern Ireland and the Republic of Ireland a table with the following information will appear. An explanation is given below of the source of the figures published. Frequent boundary and administrative changes since 1872 make a precise comparison practically impossible; nonetheless, each of the two columns stands in its own right as a picture of landownership in the area.

SOMEWHERESHIRE

	1872 <1>	2001 <2>
Total acreage		<3>
Agricultural acreage	<4>	<5>
Non agricultural acreage	<6>	<7>
Population		<8>
Owners of nothing at all	<9>	<10>
Total Dwellings		<11>
Smallholdings		
1872 owners of less than one acre	<12>	
2000 owners of 0–2ha (0–4.94 acres)		<13>
Landowners over one acre (1872)		
Landowners over 2ha (2000)		
Landowners over 500 acres		<14>
Acreage (and percentage) of county owned by owners of over 500 acres	<15>	<16>

<1> With the exception of figures at <4>, <6>, <9> and <15>, all figures in this column are taken directly from the 1872 Return.

<2> With the exception of figures at <3>, <8>, <10>, <11> and <16> figures in this column are taken directly from the MAFF Digest of Agricultural Census Statistics 1999, updated where figures were available from the Scottish Executive's Department of Rural Affairs 2001. Figures for the Republic of Ireland are taken from statistics supplied by the Irish Government statistics service.

<3> Figure from the Local Authorities Association and cross referred with *Whittaker's Concise Almanac 2001*. The total acreage of each county in Northern Ireland and the Republic of Ireland is obtained from the Irish Almanac 1997 and later.

<4> & <6> The agricultural acreage in 1872 is an estimated figure, based on historic estimates of the scale and nature of agricultural use of land in Britain in 1872. Sources for England, Wales and Scotland are *Anatomy of Agriculture* by Peter Wormell and related publications by the Royal Agricultural Society. A figure of 90% is used for England, Wales and Scotland. Sources for Ireland are the Irish Department of Agriculture, the Public Records office in Dublin, the Royal Dublin Society and the records of the Land Commission. A figure of 95% is used for both Northern Ireland and the Republic of Ireland. Urban acreage is calculated in the same way, from various historic studies of urban areas and is essentially all land not waste or agricultural, and includes industrial land.

<5> & <7> It is worth noting that there is a significant discrepancy between the overall MAFF figure for the UK and that given by the European Commission central statistics service, the latter being almost 1.4 million acres larger than the MAFF figure. Urban acreage is obtained from the DETR report on Urbanisation in England 1991–2001, as updated. This figure is in urgent need of careful study, as it is now very large and conflicts with other figures, such as those for actual road acreages and the generally unavailable figure for waste.

<8> Latest available population estimate taken from figures available from the Local Authorities Association, *Whittaker's Concise Almanac 2001* and from the Organisation of National Statistics (ONS) 1998.

<9> Figure calculated by deducting from the total population the combined figures of those who owned over one acre and those who owned under one acre.

<10> Figure calculated by subtracting number of owner-occupiers from the total population. Number of owner-occupiers calculated by taking the national average of owner-occupied dwellings (65% – DETR figures; for the Republic of Ireland the figure is 82%) multiplying that figure by two to take account of the fact that most homes are now legally owned jointly by partners and subtracting the figure from the population of each county as given above. The outcome is a crude figure, but the figure in the 1872 Return was also 'crude' in the sense that it was not broken down, by age in particular.

<11> Calculation of dwellings taken from UK Census Report 1991.

<12> From the records it is clear that this figure includes freehold owners of dwelling places as well as owners of small agricultural holdings under one acre.

<13> While the smallest defined size of landholding in 1872 was one acre, the smallest defined area in current government statistics is 2 hectares or 4.94 acres. In contrast to the 1872 figures, no non-agricultural land or dwellings are included in this figure.

<14> This figure identifies the number of farms over 500 acres in size. MAFF statistics do not necessarily identify if one or more of these farms in any given county are owned by the same landowner. While the figure of 500 acres was chosen to indicate a

significant landholding, it is also important as even using a very conservative average land value figure (£2000 per acre), an estate of this size would be worth £1million in land alone.

<15> Figure calculated by Stella Cahill and Edward Cox working directly from the 1872 Return.

<16> Figure calculated from various government publications listed at <2> above.

Details of Top Landowners 2001

For each county an attempt has been made to name the three largest confirmed owners of land. Almost without exception it was impossible during the research to confirm acreage in the various land registries, for reasons extensively covered elsewhere. Of the very few large estates which are registered, some have been broken down and registered under a vast sequence of separate titles, which in turn makes it financially prohibitive to examine as a whole.

The main sources of information on estates are listed in detail in the introduction to Part III of this book, which provides extended lists of the country's top landowners as a national picture.

Details of Significant Institutional Landowners

In many counties large institutions are an important part of the landowning picture. The largest institutional landowners are few in number; principally the Forestry Commission, followed by the Ministry of Defence, the National Trust and the Royal Society for the Protection of Birds. They can be found listed on p.147. Information on these bodies was mainly supplied by the bodies themselves, often reluctantly.

Top 10 in 1872

Because of the extraordinary state of the Land Registry, these lists of the top landowners in each county in 1872 are far more than the mere history lists they appear to be. In fact they are the starting point for locating most of the remaining large estates, especially in England, as their roots lie in this table. It is also the first attempt in at least 130 years to create some kind of digestible picture of the nature of private ownership in each county. This list was created from a computerised database of John Bateman's *Great Landowners of Great Britain & Ireland* (1883), and the output was then checked against the 1872 Return for each county.

England

The 1872 Return produced landownership figures for 42 English counties. These included Monmouthshire, treated then as part of England for administrative reasons but for the purposes of this book included among the Welsh counties, and separate listings for the East, North and West Riding of Yorkshire, which have been amalgamated here as one entry, Yorkshire. Since 1872 there have been many administrative reorganisations in England, principally to reflect changes in the population and an intensification of urban dwelling, and are not always significant in acreage terms. In 2001 there are 34 county councils in England, with slightly different boundaries used for agricultural statistics (38 separate areas) and the system of lord lieutenants and high sheriffs (47 areas). Brief explanations on changes in county structure have been given on the relevant county pages, but the changes do mean that in certain places there is no easy way to set up a like-for-like comparison between the county in 1872 and today. The map on p.225 shows the county areas used for 2001 agricultural statistics, the principal source of landownership information used on these county pages. In addition to the counties largely similar to the 1872 layout, there are a number of metropolitan areas such as Tyne & Wear, Merseyside and Greater Manchester which have not been included in the county pages which follow.

Modern landowners

There is almost no exception to the rule that most modern landed estates, and especially those which have remained in the same family since 1872, are not entered in the Land Registry. Where they are, it is usually in the form of a composite estate map, broken into sometimes hundreds of divisions, each of which would need a separate application, and a separate fee, to identify. An example of this is the Raleigh estate in Essex, which is registered with up to 700 separate titles combining to form a 4000-acre estate. To confirm the extent of this estate with the Land Registry would require 700 separate applications at a cost of some £4900.

An explanation of all figures included in the tables is given on p.219.

List of English Counties included

Bedfordshire
Berkshire
Buckinghamshire
Cambridgeshire
Cheshire
Cornwall
Cumbria
Derbyshire
Devonshire
Dorset
Durham

Essex
Gloucestershire
Hampshire (formerly Southampton)
Herefordshire
Hertfordshire
Huntingdonshire (now part of Cambridgeshire)
Kent
Lancashire
Leicestershire
Lincolnshire
Middlesex (now largely subsumed into the Greater London Council)
Norfolk
Northamptonshire
Northumberland
Nottinghamshire
Oxfordshire
Rutland
Shropshire
Somerset
Staffordshire
Suffolk
Surrey
Sussex (now East Sussex and West Sussex)
Warwickshire
Westmoreland (now divided between Northumberland and Cumbria)
Wiltshire
Worcestershire
Yorkshire (comprising North Yorkshire, South Yorkshire, West Yorkshire and the East Riding)

England and Wales 1872

England and Wales 2001

Key to English Councils

1. Hartlepool
2. Darlington
3. Stockton-on-Tees
4. Middlesbrough
5. Redcar & Cleveland
6. Blackburn with Darwen
7. Merseyside
8. Halton
9. Warrington
10. Stoke-on-Trent
11. Telford & Wrekin
12. Derby
13. Nottingham
14. Peterborough
15. Kingston-upon-Hull
16. Wokingham
17. Windsor & Maidenhead
18. Bracknell Forest
19. Poole
20. Bournemouth
21. Southampton
22. Portsmouth
23. Brighton & Hove

Key to Welsh Councils

1. Swansea
2. Neath Port Talbot
3. Bridgend
4. Rhondda Cynon Taff
5. Merthyr Tydfill
6. Blaenau Gwent
7. Vale of Glamorgan
8. Cardiff
9. Caerphilly
10. Newport
11. Torfaen
12. Monmouthshire

BEDFORDSHIRE

	1872	2001
Total acreage	286,076 acres	305,089 acres
Agricultural acreage	271,772 acres	219,271 acres
Non agricultural acreage	14,304 acres	85,818 acres
Population	146,257	543,100
Owners of nothing at all	138,573	248,000
Total Dwellings	30,506	227,000
Smallholdings: 1872 owners of less than one acre 2001 owners of 0–2ha (0–4.94 acres)	5302	81
Landowners over one acre (1872) Landowners over 2ha (2001)	2382	1035
Landowners over 500 acres	91	123
Acreage (and percentage) of county owned by owners of over 500 acres	191,792 acres (67%)	113,003 acres (37%)

Top Landowners 2001

DUKE OF BEDFORD AND HIS SON THE MARQUESS OF TAVISTOCK *13,000 acres with 20 acres in London and 10,000 acres in Cambs. No. 1 in 1872.* John Robert Russell, the 13th Duke of Bedford, who was born in 1917, has lived in exile in Monaco since the mid 1970s, having handed over the running of the estate at Woburn to his son and heir Robin, the Marquess of Tavistock. The original estate ran to over 86,000 acres, with much of the land in London, Devon, Cambridge, Northampton and Dorset. The lands were a gift from King Henry VII in 1504 and were added to by his son Henry VIII, who also made the then John Russell a Baron. The family still retain some land in Bloomsbury in London and live at Woburn, now run by Lord Howland, grandson of the duke, born in 1962.

MR SAMUEL WHITBREAD *10,800 acres. No. 2 in 1872.* The Whitbread family have been brewers in Bedfordshire for over 250 years, and have bought extensive lands in the county during that time. The first Samuel was a farmer, starting the brewery with a £2000 inheritance, the modern equivalent of perhaps £400,000. The heart of the estate is Southill Park. The family stake in the brewery was sold in the year 2000 to a Belgian company, Interbrew. The present Samuel Whitbread, born in 1937, started life wanting to be a farmer and worked on the Buccleuch Estate in Scotland as a shepherd. The family were former owners of the 32,000-acre Letterewe estate in Ross & Cromarty.

LORD ST JOHN OF BLETSO *4000 acres in trust. No. 5 in 1872.* The Bletso estates are in trust and the current peer, a financial consultant with a stockbroking company, lives in London and has a home in Wales. The family first appear in the annals of the kingdom when a Baron Beauchamp of Bletso attended Parliament in 1363. The current title was created in 1559 but the present peer, Anthony, left the House of Lords at the Blair reforms of November 1999.

Significant Institutional Landowners

1872: The largest institutional landowner was the Church of England with 21,896 acres.
2001: The diocese of Bedford still owns about 3500 acres of the original Church of England estate. The county council also owns 8894 acres of farmland.

TOP 10 IN 1872

1	Duke of Bedford (MP) of Woburn Abbey	32,269 acres	with 54,066 elsewhere
2	Mr Samuel Whitbread MP of Southill	13,257 acres	with 572 elsewhere
3	Earl Cowper of Panshanger, Herts	9105 acres	with 28,764 elsewhere
4	Mr John Crawley of Stockwood	8305 acres	with 50 elsewhere
5	Lord St John of Bletso of Melchbourne	7853 acres	with 585 elsewhere
6	Mr Edward Rhys Wingfield of Barrington Park Burford	6229 acres	with 12,562 elsewhere
7	Mr Francis Thynn of Haynes Park	4717 acres	with 10,424 elsewhere
8	Mrs Leigh of Luton Hoo	4265 acres	with 2242 elsewhere
9	Mr Arthur Macnamara of Eaton Bray	3957 acres	with 1443 elsewhere
10	Mr William Cooper of Toddington Manor, Dunstable	3388 acres	

BERKSHIRE

	1872	2001
Total acreage	430,849 acres	311,101 acres
Agricultural acreage	409,307 acres	173,609 acres
Non agricultural acreage	21,542 acres	137,492 acres
Population	196,475	769,200
Owners of nothing at all	189,235	350,000
Total Dwellings	39,638	323,000
Smallholdings: 1872 owners of less than one acre 2000 owners of 0–2ha (0–4.94 acres)	4172	83
Landowners over one acre (1872) Landowners over 2ha (2000)	3068	805
No of Landowners over 500 acres	162	93
Acreage (and percentage) of county owned by owners of over 500 acres	303,526 acres (70.4%)	101,311 acres (32.5%)

Top Landowners 2001

SIR WILLIAM BENYON *14,250 acres with 3000 acres in Essex and 2400 in Hants.* Bill Benyon, as he is better known, is the former Conservative MP for Buckingham and later for Milton Keynes. Born in 1930 he gave up his seat in the House of Commons in 1992 to concentrate on managing the family estate, which he inherited from his father, a vice admiral in the Royal Navy. His ancestor (no. 3 in 1872) was also MP for Bucks, and the estate is little changed from its size at that time, which was 16,007 acres, with 3438 acres in Essex and 2440 acres in Hampshire. He lives at the ancestral home, Englefield House, and is a director of the Peabody Trust in London.

EARL OF CARNARVON *6500 acres.* This distinguished racing man has an ancestry that travels back to 1549 when his remote ancestor, the master of Henry VIII's horse, was made Earl of Pembroke (see Wiltshire). The present Earl of Carnarvon, the 7th, Henry George Herbert, born in 1924, was made the Queen's racing manager in 1970. He is married to a daughter of the Earl of Portsmouth (see Hampshire). The bulk of the family lands in 1872 were in Somerset (12,800 acres), Hampshire (9340 acres) and Notts (13,247 acres). The lands around the family seat, Highclere Castle near Newbury, are in family hands but are not registered

LATE LORD HOWARD DE WALDEN *3000 acres.* The late Lord Howard de Walden, who died in 1999, was one of the richest men in the United Kingdom, owning through family trusts over 100 acres of central London (see London chapter). Long before his death he transferred the trusts to his four daughters. He was also a keen racing man and bought the 3000-acre Avington Manor estate in Berks in the 1950s. He was a member of the huge Howard clan, headed by the Duke of Norfolk. In 1872 the then Lord Howard owned less than 50 acres.

Other significant landowners in the county include the 3rd Baron Iliffe, with 2000 acres in the county as well as 4000 acres in Warwicks. and 25,853 acres in Sutherland. The scion of a newspaper family, Robert Peter Richard Iliffe was born in 1944 and educated at Eton and Oxford. He was High Sheriff of Warwickshire in 1983. The *Sunday Times* puts his wealth at £102 million in the 2000 Rich List.

Significant Institutional Landowners

1872: The Church of England had 18,142 acres. The Crown Estate had 10,203 acres.
2001: The National Trust own over 1700 acres at Basildon Park and are responsible for another 500 acres in the county. The Church of England still retains more than 2000 acres in the county. The Crown Estate owns 13,985 acres around Windsor.

TOP 10 IN 1872

1	Sir Robert Lloyd Lindsay Bt VC of Lockinge House, Wantage	20,538 acres	
2	Earl of Craven of Ashdown Park, Shrivenham	19,225 acres	with 11,564 elsewhere
3	Mr Richard Benyon MP of Englefield House, Reading	10,129 acres	with 5878 elsewhere
4	Mr Philip Wroughton of Woolley Park, Wantage	8692 acres	
5	Earl of Abingdon of Wytham Abbey, Oxford	7738 acres	with 13,538 elsewhere
6	Mr Charles Morrison of Basildon Park, Reading	6987 acres	with 68,745 elsewhere
7	Colonel Sir Francis Burdett Bt of Ramsbury Manor, Westbury, Wilts	6541 acres	with 14,443 elsewhere
8	Mr Charles Eyre of Welford Park, Newbury	5737 acres	with 409 elsewhere
9	Marquess of Downshire, of Hillsborough Castle, Co Down	5287 acres	with 114,902 elsewhere
10	Mr Sidney Bouverie-Pusey of Pusey, Farringdon	5022 acres	

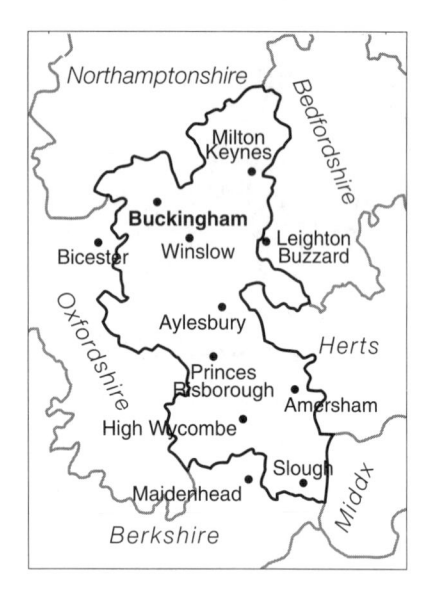

BUCKINGHAMSHIRE

	1872	2001
Total acreage	456,210 acres	465,237 acres
Agricultural acreage	433,399 acres	307,384 acres
Non agricultural acreage	22,810 acres	157,853 acres
Population	175,879	658,400
Owners of nothing at all	166,171	299,600
Total Dwellings	37,257	276,000
Smallholdings: 1872 owners of less than one acre 2000 owners of 0–2ha (0–4.94 acres)	6420	146
Landowners over one acre (1872) Landowners over 2ha (2000)	3288	1793
Landowners over 500 acres	167	151
Acreage (and percentage) of county owned by owners of over 500 acres	302,532 acres (66.3%)	124,036 acres (26.6%)

Top Landowners 2001

THE ROTHSCHILD FAMILY *12,000 acres. No. 2 in 1872.* In the late 1800s Buckinghamshire, or parts of it, became known as Rothschildshire. Members of the banking dynasty, founded in Frankfurt in the eighteenth century and developed by Nathan Rothschild in England, rapidly became members of Parliament and later of the House of Lords. They bought large amounts of land in England, including Gunnersby Park in Middlesex, but mainly at Tring Park and at Waddesdon, in Bucks. Their total landholdings by 1880 came to over 15,378 acres. Tring Park and much of the Waddesdon Estate remain in the hands of family trusts, now headed by the 4th Lord Rothschild, and by Sir Evelyn de Rothschild, head of the family bank N.M. Rothschild.

LORD CARRINGTON *4500 acres. No. 1 in 1872.* The Carington family have a long history, the title being created in 1797. The present peer, the 6th, is a former Conservative Defence Secretary and was the Foreign Secretary who resigned over the mistakes which led to the Falklands War in 1982. He subsequently became Secretary General of NATO. In 1872 the family had a massive holding of 25,809 acres, making them the biggest landowners in Bucks, with a further 9656 acres in Lincolnshire. The family are related to Baroness Willoughby de Eresby, the largest landowner in Lincolnshire. The present peer still retains residence at the family seat near Aylesbury.

EARL HOWE *4000 acres. No. 10 in 1872.* Frederick Curzon, the 7th Earl Howe, held a number of ministerial jobs in the Conservative government of John Major, including a spell at MAFF and as under secretary of state at the MoD. His current acreage is very much less than that of his ancestor in 1872. The then Earl, a major general in the army, owned 33,669 acres in Notts, Leicester, Bucks and Suffolk. A cousin was a Viceroy of India. The family seat, still the residence of the earl, is Penn House, Amersham.

Significant Institutional Landowners

1872: The largest institutional landowner was the Church of England with 21,847 acres.
2001: The National Trust has more than 20 major properties in Bucks, including Waddesdon Manor House and Stowe Gardens. Their total acreage is just under 4000, with a further 5400 acres under the protection of the Trust. The Church of England still owns over 2500 acres in the county. The county owns over 5322 acres of farmland. Stowe public school is now sited at the former home of the Duke of Buckingham (No. 3 in 1872), an extinct title.

TOP 10 IN 1872

1	Lord Carington (MP) of Wycombe Abbey, High Wycombe	16,128 acres	with 9681 elsewhere
2	Sir Nathaniel Rothschild Bt MP of Tring Park	9959 acres	with 5419 elsewhere
3	Duke of Buckingham & Chandos (MP) of Stowe	9511 acres	with 971 elsewhere
4	Mr William Selby-Lowndes of Whaddon, Stoney Stratford	7537 acres	
5	Sir Harry Verney Bt MP of Claydon House, Winslow	6890 acres	with 6868 elsewhere
6	Mr Caledon Du Pre MP of Wilton Park, Beaconsfield	6876 acres	
7	Mrs Chetwode of Chilton House, Thame	6241 acres	with 5408 elsewhere
8	Mr Thomas Tyrwhitt-Drake of Shardeloes, Amersham	5767 acres	with 12,696 elsewhere
9	Lord Overstone of Overstone Park, Northants	5072 acres	with 25,777 elsewhere
10	Earl Howe of Gopsal Park, Atherstone, Notts	4956 acres	with 28,793 elsewhere

CAMBRIDGESHIRE

(Merged with Huntingdonshire in county restructuring of 1974. For details of Huntingdonshire in 1872 see p.242)

	1872	1872 figures for Cambridgeshire and Huntingdonshire combined	2001
Total acreage	522,208 acres	747,821 acres	840,587 acres
Agricultural acreage	496,097 acres	710,429 acres	685,727 acres
Non agricultural acreage	26,111 acres	31,201 acres	154,860 acres
Population	186,903	250,611	686,900
Owners of nothing at all	173,730	233,535	300,800
Total Dwellings	40,272	54,304	297,000
Smallholdings: 1872 owners of less than one acre 2000 owners of 0–2ha (0–4.94 acres)	6677	8493	255
Landowners over one acre (1872) Landowners over 2ha (2000)	6496	8583	2792
Landowners over 500 acres	178	251	381
Acreage (and percentage) of county owned by owners of over 500 acres	275,535 acres (52.8%)	415,604 acres (55.6%)	354,776 acres (42.2%)

Top Landowners 2001

LORD DE RAMSEY *15,000 acres.* John Fellowes, the 4th Lord de Ramsey, born in 1942, is the scion of a family with MPs going back to the early nineteenth century. Ennobled, the family became courtiers to Queen Victoria. The original landholdings ran to 20,021 acres in 1872, with 15,629 acres in Hunts, 4083 in Norfolk and only 309 in Cambs. The present peer has been a president of the Country Landowners Association, a Crown Estate Commissioner and Chairman of the Environment Agency. He has the right to appoint priests to four parishes. He lives at Abbots Ripton Hall, the former home of the Roper family who were courtiers to Henry VII and VIII and later to Queen Anne.

DUKE OF BEDFORD *10,000 acres. No. 2 in 1872.* The Bedford Estates sold off vast tracts of land in north Devon and in Bloomsbury in London, but retained significant holdings in Cambridge (see Bedfordshire).

DUKE OF RUTLAND *4000 acres with 10,000 acres in Derbyshire, 12,000 acres in Leicestershire and 2000 acres in Lincolnshire. No. 4 in 1872.* Part of the Rutland Estate remains intact in Cambs. See Leicestershire (p.245).

Significant Institutional Landowners

1872: 22 of the colleges of Cambridge University and the university owned a total of 33,837 acres, with Downing College the largest landowner with 7381 acres. The Church Commissioners owned 4748 acres but the Church of England, with 16,544 acres, was the largest individual institutional landowner.
2001: The Cambridge University colleges own about 35,000 acres between them, with Downing College still the largest landowner with over 5000 acres. Cambridge County owns 34,400 acres of farmland. The Crown Estate owns 5125 acres and the National Trust owns 3748 acres, with a further 1070 acres under protection. The Church Commissioners own 4000 acres.

TOP 10 IN 1872

1	Earl of Hardwicke (MP) of Wimpole Hall, Royston, Herts	18,978	acres	with 404 elsewhere
2	Duke of Bedford (MP) of Woburn Abbey, Beds	18,800	acres	with 67,535 elsewhere
3	Mr John Walbanke Childers MP of Cantley Hall Doncaster, Yorks	7402	acres	with 5922 elsewhere
4	Duke of Rutland (MP) of Belvoir Castle, Grantham, Lincs	6585	acres	with 63,552 elsewhere
5	Mr William Hall of Six Mile Bottom, Cambs	5956	acres	with 2346 elsewhere
6	Mr John Dunn Gardner MP of Chatteris House, Cambs	3676	acres	with 16 elsewhere
7	Mr Charles Adeane of Babraham Hall Cambs	3157	acres	with 291 elsewhere
8	Hon William North of Kirtling Tower, Newmarket Suffolk	3130	acres	with 471 elsewhere
9	Mr E.J. Mortlock of Abington Cambs	2827	acres	
10	Mr George Newton of Croxton Park, St Neots	2794	acres	

CHESHIRE

	1872	2001
Total acreage	602,219 acres	576,546 acres
Agricultural acreage	572,108 acres	399,531 acres
Non agricultural acreage	30,111 acres	177,015 acres
Population	561,201	975,600
Owners of nothing at all	537,481	449,100
Total Dwellings	110,449	405,000
Smallholdings: 1872 owners of less than one acre 2000 owners of 0–2ha (0–4.94 acres)	17,691	359
Landowners over one acre (1872) Landowners over 2ha (2000)	6029	3795
Landowners over 500 acres	170	54
Acreage (and percentage) of county owned by owners of over 500 acres	416,088 acres (69.1%)	48,214 acres (8.3%)

Top Landowners 2001

THE 6TH DUKE OF WESTMINSTER, BRIGADIER GERALD GROSVENOR *15,000 acres, with 19,000 acres in Lancashire, 95,000 acres in Scotland and about 380,000 acres elsewhere in the world. No. 3 in 1872.* The Ducal ancestry is fully dealt with in the chapter on London, where he and his family own over 300 acres of the most valuable real estate in the world. The family can trace their ancestry in Cheshire back to the eleventh century.

THE 7TH MARQUESS OF CHOLMONDELEY, DAVID CHOLMONDELEY *7500 acres, with 4000 acres in Norfolk. No. 2 in 1872.* Born in 1960, it was Cholmondeley's family who saved the Westminster London lands when the seventeenth-century heiress who brought them to the family, Mary Davies, went mad and married a priest. The present peer is one of only two hereditary peers to retain a permanent seat in the House of Lords after the Blair reforms in 1999. He stays as the hereditary Lord Great Chamberlain. The original title is Irish and was created in 1628. Cholmondeley owns two magnificent palaces as well as various art treasures. He is a film producer.

THE 3RD VISCOUNT LEVERHULME *10,000 acres with 24,700 acres in Sutherland.* Philip William Bryce Lever is the heir to the vast fortune of the Lever family, creators of Port Sunlight and now part of the Unilever empire. Born in 1915, he succeeded in 1949 and is Steward of the Jockey Club as well as serving as Lord Lieutenant of Cheshire from 1949 to 1990. The main English estate is at Thornton Hough in the Wirral, with the Scottish estate at Kinbrace. He has no male heir.

Other significant landowners in the county include Peter Gilbert Greenall, the 4th Baron Daresbury, with 3500 acres in the county and 2000 acres elsewhere. He is the scion of the Greenall brewing family, based in Cheshire for over 200 years. Born in 1953 he has been both High Sheriff and Deputy Lord Lieutenant of the county. His family have been MPs in the county since 1848 and the family are reputed to have large landholdings elsewhere in the UK.

Significant Institutional Landowners

1872: The largest institutional landowner was the Church of England with 28,614 acres.
2001: The National Trust owns about 7939 acres in Cheshire, with the county owning 8730 acres of farmland.

TOP 10 IN 1872

1	Lord Tollemache of Helmingham MP of Peckforton Castle, Tarporley	28,651 acres	with 7075 elsewhere
2	Marquess of Cholmondeley (MP) of Cholmondeley Castle, Nantwich	16,992 acres	with 16,999 elsewhere
3	Duke of Westminster (MP) of Eaton Hall, Chester	15,138 acres	with 4611 elsewhere
4	Sir Henry Delves Broughton Bt of Doddington Park, Nantwich	13,832 acres	with 1322 elsewhere
5	Rev Thomas France-Hayhurst of Bostock Hall, Middlewich	10,855 acres	
6	Mr William Bromley-Davenport MP of Capesthorne, Chelford	10,166 acres	with 5481 elsewhere
7	Lord Crewe of Crewe Hall, Nantwich	10,148 acres	with 12,946 elsewhere
8	Earl of Derby (MP) of Knowsley Prescot	9500 acres	with 59,442 elsewhere
9	Lord Egerton of Tatton, MP of Tatton Park, Knutsford	8876 acres	with 2683 elsewhere
10	Sir Philip Grey-Egerton Bt of Oulton Park, Tarporley	8840 acres	

CORNWALL

	1872	2001
Total acreage	758,961 acres	880,768 acres
Agricultural acreage	721,012 acres	665,516 acres
Non agricultural acreage	37,949 acres	215,252 acres
Population	362,343	479,600
Owners of nothing at all	348,477	213,100
Total Dwellings	73,950	205,000
Smallholdings: 1872 owners of less than one acre 2000 owners of 0–2ha (0–4.94 acres)	8717	573
Landowners over one acre (1872) Landowners over 2ha (2000)	5149	6057
Landowners over 500 acres	220	122
Acreage (and percentage) of county owned by owners of over 500 acres	495,420 acres (65.3%)	91,212 acres (10.3%)

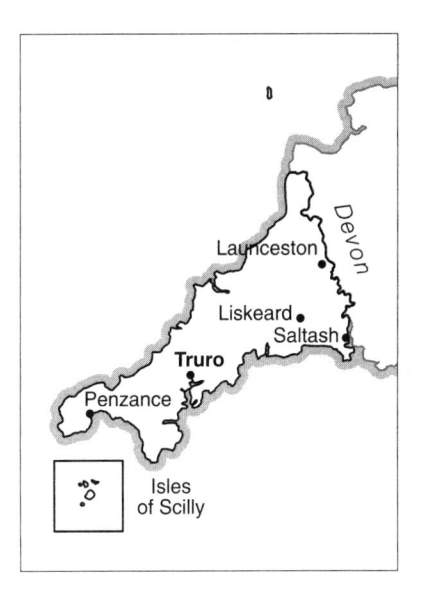

Top Landowners 2001

GEORGE HUGH BOSCAWEN, 9TH VISCOUNT FALMOUTH *42,000 acres, with 2000 acres in Kent. No. 2 in 1872.* Born in 1919, he is the owner of one of the largest landed estates in the country. According to the County Council, he is the single biggest applicant for planning consents in Cornwall and has more than twice as many official contacts with the council as the Duchy of Cornwall. A former Coldstream Guards captain he was educated at Eton and Cambridge University. He was the Lord Lieutenant from 1977 to 1994. His son and heir Evelyn now lives at the family seat, Tregothnan.

MR EDWARD FORTESCUE OF BOCONNOC *7500 acres. No. 4 in 1872.* He is the owner of the estate which has descended from the fourth largest landowner in nineteenth-century Cornwall, Cyril Fortescue. Local opinion holds that the estate is still about 20,000 acres but the owners refute this. There is a beautiful 20-acre park now open to the public on some occasions. They are relatives of the Fortescue family in Devon, who also still retain a large landholding (see Devon).

SIR RICHARD HARRY RASHLEIGH, 6TH BARONET *15,000 acres. No. 1 in 1872.* Born in 1958, Sir Harry now lives in Menabilly, the house once rented by the family to the writer Daphne du Maurier, and made famous by her. Almost all of the estate is tenanted or let, and is still huge. But the family are intensely secretive and the exact size cannot be ascertained.

Other significant landowners in the county include the Williams family with 20,000 acres. The main holdings in 1872 were too small to appear in the top 10 list, but the family have been significant landowners in the county for centuries, and still are, with homes at Burncoose, Grampound, Tredrea and Scorrier.

Significant Institutional Landowners

1872: The largest institutional landowner was the Church of England with 27,167 acres. The Duchy of Cornwall had 12,516 acres.
2001: The Duchy of Cornwall owns over 25,000 acres of the county, including the Scilly Isles. The National Trust has a similar estate amounting to about 22,000 acres, with a further 6928 acres under protection. The County Council owns 11,144 acres of farmland. The Diocese of Truro owns 2520 acres.

TOP 10 IN 1872

1	Mr Jonathan Rashleigh of Menabilly, Par	30,156 acres	with 6740 elsewhere
2	Viscount Falmouth of Mereworth Castle, Maidstone, Kent	25,910 acres	with 4696 elsewhere
3	Lord Robartes MP of Lanrhydock, Bodmin	22,234 acres	
4	Mr Cyril Fortescue of Boconnoc, Lostwithiel	20,148 acres	with 2837 elsewhere
5	Mr Gustavus Basset of Tehidy Park, Redruth	16,969 acres	
6	Earl of Mount-Edgcumbe MP of Mount Edgcumbe, Devonport	13,288 acres	with 4935 elsewhere
7	Mr Christopher Hawkins of Trewithen, Probus	12,119 acres	
8	Mr Francis Thynne of Haynes Park, Bedford	10,224 acres	with 4737 elsewhere
9	Rev Sir Vyell Vyvyan of Trelowarren, Helstone	9738 acres	
10	Colonel Arthur Tremayne MP of Carclew, Perranarworthal	8823 acres	

THE COUNTIES OF ENGLAND

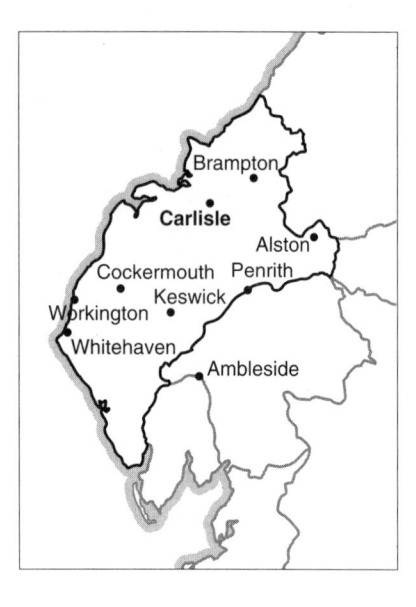

CUMBRIA

(Incorporated much of Westmoreland in 1974.)

	1872	2001
Total acreage	844,836 acres*	1,686,336 acres
Agricultural acreage	694,270 acres	1,124,285 acres
Non agricultural acreage	36,540 acres	562,051 acres
Population	220,253	682,451
Owners of nothing at all	204,740	410,751
Total Dwellings	44,061	209,000
Smallholdings: 1872 owners of less than one acre	9617	
2000 owners of 0–2ha (0–4.94 acres)		388
Landowners over one acre (1872)	5896	
Landowners over 2ha (2000)		5956
Landowners over 500 acres	189	338
Acreage (and percentage) of county owned by owners of over 500 acres	381,004 acres (45.1%)	358,203 acres (21.2%)

* In 1901 the Ordnance Survey credited Cumbria with 1,001,273 acres of land, including 261,147 acres of waste and commons (Bulmers *History & Directory of Cumberland* 1901). The 1872 Return underestimated waste significantly.

Top Landowners 2001

THE 7TH EARL OF LONSDALE *70,000 acres*. Four times married, James Lowther, the 7th Earl, born in 1922, has done much to restore and refurbish one of the very rare estates that is bigger, at least in Cumbria, than that held by his ancestor in 1872 (no. 4). The 5th Earl was described as 'almost an emperor, not quite a gentleman' by King Edward VII, such was his wealth from the coal that lay under much of the land. The present earl lives at the family seat, Askham Hall, Penrith.

SIMON HOWARD AND FAMILY *13,000 acres*. He is a descendant of the Earl of Carlisle, who heads the 1872 list of landowners. The estate, and its beautiful castle, Castle Howard, were the setting for the TV drama *Brideshead Revisited*. Simon Howard, born in 1956, is the son of the late Lord Howard of Henderskelf, a former chairman of the BBC.

THE 13TH EARL OF CARLISLE *10,000 acres*. Simon Howard's cousin, George William Beaumont Howard, the 13th Earl of Carlisle, born in 1949, lives at Naworth Castle, another of the Howard mansions in Cumbria. Educated at Eton and Oxford, he rose to the rank of major in the 9/12th Lancers.

Significant Institutional Landowners

1872: The largest institutional landowner was the Church of England with 21,216 acres. The Church Commission and Deans held almost 6000 additional acres. The Admiralty had 9432 acres.

2001: The National Trust owns 111,314 acres in Cumbria, with a further 24,420 acres protected. The Church Commissioners own 5800 acres and the County Council owns 1069 acres of farmland. The Forestry Commission owns 51,000 acres of the 153,000 acres of woodland in the county. The Crown Estate owns 3450 acres of the county.

TOP 10 IN 1872

1	Earl of Carlisle of Castle Howard, Yorks	47,730 acres	with 30,810 elsewhere
2	Earl of Lonsdale of Lowther Castle, Penrith	28,228 acres	with 39,837 elsewhere
3	Sir Frederick Graham Bt of Netherby, Carlisle	25,270 acres	with 138 elsewhere
4	Mr Henry Howard of Greystoke Castle, Penrith	15,225 acres	with 2315 elsewhere
5	Lord Leconfiled MP, of Petworth House, Sussex	11,147 acres	with 98,788 elsewhere
6	Sir Richard Musgrave Bt of Edenhall, Penrith	10,543 acres	with 4906 elsewhere
7	Sir Wilfred Lawson Bt MP of Brayton Castle, Carlisle	7730 acres	with 564 elsewhere
8	Sir Henry Vane Bt of Hutton-in-the-Forest, Penrith	7194 acres	
9	Mr Henry Curwen of Workington Hall	6011 acres	with 1107 elsewhere
10	Mr Jonas Burns-Lindow of Irton House, Whitehaven	5934 acres	

DERBYSHIRE

	1872	2001
Total acreage	620,995 acres	650,115 acres
Agricultural acreage	589,945 acres	443,134 acres
Non agricultural acreage	31,049 acres	206,981 acres
Population	379,394	954,100
Owners of nothing at all	359,528	428,900
Total Dwellings	78,309	404,000
Smallholdings: 1872 owners of less than one acre 2000 owners of 0–2ha (0–4.94 acres)	12,874	184
Landowners over one acre (1872) Landowners over 2ha (2000)	6992	3581
Landowners over 500 acres	167	89
Acreage (and percentage) of county owned by owners of over 500 acres	408,151 acres (65.7%)	110,700 acres (17%)

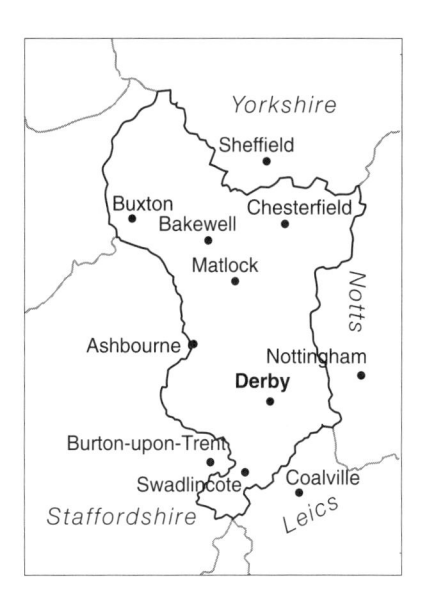

Top Landowners 2001

THE 11TH DUKE OF DEVONSHIRE AND FAMILY *35,000 acres, with 30,000 acres in Yorkshire, 8000 acres in Ireland and some land in Sussex. No. 1 in 1872*. The Devonshire estate is one of the very few estates to be fairly fully documented by a member of the family, the duchess, in her book *The Estate: A View from Chatsworth* (Macmillan 1990). The land is held in a series of trusts, as are most landed estates, mainly to avoid inheritance tax. As the duchess points out, there are still taxes to pay however. The duke, born in 1920, was decorated in World War Two. His son, the Marquess of Hartington, born in 1944, runs the estate. Father and son both went to Eton. The family live on the estate at Chatsworth.

THE 11TH DUKE OF RUTLAND *10,000 acres with 2000 acres in Lincolnshire, 4000 acres in Cambridgeshire and 12,000 acres in Leicestershire. No. 2 in 1872*. See Leicestershire (p.245) for full entry on the Duke of Rutland and family.

THE 3RD VISCOUNT SCARSDALE *10,000 acres, with 2050 acres in Scotland. No. 4 in 1872*. Francis John Nathaniel Curzon, the 3rd Viscount, was born in 1924, educated at Eton and served in the Scots Guards. The family home, Kedleston, of which he is the 30th Lord of the Manor, is now in the hands of the National Trust, with an 800-acre endowment. He lives in Ross-shire but is still the patron of three livings, which he cannot 'present' as he is a Catholic.

Significant Institutional Landowners

1872: The largest institutional landowner was the Church of England with 21,250 acres.
2001: The National Trust owns 35,137 acres in Derby, with 3751 acres protected. The Forestry Commission owns 5100 acres and the Church Commissioners own 3000 acres.

TOP 10 IN 1872

1	Duke of Devonshire (MP) of Chatsworth, Bakewell	89,462	acres	with 109,110 elsewhere
2	Duke of Rutland of Belvoir Castle, Grantham, Lincs	27,069	acres	with 43,068 elsewhere
3	Sir John Crewe Bt of Calke Abbey, Ashby-de-la-Zouche	12,923	acres	with 15,133 elsewhere
4	Rev. Lord Scarsdale of Kedleston, Derby	9606	acres	with 323 elsewhere
5	Lord Howard of Glossop (MP) of Glossop Hall, Manchester	9108	acres	with 8803 elsewhere
6	Duke of Portland of Welbeck Abbey, Worksop, Notts	8074	acres	with 175,125 elsewhere
7	Mr Thomas Evans MP of Allestree Hall, Derby	6799	acres	with 1327 elsewhere
8	Lord Vernon of Sudbury Hall, Derby	6154	acres	with 3647 elsewhere
9	Hon Mrs Fitzclarence-Hunloke of Wingworth Hall, Chesterfield	6006	acres	
10	Colonel Sir Francis Burdett Bt of Ramsbury Manor, Westbury, Wilts	5923	acres	with 15,061 elsewhere

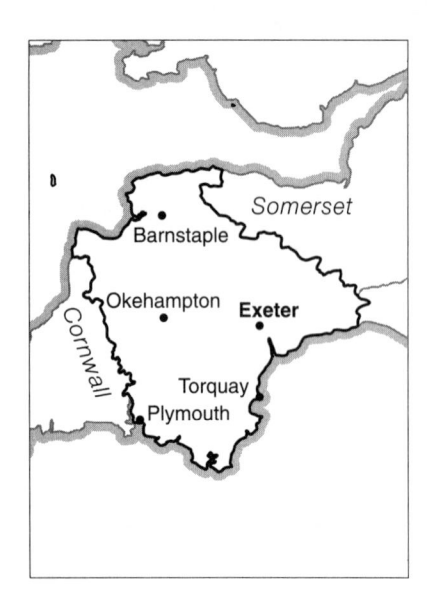

DEVONSHIRE

	1872	2001
Total acreage	1,516,981 acres	1,658,278 acres
Agricultural acreage	1,441,132 acres	1,265,853 acres
Non agricultural acreage	75,849 acres	392,425 acres
Population	601,374	1,053,400
Owners of nothing at all	569,565	469,700
Total Dwellings	105,200	449,000
Smallholdings: 1872 owners of less than one acre	21,647	
2000 owners of 0–2ha (0–4.94 acres)		871
Landowners over one acre (1872)	10,162	
Landowners over 2ha (2000)		10,985
Landowners over 500 acres	415	237
Acreage (and percentage) of county owned by owners of over 500 acres	936,726 acres (61.7%)	190,479 acres (11.4%)

Top Landowners 2001

THE 22ND BARON CLINTON *26,000 acres.* Gerard Nevile Mark Fane Trefusis, born in 1934, is the 22nd Lord Clinton, a title he re-established in 1965 after it had been in abeyance since 1957. He is a nephew of the Queen Mother and is married to Nicola Harriett Coote, a descendant of landowners from Ireland (see Laois). The estate is split in two large chunks, one portion in central and north Devon and the other around the coastal town of Budleigh Salterton. He is related to the Fortescue family, and is a descendant of Devon's largest landowners in the last century, the Rolles (see nos. 1 and 9 in table below). The family home is at Heanton Satchville, Okehampton.

SIR HUGH STUCLEY *Total holdings 15,000 acres.* Hugh George Coplestone Bampfylde Stucley, born in 1945, is the 6th baronet and the current owner of an estate that is little changed in size since his ancestor held it in 1872 (no. 7). The estate has been in the family for 600 years. In a local television programme in 1999 he admitted owning 10,000 acres and professed uncertainty about the other 5000, but said it was possible that was how much he owned. He is married to the daughter of a landowner from Berks, Angela Toller, and his four sisters are all married to landowning aristocrats, in Dorset, Shropshire, Herts and north Devon. The family seat is at Affeton Castle, near Crediton.

LADY MARGARET FORTESCUE *9000 acres. No. 3 in 1872.* Lady Margaret Fortescue, born in 1923, is, with her daughter, the only member of this once huge landowning family (see Cornwall) from the West Country still living on part of the estate. Lady Margaret is the eldest daughter of the late 5th Earl, and inherited the estate. She was divorced from Bernard van Cutsem, a Royal courtier and landowner who died in 1975. Her daughter, Eleanor, is married to the 9th Earl of Arran and they live at the original family seat, Castle Hill, Filleigh. The current Earl Fortescue, the 8th, lives in London, giving his address in *Debrett's* as the House of Lords in which he no longer sits.

Other significant landowners in the county include Henry Massey Lopes, the 3rd Baron Roborough (no. 10 in 1872), with 5000 acres in the county and 34,500 acres in Sutherland. Born in 1940 and educated at Eton he did a stint in the Coldstream Guards before succeeding to the title and the estates.

Significant Institutional Landowners

1872: The largest institutional landowner was the Church of England with 58,527 acres. The Church Commissioners owned 5390 acres. The Duchy of Cornwall owned 48,457 acres.
2001: The Duchy of Cornwall owns 72,397 acres of Devon, mostly around Dartmoor. The National Trust owns 31,764 acres, with over 3000 acres protected. The Forestry Commission owns 22,369 acres and the County Council owns 10,729 acres of farmland. The Church Commissioners own 5385 acres.

TOP 10 IN 1872

1	Hon Mr Mark George Kerr Rolle of Stephenstone, Torrington	55,592 acres	
2	Duke of Bedford (MP) of Woburn Abbey, Bedford	22,607 acres	with 63,728 elsewhere
3	Earl Fortescue (MP) of Castle Hill, South Molton	20,171 acres	with 10,716 elsewhere
4	Earl of Devon (MP) of Powderham Castle	20,049 acres	with 33,026 elsewhere
5	Lord Poltimore of Court Hall, North Molton	19,833 acres	
6	Earl of Portsmouth of Hurstborne Park, Whitechurch, Hants	16,414 acres	with 30,570 elsewhere
7	Sir George Stucley Bt MP of Moreton, Bideford	16,155 acres	with 3652 elsewhere
8	Sir Thomas Dyke Acland Bt MP of Killerton, Exeter	15,018 acres	with 24,878 elsewhere
9	Lord Clinton (MP) of Heanton Satchville, Beaford	14,431 acres	with 20,345 elsewhere
10	Sir Massey Lopes Bt MP of Maristow, Roborough	11,977 acres	with 126 elsewhere

DORSET

	1872	2001
Total acreage	573,936 acres	655,884 acres
Agricultural acreage	541,086 acres	478,375 acres
Non agricultural acreage	32,850 acres	177,509 acres
Population	195,537	673,000
Owners of nothing at all	184,634	286,900
Total Dwellings	39,410	297,000
Smallholdings: 1872 owners of less than one acre	7494	
2000 owners of 0–2ha (0–4.94 acres)		446
Landowners over one acre (1872)	3409	
Landowners over 2ha (2000)		2757
Landowners over 500 acres	191	218
Acreage (and percentage) of county owned by owners of over 500 acres	449,762 acres (78.4%)	197,867 acres (30.1%)

Top Landowners 2001

HON MRS CHARLOTTE TOWNSHEND *15,000 acres with 3000 acres in Notts and 40 acres in London. No. 6 in 1872.* Born in 1955, the daughter of the 9th Viscount Galway, who died in 1970, she inherited the first part of her estate when she was 15. Her mother, a daughter of the 7th Earl of Ilchester, died in the 1990s, leaving Mrs Townshend both the Dorset estate and the remainder of the Holland estate in west London. Divorced from her first husband, she is presently married to James Reginald Townshend, from a landowning family called Rowley in Northants, where he is a potential claimant to the dormant baronetcy of Rowley of 1786. She has one son, born in 1984.

THE 12TH BARON DIGBY *15,000 acres.* Edward Henry Kenlem Digby, born in 1924, still lives at the ancestral mansion at Minterne and still holds most of the original family acreage in trust for his son and heir Henry Noel, a banker, educated, like his father, at Eton. The most famous recent member of the family was the late Pamela Harriman who married Sir Winston Churchill's son, and later the American multimillionaire Avril Harriman. The Clinton administration made her the American ambassador to Paris in the 1990s.

THE 10TH EARL OF SHAFTSBURY *9700 acres.* Anthony Ashley Cooper, born in 1938, is the 10th Earl of Shaftsbury and continues to hold the patronage of five church of England parishes at his disposal. This is the only clear indication, apart from local wisdom, that most of the ancestral lands are still intact, if in trust and diminished. Educated at Eton and Oxford he did a stint in the 10th Hussars before taking up the baton as Chairman of the London Philharmonic Orchestra in 1966.

Other significant landowners in the county include Ivor Mervyn Vigors Guest, the 4th Viscount Wimborne, born in 1968 and educated at Eton, with 4000 acres in the county and 20,200 acres in Perthshire. Sir Richard Sutton Bt has 900 acres in the county with 1000 acres in Berks, 21 acres in London and 7574 acres in Aberdeenshire. Descended from the family of Roland de Sutton, who lived in Nottingham in the early part of the 13th century, the *Sunday Times* estimated his worth at £112 million in its 2000 list.

Significant Institutional Landowners

1872: The largest institutional landowner was the Church of England with 19,536 acres.
2001: The National Trust owns 21,918 acres in Dorset with 915 protected. The Forestry Commission owns 16,333 acres. The County Council owns 7291 acres of farmland. The Duchy of Cornwall owns 3600 acres. The Ministry of Defence owns 8760 acres.

TOP 10 IN 1872

1	Major General Fox-Pitt-Rivers of Rushmore, Salisbury, Wilts	24,942 acres	with 2762 elsewhere
2	Mr George Wingfield-Digby of Sherborne Castle	21,230 acres	with 5653 elsewhere
3	Mr Walters Bankes of Kingston Lacy, Wimbourne	19,228 acres	
4	Lord Wimborne of Canford Manor, Wimbourne	17,400 acres	with 66,130 elsewhere
5	Earl of Shaftesbury (MP) of St Giles, Cranbourne	17,317 acres	with 4468 elsewhere
6	Earl of Ilchester of Redlynch, Bruton, Somerset	15,981 acres	with 16,868 elsewhere
7	Mr Reginald Weld of Lulworth Castle, Wareham	15,478 acres	with 47 elsewhere
8	Mr John Sawbridge-Erle-Drax MP of Holnest Park, Sherborne	15,069 acres	with 8518 elsewhere
9	Lord Alington (MP) of Crichill, Wimborne	14,756 acres	with 2744 elsewhere
10	Mr Richard Brinsley Sheridan MP of Frampton Court, Dorchester	11,468 acres	

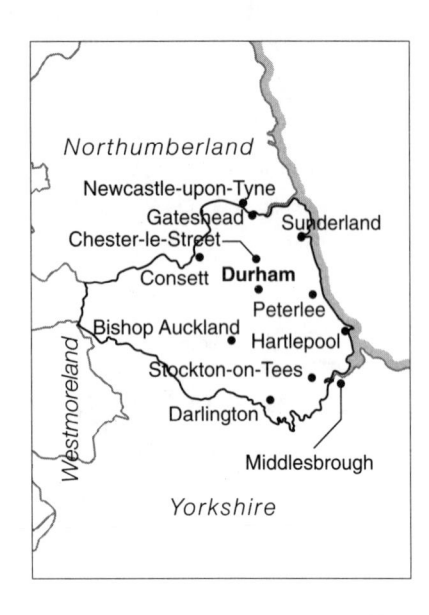

DURHAM

	1872	2001
Total acreage	517,719 acres	601,364 acres
Agricultural acreage	491,833 acres	351,423 acres
Non agricultural acreage	25,886 acres	249,941 acres
Population	685,089	607,800
Owners of nothing at all	650,772	302,300
Total Dwellings	144,705	253,000
Smallholdings: 1872 owners of less than one acre	31,205	
2000 owners of 0–2ha (0–4.94 acres)		167
Landowners over one acre (1872)	3112	
Landowners over 2ha (2000)		1790
Landowners over 500 acres	151	142
Acreage (and percentage) of county owned by owners of over 500 acres	368,046 acres (71.1%)	144,825 acres (24%)

Top Landowners 2001

THE 11TH BARON BARNARD *53,000 acres.* He is an indirect descendant of the top landowner on the list in 1872, the Duke of Cleveland. That title became extinct in 1891 and the minor title of Barnard, along with the lands, passed to the Vane family, who resurrected the Barnard peerage in 1892. Born in 1923, Barnard was Lord Lieutenant of Durham for 18 years. An honorary colonel in the TA he was also provincial grand master of the Durham Freemasons. His heir is the Hon Henry Francis, born in 1959 and, like his father, an old Etonian. He lives at the family seat, Raby Castle, Darlington.

THE 6TH EARL OF DURHAM *9500 acres. No. 3 in 1872.* Anthony Lambton, born in 1922, inherited the earldom and the family lands in 1970, but disclaimed the peerage for life in order to remain in the Commons as an MP for Berwick upon Tweed. He became a junior minister in the MoD but resigned his seat in 1973 following a minor scandal. He remains a patron of two Church of England parishes. His heir is the Hon Edward Richard, Baron Durham, who is married to a daughter of the Knight of Glin, in Ireland. He gives two residences in *Debrett's*, Biddick Hall at Chester-le-Street, and Villa Cetinale, Siena in Italy.

THE 11TH VISCOUNT BOYNE *8000 acres. No. 2 in 1872.* The Boyne estate, once the second largest in this county, is now largely concentrated in Shropshire, with almost all the Durham acreage gone. The present title holder, Gustavus Michael Stucley Hamilton-Russell born in 1965 and educated at Harrow and the Royal Agricultural College, Cirencester, farms at Bridgenorth in Shropshire. Originally an Anglo-Irish military family, his grandfather was killed during the retreat from Dunkirk in 1940. His father was Lord in Waiting to the Queen and a Director of National Westminster Bank. The present peer's son and heir, Frederick Gustavus, was born in 1997.

Significant Institutional Landowners

1872: The largest institutional landowner was the Church of England with 37,660 acres but the Church Commissioners also held 26,868 acres and the Deans held 9273 acres.
2001: The county owns 4800 acres of farmland. The Ministry of Defence owns and leases 726 acres and the Forestry Commission owns 7017 acres.

TOP 10 IN 1872

1	Duke of Cleveland (MP) of Raby Castle, Darlington	55,837 acres	with 48,357 elsewhere
2	Viscount Boyne of Brancepeth Castle, Durham	18,023 acres	with 12,182 elsewhere
3	Earl of Durham of Lambton Castle, Durham	14,664 acres	with 15,807 elsewhere
4	Marquess of Londonderry (MP) of Seaham Hall, Sunderland	12,823 acres	with 37,500 elsewhere
5	Earl of Eldon of Shirley House, Croydon	11,841 acres	with 13,920 elsewhere
6	Mr John Bowes MP of Streatlam Castle, Gateshead, Yorks	8313 acres	with 34,877 elsewhere
7	Mr Anthony Wilkinson of Hulam Castle, Eden	7940 acres	with 3250 elsewhere
8	Mr Henry Surtees MP of Redworth Hall, Darlington	7377 acres	with 2079 elsewhere
9	Sir William Eden Bt of Windlestone Hall, Bishop's Auckland	6096 acres	with 1832 elsewhere
10	Mr Edward Joicey of Newton Hall, Stocksfield-on-Tyne	5816 acres	with 2038 elsewhere

ESSEX

	1872	2001
Total acreage	950,435 acres	907,269 acres
Agricultural acreage	902,913 acres	643,670 acres
Non agricultural acreage	47,522 acres	263,599 acres
Population	466,436	1,569,900
Owners of nothing at all	444,131	704,100
Total Dwellings	92,356	666,000
Smallholdings: 1872 owners of less than one acre	14,833	
2000 owners of 0–2ha (0–4.94 acres)		449
Landowners over one acre (1872)	7472	
Landowners over 2ha (2000)		2929
Landowners over 500 acres	366	401
Acreage (and percentage) of county owned by owners of over 500 acres	555,803 acres (58.5%)	346,404 acres (38.1%)

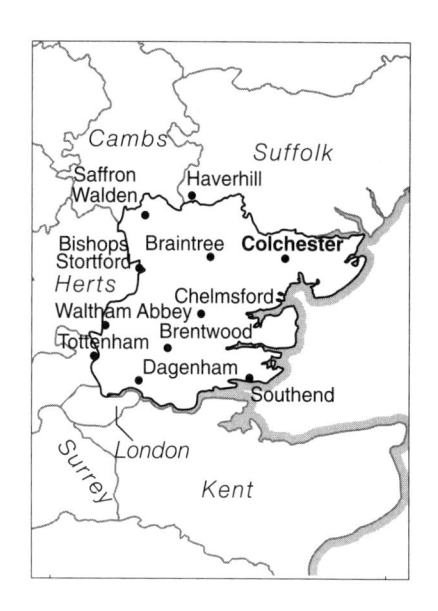

Top Landowners 2001

THE 18TH BARON PETRE *15,000 acres. No. 1 in 1872.* John Patrick Lionel Peter, the 18th Baron, was born in 1942 and educated at Eton and Oxford. He still maintains two county mansions as homes, Ingatestone Hall and Writtle Park, and became a Deputy Lord Lieutenant of the county in 1991. The title was created in 1603 but a predecessor was Henry VIII's secretary of state and was rewarded with monastic lands in Essex. He is the patron of three Church of England parishes, but being a Catholic cannot present the parish priest. His heir is the Hon Dominic William, born in 1966.

THE 10TH BARON BRAYBROOKE *7000 acres. No. 2 in 1872.* Robin Henry Charles Neville, born in 1932 and educated at Eton and Cambridge, has given the beautiful house Audley End to English heritage and it is open to the public. He lives at Abbey House, a smaller mansion on the estate. Thrice married he has seven daughters, one of whom, Caroline, is married to the Earl of Derby, a remote cousin. Although some acreage has been sold over the years most of the estate remains intact. He is a patron of three parishes and has been a deputy Lord Lieutenant of Essex since 1980.

THE 6TH BARON RAYLEIGH *4000 acres. No. 3 in 1872.* John Gerald Strutt was born in 1960 and educated at Eton and the Royal Military Academy, Sandhurst. Following a stint in the Welsh Guards he studied at the Royal Agricultural College, Cirencester, to prepare for his inheritance. The estate, which is still largely intact, was a major supplier of milk to London. The title dates to 1821 but was granted to a daughter of the Duke of Leinster. The 3rd Baron Rayleigh was a renowned physicist and won a Nobel prize. The estate and business is run from Terling Place near Chelmsford

Significant Institutional Landowners

1872: The largest institutional landowner was the Church of England with 29,529 acres. The Deans owned 4721 acres.
2001: The Ministry of Defence owns and leases 15,446 acres a huge fall from the 1973 total of 41,054 acres. The county owns 2450 acres. The National Trust owns 2504 acres and the Church Commissioners own 2248 acres.

TOP 10 IN 1872

1	Lord Petre of Thorndon Hall, Brentwood	19,085 acres	
2	Lord Braybrooke of Audley End, Saffron Walden	9820 acres	with 3691 elsewhere
3	Lord Rayleigh of Terling Place, Witham	8632 acres	
4	Lord Brooke MP of Easton Lodge, Dunmow	8617 acres	with 5227 elsewhere
5	Mr Digby Hanmer Wingfield-Baker of Orsett Hall, Romford	8545 acres	
6	Sir Thomas Western of Felix Hall, Witham	7875 acres	with 2134 elsewhere
7	Mr John Houblon of Hallingbury, Bishop's Stortford	7127 acres	with 8388 elsewhere
8	Mrs Honywood of Mark's Hall, Coggeshall	6898 acres	with 561 elsewhere
9	Mr John Jolliffe Tufnell of Langleys, Chelmsford	6582 acres	with 1002 elsewhere
10	Colonel Thomas Bramston of Skreens, Chelmsford	5426 acres	

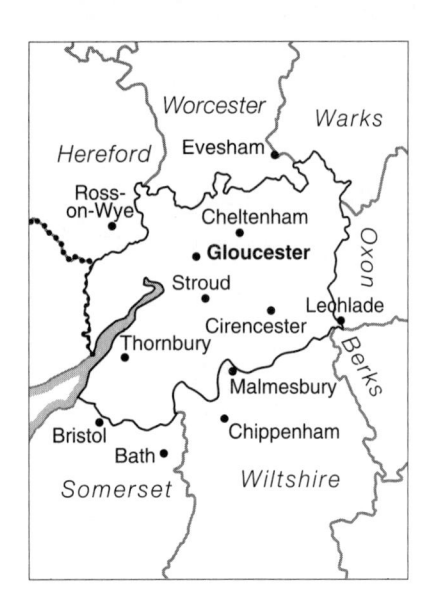

GLOUCESTERSHIRE

	1872	2001
Total acreage	733,640 acres	652,011 acres
Agricultural acreage	696,958 acres	509,908 acres
Non agricultural acreage	36,682 acres	142,103 acres
Population	534,640	549,500
Owners of nothing at all	496,935	246,600
Total Dwellings	101,474	233,000
Smallholdings:		
1872 owners of less than one acre	29,280	
2000 owners of 0–2ha (0–4.94 acres)		403
Landowners over one acre (1872)	8425	
Landowners over 2ha (2000)		3260
Landowners over 500 acres	250	215
Acreage (and percentage) of county owned by owners of over 500 acres	454,732 acres (61.9%)	211,287 acres (41.4%)

Top Landowners 2001

THE 11TH DUKE OF BEAUFORT *52,000 acres. No. 2 in 1872.* David Robert Somerset was born in 1928 and succeeded his cousin, the 10th Duke, known as Master. The estate was consolidated at the end of the nineteenth century, with sales in Wales and purchases in Gloucester, the part around the duke's Badminton House, centre of the Badminton Horse Trials, becoming known as Beaufortshire. The 10th Duke never attended the House of Lords, which took almost ten years to notice his death in 1984. The current duke is an accomplished art dealer and was once a member of the international jet set. His heir, the Marquess of Worcester, was born in 1952 and like his father was educated at Eton. Worcester is married to Tracy Ward, an aristocratic actress.

THE 8TH EARL OF BATHURST *8000 acres. No. 4 in 1872.* Henry Allen John Bathurst was born in 1927 and succeeded to the title in 1943. Educated in Canada, then at Eton and Oxford, he served as an officer in the 10th Hussars. The family still live on and around the estate which remains close to its nineteenth-century size. He is a former president of the Royal Forestry Society and of the Institute of Sales and Marketing Management. His son and heir is Lord Apsley, born in 1961, who now runs the estate from Sapperton, near Cirencester.

THE 3RD BARON VESTY AND VESTY FAMILY *4500 acres with 7000 acres in Essex, 6400 acres in Argyll and 15,000 acres in Ross & Cromarty.* Samuel George Armstrong Vesty, born in 1941, is the titular head of the once prominent meat and food distributors best known in the high street as the Dewhurst butchers chain, now sold off. Educated at Eton, he had a spell in the Scots Guards before taking on the family company. The peerage, granted in 1922, was controversial, the King himself raising objections. Despite that Lord Vesty's son and heir, the Hon William Guy, born in 1983, was a page of honour to the Queen between 1995 and 1998. The family seat is Stowell Park, near Northleach, but there are other landholdings in Essex and Scotland. Lord Vesty's brother, Edmund, owns a large estate in Sutherland (see p.301).

Significant Institutional Landowners

1872: The largest institutional landowner was the Church of England with 43,088 acres. The Deans and the Church Commissioners together owned over 7000 acres.
2001: The Forestry Commission owns 23,153 acres. The county owns 8710 acres of farmland. The National Trust owns 8156 acres with 1000 protected. The Ministry of Defence owns and leases 3093 acres. The Duchy of Cornwall owns 1863 acres and the Crown Estate owns 1972 acres. The Church Commissioners own 1506 acres.

TOP 10 IN 1872

1	Lord Fitz-Hardinge (MP) of Berkeley Castle, Gloucester	18,264 acres	with 2010 elsewhere
2	Duke of Beaufort (MP) of Badminton, Chippenham	16,610 acres	with 34,475 elsewhere
3	Lord Sherborne of Sherborne Park, Northleach	15,773 acres	with 150 elsewhere
4	Earl Bathurst (MP) of Oakley Park, Cirencester	10,320 acres	with 3343 elsewhere
5	Mr Robert Stayner Holford MP of Weston Birt, Tetbury	9332 acres	with 6987 elsewhere
6	Rt Hon Sir Michael Hicks-Beach Bt MP of Williamstrip Park, Fairford	7199 acres	with 4135 elsewhere
7	Mr Thomas William Master MP of the Abbey, Cirencester	7190 acres	
8	Earl of Eldon of Shirley House, Croydon	6664 acres	with 19,097 elsewhere
9	Lord Sudeley (MP) of Gregynog, Newtown, Montgomery	6620 acres	with 17,333 elsewhere
10	Earl of Ducie (MP) of Tortworth Court, Falfield	5193 acres	with 8799 elsewhere

HAMPSHIRE

(Known in 1872 as Southampton county)

	1872	2001
Total acreage	884,649 acres	934,092 acres
Agricultural acreage	840,416 acres	549,201 acres
Non agricultural acreage	44,232 acres	384,891 acres
Population	544,684	1,605,700
Owners of nothing at all	517,213	729,500
Total Dwellings	98,283	674,000
Smallholdings: 1872 owners of less than one acre 2000 owners of 0–2ha (0–4.94 acres)	21,236	383
Landowners over one acre (1872) Landowners over 2ha (2000)	6235	2675
Landowners over 500 acres	301	307
Acreage (and percentage) of county owned by owners of over 500 acres	655,439 acres (74%)	331,946 acres (35.5%)

Top Landowners 2001

BRIGADIER GENERAL THE 8TH DUKE OF WELLINGTON *7000 acres with 4700 acres in Ayr and 20,000 acres elsewhere. No. 2 in 1872.* Arthur Valerian Wellesley, born in 1915, is an English duke, a Dutch prince, the duke of both Ciudad Rodrigo and of Vittoria, both in Spain, the Marquess of Torres Vedras, also in Spain, and a count in Portugal. All the titles descend to him from the 1st Duke, the victor at Waterloo over Napoleon in 1812 – an event which shaped European history for a century. A decorated brigadier in the modern British army, the present duke still holds lands granted to his ancestor in Belgium and Spain. He lives at the family seat in Hampshire, at Stratfield Saye near Basingstoke, and the family have become much more active in the management of the London property at Apsley House on Hyde Park. His son and heir, the Marquess of Duoro, a former MEP, is chairman or director of a series of large international corporations.

THE 6TH EARL OF NORMANTON *6000 acres. No. 10 in 1872.* Shaun James Christian Welbore Ellis Agar, born in 1945, was educated at Eton and was a captain in the Blues and Royals, the most prestigious of the British cavalry regiments. His estate is much reduced from that of his ancestor in 1872, but he remains a patron of three Church of England parishes. His heir, Viscount Somerton, was born in 1982. They continue to live at the family seat at Somerley near Ringwood.

THE 10TH EARL OF PORTSMOUTH *3000 acres. No. 1 in 1872.* Quentin Gerard Carew Wallop, the present Earl, was born in 1954 and educated at Eton and Millfield. An astute businessman, he sold property in the 1980s and created a property trust with the proceeds. He is the hereditary Bailiff of Burley, New Forest. His son and heir is Viscount Lymington, born in 1981. The Earl is president of his local Conservative Association and lives at the Farleigh House, the family seat near Basingstoke.

Significant Institutional Landowners

1872: The largest institutional landowner was the Church of England with 22,484 acres. The Deans and Church Commissioners owned over 10,000 acres. Winchester School owned 7629 acres and the Oxford Colleges owned 6000 acres.
2001: The Forestry Commission owns 49,756 acres. The Ministry of Defence owns and leases 24,040 acres. The National Trust owns 8130 acres. The county owns 4850 acres of farmland. The Church Commissioners own 2903 acres.

TOP 10 IN 1872

1	Earl of Portsmouth of Hurstborne Park, Whitchurch	17,460	acres	with 29,524 elsewhere
2	Lt Gen the Duke of Wellington (MP) of Stratfield Saye, Basingstoke	15,847	acres	with 3269 elsewhere
3	Lord Ashburton (MP) of The Grange, Alresford	15,330	acres	with 21,442 elsewhere
4	Sir William Perceval Heathcote Bt of Hursley Park, Winchester	14,189	acres	
5	Lord Bolton of Hackwood Park, Basingstoke	13,808	acres	with 15,413 elsewhere
6	Mr John Edward Arthur Willis-Fleming of Stoneham Park, Southampton	11,610	acres	
7	Mr Tankerville Chamberlayne of Cranbury Park, Winchester	11,000	acres	with 1363 elsewhere
8	Mr Melville Portal MP of Laverstoke House, Overton	10,966	acres	
9	Mr William George Ward of Weston Manor, Freshwater	10,000	acres	
10	Earl of Normanton (MP) of Somerley, Ringwood	9468	acres	with 33,493 elsewhere

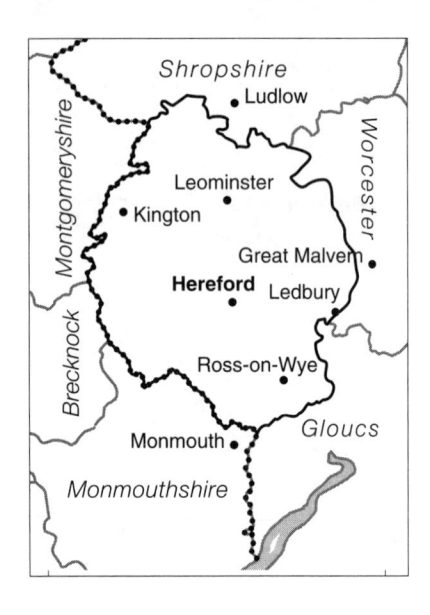

HEREFORDSHIRE

(Merged with Worcestershire in the 1974 restructuring of the counties. 2001 figures are for the merged entity. For details of Worcester in 1872 see p.000)

	1872	1872 figures for Hereford & Worcester combined	2001
Total acreage	506,559 acres	947,620 acres	970,238 acres
Agricultural acreage	487,543 acres	906,550 acres	748,636 acres
Non agricultural acreage	25,660 acres	47,713 acres	221,602 acres
Population	125,370	464,207	699,900
Owners of nothing at all	111,639	428,672	324,200
Total Dwellings	26,371	96,369	289,000
Smallholdings: 1872 owners of less than one acre 2000 owners of 0–2ha (0–4.94 acres)	9085	25,093	547
Landowners over one acre (1872) Landowners over 2ha (2000)	4646	10,442	6114
Landowners over 500 acres	178	379	214
Acreage (and percentage) of county owned by owners of over 500 acres	319,931 acres (63.2%)	629,040 acres (66.3%)	161,697 acres (21.5%)

Top Landowners 2001

THE 10TH VISCOUNT PORTMAN AND PORTMAN FAMILY TRUSTS *9000 acres with 100 acres in London*. The present Viscount Portman was born in 1958 and succeeded in 1999, just in time to lose his seat to the Blair reforms. The family were badly hit for inheritance tax in the twentieth century and all the assets were placed in trust, including the residue of the land in the West Country, which was centred around Clifford in Hereford during the life of the 9th Viscount, the land in Somerset having been sold off earlier to meet the revenue claims on the 7th Viscount's estate (see landowners in London, p.158).

THE LUCAS SCUDAMORE FAMILY OF KENTCHURCH *5000 acres.* Landed gentry rather than aristocracy, this is one of the oldest estates in the country. The family lineage occupies almost six pages of *Burke's Landed Gentry*, starting with a grant of land in 1086 by Alfred of Marlborough, a tenant-in-chief of William the Conqueror. The family is headed by John Edward, born in 1953 as the son of Lt Cdr John Harford Lucas Scudamore who became Deputy Lieutenant of the county in 1958.

THE VAUGHAN FAMILY OF COURTFIELD *2000 acres.*
This is another very ancient family, with the first recorded holding in the area in 1436. The family is currently headed by Patrick Charles More Vaughan, born in 1943, who is a London-based chartered surveyor. Francis Fulford notes in *The Field* that this Catholic family produced one cardinal, Vaughan, who was a leader of the Catholic revival and the 3rd Archbishop of Westminster. He was also responsible for the building of Westminster Cathedral, close to Parliament in London, at the end of the nineteenth century.

Significant Institutional Landowners

1872: The largest institutional landowner was the Church of England with 30,811 acres. The Deans and the Church Commissioners owned an additional 5000 acres.
2001: The National Trust owns 7377 acres with 2500 protected. The county owns 4927 acres of farmland. The Dioscese of Hereford owns 1534 acres and the Church Commissioners 1132 acres. The Ministry of Defence owns and leases 2075 acres.

TOP 10 IN 1872

1	Mr John Hungerford Arkwright of Hampton Court, Leominster	10,559 acres	
2	Mr Andrew Johnes Rouse-Boughton-Knight of Downton Castle	10,348 acres	with 170 elsewhere
3	Mr Robert Daker Harley of Brampton Bryan, Presteign	9901 acres	with 320 elsewhere
4	Lord Bateman of Shobdon Court, Leominster	7200 acres	with 53 elsewhere
5	Mr Charles Meysey Bolton Clive of Whitfield, Hereford	7000 acres	with 6560 elsewhere
6	Rev Sir George Henry Cornewall Bt of Moccas Court, Hereford	6946 acres	with 368 elsewhere
7	Earl Somers of Eastnor Castle, Ledbury	6668 acres	with 6399 elsewhere
8	Lord Ashburton of The Grange, Alresford, Hants	6583 acres	with 30,189 elsewhere
9	Mrs Symons of Mynde Park, Hereford	6056 acres	
10	The Lady Emily Foley of Stoke Edith Park, Hereford	5561 acres	with 2644 elsewhere

HERTFORDSHIRE

	1872	2001
Total acreage	384,809 acres	404,258 acres
Agricultural acreage	365,568 acres	249,106 acres
Non agricultural acreage	19,240 acres	155,152 acres
Population	192,226	1,005,400
Owners of nothing at all	179,839	457,852
Total Dwellings	39,056	421,000
Smallholdings: 1872 owners of less than one acre	9556	
2000 owners of 0–2ha (0–4.94 acres)		145
Landowners over one acre (1872)	2831	
Landowners over 2ha (2000)		1103
Landowners over 500 acres	164	158
Acreage (and percentage) of county owned by owners of over 500 acres	266,568 acres (69.3%)	137,545 acres (34%)

Top Landowners 2001

THE 6TH MARQUESS OF SALISBURY *3500 acres with 3500 acres in Dorset and land in London. No. 1 in 1872.* Born in 1916, Robert Edward Peter Gascoyne-Cecil was educated at Eton and served as Tory MP for Bournemouth in 1950–54. His family have been at the top of politics since an ancestor served Elizabeth I as her secretary of state and spymaster. The 6th Marquess's son and heir Viscount Cranbourne, born in 1946 and also Eton-educated, was leader of the House of Lords during the Major government and essentially failed to halt the Blairite eviction of the hereditaries in 1999. He is a patron of seven Church of England parishes which suggests that the estimate of the size of the estate above is inadequate. The family continue to live at the beautiful Elizabethan house at Hatfield.

THE 7TH EARL OF VERULAM *2000 acres. No. 4 in 1872.* John Duncan Grimston, educated at Eton and Oxford, was born in 1951. A City banker, he lives at the family seat at Gorehambury. Much of the Crown Estate land, below, was bought from the Grimston family. Educated at Eton and Oxford, he has an entry in the *Sunday Times* Rich List at £30 million based on the old master paintings at Gorehambury. His heir is Viscount Grimston born in 1978.

THE 2ND BARON COBBOLD *2000 acres.* David Anthony Fromanteel Lytton Cobbold, born in 1937, was educated at Eton and Cambridge, and has his family seat at the original home of the Earls of Lytton at Knebworth. His mother was a daughter of the 2nd Earl of Lytton. A banker, he has had a series of high profile City appointments at BP, Close Brothers, TSB and is a Deputy Lieutenant of the county.

Significant Institutional Landowners

1872: The largest institutional landowner was the Church of England with 12,249 acres.
2001: The National Trust owns 4155 acres. The diocese of St Albans owns 3734 acres. The county owns 4927 acres of farmland. The Crown Estate owns 6922 acres.

TOP 10 IN 1872

1	Marquess Salisbury (MP) of Hatfield House	13,389 acres	with 6813 elsewhere
2	Mr Abel Smith MP of Woodhall Park, Ware	11,212 acres	
3	Earl Cowper of Panshanger (Lord Lieutenant of Ireland)	10,122 acres	with 27,747 elsewhere
4	Earl of Verulam (MP) of Gorhambury, St Albans	8625 acres	with 1492 elsewhere
5	Earl Brownlow (MP) of Belton House, Grantham, Lincs	8551 acres	with 49,784 elsewhere
6	Mr Charles Cholmeley Hale of Kings Walden Park, Hitchin	6905 acres	with 1094 elsewhere
7	Lord Dacre (MP) of The Hoo, Welwyn	6658 acres	with 6659 elsewhere
8	Earl of Essex of Cashiobury Park, Watford	5545 acres	with 9325 elsewhere
9	Earl of Lytton of Knebworth Park, Stevenage Viceroy of India	4863 acres	
10	Mr William Baker of Bayfordbury, Hertford	3911 acres	

HUNTINGDONSHIRE

(Merged with Cambridgeshire in county restructuring of 1974. Details for the new county are given in Cambridgeshire entry on p.229.)

	1872
Total acreage	225,613 acres
Agricultural acreage	214,332 acres
Non agricultural acreage	5090 acres
Population	63,708
Owners of nothing at all	59,805
Total Dwellings	14,032
Smallholdings: 1872 owners of less than one acre 2000 owners of 0–2ha (0–4.94 acres)	1816
Landowners over one acre (1872) Landowners over 2ha (2000)	2087
Landowners over 500 acres	73
Acreage (and percentage) of county owned by owners of over 500 acres	140,069 acres (62%)

Top Landowners 2001

See Cambridgeshire (p.229)

Where they are now:
The 4th Baron de Ramsey is a direct descendant of the head of the list of 1872 landowners below, and lives on another part of the original estate (see Cambs).

The present Duke of Manchester (no. 2 in 1872) has had a chequered business career and spent some time in jail in America. His ancestors had an equally rough time and their vicissitudes are colourfully recounted by Cannadine in *Decline and Fall of the British Aristocracy*.

Significant Institutional Landowner

1872: The largest institutional landowner was the Church of England with 13,803 acres.

TOP 10 IN 1872

1	Mr Edward Fellowes MP of Ramsey Abbey	15,629	acres	with 4392 elsewhere
2	Duke of Manchester (MP) of Kimbolton Castle, St Neots	13,835	acres	with 13,477 elsewhere
3	Mr John Moyer Heathcote MP of Connington Castle, Stilton	7144	acres	
4	Mr William Wells MP of Holme Wood, Stilton	6000	acres	
5	Marquess of Huntly of Aboyne Castle, Aberdeen	5711	acres	with 80,000 elsewhere
6	Mr George Fitzwilliam of Milton Park, Peterborough, Northants	5202	acres	with 18,116 elsewhere
7	Earl of Carysfort of Glenart Castle, Arklow, Wicklow	3972	acres	with 21,942 elsewhere
8	Lord Chesham of Latimer, Chesham, Bucks	3787	acres	with 7700 elsewhere
9	Mr William Duberly of Gaynes Hall, St Neot's	3712	acres	with 992 elsewhere
10	Mr Walter Duncombe of Waresley Park, St Neot's	3407	acres	

KENT

	1872	2001
Total acreage	950,607 acres	921,838 acres
Agricultural acreage	903,076 acres	596,815 acres
Non agricultural acreage	47,530 acres	325,023 acres
Population	630,127	1,546,300
Owners of nothing at all	592,444	1,126,400
Total Dwellings	117,388	646,000
Smallholdings: 1872 owners of less than one acre	26,925	
2000 owners of 0–2ha (0–4.94 acres)		432
Landowners over one acre (1872)	7758	
Landowners over 2ha (2000)		3671
Landowners over 500 acres	330	293
Acreage (and percentage) of county owned by owners of over 500 acres	590,755 acres (62.1%)	287,532 acres (31%)

Top Landowners 2001

THE 7TH MARQUESS OF CONYNGHAM *5000 acres. No. 4 in 1872.* Frederick William Henry Francis Conyngham was born in 1924. Educated at Eton he served in the Irish Guards before eventually settling in the Isle of Man, leaving the family acreage at Bifrons near Canterbury and the patronage of one parish in family trusts. Four times married, his son and heir is the Earl of Mount Charles, born in 1951.

THE 6TH BARON SACKVILLE *2000 acres.* Lionel Bertrand Sackville-West was born in 1913 and educated at Winchester and Oxford University. The family acres in Kent were just under 2000 in 1872, with 6500 acres in Sussex and Gloucester. He is currently a patron of 11 parishes, suggesting that the acreage was seriously expanded in the interval. He has four daughters and no direct heir. His grandfather will be remembered for the gift to the National Trust of Knole, described as 'one of the largest private houses in England'. It is stuffed with treasures and with paintings on loan from Lord Sackville. (See also De La Warr in Sussex.)

THE 2ND VISCOUNT D'LISLE *2500 acres.* Philip John Algernon Sidney, born in 1945, is an indirect descendant of the family of the Earls of Leicester. The family seat, Penshurst Place, was surrounded by 4500 acres of land in 1872 and some of this was sold off at various times since. He is a former major in the Grenadier Guards and is active in the City of London. His father was a Governor General of Australia and was created a Viscount in 1956. His son and heir, the Hon Philip, was born in 1985.

Significant Institutional Landowners

1872: The largest institutional landowner was the Church of England with 31,425 acres. The Deans and the Church Commissioners owned over 18,000 acres. The War Office (MoD) had 5767 acres.
2001: The Ministry of Defence owns and leases 12,394 acres (10,815 acres in 1973) of Kent. The National Trust owns 4624 acres with 529 protected. The Church Commissioners own 12,262 acres. The Crown Estate owns 10,023 acres.

TOP 10 IN 1872

1	Viscount Holmesdale (MP) of Linton Park, Maidstone	16,209 acres	with 1856 elsewhere
2	Earl Sondes (MP) of Lee Court, Faversham	14,157 acres	with 4939 elsewhere
3	Lord Hothfield of Hothfield Place, Ashford	10,144 acres	with 29,132 elsewhere
4	Marquess Conyngham of Bifrons, Canterbury	9737 acres	with 156,973 elsewhere
5	Earl of Darnley of Cobham Hall, Gravesend	9309 acres	with 25,463 elsewhere
6	Earl of Guildford of Waldershare Park, Dover	8065 acres	with 2864 elsewhere
7	Rt Hon Sir William Hart Dyke Bt MP of Lullingstone Castle, Dartford	7951 acres	with 914 elsewhere
8	Sir Edward Cholmeley Dering Bt MP of Surrenden Dering, Pluckley	7280 acres	
9	Marquess of Camden of Wilderness Park, Sevenoaks	7214 acres	with 10,185 elsewhere
10	Sir Edmund Filmer Bt MP of East Sutton Park, Staplehurst	6596 acres	with 12 elsewhere

LANCASHIRE

	1872	2001
Total acreage	947,464 acres	758,490 acres
Agricultural acreage	900,090 acres	520,691 acres
Non agricultural acreage	47,373 acres	237,790 acres
Population	2,819,495	1,424,000
Owners of nothing at all	2,730,760	1,043,500
Total Dwellings	530,490	585,000
Smallholdings: 1872 owners of less than one acre 2000 owners of 0–2ha (0–4.94 acres)	76,177	717
Landowners over one acre (1872) Landowners over 2ha (2000)	12,558	4590
Landowners over 500 acres	275	106
Acreage (and percentage) of county owned by owners of over 500 acres	571,319 acres (60.3%)	113,379 acres (14.9%)

Top Landowners 2001

THE 6TH DUKE OF WESTMINSTER *19,000 acres with 15,000 acres in Cheshire, 95,000 acres in Scotland and 380,000 acres in other parts of the world.* A fuller account of the Ducal lands is given in the London chapter (see p.148). The Abbeystead estate is based in deep fell country in what was the ancient Forest of Bowland, adjacent to landholdings of the Duchy of Lancaster. It is essentially a shooting estate, north of a huge 14,000 acre estate that once belonged to the Towneley family (no. 4 in 1872).

SIR RICHARD BERNARD CUTHBERT DE HOGHTON BT, 14TH BARONET *4000 acres.* The Hoghton estates were first formed in the time of King Stephen (1135-1154) and the Hoghtons were sheriffs of Lancaster in the thirteenth century. They have been in Parliament on and off since the mid fourteenth century. The current baronet, born in 1945 and Ampleforth educated, and his Italian wife have opened the family seat, Hoghton Tower, to the public.

THE FLEETWOOD HESKETH FAMILY OF MEOLS HALL *6000 acres.* The family held over 13,000 acres of Lancaster at the time of the 1872 Returns, in two lots of less than 7000 acres. The first of 4128 acres at Meols owned by Edward Fleetwood Hesketh consisted of a large part of Southport and yielded over £31,000, the modern equivalent of £2.1 million. The second holding, of 9394 acres, with 5784 acres in Northants, was at Ormskirk, held by Sir Thomas Fermor Heketh, a cousin. The family seat at Meols was recently rebuilt by the family of Roger Fleetwood, the last recorded holder of the estate in the *Burke's Landed Gentry* of 1963.

*THE TOWNELEY FAMILY OF DYNELEY *(see below)*
The four daughters of Colonel John Towneley were: Theresa, who married Capt John Delcour; Lucy, who married John Murray of Touchadam and Polmaise; Mary who became a nun in Belgium; and Mabel who married Baron Clifford of Chudleigh. The family trace their descent and the lands from Spartlingus, the first dean of Whalley who was alive around 896. The last incumbent of the estates was Simon Towneley, born in 1921, who lectured on music at Oxford. The 1963–72 *Burke's* records him living at Dyneley, the family seat, near Burnley.

Significant Institutional Landowners

1872: The largest institutional landowner was the Church of England with 27,904 acres.
2001: The Duchy of Lancaster owns 11,648 acres. The Ministry of Defence owns and leases 1541 acres (2312 acres in 1973). The county owns 511 acres of farmland. The Church Commissioners own 5670 acres.

TOP 10 IN 1872

1	Earl of Derby (MP) of Knowsley, Prescot	57,000 acres	with 11,942 elsewhere
2	Earl of Sefton of Croxteth Hall, Liverpool	20,250 acres	
3	Mr John Talbot Clifton of Lytham Hall, Lytham	15,802 acres	
4	Marquis de Casteja of Scarisbrick Hall, Ormskirk	14,764 acres	
5*	4 Daughters of John Towneley of Burnley (Note: Shown in Bateman as Yorks, but the 14,086 acres here are in the Returns for Lancs.)	14,086 acres	with 10,081 elsewhere
6	Duke of Devonshire (MP) of Chatsworth, Bakewell	12,681 acres	with 185,891 elsewhere
7	Mr William Foster of Hornby Castle	10,841 acres	with 1884 elsewhere
8	Mr Thomas Weld-Blundell of Ince-Blundell, Liverpool	10,400 acres	
9	Earl of Ellesmere of Worsley Hall, Manchester	10,080 acres	with 3142 elsewhere
10	Sir Thomas George Fermor-Hesketh Bt of Rufford Hall, Ormskirk	9394 acres	with 5799 elsewhere

LEICESTERSHIRE

(2001 figures include Rutland. Rutland has, however, been restored as a separate county and will produce separate figures soon. See also p.253)

	1872	1872 figures for Leicestershire & Rutland combined	2001
Total acreage	519,227 acres	612,305 acres	630,838 acres
Agricultural acreage	493,265 acres	581,699 acres	468,118 acres
Non agricultural acreage	26,959 acres	31,612 acres	162,720 acres
Population	269,311	291,384	916,900
Owners of nothing at all	255,463	276,111	434,600
Total Dwellings	58,606	63,372	371,000
Smallholdings: 1872 owners of less than one acre	8921	9782	
2000 owners of 0–2ha (0–4.94 acres)			134
Landowners over one acre (1872)	4927	5491	
Landowners over 2ha (2000)			2654
Landowners over 500 acres	167	203	212
Acreage (and percentage) of county owned by owners of over 500 acres	306,097 acres (58.9%)	390,720 acres	180,417 acres (28.5%)

Top Landowners 2001

THE 11TH DUKE OF RUTLAND *12,000 acres with 10,000 acres in Derbyshire, 2000 acres in Lincolnshire and 4000 acres in Derbyshire. No. 1 in 1872.* Descended from one of the oldest families in the UK, De Ros, who obtained their first peerage in 1264, the 11th Duke has manged to hold on to much of the family acreage and art treasures. David Robert Charles Manners was born in 1959 and succeeded to the dukedom in 1999. He is a patron of 11 parishes, but being a Catholic cannot present the parish priest to the congregation. He is active in the City of London where he is a freeman and a Liveryman of the Gunmakers. His heir, born in 1999, is the Marquess of Granby. The family seat is Belvoir Castle in Lincs, with another occupied mansion at Haddon Hall, Bakewell, Derby.

THE 2ND BARON HAZLERIGG (AND 14TH BARONET) *2000 acres.* The baronetcy, the 14th, is much older than the title, which was granted to the present peer's father in 1945. The family was established in Leicester in the eleventh century by Roger de Hesilrige, a knight in the Conqueror's army, according to *Burke's*. The knighthood was from James I in 1622 but the family achieved fame as commanders in the Parliamentary army, and were governors of Newcastle for Cromwell. The land is much as stated in the 1872 Returns, and was too small for inclusion in Bateman. The seat is at Noseley Hall, Billesdon.

THE 1ST BARON KIMBALL *1500 acres.* Lord Kimball, born in 1928, is the former Conservative MP for Gainsborough, Marcus Richard Kimball, who was enobled as a life peer in 1985. He is the son of a soldier landowner from Hants, who married into the Leics landed gentry (Ratcliff of Stanford Hall). Educated at Eton and Cambridge, he rose to the rank of major in the local TA regiment, the Leicester Yeomanry. He has been the Deputy Lieutenant of the county since 1984 and is married to June Mary, the daughter of another landowner, Montague Fenwick, of Great Stucley Hall in Hunts. The family seat is at Great Easton Manor, near Market Harborough.

Significant Institutional Landowners

1872: The largest institutional landowner was the Church of England with 39,078 acres.
2001: The Church Commissioners own 1727 acres. The Ministry of Defence owns and leases 2550 acres (539 acres in 1973). The county owns 7526 acres of farmland. The Crown Estate owns 8080 acres.

TOP 10 IN 1872

1	Duke of Rutland (MP) of Belvoir Castle, Grantham	30,188	acres	with 30,188 elsewhere
2	Major General the Earl Howe of Gopsal Hall, Atherstone	9755	acres	with 23,914 elsewhere
3	Earl of Stamford and Warrington of Enville Hall, Stourbridge	9012	acres	with 21,950 elsewhere
4	Earl of Dysart of Buckminster Park, Grantham	8420	acres	with 18,770 elsewhere
5	Mr Ambrose Charles Phillips De L'Isle of Garendon Park, Loughborough	7358	acres	
6	Mrs Perry-Herrick of Beaumanor Park, Loughborough	6560	acres	with 7187 elsewhere
7	Mr Harry Leycester Powys-Keck of Stoughton Grange, Leicester	6529	acres	
8	Mr William Ann Pochin of Edmonthorpe Hall, Oakham	5865	acres	with 1956 elsewhere
9	Hon Mr Harry Tyrwhitt-Wilson of Keythorpe Hall, Leicester	5758	acres	with 1164 elsewhere
10	Mr Edward Bourchier Hartopp (MP) of Dalby Hall, Melton Mowbray	5423	acres	with 28,767 elsewhere

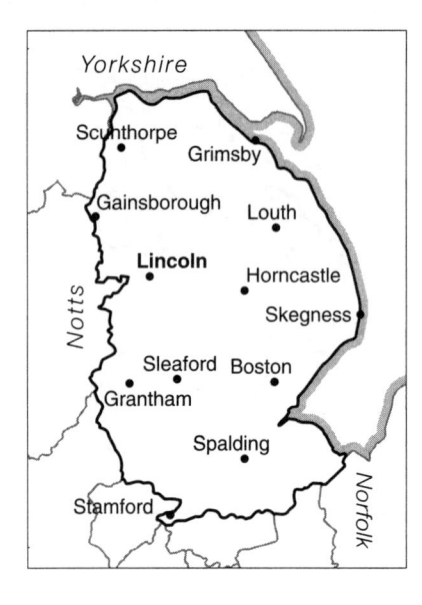

LINCOLNSHIRE

	1872	2001
Total acreage	1,606,543 acres	1,462,315 acres
Agricultural acreage	1,526,215 acres	1,278,678 acres
Non agricultural acreage	80,327 acres	183,637 acres
Population	436,599	605,600
Owners of nothing at all	406,102	265,000
Total Dwellings	94,212	262,000
Smallholdings: 1872 owners of less than one acre 2000 owners of 0–2ha (0–4.94 acres)	13,768	505
Landowners over one acre (1872) Landowners over 2ha (2000)	16,729	4814
Landowners over 500 acres	435	739
Acreage (and percentage) of county owned by owners of over 500 acres	1,007,742 acres (62.7%)	766,178 acres (52.3%)

Top Landowners 2001

THE 27TH BARONESS WILLOUGHBY DE ERESBY *15,000 acres, with 63,200 acres in Perthshire.* Nancy Jane Marie Heathcote-Drummond-Willoughby is the 27th holder of a title created in 1313 for Roger Willoughby, a soldier with Edward I in his wars with the Scots and the French. She was born in 1934 and still has a potential seat in the reformed House of Lords. She is the joint hereditary Lord Great Chamberlain of England with the Marquess of Cholmondeley, who has retained his seat, and she or her heirs take it in turns with his family to hold the honour. She is heiress to the Aveland barony, which together with her Barony, owned 163,000 mostly English acres, in 1872. She has two palatial homes, Grimsthorpe Castle at the estate in Lincs and Drummond Castle in Perthshire.

THE 7TH BARON BROWNLOW *10,000 acres with 12,000 acres elsewhere.* Edward John Peregrine Cust was born in 1936. Educated at Eton he did a stint in the Grenadier Guards before occupying a number of senior positions in the City of London. The family seat, Belton House, is now with the National Trust and the peer lives in Jersey. A patron of ten livings, the estate was retained when the house was given to the Trust in 1984. His family gold and silver plate was lent to 10 Downing Street for Margaret Thatcher's premiership, she being the local girl made good. Local rumours exist that she is a descendant of the family by an irregular liaison – rumour based entirely on her fine complexion, this being a characteristic of the Cust family.

THE 11TH BARON MONSON *3000 acres.* John Monson, born in 1932, was educated at Eton and Cambridge. The estate came to almost 8100 acres in 1872, with an additional 2000 acres in Surrey. The first knight in the family, Sir Thomas (1611), had been an MP for Castle Rising and other parts of Lincolnshire since 1597. They were prominent courtiers in the reign of Victoria. The present baron still retains a home on the original estate lands at South Carlton.

Significant Institutional Landowners

1872: The largest institutional landowner was the Church of England with 99,264 acres. The Church Commissioners and Deans owned an additional 14,000 acres. The Crown Estate owned 12,745 acres. London Bridge Hospital owned 6145 acres. Christ's Hospital owned 6477 acres.

2001: The Crown Estate owns 49,400 acres. The diocese of Lincolnshire owns 15,266 acres. The Ministry of Defence owns and leases 14,662 acres (21,739 acres in 1973). The National Trust owns 2574 acres. The county owns 22,557 acres of farmland. The Church Commissioners own 11,748 acres. The Duchy of Cornwall owns 1936 acres.

TOP 10 IN 1872

1	Earl of Yarborough of Brocklesby Park, Ulceby	56,795 acres	with 98 elsewhere
2	Baroness Willoughby D'Eresby of Grimsthorpe, Bourne	24,696 acres	with 107,524 elsewhere
3	Mr Henry Chaplin MP of Blakeney Hall, Sleaford	23,370 acres	
4	Mr Christopher Turnor MP of Stoke Rochford, Grantham	20,664 acres	
5	Earl Brownlow (MP) of Belton House, Grantham	20,233 acres	with 38,102 elsewhere
6	Earl of Dysart of Buckminster Park, Grantham	18,025 acres	with 9084 elsewhere
7	Lord Aveland (MP) of Normanton Park, Stamford	17,637 acres	with 13,638 elsewhere
8	Mr Ernest Richard Cust of Arthingworth, Northants	14,868 acres	with 2254 elsewhere
9	Mr Henry Frederick Clare Viner and Lady Viner of Newby Hall, Ripon, Yorks	14,443 acres	with 12,262 elsewhere
10	Marquess of Bristol of Ickworth Park, Bury St Edmunds, Suffolk	13,745 acres	with 18,269 elsewhere

MIDDLESEX

(Middlesex no longer appears as an entity in local government. The figures for 2001 below are those for the area now defined as Greater London. The county appears here because of the large landholdings still retained in Middlesex by the Duke of Northumberland and the Earl of Jersey.)

	1872 (Middlesex)	2001 (Greater London)
Total acreage	143,014 acres	429,954 (including other counties)
Agricultural acreage	135,863 acres	32,861 acres
Non agricultural acreage	2045 acres	397,093
Population	253,197	7,300,000
Owners of nothing at all	241,316	3,320,700
Total Dwellings	44,383	3,061,000
Smallholdings: 1872 owners of less than one acre 2000 owners of 0–2ha (0–4.94 acres)	9006	74
Landowners over one acre (1872) Landowners over 2ha (2000)	2875	328
Landowners over 500 acres	50	9
Acreage (and percentage) of county owned by owners of over 500 acres	52,684 acres (36.8%)	6953 acres (9.2%)

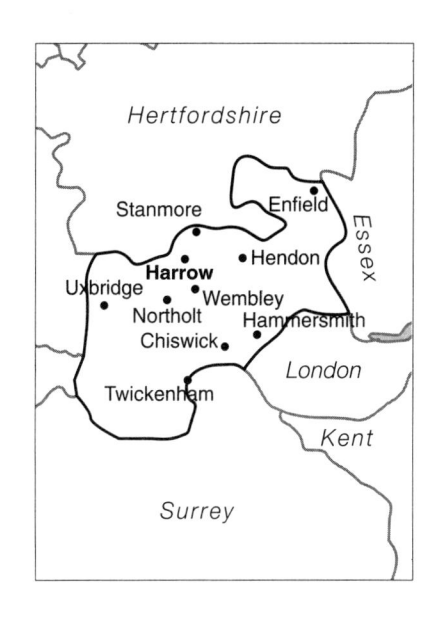

Top Landowners 2001

THE 10TH EARL OF JERSEY *1900 acres. No. 3 in 1872.* George Francis William Child Villiers was born in 1976 and is an actor. He succeeded his grandfather to the title in 1998, his father having died. Both his father and grandfather lived on the tax efficient island of Jersey. The family are descended from Viscount Grandison, who was either the father or uncle of Barbara Villiers (see entry for the Duke of Grafton in Norfolk, p.248) depending on whose version of her ancestry you believe (*Debrett's* and *Burke's* offer different lineage). They were connected to the bank of Child & Co. Osterley Park, the family estate, is the last big open space in Middlesex and any development would yield a new fortune for the family. Each acre of development land in Middlesex is worth about £2.2 million, giving the estate a theoretical value of £3.8 billion in the unlikely event of permission being granted for development. He lives in London.

12TH DUKE OF NORTHUMBERLAND, Sion House and park, Middlesex *550 acres, with 120,000 acres elsewhere.* See Northumberland (p.250) for details on the Duke of Northumberland.

Significant Institutional Landowners

1872: the Church of England owned 1749 acres. The Church Commissioners and Deans owned 2102 acres. Oxford colleges owned 3074 acres. Cambridge colleges owned 2075 acres. The Crown owned 2382 acres. The Duchy of Lancaster owned 2273 acres. The three hospitals, Bart's, Thomas's and Christ's owned 1800 acres.
2001: The National Trust owns 885 acres around London.

TOP 10 IN 1872

1	Earl of Strafford (MP) of Wrotham Park, Barnet	4436	acres	with 10,558 elsewhere
2	Sir Charles Mills Bt of Hillingdon Court Middlesex	2709	acres	
3	Earl of Jersey of Middleton Park, Bicester	1982	acres	with 17,407 elsewhere
4	Mr Thomas Wood of Littleton, Chertsey	1571	acres	with 8409 elsewhere
5	Mr Charles Newdegate MP of Arbury Nuneaton	1491	acres	with 5318 elsewhere
6	Mr Francis Deane of Middlesex	1448	acres	
7	Mr Frederick Cater of Middlesex	1363	acres	
8	Lord Northwick MP of Northwick Park, Moreton-in-the-Marsh, Glos	1260	acres	with 8635 elsewhere
9	Mr D.A. Hambrough of Middlesex	1252	acres	
10	Lady Delpierre of Middlesex	1051	acres	

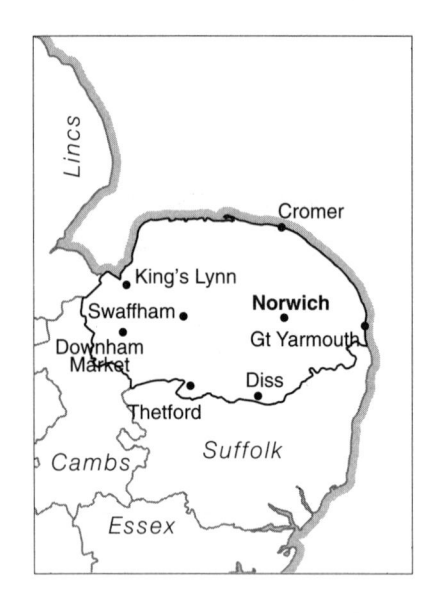

NORFOLK

	1872	2001
Total acreage	1,234,884 acres	1,328,118 acres
Agricultural acreage	1,173,139 acres	1,063,256 acres
Non agricultural acreage	61,745 acres	264,862 acres
Population	438,656	768,500
Owners of nothing at all	412,008	331,700
Total Dwellings	99,428	336,000
Smallholdings: 1872 owners of less than one acre	16,552	
2000 owners of 0–2ha (0–4.94 acres)		589
Landowners over one acre (1872)	10,096	
Landowners over 2ha (2000)		4250
Landowners over 500 acres	395	632
Acreage (and percentage) of county owned by owners of over 500 acres	852,504 acres (69%)	658,911 acres (49.6%)

Top Landowners 2001

THE 7TH EARL OF LEICESTER *26,000 acres. No. 1 in 1872.*
Edward Douglas Coke was born in 1934 and educated in South Africa. Most of his training was in agriculture, to prepare him for his vast inheritance at Holkham Hall near Wells. It is one of the most beautiful houses in England and he is the president of the Historic Houses Association. He is descended from a family of MPs first enobled in 1837. His son, Viscount Coke, was a page of honour to the queen from 1991–1993, maintaining a royal connection that goes back to the mid 1800s. The family were significant agricultural reformers in the nineteenth century.

THE QUEEN *20,100 acres, with 50,000 acres elsewhere.* The Queen has a private family estate at Sandringham. See Chapter 4 for further details.

THE 11TH DUKE OF GRAFTON *11,000 acres.* Hugh Denis Charles Fitzroy was born in 1919 and in 1970 succeeded to the title which was created for the second son of King Charles II by Barbara Villiers in 1675. In 1872 the estate of 25,000 acres included parts of London around Euston station but had no acreage in Norfolk. The duke is currently patron of four parish livings and of almost everything to do with the national heritage both locally in Norfolk and nationally over the years. His wife, Fortune, has been Mistress of the Robes to the Queen for many years. His son and heir is the Earl of Euston, born in 1947 and like his father educated at Eton. The family live at Euston Hall.

Where they are now:
There are a number of old landed families still living in the county. They were all too small to appear in the top 10 list for 1872 but include the Walpoles, descendants of the Prime Minister, the Le Stranges of Hunstanton, the De Grays of Merton and the Berneys of Hocking, who have recently built a new family seat (according to Francis Fulford in the *Field*). In addition there are the Buxtons and the Gurneys, landowners and one time hereditary directors of Barclays Bank.

Significant Institutional Landowners

1872: The largest institutional landowner was the Church of England with 56,240 acres. The Church Commissioners and Deans owned over 8000 acres.
2001: The Forestry Commission owns 34,176 acres. The Ministry of Defence owns 27,116 acres (19,400 acres in 1973). The county owns 18,780 acres of farmland. The National Trust owns 17,211 acres with over 1200 acres protected. The Crown Estate owns 14,011 acres.

TOP 10 IN 1872

1	Earl of Leicester of Holkham Park, Wells	44,090 acres	
2	Marquess Townshend (MP) of Rainham Hall, Fakenham	18,343 acres	with 1567 elsewhere
3	Marquess of Cholmondeley of Cholmondeley Castle, Natwich, Cheshire	16,995 acres	with 16,996 elsewhere
4	Mr Henry Evans-Lombe of Bylaugh Park, East Derham	13,832 acres	
5	Lord Hastings of Melton Constable, Dereham	12,737 acres	with 6821 elsewhere
6	Earl of Orford (MP) of Wolterton Park, Aylsham	12,341 acres	
7	Lord Walshingham (MP) of Merton Hall, Thetford	12,120 acres	with 7028 elsewhere
8	Lord Suffield of Gunton Park, Norwich	11,828 acres	
9	Sir George Ralph Leigh Hare Bt of Stow Hall, Downham Market	11,310 acres	
10	Earl of Kimberley of Kimberley Hall, Wymondham, Lord Lieutenant of Ireland	10,805 acres	with 342 elsewhere

NORTHAMPTONSHIRE

	1872	2001
Total acreage	592,771 acres	584,937 acres
Agricultural acreage	563,132 acres	452,929 acres
Non agricultural acreage	29,638 acres	132,008 acres
Population	243,891	594,800
Owners of nothing at all	229,335	272,100
Total Dwellings	52,539	249,000
Smallholdings: 1872 owners of less than one acre	10,101	
2000 owners of 0–2ha (0–4.94 acres)		102
Landowners over one acre (1872)	4455	
Landowners over 2ha (2000)		1890
Landowners over 500 acres	182	263
Acreage (and percentage) of county owned by owners of over 500 acres	377,790 acres (63.7%)	230,042 acres (39.3%)

Top Landowners 2001

THE 9TH DUKE OF BUCCLEUCH AND QUEENSBURY *11,000 acres with 266,000 elswhere. No. 1 in 1872.* Boughton House at Kettering is the fourth of the Duke's mansion-palaces, and is attached to the smallest of his various landholdings, overall down 50% since 1872. For a fuller account of the duke's landholdings see Dumfriesshire (p.280).

THE 9TH EARL SPENCER *13,000 acres. No. 2 in 1872.* Charles Edward Maurice Spencer, born in 1964, is probably best known as the brother of the late Diana, Princess of Wales. He is also owner of an ancient estate and mansion, Althorp. The estate, though only about half its 1872 size, is highly profitable, and may soon benefit from the sale of some derelict acres as development land, at £550,000 per acre. 'Enough to keep the estate going for another two generations' according to the earl, quoted in the *Sunday Times'* Rich List for 2000. Patron of 12 livings or parishes, his heir is Viscount Althorp, born in 1994.

THE 7TH MARQUESS OF NORTHAMPTON *15,000 acres with 10,000 acres in Warwick and 5000 acres in Surrey. No. 6 in 1872.* The four-times married Spencer Douglas David Compton, born in 1946, owns two princely homes, Castle Ashby in Northants and Compton Wynyates in Warwick. Educated at Eton he is patron of nine parishes. His has children by three of his marriages and his heir is the Earl Compton, born in 1973.

Other significant landowners in the county include Major Sir Hereward Wake Bt, 14th Baronet, with 2000 acres, part of a family which has been residents of Bourne and Deeping since the time of King Stephen (1135-1154). Descendants of Hereward Wac, an heroic figure in Anglo Saxon literature, they convey an aura of military prowess, maintained by the present holder, a major decorated for bravery with the Military Cross in World War Two. His father was a major general. In 1970 they owned the 63,000 acre Amhuinnsuidhe in Inverness, but have since sold it to the Bulmer cider family from Somerset.

Significant Institutional Landowners

1872: The largest institutional landowner was the Church of England with 57,612 acres. The Church Commissioners and the Deans owned over 8000 acres.
2001: The Forestry Commission owns 9995 acres. The diocese of Peterborough owns 5016 acres. The Church Commissioners own 3081 acres.

TOP 10 IN 1872

1	Duke of Buccleuch & Queensbury of Dalkeith Palace, Edinburgh	17,965 acres	with 442,143 elsewhere
2	Earl Spencer (MP) of Althorp Park. Lord Lieutenant of Ireland	16,800 acres	with 10,385 elsewhere
3	Marquess of Exeter of Burghley House, Stamford	15,625 acres	with 12,646 elsewhere
4	Lord Overstone (MP) of Overstone Park	15,045 acres	with 15,804 elsewhere
5	Duke of Grafton (MP) of Euston Hall, Thetford	14,507 acres	with 11,226 elsewhere
6	Vice Admiral the Marquess of Northampton of Castle Ashby	9,649 acres	with 13,852 elsewhere
7	Sir James Hay Langham of Cottesbrook Park	9,118 acres	with 551 elsewhere
8	Sir Rainald Knightley Bt MP of Fawsley, Daventry	8,041 acres	
9	Lord Lilford of Lilford Hall, Oundle	7,998 acres	with 7556 elsewhere
10	Countess of Cardigan (and de Lancastre of Portugal) of Deane Park, Wandsford	7,210 acres	with 8514 elsewhere

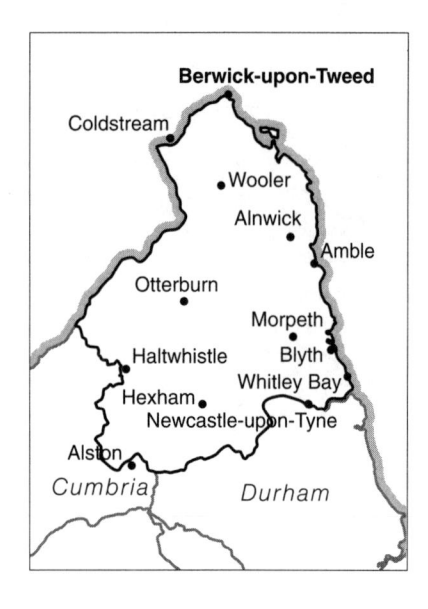

NORTHUMBERLAND

	1872	2001
Total acreage	1,190,044 acres	1,243,320 acres
Agricultural acreage	1,130,541 acres	928,663 acres
Non agricultural acreage	59,502 acres	314,657 acres
Population	386,646	307,700
Owners of nothing at all	374,389	141,300
Total Dwellings	62,436	128,000
Smallholdings: 1872 owners of less than one acre 2000 owners of 0–2ha (0–4.94 acres)	10,036	111
Landowners over one acre (1872) Landowners over 2ha (2000)	2221	2249
Landowners over 500 acres	267	568
Acreage (and percentage) of county owned by owners of over 500 acres	1,066,144 acres (89.5%)	620,870 acres (49.9%)

Top Landowners 2001

THE 12TH DUKE OF NORTHUMBERLAND *120,000 acres with 9000 acres in Berwickshire, 3750 acres in Surrey and 550 acres in Middlesex. No. 1 in 1872.* Ralph George Algernon Percy was born in 1956 and succeeded his unmarried brother, the 11th Duke, who died at the age of 42 in 1995. His estate is a ducal one in the old-fashioned sense, with two thirds of the 1872 lands still in the possession of the family. The gardens at Alnwick Castle, the family seat, are being refurbished at a cost of £30 million. Educated at Eton and Oxford, his heir, the Earl Percy, was born in 1984. The earl was a page of honour to the Queen between 1996 and 1998. The family can trace its ancestry back to Harry Hotspur and, despite breaks in the succession, there is still Plantagenet blood in the Percy veins.

THE 3RD VISCOUNT ALLENDALE *20,000 acres.* Wentworth Hubert Charles Beaumont, born in 1922, was educated at Eton and was a Steward of the Jockey Club. He owns two estates, both inherited from ancestors in the nineteenth century, neither of which were large enough to be amongst the top 10 in 1872. One is sited at Bywell Hall near Stockfields-on-Tyne and the other is at Allenheads Hall, at Allenhead. He was a prisoner of war during World War Two. His son and heir is the Hon Wentworth Peter Ismay, born in 1948. He lives at Bywell Castle and has taken over the estate.

THE 4TH VISCOUNT RIDLEY *9000 acres.* Matthew White Ridley has all the qualifications for a large landowner from the nineteenth century. Born in 1925, he was educated at Eton and Oxford and served as an officer in the Coldstream Guards in World War Two. He has been the Lord Lieutenant of Northumberland since 1984 and is also the Lord Steward of the Queen's household. He married a daughter of the Earl of Scarborough, a large landowner from Yorkshire. The family were MPs in Northumberland from the middle of the eighteenth century. The family seat is at Blagdon, on Seaton Burn near Newcastle–upon-Tyne.

Significant Institutional Landowners

1872: The largest institutional landowner was the Church of England with 39,580 acres. The Admiralty had 20,642 acres.
2001: The Forestry Commission owns 117,696 acres. The Ministry of Defence owns and leases 56,905 acres. The National Trust owns 22,677 acres with 1155 acres protected. The county owns 1672 acres of farmland.

TOP 10 IN 1872

1	Duke of Northumberland (MP) of Alnwick Castle	181,616 acres	with 4781 elsewhere
2	Mr Walter Charles Selby of Biddlestone, Rothbury	30,000 acres	
3	Earl of Tankerville (MP) of Chillingham Castle, Alnwick	28,930 acres	with 2493 elsewhere
4	Commander Sir John Swinburne Bt RN of Capheaton, Newcastle-upon-Tyne	28,902 acres	
5	Mr William Oswald Charlton of Hesleyside, Bellingham	21,200 acres	
6	Mr Thomas Leyland	17,644 acres	with 3426 elsewhere
7	The Earl Grey (MP)	17,599 acres	
8	Earl of Redesdale	17,204 acres	with 9293 elsewhere
9	Mrs Blackett-Ord	15,868 acres	
10	Sir Edward Blackett Bt	15,345 acres	with 2122 elsewhere

NOTTINGHAMSHIRE

	1872	2001
Total acreage	507,337 acres	533,958 acres
Agricultural acreage	481,970 acres	371,156 acres
Non agricultural acreage	25,366 acres	162,772 acres
Population	319,758	1,030,900
Owners of nothing at all	305,239	470,600
Total Dwellings	68,419	431,000
Smallholdings: 1872 owners of less than one acre	9891	
2000 owners of 0–2ha (0–4.94 acres)		155
Landowners over one acre (1872)	4628	
Landowners over 2ha (2000)		1726
Landowners over 500 acres	125	187
Acreage (and percentage) of county owned by owners of over 500 acres	360,387 acres (71.0%)	170,081 acres (31.8%)

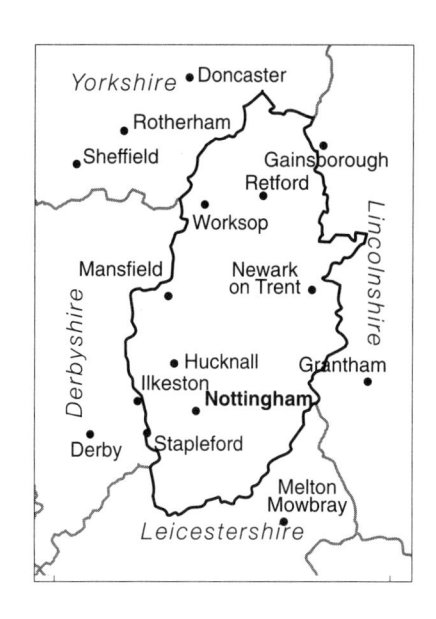

Top Landowners 2001

LADY ANNE CAVENDISH BENTINCK *17,000 acres with 45,000 in Caithness.* Lady Alexandra Margaret Anne Cavendish Bentinck was born in 1916, a daughter of the 7th Duke of Portland (no. 1 in 1872), a title that is now extinct. The Portland dukedom and lands arise from the grants made to Baron Bentinck, a Dutch courtier and soldier who came to England with William of Orange in 1688. In the Victorian era when coal mining in Nottingham was at its height, the duke was one of the richest people in England. The heiress still owns four homes, Welbeck Abbey and Welbeck Woodhouse in Notts, Langwell in Caithness and Bothal Castle in Northumberland. Much of the estate is in trust and some of the shares are held abroad.

THE 4TH BARON BELPER *5000 acres.* Alexander Ronald George Strutt was born in 1912. He served as a major in the Coldstream Guards in World War Two. He is descended from a long line of Members of Parliament, who acquired a peerage and lands in the mid nineteenth century. One of his ancestors was a leading courtier towards the end of Victoria's reign. His son and heir the Hon Richard Henry was born in 1941 and lives in a large house on the estate, which he runs. The family are patrons of two Church of England parishes.

THE HILDYARD FAMILY *2100 acres.* This family are landed gentry, with an estate at Flintham that goes back to 1815, when the niece and heiress of the family married Colonel Thoroton of the Coldstream Guards and swapped the original Yorkshire estate for that at Flintham. The family still hold the estate and the last recorded incumbent was Myles Thoroton Hildyard, born in 1914, a barrister who won a Military Cross in World War Two. As of 1963 he had not married. The entire male line of the family were educated at Eton.

Significant Institutional Landowners

1872: The largest institutional landowner was the Church of England with 21,551 acres. The Deans and Church Commissioners owned 7890 acres.
2001: The Forestry Commission owns 15,305 acres. The Crown Estate owns 10,433 acres. The National Trust owns 3784 acres. The Ministry of Defence rents and leases 3573 acres.

TOP 10 IN 1872

1	Duke of Portland of Welbeck Abbey, Worksop	43,036 acres	with 140,163 elsewhere
2	Duke of Newcastle of Clumber Park, Ollerton	34,467 acres	with 1080 elsewhere
3	The Earl Manvers (MP) of Thoresby Park, Ollerton	26,771 acres	with 11,265 elsewhere
4	Mr Augustus Savile of Rufford Abbey, Ollerton	17,820 acres	with 16,000 elsewhere
5	Lord Middleton of Wollaton Hall, Nottingham	15,015 acres	with 84,561 elsewhere
6	Major General the Earl Howe of Gopsal Hall, Atherstone	11,600 acres	with 22,069 elsewhere
7	Mr Francis John Savile Foljambe MP of Osberton Hall, Worksop	9289 acres	with 5209 elsewhere
8	Mr John Chaworth Musters of Annesley Park	8211 acres	
9	Mr William Webb of Newstead Abbey	5859 acres	with 3677 elsewhere
10	Sir William Fitz-Herbert Bt of Tissington Hall, Ashbourne	5846 acres	with 3339 elsewhere

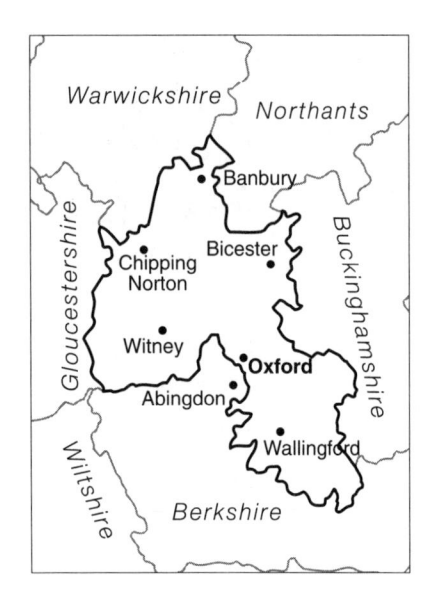

OXFORDSHIRE

	1872	2001
Total acreage	449,283 acres	644,431 acres
Agricultural acreage	426,818 acres	493,253 acres
Non agricultural acreage	22,464 acres	151,178 acres
Population	177,975	590,200
Owners of nothing at all	167,798	273,000
Total Dwellings	37,849	244,000
Smallholdings: 1872 owners of less than one acre 2000 owners of 0–2ha (0–4.94 acres)	6833	171
Landowners over one acre (1872) Landowners over 2ha (2000)	3344	2177
Landowners over 500 acres	165	304
Acreage (and percentage) of county owned by owners of over 500 acres	300,829 acres (66.9%)	280,631 acres (43.5%)

Top Landowners 2001

THE 11TH DUKE OF MARLBOROUGH *11,500 acres. No. 1 in 1872.* John George Vanderbilt Henry Spencer-Churchill was born in 1926 to a title that for a very short while might have gone to his cousin Winston Churchill, the wartime leader of Britain. In turn, Winston Churchill was one of the few people in the twentieth century to be offered (and to refuse) a real dukedom. The Marlborough Estate is about half its 1872 size, with few treasures left in Blenheim Palace, the family seat, built for the 1st Duke by the king after his many military victories in the early eighteenth century. The estate is in trust and will not be inherited by the duke's son and heir the Marquess of Blandford, born in 1955.

THE HARCOURT FAMILY *7000 acres. No. 6 in 1872.* The 2nd Viscount Harcourt, who died in 1979 and with whom the title became extinct, was a diplomat, banker and master of most of the county appointments available in Oxford. His daughter, the Hon Mrs Elizabeth Ann Gascoigne, now occupies the family home at Stanton Harcourt, which has been in the family for over 500 years.

THE 7TH BARON CAMOYS *1000 acres.* This title and the family holding, which has been in the family since at least 1383, is dealt with in the preface of this book (see p.3).

Other significant landowners in the county include the 4th Viscount Astor with 2000 acres (as well as 19,500 acres on the island of Jura in Argyll). William Waldorf Astor, born in 1951, is an old Etonian and was a government minister in the Conservative government of John Major. He lives at Ginge Manor near Wantage and owns most of the island of Jura not owned by Lindsay Bury.

Significant Institutional Landowners

1872: The largest single institutional landowner was the Church of England with 35,822 acres. The Oxford colleges owned 31,000 acres.
2001: The Oxford colleges still own about 30,000 acres. The National Trust owns 9206 acres with 2516 acres protected. The Ministry of Defence owns and leases 8502 acres. The Church Commissioners own 4000 acres. The Crown Estate owns 1251 acres. The Forestry Commission owns 1554 acres.

TOP 10 IN 1872

1	Duke of Marlborough (MP) of Blenheim Palace, Woodstock	21,944 acres	with 1567 elsewhere
2	Earl of Ducie (MP) of Tortworth Court, Falfield, Glos	8798 acres	with 5193 elsewhere
3	Earl of Abingdon (MP) of Wytham Abbey, Oxford	8173 acres	with 13,103 elsewhere
4	Mr Matthew Piers Watt Boulton of Haseley Court, Tetsworth	7945 acres	with 370 elsewhere
5	Sir Henry William Dashwood Bt of Kirtlington Park, Oxford	7515 acres	with 115 elsewhere
6	Mr Edward William Harcourt MP of Nuneham Park, Abingdon	7250 acres	with 686 elsewhere
7	Earl of Jersey of Middleton Park, Bicester	5735 acres	with 13,654 elsewhere
8	Earl of Macclesfield (MP) of Shirburn Castle, Tetsworth	5518 acres	with 9035 elsewhere
9	Viscount Dillon of Dytchley Park, Charlbury	5444 acres	with 89,320 elsewhere
10	Lord Churchill of Cornbury Park, Charlbury	5352 acres	with 3760 elsewhere

RUTLAND

(Rutland became part of Leicestershire in 1974 and was recreated a county in 2000. There are no agricultural statistics or other statistics for 2001 available as yet.)

	1872
Total acreage	93,078 acres
Agricultural acreage	88,434 acres
Non agricultural acreage	4,653 acres
Population	22,073
Owners of nothing at all	20,648
Total Dwellings	4766
Smallholdings: 1872 owners of less than one acre 2000 owners of 0–2ha (0–4.94 acres)	861
Landowners over one acre (1872) Landowners over 2ha (2000)	564
Landowners over 500 acres	25
Acreage (and percentage) of county owned by owners of over 500 acres	73,073 acres (80.6%)

Top Landowners 2001

THE 5TH EARL OF GAINSBOROUGH *4500 acres. No. 1 in 1872.* Anthony Gerard Edward Noel, born in 1923, was educated at Worth Abbey and in the USA. He had been chairman of the Rutland County Council before its dissolution in 1974. Many of the 18,000 acres of 1872 are gone but a substantial estate remains and his son and heir Viscount Campden, born in 1950 and educated at Ampleforth, now runs the estate from the family seat at Exton Park. The family are patrons of two Church of England parishes, but being Catholics cannot present the parish priest.

SIR JOHN EARNEST MICHAEL CONANT BT, 2ND BARONET *2000 acres.* The Conant family have held land in Rutland since the mid-eighteenth century. He was high sheriff of the county in 1960 and succeeded his father, who was knighted and awarded a CVO by the Palace (1954). Sir John's brother Guy was the High Sheriff of Northamptonshire and Deputy Lieutenant of the county. Sir John's son and heir, Simon Edward, was born in 1958 and educated at Eton (like his father) and went to the Royal Agricultural College, Cirencester. The family estate is near Oakham.

Significant Institutional Landowners

1872: The Church of England was the largest institutional landowner with 7349 acres.
2001: The Ministry of Defence owns 847 acres.

TOP 10 IN 1872

1	Earl of Gainsborough of Exton Park, Oakham	15,076 acres	with 3492 elsewhere
2	Lord Aveland (MP) of Normanton Park, Stamford	13,633 acres	with 17,642 elsewhere
3	Mr George Henry Finch MP of Burley-on-the-Hill, Oakham	9183 acres	with 8149 elsewhere
4	Marquess of Exeter MP of Burghley House, Stamford	8998 acres	with 19,273 elsewhere
5	Mr John Maurice Wingfield of Tickencote Hall, Stamford	2905 acres	with 502 elsewhere
6	Mr Edward Monckton of Fineshade, Wansford	2183 acres	with 928 elsewhere
7	Mr Calcraft Kennedy of Rutland	1950 acres	
8	Lord Northwick (MP) of Northwick Park, Moreton-in-the-Marsh	1885 acres	with 8010 elsewhere
9	Mr John Handley of Clipsham (Includes Notts & Lincs)	1736 acres	
10	Mr Richard Lucas of Edithweston Hall, Stamford	1631 acres	with 2116 elsewhere

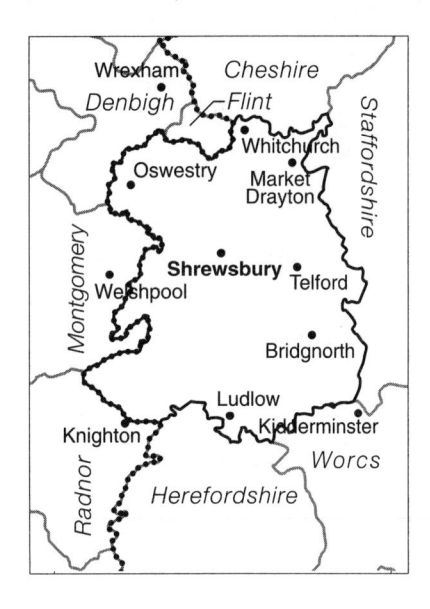

SHROPSHIRE

	1872	2001
Total acreage	791,911 acres	862,411 acres
Agricultural acreage	752,315 acres	692,680 acres
Non agricultural acreage	39,596 acres	169,731 acres
Population	248,111	416,500
Owners of nothing at all	235,992	190,300
Total Dwellings	50,804	174,000
Smallholdings: 1872 owners of less than one acre 2000 owners of 0–2ha (0–4.94 acres)	7281	327
Landowners over one acre (1872) Landowners over 2ha (2000)	4838	4520
Landowners over 500 acres	254	239
Acreage (and percentage) of county owned by owners of over 500 acres	584,181 acres (73.7%)	181,942 acres (21%)

Top Landowners 2001

THE CORBETT FAMILY *15,000 acres*. In the 1872 Returns eleven members of this Shropshire family owned over 30,000 acres. The family still owns land in Shropshire at Longnor and at Acton Reynold. The last knight, Sir John Vincent Corbet, of Moreton Corbet, died in 1996 and the title became extinct.

THE 7TH EARL OF BRADFORD FAMILY TRUSTS *10,000 acres. No. 8 in 1872.* Richard Thomas Orlando Bradford, born in 1947 and educated at Harrow and Cambridge, is a successful London restaurateur and businessman. Faced with death duties of £8 million on his father's estate in 1981, some land and art was sold but about half the original estate remains in trusts for the family. His heir is Viscount Newport, born in 1980. The family are patrons of five church of England parishes. The family live on the estate, but not in the seat at Weston Park, Shifnal.

THE 8TH BARON FORESTER *7500 acres with 12,000 acres in Zimbabwe. No. 6 in 1872.* The *Debrett's* 'predecessors' for this title begins in 1811 with the creation of the peerage. But, as the peer has noted to *Debrett's*, he holds a licence given by Henry VIII to John Forester of Watling St, Shropshire, allowing that man to wear a hat in the royal presence. The present peer is Deputy Lieutenant of the county and his wife, a daughter of the 10th Viscount Cobham, is High Sheriff. He is keenly involved in the CLA, the Forestry Commission, the county show and many other rural activities. Born George Cecil Brooke Weld-Forester in 1938, he was educated at Eton and the Royal Agricultural College. The estate is still very large and he lives at the family seat, Willey Park, Broseley.

Other significant landowners in the county include the 3rd Earl of Plymouth, Robert Ivor Windsor Clive, with 4500 acres, a much diminished estate from their 1872 holding (see Lord Windsor, no. 7 below), but the family continue to live in Shropshire at Oakly Park near Ludlow and are active in county affairs. His son and heir is Viscount Windsor, who now runs the estate from the family seat. Lindsay Claude Neils Bury, with 2500 acres in the county, is a financier and former director of Singer & Friedlander Bank in London. He owns the beautiful Millichope estate and Elizabethan manor of the Childe family at Craven Arms, and a sizable portion of Jura. An old Etonian he is one of the most successful hi-tech investors of his era.

Significant Institutional Landowners

1872: The largest institutional landowner was the Church of England with 25,005 acres.
The National Trust owns 13,960 acres. The Forestry Commission owns 10,593 acres.
2001: The county owns 4447 acres of farmland. The Ministry of Defence owns and leases 4571 acres (1185 acres in 1973).

TOP 10 IN 1872

1	Earl of Powis (MP) of Powis Castle, Welshpool	26,986 acres	with 33,573 elsewhere
2	Duke of Cleveland (MP) of Raby Castle, Darlington	25,604 acres	with 78,590 elsewhere
3	Earl Brownlow (MP) of Belton House, Grantham, Lincs	20,233 acres	with 38,102 elsewhere
4	Duke of Sutherland (MP) of Dunrobin Castle, Golspie	17,495 acres	with 134,1050 elsewhere
5	Viscount Hill (MP) of Hawkstone, Shrewsbury	16,554 acres	
6	General the Lord Forester (MP) of Willey Park, Broseley	14,891 acres	with 724 elsewhere
7	Lord Windsor of Oakley Park, Bromfield	11,204 acres	with 26,250 elsewhere
8	Earl of Bradford (MP) of Weston Park, Shifnal	10,883 acres	with 10,827 elsewhere
9	Mr Henry Reginald Corbet of Adderley Hall, Market Drayton	8856 acres	with 127 elsewhere
10	Mr William Orme Foster MP of Apley Park, Bridgnorth	8547 acres	with 12,515 elsewhere

SOMERSET

	1872	2001
Total acreage	940,483 acres	853,070 acres
Agricultural acreage	893,458 acres	657,711 acres
Non agricultural acreage	47,024 acres	195,359 acres
Population	463,483	477,900
Owners of nothing at all	430,718	251,000
Total Dwellings	92,205	203,000
Smallholdings: 1872 owners of less than one acre	20,370	
2000 owners of 0–2ha (0–4.94 acres)		738
Landowners over one acre (1872)	12,395	
Landowners over 2ha (2000)		5372
Landowners over 500 acres	256	172
Acreage (and percentage) of county owned by owners of over 500 acres	636,081 acres (67.6%)	131,044 acres (15.3%)

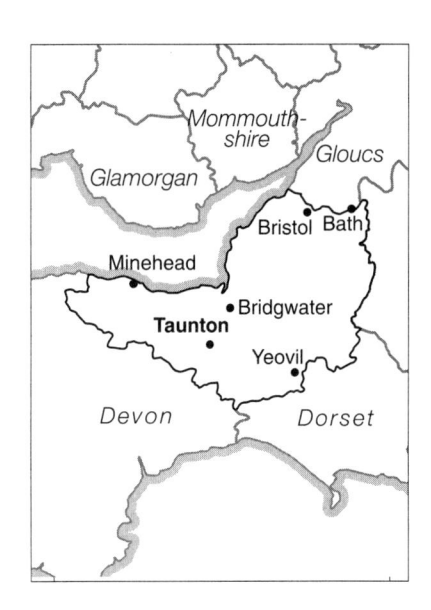

Top Landowners 2001

THE 13TH EARL WALDEGRAVE *4500 acres*. The Waldegrave estate was some 15,425 acres in 1872 and was based, with the Countess, at Navestock in Essex, where she was married to Lord Carlingford. They were important courtiers and government officials in the court of Queen Victoria. In 1872 only 5321 of the acres were in Somerset, but the family were by then Governors of Plymouth and had married into the Devon landowning family of Bastard. The current earl, John Sherbrooke Waldegrave, was born in 1940 and educated at Eton and Cambridge. His brother, William, now a life peer, was Chief Secretary of the Treasury in the Major cabinet 1995–1997. The family seat is at Chewton Mendip, near Bath

THE LUTTRELL FAMILY *10,000 acres. No. 4 in 1872*. The Luttrell family put down roots at Dunster in 1337, when the family, which arrived with the Conqueror, had acquired by marriage the first Somerset estate of Quantoxhead. The Dunster estate was added later The family gave the fortified family home, Dunster Castle, to the National Trust in 1976 and it is open to the public. The estate was retained. The last recorded head of the family was Colonel Sir Geoffrey Walter Fownes Luttrell, born in 1919 and living at both family homes in 1963. He was knighted in 1993. He has no direct heirs but the family are cousins to virtually every landowner in the west country.

THE 8TH EARL OF CASTLE STEWART *2000 acres*. Arthur Patrick Avondale Stuart, the present earl, born in 1928, who describes himself as a farmer, now lives at Babcary in Somerset. The family seat is at Stewartstown in County Tyrone. The title was originally granted as a Scottish barony in 1459. The family owned 32,615 acres of Tyrone and 2260 acres of Cavan in 1872. His son and heir Viscount Stuart was born in 1953 and farms in Devon.

Significant Institutional Landowners

1872: The largest institutional landowner was the Church of England with 36,628 acres. The Church Commissioners owned 8464 acres.
2001: The Crown Estate owns 19,881 acres. The National Trust owns 17,904 acres. The Forestry Commission owns 9614 acres. The County Council owns 8900 acres of farmland. The Duchy of Cornwall owns 7752 acres. The Ministry of Defence owns and leases 2359 acres. The Church Commissioners own 4179 acres.

TOP 10 IN 1872

1	Viscount Portman (MP) of Bryanston, Blandford	24,339 acres	with 9552 elsewhere
2	Earl Poulett of Hinton House, Crewkerne	22,123 acres	with 6 elsewhere
3	Sir Thomas Dyke Acland Bt MP of Killerton, Exeter	20,300 acres	with 19,596 elsewhere
4	Mr George Fownes Luttrell of Dunster Castle	15,374 acres	with 154 elsewhere
5	Sir John Henry Greville Smyth Bt of Ashton Court, Bristol	13,542 acres	with 1432 elsewhere
6	Earl of Ilchester of Redlynch, Bruton	13,169 acres	with 19,680 elsewhere
7	Earl of Carnarvon of Highclere Castle, Newbury	12,800 acres	with 22,783 elsewhere
8	Sir Alexander Bateman Fullerton-Acland-Hood Bt MP of St Audries, Bridgwater	11,337 acres	
9	Marquess of Bath of Longleat, Warminster, Wilts	8212 acres	with 47,362 elsewhere
10	Mr James Harvey Insole of Ely Court, Llandaff	7201 acres	with 1107 elsewhere

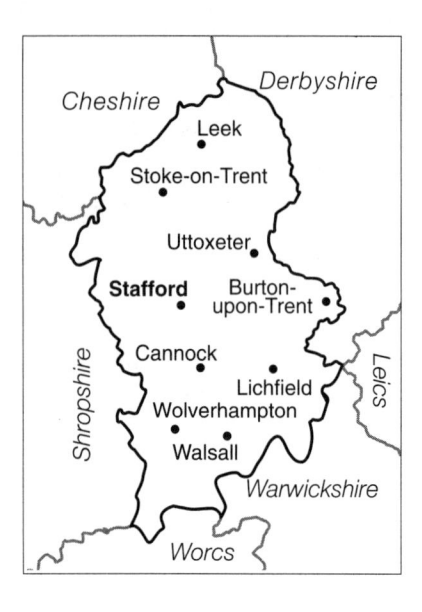

STAFFORDSHIRE

	1872	2001
Total acreage	638,084 acres	671,187 acres
Agricultural acreage	606,179 acres	472,707 acres
Non agricultural acreage	31,904 acres	198,480 acres
Population	858,326	1,054,400
Owners of nothing at all	814,955	498,000
Total Dwellings	167,614	428,000
Smallholdings: 1872 owners of less than one acre	33,672	
2000 owners of 0–2ha (0–4.94 acres)		379
Landowners over one acre (1872)	9699	
Landowners over 2ha (2000)		4306
Landowners over 500 acres	188	458
Acreage (and percentage) of county owned by owners of over 500 acres	424,330 acres (66.5%)	210,744 acres (31.3%)

Top Landowners 2001

TRUSTEES OF THE 5TH EARL OF LICHFIELD *4500 acres. No. 1 in 1872.* Thomas Patrick John Anson, born in 1939, did everything a good landowning aristocrat should do. He was educated at Harrow, the Royal Military Academy Sandhurst and was a lieutenant in the Grenadier Guards. He married a sister of the richest man in the kingdom, the Duke of Westminster and has been a Deputy Lieutenant of Staffordshire since 1996. But he has actually made his career as a photographer of international distinction. The family home, Shugborough Hall, was given to the National Trust with an endowment of 900 acres. But the trustees have retained some of the acreage, estimated at 4500 acres. His heir is Viscount Anson, born in 1978. He was divorced from Lady Leonora Grosvenor in 1986.

TRUSTEES OF THE 6TH BARON BAGOT *6000 acres. No. 6 in 1872.* The current Lord Bagot, the 9th, is Heneage Charles Bagot, born in 1914. He lives in North Wales. He acquired the peerage through a descent via a cousin and a half brother, leaving the family estate for the benefit of the heirs of the 6th baron, a wife and adopted daughter who live at the family home of Blithfield Hall near Rugeley. The estate goes back to Bagod, a sub-tenant of Robert de Stafford at the time of the first Domesday in 1086.

THE 15TH BARON STAFFORD *2500 acres.* Francis Melford William Fitzherbert was born in 1954 and was educated at Ampleforth. The estate in 1872 was based at Costessy Park in Norfolk and ran to 10,050 acres, 1710 of those in Stafford. Though much reduced, the estate is still big enough to be the patron to one Church of England parish, though as a Catholic the peer is unable to present. His heir is the Hon Benjamin John, born in 1983. The original family of Fitzherberts of Swynnerton held the Staffordshire lands for over 500 years.

Other significant landowners in the county include the 3rd Baron Burton with 5000 acres (as well as 31,000 acres in Inverness and 17,000 acres in Ross & Cromarty). Michael Evan Victor Baillie, born in 1924 and heir to the Burton brewery fortune, has a large estate around Burton on Trent. He has three surviving daughters.

Significant Institutional Landowners

1872: The largest institutional landowner was the Church of England with 13,999 acres.
2001: The Forestry Commission owns 10,667 acres. The county owns 8589 acres of farmland. The Ministry of Defence owns and leases 3501 acres (4502 acres in 1973). The Crown Estate owns 3853 acres. The National Trust owns 1786 acres. The Church Commissioners own 1700 acres.

TOP 10 IN 1872

1	Earl of Lichfield (MP) of Shugborough Park	21,443 acres	with 97 elsewhere
2	Marquess of Anglesey of Beaudesert Park, Lichfield	17,444 acres	with 16,798 elsewhere
3	Lord Hatherton (MP) of Teddesley Park, Penkridge	14,901 acres	
4	Sir John Harpur Crewe Bt of Calke Abbey, Ashby-de-la-Zouche	14,256 acres	with 13,800 elsewhere
5	Duke of Sutherland (MP) of Dunrobin Castle, Golspie, Sutherland	12,744 acres	with 1,345,801 elsewhere
6	Lord Bagot (MP) of Blithfield House, Rugeley	10,841 acres	with 19,702 elsewhere
7	Sir Thomas Fletcher Fenton-Boughey Bt of Aqualate Hall, Newport	10,505 acres	with 470 elsewhere
8	Hon Mr Edward Swynfen Parker-Jervis of Aston Hall, Sutton Coldfield	8020 acres	with 164 elsewhere
9	Earl of Stamford and Warrington of Enville Hall, Stourbridge	7339 acres	with 23,623 elsewhere
10	Mr Walter Thomas Courtenay Giffard of Chillington Hall, Wolverhampton	7069 acres	with 718 elsewhere

SUFFOLK

	1872	2001
Total acreage	912,237 acres	938,149 acres
Agricultural acreage	866,625 acres	746,639 acres
Non agricultural acreage	45,611 acres	191,510 acres
Population	348,869	649,500
Owners of nothing at all	329,593	288,100
Total Dwellings	76,501	278,000
Smallholdings: 1872 owners of less than one acre	12,511	
2000 owners of 0–2ha (0–4.94 acres)		332
Landowners over one acre (1872)	6765	
Landowners over 2ha (2000)		3104
Landowners over 500 acres	281	410
Acreage (and percentage) of county owned by owners of over 500 acres	574,806 acres (63%)	416,865 acres (44.4%)

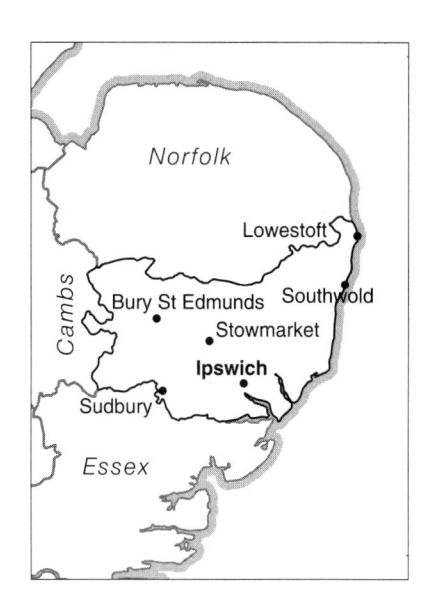

Top Landowners 2001

THE 4TH EARL OF IVEAGH *25,000 acres with 2270 acres in Berwickshire.* The estate once vested in the unhappy Indian Maharajah, Duleep Singh, at Elveden, is now in the possession of a family at least as wealthy, if not more so, than any maharajah. Arthur Edward Rory Guinness, the 4th Earl, born in 1969, who succeeded his father in 1992, is the titular head of the Guinness brewing family, little of whose wealth is now in the brewery, but which draws an income from Swiss trusts, which in turn control a huge investment portfolio. He has, however, taken on the running of the Elvenden estate and it remains a huge part of the Guinness inheritance. He had just begun to make a name for himself in the Lords when the Blair reformers arrived and he is now seatless but well ensconced in Suffolk.

TRUSTEES OF THE ESTATE OF THE MARQUESS OF BRISTOL *20,000 acres. No. 4 in 1872.* The 8th Marquess of Bristol, Frederick William Augustus Hervey, born in 1979, succeeded his half brother, the 7th Marquess, in 1999. While the tabloids gave the impression that his half brother had squandered the Bristol inheritance they failed to understand quite how it worked, which was mostly through trustees. For that reason, much of the inheritance was saved from the profligate 7th Marquess. The family seat is Ickworth, near Bury St Edmunds

TRUSTEES OF THE 4TH EARL OF STRADBROKE *3750 acres. No. 6 in 1872.* The 6th Earl of Stradbroke, Robert Keith Rous, is, in the words of Francis Fulford writing in *The Field*, 'a colourful Australian'. He lives in Australia, but the remaining family lands around Beccles are still with trustees. The earl is currently planning to build a new stately home at or near the current one at Henham, near Beccles.

Other significant landowners in the county include the Cayzer family with 3000 acres (as well as 8000 acres in Angus and 35,200 acres in Ross & Cromarty). Lord Cayzer died in 1999 and the title became extinct. The estate at Walsham-le-Willows was split between his two daughters, Nicola, wife of Michael Colvin, MP for Andover in Hants, and Elizabeth. Nicola and her husband were killed in 2000 in an as yet unexplained fire at their beautiful home at Tangley near Romsey in Hants. The main members of the family are her eldest son, James Cayzer Colvin, and cousins Patrick Colvin and Sir James Arthur Cayzer Bt.

Significant Institutional Landowners

1872: The largest institutional landowner was the Church of England with 61,802 acres.
2001: The Forestry Commission owns 22,352 acres. The county owns 13,526 acres. The Jockey Club owns over 9000 acres. The National Trust owns 3892 acres. The Ministry of Defence owns and leases 7195 acres (1262 acres in 1973).

TOP 10 IN 1872

1	Lord Rendlesham (MP) of Rendlesham Hall, Woodbridge	19,896 acres	with 4159 elsewhere
2	Colonel George Tomline MP of Orwell Park, Woodbridge	18,473 acres	with 8441 elsewhere
3	Maharajah, His Highness Duleep-Singh of Elveden Hall, Thetford	17,210 acres	
4	Marquess of Bristol MP of Ickworth, Bury St Edmunds	16,981 acres	with 15,033 elsewhere
5	Lord Huntingfield of Heveningham Hall, Yoxford	16,869 acres	
6	Earl of Stradbroke of Henham Hall, Wangford	12,203 acres	
7	Sir Richard Wallace Bt KCB MP of Sudbourn Hall, Wickham Market	11,224 acres	with 61,083 elsewhere
8	Duke of Grafton (MP) of Euston Hall, Thetford	11,127 acres	with 14,646 elsewhere
9	Lord Waveney (MP) of Flixton Hall, Bungay	10,930 acres	with 8322 elsewhere
10	Lord Henniker (MP) of Thornham Hall, Eye	10,910 acres	with 130 elsewhere

SURREY

	1872	2001
Total acreage	398,746 acres	414,940 acres
Agricultural acreage	378,808 acres	156,735 acres
Non agricultural acreage	19,937 acres	258,205 acres
Population	342,113	1,041,200
Owners of nothing at all	324,820	478,300
Total Dwellings	61,482	433,000
Smallholdings: 1872 owners of less than one acre 2000 owners of 0–2ha (0–4.94 acres)	12,712	191
Landowners over one acre (1872) Landowners over 2ha (2000)	4581	1531
Landowners over 500 acres	171	61
Acreage (and percentage) of county owned by owners of over 500 acres	239,884 acres (60.1%)	48,315 acres (11.6%)

Top Landowners 2001

THE 7TH MARQUESS OF NORTHAMPTON *5000 acres with 25,000 elsewhere.* Fuller details of the Northampton acreage, which includes a small acreage near the City in London, are given with the Northamptonshire entry (see p.249). The estate in Surrey is worth a minimum of £15 million.

THE 12TH DUKE OF NORTHUMBERLAND *3750 acres with 120,000 elsewhere.* The Albury estate in Surrey is small in acreage compared with the rest of the ducal lands, but would be worth around £10 million to £12 million, excluding any development land attached. Further details are given in the Northumberland entry (see p.250).

THE 7TH EARL OF ONSLOW *2500 acres.* Michael William Coplestone Dillon Onslow, born in 1938 and educated at Eton and the Sorbonne, is an insurance broker. He was one of the few to try and make a stand against the Blair reforms of the House of Lords. A small estate in trust is all that remains of what was the largest estate in Surrey in 1872.

Significant Institutional Landowners

1872: The largest institutional landowner was the Church of England with 12,546 acres. The Crown Estate had 7465 acres.
2001: The National Trust owns 13,458 acres. The Forestry Commission owns 3916 acres. The county owns 2174 acres of farmland. The Crown Estate owns 1625 acres. The Ministry of Defence owns and leases 13,079 acres (1053 acres in 1973).

TOP 10 IN 1872

1	Earl of Onslow of Clandon Park, Guildford	11,761 acres	with 1727 elsewhere
2	Earl of Lovelace of East Horsley Towers, Leatherhead	10,214 acres	with 8267 elsewhere
3	Mr Granville William Gresham Leveson-Gower MP of Titsey Place, Limpsfield	6930 acres	with 183 elsewhere
4	Sir William Clayton Bt of Harleyford Manor, Great Marlow	6505 acres	with 4660 elsewhere
5	Lord Hylton MP of Merstham House, Redhill	4445 acres	with 5613 elsewhere
6	Mrs Wigsell of Sanderstead Court, Croydon	4196 acres	
7	Mr Robert Cloyne Godwin-Austen FRS of Shalford House, Guildford	4100 acres	
8	Rt Hon Mr George Cubbitt MP of Denbies, Dorking	3989 acres	with 2800 elsewhere
9	Mrs Hope of Deepdene, Dorking	3931 acres	with 17,842 elsewhere
10	Mr W.J. Evelyn of Sutton (Includes Sussex)	3601 acres	

SUSSEX

(Divided into East and West Sussex in 1974. For 2001 the figures from these two areas are merged.)

	1872	2001
Total acreage	869,423 acres	935,187 acres
Agricultural acreage	825,780 acres	577,677 acres
Non agricultural acreage	43,462 acres	357,510 acres
Population	417,456	1,448,600
Owners of nothing at all	397,722	601,000
Total Dwellings	75,385	652,000
Smallholdings: 1872 owners of less than one acre	14,675	
2000 owners of 0–2ha (0–4.94 acres)		449
Landowners over one acre (1872)	5059	
Landowners over 2ha (2000)		4084
Landowners over 500 acres	297	259
Acreage (and percentage) of county owned by owners of over 500 acres	630,018 acres (72.4%)	226,939 acres (24.2%)

Top Landowners 2001

THE 17TH DUKE OF NORFOLK AND FAMILY TRUSTS *16,000 acres with 30,000 acres elsewhere including 4 in London. No. 2 in 1872.* The full Howard portfolio of land, including the Norfolk lands, has never been documented, but it might yet emerge as the largest connected family holding in the country. In the meantime, Major General Miles Francis Stapleton Fitzalan Howard, born in 1915, retains his hereditary seat in the House of Lords as Earl Marshal and hereditary Marshal of England. He is also the country's leading Catholic layman. The Sussex estates surround Arundel Castle, and his heir, the Earl of Arundel and Surrey, born in 1956, runs the trusts from there.

VISCOUNT COWDRAY AND FAMILY *17,000 acres with 65,600 acres in Aberdeenshire.* See Aberdeenshire (p.270).

THE 10TH DUKE OF RICHMOND AND GORDON AND FAMILY TRUSTS *12,000 acres. No. 4 in 1872.* Charles Henry Gordon Lennox, the current duke, was born in 1929. A chartered accountant by profession he owns the Goodwood car racing circuit, now a part of the burgeoning Formula 1 empire. There is further development planned in the area and his shrewd retention of the Sussex land looks like vastly increasing the value of his assets put at £30 million by the *Sunday Times* in its 2000 Rich List. His son and heir is the Earl of March and Kinrara, born in 1955.

Other significant landowners in the coutny include the 11th Earl de la Warr with 6500 acres (no. 3 in 1872). This horse-racing peer, William Herbrand Sackville, was born in 1948 and educated at Eton. He still lives at the family seat, Buckhurst Park, and is the patron of four church of England parishes. His heir, born in 1979, is Lord Buckhurst.

Significant Institutional Landowners

1872: The largest institutional landowner was the Church of England with 17,508 acres.
2001: The Forestry Commission owns 15,692 acres. The National Trust owns 14,650 acres with 4100 protected. The Church Commissioners own 6846 acres. The Ministry of Defence owns and leases 2411 acres (3853 acres in 1973). The county owns 1299 acres of farmland.

TOP 10 IN 1872

1	Lord Leconfield (MP) of Petworth House	30,221 acres	with 79,813 elsewhere
2	Duke of Norfolk of Arundel Castle, Arundel	21,446 acres	with 28,420 elsewhere
3	Earl De La Warr of Buckhurst Park, Tunbridge Wells	17,185 acres	with 6181 elsewhere
4	Duke of Richmond and Gordon (MP) of Goodwood, Chichester	17,117 acres	with 269,294 elsewhere
5	Earl of Chichester of Stanmer, Lewes	16,232 acres	
6	Marquess of Abergavenny of Eridge Castle, Tunbridge Wells	15,364 acres	with 13,170 elsewhere
7	Rev John Goring of Wiston Manor, Steyning	14,139 acres	
8	Earl of Ashburnham of Ashburnham Place, Battle	14,051 acres	with 10,438 elsewhere
9	Earl of Egmont (MP) of Nork House, Epsom	14,021 acres	with 2745 elsewhere
10	Viscount Gage of Firle Place, Lewes	12,352 acres	

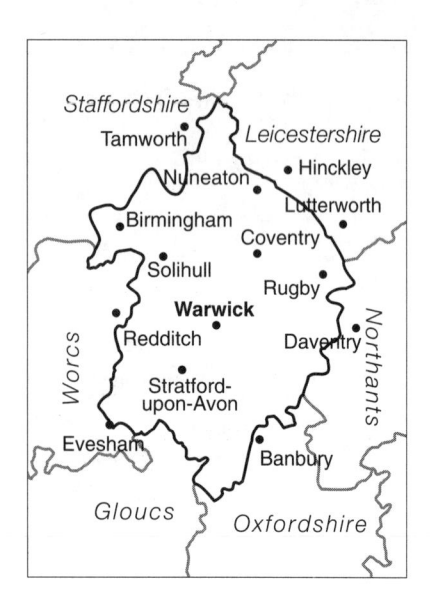

WARWICKSHIRE

	1872	2001
Total acreage	541,022 acres	489,386 acres
Agricultural acreage	513,970 acres	376,380 acres
Non agricultural acreage	27,051 acres	113,006 acres
Population	634,189	496,300
Owners of nothing at all	582,673	224,600
Total Dwellings	131,442	209,000
Smallholdings: 1872 owners of less than one acre	46,894	
2000 owners of 0–2ha (0–4.94 acres)		220
Landowners over one acre (1872)	4622	
Landowners over 2ha (2000)		2269
Landowners over 500 acres	170	167
Acreage (and percentage) of county owned by owners of over 500 acres	320,864 acres (59.1%)	136,253 acres (27.8%)

Top Landowners 2001

THE 7TH MARQUESS OF NORTHAMPTON *10,000 acres with 10,000 in Northants and 5000 acres in Surrey.* See Northamptonshire (p.249) for further details. The Warwick estate is at Compton Wynyates, Tysoe.

THE 21ST BARON WILLOUGHBY DE BROKE *4000 acres. No. 2 in 1872.* Born in 1938, Leopold David Verney succeeded his father, a keen fan of the turf, in 1986. He was educated at the international school Le Rosey in Switzerland and then Oxford. He is a patron of two parishes of the Church of England. He farms at Moreton-in-Marsh. The seat is at Compton Verney, near Stratford-on-Avon.

THE 5TH BARON LEIGH AND FAMILY TRUSTS *2000 acres. No. 1 in 1872.* John Piers Leigh, born in 1935, gives his address in *Debrett's* as the House of Lords, in which he no longer has a seat. Most of the family lands are gone, but the family trustees have retained at least 2000 acres, maybe more. His son and heir is the Hon Christopher, educated at Eton like his father, then the Royal Agricultural College, who now farms in Gloucester. The family seat was Stoneleigh Abbey at Kenilworth.

Significant Institutional Landowners

1872: The largest institutional landowner was the Church of England with 29,253 acres.
2001: The county owns 5070 acres of farmland. The Ministry of Defence owns and leases 4005 acres. The diocese of Coventry owns 3700 acres. The National Trust owns 1287 acres. The Forestry Commission own 1359 acres.

TOP 10 IN 1872

1	Lord Leigh of Stoneleigh Abbey	14,891 acres	with 6074 elsewhere
2	Lord Willoughby de Broke of Compton Verney	12,621 acres	with 5524 elsewhere
3	Earl of Aylesford of Packington Hall, Coventry	12,543 acres	with 7038 elsewhere
4	Marquess of Hertford of Ragley Hall, Alcester	10,281 acres	with 2008 elsewhere
5	Mr John Wingfield Digby of Coleshill Park, Birmingham	8904 acres	with 182 elsewhere
6	Earl of Craven of Ashdown Park, Shrivenham	8447 acres	with 22,342 elsewhere
7	Earl of Warwick and Brooke (MP) of The Castle, Warwick	8262 acres	with 1840 elsewhere
8	Sir Nicholas William Throckmorton Bt. of Coughton Court, Alcester	7618 acres	with 14,767 elsewhere
9	Mr Thomas Walker of Berkswell Hall, Coventry	6117 acres	with 1477 elsewhere
10	Mr Henry Spencer Lucy of Charlcote Park, Warwick	5765 acres	with 118 elsewhere

WESTMORELAND

(This county disappeared in the local government reorganisation of 1974 and became part of the neighbouring counties of Northumberland and Cumbria.)

	1872
Total acreage	335,160 acres
Agricultural acreage	318,402 acres
Non agricultural acreage	16,758 acres
Population	65,010
Owners of nothing at all	60,634
Total Dwellings	12,671
Smallholdings: 1872 owners of less than one acre 2000 owners of 0–2ha (0–4.94 acres)	1714
Landowners over one acre (1872) Landowners over 2ha (2000)	2662
Landowners over 500 acres	87
Acreage (and percentage) of county owned by owners of over 500 acres	192,622 acres (42.8%)

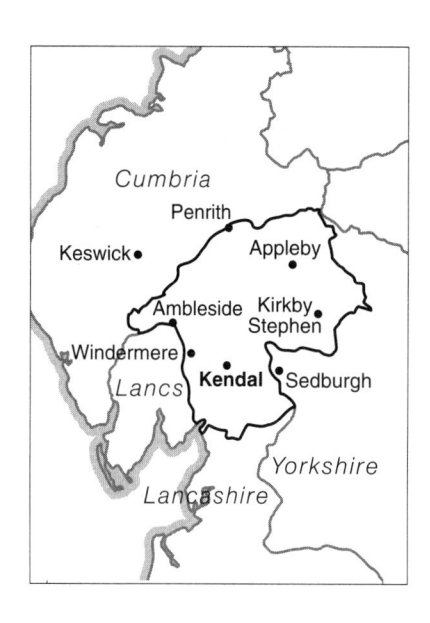

Significant Institutional Landowners

1872: The largest institutional landowner was the Church of England with 15,757 acres. In 1973 the Ministry of Defence owned 14,789 acres in the county.

TOP 10 IN 1872

1	Earl of Lonsdale of Lowther Castle, Penrith	39,229 acres	with 28,836 elsewhere
2	Marquess of Headfort of Headfort House, Kells, Co Meath	12,851 acres	with 29,903 elsewhere
3	Gen the Hon Arthur Upton of Levens Hall, Milnthorpe	9252 acres	
4	Mr Christopher Wyndham Wilson of Rigmaden, Kirkby Lonsdale	8730 acres	
5	Mr Edward Hugh Wilson of Dallam Tower, Milnthorpe	8690 acres	with 1167 elsewhere
6	Mr William Henry Wakefield of Sedgwick, Kendal	6024 acres	with 1065 elsewhere
7	Hon Mr E.M. Pakenham of Cookesboro	4557 acres	
8	Mrs Thompson of Stobars, Kirkby-Stephen	4543 acres	
9	Mr Stanley Hughes Le Fleming of Rydal Hall, Ambleside	3617 acres	with 1825 elsewhere
10	Sir Richard Musgrave of Edenhall Penrith	3121 acres	with 12,328 elsewhere

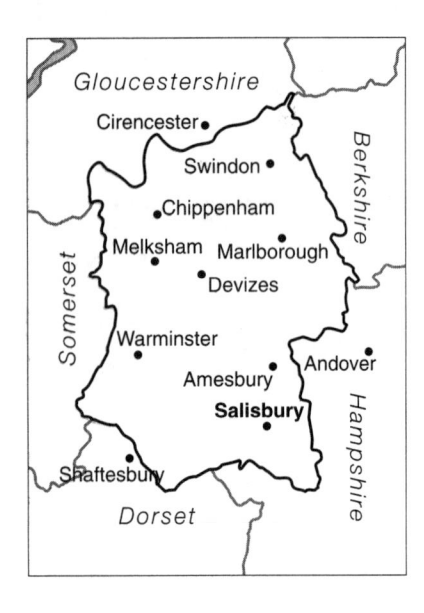

WILTSHIRE

	1872	2001
Total acreage	828,984 acres	859,658 acres
Agricultural acreage	787,534 acres	664,103 acres
Non agricultural acreage	41,449 acres	195,555 acres
Population	257,177	586,300
Owners of nothing at all	243,164	266,500
Total Dwellings	54,874	246,000
Smallholdings: 1872 owners of less than one acre	9635	
2000 owners of 0–2ha (0–4.94 acres)		364
Landowners over one acre (1872)	4378	
Landowners over 2ha (2000)		2918
Landowners over 500 acres	283	375
Acreage (and percentage) of county owned by owners of over 500 acres	662,259 acres (79.8%)	372,268 acres (43.3%)

Top Landowners 2001

THE 17TH EARL OF PEMBROKE AND MONTGOMERY *14,000 acres. No. 1 in 1872.* Henry George Charles Alexander Herbert, the present earl, was born in 1939 and succeeded to the title in 1969. Educated at Eton and Oxford, he rounded off his training with a stint as an officer in the Royal Horse Guards, the top cavalry regiment in the army. Twice married he has six daughters but his heir, Lord Herbert, was born in 1978. The acreage, based around Wilton House, Salisbury, is in trust. Relatively small parcels have been sold off for housing in recent years, raising £500,000 an acre.

THE 7TH MARQUESS OF BATH AND FAMILY TRUSTS *10,000 acres. No. 3 in 1872.* The figure in monogrammed slippers, fulsome beard and flying cape, striding into the House of Lords to sit for the last time in 1999, is a far cry from Lieutenant the Viscount Weymouth, Her Majesty's Life Guards. But such is the marquess's background. Born in 1932, educated at Eton and Oxford, followed by the Life Guards, he eventually rebelled, becoming a Wessex regionalist and a man with many 'wifelets', though never divorcing his original wife, the model Anna Gael Gyarmarthy. He succeeded to the title in 1992. The estate is the home of the famous lions of Longleat and is about one quarter of its original size. His heir, Viscount Weymouth, born in 1974, is a neat, suited businessman.

THE 8TH MARQUESS OF AILESBURY *4500 acres. No. 2 in 1872.* Born in 1926, Michael Sydney Cedric Brudenell-Bruce, the present marquess, was a working member of the London Stock Exchange for most of his life. Educated at Eton, then as a lieutenant in the Royal Horse Guards, he succeeded to the title in 1974. Three times divorced, his heir is the Earl of Cardigan, born in 1952. The earl is the 31st Hereditary Warden of Savernake Forest, most of which now belongs to the Forestry Commission (see below). He now lives at Luton Lye, Savernake Forest.

Other significant landowners in the county include Lord Margadale, with 5000 acres in Wiltshire and 49,600 acres in Argyll (see Argyllshire, p.272) for details.

Significant Institutional Landowners

1872: The largest institutional landowner was the Church of England with 21,140 acres. The Deans and Church Commissioners owned over 8400 acres.
2001: The Ministry of Defence owns and leases 107,125 acres (98,820 acres in 1973). The Crown Estate owns 20,467 acres. The Forestry Commission owns 9206 acres. The county owns 8759 acres of farmland. The National Trust owns 7420 acres. The Duchy of Cornwall owns 3768 acres. The Church Commissioners own 3102 acres. The Diocese of Salisbury owns 2064 acres.

TOP 10 IN 1872

1	Earl of Pembroke of Wilton House, Salisbury	42,244 acres	with 2562 elsewhere
2	Marquess of Ailesbury (MP) of Savernake, Marlborough	37,993 acres	with 17,058 elsewhere
3	Marquess of Bath of Longleat, Warminster	19,984 acres	with 32,812 elsewhere
4	Earl of Radnor of Longford Castle, Salisbury	17,000 acres	with 7870 elsewhere
5	Mr Simon Watson-Taylor MP of Erlestoke, Westbury	15,000 acres	
6	Mr Walter Long MP of Wraxall, Trowbridge	13,829 acres	with 1575 elsewhere
7	Sir John Neeld Bt MP of Grittleton, Chippenham	13,112 acres	with 700 elsewhere
8	Sir Henry Meux Bt MP of Theobalds, Cheshunt	11,895 acres	with 3215 elsewhere
9	Marquess of Lansdowne of Bowood Park, Calne	11,145 acres	with 131,771 elsewhere
10	Earl of Suffolk and Berkshire (MP) of Charlton Park, Malmsbury	11,098 acres	

WORCESTERSHIRE

(Merged with Herefordshire in the local government reorganisation of 1974. Details for the new county are given in Herefordshire entry on p.240. However, agricultural statistics continue to be produced for Worcester alone and are given here.)

	1872	2001
Total acreage	441,061 acres	
Agricultural acreage	419,007 acres	305,460 acres
Non agricultural acreage	22,053 acres	
Population	338,837	
Owners of nothing at all	317,033	
Total Dwellings	69,998	
Smallholdings: 1872 owners of less than one acre	16,008	
2000 owners of 0–2ha (0–4.94 acres)		282
Landowners over one acre (1872)	5796	
Landowners over 2ha (2000)		2807
Landowners over 500 acres	123	92
Acreage (and percentage) of county owned by owners of over 500 acres	231,888 acres (52.1%)	70,386 acres (23% of agric. acreage)

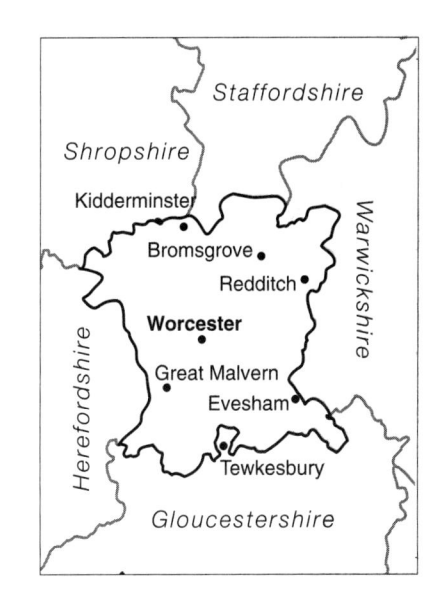

Top Landowners 2001

See Herefordshire (p.240)

Significant Institutional Landowners

1872: The largest institutional landowner was the Church of England with 19,301 acres.

TOP 10 IN 1872

1	Earl of Dudley, of Witley Court, Stourport	14,698 acres	with 10,856 elsewhere
2	Earl of Coventry, of Croome Court, Worcester	13,021 acres	with 13,98 elsewhere
3	Earl Beauchamp of Madresfield Court, Great Malvern	10,624 acres	with 7010 elsewhere
4	Lord Windsor of Oakley Park, Bromfield, Salop	8530 acres	with 28,957 elsewhere
5	Mr Harry Foley Vernon MP of Hanbury Hall, Droitwich	7447 acres	
6	Earl Somers (MP) of Eastnor Castle, Ledbury	6265 acres	with 6802 elsewhere
7	Lord Lyttleton (MP) of Hagley Hall, Stourbridge	5907 acres	with 1032 elsewhere
8	Lord Hampton of Westwood Park, Droitwich	4867 acres	with 633 elsewhere
9	Mr Robert Berkeley of Spetchley Park, Worcester	4811 acres	
10	HRH le Duc D'Aumale of Woodnorton, Evesham	4604 acres	

YORKSHIRE

(In 1872 Yorkshire was divided into three ridings, East, North and West. In the local government reorganisation of 1974, only North Yorkshire survived as a county. The current agricultural statistics, however, are divided into four areas, North, East, South and West Yorkshire. For simplicity's sake and because it gives the most reasonable overall picture, the county has been grouped, for both 1872 and for 2001, into one area, Yorkshire.)

	1872	2001
Total acreage	3,256,505 acres	3,678,095 acres (est)
Agricultural acreage	3,093,679 acres	3,171,041 acres
Non agricultural acreage	192,826 acres	507,054 acres
Population	2,436,355	3,821,570
Owners of nothing at all	2,323,853	1,094,170
Total Dwellings	507,040	2,098,000
		(All Yorks plus Humberside.)
Smallholdings:		
1872 owners of less than one acre	84,623	
2000 owners of 0–2ha (0–4.94 acres)		1540
Landowners over one acre (1872)	27,879	
Landowners over 2ha (2000)		14,644
Landowners over 500 acres	864	1145
Acreage (and percentage) of county owned by owners of over 500 acres	2,155,159 acres (66.1%)	1,062,206 acres (33.4% of agric. acreage)

Top Landowners 2001

In 1872 there were over 240 owners of estates larger than 3000 acres and yielding over £3000 a year, the modern equivalent of £210,000 p.a. Yorkshire remains the redoubt of most of the survivors from the 1872 list many of whom appear in the list below.

ROBERT MILLER *32,000 acres.* Miller, an American entrepreneur specialising in duty free shops, bought the Gunnerside estate from the 3rd Earl Peel in 1995. The earldom was created in 1929 and this estate does not figure in the 1872 Return. The estate is based at Gunnerside near Richmond. Miller, a self made billionaire was educated at Cornell University in New York, has seen his daughters marry a Grand Duke, the heir to the throne of Greece and a member of the Getty family.

THE 11TH VISCOUNT DOWNE AND FAMILY TRUST *20,000 acres.* The Eton educated 11th Viscount Downe, born John Christian George Dawnay in 1935, still retains 20,000 of the family acres near Scarborough. The title, originally Irish, is an old one dating to 1681 but the family are Yorkshire and always have been. To get the size of the original estate the two entries (nos. 9 and 20) below should be considered. While a member of the Lords he sat as Baron Dawnay. He lives in London.

THE 7TH BARON BOLTON *17,500 acres. No. 22 in 1872.* Born Richard William Algar Orde Powlett in 1929, he is one of the biggest farmers in Yorkshire, holding 17,500 acres at Leyburn, an increase of over 2000 acres on the 1872 estate, of which 13,808 acres were in Hants. Married three times, he is a keen racing man and lists the Central African Deep Sea Fishers as one of his clubs.

THE 5TH MARQUESS OF NORMANBY *15,000 acres.* Constantine Edmund Walter Phipps, the 5th Marquess, born in 1954, is a Guinness heir through his mother. The estate at Whitby is more than twice its size in 1872 (6834 acres). It was slimmed down considerably in recent years when a large portion at Pocklington was sold off for development. The *Sunday Times* rates him worth £140 million in the 2000 Rich List.

THE 3RD EARL OF HALIFAX *15,000 acres.* Charles Edward Peter Neil Brown, the 3rd Earl, born in 1944, is a Deputy Lieutenant of Humberside, and Vice Lord Lieutenant of the East Riding. The estate at 15,000 acres around Garrowby, is now half as big again as it was in 1872 (10,142 acres). Educated at Eton and Oxford, he is a Knight of the Order of St John of Jerusalem. His heir is Lord Irwin, born in 1977.

THE 4TH MARQUESS OF ZETLAND *14,000 acres.* Lawrence Mark Dundas, born in 1937, is a steward of the Jockey Club and a director of the British Horseracing Board since 1993. While the Scottish acres have all but vanished – they came to over 50,000 acres in 1872 – the Yorkshire estate has increased by over 3000 acres. He receives regular mention in the diaries of Lord Woodrow Wyatt. He was educated at Eton and Cambridge and was a second lieutenant in the Grenadier Guards. His heir is the Earl of Ronaldshay, betraying the real origin of the title which is with the Shetland islands.

SIR TATTON CHRISTOPHER MARK SYKES, 8TH BARONET *13,000 acres.* Born in 1943, he runs a very successful racing stable from the family seat at Sledmere. The estate was over 34,000 acres in 1872 (no. 4 below), and though much reduced in size is thriving once more. The family have been MPs in York for two centuries, dominant figures in its racing world and often played a role in international affairs. The Sykes–Picot agreement, which placed Syrian and Lebanon in the French sphere of influence in 1916, was drafted and signed by an ancestor.

THE 6TH BARON FEVERSHAM *12,000 acres.* Charles Anthony Peter Duncombe was born in 1945 and educated at Eton. He is a major figure in the Yorkshire arts world and was also president of the National Association of Local Councils from 1986 to 1999. The estate is in trust and much reduced from its size in 1872, when it was the second largest estate in the county (no. 2 below). His son and heir, Jason Orlando, was born in 1968

THE 7TH EARL OF HAREWOOD *10,000 acres. No. 5 in 1872.* George Henry Hubert Lascelles, a cousin of the Queen, was born in 1923 and educated at Eton and Cambridge University. He was wounded in Italy where he served during World War Two as a captain in the Grenadier Guards. Physically distinguished in appearance, he was the very model of a modern aristocrat, serving as a Counsellor of State in the 1940s and 1950s when King George VI and later Queen Elizabeth were abroad. He was a noted director and administrator of opera, founding the magazine *Opera* and running both the Royal Opera House and later Sadlers Wells, now English National Opera. He is credited with paving the way for the huge popularisation of classical music that is a feature of modern life. The estate is much reduced from its 1872 acreage of 29,078 acres. Harewood House is stuffed with treasures but, like the land, is in trust. He and his son and heir Viscount Lascelles, born in 1950, live on the estate.

Significant Institutional Landowners

1872: The largest institutional landowner was the Church of England with 140,979 acres. The Church Commissioners owned over 11,400 acres.
2001: The Forestry Commission owns 49,041 acres. The Ministry of Defence owns and leases 34,282 acres (28,377 acres in 1973). The Crown Estate owns 26,371 acres. The National Trust owns 21,400 acres. The Duchy of Lancaster owns 17,270 acres. The county owns 17,111 acres of farmland. The Church Commissioners own 15,429 acres. The diocese of Ripon and Leeds owns 800 acres.

TOP 30 IN 1872

1	Lord Londesborough (MP) of Londesborough Lodge, Scarsborough	52,655	acres	
2	Earl of Feversham (MP) of Duncombe Park, Helmsley	39,312	acres	
3	Mr. John Bowes MP of Streatlam Castle, Gateshead	34,887	acres	with 8313 elsewhere
4	Sir Tatton Sykes Bt of Sledmere House, Malton	34,010	acres	
5	Earl of Harewood of Harewood House, Leeds	29,078	acres	with 542 elsewhere
6	Lord Leconfield (MP) of Petworth House, Sussex	24,753	acres	with 85,202 elsewhere
7	Mr Samuel Cunliffe-Lister of Swinton Park, Bedale	24,240	acres	with 329 elsewhere
8	Earl of Wharncliffe of Wortley Hall, Sheffield	22,544	acres	with 10,905 elsewhere
9	Dowager Viscountess of Downe of Baldersby Park, Thirsk	22,237	acres	
10	Earl Fitzwilliam (MP) of Wentworth House, Rotherham	22,192	acres	with 93,551 elsewhere
11	The 4 Misses Towneley of Burnley (See Lancs)	21,341	acres	with 2826 elsewhere
12	Lord Wenlock (MP) of Escrik Park, York	20,853	acres	with 5227 elsewhere
13	Mr Andrew Montague of Ingmunthorpe, Wetherby	20,700	acres	with 7265 elsewhere
14	Lord Hotham of Dalton Hall, Beverley	20,353	acres	
15	Duke of Norfolk (MP) of Arundel Castle, Sussex	19,440	acres	with 30,426 elsewhere
16	Duke of Devonshire (MP) of Chatsworth House, Bakewell	19,239	acres	with 179,333 elswhere
17	Sir Frederick Augustus Talbot Clifford-Constable Bt of Burton Constable, Hull	18,666	acres	with 48 elsewhere
18	Sir Charles William Strickland Bt of Hildenley, Malton	16,000	acres	
19	Mr Augustus William Savile of Rufford Abbey, Ollerton	16,000	acres	with 17,820 elsewhere
20	Viscount Downe of Danby Lodge, Yarmouth	15,515	acres	with 3 elsewhere
21	Marquess of Aylesbury (MP) of Savernake, Marlborough, Wilts	15,502	acres	with 39,999 elsewhere
22	Lord Bolton of Hackwood Park, Basingstoke, Hants	15,413	acres	with 13,808 elsewhere
23	Mr George Lane-Fox of Bramham Park, Tadcaster	15,000	acres	with 24,069 elsewhere
24	Mr William Henry Harrison-Broadley MP of Welton Brough, Hull	14,877	acres	
25	Duke of Leeds of Gogmagog Hills, Cambridge	14,772	acres	with 9465 elsewhere
26	Marquess of Ripon (MP) of Studley Royal, Ripon Viceroy of India	14,668	acres	with 7102 elsewhere
27	Mr John Yorke of Bewerley Hall, Ripon	14,499	acres	
28	Lord Middleton of Wollaton Hall, Nottingham	14,045	acres	with 85,531 elsewhere
29	Mr Walter Morrison MP of Malham Tarn, Leeds	13,705	acres	with 5 elsewhere
30	Mr William Bethell of Rise Park, Hull	13,395	acres	

Scotland

Scotland is unique in having as a record of landownership not only the 1872 Return, but those of the great chroniclers John MacEwen and Andy Wightman. This has given a degree of continuity to the evolving picture which no other part of the United Kingdom can match. In practice, what the Scottish pages here do is unite the 1872 record with that of Andy Wightman, which itself includes that of John MacEwen. In so doing the author hopes that readers will begin to understand fully the gap in the historic record, and its potential economic importance, created by the disappearance of the 1872 Return.

The 34 counties of 1872 Scotland were reorganised in 1975 into nine regions and 53 district councils. In 1996 this system was again reorganised into 32 'unitary authorities', including 3 island councils and 29 mainland administrative areas. It was interesting to note the survival within the new system of much of the original county structure, meaning that there were available agricultural, housing and population statistics for most of the old counties. Where this was not the case, the old counties, such as Caithness, Ross & Cromarty and Sutherland, are left to stand on their own as part of the historic record.

Modern landowners

With the work of John MacEwen and Andy Wightman to rely upon the list of modern landowners is the best available for all four countries. Where major changes have occurred, such as in the Lovat and Atholl estate, they have been recorded. In the main, however, the landowners and figures are adopted from Andy Wightman's masterly work (Wightman, Andy, *Who Owns Scotland*, Canongate Books), and any reader seeking further detail is directed to it.

Institutional landowners

Very few institutional landowners of any consequence appeared in the 1872 Return. While it is possible that there were very few institutional landowners (the Church of Scotland, for example, did not have landholdings on nearly the scale of the Church of England), another explanation is that the compilers of the Return failed to report as they should have.

In 1995 Andy Wightman recorded significant landholdings belonging to the then regional authorities. It is assumed that these are now owned by the successor institutions – there are no details of any big selloffs by the Scottish institutions in recent years.

An explanation of all figures included in the tables is given on p.219.

List of Scottish Counties included

Aberdeenshire
Angus (formerly Forfarshire)
Argyllshire
Ayrshire
Banffshire
Berwickshire
Bute
Caithness
Clackmannanshire
Cromarty (now part of Ross & Cromarty)
Dumfriesshire
Dunbartonshire
East Lothian (formerly Haddington)
Fife
Inverness-shire
Kincardineshire
Kinross-shire
Kirkcudbrightshire
Lanarkshire
Midlothian (formerly the County of Edinburgh)
Moray (formerly Elgin)
Nairnshire
Orkney
Peeblesshire
Perthshire
Renfrewshire
Ross-shire (now part of Ross & Cromarty)
Roxburghshire
Selkirkshire
Shetland (Zetland)
Stirlingshire
Sutherland
West Lothian (formerly Linlithgow)
Wigtownshire

Scotland 1872

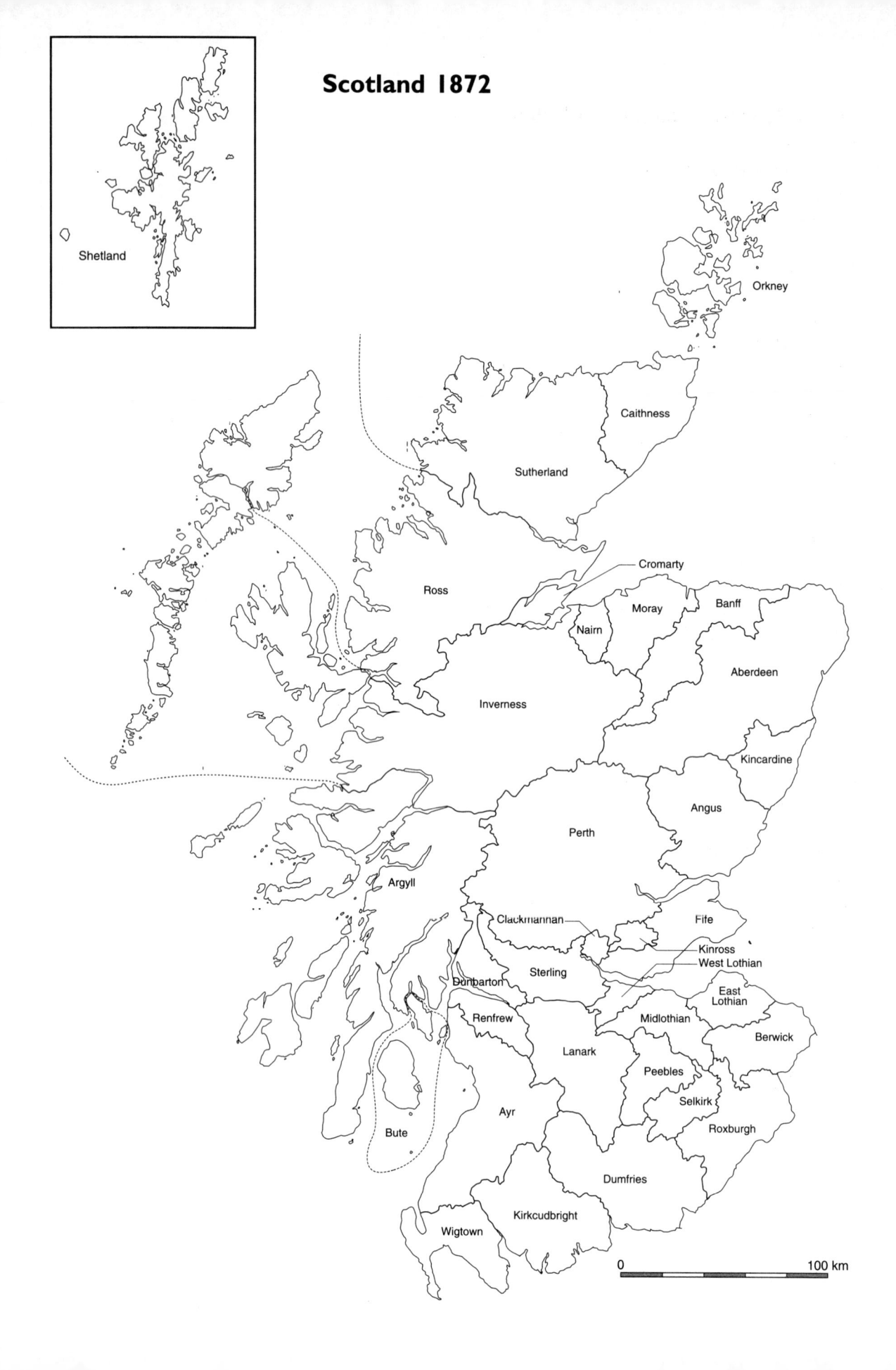

Scotland 2001

Shetland

Orkney

Western Isles
(Na H Eileanan An Iar)

Highland

Moray

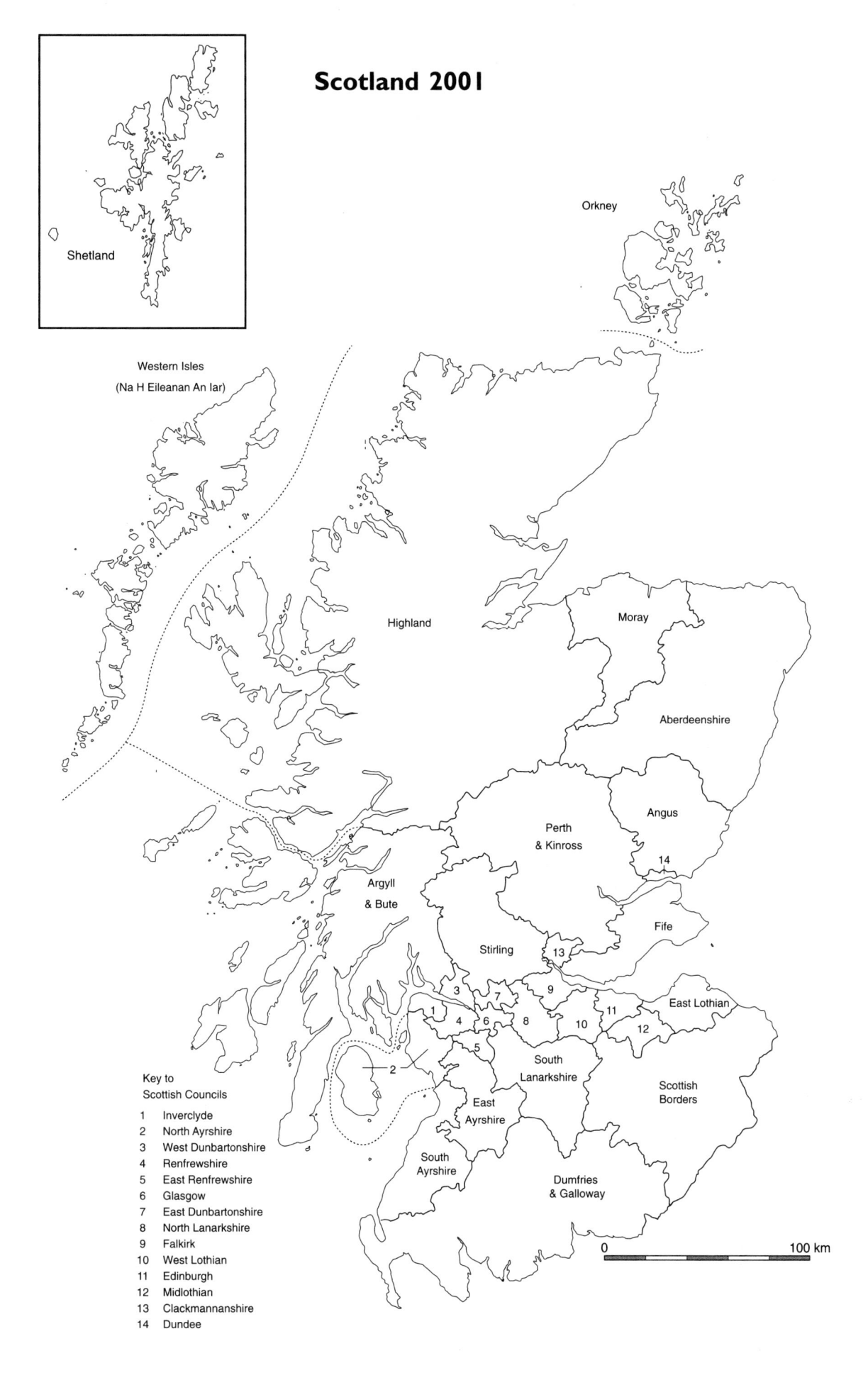

Aberdeenshire

Angus

Perth & Kinross

Fife

Argyll & Bute

Stirling

East Lothian

South Lanarkshire

East Ayrshire

Scottish Borders

South Ayrshire

Dumfries & Galloway

Key to Scottish Councils

1. Inverclyde
2. North Ayrshire
3. West Dunbartonshire
4. Renfrewshire
5. East Renfrewshire
6. Glasgow
7. East Dunbartonshire
8. North Lanarkshire
9. Falkirk
10. West Lothian
11. Edinburgh
12. Midlothian
13. Clackmannanshire
14. Dundee

0   100 km

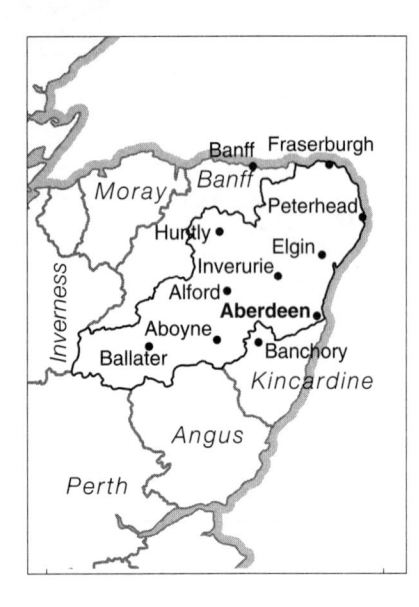

ABERDEENSHIRE

	1872	2001
Total acreage	1,255,138 acres	1,261,333 acres
Agricultural acreage	1,129,624 acres	993,927 acres
Non agricultural acreage	125,513 acres	267,406 acres
Population	264,603	228,610
Owners of nothing at all	257,127	92,500
Total Dwellings	34,589	104,700
Smallholdings: 1872 owners of less than one acre 2000 owners of 0–2ha (0–4.94 acres)	6496	586
Landowners over one acre (1872) Landowners over 2ha (2000)	980	4967
Landowners over 500 acres	63	330
Acreage (and percentage) of county owned by owners of over 500 acres	793,013 acres (63.3%)	524,121 acres (41.5%).

Top Landowners 1995/2001

CAPTAIN A.A.C. FARQUHARSON, THE 16TH FARQUHARSON OF INVERCAULD *87,500 acres with 19,000 acres elsewhere (mainly Perthshire). No. 2 in 1872.* If British Aluminium (Alcan) are excluded, Captain Farquharson is the sixth largest landowner in Scotland, and the biggest in Aberdeenshire. He also boasts one of the most distinguished lineages in that country. It begins, 'Shaw of Rothiemurcus, or John with the bucktooth, had issue, a son, James who was killed at Harlaw, 1411, leaving a son, etc'. That was 1411. The record actually commences in 1345. The present incumbent was born in 1919 and educated at Eton. He won a Military Cross in World War Two. He still owns almost exactly the same acreage as his ancestor in the Returns.

THE 4TH VISCOUNT COWDRAY *65,600 acres with 17,000 acres in Sussex.* Michael Orlando Weetman Pearson, the 4th Viscount, was born in 1944 and educated at Gordonstoun in Scotland. With his family he was ranked the 12th richest person in the UK, with a fortune of £1.3 billion, in the *Sunday Times* Rich List for 2000. Although the landholdings are huge and enormously valuable, especially the Sussex acres at Cowdray Park, his wealth comes from shares in Pearson plc, the media conglomerate best known for its flagship publication the *Financial Times*. He has two sons and three daughters.

THE QUEEN AND TRUSTEES OF BALMORAL *50,370 acres with 23,000 acres elsewhere.* Prince Charles has volunteered Balmoral, which he does not own, to the Scottish nation, when he becomes King. His mother, the Sovereign of Scotland, who does own it, has not expressed a view. It is clear from the frequency of their visits that the Royals do love their Scottish spread, a great deal of which is open to the public. For further information see Chapter 4.

Significant Institutional Landowners

The National Trust for Scotland has 73,582 acres. The Forestry Commission owns 59,135 acres.

TOP 10 IN 1872

1	Earl of Fife (MP) of Duff House, Banff	135,829	acres	with 113,391 elsewhere
2	Colonel James Ross Farquharson of Invercauld, Ballater	87,745	acres	with 21,816 elsewhere
3	Marquess of Huntly of Aboyne Castle	80,000	acres	with 5711 elsewhere
4	Duke of Richmond & Gordon (MP) of Goodwood, Chichester	69,660	acres	with 216,751 elsewhere
5	Earl of Aberdeen of Haddo House,	62,422	acres	
6	Mr James Mackenzie of Glenmuick, Ballater	29,500	acres	with 43,229 elsewhere
7	Sir Charles John Forbes Bt of Newe, Strathdon	29,238	acres	
8	Queen Victoria I of Balmoral and Buckingham Palace	25,350	acres	with 2091 elsewhere
9	Mr Alexander Dingwall Fordyce of Brucklay Castle	20,903	acres	with 46 elsewhere
10	Lady Cathcart of Cluny	20,395	acres	with 105,077 elsewhere

ANGUS

(Known in 1872 as Forfarshire)

	1872	2001
Total acreage	555,994 acres	559,090 acres
Agricultural acreage	500,394 acres	476,974 acres
Non agricultural acreage	55,599	82,116 acres
Population	257,567	110,070
Owners of nothing at all	248,224	45,340
Total Dwellings	25,663	50,100
Smallholdings: 1872 owners of less than one acre 2000 owners of 0–2ha (0–4.94 acres)	8184	141
Landowners over one acre (1872) Landowners over 2ha (2000)	1159	1179
Landowners over 500 acres	176	200
Acreage (and percentage) of county owned by owners of over 500 acres	441,976 acres (79.4%)	327,424 acres (58.5%)

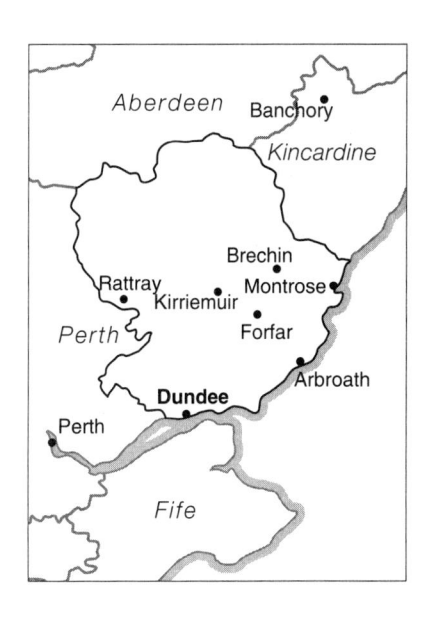

Top Landowners 2001

THE 17TH EARL OF DALHOUSIE *47,200 acres. No. 1 in 1872.* The 16th Earl, one of Scotland's most distinguished statesmen and a holder of the Military Cross from World War Two, was a former Governor General of Rhodesia and Nyasaland. He died in 1999 and was succeeded by his son, James Hubert Ramsay, born in 1948 and educated at the Catholic Eton, Ampleforth. A lieutenant in the Coldstream Guards, he lives at Brechin Castle, the second of the two family homes. The other is Dalhousie Castle at Bonnyrigg in Midlothian although the chroniclers, MacEwen and Wightman could find no modern acreage there. The 17th Earl is married with a son and daughter.

THE 13TH EARL OF AIRLIE *37,300 acres. No. 2 in 1872.* Born in 1926, David George Coke Patrick Ogilvy, the 13th Earl, was Lord Chamberlain of the Queen's Household during some of its most traumatic modern events, including the death of the Princess of Wales and the divorce of Sarah and the Queen's second son Prince Andrew. He was High Commissioner in post World War Two Austria. The earldom, granted in 1639, precedes the union, but the first Ogilvy of record, Sir James, was Ambassador from Scotland to Denmark in 1491. The present earl has two homes, both close to Kirriemuir in Angus, Cortachy Castle and Airlie Castle.

THE 18TH EARL OF STRATHMORE *17,300 acres.* Michael Fergus Bowes Lyons, the 18th Earl of Strathmore and Kinghorn, was born in 1957, is married with three sons and lives at Glamis Castle near Forfar. The Returns for 1872 show less than 5000 acres, while the Bateman correction ups that to 22,000 acres. His great aunt, the Queen Mother, owns the Castle of Mey in Caithness, but the chroniclers MacEwen and Wightman could find no significant landholding there.

Significant Institutional Landowners

The Forestry Commission owns 10,122 acres. The successors to Tayside Regional Council own 9970 acres and the Ministry of Defence 3418 acres.

TOP 10 IN 1872

1	Earl of Dalhousie RN (MP) of Panmure House, Muirdrum	136,602 acres	with 1419 elsewhere
2	Earl of Airlie of Cortachy Castle, Kirriemuir	65,059 acres	with 4647 elsewhere
3	Earl of Southesk of Kinnaird Castle, Brechin	22,699 acres	
4	Mr Donald Ogilvie of Clova, of Balnaboth, Kirriemuir	21,893 acres	
5	Earl of Glamis of Glamis (not in Bateman)	17,034 acres	
6	Captain T.S.F. Fotheringham of Fotheringham	12,529 acres	
7	Mr James Small of Dirnanean, Pitlochrie	11,261 acres	with 9193 elsewhere
8	Mr James MacKenzie of Glenmuick, Ballater	7129 acres	with 65,600 elsewhere
9	Hon Mrs Elizabeth Maule of Maulesden, Brechin	6992 acres	
10	Earl of Camperdown of Camperdown House, Dundee	6770 acres	with 7122 elsewhere

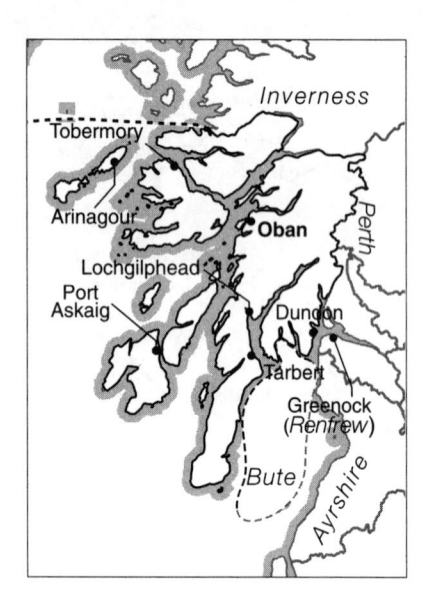

ARGYLLSHIRE

	1872	2001
Total acreage	2,030,948 acres	1,990,522 acres
Agricultural acreage	1,827,853 acres	1,339,605 acres
Non agricultural acreage	203,948 acres	650,917 acres
Population	75,679	89,730
Owners of nothing at all	72,833	36,300
Total Dwellings	13,497	41,100
Smallholdings: 1872 owners of less than one acre	2283	
2000 owners of 0–2ha (0–4.94 acres)		366
Landowners over one acre (1872)	581	
Landowners over 2ha (2000)		1868
Landowners over 500 acres	81	408
Acreage (and percentage) of county owned by owners of over 500 acres	1,563,104 acres (76.9%)	1,197,953 acres (60.1%)

Top Landowners 2001

ROBERT FLEMING AND TRUSTS *88,900 acres.* Robert Fleming, born in 1933, is the recently retired chairman of the London merchant bank of Robert Fleming, founded in 1900 in an office beside the Bank of England. He has been succeeded as chairman by his cousin. The *Sunday Times* made the family the 22nd richest in the UK and assessed them as worth £1 billion in 2000. The family have built up the estate in the twentieth century, not being either aristocrats or landed gentry prior to that. The family are close to the Royals and are thought to have inherited what royal banking they did not already have when Barings went bust in the 1990s. The estate is centred around Blackmount and Glen Etive. His cousins own a further 23,200 acres at Glenkinglass.

TRUSTEES OF 10TH DUKE OF ARGYLL *60,800 acres. No. 2 in 1872.* The late Ian Campbell, the Hereditary Master of the Queen's Household in Scotland, was born in 1937 and eschewed the standard educational drill for an aristocratic landowner by going to Le Rosy, the international school in Switzerland, and then McGill University in Canada. He didn't maintain the unconventionality for long, however. He married the only daughter of Sir Ivar Colquhoun of Luss, who owns 50,000 acres in Dumbarton. The Duke was the Lord Lieutenant of Argyll and Bute and Keeper of the Great Seal of Scotland. The 10th Duke died suddenly in 2001. He has been succeeded by his heir the Marquess of Lorne, born in 1968. The 11th Duke was educated at Glenalmond and the Royal Agricultural College, Cirencester. He was Page of Honour to the Queen between 1981 and 1983. The family home is Inveraray Castle.

LORD MARGADALE *49,500 acres with 5000 acres in Wiltshire.* The 2nd Lord Margadale, James Ian Morrison, was born in 1930 and succeeded his father in 1996. Two of his three brothers were prominent MPs in the Thatcher era. He owns the beautiful Fonthill House in Wiltshire and had the standard education package for the aristocratic rich, Eton, the Royal Agricultural College at Cirencester and a stint as a second lieutenant in the Life Guards. He was High Sheriff and later Deputy Lieutenant of Wilts, as well a member of the Queen's Bodyguard for Scotland. The *Sunday Times* rated him worth £35 million in the 2000 Rich List. The estate is on Islay.

Significant Institutional Landowners

The Forestry Commission has 415,045 acres. SOAFED has 8144. SNH has 7872 acres.

TOP 10 IN 1872

1	Earl of Breadalbane of Taymouth Castle, Aberfeldy	204,192 acres	with 234,166 elsewhere
2	Duke of Argyll of the Castle, Inverary	168,351 acres	with 6799 elsewhere
3	Mr John Malcolm of Poltalloch, Lochgilphead	83,279 acres	with 2332 elsewhere
4	Mr Charles Morrison of Reading and Islay	67,000 acres	with 8732 elsewhere
5	Mr John James Dalgleish of Westgrange, Culross	55,000 acres	with 2400 elsewhere
6	Mr James Campbell of Jura	55,000 acres	
7	Sir Thomas Milles Riddell Bt of Strontian, Bonaw	54,418 acres	
8	Mr John Ramsay MP of Kildalton, Greenock	54,250 acres	
9	Mr George Frederick Callander of Ardkinlglas, Cairndow, Glasgow	51,670 acres	with 601 elsewhere
10	Earl of Morton of Dalmahoy, Midcalder	49,814 acres	with 15,347 elsewhere

AYRSHIRE

	1872	2001
Total acreage	721,947 acres	743,234 acres
Agricultural acreage	649,752 acres	509,233 acres
Non agricultural acreage	72,194 acres	234,001 acres
Population	220,908	377,010
Owners of nothing at all	211,532	158,610
Total Dwellings	26,798	168,400
Smallholdings: 1872 owners of less than one acre	8050	
2000 owners of 0–2ha (0–4.94 acres)		214
Landowners over one acre (1872)	1326	
Landowners over 2ha (2000)		2275
Landowners over 500 acres	48	196
Acreage (and percentage) of county owned by owners of over 500 acres	610,234 acres (84%)	245,647 acres (33%)

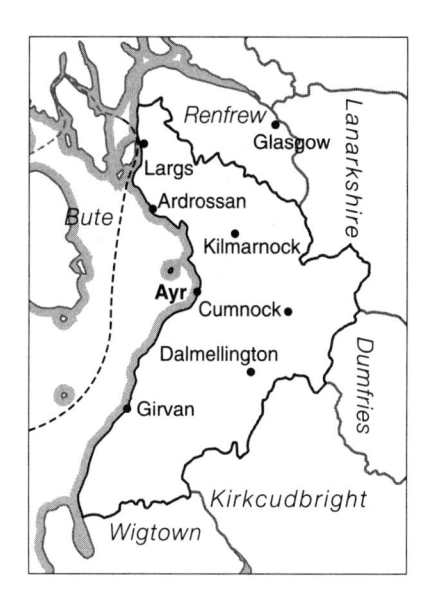

Top Landowners 2001

THE 7TH MARQUESS OF BUTE *19,600 acres with 30,100 in Bute and 25,000 in Spain. No. 2 in 1872*. Better known as racing driver Johnny Dumfries, the joint Le Mans winner in 1988 and the Formula 3 champion in the 1980s, his real name is John Colum Crichton-Stuart, born in 1958. He is entitled to act as hereditary Sheriff and Coroner of Bute and according to *Debrett's* is the patron of nine parishes. He was educated at Ampleforth, the Catholic Eton. The family sold treasures and land to make a series of inspired purchases of land in Spain around Soto Grande, which have escalated in value. The *Sunday Times* credits him with a value of £110 million in its 2000 Rich List. He is married for a second time, with one son and three daughters.

THE 4TH EARL OF INCHCAPE *13,000 acres*. Kenneth Peter Lyle Mackay, the 4th Earl, was born in 1943, heir to a great shipping fortune created by his ancestor in India in the late 1800s. The *Sunday Times* rates him worth £50 million, with £10 million allowed for the Glenapp Estate company, which holds various real estate assets as well as the Scottish land. He is a director of many companies. His heir, Viscount Glenapp, was born in 1979. The family live in Wiltshire.

THE 8TH MARQUESS OF AILSA *10,000 acres in family trust. No. 1 in 1872*. Archibald Angus Charles Kennedy, the 8th Marquess, born in 1956, attended all but one of the sitting days in the last year of the House of Lords before reform (1997/1998). He lives in the home counties and the family seat is Cassillis near Maybole. He is divorced with two daughters.

Significant Institutional Landowner

The Forestry Commission owns 95,362 acres.

TOP 10 IN 1872

1	Marquess of Ailsa of Cassilis House, Maybole	76,015 acres	
2	Marquess of Bute of Mount Stuart, Rothesay	43,734 acres	with 72,934 elsewhere
3	Earl of Glasgow MP of Crauford Priory, Fife	25,613 acres	with 12,212 elsewhere
4	Earl of Eglinton and Winton of Eglinton Castle, Irvine	23,631 acres	with 6537 elsewhere
5	Rt Hon Sir James Fergusson KCMG, MP Bt of Kilkerran, Maybole	22,630 acres	
6	Earl of Stair (MP) of Oxenfoord Castle, Dalkeith (Held in the name of the Countess)	19,758 acres	with 96,612 elsewhere
7	Mrs Baird of Cambustoon	19,599 acres	
8	Earl of Loudoun of Rowallen Castle, Kilmarnock	18,638 acres	with 14,272 elsewhere
9	Duke of Portland of Welbeck Abbey, Worksop	17,244 acres	with 165,955 elsewhere
10	Mr Frederick Macadam of Craigengillan	15,000 acres	with 20,000 elsewhere

THE COUNTIES OF SCOTLAND

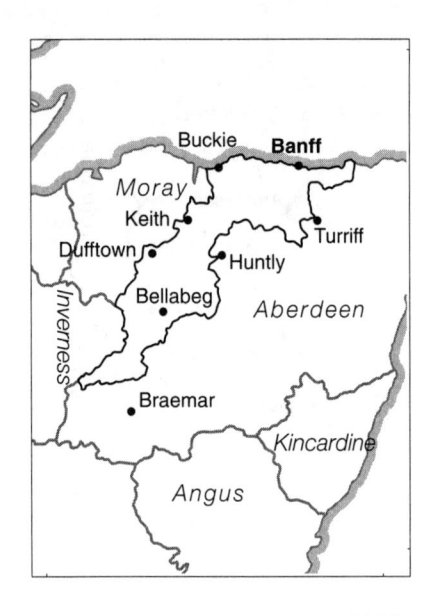

BANFFSHIRE

	1872	2001
Total acreage	407,501 acres	403,054 acres
Agricultural acreage	366,750 acres	285,477 acres
Non agricultural acreage	40,750 acres	117,577 acres
Population	62,032	43,503
Owners of nothing at all	58,007	-
Total Dwellings	11,603	-
Smallholdings: 1872 owners of less than one acre 2000 owners of 0–2ha (0–4.94 acres)	3883	139
Landowners over one acre (1872) Landowners over 2ha (2000)	142	1174
Landowners over 500 acres	36	113
Acreage (and percentage) of county owned by owners of over 500 acres	191,104 acres (46.8%)	155,490 acres (38.5%)

Top Landowners 2001

THE 13TH EARL OF SEAFIELD *35,000 acres with 50,000 acres in Inverness and 16,000 acres in Moray.* In the 1872 Returns the Seafield Estate was the 6th largest estate in Great Britain. It remains one of the largest in the UK today, but it is not clear how it is held, or on whose behalf. Ian Derek Francis Ogilvie-Grant, the 13th Earl, born in 1939, succeeded his mother to the title in 1969, she having succeeded in 1915. A Conservative, the 13th Earl attended the House of Lords on only two days in the final year before reform (1997/98). His current countess, the second, is from Egypt. The family seat is at the Old Cullen, Cullen.

C. MACPHERSON GRANT RUSSELL AND BALLINDALLOCH TRUSTS *14,200 acres.* These are the lands of Sir George Macpherson Grant, shown below from the 1872 Returns (no. 4). There is no further information available on the owners. The estate is at Ballindalloch.

L.A. AND P.M. GORDON DUFF *7400 acres.* Like the previous estate, this is the residue of the lands of Major Gordon Duff, the local MP when Bateman was reviewing the Return in 1883. The estate is at Drummuir.

Significant Institutional Landowners

The Crown Estate owns 57,700 acres. The Forestry Commission owns 19,977 acres.

TOP 10 IN 1872

1	Duke of Richmond and Gordon (MP) of Goodwood, Chichester, Sussex	159,925	acres	with 126,459 elsewhere
2	Earl of Fife of Duff House, Banff	72,432	acres	with 176,788 elsewhere
3	Earl of Seafield of Castle Grant, Grantown, Inverness	48,936	acres	with 256,984 elsewhere
4	Sir George Macpherson-Grant of Ballindalloch Castle, Elgin	14,223	acres	with 111,220 elsewhere
5	Major Lachlan Duff Gordon-Duff MP of Drummuir Castle, Keith	13,053	acres	with 4885 elsewhere
6	Lt Col George Fergueson of Pitfour, Mintlaw	10,845	acres	with 12,305 elsewhere
7	Mr Francis William Garden-Campbell of Troup House	9547	acres	with 10,516 elsewhere
8	Sir Robert John Abercromby MP of Forglen House, Turriff	8053	acres	with 3715 elsewhere
9	Mr Andrew Stuart MP of Auchlunkart House, Keith	6329	acres	with 483 elsewhere
10	Colonel Grant-Kinloch, HM Inspector of Foreign Legions. of Logie, Kirriemuir	5894	acres	with 2800 elsewhere

BERWICKSHIRE

	1872	2001
Total acreage	292,139 acres	292,535 acres
Agricultural acreage	262,925 acres	272,242 acres
Non agricultural acreage	29,213 acres	20,293 acres
Population	36,486	20,779
Owners of nothing at all	34,743	-
Total Dwellings	6491	-
Smallholdings: 1872 owners of less than one acre 2000 owners of 0–2ha (0–4.94 acres)	1290	66
Landowners over one acre (1872) Landowners over 2ha (2000)	453	646
Landowners over 500 acres	123	194
Acreage (and percentage) of county owned by owners of over 500 acres	201,126 acres (68.8%)	201,564 acres (68.9%)

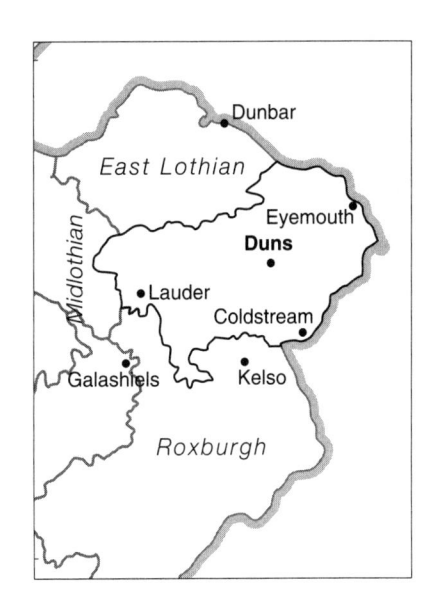

Top Landowners 2001

THE 10TH DUKE OF ROXBURGHE *10,100 acres with 55,500 acres in Roxburghshire.* This small portion of the Roxburghe estate remains little changed from when the ancestor of Guy David Innes-Ker held it in 1872. He is the 10th Duke, born in 1954 and educated at Eton, Cambridge and the Royal Military Academy, Sandhurst. He met his first wife, Lady Jane Grosvenor, when he was serving as a lieutenant in the Blues and Royals in Northern Ireland in 1976. They were divorced in 1990 but she lives on the Floors estate, not far from Floors Castle. The Roxburghshire Estate, like many landed estates, is held in an offshore trust, in this case in Jersey. He has five children, three sons and two daughters. The *Sunday Times* assigns him a value of £70 million in the 2000 Rich List.

THE 12TH DUKE OF NORTHUMBERLAND *9000 acres with 120,000 acres in Northumberland, 550 acres in Middlesex and 3000 acres in Surrey.* See Northumberland (p.250).

THE 13TH EARL OF HADDINGTON *7000 acres with 6000 acres in East Lothian. No. 4 in 1872.* The estate, the East Lothian portion held in his son and heir Lord Tyninghame's name, is about half what it was in 1872. The earl, John George Baillie-Hamilton, was born in 1941 and educated at Ampleforth. Twice married, his heir is Lord Binning, born in 1985. The family seat is at Mellerstain. He attended about one third of the sitting days in the last year of the old House of Lords before reform (1997/1998) but was not elected as a hereditary representative.

Significant Institutional Landowners

None known.

TOP 10 IN 1872

1	Earl of Lauderdale of Thirlestane Castle, Lauder	24,681	acres	with 831 elsewhere
2	Sir Hugh Hume-Campbell Bt MP of Marchmount House, Dunse	20,180	acres	
3	Marquess of Tweedale (MP) of Yester House, Haddington	18,116	acres	with 25,401 elsewhere
4	Earl of Haddington of Arderne Hall, Tarporley, Cheshire	14,279	acres	with 19,767 elsewhere
5	Lady John Douglas-Montague-Scott-Spottiswoode of Lauder	11,412	acres	
6	Mr David Milne-Home MP of Paxton House	9144	acres	
7	Lady E. Pringle of Langton House, Duns	8121	acres	with 12 elsewhere
8	Sir Basil Hall of Dunglass, Dunbar	7948	acres	with 887 elsewhere
9	Lady Marjoribanks of Ladykirk	6832	acres	
10	Lt. Col Trotter of Mortonhall, Liberton	6796	acres	with 2515 elsewhere

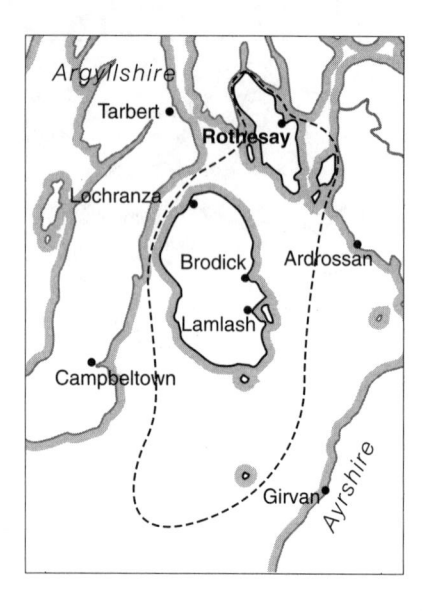

BUTE
(includes the island of Arran)

	1872	2001
Total acreage	138,972 acres	139,711 acres
Agricultural acreage	125,074 acres	96,356 acres
Non agricultural acreage	13,897 acres	43,355 acres
Population	16,977	89,730
Owners of nothing at all	16,240	36,430
Total Dwellings	2433	41,100
Smallholdings: 1872 owners of less than one acre	648	
2000 owners of 0–2ha (0–4.94 acres)		22
Landowners over one acre (1872)	89	
Landowners over 2ha (2000)		245
Landowners over 500 acres	11	33
Acreage (and percentage) of county owned by owners of over 500 acres	99,876 acres (65.3%)	70,590 acres (50.5%)

Top Landowners 2001

THE 7TH MARQUESS OF BUTE *31,100 acres* with 19,600 acres in Ayrshire. No. 2 in 1872. See Ayrshire (p.273).

STEPHEN GIBBS *24,908 acres.* The Scottish chronicler Andy Wightman records that Stephen Gibbs was reported in the local papers to have charged geology students to study the unusual rock formations in the Arran granite. He is said to have been especially forceful over feudal dues, the anarchic system of tiered ownership. Mr Gibbs has become the owner of much of what were the lands of the Hamilton dukedom (no. 1 in 1872). The present duke, the 15th, still has some land on Arran and lives in Haddington, where there are 5000 acres. The family seat, Lennoxlove, is in Haddington, but Brodick Castle on Arran is with the National Trust for Scotland and open to the public.

CHARLES JG FORDE *16,300 acres.* He is the son of Lady Jean Fforde, aunt of the present Duke of Montrose, and sister of the late 6th Duke of Montrose. She was Deputy Lieutenant of Ayrshire and Arran. Born in 1948, he lives at Brodick on Arran. The chronicler John MacEwen identified two Montrose families in Bute, Lady Jean's and Lady Mary Dunn, holding a total of 56,000 acres between them.

Other significant landowners include Sir David Attenborough, the noted wildlife filmmaker, who has a small estate of 2000 acres in Bute at Rhubodach.

Significant Institutional Landowner
The Forestry Commission has 27,170 acres.

TOP 10 IN 1872

1	Duke of Hamilton and Brandon of Hamilton Palace, Glasgow	102,210 acres	with 55,176 elsewhere
2	Marquess of Bute of Mount Stuart, Rothesay	29,279 acres	with 87,389 elsewhere
3	Mrs Jane A Fullarton Bowden of Kilmichael, of 150 Bath St. Glasgow	3632 acres	
4	Earl of Glasgow of Crauford Priory, Fife	1833 acres	with 35,992 elsewhere
5	Earl of Eglinton & Winton	671 acres	with 29,497 elsewhere
6	Mr Robert Thom, of Ascog, Rothesay	300 acres	
7	Mr Arthur Campbell of Ardbeg, Rothesay	99 acres	
8	Mrs Elizabeth MacKay of South Garrochty, Rothesay	65 acres	
9	Mr John MacKirdy of Rothesay	37 acres	
10	Mr Charles Dalrymple of Hailes MP of Ardencraig, Rothesay	33 acres	

CAITHNESS

	1872	2001
Total acreage	471,763 acres	438,943 acres
Agricultural acreage	424,586 acres	344,010 acres
Non agricultural acreage	47,176 acres	94,933 acres
Population	39,992	27,781
Owners of nothing at all	38,962	-
Total Dwellings	7474	-
Smallholdings: 1872 owners of less than one acre 2000 owners of 0–2ha (0–4.94 acres)	809	154
Landowners over one acre (1872) Landowners over 2ha (2000)	221	1193
Landowners over 500 acres	93	124
Acreage (and percentage) of county owned by owners of over 500 acres	361,090 acres (76.5%)	247,700 acres (56.4%)

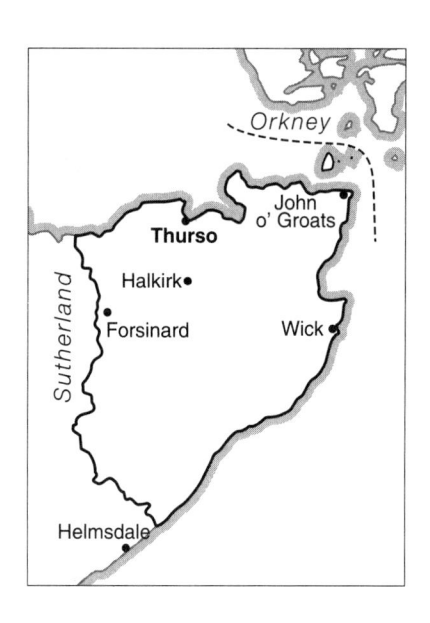

Top Landowners 2001

LADY ANNE CAVENDISH BENTINCK *45,000 acres with 17,000 acres in Notts.* See Notts (p.251). The land in Caithness is owned by the Welbeck Estates Company Ltd, and some of the shares in the company, like those of the Roxburgh estate, are held in an offshore financial centre.

STUART MURRAY TREIPLAND FAMILY *45,000 acres.* The Dunbeath & Glutt Estate, once the possession of the Earls of Caithness and later the Bute family, was sold in 1995 to the Stuart Murray Treipland family. The size of the estate is a source of confusion. The current home web site describes it as being 45,000 acres. The Scottish Estates marketing site describes it as 33,000 acres. Stuart Murray Treipland also purchased the 10,000-acre Strathmore estate at Mey from Clare College, Cambridge.

THE 3RD VISCOUNT THURSO *36,800 acres.* John Archibald Sinclair, the 3rd Viscount and heir to some of the Sinclair lands shown below, was born in 1953. His ancestor, Sir John (no. 2 in 1872) was a royal courtier, but it was for services to the Liberal party, as Secretary of State for Scotland in the National Government in 1931 and leader of the Liberals in the House of Commons during World War Two, that he was eventually made a Viscount. His grandson was an active Liberal working peer attending 43 of the 79 days in the final session of the House of Lords before reform (1997/1998). He was not elected to represent the hereditaries nor given a life peerage. He is a director of several companies including the Savoy Hotel. The estate is at Dalnawillan and Thurso and has some excellent salmon fishing.

During the 1990s Dame Shirley Porter, the controversial former head of Westminster City Council who was surcharged millions for alleged gerrymandering, had a 1000 acre estate in Caithness at Moss of Quintfall.

Significant Institutional Landowner

The Forestry Commission owns 18,912 acres.

TOP 10 IN 1872

1	Duke of Portland of Welbeck Abbey, Worksop	101,000 acres	with 82,199 elsewhere
2	Sir John George Tollemache Sinclair Bt MP of Thurso Castle	78,053 acres	
3	Mr William Sinclair Thomson-Sinclair of Dunbeath Castle	57,757 acres	
4	Mr Garden Duff-Dunbar of Hempriggs Castle, Wick	26,880 acres	
5	Sir Robert Anstruther Bt MP of Balcaskie, Pittenween, Fife	22,597 acres	with 2121 elsewhere
6	Sir Robert Charles Sinclair Bt of Stevenson, Haddington	18,874 acres	with 473 elsewhere
7	Mr James Christie Traill of Castle Hill	15,263 acres	with 5201 elsewhere
8	Earl of Caithness of Barrowgill Castle, Wick	14,460 acres	with 613 elsewhere
9	Mr C.S. Guthrie of Scotscalder	13,934 acres	
10	Major Michael Stocks of Latheronwheel	13,600 acres	with 2860 elsewhere

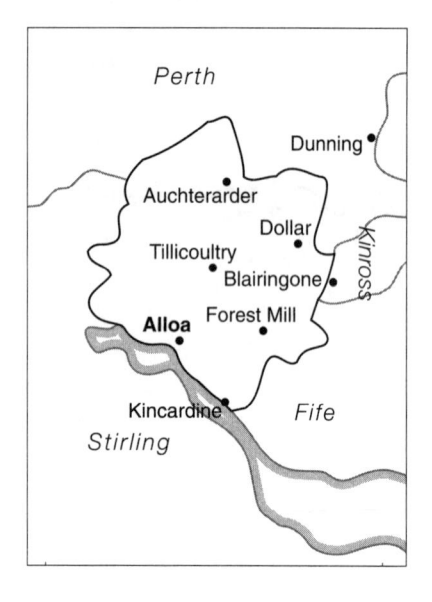

CLACKMANNANSHIRE

	1872	2001
Total acreage	30,189 acres	34,860 acres
Agricultural acreage	27,170 acres	25,352 acres
Non agricultural acreage	3018 acres	9508 acres
Population	23,747	48,560
Owners of nothing at all	22,520	20,310
Total Dwellings	3316	22,500
Smallholdings: 1872 owners of less than one acre	1137	
2000 owners of 0–2ha (0–4.94 acres)		10
Landowners over one acre (1872)	90	
Landowners over 2ha (2000)		88
Landowners over 500 acres	13	10
Acreage (and percentage) of county owned by owners of over 500 acres	18,657 acres (61.8%)	16,577 (47.5%)

Top Landowners 2001

Neither of the two chroniclers, John MacEwen and Andy Wightman, were able to establish the ownership of any except two estates in this tiny county, the smallest in Scotland. The county was heavily mined for coal during Scottish industrialisation and the five aristocratic families showing in the 1872 list were said to have made a great fortune out of the 'blood, sweat and tears of the men, women and children slaving in the mines.' MacEwen, who made the comment, reckoned that the five raised the equivalent of £1.4 million from the acreage. Part of Lord Abercromby's land is now part of Stirling University.

Known estates in 1995:
Mr J Miller of Rodders	5000 acres
Glencarse & Harvieston estate	4200 acres
Tillycoultry estate	2000 acres
Colin Campbell	1350 acres

TOP 10 IN 1872

1	Earl of Mar and Kellie of Alloa Park, Alloa	6163 acres	with 149 elsewhere
2	Mr James Orr of Harvistoun Castle, Dollar	4726 acres	with 475 elsewhere
3	Mr Robert Balfour Wardlaw Ramsay of Whitehill, Edinburgh	4147 acres	with 3353 elsewhere
4	Lord Abercromby of Airthrey Castle, Stirling	3707 acres	with 11,557 elsewhere
5	Earl of Zetland MP of Aske Hall, Richmond	2726 acres	with 65,444 elsewhere
6	Earl of Mansfield MP of Scone Palace, Perth	1705 acres	with 47,369 elsewhere
7	Mr James Johnstone MP of Alva, Stirling	1587 acres	with 13,927 elsewhere
8	Lord Burleigh of Kennet House	943 acres	
9	Mr John Moir of Hillfoot, Dollar	637 acres	
10	Mrs Mary Wedderburn Morries Stirling of Northfield & Garnal of 9 South Eaton Place, London	578 acres	

CROMARTY

(Joined with Ross-shire in 1889 to form Ross & Cromarty. See Ross-shire, p.296)

	1872
Total acreage	18,206 acres
Agricultural acreage	16,385 acres
Non agricultural acreage	1820 acres
Population	3362
Owners of nothing at all	3117
Total Dwellings	685
Smallholdings: 1872 owners of less than one acre 2000 owners of 0–2ha (0–4.94 acres)	217
Landowners over one acre (1872) Landowners over 2ha (2000)	14
Landowners over 500 acres	5
Acreage (and percentage) of county owned by owners of over 500 acres	17,503 acres (96.1%)

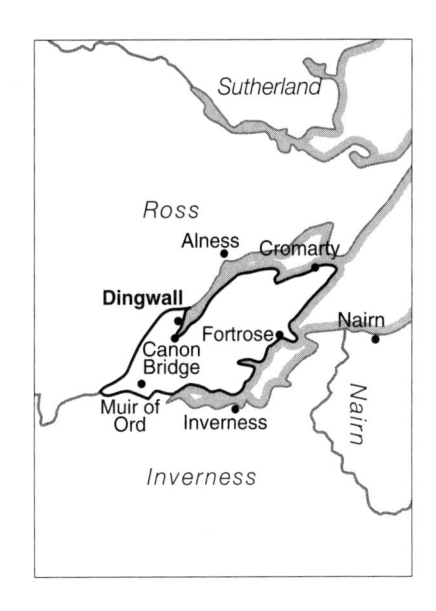

Top Landowners 2001

See Ross-shire (p.296).

TOP 10 IN 1872

1	Colonel George Ross of Cromarty House	7437 acres	with 1646 elsewhere
2	Mr John A Shaw Mackenzie of New Hall	6590 acres	
3	Mr George Munro of Poyntzfield House, Invergordon	1776 acres	
4	Mr James Fletcher of Rosehaugh House, Inverness	880 acres	
5	Mr Hugh Frazer of Braelangwell	820 acres	
6	Mr William Ord Mackenzie of Culbo, Invergordon	371 acres	
7	Mr Colin Lyon Mackenzie of St Martins, Inverness	191 acres	
8	Rev Mr Robert Macdougall of The Manse, Resolis, Invergordon	49 acres	
9	Mr Hugh Noble of Gordonmill, Invergordon	43 acres	
10	Rev Mr George Russel of The Manse, Cromarty	14 acres	

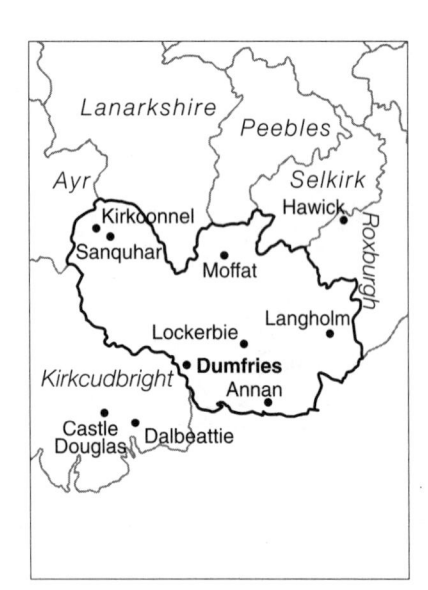

DUMFRIESSHIRE

	1872	2001
Total acreage	676,971 acres	688,112 acres
Agricultural acreage	609,273 acres	510,150 acres
Non agricultural acreage	67,687 acres	177,962 acres
Population	74,808	147,300
Owners of nothing at all	70,631	67,290
Total Dwellings	13,646	67,700
Smallholdings: 1872 owners of less than one acre 2000 owners of 0–2ha (0–4.94 acres)	3291	208
Landowners over one acre (1872) Landowners over 2ha (2000)	886	1549
Landowners over 500 acres	97	241
Acreage (and percentage) of county owned by owners of over 500 acres	410,876 acres (60.6%)	322,094 acres (46.8%)

Top Landowners 2001

THE 9TH DUKE OF BUCCLEUCH AND 11TH OF QUEENSBURY *167,200 acres with 49,200 in Roxburghshire, 37,500 in Selkirk and 17,000 in England. No. 1 in 1872.* The Duke, born in 1923 and whose full name is Walter John Francis Douglas Montague-Scott, is the largest individual landowner in the United Kingdom (excluding the indirect ownerships of his great friend the Queen and her family). Once rated worth £300 million by the *Sunday Times*, he has now been reduced to a mere £50 million. This valuation, which ignores the fact that one of his paintings alone, a Leonardo da Vinci, is worth over £50 million, is based on the fact that the vast ducal acreage is in trust. Though this is a fact, as it is for almost every modern estate in this book, the duke's family are the ultimate beneficiary of the trusts, and ultimately, they do own the 270,700 acres that can be accounted for, to date. His heir is the Earl of Dalkeith, an active public figure in both Scotland and England. He lives at Thornhill, the third of the family seats.

SIR ANDREW RUPERT JOHN BUCHANAN-JARDINE, 4TH BARONET, FAMILY TRUSTS *24,500 acres*. Born in 1923 he is the direct descendant of the first of the Jardine Taipans – heads of great commercial empires, in this case the Jardine Matheson company in Hong Kong. The 1st and 3rd of his predecessors, headed the family firm. He was educated at Harrow and the Royal Agricultural College, Cirencester, but chose the Royal Horse Guards cavalry regiment for a career, where he rose to the rank of major. The family home is at Castle Milk, near Lockerbie. His son, born in 1952, runs the estate.

THE 11TH EARL OF ANNANDALE AND HARTFELL *12,500 acres*. The hereditary chief of the Clan Johnstone, Patrick Andrew Wentworth Hope Johnston, born in 1941, is also keeper of Lochmaben Castle and the Vice Lord Lieutenant of Nithsdale, Annandale and Eskdale districts. He was admitted to the House of Lords as an earl after a special application to the Committee of Privileges in 1985. Having obtained entry, however, he failed to make a single appearance in the final year before reform and ejection. He has been a professional underwriting member of Lloyds since 1976. It is not clear who runs the estate or how it is held. The family seat is Lochwood Castle.

Significant Institutional Landowners

The Crown Estate owns 17,493 acres. The Forestry Commission owns 55,938 acres.

TOP 10 IN 1872

1	Duke of Buccleuch & Queensbury of Dalkeith Palace, Edinburgh	254,179	acres	with 205,929 elsewhere
2	Mr John James Hope-Johnstone MP of Raehills, Annandale, Lockerbie	64,079	acres	with 1287 elsewhere
3	Sir Frederick John Johnstone Bt MP of Westerhall, Langholme	17,064	acres	with 200 elsewhere
4	Earl of Mansfield (MP) of Scone Palace, Perth	14,342	acres	with 34,732 elsewhere
5	Mr Frederick Ernest Villiers of Closeburn, Thornhill	13,573	acres	
6	Captain Sir John Heron-Maxwell Bt RN MP of Springkell, Ecclefechan	13,391	acres	
7	Marquess of Queensbury of Kinmount, Annan	13,243	acres	
8	Miss Mary Stewart-Beattie of Crieve, Lockerbie	11,159	acres	with 9354 elsewhere
9	Mr James Alexander Rogerson of Gillesbie, Lockerbie	9284	acres	
10	Mr Andrew Jardine of Lanrick Castle, Doune	9131	acres	

DUNBARTONSHIRE

	1872	2001
Total acreage	153,736 acres	154,562 acres
Agricultural acreage	138,362 acres	101,849 acres
Non agricultural acreage	15,373 acres	52,713 acres
Population	58,857	204,980
Owners of nothing at all	56,511	91,140
Total Dwellings	7638	87,600
Smallholdings: 1872 owners of less than one acre 2000 owners of 0–2ha (0–4.94 acres)	1640	34
Landowners over one acre (1872) Landowners over 2ha (2000)	706	313
Landowners over 500 acres	26	39
Acreage (and percentage) of county owned by owners of over 500 acres	83,400 acres (54.2%)	72,837 acres (47.1%)

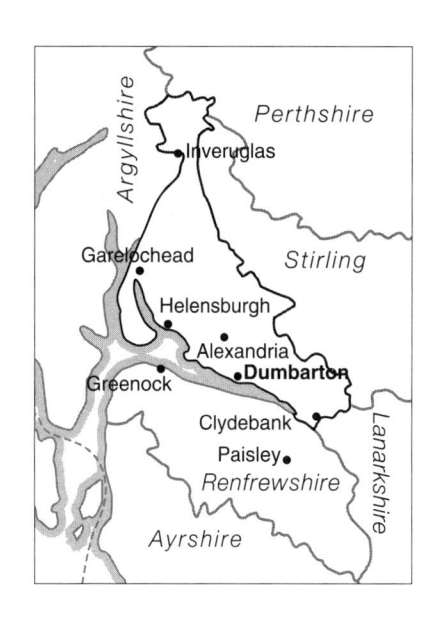

Top Landowners 2001

SIR IVAR COLQUHOUN AND LUSS ESTATES COMPANY *50,000 acres. No. 1 in 1872*. Sir Ivar, the 8th Baronet, is chief of the Clan Colquhoun, and remains in possession of most of the 1872 lands. Born in 1916, he succeeded to the title and the estate over 50 years ago. His daughter Iona is the Duchess of Argyll. The family trace their ancestry back to Robert Colquhoun, the 1st laird of Camstradden, who was the second son of Sir Robert Colquhoun, the laird of Colquhoun. Robert got the lands at Camscadden, which is still the site of the family seat, by way of a charter from his elder brother, the heir, dated 4 July 1395.

Andy Wightman in *Who Owns Scotland* notes that apart from the Luss estate and the three below, the rest of the county is farmed, by farmers.

Dr Frischman	4118 acres at Garabal
D. Fisher	2700 acres at Stuckindroin
Lowe brothers	2700 acres at Ardlesish lodge

Significant Institutional Landowners

Forestry Commission owns 5327 acres. The Ministry of Defence owns 10,870 acres.

TOP 10 IN 1872

1	Sir James Colquhoun Bt of Rossdhu House Luss	67,041 acres	
2	Mrs Jane T Ewing of Strathleven	9180 acres	
3	Duke of Argyll of The Castle, Inverary, Argyll	6799 acres	with 168,315 elsewhere
4	Mr John William Burns of Kilmahew, Cardross	5568 acres	
5	The Hon Cornwallis Fleming of Cumbernauld House	3520 acres	
6	Lord Blantyre of Erskine, Renfrew	2946 acres	with 11,115 elsewhere
7	Miss Grace Hamilton of Cochno House, Duntocher	2615 acres	
8	Duke of Montrose of Buchanan Castle, Glasgow	2588 acres	with 100,859 elsewhere
9	Lady Campbell of Succoth of Garscube, Glasgow	2478 acres	with 8123 elsewhere
10	Mr Colin Campbell of Camiesseskan, Cardross	2124 acres	

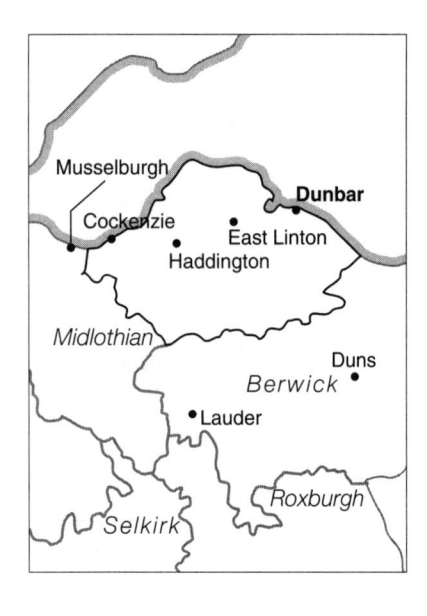

EAST LOTHIAN
(Known in 1872 as Haddington)

	1872	2001
Total acreage	171,739 acres	171,044 acres
Agricultural acreage	154,565 acres	141,996 acres
Non agricultural acreage	17,173 acres	29,048 acres
Population	37,771	90,430
Owners of nothing at all	36,260	41,680
Total Dwellings	7179	37,500
Smallholdings: 1872 owners of less than one acre	1191	
2000 owners of 0–2ha (0–4.94 acres)		53
Landowners over one acre (1872)	320	
Landowners over 2ha (2000)		430
Landowners over 500 acres	51	100
Acreage (and percentage) of county owned by owners of over 500 acres	121,273 acres (71%)	96,317 acres (56%)

Top Landowners 2001

LORD BINNING (HEIR TO THE EARL OF HADDINGTON) *6000 acres with 7000 acres in Berwickshire.* Born in 1985 George Edmund Baldred Baillie-Hamilton is the son and heir of the 13th Earl of Haddington (see Berwickshire p.275).

THE 15TH DUKE OF HAMILTON AND 12TH DUKE OF BRANDON *5200 acres*. Once one of the richest dukedoms in Scotland, with over 157,000 acres at its disposal, this may be all that is left of that gigantic inheritance. The present Duke, Angus Alan Douglas-Hamilton, was born in 1938, educated at Eton and Oxford and was a test pilot for Scottish Aviation following a stint in the RAF. He is the premier peer of Scotland and the Hereditary Keeper of Holyrood Palace. Three times married his son and heir is the Marquess of Douglas & Clydesdale, born in 1978.

THE EARL OF WEMYSS & MARCH *4700 acres with 21,000 acres in Selkirk, 5000 acres in Fife and 5000 acres near Cheltenham. No. 4 in 1872. See Fife (p.283).*

Significant Institutional Landowners
None known.

TOP 10 IN 1872

1	Marquess of Tweedale (MP) of Yester House	20,468 acres	with 23,049 elsewhere
2	Lady Mary Nisbet-Hamilton of Biel, Prestonkirk	16,664 acres	with 9032 elsewhere
3	Mr Arthur James Balfour MP of Whittinghame, Prestonkirk	14,198 acres	with 72,998 elsewhere
4	Earl of Wemyss & March of Amisfield	9167 acres	with 52,861 elsewhere
5	Sir George Grant Suttie Bt of Prestongrange	8788 acres	with 2275 elsewhere
6	Earl of Hopetoun of Hopetoun House, South Queensferry	7967 acres	with 34,540 elsewhere
7	Mr Richard Hunter of Thurston, Dunbar	6492 acres	
8	Colonel Alexander Houston of Clerkington	5148 acres	
9	Duke of Roxburghe MP of Floors Castle, Roxburgh	3863 acres	with 56,280 elsewhere
10	Captain Henry Walter Hope of Lufness, Drem	3201 acres	with 2509 elsewhere

FIFE

	1872	2001
Total acreage	304,363 acres	322,856 acres
Agricultural acreage	273,926 acres	243,442 acres
Non agricultural acreage	30,436 acres	79,414 acres
Population	160,735	348,900
Owners of nothing at all	150,325	139,340
Total Dwellings	27,056	161,200
Smallholdings: 1872 owners of less than one acre	8638	
2000 owners of 0–2ha (0–4.94 acres)		245
Landowners over one acre (1872)	1772	
Landowners over 2ha (2000)		1139
Landowners over 500 acres	97	129
Acreage (and percentage) of county owned by owners of over 500 acres	196,000 acres (64.3%)	99,351 acres (30.7%)

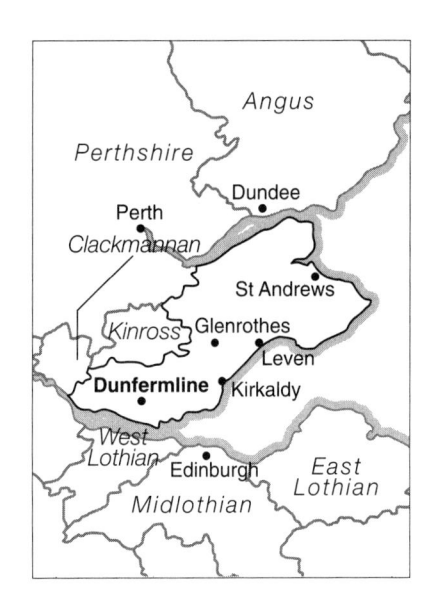

Top Landowners 2001

In his book *Who Owns Scotland*, the chronicler John MacEwen noted that Fife was unusual, even in 1872. It had no 'grotesque' landowner, someone who owned so much of the county that they jumped off the page. The county is medium to small in size, but is markedly different from most other Scottish counties both in 1872 and today in having a list of such relatively small landowners. Andy Wightman fared little better than MacEwen, establishing a mere 13% of the ownership of the county.

MS JEAN BALFOUR OF BALBIRNIE *5000 acres. No. 1 in 1872.* The estate is a very old one, first coming into the hands of the Balfours in 1483, to a then Andrew Balfour Sheriff, depute of Fife. Over the years the estate was forfeited to creditors on several occasions, but always came back to the Balfours. They are prolific in the peerage. There is one Earl Balfour and two lords Balfour, while the family name of Baron Kinross and of Baron Riverdale is Balfour. All are related.

THE 12TH EARL OF WEYMSS & MARCH *5000 acres in trust with 32,700 acres elsewhere in Scotland and 5000 acres in the Cotswold area of England.* Born in 1912, David Charteris succeeded his grandfather, the 11th Earl, in 1937. His father, Lord Neidpath was killed in action in 1916 during World War One. His first wife, Mavis Gordon, died in 1988 and he remarried in 1995, at the age of 83. His landholdings are scattered around Scotland, but there is an estate in the Cotswolds of over 5000 acres. The *Sunday Times* rates him worth only £20 million. The family seat is at Gosford House in Longniddry, East Lothian. His heir is Lord Neidpath, born in 1948.

LORD BALNEIL *4000 acres.* Anthony Robert Lindsay, born in 1958 and educated at Eton and Edinburgh, is the eldest son of the Earl of Crawford & Balcarres, a former Conservative MP and minister, who has been the Lord Chamberlain to the Queen Mother since 1992. The original Scottish estate was in Aberdeen though no trace of it was found by either of the chroniclers.

Significant Institutional Landowners

The Forestry Commission owns 9323 acres. The Ministry of Defence has 2983 acres.

TOP 10 IN 1872

1	Mr John Balfour of Balbirnie, Markinch	10,590 acres	with 10 elsewhere
2	Mr George Johnstone of Lathrisk, Falkland	10,005 acres	with 5131 elsewhere
3	Earl of Moray of Doune Lodge, Perth	7463 acres	with 74,166 elsewhere
4	Colonel Robert Munro Ferguson of Raith, Kirkcaldy	7135 acres	with 18,371 elsewhere
5	Lt Col W.H. Tyndall-Bruce of Falkland	7058 acres	with 445 elsewhere
6	Mr James Hay Erskine-Wemyss of Wemyss Castle	6925 acres	
7	Mr George Clerk Cheape of Wellfield, Strathmiglo	5230 acres	
8	Sir Thomas Coutts Lindsay Bt pf Balcarres, Colinsburgh	4672 acres	with 616 elsewhere
9	Mr Lawrence Dalgleish of Pitfarrine, Dunfermline	4563 acres	
10	Mr John Anstruther-Thomson of Charleton, Colinsburgh	4034 acres	

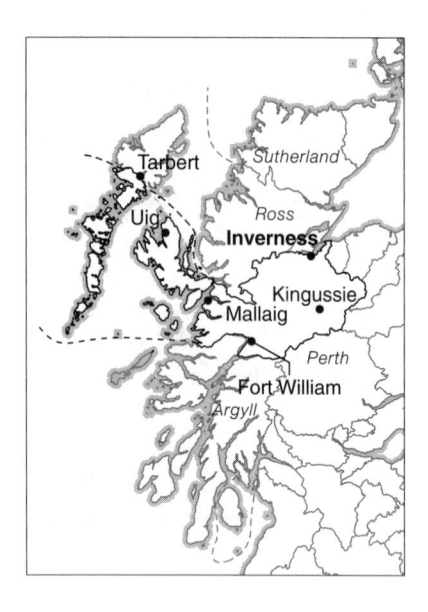

INVERNESS-SHIRE

	1872	2001
Total acreage	2,589,152 acres	2,695,094 acres
Agricultural acreage	2,330,023 acres	1,817,791 acres
Non agricultural acreage	258,915 acres	877,303 acres
Population	87,531	89,659
Owners of nothing at all	85,664	-
Total Dwellings	16,575	-
Smallholdings: 1872 owners of less than one acre 2000 owners of 0–2ha (0–4.94 acres)	1575	917
Landowners over one acre (1872) Landowners over 2ha (2000)	292	4908
Landowners over 500 acres	199	322
Acreage (and percentage) of county owned by owners of over 500 acres	1,990,321 acres (76.8%)	1,634,042 acres (61%)

Top Landowners 2001

Despite being the biggest county in Scotland, Inverness gets just three and one quarter pages in the Return of 1872, such is the extraordinary extent of landholdings of over 100,000 acres, seven in all, with no one among the top ten owning less than 81,000 acres. The economic and demographic bottleneck this created is hard to imagine, despite the bleakness of much of this very beautiful area.

COLONEL SIR HAMISH CAMERON OF LOCHIEL *76,000 acres. No. 6 in 1872.* Styled Sir, he does not occur in *Debrett's*, the title being a Scottish one which does appear in *Douglas's*, the Scottish Baronage. He is the 26th Chief of the Clan Cameron. The family has a spectacular history, including a record of the 6th chief, John Ochtery, leading a body of men from Lochiel in David II's cause at the battle of Halidon Hill in 1333. The 9th chief began a feud with the Clan Chattan which lasted hundreds of years. The 17th chief distinguished himself at the battle of Ben Nevis in 1658 by biting the throat out of one of his English adversaries and killing him. He took part in the battle of Killicrankie when in his eighties. The estate was confiscated several times, and is down on its 1872 size, but remains one of the largest in the country.

THE 6TH EARL OF GRANVILLE AND FAMILY *62,200 acres.* Granville George Fergus Leveson Gower was born in 1959 and educated at Eton. He was a page of honour to the Queen in 1973–74. The family estate is not in the 1872 Return or Bateman. The nearest the Return gets is Sir John Orde (no. 10 in 1872), whose acreage was in North Uist, around Lochmaddy, where the Grenville seat now is.

THE EARL OF SEAFIELD *50,000 acres with 41,000 acres elsewhere in Scotland.* See Banff (p.274).

Significant Institutional Landowners

The Forestry Commission owns 316,887 acres. SOAFED owns 190,709 acres. SNH owns 49,894 acres. The Ministry of Defence has 3116 acres. The Alcan company owns 112,400 acres and South Uist Estates has 92,000 acres.

TOP 10 IN 1872

1	Lord Lovat of Beaufort Castle, Beauly	181,791 acres	
2	Earl of Seafield of Castle Grant, Grantown	160,224 acres	with 145,706 elsewhere
3	The Macleod, Norman Macleod, of Dunvegan Castle, Skye	141,679 acres	
4	Lord Macdonald of Armadale Castle, Isle of Skye	129,919 acres	with 2500 elsewhere
5	The Mackintosh, Alfred Donald Mackintosh of Moy Hall, Inverness	124,181 acres	with 2114 elsewhere
6	Mr Donald Cameron of Lochiel MP of Achnacarry Castle, Fort William	109,574 acres	with 16,434 elsewhere
7	Sir George Macpherson Grant Bt of Ballindalloch Castle, Elgin	103,372 acres	with 22,071 elsewhere
8	Mr Edward Ellice MP (Mrs Ellice in Bateman) of Glenquoich	99,545 acres	with 14 elsewhere
9	The Chisholm, James Sutherland of Erchless Castle	94,328 acres	
10	Sir John William Campbell Orde of Kilmory, Loughilphead	81,098 acres	with 4646 elsewhere

KINCARDINESHIRE

	1872	2001
Total acreage	244,585 acres	244,248 acres
Agricultural acreage	220,126 acres	167,303 acres
Non agricultural acreage	24,458 acres	76,945 acres
Population	34,630	26,059
Owners of nothing at all	33,246	-
Total Dwellings	6661	-
Smallholdings: 1872 owners of less than one acre 2000 owners of 0–2ha (0–4.94 acres)	1189	94
Landowners over one acre (1872) Landowners over 2ha (2000)	195	824
Landowners over 500 acres	31	66
Acreage (and percentage) of county owned by owners of over 500 acres	178,177 acres (73%)	75,526 acres (31%)

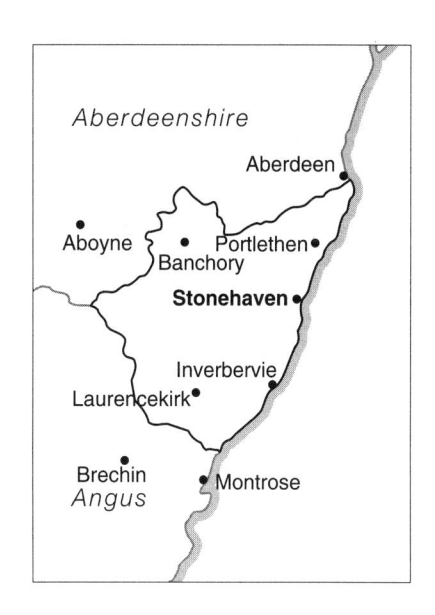

Top Landowners 2001

SIR WILLIAM GLADSTONE BT *47,700 acres with 7000 acres in Clwyd. No. 1 in 1872.* His great grandfather was the great Liberal Prime Minster, William Ewart Gladstone, and he lives at the former Prime Minister's home in Hawarden Castle, Deeside in Clwyd, as well as having a home at Fasque, near Laurencekirk in Kincardine. Gladstone the Prime Minister was, in turn, the youngest son of the 1st Baronet, who came by the title in 1846. The present Sir William was born in 1925 and has been the Deputy Lieutenant of Clwyd since 1985, and was the Chief Scout of the UK for 10 years. Educated at Eton he was also a housemaster there in the 1960s. He and the family are active managers of the two estates.

VISCOUNT COWDRAY AND TRUSTS *11,000 acres with 65,600 acres in Aberdeenshire and 17,000 acres in Sussex.* See Aberdeenshire (p.270). MacEwen found another 10,000 acres of Cowdray land in Kincardine, but it was not visible to Wightman.

MRS M.C. MILLER *6200 acres.* There are no details of this estate, although it appears in MacEwen's *Who Owns Scotland* in 1970.

Significant Institutional Landowners

The Forestry Commission owns 24,506 acres. SOAFED have 3952 acres.

TOP 10 IN 1872

1	Sir Thomas Gladstone Bt MP of Fasque, Fettercairn	45,062 acres	
2	Mr James Young of Durris House, Aberdeen	16,804 acres	
3	Captain the Viscount Arbuthnott of Arbuthnott House, Fordoun	13,560 acres	
4	Sir Robert Burnett, Bt of Crathes, Aberdeen	12,025 acres	with 84 elsewhere
5	Mr James Nicolson of Glenbervie House, Drumlithie, Fordoun	9642 acres	
6	Mr Robert William Duff MP of Fetteresso Castle, Stonehaven	8922 acres	with 4259 elsewhere
7	Earl of Kintore of Keith Hall, Inverurie	8325 acres	with 17,108 elsewhere
8	Mr Alexander Baird of Urie, Stonehaven	8000 acres	with 3018 elsewhere
9	Mr Alexander Innes of Raemoir House, Banchory	6998 acres	
10	Mr William Nathaniel Forbes of Dunnottar, Stonehaven	6528 acres	with 1300 elsewhere

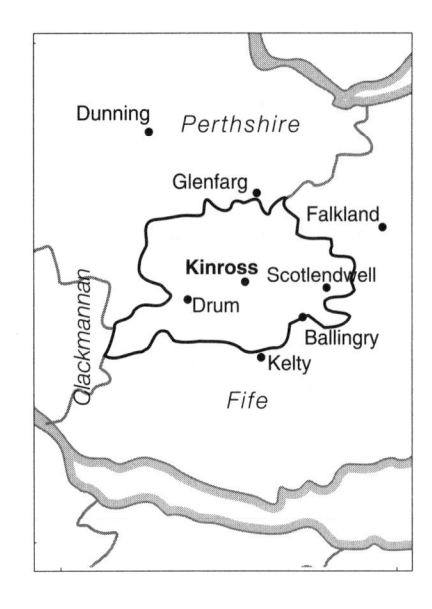

KINROSS-SHIRE

	1872	2001
Total acreage	44,888 acres	52,392 acres
Agricultural acreage	40,399 acres	42,889 acres
Non agricultural acreage	4488 acres	9503 acres
Population	7198	Not avail for county
Owners of nothing at all	6473	-
Total Dwellings	1517	-
Smallholdings: 1872 owners of less than one acre	468	
2000 owners of 0–2ha (0–4.94 acres)		40
Landowners over one acre (1872)	257	
Landowners over 2ha (2000)		227
Landowners over 500 acres	16	26
Acreage (and percentage) of county owned by owners of over 500 acres	23,040 acres (51%)	17,489 acres (33%)

Top Landowners 2001

This is the second smallest county in Scotland. According to Andy Wightman this is now almost entirely farmed, with only the small estates mentioned below still in existence.

THE HERRIOT-MAITLAND FAMILY TRUSTS *1500 acres.* No information is available on this estate.

SIR DAVID MONTGOMERY BT *1100 acres.* The present, 9th Baronet, Basil Henry David Montgomery, was born in 1931. He was educated at Eton, is a Justice of the Peace and has been Lord Lieutenant of Perth and Kinross since 1996. He lives on the home farm while his son, James, born in 1957 and educated at Eton like his father, runs the estate from the family seat, Kinross House. The family records begin with a grant of land in 1413–1414 in Ayr. Over the years the family estates became concentrated at Kinross, though the second family seat is Stobo Castle in Peebles.

WILLIAM AND JEAN S. PATERSON *1100 acres.* No information is available on this estate.

Significant Institutional Landowner

The Forestry Commission has 808 acres.

TOP 10 IN 1872

1	Rt Hon Mr William Adam MP of Blair Adam (Not in Bateman)	2896	acres	with 1408 elsewhere
2	Sir Graham Montgomery Bt MP of Stobo Castle, Stobo	2454	acres	with 18,180 elsewhere
3	Mr Harry Young of Cleish Castle (Not in Bateman)	1910	acres	
4	Mr James Haig of Blairhill, Dollar (Not in Bateman)	1690	acres	
5	Mr John Horn of Thomanean, Milnathort (Not in Bateman)	1431	acres	
6	Dowager Marchioness of Lansdowne of Bowood Park, Calne	1348	acres	with 9070 elsewhere
7	Captain Lawrence Oliphant of Condie, Bridge of Earn	1210	acres	with 2660 elsewhere
8	Mr David Syme of Warrock	1168	acres	
9	Vice Admiral the Marquess of Northamptonshire of Castle Ashby, Northants	864	acres	with 22,637 elsewhere
10	Mr James Walker of 10 Grosvenor Crescent, Edinburgh (Not in Bateman)	736	acres	

KIRKCUDBRIGHTSHIRE

	1872	2001
Total acreage	571,950 acres	574,024 acres
Agricultural acreage	514,755 acres	341,593 acres
Non agricultural acreage	57,195 acres	232,431 acres
Population	41,859	27,631
Owners of nothing at all	39,473	-
Total Dwellings	7457	-
Smallholdings: 1872 owners of less than one acre 2000 owners of 0–2ha (0–4.94 acres)	1908	70
Landowners over one acre (1872) Landowners over 2ha (2000)	478	1075
Landowners over 500 acres	111	176
Acreage (and percentage) of county owned by owners of over 500 acres	321,957 acres (56.%)	207,690 acres (36%)

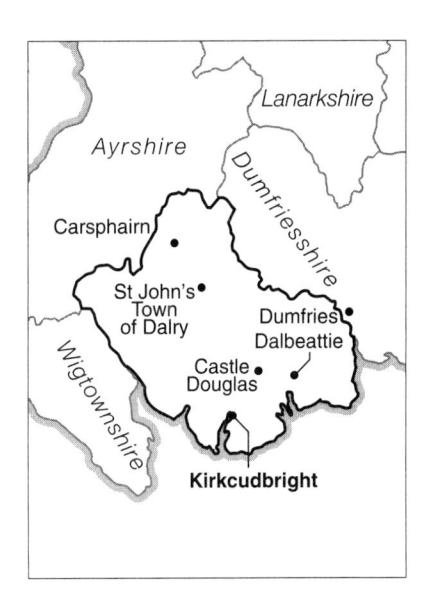

Top Landowners 2001

Although he managed to identify 54 owners or estates, the chronicler Andy Wightman could still only account for the acreage of 51% of the county. There was no sign of the owner who had intrigued his predecessor, John MacEwen. This was the Duke of Norfolk, who had been written off as a landowner in England by Masters in his book *The Dukes*. (See also Sussex, p.259.) MacEwen attributed 17,500 Scottish acres to the duke's estates. The county is notable for the number of female owners among the top 10 in 1872.

MR FRED OLSEN *11,568 acres*. Fred Olsen, born in 1929, is a Norwegian shipowner, and one of the world's seriously rich people. He retired in 2001 as Chairman of Harland & Wolf, the Belfast shipyard which built the Titanic. Olsen, who took over the company in the early 1990s, reduced its debt by half by selling property for a development he has named Titanic Park. He is also the owner of Timex, the biggest watch company in the world. The company was the focus of a bitter strike at its Scottish factory in the 1980s.

R.W. RAINSFORD-HANNAY *7500 acres*. The Rainsford Hannays first took up residence at Kirkdale in 1532. One of the family is recorded as having been killed at the Cruives of Cree in 1610, as he assisted the Earl of Galloway in battle against the Kennedy of Blairquahan The estate is in Bateman at 3978 acres in 1872 and was passed to Colonel Frederick Rainsford Hannay by deed of gift from his father at the turn of the last century.

MR HENRY KESWICK *5681 acres*. Henry Keswick is the older of the two Keswick brothers who continue an involvement in the affairs of the family company Jardine Matheson. Originally based in Hong Kong, the company has moved offshore to Bermuda. Henry, born in 1938, chaired the company in succession to his brother Simon. The *Sunday Times* valued them at £220 million in its 2000 Rich List. He was educated at Eton, Cambridge and did a stint in the Scots Guards before joining the company. The family have an estate in Gloucestershire.

Significant Institutional Landowners

The Forestry Commission owns 146,506 acres. SNH owns 3247 acres. The Ministry of Defence has 4716 acres.

TOP 10 IN 1872

1	Earl of Galloway MP of Galloway House, Garlieston	55,981 acres	with 23,203 elsewhere
2	Mr Horatio Granville Murray–Stewart of Cally, Gatehouse	45,867 acres	with 52,402 elsewhere
3	Mr William Forbes of Callendar House, Falkirk	40,445 acres	with 16,259 elsewhere
4	Mrs Jean Cathcart (Not in Bateman) of Berbeth House, Calmington	39,889 acres	
5	Mr Richard Alexander Oswald of Auchincruive, Ayr	24,556 acres	with 11,564 elsewhere
6	Earl of Selkirk of St Mary's Isle, Kirkcudbright	20,823 acres	
7	Hon Mrs Louisa Bellamy-Gordon of Kenmure Castle, New Galloway	14,093 acres	
8	Mrs Eliza Esther Murray-Dunlop of Corsock, Dalbeattie	12,774 acres	
9	Mr Alfred Peter Constable-Maxwell of Terregles, Dumfries	12,396 acres	
10	Mr John Maxwell Heron-Maxwell MP of Kirrouchtree, Newton Stewart	12,300 acres	

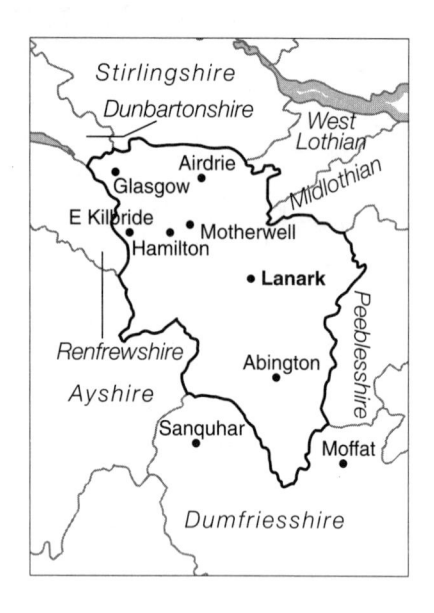

LANARKSHIRE

	1872	2001
Total acreage	557,919	574,473
Agricultural acreage	502,127	380,291
Non agricultural acreage	55,791	194,192
Population	785,339	626,790
Owners of nothing at all	765,231	-
Total Dwellings	47,962	-
Smallholdings: 1872 owners of less than one acre	17,908	
2000 owners of 0–2ha (0–4.94 acres)		220
Landowners over one acre (1872)	2200	
Landowners over 2ha (2000)		1850
Landowners over 500 acres	87	149
Acreage (and percentage) of county owned by owners of over 500 acres	289,431 acres (52%)	187,452 acres (33%)

Top Landowners 2001

THE 15TH EARL OF HOME *30,000 acres. No. 1 in 1872*. David Alexander Cospatrick Douglas-Home, born in 1943, is the son of the former Prime Minister, Alec Douglas Home, and has recovered and uses the titles his father eschewed for life in 1963. The present earl was educated at Eton and Oxford and is presently chairman of Coutts Bank and of the Commonwealth Institute. The family home is at the Hirsel, near Coldstream. The estate is half its 1872 size but remains with the family and is well managed.

THE 4TH MARQUESS OF LINLITHGOW *18,300 acres*. Adrian John Charles Hope was born in 1946 and educated at Eton. The family holdings in the county in 1872 were shown as those of the Earl of Hopetoun (no. 5 in 1872). Prior to the upgrading of the Earldom to the rank of Marquess in 1902, the then holder of the title was a Lord Chamberlain to Queen Victoria. The current Marquess's son, the Earl of Hopetoun, born in 1969, was a page of honour to the Queen Mother in the 1970s. The estate is at Leadhills and Glencaple.

A.M. MACDONALD LOCKHART *12,500 acres. No. 3 in 1872*. The title is extinct – see below, but a member of the family still holds the lands that Sir Simon held in 1872. MacEwen only identified six owners, including MacDonald Lockhart, who then had 20,000 acres, in this fairly large county in 1970. Andy Wightman upped that considerably to 37 estates and owners, but still only accounted for the ownership of 29.2% of the county. The MacDonald Lockhart estate is at Lee and Carnwath.

Significant Institutional Landowners

The Forestry Commission owns 6660 acres. The successors of Strathclyde Regional Council owns 12,000 acres.

TOP 10 IN 1872

1	Earl of Home of The Hirsel, Coldstream	61,943	acres	with 44,607 elsewhere
2	Duke of Hamilton and Brandon of Hamilton Palace, Glasgow	45,731	acres	with 111,655 elsewhere
3	Sir Simon Macdonald-Lockhart Bt of Lee Castle, Lanark	31,566	acres	with 708 elsewhere
4	Sir Thomas Edward Colebrooke Bt MP of Abington House	29,604	acres	with 419 elsewhere
5	Earl of Hopetoun of Hopetoun House, South Queensferry	19,180	acres	with 23,327 elsewhere
6	Sir Windham Charles James Anstruther Bt MP	11,184	acres	with 584 elsewhere
7	Lord Lamington MP	10,833	acres	with 1875 elsewhere
8	Mrs Louisa Catterson of Birkcleugh, Abington (Not in Bateman)	6870	acres	
9	Mr James Hope-Vere of Blackwood, Lanark	6440	acres	with 1849 elsewhere
10	Mr William Bertram of Kersewell, Carnwath (Not in Bateman)	5863	acres	

MIDLOTHIAN

(Known in 1872 as The County of Edinburgh)

	1872	2001
Total acreage	226,223 acres	234,389 acres
Agricultural acreage	203,600 acres	172,757 acres
Non agricultural acreage	22,600 acres	61,632 acres
Population	328,379	80,860
Owners of nothing at all	325,142	41,340
Total Dwellings	27,856	31,800
Smallholdings: 1872 owners of less than one acre	2541	
2000 owners of 0–2ha (0–4.94 acres)		84
Landowners over one acre (1872)	696	
Landowners over 2ha (2000)		602
Landowners over 500 acres	90	105
Acreage (and percentage) of county owned by owners of over 500 acres	204,690 acres (90%)	124,632 acres (53%)

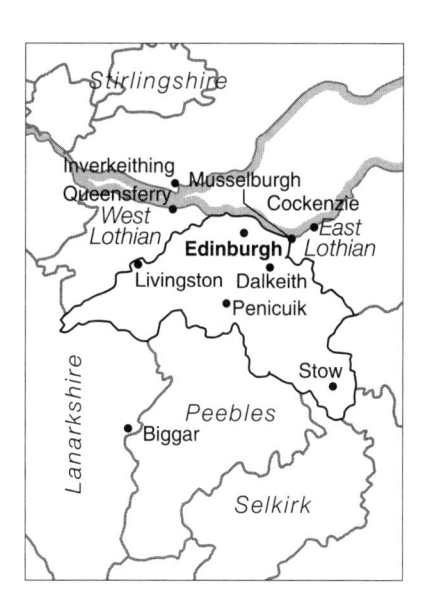

Top Landowners 2001

THE 7TH EARL OF ROSEBERY OF DALMENY *11,000 acres. No. 1 in 1872.* See Peeblesshire (p.293).

BORTHWICK FAMILY *10,400 acres. No. 8 in 1872.* These are the lands of the Borthwicks, lairds of Crookston and Heriotmuir. The present Lord Borthwick, the 25th, John Hugh Borthwick of that ilk, was born in 1940. The title goes back to 1450 and originated with Sir William Borthwick, a substitute hostage for James I in the early 1400s. The lands appear in both the Returns and Bateman as the property of John Borthwick. The title is not used in either, being in abeyance, and was only admitted by the Lord Lyon in 1986. The 24th laird, Malcolm Borthwick, died in 1996 and was succeeded by his twin brother John.

MRS BEKKER-DUNDAS OF ARNISTON *10,100 acres.* Mrs Bekker-Dundas holds the lands, almost to the acre, of Robert Dundas in 1872 (no. 4). There is, however, no entry in *Burke's Landed Gentry* for this branch of the Dundas family, despite the considerable value of the acreage.

Significant Institutional Landowners

The Crown Estate owns 3641 acres. The Forestry Commission owns 2663 acres. The Ministry of Defence owns 2176 acres. The successors to Lothian Regional Council and SOAFED own 1649 acres.

TOP 10 IN 1872

1	Earl of Rosebery of Dalmeny Park	15,568 acres	with 13,871 elsewhere
2	Sir George Douglas Clerk Bt of Penicuick House, Penicuik	12,696 acres	with 500 elsewhere
3	Earl of Morton of Dalmahoy, Ratho	10,411 acres	with 54,750 elsewhere
4	Mr Robert Dundas of Arniston House, Gorebridge	10,184 acres	with 329 elsewhere
5	Mr (Heirs of) Alexander Mitchell of Stow (Not in Bateman)	9038 acres	
6	Mr George Fairholme of Old Melrose	6200 acres	with 1300 elsewhere
7	Mr Charles Cowan of Logan House, Wester Lea	5677 acres	with 1252 elsewhere
8	Mr John Borthwick of Crookston House, Edinburgh	5239 acres	with 4484 elsewhere
9	Mr Henry Callander of Prestonhall	4869 acres	with 1014 elsewhere
10	Marquess of Lothian of Newbattle Abbey	4548 acres	with 27,813 elsewhere

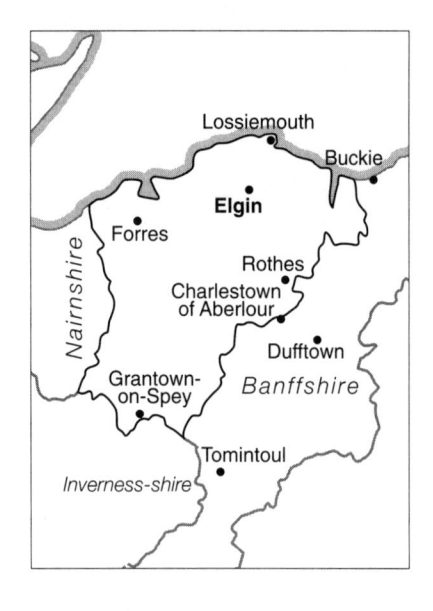

MORAY

(Known in 1872 as Elgin)

	1872	2001
Total acreage	303,168 acres	304,931 acres
Agricultural acreage	272,851 acres	190,252 acres
Non agricultural acreage	30,316 acres	114,679 acres
Population	43,612	85,870
Owners of nothing at all	41,048	39,330
Total Dwellings	8452	35,800
Smallholdings: 1872 owners of less than one acre	2313	
2000 owners of 0–2ha (0–4.94 acres)		68
Landowners over one acre (1872)	251	
Landowners over 2ha (2000)		533
Landowners over 500 acres	34	84
Acreage (and percentage) of county owned by owners of over 500 acres	243,105 acres (80%)	130,419 acres (42.7%)

Top Landowners 2001

LEON G. LITCHFIELD *20,000 acres.* Leon G. Litchfield is an industrialist, presently chairman of L.B. Plastics. His home base is Derbyshire. The Sunday Times' Rich List for 2001 estimated his wealth at £75 million. He owns the Tulchan estate which was originally part of the vast Seafield estate shown below. According to Andy Wightman, it was first sold to Ennessy Co, former owners of Mar Lodge Estate in Aberdeenshire and Amhuinnsuidhe Estate on Harris.

THE CAYZER FAMILY AND JOHN GUTHERIE *16,861 acres.* The Rothes Estate was sold by the Eagle Star insurance company in 1994 for £4,797,000. It went to a joint enterprise owned by the Cayzer family and a director of some of the Cayzer companies, John Gutherie, who owned land in Argyll (Conaglen). According to Andy Wightman the buyers, who acted through two companies, Broadland Properties Ltd and Edinmore Ltd, then sold off 2093 acres and obtained £1,690,289 for the detached plot. The Cayzer family were struck by tragedy in 2000 when the late Lord Cayzer's daughter, Nicola Colvin, was killed with her Tory MP husband Michael by a fire at their palatial family home near Romsey. (See also Suffolk p.257 for other details of the Cayzer family.)

THE 20TH EARL OF MORAY AND FAMILY TRUSTS *16,500 acres with 12,900 acres in Perthshire. No. 4 in 1872.* The 20th Earl of Moray, Douglas John Moray Stuart, was born in 1928 and is married to Lady Malvina Dorothea Murray, a daughter of the late 7th Earl of Mansfield, whose estates now vest in her brother, the 8th Earl of Mansfield (see Perth, p.294). The earl was educated in South Africa and at Cambridge University. His son and heir, Lord Doune, was born in 1966. The family have a seat in Perth, Doune Park, surrounded by 12,900 acres, where Lord Doune lives. His father and mother live at Darnaway Castle near Forres.

Significant Institutional Landowners

The Forestry Commission owns 29,567 acres. The Ministry of Defence has 3570 acres.

TOP 10 IN 1872

1	Earl of Seafield of Castle Grant, Grantown	96,721	acres	with 209,170 elsewhere
2	Earl of Fife (MP) of Duff House, Banff	40,959	acres	with 208,261 elsewhere
3	Sir William Gordon Gordon-Cummings Bt of Altyre, Forres	36,387	acres	with 2112 elsewhere
4	Earl of Moray of Doune Lodge, Perth	21,669	acres	with 59,960 elsewhere
5	Mr Henry Alexander Grant of Wester Elchies, Craigellachie	20,462	acres	with 4212 elsewhere
6	Duke of Richmond and Gordon (MP) of Goodwood, Sussex	12,271	acres	with 274,140 elsewhere
7	Mr Charles Lennox Cummings Bruce of Dunphail, Forres (Not in Bateman)	10,518	acres	
8	Sir George Macpherson Grant Bt of Ballindalloch Castle, Elgin	7848	acres	with 117,595 elsewhere
9	Mr Hugh Brodie of Brodie Castle, Forres	4728	acres	with 4407 elsewhere
10	Mr Robert McKissack of Ardgye, Alves	4165	acres	with 28 elsewhere

NAIRNSHIRE

	1872	2001
Total acreage	120,795 acres	104,252 acres
Agricultural acreage	108,715 acres	71,999 acres
Non agricultural acreage	12,079 acres	32,253 acres
Population	10,225	11,051
Owners of nothing at all	9688	-
Total Dwellings	2029	-
Smallholdings: 1872 owners of less than one acre 2000 owners of 0–2ha (0–4.94 acres)	467	8
Landowners over one acre (1872) Landowners over 2ha (2000)	70	169
Landowners over 500 acres	12	27
Acreage (and percentage) of county owned by owners of over 500 acres	101,122 acres (83.7%)	49,743 acres (47.7%)

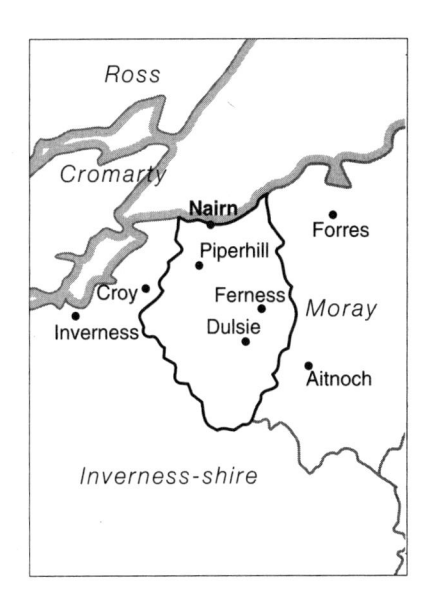

Top Landowners 2001

THE 7TH EARL OF CAWDOR *49,400 acres with 7000 acres elsewhere. No. 1 in 1872.* He is the 25th Thane of Cawdor, and is a direct descendant of the Thane mentioned in Shakespeare's *Macbeth*. Born Colin Robert Vaughan Campbell in 1962, he was educated at Eton and Oxford, and succeeded in 1993. An ancestor accepted the surrender of the last army to invade Britain when he met a French force at Fishguard in 1797. He attended the Lords just once in the year before reform ended his right to a seat. His father sold 36,000 acres in Wales in 1976 to pay death duties. His wife is a daughter of the Earl Harrington – see Limerick County in Ireland (p.341). The estate is at Cawdor.

E.J. BRODIE *12,800 acres.* The Brodie lands in Nairn have been in the family since 1634 when an ancestor bought them on 14 March that year from Sir John Grant of Freuchie. The present incumbent, Ewen John Brodie, was born in 1942 and is the 16th Laird of Lethen, of Culmony House, Dunphaile and of Dunearn Lodge, Nairn.

LORD BALGONIE *6500 acres. No. 4 in 1872.* He is the eldest son of the 14th Earl of Leven & Melville, and was born in 1954. The lands are not all that much changed since 1872 and he lives at the family seat, Glenferness House. His father has been Lord Lieutenant of Nairn since 1969. Father and son are old Etonians.

Significant Institutional Landowner

The Forestry Commission owns 3463 acres.

TOP 10 IN 1872

1	Earl of Cawdor (MP) of Stackpoole, Pembroke and Cawdor	46,176	acres	with 55,481 elsewhere
2	Mr James Campbell Brodie of Lethen House (Not in Bateman)	22,378	acres	
3	Mr Neil John MacGillivary of Dumnaglass of Glengarry, Canada (Not in Bateman)	12,600	acres	
4	Earl of Leven and Melville of Glenferness, Dunphail	7805	acres	with 1019 elsewhere
5	Mr Hugh Davidson of Cantray House, Croy, Inverness (Not in Bateman)	6363	acres	with 3228 elsewhere
6	Mr Hugh Brodie of Brodie Castle, Forres	4407	acres	with 4728 elsewhere
7	Major James Rose of Kilravock	4395	acres	
8	Rev Mr Hugh Rose of Holme Rose House, Croy, Inverness (Not in Bateman)	3672	acres	
9	Mr John Gordon of Cluny Castle, Aberdeen	3635	acres	
10	Sir William Armstrong Cummings Gordon Gordon Bt of Altyre, Forres	2112	acres	with 36,387 elsewhere

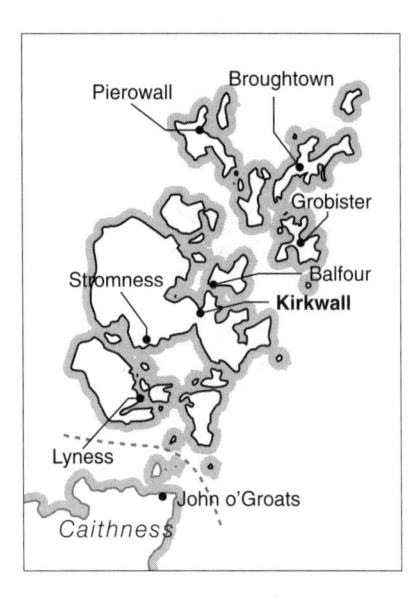

ORKNEY

	1872	2001
Total acreage	220,873 acres	240,848 acres
Agricultural acreage	198,785 acres	226,612 acres
Non agricultural acreage	22,087 acres	14,236 acres
Population	31,274	19,550
Owners of nothing at all	29,966	7330
Total Dwellings	6288	9400
Smallholdings: 1872 owners of less than one acre	546	
2000 owners of 0–2ha (0–4.94 acres)		236
Landowners over one acre (1872)	762	
Landowners over 2ha (2000)		1652
Landowners over 500 acres	41	68
Acreage (and percentage) of county owned by owners of over 500 acres	147,200 acres (67%)	91,785 acres (38.1%)

Top Landowners 2001

Orkney defeated both of the chroniclers and the great map maker Dr Millman, upon whose shoulders both have stood, as has this author. The island is strategically important because of the oil industry.

Both MacEwen and Wightman believed that the big estates had broken up but there is no evidence available to see what the situation is and how it has changed since 1872.

Significant Institutional Landowner

The Royal Society for the Protection of Birds owns 15,056 acres

TOP 10 IN 1872

1	Mr John Heddle of Melsetter House, Kirkwall	50,410 acres	
2	Mr David Balfour of Balfour Castle, Kirkwall	30,000 acres	
3	Earl of Zetland MP of Aske Hall, Richmond, Yorks	29,846 acres	with 38,864 elsewhere
4	Mr Robert Baikie of Tankerness, of Edinburgh (Not in Bateman)	7846 acres	
5	Mr Robert Hebden of Eday (Not in Bateman)	7500 acres	
6	General Traill Burroughs of Rousay	6693 acres	
7	Mr Alexander Sutherland Graeme of Graemshall (The Dome House, Brighton, Sussex) (Not in Bateman)	6444 acres	
8	Mr James Stewart of Fribo House, Westray (Not in Bateman)	6243 acres	
9	Mr Thomas Traill of Ratter, Thurso	5780 acres	
10	Mr George Traill of Holland, Kirkwall	5031 acres	

PEEBLESSHIRE

	1872	2001
Total acreage	232,410 acres	222,240 acres
Agricultural acreage	209,169 acres	174,173 acres
Non agricultural acreage	23,241 acres	48,067 acres
Population	12,330	13,676
Owners of nothing at all	11,622	-
Total Dwellings	2187	-
Smallholdings: 1872 owners of less than one acre 2000 owners of 0–2ha (0–4.94 acres)	532	17
Landowners over one acre (1872) Landowners over 2ha (2000)	176	302
Landowners over 500 acres	57	95
Acreage (and percentage) of county owned by owners of over 500 acres	177,263 acres (76%)	151,551 acres (68.%)

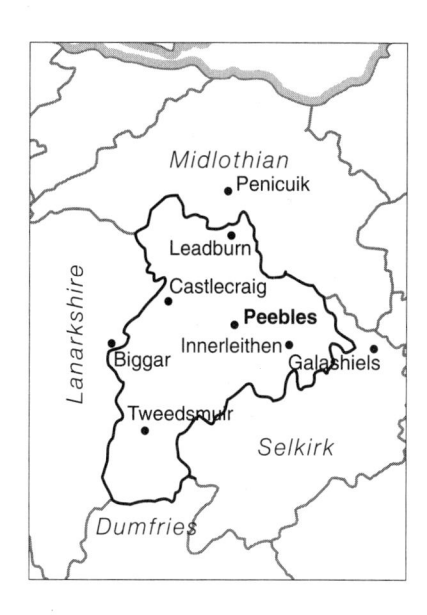

Top Landowners 2001

THE 7TH EARL OF ROSEBERY *9900 acres with 11,000 acres elsewhere.* Neil Archibald Primrose, born in 1929, is a successful entrepreneur, and the *Sunday Times* rates his land, art and lighting company at a collective value of £65 million. His entry in *Debrett's* indicates that he still has patronage of three parishes. He lives at Dalmeny House, Dalmeny and is the Deputy Lieutenant of Midlothian. His son and heir is Lord Dalmeny, born in 1967.

EARL OF WEMYSS & MARCH *9400 acres with 5500 acres in Fife, 22,800 acres elsewhere in Scotland and 5000 acres in the Cotswolds in England.* See Fife (p.283).

MARY COLTMAN *6700 acres.* This estate was owned by Lt. Colonel Sprot in MacEwen's 1970 lists.

Significant Institutional Landowners

The Forestry Commission owns 15,716. The successors to Lothian Regional Council own 5800 acres.

TOP 10 IN 1872

1	Earl of Wemyss and March of Amisfield, Haddington	41,247	acres	with 20,771 elsewhere
2	Sir Graham Montgomery MP of Stobo Castle, Stobo	18,172	acres	with 2462 elsewhere
3	Sir James Naesmyth Bt of Posso of Dalwick, Stobo	15,485	acres	
4	Mr John Miller of Leithin Lodge, Innerleithin	13,000	acres	with 2750 elsewhere
5	Mr James Tweedie of Quarter, of Rachan, Biggar	13,151	acres	
6	Earl of Traquair of Edinburgh (Not in Bateman)	10,778	acres	with 11,443 elsewhere
7	Sir Robert Hay Bt of Kings Meadows, Haystoune	9155	acres	with 600 elsewhere
8	Rev Sir William Gibson-Carmichael Bt of Castle Craig, Dolphington	8756	acres	with 732 elsewhere
9	Mr George Bell of Crurie, of Castle'er, Langholm	6600	acres	
10	Miss White of Netherurd House, Dolphington	6376	acres	

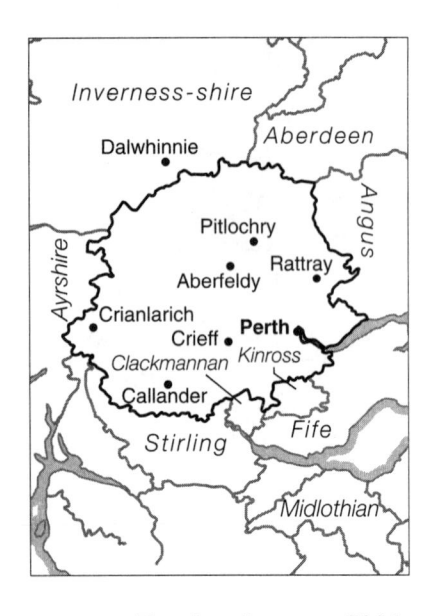

PERTHSHIRE

	1872	2001
Total acreage	1,612,840 acres	1,595,804 acres
Agricultural acreage	1,451,556 acres	329,802 acres
Non agricultural acreage	161,284 acres	1,266,002 acres
Population	147,768	133,040
Owners of nothing at all	140,125	51,400
Total Dwellings	22,134	62,800
Smallholdings: 1872 owners of less than one acre	6539	
2000 owners of 0–2ha (0–4.94 acres)		246
Landowners over one acre (1872)	1104	
Landowners over 2ha (2000)		2128
Landowners over 500 acres	120	393
Acreage (and percentage) of county owned by owners of over 500 acres	1,166,890 acres (72%)	1,044,363 acres (65%)

Top Landowners 2001

TRUSTS OF THE 10TH DUKE OF ATHOLL (SARAH TROUGHTON AND BLAIR TRUST) *148,000 acres with 16,400 acres in Argyll. No. 2 in 1872.* The 10th Duke of Atholl, the six foot seven inch-tall 'Wee Ian', didn't much like the look of his successor, the 11th Duke to be, a cousin from South Africa, and placed the huge estate in trust. Sarah Troughton, described (a little unclearly) in *Debrett's* as the 10th Duke's half sister, along with her son, are the senior trustees of this huge landholding. The 11th Duke, John Murray, born in 1929, succeeded in 1996, but did not make a single appearance in the Lords in the year before the 1999 reforms deprived him even of that small consolation for the loss of his ancestral acres.

BARONESS WILLOUGHBY DE ERESBY *63,200 acres with 15,000 acres elsewhere. No. 4 in 1872.* See Lincolnshire (p.246).

BEVERLEY JANE MALIM *36,500 acres.* This is the former estate of Sir Edward Wills Bt, an heir to the Player Wills tobacco fortune. He and his family owned 263,000 acres of Scotland in 1970, making them the second largest landowners in the country after the Duke of Buccleuch. In the 25 years between MacEwen and Wightman almost the entire landholding was sold off.

THE 8TH EARL OF MANSFIELD AND MANSFIELD *33,800 acres. No. 10 in 1872.* This Scottish aristocrat, educated at Eton, has had a distinguished career, including a spell as First Crown Commissioner at the Crown Estate from 1985-1995. The revenues from the Crown Estate improved a good deal under his regime and there was talk of privatisation, which he denied. The estate is held in trust with his son and heir Viscount Stormont, born in 1956. The peer himself, William David Mungo James Murray, was born in 1930 and served during the Malaysian emergency as a lieutenant in the Scots Guards. The estate is very little changed from 1872.

Perthshire is a very large county, and has attracted a wide range of new owners following first the breakup of the Breadalbane estate in the early 1900s and then the sale of the Menzies estate. Many aristocrats from the south, and from abroad, including the Al Tajir family from Dubai, have taken up residence here. Others who have bought estates in the county include Viscount Wimborne, Lord Pearson of Rannoch, Earl Cadogan, Viscount Chelsea and the Earl of Shelbourne.

Significant Institutional Landowners

The Forestry Commission owns 150,726 acres. The successors of Strathclyde Regional Council own 21,000 acres.

TOP 10 IN 1872

1	Earl of Breadalbane of Taymouth Castle, Aberfealdy	234,166 acres	with 204,192 elsewhere
2	Duke Atholl of the Castle, Blair Atholl	201,640 acres	
3	Sir Robert Menzies Bt of Menzies, Aberfeldy (Does not appear in the Original Return)	98,284 acres	
4	Baroness Willoughby de Eresby of Grimsthorpe Castle, Lincs	76,837 acres	with 55,383 elsewhere
5	Earl of Moray of Doune Lodge, Perth	40,553 acres	with 41,076 elsewhere
6	Mr Charles Stirling Home-Drummond-Moray of Blair Drummond, Stirling	38,797 acres	with 1871 elsewhere
7	Sir Archibald Stewart Bt of Grandtully of Murtly Castle, Murtly (Land held since 1417)	33,274 acres	
8	Mr William George Steuart-Menzies of Meggernie Castle, Glenlyon	33,000 acres	
9	Duke of Montrose of Buchanan Castle, Glasgow	32,294 acres	with 71,153 elsewhere
10	Earl of Mansfield MP of Scone Castle, Perth	31,197 acres	with 17,877 elsewhere

RENFREWSHIRE

	1872	2001
Total acreage	155,321 acres	143,829 acres
Agricultural acreage	139,788 acres	96,089 acres
Non agricultural acreage	15,532 acres	47,740 acres
Population	256,947	265,810
Owners of nothing at all	251,209	93,170
Total Dwellings	13,551	132,800
Smallholdings: 1872 owners of less than one acre 2000 owners of 0–2ha (0–4.94 acres)	4842	40
Landowners over one acre (1872) Landowners over 2ha (2000)	896	552
Landowners over 500 acres	11	33
Acreage (and percentage) of county owned by owners of over 500 acres	46,003 acres (33%)	39,919 acres (28%)

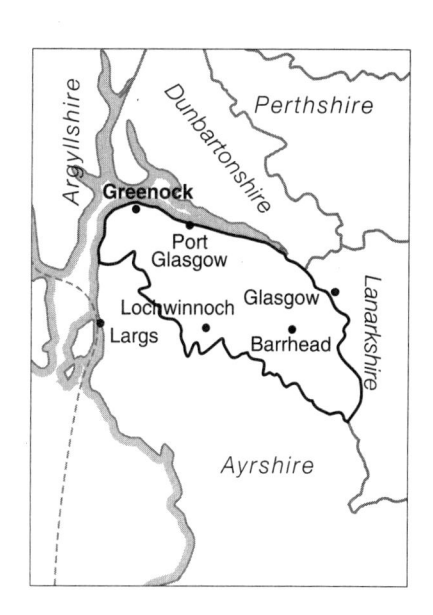

Top Landowners 2001

H. SHAW STEWART *9200 acres*. These lands belonged to the family of Shaw Stewart since the time of King Robert III (1390–1406), from whom they claim direct descent. The present baronet, Major Sir Houston Mark Shaw Stewart MC, born in 1931, is not shown as the owner but the lands may have passed to him before his brother Sir Guy died in 1980. The family seat is given as Ardgowan, Inverkip, in *Debrett's*.

MARK A. CRICHTON-MAITLAND *5000 acres*. No details are available on this estate or family.

Significant Institutional Landowners

The Forestry Commission owns 2131 acres. The successors to Strathclyde Regional Council own 19,000 acres.

TOP 10 IN 1872

1	Sir William Shaw-Stewart Bt MP of Blackhall, of Ardgown, Greenock	26,376	acres	with 92 elsewhere
2	Mr Allan Gilmour of Eaglesham House, Glasgow	16,931	acres	
3	Mr Alexander Archibald Speirs of Elderslie, Paisley	11,287	acres	with 206 elsewhere
4	Mr Henry Lee-Harvey of Castle Semple, Lochwinnoch	6500	acres	
5	Sir William Stirling Maxwell Bt of Keir, Dunblane	4773	acres	with 16,041 elsewhere
6	Earl of Glasgow MP of Crauford Priory, Fife	4579	acres	with 33,246 elsewhere
7	Lord Blantyre of Erskine	4449	acres	with 9612 elsewhere
8	Mr Thomas Greig of Glecarse	3798	acres	with 662 elsewhere
9	Mr John Broom Pollock of Glasgow	3761	acres	with 35,375 elsewhere
10	Colonel William Mure of Caldwell, Beith	3624	acres	

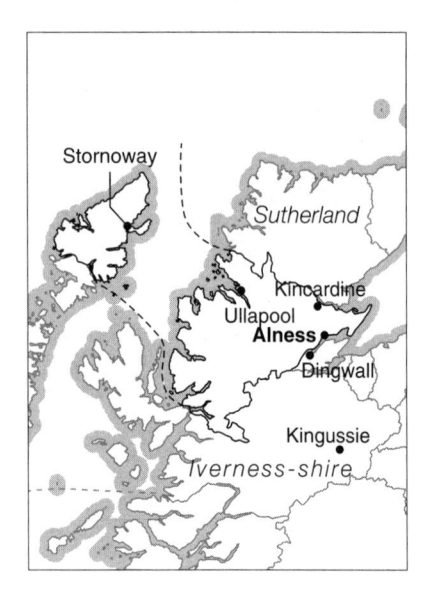

ROSS-SHIRE
(Now merged with Cromarty to form Ross & Cromarty)

	1872	1872 figure for Ross and Cromarty combined	2001
Total acreage	1,971,309 acres	1,989,515 acres	1,977,254 acres
Agricultural acreage	1,774,178 acres	1,790,563 acres	1,345,019 acres
Non agricultural acreage	197,130 acres	198,950 acres	632,235 acres
Population	77,593	80,955	58,287
Owners of nothing at all	75,550	78,667	-
Total Dwellings	15,028	15,713	-
Smallholdings: 1872 owners of less than one acre 2000 owners of 0–2ha (0–4.94 acres)	1719	1936	2702
Landowners over one acre (1872) Landowners over 2ha (2000)	324	338	3802
Landowners over 500 acres	91	96	214
Acreage (and percentage) of county owned by owners of over 500 acres	1,601,109 acres (81.2%)	1,618,612 acres (81.4%)	1,212,771 acres (61.3%)

Top Landowners 2001

PAUL FENTENER VAN VLISSINGEN *81,000 acres.* He is a Dutch businessman and the 99th richest person in Europe (*Eurobusiness* Richest 400 Europeans, 2000), with a fortune estimated at just under £1.3 billion. He is retired but his brother, now worth over £2 billion, still runs a huge travel company World Travel Partners. According to the magazine *Eurobusiness*, Paul van Vlissingen supports the Countryside Alliance and is into philosophy. He bought Letterewe from the late Colonel Whitbread, one of the Whitbread brewing family (see Herts, p.241)

SHEIK MOHAMMED BIN RASHID AL MAKTOUM *63,100 acres.* He is one of three brothers who rule the oil rich sheikdom of Dubai and who are now the breeders of the world's top racehorses. The estate was constructed from others bought in over the years, including Killian from Miss E.J.M. Douglas, West Benula, and Glomach. Local sensitivities were not assisted when the Maktoums' factor pointed out in a Scottish TV programme that it was people who disturbed the environment and the best way to preserve the environment was to keep them out.

CAPTAIN FRED WILLS *62,000 acres.* He is the last representative of the family who as recently as 1970 owned 263,000 acres of Scotland and were its second biggest landowners after the Duke of Buccleuch. He is a descendant of the family behind the immensely rich Player Wills tobacco company, once based in Bristol.

Significant Institutional Landowners

The Forestry Commission owns 98,825 acres. Scottish Natural Heritage owns 16,076 acres.

TOP 10 IN 1872

1	Lady James Matheson of Lews Castle, Stornoway	406,070 acres	with 18,490 elsewhere
2	Sir Charles William Augustus Ross Bt of Ballnagown Castle, Tain	300,000 acres	with 56,500 elsewhere
3	Sir Alexander Matheson of Ardross, Alness	220,433 acres	with 230 elsewhere
4	Sir Kenneth Smith Mackenzie Bt of Gairloch, Dingwall	164,680 acres	
5	Duchess of Sutherland of Dunrobin Castle, Golspie	149,999 acres	
6	Mr Arthur Balfour MP of Whittinghame, Preston-Kirk	71,778 acres	with 15,418 elsewhere
7	Mr William Meyrick Bankes of Winstanley Hall, Wigan	69,800 acres	with 4065 elsewhere
8	Mr Hugh Mackenzie of Dundonnell, Ullapool	64,335 acres	
9	Lord Middleton of Wollaton Hall, Nottingham	63,000 acres	with 36,576 elsewhere
10	Mr John Fowler of Braemore, Loch Broom	39,530 acres	with 7718 elsewhere

ROXBURGHSHIRE

	1872	2001
Total acreage	423,463 acres	425,564 acres
Agricultural acreage	381,116 acres	325,403 acres
Non agricultural acreage	42,346 acres	100,161 acres
Population	53,974	58,287
Owners of nothing at all	51,519	-
Total Dwellings	7829	-
Smallholdings: 1872 owners of less than one acre 2000 owners of 0–2ha (0–4.94 acres)	1880	71
Landowners over one acre (1872) Landowners over 2ha (2000)	575	822
Landowners over 500 acres	88	220
Acreage (and percentage) of county owned by owners of over 500 acres	324,069 acres (76%)	250,171 acres (59%)

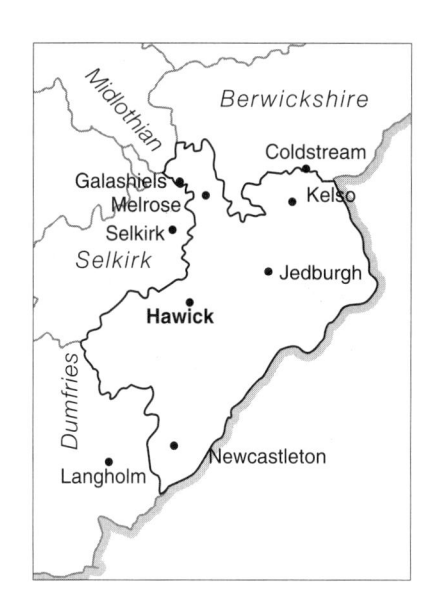

Top Landowners 2001

THE 10TH DUKE OF ROXBURGHE *55,500 acres with 10,100 acres in Berwickshire. No. 2 in 1872.* See Berwickshire (p.275).

THE 9TH DUKE OF BUCCLEUCH *49,200 acres with 167,200 acres in Dumfries, 37,500 acres in Selkirk and 17,000 acres in England. No. 1 in 1872.* See Dumfriesshire (p.280).

THE 12TH MARQUESS OF LOTHIAN *18,000 acres. No. 4 in 1872.* Peter Francis Walter Kerr, the 12th Marquess, was born in 1922, went to Ampleforth, Oxford and was a lieutenant in the Scots Guards. He followed up that rigidly regimented aristocratic background with a spell as a Conservative minister and whip in the 1960s and 1970s. He was also Lord Warden of the Stannaries and keeper of the Privy Seal to the biggest landowner in England, the Duke of Cornwall. His son and heir, the Earl of Ancram, better known as Michael Ancram, is a Conservative MP, front bench spokesman and is married to a daughter of the Duke of Norfolk (See Sussex, p.259). The family estate is near Newbattle Abbey at Dalkeith.

Significant Institutional Landowner

The Forestry Commission owns 33,297 acres.

TOP 10 IN 1872

1	Duke of Buccleuch and Queensbury of Dalkeith Palace, Edinburgh	104,461 acres	with 355,467 elsewhere
2	Duke of Roxburghe (MP) of Floors Castle	50,459 acres	with 9959 elsewhere
3	Countess of Home of The Hirsel, Coldstream, Lanark	25,380 acres	
4	Marquess of Lothian of Newbattle Abbey, Dalkeith	19,740 acres	with 12,621 elsewhere
5	Sir William Francis Augustus Eliott Bt of Stobs Castle, Hawick	19,345 acres	
6	Miss Malcolm-Douglas of Cavers, Hawick	9840 acres	
7	Earl of Minto (MP) of Minto House, Hawick	8663 acres	with 7408 elsewhere
8	Mr William Oliver-Rutherfurd of Edgerston, Jedburgh	7723 acres	with 756 elsewhere
9	Mr James Jardine of Dryfeholme (with Dumfries)	5684 acres	
10	Sir George Henry Scott-Douglas Bt MP of Springwood Park, Kelso	5568 acres	

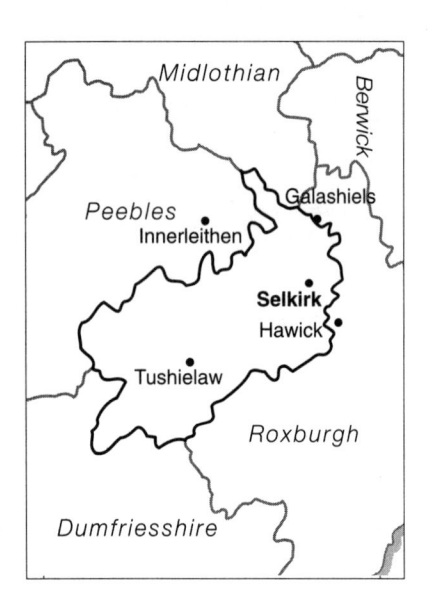

SELKIRKSHIRE

	1872	2001
Total acreage	161,815 acres	171,209 acres
Agricultural acreage	145,633 acres	128,094 acres
Non agricultural acreage	16,185 acres	43,115 acres
Population	14,005	20,868
Owners of nothing at all	13,299	-
Total Dwellings	1741	-
Smallholdings: 1872 owners of less than one acre 2000 owners of 0–2ha (0–4.94 acres)	538	21
Landowners over one acre (1872) Landowners over 2ha (2000)	168	187
Landowners over 500 acres	27	81
Acreage (and percentage) of county owned by owners of over 500 acres	130,345 acres (80%)	118,612 acres (69%)

Top Landowners 2001

THE 9TH DUKE OF BUCCLEUCH *37,500 acres*. No. 1 in 1872. See Dumfries (p.280).

THE 12TH EARL OF WEYMSS & MARCH TRUSTS *21,000 acres*. See Fife (p. 283).

SIR MICHAEL STRANG STEEL BT *6200 acres*. He is a prominent figure in Scottish public life, having been a Forestry Commissioner and Deputy Lieutenant of the Borders Region since 1990. Eton educated, he was a major in the 17th/21st Lancers, a cavalry regiment. The family seat is at Philipshaugh, where the family have been established since at least 1743. The estate is missed in the 1872 Return.

Significant Institutional Landowner

The Forestry Commission owns 7991 acres.

TOP 10 IN 1872

1	Duke of Buccleuch and Queensbury of Dalkeith Palace, Edinburgh	60,428 acres	with 399,680 elsewhere
2	Earl of Traquair (Not in Bateman) See Peebles	9765 acres	
3	Mr James Johnstone MP of Alva, Stirling	8614 acres	with 6927 elsewhere
4	Lord Napier and Ettrick of Selkirk, Midlothian	6991 acres	
5	Mr George Pott of Potburn, of Linthaughlee, Jedburgh (Not in Bateman)	5660 acres	
6	Mr James Pringle of Torwoodleigh of Galasheils	5401 acres	with 2500 elsewhere
7	Mrs Ann Pringle Pattison of The Haining, Selkirk	4800 acres	with 2527 elsewhere
8	Mr Hugh Scott of Gala House, Galasheils	3600 acres	with 190 elsewhere
9	Sir John Murray Bt of Philipshaugh, Selkirk	2799 acres	
10	Mrs Corse-Scott of Sinton House, Hawick (Incl Roxburgh)	2531 acres	

SHETLAND
(Known as Zetland in 1872)

	1872	2001
Total acreage	305,383 acres	352,337 acres
Agricultural acreage	274,844 acres	193,316 acres
Non agricultural acreage	30,538 acres	159,021 acres
Population	31,608	22,375
Owners of nothing at all	31,059	9375
Total Dwellings	5667	10,000
Smallholdings: 1872 owners of less than one acre 2000 owners of 0–2ha (0–4.94 acres)	240	159
Landowners over one acre (1872) Landowners over 2ha (2000)	309	1917
Landowners over 500 acres	22	86
Acreage (and percentage) of county owned by owners of over 500 acres	230,130 acres (75%)	71,903 acres (20%)

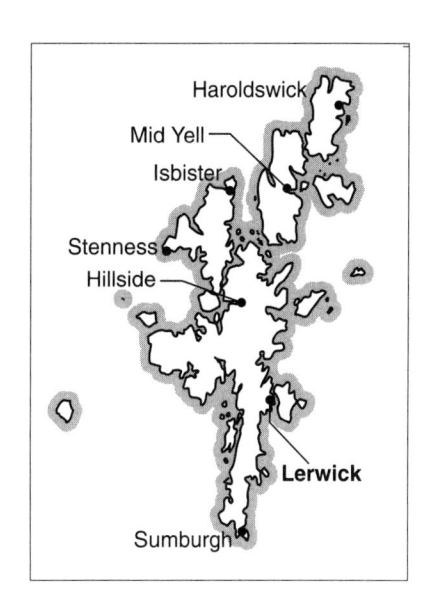

Top Landowners 2001

Shetland is unique in the 1872 survey. The ratable values were so low that Bateman, as can be seen below, picked up only one landowner, the Earl of Zetland in Yorkshire, and that only because the earl had other lands. The ratable value of his Zetland acres, £858 (£60,000 in 2001 money) would not have qualified him for Bateman's lists.

Shetland was unmapped by Dr John Millman, upon whose maps John MacEwen relied. As a result there is no 1970 list for Shetland. Andy Wightman manged to establish the ownership of 39.4% of the county, establsihing amongst other things that the Marquess of Zetland's holding was now down to 1000 acres. The Royal Society for the Protection of Birds and the National Trust have two small holdings. One interesting aspect of the 1872 list is the number of smallholdings, 90 acres or less, which have owners living in places like Australia, India and the USA. Shetland started losing its population a long time ago.

JOHN AND WENDY SCOTT *14,000 acres*. No information is available on this estate.

MRS O. BORLAND *10,000 acres*. This is the residue of the estate of Lady Nicholson, who lived in Cheltenham at the time of the 1872 survey.

HENRY ANDERTON *10,000 acres*. No information is available on this estate.

Significant Institutional Landowners

The Shetland Island Council owns 65,400 acres. The Royal Society for the Protection of Birds owns 4885 acres. The National Trust owns 1933 acres.

TOP 10 IN 1872

1	Mr Thomas Gifford of Busta (Busta Trustees) (Not in Bateman)	30,960 acres	
2	Mr William Bruce of Symbester, Lerwick (Not in Bateman)	25,180 acres	
3	Lady Nicolson of Shelbourne House, Cheltenham, Glos (Not in Bateman)	24,785 acres	
4	Major Thomas Mouat Cameron of Annsbrae, Lerwick (Not in Bateman)	24,363 acres	
5	Mr Andrew Grierson of Quendale House, Lerwick (Not in Bateman)	22,006 acres	
6	Mrs Babara Robertson of Lerwick (Not in Bateman)	13,700 acres	
7	Earl of Zetland (MP) of Aske Hall, Richmond, Yorks	13,600 acres	with 54,570 elsewhere
8	Mr Robert Scott of Melby, of Melby House, Walls (Not in Bateman)	13,020 acres	
9	Mr John Bruce of Sand Lodge, Sandwick (Not in Bateman)	12,338 acres	
10	Mr Joseph Leask of Sand, of Sound, Lerwick (Not in Bateman)	11,847 acres	

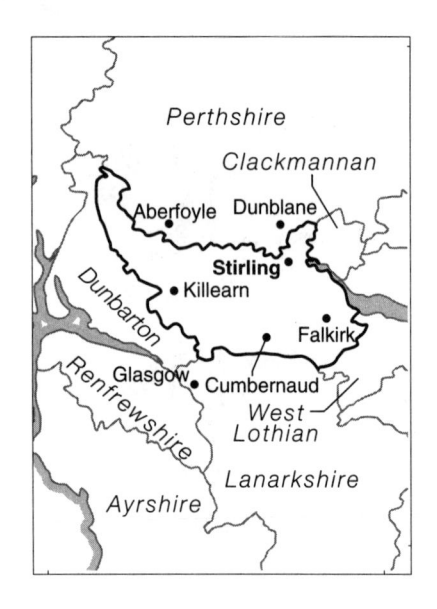

STIRLINGSHIRE

	1872	2001
Total acreage	284,751 acres	288,345 acres
Agricultural acreage	256,275 acres	221,895 acres
Non agricultural acreage	28,475 acres	66,450 acres
Population	98,218	83,130
Owners of nothing at all	93,961	33,340
Total Dwellings	13,275	38,300
Smallholdings: 1872 owners of less than one acre	3409	
2000 owners of 0–2ha (0–4.94 acres)		94
Landowners over one acre (1872)	848	
Landowners over 2ha (2000)		923
Landowners over 500 acres	41	86
Acreage (and percentage) of county owned by owners of over 500 acres	173,271 acres (61%)	130,827 acres (45%)

Top Landowners 2001

THE 8TH DUKE OF MONTROSE *8800 acres. No. 1 in 1872.* James Graham, born in 1935 and educated, unlike most of the Scottish aristocracy, at a Scottish school, Loretto, is the Hereditary Sheriff of Dumbarton. An active farmer, he sat on the Council of the Scottish National Farmers Union between 1981 and 1986. The dukedom is post union, 1707, but the peerage goes back to 1445, and the earldom, still potentially carried by the Duke's heir's son, was created in 1505. The 5th Earl, the famous military leader, was hanged after losing to the Parliamentarians at Strachan in 1650. The family seat is at Auchmar, Drymen near Glasgow.

CAPTAIN W.F.E. FORBES *7000 acres.* The Forbes are landed gentry, having bought the Callander estate in 1783. Captain William Frederick Eustace Forbes, born in 1932 and educated, like his father at Eton, is now the owner. His father was a lieutenant colonel in the Coldstream Guards and his mother was a cousin of the De Vecis, landowners in Ireland (see County Laois p.339).

SIR ARCHIBALD B.C. EDMONSTONE BT *5600 acres. No. 3 in 1872.* The 7th Baronet, Sir Archibald Bruce Charles Edmonstone, was born in 1934 and educated at Stowe, in England. The family descent is the most ancient claimed in the baronetage, going back to 'Edmondus, of the race of Seton, which resided in Scotland, fado, fado' (long, long ago, in Gaelic). Mary, a daughter of King Robert III, married an ancestor in 1445 and the Duntreath lands came into the family. They have land there still.

Significant Institutional Landowners

The Forestry Commission owns 23,707 acres. The successors to Strathclyde Regional Council own 7700 acres.

TOP 10 IN 1872

1	Duke of Montrose of Buchanan Castle, Glasgow	68,565 acres	with 34,882 elsewhere
2	Mr William Forbes of Callendar House, Falkirk	13,041 acres	with 43,663 elsewhere
3	Vice Admiral Sir William Edmonstone Bt MP of Colzium, Kilsyth	9778 acres	
4	Hon Mr Charles Spencer Hanbury-Kincaid-Lennox MP of Lennox Castle, Lennoxtown	7606 acres	with 80 elsewhere
5	Sir George Home-Speirs Bt of Culcreuch, Fintry	7270 acres	
6	Mr William Graham-Bontine of Ardoch, Cardross	6931 acres	with 3949 elsewhere
7	Lt.Colonel John Murray of Polmaise Castle, Stirling	6813 acres	
8	Mr Archibald Orr-Ewing MP of Ballykinrain, Killearn	5840 acres	with 201 elsewhere
9	Captain Henry Fletcher-Campbell RN of Bolquhan House, Stirling	5679 acres	
10	Sir James Ramsay-Gibson-Maitland Bt of Clifton Hall, Edinburgh	5678 acres	with 4550 elsewhere

SUTHERLAND

	1872	2001
Total acreage	1,299,253 acres	1,297,803 acres
Agricultural acreage	1,169,327 acres	779,042 acres
Non agricultural acreage	129,925 acres	518,761 acres
Population	24,317	13,055
Owners of nothing at all	23,884	-
Total Dwellings	4914	-
Smallholdings: 1872 owners of less than one acre 2000 owners of 0–2ha (0–4.94 acres)	348	451
Landowners over one acre (1872) Landowners over 2ha (2000)	85	1232
Landowners over 500 acres	12	96
Acreage (and percentage) of county owned by owners of over 500 acres	999,103 acres (77%)	729,216 acres (56%)

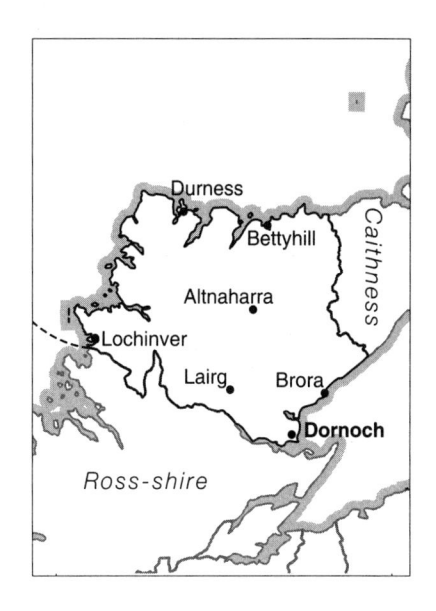

Top Landowners 2001

THE 6TH DUKE OF WESTMINSTER *95,100 acres, with 34,000 acres in England and about 380,000 elsewhere in the world.* See Cheshire (p.230) and London chapter (p.148) for fuller details.

THE COUNTESS OF SUTHERLAND *83,239 acres.* Born in 1921, she held one of the oldest titles in the House of Lords, second only to her neighbour in the precedence list, Margaret of Mar, a title created in 1114. The Sutherland earldom was accepted as being created in 1235, although the family claim descent from William of Moray, who ruled Moray in the twelfth century. The family history defies fiction. From it came kings and queens, idiots, 'The Wolf of Badenoch', a string of poisonings that would make a Borgia envious, wars, rebellions and endless intrigue. The title is separate from the dukedom, and had a separate seat in the Lords. In 1785 the 20th Countess married the 1st Duke of Sutherland and the title of Countess only separated from the Dukedom with the death of the 5th Duke in 1963, when Elizabeth Millicent Sutherland succeeded to her title and her seat in the Lords. She married, in 1946, Noel Janson, an officer in the Welsh Guards. Neither she nor her cousin the Duke attended the House of Lords in the year before they lost their seats. The estate is at Golspie. In 1872 her direct ancestor owned the largest estate by several magnitudes, in the whole of the four countries of the United Kingdom. What that meant for the rest of the population of the county can be seen in the above table.

MR EDMUND VESTY *70,500 acres.* Edmund is a brother of Baron Vesty (see Gloucestershire, p.238).

Significant Institutional Landowners

The Forestry Commission owns 57,004 acres. SOAFED owns 58,269 acres.

TOP 10 IN 1872

1	Duke of Sutherland MP of Dunrobin Castle, Golspie	1,176,343	acres	with 182,091 elsewhere
2	Sir Charles Ross Bt of Balnagown Castle, Parkhill	55,000	acres	with 301,500 elsewhere
3	Mr Evan Sutherland-Walker of Skibo, of Skibo Castle, Dornoch	20,000	acres	with 7072 elsewhere
4	Lady James Matheson of Achany, Lairg	18,490	acres	with 406,070 elsewhere
5	Mr Gordon MacLeod of Glencassley, Rosehall, Ardgay (Not in Bateman)	11,000	acres	
6	Mr Dougald Gilchrist of Ospisdale House, Dornoch (Not in Bateman)	3600	acres	
7	Mr Sidney Hadwen of Balblair, of West Garty, Helmsdale (Not in Bateman)	2991	acres	
8	Mr Robert Tennant of Rosehall, of Scarcroft Lodge, Leeds	2080	acres	
9	Mr Charles Stewart	2000	acres	
10	Rev Mr David Williamson of The Manse of Assynt, Lairg	1800	acres	

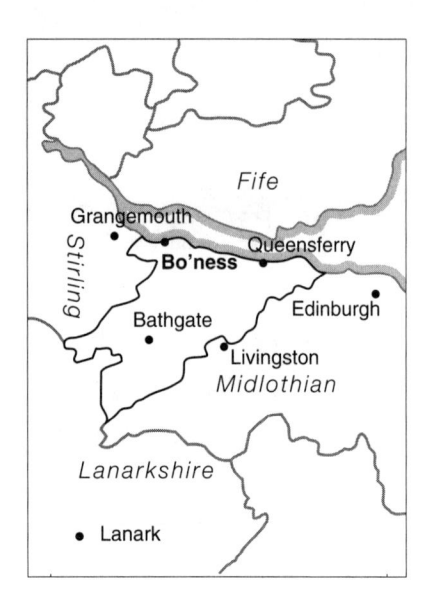

WEST LOTHIAN
(Known in 1872 as Linlithgow)

	1872	2001
Total acreage	75,785 acres	76,855 acres
Agricultural acreage	68,206 acres	48,987 acres
Non agricultural acreage	7578 acres	27,826 acres
Population	40,695	153,090
Owners of nothing at all	39,160	111,900*
Total Dwellings	6255	63,400
Smallholdings: 1872 owners of less than one acre 2000 owners of 0–2ha (0–4.94 acres)	1248	31
Landowners over one acre (1872) Landowners over 2ha (2000)	287	355
Landowners over 500 acres	12	20
Acreage (and percentage) of county owned by owners of over 500 acres	34,211 acres (45%)	14929 acres (19%)

*Figs for population and households are from official Statistics, but the figure for persons per household is unusually high and this figure may not be reliable.

Top Landowners 2001

THE 4TH MARQUESS OF LINLITHGOW *3000 acres*. Adrian John Charles Hope, the 4th Marquess, is the descendant and successor to the largest estate owner in this tiny county in 1872. This was the Earl of Hopetoun and the present Marquess gives the address below as his seat. Born in 1946 and educated at Eton he has been married three times. His son and heir is the Earl of Hopetoun, born in 1969 and educated like his father at Eton. The Earl was a page of honour to the Queen mother from 1984 to 1986.

THE EARL OF ROSEBERY *1500 acres with 9900 acres in Peeblesshire*. See Peeblesshire (p.293).

The only other significant landholding that Andy Wightman was able to identify was that of a farmer, Roy McNee at Woodend Farm with 2300 acres.

Significant Institutional Landowners

The Forestry Commission owns 808 acres and the successors to Lothian Regional Council own 488 acres.

TOP 10 IN 1872

1	Earl Hopetoun of Hopetoun House, South Queensferry	11,870 acres	with 30,637 elsewhere
2	Earl of Rosebery of Dalmeny park, Queensferry	5680 acres	with 26,731 elsewhere
3	Sir William Baillie Bt of Polkemmet	4320 acres	
4	Duke of Hamilton of Hamilton Palace, Glasgow	3694 acres	with 153,692 elsewhere
5	Lord Cardross of Amondell, Broxburn	2995 acres	with 76 elsewhere
6	Mr R.J.A. Hay of Nunraw (Not in Returns)	2593 acres	
7	Colonel Hare of Calder (111 acres in Returns)	2484 acres	
8	Mr William Cowan of Boghall	2231 acres	
9	Mr James Dundas of Arniston, Gorebridge	2094 acres	
10	Earl of Selkirk of St Mary's Isle, Kirkcudbright	1441 acres	with 20,823 elsewhere

WIGTOWNSHIRE

	1872	2001
Total acreage	309,087 acres	311,984 acres
Agricultural acreage	278,178 acres	247,006 acres
Non agricultural acreage	30,908 acres	64,978 acres
Population	38,830	27,341
Owners of nothing at all	37,010	-
Total Dwellings	6739	-
Smallholdings: 1872 owners of less than one acre 2000 owners of 0–2ha (0–4.94 acres)	1674	65
Landowners over one acre (1872) Landowners over 2ha (2000)	146	784
Landowners over 500 acres	32	128
Acreage (and percentage) of county owned by owners of over 500 acres	210,080 acres (68%)	127,083 acres (41%)

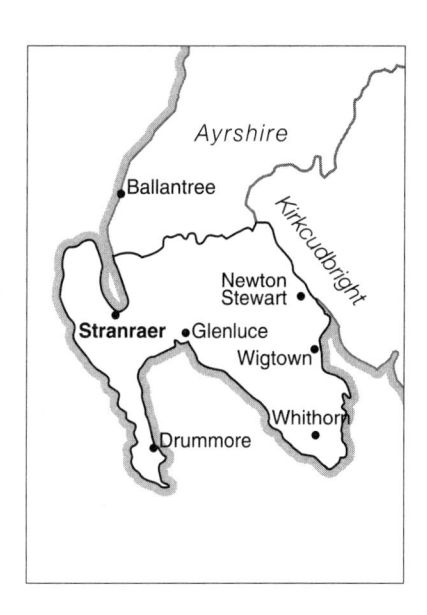

Top Landowners 2001

THE 14TH EARL OF STAIR *43,674 acres. No. 1 in 1872.* John David James Dalrymple, born in 1961, was educated at Harrow. He inherited the title in 1996 and was an officer in the Scots Guards, as was his father. He is a cousin of the Queen Mother through his mother. The estate is about half the size it was in 1872, parts having been sold to the Wemyss family. MacEwen put its size at 105,000 acres in 1970, but Andy Wightman does not believe that this was accurate. An ancestor resigned as Principal Secretary of State for Scotland over his involvement in the Glencoe massacre. The family seat is at Lochinch Castle, Stranraer.

ANDREW GLADSTONE *7362 acres.* This estate at Craiglaw was owned in 1872 by William Charles Stewart Hamilton, at a little under its present size. MacEwen describes it as owned by the Craiglaw trust in 1970. Andrew Gladstone is a descendant of the Hamiltons, via his mother, Diana Rosemund Fleming, who married John Gladstone, eldest son of Sir Hugh Gladstone of Capenoch in 1950. The Hamiltons bought the land from the Abbott of Kilwinning in 1543.

THE HON MRS FLORA STUART *5501 acres.* The Mochrum estate was the ancestral lands of the Dunbars, who still held them in MacEwen's 1970 list. They came into the family in 1564, through a strategic marriage. The family seat is Mochrum Park, but the present baronet, the 14th, lives in America, where his father, the 13th Baronet, was a sergeant in the Mountain Engineers. The present owner could not be found in *Debrett's*.

Significant Institutional Landowners

The Forestry Commission owns 22,375 acres. The Ministry of Defence owns 4569 acres.

TOP 10 IN 1872

1	Earl of Stair (MP) of Oxenfoorde Castle, Dalkeith	82,666 acres	with 33,704 elsewhere
2	Mr Edward James Stopford-Blair of Penninghame, Newton-Stewart	37,268 acres	
3	Earl of Galloway (MP) of Galloway House, Garliston	23,203 acres	with 55,981 elsewhere
4	Marquess of Bute of Mount Stuart, Rothesay	20,157 acres	with 96,511 elsewhere
5	Sir Herbert Eustace Maxwell Bt MP of Monreith, Whauphill. (Land held since 1481)	16,877 acres	
6	Mr James McDouall of Logan, Stranraer	16,290 acres	with 5643 elsewhere
7	Sir Andrew Agnew Bt MP of Lochnaw Castle, Stranraer	14,000 acres	
8	Mr John Charles Cunninghame of Craigends, Paisley	8306 acres	with 25,642 elsewhere
9	Sir Edward Hunter-Blair Bt of Blairquahan, Maybole	8255 acres	with 13,417 elsewhere
10	Rear Admiral Sir John Hay Bt MP of Dunragit House, Dunluce and 108 St George's Square, London (Not in Bateman)	7400 acres	

Wales

Wales presents unique difficulties. The 12 counties of 1872 have been significantly changed twice – the map on p.225 shows the most recent structure of Wales with just seven 'administrative units', reduced from eight after the 1974 reorganisation of local government. Three of the 1872 counties, Radnor, Montgomery and Brecknock, have been absorbed into what is broadly Powys but not precisely enough to combine the three for comparison with Powys. For this reason, the three counties are simply shown as they stood in 1872. The second difficulty with Wales is that there was an element of Irish-style land redistribution in progress in the 1800s and 1900s and far more of the 1872 estates have vanished altogether than is the case in England or Scotland.

Modern landowners

As with England most modern landed estates, especially those that have remained in the same family since 1872, are not entered in the Land Registry. In Wales too there has in fact been an even poorer recording of the landed estates than in England, and Wales shares the same central defect of the English element of the Land Registry, that of having perhaps 50% of the country unrecorded. This is a malign tribute to the same bad legislation of 1925 which created the registry. Wales, like Scotland, had very few large institutional landowners in 1872.

An explanation of all figures included in the tables is given on p.219.

List of Welsh Counties included

Anglesey
Brecknock (or Breconshire)
Caernarvonshire
Cardiganshire
Carmarthenshire
Denbighshire
Flintshire
Glamorganshire
Merionethshire
Monmouthshire
Montgomeryshire
Pembrokeshire
Radnorshire

For map see pages 224 & 225.

ANGLESEY

	1872	2001
Total acreage	161,936 acres	176,429 acres
Agricultural acreage	153,839 acres	122,200 acres
Non agricultural acreage	8096 acres	54,229 acres
Population	51,040	67,055
Owners of nothing at all	46,899	30,655
Total Dwellings	12,170	28,000
Smallholdings: 1872 owners of less than one acre	3015	
2000 owners of 0–2ha (0–4.94 acres)		234
Landowners over one acre (1872)	1126	
Landowners over 2ha (2000)		1211
Landowners over 500 acres	43	24
Acreage (and percentage) of county owned by owners of over 500 acres	117,968 acres (70.3%)	17,687 acres (10%)

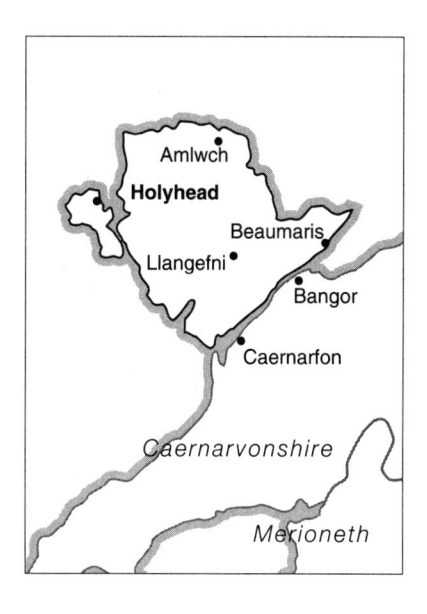

Top Landowners 2001

THE 7TH MARQUESS OF ANGLESEY *8000 acres. No. 3 in 1872.* George Henry Victor Paget, born in 1922, was educated at Eton and was a major in the Royal Horse Guards. The family have moved from Litchfield and now live at Plas Newydd, near Llanfair in Anglesey. The *Sunday Times* has reduced the acreage to just 4000 acres, but with the patronage of four parishes retained, it is estimated that the holding is double that. He is an authority on Welsh affairs and is a military historian, having written extensively on cavalry matters. His heir is the Earl of Uxbridge, Eton educated like his father, born in 1950.

SIR RICHARD WILLIAMS-BULKELEY, 14TH BARONET *2000 acres. No. 1 in 1872.* The baronetcy was by gift of the Lord Protector, Cromwell in 1658, confirmed by Charles II in 1661. The family lineage prior to that is of enormous antiquity, going back to Ednyfed Vychan, Chief Minister of Llywelyn the Great, William ap Griffith of Cochwillan, Caernarvonshire. The 10th male is cited in *Debrett's* as an assistant to Henry VII at Bosworth, and to being a member of Henry's family, that of Tudor. The family seat is identified as Baron Hill, as in 1872, with residence at Red Hill, Beaumaris. Francis Fulford names it as Plas Meigan in *The Field*. The present Baronet is Sir Richard Thomas Williams-Bulkeley, born in 1939, educated at Eton and with stint in the Welsh Guards. He has been Deputy Lieutenant of the county since 1998. The family holding is much reduced but is still a large estate by modern standards.

The descendants of both Baron Boston (no. 2 in 1872), currently Timothy Irby, the 10th Baron, and Baron Stanley of Alderley Edge (no. 4 in 1872), Timothy Stanley, the 8th Baron (who is also Baron Sheffield), live in Anglesey. The 13th Reade Baronet (no. 10 in 1872), Sir Kenneth Ray Reade, lives in America.

Significant Institutional Landowner

The National Trust owns 1268 acres with 482 protected.

TOP 10 IN 1872

1	Sir Richard Mostyn Williams-Bulkeley Bt of Baron Hill, Beaumaris	16,516 acres	with 13,362 elsewhere
2	Lord Boston of Llanidan	9507 acres	with 2967 elsewhere
3	Marquess of Anglesey of Beaudesert Park, Lichfield	8485 acres	with 20,117 elsewhere
4	Lord Stanley of Alderley Park, Crewe	5960 acres	with 5011 elsewhere
5	Hon Mr William Owen Stanley MP of Penrhos	5808 acres	
6	Sir Thomas Lewis Arundel Neave Bt of Dagenham Park, Essex	5739 acres	
7	Mr William Bulkeley Hughes MP of Plas Coch	5404 acres	
8	Captain E.H. Verney of Rhianfa	5078 acres	
9	Mr Robert Davies of Bodlowdeb	3926 acres	with 924 elsewhere
10	Sir Chandos Stanhope Hoskyns Reade Bt of Carreglwyd	3764 acres	

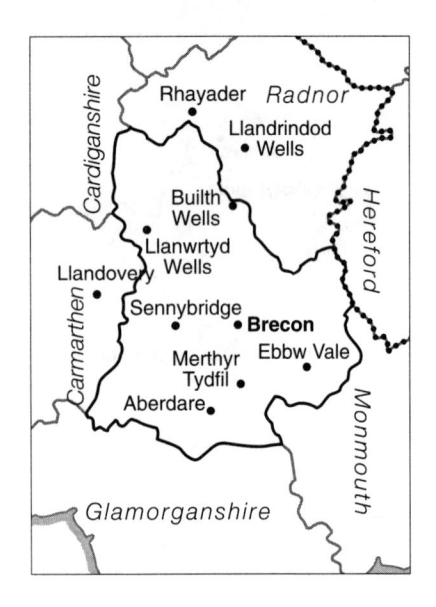

BRECKNOCK

(No modern equivalent. This 1872 county now takes up about one third of Powys.)

	1872
Total acreage	302,237 acres
Agricultural acreage	287,125 acres
Non agricultural acreage	15,111 acres
Population	59,901
Owners of nothing at all	57,487
Total Dwellings	12,647
Smallholdings: 1872 owners of less than one acre 2000 owners of 0–2ha (0–4.94 acres)	1195
Landowners over one acre (1872)	
Landowners over 2ha (2000)	1219
Landowners over 500 acres	103
Acreage (and percentage) of county owned by owners of over 500 acres	119,384 acres (47.7%)

Top Landowners 2001

THE 3RD BARON MILFORD *3000 acres*. Like his father, Hugo John Lawrence Phillips describes himself as a farmer and lives at the family seat, Llanstephan House, Llanstephan. Like his father, he was educated at Eton. However, his father Wogan Phillips was the only communist peer in the House of Lords, having fought in the Spanish Civil war on the side of the Republic, served as a communist counsellor on Cirencester Rural District Council and married as his third wife the widow of William Rust, the editor of the Daily Worker. The present peer's mother was the distinguished writer Rosamond Lehmann, his father's first wife. Francis Fulford attributes the acreage to an inheritance from the Wogan family, not in Bateman or *Burke's* but possibly a now extinct Irish family found in *Debrett's*.

Significant Institutional Landowners

None known.

TOP 10 IN 1872

1	Sir Joseph Russell Bailey Bt MP of Glanusk Park Crickhowell	21,979	acres	with 6329 elsewhere
2	Miss Clara Thomas of Llwynmadoc Builth	9235	acres	with 5021 elsewhere
3	Mr W.E. Powell of Nanteos, Cardigan	8055	acres	
4	Lord Tredegar (MP) of Tredegar Park, Mons	7300	acres	with 31,857 elsewhere
5	Mr Penry Williams of Penpont, Brecon	7042	acres	with 1094 elsewhere
6	Mr E. Thomas of Welfield	5472	acres	
7	Mr John Morgan Harris of Treferig House, Pontypridd	3996	acres	with 4153 elsewhere
8	Miss Susan Williams of Trephilip, Brecon	2917	acres	
9	Rev Ven Archdeacon Davies of Court-y-Gollen	2813	acres	
10	Mr John Williams-Vaughan of Velinnewydd	2703	acres	with 2647 elsewhere

CAERNARVONSHIRE
(Now part of Gwynedd)

	1872	2001
Total acreage	301,223 acres	629,610 acres
Agricultural acreage	286,161 acres	464,842 acres
Non agricultural acreage	15,061 acres	164,768 acres
Population	106,121	117,000
Owners of nothing at all	99,881	55,900
Total Dwellings	23,298	47,000
Smallholdings: 1872 owners of less than one acre 2000 owners of 0–2ha (0–4.94 acres)	4610	264
Landowners over one acre (1872) Landowners over 2ha (2000)	1630	2165
Landowners over 500 acres	61	247
Acreage (and percentage) of county owned by owners of over 500 acres	246,141 acres (77.9%)	230,927 acres (37%)

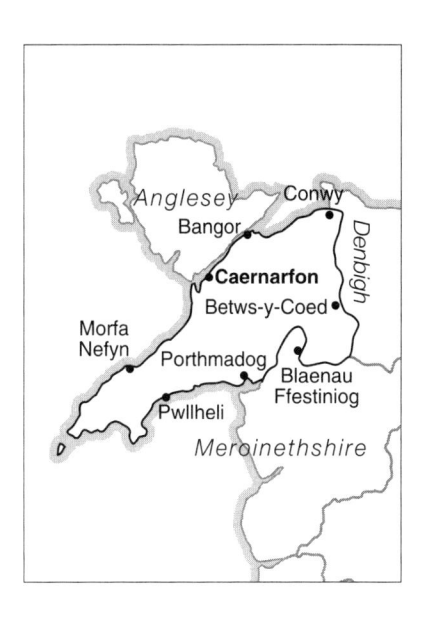

Top Landowners 2001

THE 8TH BARON NEWBOROUGH *20,000 acres with 2000 acres in Shropshire*. The 8th Baron's father, who died in 1998, was almost a figure out of romantic fiction. Educated at Oundle, he was a cavalry officer in the 16th/5th Lancers invalided in action in 1940. Months later he was back at Dunkirk as a reserve officer in the RN, commanding MTB 74 and rescuing parts of the army that later defeated Hitler. At Dunkirk he was awarded a Distinguished Service Cross, was wounded again, captured and incarcerated in Colditz, from which he escaped. His son, the present peer, lives in Shropshire, but his widow, his second wife, Jennie, lives at the family home at Rug. She is a relative of the Aclands, landowners in Devon. The 7th Baron's first wife Rosemund Barbour was the daughter of landowners from Cheshire.

Where they are now:
THE 6TH BARON PENRHYN The vast estate of the Penrhyns (no. 1 in 1872), was donated almost whole, to the National Trust, through the National Land Fund, in 1951. The total estate at Penrhyn is 36,718 acres, the largest single property of the National Trust. The present Baron Penrhyn, a former Colonel in the Kings Royal Rifle Corps, with an MBE and a DSO, born in 1908, lives near Winchester in Hants. The land originally belonged to the Pennant family, going back to medieval times, and came to the Penrhyns in 1833 when the future 1st Baron married the co-heiress to the estate.

Significant Institutional Landowners

The National Trust owns 48,503 acres in Gwynedd.

TOP 10 IN 1872

1	Lord Penrhyn (MP) of Penrhyn Castle, Bangor	41,348 acres	with 8200 elsewhere
2	Mr George Duff-Assheaton-Smith of Vaynol	33,752 acres	with 730 elsewhere
3	Baroness Willoughby De Eresby of Grinsthorpe, Lincs	30,391 acres	with 101,829 elsewhere
4	Lord Newborough of Glynnllivon Park	22,063 acres	with 6737 elsewhere
5	Sir Richard Mostyn Williams-Bulkeley Bt of Baron Hill, Beaumaris	13,362 acres	with 16,516 elsewhere
6	Mr Thomas Love Duncombe Jones-Parry MP of Madryn, Pwllheli	10,025 acres	
7	Mr John R.O. Gore of Porkington, Salop (Not in Bateman)	8570 acres	
8	Mr Hugh John Ellis-Nanney of Gwynfryn, Criccith	7587 acres	with 4485 elsewhere
9	Mr George Augustus Huddart of Brynkir, Tremadoc	7555 acres	with 237 elsewhere
10	Mr Francis William Lloyd Edwards of Nanhoron, Pwllheli	6769 acres	with 2240 elsewhere

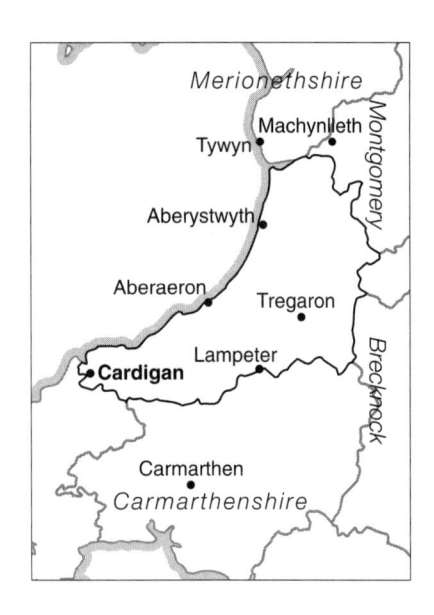

CARDIGANSHIRE

	1872	2001
Total acreage	391,685 acres	443,544 acres
Agricultural acreage	372,100 acres	343,431 acres
Non agricultural acreage	19,584 acres	100,113 acres
Population	73,441	69,545
Owners of nothing at all	70,125	-
Total Dwellings	16,420	-
Smallholdings: 1872 owners of less than one acre	1278	
2000 owners of 0–2ha (0–4.94 acres)		336
Landowners over one acre (1872)	2038	
Landowners over 2ha (2000)		2634
Landowners over 500 acres	98	92
Acreage (and percentage) of county owned by owners of over 500 acres	270,975 acres (67.9%)	93,109 (21%)

Top Landowners 2001

THE 8TH EARL OF LISBURNE *2000 acres. No. 1 in 1872.* John David Malet Vaughan was born in 1918 and served in World War Two as a Captain in the Welsh Guards. Educated in the traditional fashion at Eton and Oxford, he trained as a barrister. The title being Irish he was not able to sit in the Lords. The acreage in the 1872 Return is vast, but he now lives at The Manor House, Hopton Wafers in Worcs, and neither his heir, David, born in 1945, nor his other two sons, live in Wales. All three sons were educated at Ampleforth, and the family still retain the patronage of one Church of England parish.

Significant Institutional Landowner

The National Trust owns 1513 acres.

TOP 10 IN 1872

1	Earl of Lisburne of Crosswood, Aberystwyth	42,720 acres	with 41 elsewhere
2	Sir Pryse Pryse Bt of Gogerddan, Aberystwyth	28,684 acres	with 3673 elsewhere
3	Mr George Ernest John Powell of Nanteos, Aberystwyth	21,933 acres	with 11,741 elsewhere
4	Mr John Waddingham of Hafod, Aberystwyth	10,963 acres	with 2362 elsewhere
5	Mr L.P. Pugh of Abermaed	6894 acres	
6	Mr Haworth Peel Massey of Blaendyffryn	5417 acres	with 1459 elsewhere
7	Mr J Loxdale of Castle Hill (incl Staffs)	4915 acres	
8	Mr T.E. Lloyd of Coedmore (incl Carm & Pem)	4872 acres	
9	Miss Jones of Derry Ormond (may be Bettws Bledrws)	4782 acres	
10	Mrs M.A. Lewis of Lanaeron	4397 acres	

CARMARTHENSHIRE

	1872	2001
Total acreage	510,574 acres	591,804 acres
Agricultural acreage	485,045 acres	426,183 acres
Non agricultural acreage	25,528 acres	165,621 acres
Population	115,710	169,000
Owners of nothing at all	107,644	-
Total Dwellings	24,333	-
Smallholdings: 1872 owners of less than one acre	5168	
2000 owners of 0–2ha (0–4.94 acres)		547
Landowners over one acre (1872)	2898	
Landowners over 2ha (2000)		4250
Landowners over 500 acres	161	39
Acreage (and percentage) of county owned by owners of over 500 acres	306,788 acres (58%)	25,943 (4%)

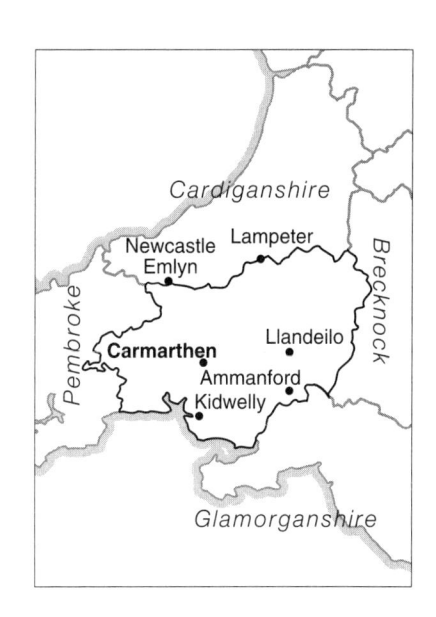

Top Landowners 2001

Where they are now:
THE EARL OF CAWDOR'S ESTATE *(no. 1 in 1872)* was sold in 1976. See Nairn p.291.

THE 9TH BARON DYNEVOR *(no. 8 in 1872)* Richard Charles Uryan Rhys, the 9th Baron was born in 1935 and succeeded in 1962. He does not appear on the roll of the House of Lords for the final year before reform and ejection and gives no address in *Debrett's*.

Significant Institutional Landowner

The National Trust owns 3573 acres.

TOP 10 IN 1872

1	Earl of Cawdor (MP) of Stackpool, Pembs	33,782	acres	with 67,875 elsewhere
2	Mr Morgan Jones of Llanmilo, St Clear	11,031	acres	with 1030 elsewhere
3	Sir Arthur Keppel Cowell-Stepney Bt MP of Llanelly	9841	acres	with 6 elsewhere
4	Sir James Hamlyn Williams-Drummond Bt of Edswinford, Llandilo	9281	acres	with 482 elsewhere
5	Mr Frederick Arthur Jones of Pantglas	8280	acres	
6	Mr A.H.C. Jones (Not in Bateman)	7662	acres	
7	Mr David Pugh MP of Manoravon, Llandilo	7292	acres	with 884 elsewhere
8	Lord Dynevor of Dynevor Castle, Llandilo	7208	acres	with 3520 elsewhere
9	Mr Alan James Gulston of Dirleton, Landilo	7145	acres	
10	Mr John William Gwynne Hughes of Tregib, Llandilo	6797	acres	

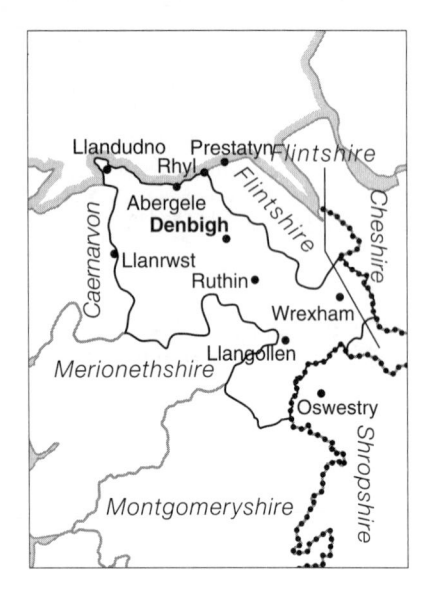

DENBIGHSHIRE

	1872	2001
Total acreage	348,417 acres	207,069 acres
Agricultural acreage	330,996 acres	140,790 acres
Non agricultural acreage	17,420 acres	66,279 acres
Population	105,102	91,000
Owners of nothing at all	99,394	42,900
Total Dwellings	22,500	37,000
Smallholdings: 1872 owners of less than one acre	3436	
2000 owners of 0–2ha (0–4.94 acres)		157
Landowners over one acre (1872)	2272	
Landowners over 2ha (2000)		928
Landowners over 500 acres	112	40
Acreage (and percentage) of county owned by owners of over 500 acres	237,121 acres (64.5%)	36,499 acres (18%)

Top Landowners 2001

SIR (DAVID) WATKIN WILLIAMS-WYNN, THE 11TH BARONET *17,000 acres. No. 1 in 1872.* Quite a reduction on the vast tracts they owned at the time of the 1872 Return, but a major modern estate all the same. The original family claim descent from Cadrodd Hardd (the Handsome) who was a tribal Chief and Lord of Talybolion in Anglesey in 1100AD. The 1st Baronet was the Speaker in the House of Commons from 1679 to 1685 and helped to create the tradition that MPs cannot be sued for libel, by overturning a libel verdict that had cost him a £10,000 fine (about £1 million nowadays). The present Baronet, born in 1940, was a major in the 1st Royal Dragoons and lost a brother in Northern Ireland in 1972. His father, a lieutenant colonel, spent three and a half years working on the death railway in Burma as a prisoner of the Japanese in 1941-5. The family seat is Wynnstay, but the present baronet lives at Plas-yn-Cefn at St Aseph.

THE 3RD BARON ABERCONWAY *6700 acres.* Charles Melville McLaren, born in 1913, and his family have left an enduring mark on modern Wales. His father gave the gardens at the family seat, Bodnant, to the National Trust in 1949. The gardens are described as amongst the finest in the country. He has continued to add to his father's legacy and was president of the Royal Horticultural Society from 1961 to 1984. The family are essentially Scottish, and came to Wales at the turn of the twentieth century. His son and heir, Charles, born in 1948, was, like his father educated at Eton.

THE 9TH LORD BAGOT *4000 acres with 1700 acres in Staffs.* Heneage Charles Bagot, born in 1914, was educated at Harrow and served as a major in the Gurkhas. He claims descent from Bagod, a Norman follower of William the Bastard, who held land at Bramshall in Stafford from Robert de Stafford, whose family were later Dukes of Buckingham. The widow of the 6th Baron still lives at the family seat in Staffs, Blithfield Hall. The present peer lives at Tyne-y-Mynydd. The 1872 estate (no. 2 below) was based at Pool Park, near Ruthin. His son and heir, the Hon Shaun, born in 1944, lives in London.

Significant Institutional Landowners

None known.

TOP 10 IN 1872

1	Sir Watkin Williams-Wynn Bt MP of Wynnstay, Ruabon	28,721 acres	with 117,049 elsewhere
2	Lord Bagot MP of Blithfield House Rugley Staffs	18,044 acres	with 12,499 elsewhere
3	Mr Hugh Robert Hughes of Kinmel Park, Abergele	13,287 acres	
4	Mr Townshend Mainwaring MP of Galltfaenan	10,685 acres	
5	Mr John Lloyd Wynne of Coed Coch, Abergele	9000 acres	
6	Mr H.R. Hughes of St Asaph (not in Bateman)	8561 acres	
7	Mr Charles Arthur Wynne-Finch of Voelas	8025 acres	with 7133 elsewhere
8	Mr Brownlow Wynne of Garthewin, Abergele	6495 acres	
9	Mr Richard Myddleton-Biddulph of Chirk Castle Ruabon	5781 acres	with 2557 elsewhere
10	Mr William Cornwallis West of the Castle, Ruthin	5457 acres	with 2404 elsewhere

FLINTSHIRE

	1872	2001
Total acreage	142,286 acres	108,229 acres
Agricultural acreage	135,171 acres	64,709 acres
Non agricultural acreage	7114 acres	43,520 acres
Population	76,312	144,900
Owners of nothing at all	72,802	71,200
Total Dwellings	16,636	56,000
Smallholdings: 1872 owners of less than one acre	2048	
2000 owners of 0–2ha (0–4.94 acres)		141
Landowners over one acre (1872)	1462	
Landowners over 2ha (2000)		694
Landowners over 500 acres	46	9
Acreage (and percentage) of county owned by owners of over 500 acres	81,558 acres (55.6%)	7,338 acres (7%)

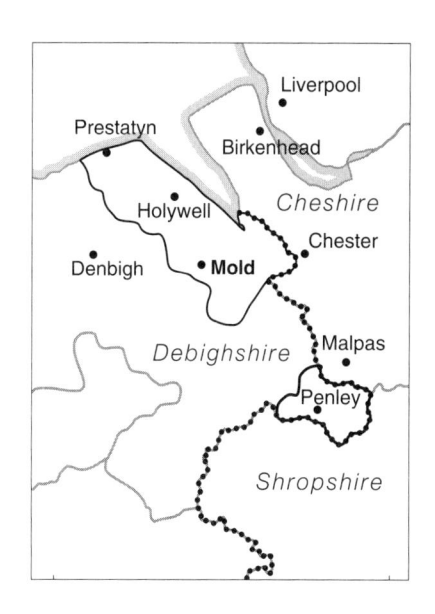

Top Landowners 2001

THE BANKES FAMILY OF SOUGHTON HALL *2500 acres.* The last incumbent recorded at Soughton Hall in *Burke's Landed Gentry* in 1972 was Robert Wynn Bankes CBE, a one-time secretary of the Institute of Chartered Accountants and later private secretary to successive Lord Chancellors for the period 1919–29. His eldest son John was a solicitor in London at the time of the last BLG in 1972. The family are close relatives of the Bankes of Kingston Lacey in Dorset.

THE 9TH BARON LANGFORD, COLONEL THE LORD LANGFORD OBE *2000 acres. No. 3 in 1872.* Geoffrey Alexander Rowley-Conwy was born in 1912. He lives at the family seat Bodrhyddan, Rhuddlan, where his untitled ancestor lived in 1872. The peerage was in Ireland at that time, based in Meath. Like his neighbour, the late 7th Lord Newborough, he had an extraordinary war career, avoiding capture when Singapore fell to the Japanese in 1941, leading a battery of Indian artillery in the counter attack in Burma and taking part in the Berlin airlift during the cold war. He and his three sons, including his heir the Hon Peter Alexander, born in 1951, were educated at Marlborough.

THE 5TH BARON MOSTYN MC *2000 acres.* The lands of the peerage do not appear in Bateman, where Mostyn is recorded as being an estate added to a larger, unidentified one. Roger Edward Lloyd Lloyd Mostyn, the present peer, was born in 1920, and like his neighbours Langford and the late Lord Newborough, was decorated for courage in World War Two as a captain in the Queen's Royal Lancers. He is recorded by Francis Fulford as landed gentry, though *Burke's* does not list the family as such, probably because of the peerage. He was educated at Eton as was his son and heir, the Hon Llewellyn Roger, born in 1948, who did a stint in the army legal service as a captain.

Significant Institutional Landowners
None known.

TOP 10 IN 1872

1	Sir Wyndham Edward Hanmer Bt of Bettisfield Park, Whitchurch, Salop	7318	acres	with 4342 elsewhere
2	Rt Hon Mr William Ewart Gladstone MP of Hawarden Castle. (Prime Minister)	6908	acres	with 10 elsewhere
3	Captain Conwn Grenville Hercules Rowley-Conwy of Boddrhyddan, Rhyl	5526	acres	
4	Mr Llewelyn Nevill Vaughan Lloyd-Mostyn of Gloddaeth, Llandudno	5462	acres	with 2317 elsewhere
5	Sir Pyres William Mostyn Bt of Talacre, Rhyl	4184	acres	
6	Lord Kenyon of Gredington Hall, Whitchurch, Salop	4004	acres	with 3937 elsewhere
7	Earl of Denbigh of Newnham Paddox, Lutterworth, Leics	2848	acres	
8	Mr Edmund Peel of Bryn-y-Pys, Ruabon	2897	acres	with 5569 elsewhere
9	Mr T.B.D. Cooke of Owston, Doncaster	2267	acres	
10	Mr P.L. Fletcher of Nerquis Hall	1744	acres	

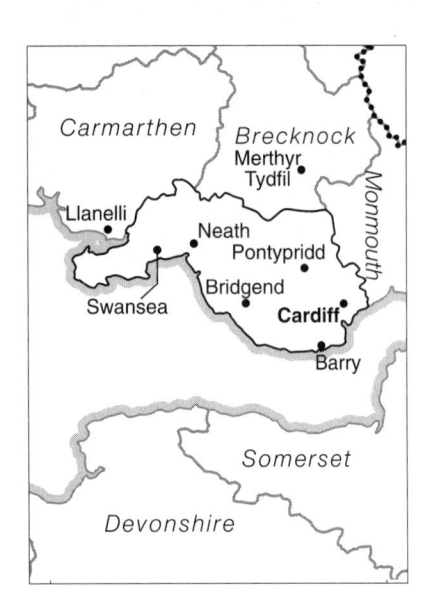

GLAMORGANSHIRE

	1872	2001
Total acreage	428,386 acres	82,778 acres
Agricultural acreage	406,966 acres	55,738 acres
Non agricultural acreage	21,419 acres	27,040 acres
Population	397,859	119,200
Owners of nothing at all	389,433	59,400
Total Dwellings	72,905	46,000
Smallholdings: 1872 owners of less than one acre	6570	
2000 owners of 0–2ha (0–4.94 acres)		54
Landowners over one acre (1872)	1856	
Landowners over 2ha (2000)		391
Landowners over 500 acres	121	21
Acreage (and percentage) of county owned by owners of over 500 acres	323,781 acres (68.1%)	18,638 acres (23%)

Top Landowners 2001

Where they are now:
THE MARQUESS OF BUTE *(no. 3 in 1872)*. See Ayrshire (p.273).

THE EARL OF JERSEY *(no. 5 in 1872)*. See Middlesex (p.247).

THE EARL OF DUNRAVEN AND MOUNT-EARL *(no. 2 in 1872)*. The 7th Earl, Thady Windham Thomas Wyndham-Quin, born in 1939 and educated at Le Rosy in Switzerland, lives in Limerick in Ireland. He has no male heir. His sister is the Marchioness of Waterford (see Waterford, p.351)

THE BARONY OF TREDEGAR *(no. 9 in 1872)* became extinct when the 6th Baron died in 1962.

Significant Institutional Landowners

1872: The railway companies owned 3289 acres. The coal companies owned 33,441 acres. Jesus College, Oxford, owned 1496 acres.

TOP 10 IN 1872

1	Mr Christopher Rice Mansel Talbot MP of Margam Abbey, Taibach	33,920 acres	
2	Earl of Dunraven of Adare Manor, Limerick	23,751 acres	with 16,004 elsewhere
3	Marquess of Bute of Mount Stuart, Rothesay	21,402 acres	with 95,266 elsewhere
4	Lord Windsor of Oakly Park, Bromfiled, Salop	17,355 acres	with 20,099 elsewhere
5	Earl of Jersey of Middleton Park, Bicester, Oxford	10,000 acres	with 9389 elsewhere
6	Mr Vaughan Hanning Vaughan-Lee MP of Dillington Park, Somerset	9222 acres	with 5956 elsewhere
7	Mr John Dillwyn-Llewelyn of Penllergare, Swansea	8797 acres	with 6070 elsewhere
8	Mr Edward Rhys Wingfield of Barrington Park, Burford, Beds	6463 acres	with 12,328 elsewhere
9	Lord Tredegar MP of Tredegar Park, Newport, Mons	6157 acres	with 33,000 elsewhere
10	Mrs John Blandy-Jenkins of Kingston Bagpuize, Abingdon, Berks	6128 acres	with 1142 elsewhere

MERIONETHSHIRE

(No modern equivalent. Various parts of this 1872 county are now in Dyfed, Powys and Gwynedd.)

	1872
Total acreage	303,073 acres
Agricultural acreage	287,524 acres
Non agricultural acreage	15,132 acres
Population	46,598
Owners of nothing at all	44,903
Total Dwellings	10,006
Smallholdings: 1872 owners of less than one acre 2000 owners of 0–2ha (0–4.94 acres)	1044
Landowners over one acre (1872) Landowners over 2ha (2000)	651
Landowners over 500 acres	109
Acreage (and percentage) of county owned by owners of over 500 acres	239,110 acres (78.8%)

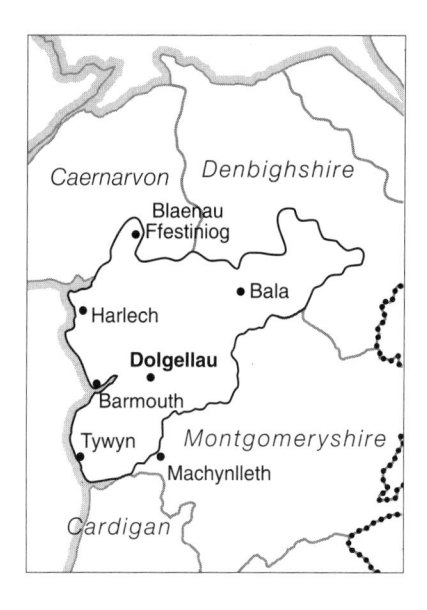

TOP 10 IN 1872

1	Sir Watkin Williams Wyn Bt MP of Wynnstay, Ruabon	42,044 acres	
2	Mr Richard John Lloyd Price of Rhiwlas, Bala	40,500 acres	with 764 elsewhere
3	Mr T. Price-Lloyd of Trawsfynnyd	16,974 acres	
4	Mr John Vaughan of Nannau, Dolgelly	16,443 acres	with 145 elsewhere
5	Mrs Kirby of Maesyneuadd-Talsarnau, Harlach	13,409 acres	
6	Hon Mr Charles Henry Wynn of Rug, Corwen	10,504 acres	
7	Mr Athelstan J.G. Corbet of Towyn (Not in Bateman)	9347 acres	
8	Sir E. Buckley Bt	8737 acres	
9	Mr William Edward Oakeley of Tan-y-Bwlch, Harlach	7169 acres	
10	Mr W.O. Gore of Porkington, Salop (Not in Bateman)	5496 acres	

MONMOUTHSHIRE

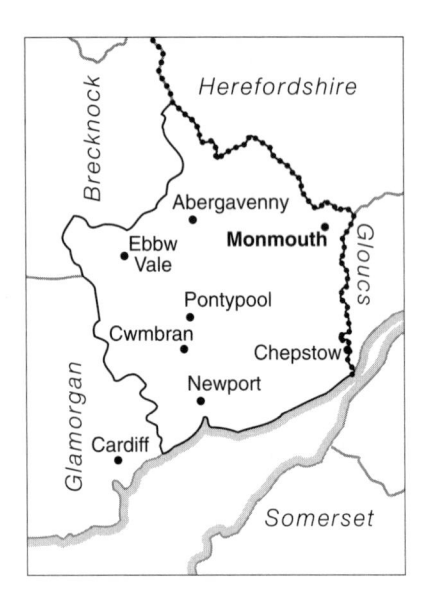

(Monmouthshire was treated for administrative purposes as an English county in 1872. It is now part of South Wales (Gwent).)

	1872	2001
Total acreage	289,377 acres	209,185 acres
Agricultural acreage	274,908 acres	142,089 acres
Non agricultural acreage	14,468 acres	67,096 acres
Population	195,448	86,248
Owners of nothing at all	187,634	43,348
Total Dwellings	36,169	33,000
Smallholdings: 1872 owners of less than one acre 2000 owners of 0–2ha (0–4.94 acres)	4970	197
Landowners over one acre (1872) Landowners over 2ha (2000)	2844	1387
Landowners over 500 acres	76	20
Acreage (and percentage) of county owned by owners of over 500 acres	171,258 acres (59.2%)	12,649 acres (6%)

Top Landowners 2001

THE 5TH LORD RAGLAN *2500 acres*. Fitzroy John Somerset, born in 1927, is a Plantagenet, related to the family of the Duke of Beaufort. The estate appears in Bateman, although at the time of the 1872 Return Cefntilla Park, now the family seat, was not shown as the seat of any estate in Mons. The present peer was Deputy Lieutenant for Mons and a Captain in the Welsh Guards. He was chairman of the Cwmbran New Town Development Corporation. Both he and his son went to Westminster School and his son the Hon Geoffrey, born in 1932, farms in Oxfordshire.

Where they are now:

THE DUKE OF BEAUFORT'S FAMILY *(no. 1 in 1872)* sold out the Welsh holdings and added a slightly larger number of acres in Gloucestershire (see p.238).

THE BARONY OF TREDEGAR *(no. 2 in 1872)* became extinct in 1962 when the 6th Baron Tredegar died without an heir. His widow, Joanna, née Law-Smith, of Adelaide, South Australia, survived him, married the 9th Baron Wharton, was widowed again and now lives in Marebella, Spain, with her fourth husband, Bruce York. There is no current record of the estate.

THE HANBURYS *(no. 3 in 1872)* live on in the shape of the Hanbury Tenisons, who have left the family seat at Pont-y-Pool and farm at Tycadno near Panteg and have given the world the old Etonian countryside campaigner, Richard Hanbury Tenison. They are descendants of the family of Lord Sudeley, of Sudeley Castle (see Montgomery 1872).

Significant Institutional Landowners

1872: The largest institutional landowner in 1872 was the Church of England with 13,083 acres.
2001: The National Trust owns 3269 acres.

TOP 10 IN 1872

1	Duke Beaufort (MP) of Badminton, Chippenham, Wilts	27,299 acres	with 23,786 elsewhere
2	Lord Tredegar (MP) of Tredegar Park, Newport	25,500 acres	with 13,657 elsewhere
3	Mr John Capel Hanbury of Pontypool Park	10,210 acres	with 763 elsewhere
4	Lady Llanover of Llanover, Abergavenny	6312 acres	with 221 elsewhere
5	Colonel Kemeys-Tynte of Halswell, Bridgewater	4753 acres	with 15,956 elsewhere
6	Mr John Herbert of Llanarth Court, Raglan	4641 acres	
7	Mr William Herbert of Clytha House Usk	4542 acres	
8	Mr Charles Edward Lewis of St Pierre, Chepstow	4504 acres	
9	Mr John Allan Rolls MP of The Hendre	4082 acres	
10	Sir Henry Mather Jackson Bt of Llantilio	3137 acres	

MONTGOMERYSHIRE

(No modern equivalent. Various parts of this 1872 county are now in Dyfed, Powys and Gwynedd.)

	1872
Total acreage	380,384 acres
Agricultural acreage	361,364 acres
Non agricultural acreage	19,019 acres
Population	67,623
Owners of nothing at all	64,382
Total Dwellings	13,911
Smallholdings: 1872 owners of less than one acre 2000 owners of 0–2ha (0–4.94 acres)	1314
Landowners over one acre (1872) Landowners over 2ha (2000)	1927
Landowners over 500 acres	120
Acreage (and percentage) of county owned by owners of over 500 acres	256,501 acres (66.2%)

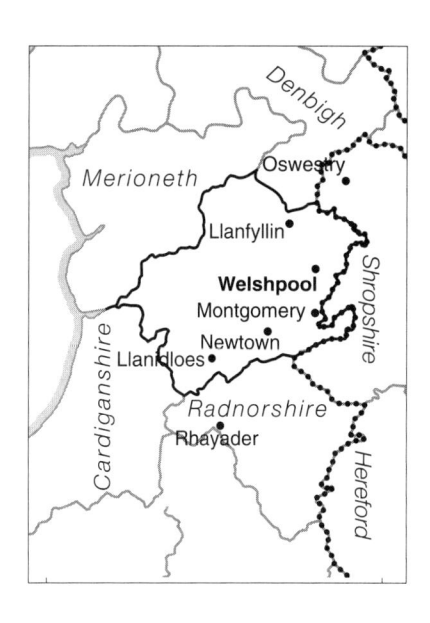

Top Landowners 2001

THE 8TH EARL OF POWIS *30,000 acres in trust. No. 2 in 1872.* The beautiful red castle, with its splendid gardens, was given to the National Trust in 1952 by the 4th Earl, with an endowment, but only 55 acres of land. The present earl, John George Herbert, born in 1952, is a former Assistant Professor of English at Redeemer College Ontario, and has a doctorate in literature from McMaster University. The earl describes Powis castle as his seat, and remains the patron of 12 Church of England parishes, implying that much of the estate is still intact. This is indirectly confirmed by local opinion. His son, Viscount Clive, born in 1979, carries the name of the most illustrious member of the family, Robert Clive, President of Bengal and the man who largely created British India in the eighteenth century by defeating Surajah Dowla at Plassy. This ended the Surajah's habit of throwing his British captives into the Black Hole of Calcutta and founded the Raj.

TOP 10 IN 1872

1	Sir Watkin Williams-Wynn Bt MP	70,559	acres	with 75,211 elsewhere
2	Earl of Powis (MP) of Powis Castle, Weshpool	33,545	acres	with 27,014 elsewhere
3	Lord Sudeley MP of Gregynog, Newtown	17,158	acres	with 6795 elsewhere
4	Mr John Naylor of Leighton Hall, Welshpool	11,257	acres	with 467 elsewhere
5	Marquess of Londonderry MP of Seaham Hall, Sunderland	7399	acres	with 42,924 elsewhere
6	Mr James Walton of Dolforgan, Newtown	5123	acres	with 746 elsewhere
7	Major Corbett-Corbett-Winder of Vaynor Park, Berriew	5116	acres	
8	Mr Arthur Charles Humphreys-Owen of Glanseveren, Garthymyll	4482	acres	
9	Lt Colonel George Edward Herbert of Glan Hafren, Newtown	4031	acres	with 1514 elsewhere
10	Mr Charles John Morris of Berth Lloyd	3923	acres	with 3043 elsewhere

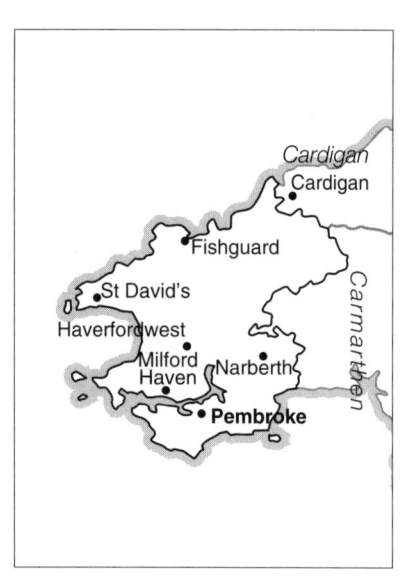

PEMBROKESHIRE

	1872	2001
Total acreage	356,699 acres	392,641 acres
Agricultural acreage	338,864 acres	302,536 acres
Non agricultural acreage	17,834 acres	90,105 acres
Population	91,998	114,400
Owners of nothing at all	88,877	55,900
Total Dwellings	19,583	45,000
Smallholdings: 1872 owners of less than one acre 2000 owners of 0–2ha (0–4.94 acres)	1492	325
Landowners over one acre (1872) Landowners over 2ha (2000)	1629	2612
Landowners over 500 acres	116	42
Acreage (and percentage) of county owned by owners of over 500 acres	237,777 acres (64.6%)	29,884 acres (8%)

Top Landowners 2001

THE 3RD EARL LLOYD GEORGE OF DWYFOR *2500 acres*. He is the grandson of the World War One Prime Minister, David Lloyd George and has been an active figure in Welsh public life for many years, carrying the Sword of Investiture at Prince Charles' investiture as Prince of Wales in 1969. Born in 1924, he was educated at Oundle – his sons went to Eton – and served in World War Two as a captain in the Welsh Guards. He is a Deputy Lieutenant for Dyfed and has been an underwriting member of Lloyds most of his working life. The estate is shown below as being the property of Mrs Colby (no. 4) and he lives at Fynone.

THE 4TH BARON MERTHYR *2000 acres*. The 4th Baron, Trevor Oswin Lewis, born in 1935, has disclaimed his peerage and baronetcy for life. Educated at Eton and Cambridge, he has been a member of the Countryside Commission since 1973 and Chairman of the Countryside Commission in Wales 1973-80. He is a Deputy Lieutenant for Pembroke and was awarded the CBE in 1983. The family are descendants of the Welsh Iron masters of the nineteenth century and he lives at Hean Castle, Saudersfoot.

Significant Institutional Landowners

1872: The Bishop of St Davids owned 4972 acres.
2001: The National Trust owns 9122 acres with 7828 acres protected.

TOP 10 IN 1872

1	Mr Charles Edward Gregg Philipps of Picton Castle, Haverfordwest	19,745 acres	with 3360 elsewhere
2	Earl of Cawdor MP of Stackpoole	17,735 acres	with 83,922 elsewhere
3	Sir Owen Henry Phillips Scourfield Bt	11,243 acres	with 2196 elsewhere
4	Mrs Colby of Fynone, Newcastle-Emlyn	6663 acres	with 2589 elsewhere
5	Lord Kensington (MP) of St Bride's, Haverfordwest	6537 acres	with 934 elsewhere
6	Mr John Frederick Lort Phillips of Lawrenny	6522 acres	
7	Mr Mark Anthony Saurin of Orielton	5752 acres	with 140 elsewhere
8	Mr William Francis Roch of Butter Hill, Haverfordwest	5665 acres	
9	Baron de Rutzen of Slebech Park, Haverfordwest	5573 acres	
10	Mr George Harries of Rickstone, Milford Haven	5173 acres	

RADNORSHIRE

(No modern equivalent. The 1872 county makes up about one third of Powys.)

	1872
Total acreage	207,394 acres
Agricultural acreage	197,024 acres
Non agricultural acreage	10,369 acres
Population	25,430
Owners of nothing at all	23,788
Total Dwellings	4925
Smallholdings: 1872 owners of less than one acre 2000 owners of 0–2ha (0–4.94 acres)	452
Landowners over one acre (1872) Landowners over 2ha (2000)	1190
Landowners over 500 acres	61
Acreage (and percentage) of county owned by owners of over 500 acres	128,241 acres (44.9%)

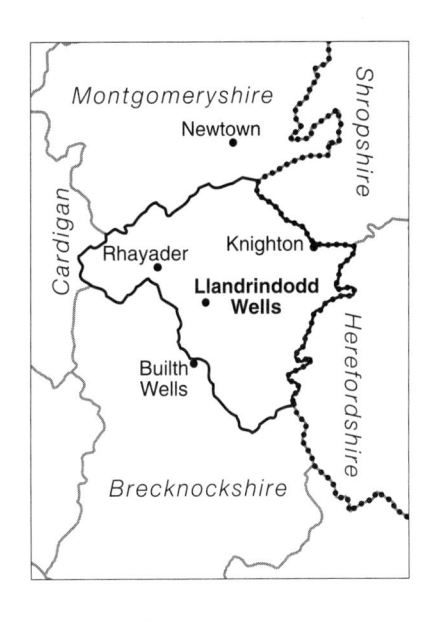

Top Landowners 2001

THE ARKWRIGHTS OF KINSHAM COURT, PRESTEIGNE, RADNOR *2000 acres in 1972*. This family were still living at the family seat when the last edition of *Burke's Landed Gentry* was completed in 1972.

TOP 10 IN 1872

1	Lord Ormathwaite MP of Newcastle Court, Radnor	12,428 acres	with 13,833 elsewhere
2	Rev Sir Gilbert Frankland Lewis Bt of Harpton Court, Kington	10,000 acres	
3	Sir Richard Green-Price Bt MP of Norton Manor, Presteigne	8774 acres	
4	Mr John Percy Chesment-Severn of Penybont, Radnor	8471 acres	with 65 elsewhere
5	Mr James Gibson-Watts of Doldowlod, Rhayader	8200 acres	with 2836 elsewhere
6	Mr Robert Baskerville Mynors of Evancoed, Kington	7000 acres	with 1041 elsewhere
7	Mr Walter De Winton of Maesllwych Castle, Hay	4955 acres	with 4945 elsewhere
8	Mrs M.M. Prickard of Dderw, Rhayader	4083 acres	
9	Mr Walter Thomas Mynors Baskerville of Clyro Court, Hay	3900 acres	with 2497 elsewhere
10	Mr Charles Coltman Rogers of Stanage Park, Knighton	3217 acres	with 2471 elsewhere

Northern Ireland

There have been almost no changes whatsoever since 1872 to the boundaries of the six counties which now make up Northern Ireland. This makes some of the comparisons very easy to establish. But the 'Troubles' have added their own small cloud to this exercise. There was a great reluctance on the part of anybody to name or indicate the location of the residual estates or of the modern landowners, for fear of potential agitation against the landowners. This is one reason why any analysis inevitably flows back to what was set out in the 1872 Return. While there is some evidence that the Land Commission established by the Imperial authorities in London in the 1880s redistributed Northern Irish land much as it did in what later became the Republic, there is a need to establish whether that process ceased at partition and to establish the economic consequences. The significant changes are the same as those which occurred in most other parts of the United Kingdom; the population has grown and most of that growth has been concentrated in urban areas around Belfast, Derry and other towns and cities.

Modern landowners

The Northern Irish Land Registry suffers from essentially the same problem as that of England and Wales. There is no accessible record of the estates which have not changed ownership and those which are in the Registry are economically inaccessible because of the cost of having to obtain each record of the many that can constitute an estate. The landowners shown are those whose existence and estates are widely and publicly known despite the reasons stated above.

An explanation of all figures included in the tables is given on p.219.

List of Northern Irish Counties included

Antrim
Armagh
Down
Fermanagh
Londonderry
Tyrone

Ireland 1872 & 2001

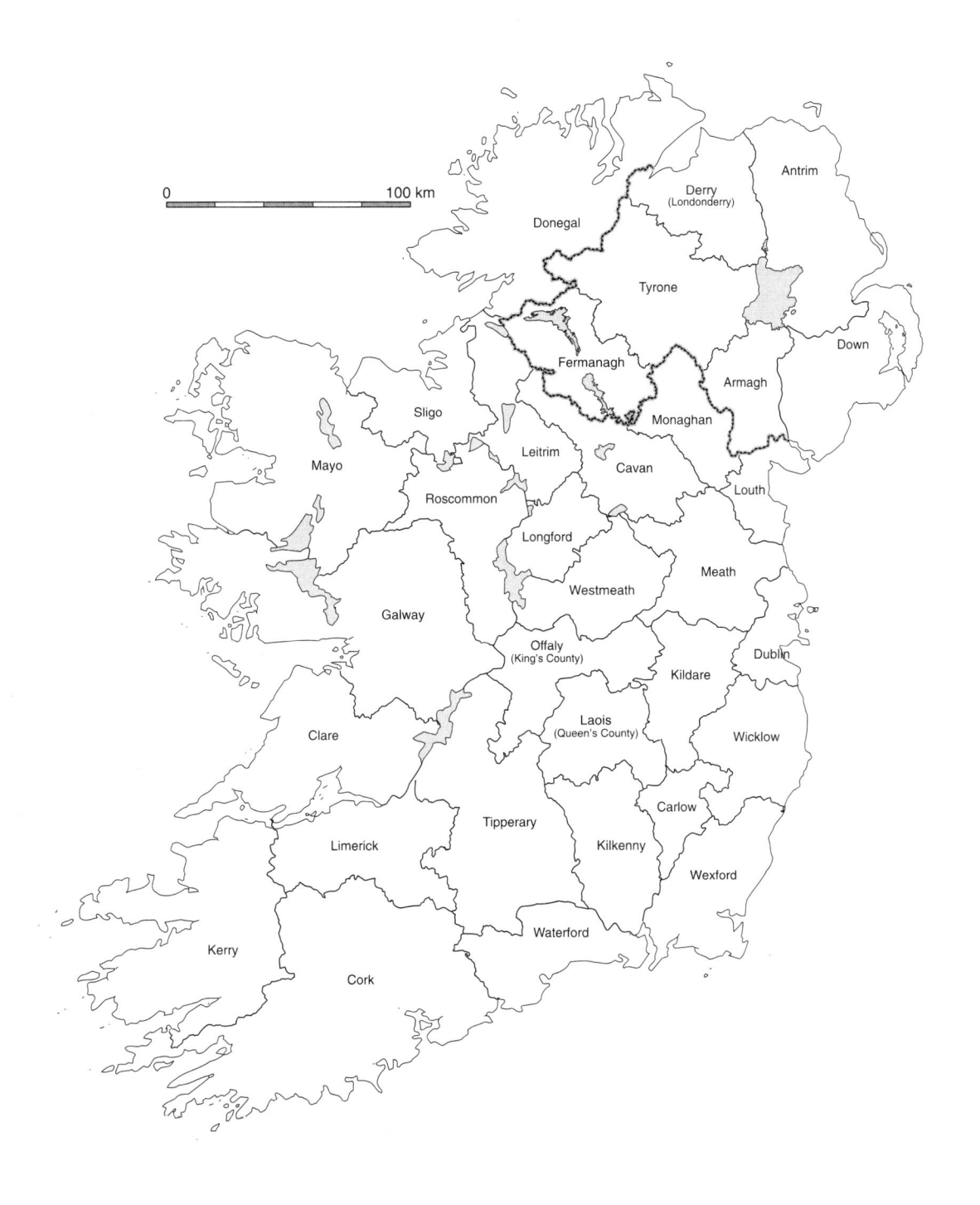

ANTRIM

	1872	2001
Total acreage	708,405 acres	715,520 acres
Agricultural acreage	637,564 acres	560,257 acres
Non agricultural acreage	70,084 acres	156,662 acres
	(excluding Belfast city)	
Population	404,070	388,081
Owners of nothing at all	398,500	169,724
Total Dwellings	71,229	168,890
Smallholdings:		
1872 owners of less than one acre	3321	
2000 owners of 0–2ha (0–4.94 acres)		154
Landowners over one acre (1872)	2249	
Landowners over 2ha (2000)		5040
Landowners over 500 acres	171	88
Acreage (and percentage) of county owned by owners of over 500 acres	413,404 acres (58.3%)	70,575 acres (9.8%)

Top Landowners 2001

THE 4TH BARON O'NEILL *15,000 acres in trust.* Raymond Arthur Clanaboy O'Neill, born in 1933 and educated at Eton, is the nephew of the former Prime Minister of Northern Ireland, the late Baron O'Neill of the Maine. The great estate shown below came to the family when the Earldom of O'Neill became extinct in 1855. The family name was Chichester, huge landowners in both Devon and Northern Ireland. Baron O'Neill is Lord Lieutenant of the county and still farms extensively, for which he was trained at the Royal College of Agriculture at Cirencester. His heir, Shane, was born in 1965. The original O'Neill family holders of the title were the second oldest recorded family in Ireland, or indeed the British Isles. According to *Burke's Peerage and Gentry* in 1896, 'Hugh O'Neill, Prince of Tir Owen, descended from Niall the Great, King of Ireland in AD 388.' There follows a slight gap before we catch up with the first mentioned Hugh O'Neill. 'Hugh Dubh O'Neill was elected King of Ulster in 1230, leaving a son Domhnel Oge whose son Hugh Boy O'Neill or Yellow Hugh, was King of Ulster in 1260. He recovered from the English the territories in the counties of Antrim and Down called Clan-aedh-buidh or Clanaboy, and had his chief seat at Edenduffcarrig, now called Shane's Castle.' The family seat and home remains Shane's Castle.

THE 9TH EARL OF ANTRIM *7500 acres in trust.* Alexander Randal Mark McDonnell was born in 1935 and retains a home on the family estate at Glenarm. He was educated at Downside and Oxford, and is Keeper of Conservation at the Tate Gallery in London. He was a director of Ulster TV. His son, Randal, born in 1967, lives at the family home, Glenarm Castle, and runs the estate. The estimate above, like that of the O'Neill estate, is believed to be a serious underestimate.

DOBBS FAMILY AT CASTLE DOBBS CARRICKFERGUS *5000 acres.* The Dobbs family of Castle Dobbs, Carrickfergus, appear in Bateman, credited with 5060 acres, all of which they are believed to have retained. The heir to the estate, Richard Francis Dobbs, married Lady Jane Alexander in 1990. They were divorced in 1999. She is a sister of the Earl of Caledon, a landowner in Tyrone (see Tyrone p.325).

Significant Institutional Landowners

1872: The Church of Ireland owned 634 acres. The railway companies owned 1021 acres. The Moravians at Gracehill owned 351 acres.
2001: The National Trust owns 5191 acres. The Forestry Service owns 32,730 acres.

TOP 10 IN 1872

1	Rev Lord O'Neill of Shane's Castle, Antrim	65,919 acres	
2	Sir Richard Wallace Bt MP of Antrim Castle, Co Antrim	58,365 acres	with 13,942 elsewhere
3	Earl of Antrim of Glenarm Castle, Antrim	34,292 acres	with 112 elsewhere
4	Rev Mr Arthur Hercules Pakenham of Longford Lodge, Crumlin	14,629 acres	
5	Marquess of Donegall (MP) of Grosvenor Sq, London and The Castle, Belfast	14,617 acres	with 8379 elsewhere
6	Lord Herbert Lionel Vane-Tempest of Co Antrim	13,781 acres	
7	Mr Carthenac George Macartney of Lisanoure Castle	12,532 acres	with 586 elsewhere
8	General the Viscount Templetown MP of Castle Upton, Templepatrick, Belfast	11,924 acres	with 12,845 elsewhere
9	Viscount Massereene and Ferrard of Oriel Temple, Co Louth	11,777 acres	with 9247 elsewhere
10	Mr William Agnew of Kilwaughter, Larne	9770 acres	

ARMAGH

	1872	2001
Total acreage	309,561 acres	309,760 acres
Agricultural acreage	278,604 acres	255,380 acres
Non agricultural acreage	30,956 acres	54,380 acres
Population	179,221	212,083
Owners of nothing at all	176,754	127,583
Total Dwellings	34,429	65,000
Smallholdings: 1872 owners of less than one acre 2000 owners of 0–2ha (0–4.94 acres)	925	159
Landowners over one acre (1872) Landowners over 2ha (2000)	1542	4348
Landowners over 500 acres	68	3
Acreage (and percentage) of county owned by owners of over 500 acres	123,141 acres (39.7%)	1645 acres (0.53%)

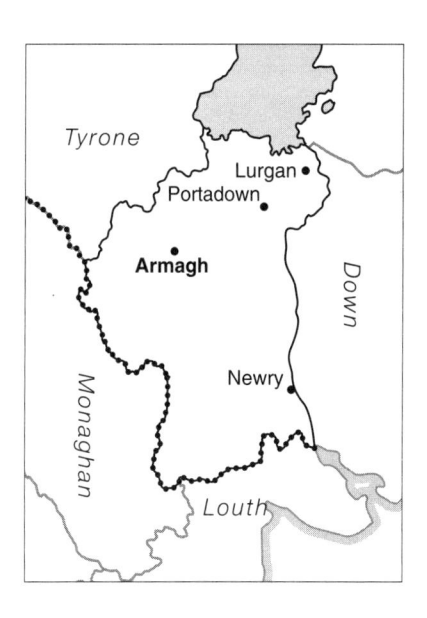

Top Landowners 2001

THE 7TH EARL OF GOSFORD *3000 acres in settled estate trust. No. 4 in 1872.* Charles Acheson Sparrow, born in 1942, trained as an artist at the Royal Academy schools. The family seat is at Gosford Castle in Markethill but the earl gives his address in *Debrett's* as the House of Lords where he lost his seat in 1999. He did not attend on any day in the final year before reform. He was married in 1983 to Lynette Redmond from Sydney, Australia. Local sources say that the estate is still run for a family trust.

THE 7TH EARL OF CALEDON *2000 acres with 7400 in Tyrone.* Nicholas James Alexander, born in 1955, is Lord Lieutenant of the county and has a landholding of about 2000 acres at Caledon House, in Caledon, Armagh. The family home is at Caledon Castle in Tyrone, where most of the estate is concentrated. Educated at the Jesuit school of Stonyhurst in England, his heir is Viscount Alexander, born in 1990.

Where they are now:
EARL OF CHARLEMONT, now the 14th Viscount. The earldom became extinct in 1892, but the family remained active in Northern Ireland until after World War Two. The viscount lives in Canada.

Significant Institutional Landowners

1872: The Church of Ireland owned 8548 acres.
2001: The Forestry Commission owns 8146 acres. The National Trust owns 580 acres.

TOP 10 IN 1872

1	Earl of Charlemont (MP) of The Moy, Charlemont	20,695 acres	with 6123 elsewhere
2	Lord Lurgan of Brownlow House, Lurgan	15,166 acres	with 110 elsewhere
3	Duke of Manchester (MP) The Castle, Tandragee and Kimbolton, Herts	12,298 acres	with 15,014 elsewhere
4	Earl of Gosford of The Castle, Markethill	12,177 acres	with 6417 elsewhere
5	Mr Francis Robert Cope of Loughall	9367 acres	
6	Mr Maxwell Charles Close MP of Drumbangher, Newry	9087 acres	with 3678 elsewhere
7	Mr Granville Henry Jackson Alexander of Forkhill, Dundalk	8324 acres	
8	Mr Mark Seton Synnot of Ballymower House, Newtownhamilton	7321 acres	
9	Mr Robert John Macgeough of Silverbridge, Newtownhamilton	7213 acres	
10	Mrs Bacon of The Castle, Richill	6878 acres	

DOWN

	1872	2001
Total acreage	608,214 acres	604,800 acres
Agricultural acreage	547,392 acres	456,638 acres
Non agricultural acreage	60,821 acres	148,162 acres
Population	293,449	299,431
Owners of nothing at all	289,844	108,916
Total Dwellings	58,343	146,550
Smallholdings: 1872 owners of less than one acre	1460	
2000 owners of 0–2ha (0–4.94 acres)		191
Landowners over one acre (1872)	2145	
Landowners over 2ha (2000)		5850
Landowners over 500 acres	141	41
Acreage (and percentage) of county owned by owners of over 500 acres	263,106 acres (43.2%)	30,808 acres (5.0%)

Top Landowners 2001

THE 6TH EARL OF KILMOREY *12,000 acres. No. 2 in 1872.* The Rt Hon Sir Richard Needham, MP for Chippenham and Wiltshire North and a minister in both the Thatcher and Major governments (1985–1995) was born in 1942 and educated at Eton. He did not use his title and did not sit in the House of Lords as he had no UK peerage. He is the Hereditary Abbot of the exempt jurisdiction of Newry and Mourne and his heir Robert, born in 1966, is styled Viscount Newry and Mourne. The Kilmorey estate escaped the Land Commission and was placed in trust in the 1930s. The personal connection with Northern Ireland ended with the death of the 4th Earl in 1961. He was Vice Admiral of Ulster and Lord Lieutenant of Co Down.

THE BLACKWOOD FAMILY OF CLANDEBOYE *10,000 acres in trust.* The earldom, later the Marquessate, of Dufferin and Ava became extinct in 1988 with the death of the 5th Marquess. His wife, the Dowager Marchioness Serena Belinda (Lindy), is a Guinness heiress and still maintains a residence at the family seat at Clandeboye. Perdita Maureen Blackwood, a daughter of the 4th Marquess, runs a stud farm on the estate.

THE 8TH VISCOUNT BANGOR *5000 acres in trust.* William Maxwell David Ward, born in 1948, now lives in London. Castle Ward, the family seat, is with the National Trust, which acquired it from the Ulster Government which had in turn accepted it in lieu of death duties on the estate of the 6th Viscount.

Where they are now:
THE 8TH MARQUESS OF DOWNSHIRE, Arthur Robin Hill was born in 1929 and educated at Eton. He is the Hereditary Constable of Hillsborough Fort and sat in the House of Lords until evicted in 1999 as the Earl of Hillsborough. He took Conservative whip in the Lords and was a regular attender, signing in 39 times in the last session (1996/97) before the Blair government arrived and reform began. He did not retain a seat despite his attendance record. Twice widowed, his first wife Juliet Weld-Forester, who died in 1986, was a daughter of the Shropshire landowner, the 7th Baron Forester. His heir is the Earl of Hillsborough, born in 1959. The family farm a 2000-acre estate at Ripon in Yorkshire and still retain a residence in Northern Ireland.

Significant Institutional Landowners

1872: The trustees of the Kilmorey estate, of Chertsey in Surrey, owned 37,457 acres. The Church owned 5334 acres.
2001: The National Trust owns 13,285 acres. The Forestry Commission owns 12,710 acres.

TOP 10 IN 1872

1	Marquess of Downshire of The Castle, Hillsborough	78,051	acres	with 42,138 elsewhere
2	Earl of Kilmorey, Mourne Park, Newry	40,902	acres	with 11,510 elsewhere
3	Earl of Annesley (MP) of Castlewellan	24,221	acres	with 26,839 elsewhere
4	Marquess of Londonderry (MP) Mountstewart, Newtownards	23,554	acres	with 26,769 elsewhere
5	Mr Richard William Blackwood Ker of Montalto, Ballynahinch	20,544	acres	
6	Colonel William Brownlow Forde MP of Seaforde	20,106	acres	
7	Earl Dufferin (and Ava) of Clandeboy, Bangor	18,238	acres	
8	Mr John Mulholland MP of Ballywalter Park, Belfast	13,506	acres	with 1182 elsewhere
9	Hon Mr Robert Henry Meade of Co Down	13,492	acres	
10	Mr Robert Narcissus Batt of Purdysburn, Belfast	12,010	acres	

FERMANAGH

	1872	2001
Total acreage	408,942 acres	414,080 acres
Agricultural acreage	368,047 acres	321,153 acres
Non agricultural acreage	40,895 acres	92,927 acres
Population	92,688	54,446
Owners of nothing at all	91,991	28,394
Total Dwellings	17,516	20,040
Smallholdings: 1872 owners of less than one acre	130	
2000 owners of 0–2ha (0–4.94 acres)		36
Landowners over one acre (1872)	567	
Landowners over 2ha (2000)		3525
Landowners over 500 acres	77	27
Acreage (and percentage) of county owned by owners of over 500 acres	201,321 acres (54.6%)	18,117 acres (4.3%)

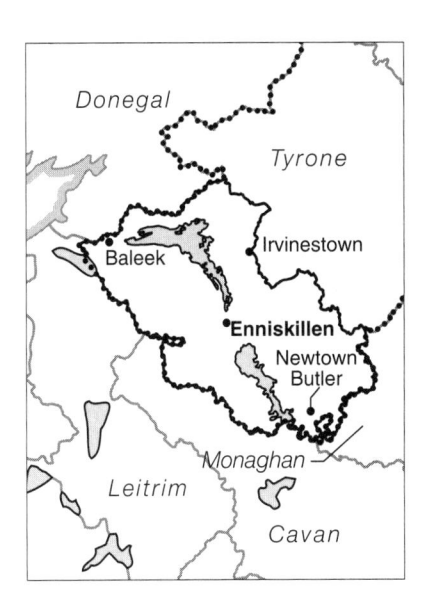

Top Landowners 2001

THE 6TH EARL OF ERNE *15,000 acres. No. 2 in 1872.* Henry George Victor John Crighton, the 6th Earl, was born in 1937 and was a page of honour to Queen Elizabeth just after her coronation in 1952. Educated at Eton, he was an officer in the North Irish Horse, a TA unit. The family seat is Crom Castle. Twice married, he is Lord Lieutenant of the county. The family remain one of the largest landowners in Northern Ireland. He attended the House of Lords as a Conservative. He did not retain his seat despite attending on 40 of the 79 sitting days in 1997–1998 session.

THE 8TH EARL OF BELMORE *6500 acres.* John Armar Lowrey-Corry, born in 1951, still lives on the family estate, although the family home, Castle Coole, was donated to the National Trust in 1951. The furniture in the house belongs to the present earl, who is married to a daughter of the 6th Earl of Clanwilliam, a landowning family from Co Down who now live in Wilts.

THE 7TH EARL OF ENNISKILLEN *5000 acres in trust. No. 3 in 1872.* Andrew John Galbraith Cole, the 7th Earl, born in 1942, was educated at Eton and was a captain in the Irish Guards. His father gave the family home, the beautiful Florence Court, to the National Trust in 1954, with an endowment. The family lands survived the Land Commission to an extent, and are retained in trust for the family. The present earl gives his address as the House of Lords but lost his seat in 1999 in the Blair reforms. He had attended just 10 times in the 79 days of the 1997–8 session.

THE GROSVENOR/ELY FAMILY *5000 acres. No. 1 in 1872.* The mother of the present Duke of Westminster, the Dowager Duchess, was killed in a car accident near the family home of Ely Court in 1987. Most of the family land, which was still over 20,000 acres, was sold to the tenants. Local sources say that the family retained some land. The 8th Marquess of Ely, born in 1913, whose family name is Tottenham, and whose family owned huge tracts of Ireland in the 1872 Return, was a headmaster in Canada.

Significant Institutional Landowners

1872: The Church of Ireland owned 10,357 acres. The Commissioners of Education owned 5656 acres.
2001: The National Trust owns 2380 acres. The Forestry Commission owns 58,599 acres.

TOP 10 IN 1872

1	Marquess of Ely of Ely Lodge, Enniskillen	34,879 acres	with 14,113 elsewhere
2	Earl of Erne of Crom Castle	31,389 acres	with 8976 elsewhere
3	Earl of Enniskillen (MP) of Florence Court, Enniskillen	29,635 acres	with 596 elsewhere
4	Sir Victor Brooke Bt of Colebrooke Park, Brookboro	27,994 acres	
5	Mr William Humphrys Archdale MP of Castle Archdale, Enniskillen (Qualified in Bateman down to 5627 acres, but Archdale still the freeholder of the 27,410 acres)	27,410 acres	
6	Rev Mr John Grey Porter of Belleisle, Lisbellaw	11,880 acres	
7	Mr John Gerard Irvine of Killadeas, Enniskillen	11,602 acres	with 2512 elsewhere
8	Mr John Madden of Roslea Manor, Roslea	10,498 acres	with 628 elsewhere
9	Mr Hugh Montgomery De Fellenberg of Fivemiletown	7996 acres	
10	Mr Richard Hall of Park Lane, London and Inismore, Lisbellow	6540 acres	with 2418 elsewhere

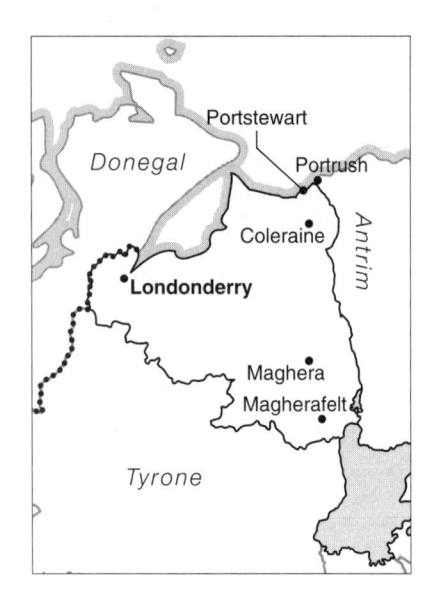

LONDONDERRY/DERRY

	1872	2001
Total acreage	511,838 acres	512,640 acres
Agricultural acreage	460,654 acres	420,072 acres
Non agricultural acreage	51,183 acres	92,372 acres
Population	179,932	220,968
Owners of nothing at all	177,754	115,681
Total Dwellings	32,601	80,990
Smallholdings: 1872 owners of less than one acre 2000 owners of 0–2ha (0–4.94 acres)	798	86
Landowners over one acre (1872) Landowners over 2ha (2000)	1380	3902
Landowners over 500 acres	213	71
Acreage (and percentage) of county owned by owners of over 500 acres	389,010 acres (76%)	54,869 acres (10.7%)

Top Landowners 2001
None of record.

Significant Institutional Landowners
1872: The Church Commissioners owned 13,413 acres. The Drapers Livery Company owned 27,025 acres. The Fishmongers Livery Company owned 20,509 acres. The Grocers Livery Company owned 11,638 acres. The Mercers Livery Company owned 21,241 acres. The Salters Livery Company owned 19,445 acres. The Skinners Livery Company owned 34,772 acres. The Honourable Irish Society owned 6075 acres.
2001: The National Trust owns 451 acres. The Forestry Commission owns 29,414 acres.

TOP 10 IN 1872

1	Sir Henry Hervey Bruce Bt MP of Downhill, Coleraine	20,801 acres	with 713 elsewhere
2	Mr Thomas Richardson of Somerset, Coleraine	18,159 acres	
3	Mr Stewart C. Bruce, The Cedars, Putney, London	13,651 acres	
4	Mr Connoly Thomas McCausland of Dreenagh, Newtown-Limavady	12,886 acres	with 4799 elsewhere
5	Mr John Barre Beresford of Ashbrook	10,420 acres	with 2453 elsewhere
6	Mr Robert Alexander Ogilby of Ardnargle, Newtown-Limavady	9735 acres	
7	Dowager Lady Charlotte Garvagh of Garvagh House, Garvagh	8427 acres	with 6979 elsewhere
8	Lord Charles Beresford (Not in Bateman for Derry)	7946 acres	
9	Earl of Stafford MP of London (Not in Bateman)	7647 acres	
10	Miss Catherine Downing Nesbitt and Count Susi. Of Leixlip, Co Dublin	5638 acres	with 6553 elsewhere

TYRONE

	1872	2001
Total acreage	775,285 acres	775,040 acres
Agricultural acreage	697,756 acres	620,776 acres
Non agricultural acreage	77,528 acres	145,986 acres
Population	215,668	158,384
Owners of nothing at all	212,881	85,662
Total Dwellings	41,263	55,940
Smallholdings: 1872 owners of less than one acre	1070	
2000 owners of 0–2ha (0–4.94 acres)		135
Landowners over one acre (1872)	1717	
Landowners over 2ha (2000)		7072
Landowners over 500 acres	108	55
Acreage (and percentage) of county owned by owners of over 500 acres	401,236 acres (51.7%)	42,854 acres (5.5%)

Top Landowners 2001

THE 5TH DUKE OF ABERCORN *15,000 acres in trust. No. 1 in 1872.* James Hamilton, born in 1934, was educated at Eton and then at the Royal Agricultural College at Cirencester to prepare him for his role as heir to a significant part of the estates of 1872 given below. He is Lord Lieutenant of the county, a former Unionist MP and former President of the Building Societies Association. He is a cousin of the Queen and is married to the elder sister of the Duchess of Westminster. The entire family, including his son and heir the Marquess of Hamilton, live in the area.

THE 7TH EARL OF CALEDON *7400 acres. No. 3 in 1872.* See Armagh (p.321).

THE 8TH EARL OF CASTLE STEWART *3500 acres in trust. No. 2 in 1872.* Arthur Patrick Avondale Stuart, born in 1928, was educated at Eton, Cambridge and was a Lieutenant in the Scots Guards. He farms in Somerset, and his heir, Viscount Stuart, farms in Devon. The settled estates at Stuart Hall are still recorded in the county, but they may have been sold. His father was a major in the Machine Gun Corps and was MP for Harborough in Leicester.

Significant Institutional Landowners

1872: The Church of Ireland had 28,002 acres.
2001: The Forestry Commission has 45,026 acres.

TOP 10 IN 1872

1	Duke of Abercorn. Lord Lieutenant of Ireland (Twice) Of Baronscourt, Newtownstewart	60,000 acres	with 18,662 elsewhere
2	Earl of Castlestuart of Stuart Hall, Stuartstown	32,615 acres	with 2260 elsewhere
3	Earl of Caledon of Caledon House, Caledon	29,236 acres	with 4824 elsewhere
4	Sir John Marcus Stewart Bt Ballygawley House, Ballygawley	27,905 acres	with 629 elsewhere
5	Major Arthur William Cole-Hamilton of Beltrim, Gortin, Newtownstewart	16,811 acres	
6	Sir William Samuel McMahon Bt of Fecarry House, Omagh	16,326 acres	with 4703 elsewhere
7	Earl of Belmore of Castle Coole, Enniskillen	14,521 acres	with 5041 elsewhere
8	Mr Thomas Arthur Hope of Wavertree, Lancs	14,006 acres	with 2685 elsewhere
9	Mrs Louisa Elizabeth De Bille of Slaghtfreedan, Cookstown	12,680 acres	
10	Lord Dorchester of Greywell Hall, Hants, England	12,607 acres	with 1914 elsewhere

The Republic of Ireland

The 26 counties of the Irish Republic, created in 1922 as a Free State and as a full Republic in 1949, have boundaries almost identical in every respect to those of 1872. This enables an extraordinary picture to emerge in two respects. The first is the almost total lack of estates over 500 acres in modern Ireland. This is despite the shrinking of the farming community from about 450,000 farms shortly after independence, to about 145,000 farms today (and still falling fast, by 7% in 2000/1). It pays homage to the operation of a partially free market in land, but one which has evolved naturally from a significant redistribution via the Land Commission, and which does not remain bottlenecked by huge estates protected by biased statutes. It may be a major contributor to Ireland's decade of 10% per annum growth in GDP. The other picture is even more startling. Just by looking at the population figures in 1872 and now, with but a few exceptions, the terrible shadow of the famine can still be seen in huge, fertile but under-populated areas like Laois, Offaly, Mayo, Sligo and Donegal. The 1872 record was made more than a quarter of a century after the famine, but the underlying cause of the destruction invoked by the loss of the staple food, the potato, is there for all to see. Over 98% of the rapidly declining population owned nothing at all. They were strangers in their own land, a land owned by strangers. In some counties the population is declining still and has never recovered.

Modern landowners

Ireland has both a Land Registry and a Registry of Deeds, both now being computerised. In practice all land in Ireland is in one or the other institution. Having said that, the problem that defeats an attempt to extract the identity and size of any estate in England or Scotland applies here too, and the cost of assembling an estate's full records is all but prohibitive to an outsider. In stark contrast to the situation in the United Kingdom, however, there are almost no large estates in modern Ireland. Therefore, the overall portrait of large landowners is radically different to that displayed in the county records for England, Wales, Scotland and Northern Ireland. Those large landowners which do remain, particularly aristocrats, have been mostly identified. Below these, however, the distinction between significant land holdings of, say 500 acres, and large farms, becomes blurred. For further details on the pattern of landownership and farming in the Republic, see chapter 14.

An explanation of all figures included in the tables is given on p.219.

List of counties in the Republic of Ireland included
Carlow
Cavan
Clare
Cork

Donegal
Dublin
Galway
Kerry
Kildare
Kilkenny
Laois (Queens)
Leitrim
Limerick
Longford
Louth
Mayo
Meath
Monaghan
Offaly (Kings)
Roscommon
Sligo
Tipperary
Waterford
Westmeath
Wexford
Wicklow

Ireland 1872 & 2001

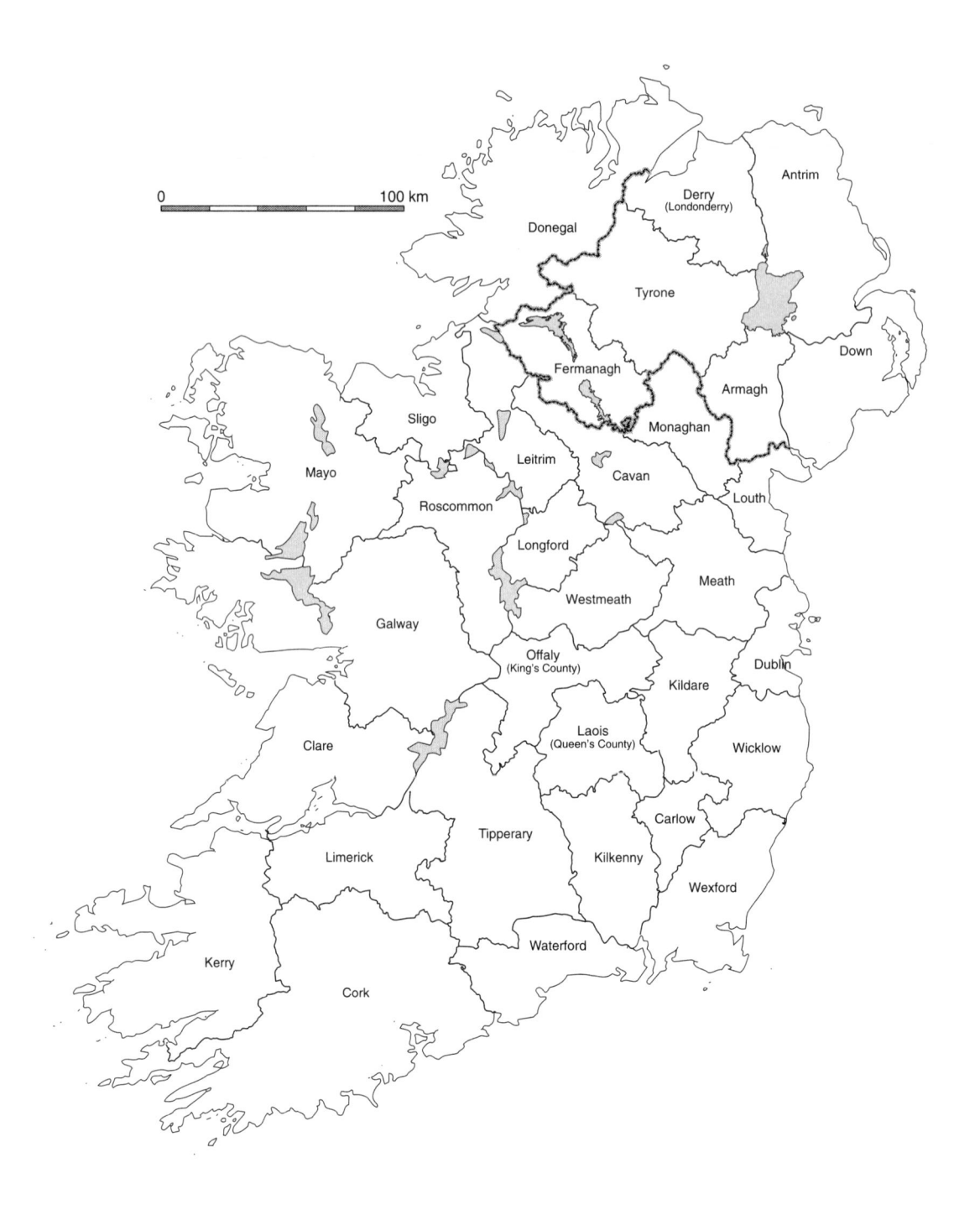

CARLOW

	1872	2001
Total acreage	221,572 acres	221,440 acres
Agricultural acreage	199,414 acres	192,530 acres
Non agricultural acreage	21,572 acres	28,910 acres
Population	51,650	40,946
Owners of nothing at all	50,074	21,110
Total Dwellings	9701	11,135
Smallholdings: 1872 owners of less than one acre	995	
2000 owners of 0–2ha (0–4.94 acres)		40
Landowners over one acre (1872)	581	
Landowners over 2ha (2000)		2090
Landowners over 500 acres	41	7
Acreage (and percentage) of county owned by owners of over 500 acres	134,100 acres (60.5%)	

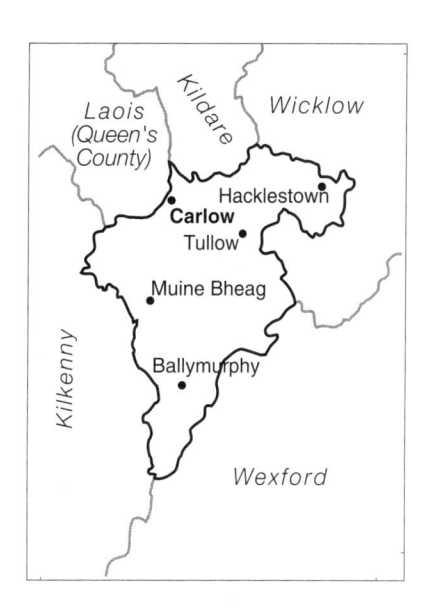

Top Landowners 2001

Carlow is the home of a number of religious orders, most with some landholdings. It has also become a favourite country retreat for many Dubliners, especially wealthy ones. There are only seven farms over five hundred acres, a comparatively high number for so small a county, but horse-breeding and -training is of growing importance in the county. The population is fast approaching its 1872 level.

WILLIAM MULLINS. He is the six-times champion amateur rider in Ireland, and his stud at Closutton near Muine Bheag has produced five winners at the Cheltenham race week over the years. He comes from a horse-breeding family and was assistant to his father Pat Mullins, a well-known trainer, in the 1980s. He is the recent Chairman of the Irish Racehorse Trainers Association.

Where they are now:
THE 11TH EARL OF BESSBOROUGH (no. 3 in 1872), born in 1912, lives in Wiltshire. Widowed, remarried, divorced and remarried he has five sons and two daughters.

THE 9TH EARL OF COURTOWN (no. 5 in 1872), born in 1954, educated at Eton, was a government whip in the last days of the Major government (1995–1997). He attended on 75 of the 79 days that the Lords sat in the year before reform (1997–1998). He farms in Gloucester.

SIR RICHARD BUTLER (no. 6 in 1872), the 12th Baronet, born in 1940 was educated at Eton and New York University and is an accountant in England.

Significant Institutional Landowners

1872: The Bishop of Ossory owned 3769 acres. The Court of Chancery owned 2617 acres.
2001: Coillte owns 8922 acres.

TOP 10 IN 1872

1	Rt Hon Mr Henry Bruen MP of Oak Park	16,477 acres	with 7140 elsewhere
2	Mr Arthur McMurrough Kavanagh MP of Borris House	16,051 acres	with 12,974 elsewhere
3	Earl of Bessborough of Bessborough House, Piltown, Kilkenny	10,578 acres	with 24,862 elsewhere
4	Mr Denis Robert Pack-Beresford of Fenagh House, Bagnalstown	7679 acres	
5	Earl of Courtown of Courtown House, Gorey	7395 acres	
6	Sir Thomas Butler Bt of Ballin Temple, Tullow	6538 acres	
7	Mr William Fitz-William Burton of Burton Hall, Carlow	5964 acres	with 1406 elsewhere
8	Mr Dare Hall of Newtownbarry	5627 acres	
9	Mr Philip Jocelyn Newton of Dunleckeny, Bagnalstown	5134 acres	
10	Mr William Duckett of Duckett's Grove, Carlow	4923 acres	with 6723 elsewhere

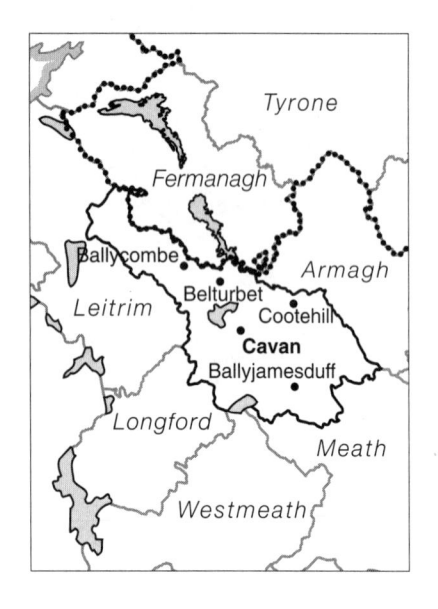

CAVAN

	1872	2001
Total acreage	454,048 acres	467,200 acres
Agricultural acreage	408,643 acres	318,902 acres
Non agricultural acreage	45,400 acres	148,298 acres
Population	140,555	52,796
Owners of nothing at all	139,511	24,870
Total Dwellings	26,372	15,446
Smallholdings: 1872 owners of less than one acre 2000 owners of 0–2ha (0–4.94 acres)	328	46
Landowners over one acre (1872) Landowners over 2ha (2000)	716	6673
Landowners over 500 acres	87	3
Acreage (and percentage) of county owned by owners of over 500 acres	230,160 acres (56.3%)	

Top Landowners 2001

THE LATE 12TH LORD FARNHAM *3000 acres in trust.* Barry Owen Somerset Maxwell, born in 1931, died in 2001 without a direct male heir. Eton and Harvard educated, he was prominent in the City of London and chaired Brown Shipley, the merchant bank. His wife has been a Lady of the Bedchamber to Queen Elizabeth II since 1987.

BUDDY KIERNAN, 70. *2000 acres.* Unusually, Kiernan was educated first in New York and then returned to Ireland starting a series of businesses in and around his native Cavan. He farms the largest pig unit in Northern Europe producing over 300,000 animals annually. His landholdings are conservatively put at 2000 acres and are not confined to Cavan but are scattered across five other counties, including Longford, Sligo, Tipperary and Westmeath. He chaired the County Council, and is Chairman of the trustees of the Fine Gael Party.

MR AND MRS BRIAN MILLS *900 acres.* The owners of the house (Coothill) and residual estate of the Cootes at Bellamont forest. In 1872 the owner was Richard Coote, who had 5321 acres, stated in the Returns, but not Bateman.

Where they are now:
THE 10TH EARL OF ANNESLEY was born in 1924 and succeeded to the title in 1979. Educated at Strode's Grammar school in Egham, Surrey, he has four daughters all living in the local area. He served in the Royal Navy and did not sit in the Lords as his is an Irish title.

THE 6TH MARQUESS OF HEADFORT, Thomas Geoffrey Charles Taylour, was born in 1932 and lives in the Philippines with an additional address in the Isle of Man. A professional pilot, he was educated at Stowe and Cambridge but spent most of his life in the Far East. He retains an Irish link through his membership of the Kildare St Club. His heir is the Earl of Bective who lives in Mayfair, London. He sat in the Lords as Baron Kenlis but was ejected with the other hereditaries in 1999. He was a cross-bencher who attended once in 1997–1998.

Significant Institutional Landowners

1872: The Church of Ireland owned 10,751 acres.
2001: Coillte owns 15,989 acres.

TOP 10 IN 1872

1	Lord Farnham of Farnham Co Cavan (MP)	25,920	acres	
2	Earl of Annesley (MP)	24,221	acres	with 26,839 elsewhere
3	Marquess of Headfort of Headfort House, Kells (MP)	14,220	acres	with 28,503 elsewhere
4	Mr Edward Saunderson of Castle Saunderson Belturbet MP	12,362	acres	
5	Miss Harriett Parker of Devon (not in Bateman)	10,540	acres	
6	Mr Alexander Nesbitt of Lismore	9735	acres	
7	Mr Robert James Burrowes of Stradone House	9572	acres	
8	Lady Lisgar and Sir Francis Turville of Lisgar House, Baillieborough	8924	acres	
9	Lord Charles Beresford of Curraghmore, Waterford	8817	acres	with 2243 elsewhere
10	Mr Mervyn Pratt of Cabra Castle, Kingscourt	8095	acres	with 18,969 elsewhere

CLARE

	1872	2001
Total acreage	759,775 acres	807,680 acres
Agricultural acreage	683,797 acres	533,328 acres
Non agricultural acreage	75,975 acres	274,352 acres
Population	147,864	90,918
Owners of nothing at all	146,839	44,585
Total Dwellings	26,069	26118
Smallholdings: 1872 owners of less than one acre	243	
2000 owners of 0–2ha (0–4.94 acres)		37
Landowners over one acre (1872)	782	
Landowners over 2ha (2000)		8192
Landowners over 500 acres	41	25
Acreage (and percentage) of county owned by owners of over 500 acres	516,879 acres (68%)	

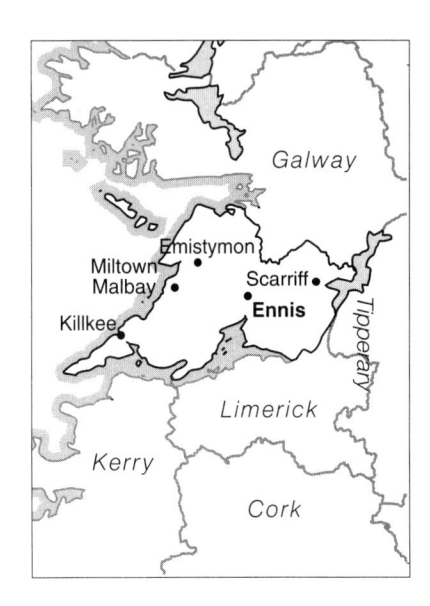

Top Landowners 2001

THE 18TH BARON INCHQUIN. Conor O'Brien, who is the Chief of the name O'Brien, was born in 1943 and educated at Eton followed by a stint in the 14th/20th Hussars, a smart cavalry regiment. His title is Irish and he did not sit in the House of Lords. He married Helen O'Farrell, daughter of a landowner in Longford in 1988 and he has two daughters. The family still retain land in County Clare around Dromoland, where the family seat stands.

IEVERS FAMILY OF MOUNT IEVERS COURT *500 acres*. This is the small estate surrounding a notable house which survived the War of Independence intact. It was still owned by the Ievers family in the 1970s.

Where they are now:

BARON LECONFIELD, who also holds the title Baron Egremont. Max Henry Scawen Wyndham, born in 1948 is the 7th Baron Leconfield and the 2nd Baron Egremont and is best known as the author Max Egremont. He has two homes, Petworth House in West Sussex which has been donated to the National Trust and Cockermouth Castle in Cumbria. He is still reckoned to be the owner of about 22,000 acres in Cumbria and Sussex and is the UK's 112th largest landowner. He was educated at Eton and Oxford and is a trustee of the British Museum and sits on other public bodies. His heir is the Hon. George Wyndham born in 1983. He lost his seat in the Lords in 1999, having been an infrequent attender who took the Tory whip.

THE 7TH MARQUESS OF CONYNGHAM. See County Meath and the Earl and Countess of Mount Charles.

Significant Institutional Landowner

Coillte owns 50,531 acres.

TOP 10 IN 1872

1	Lord Leconfield MP of Petworth House Sussex	37,292 acres	with 72,643 elsewhere
2	Major General the Marquess of Conyngham of Bifrons, Canterbury, Kent	27,613 acres	with 139,097 elsewhere
3	Lord Inchiquin of Dromoland, Newmarket-on-Fergus	20,321 acres	
4	Colonel Hector Stewart Vandeleur of Kilrush	19,790 acres	with 416 elsewhere
5	Mr Henry Valentine Macnamara of Doolin, Ennis	15,246 acres	
6	Sir Augustine Fitzgerald Bt of Carrigoran, Ennis	14,915 acres	with 1436 elsewhere
7	Mr Horace Stafford O'Brien of Blatherwycke Park, Wansford, England	11,630 acres	with 15,764 elsewhere
8	The Misses Anna, Sophia & Henrietta Butler of Castlecrine	11,389 acres	
9	Mr Arthur Francis of Dublin	10,534 acres	
10	Major William Wills Moloney of Kiltanon, Tulla	10,095 acres	

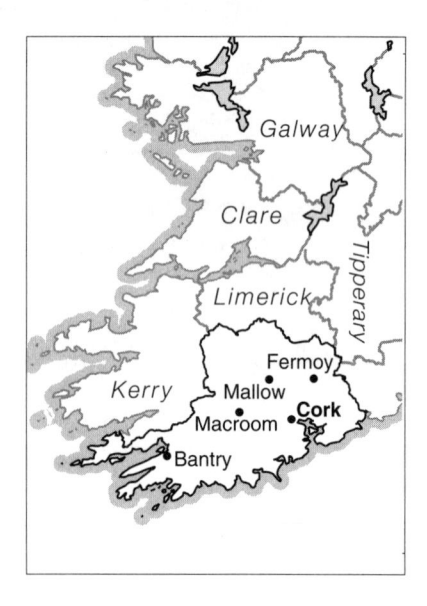

CORK

	1872	2001
Total acreage	1,822,739 acres	1,841,920 acres
Agricultural acreage	1,640,465 acres	1,357,619 acres
Non agricultural acreage	182,273 acres	484,301 acres
Population	438,434	412,623
Owners of nothing at all	432,545	269,019
Total Dwellings	74,399	80,226
Smallholdings: 1872 owners of less than one acre	3091	
2000 owners of 0–2ha (0–4.94 acres)		201
Landowners over one acre (1872)	2798	
Landowners over 2ha (2000)		17,097
Landowners over 500 acres	189	82
Acreage (and percentage) of county owned by owners of over 500 acres	675,005 acres (37%)	

Top Landowners 2001

THE SHELSWELL-WHITE FAMILY *2500 acres (woodland)*. This family are the descendants of the Earl of Bantry, the largest Cork landowner in 1872. The house is beautifully preserved and was the first country house opened to the public in the Irish Republic. The title is long extinct.

LIAM CASHMAN is the owner of the Rathbarry Stud at Fermoy founded by his father in 1935. In addition to the stud there is an extensive farm. Cashman is a long-term member of the now-thriving Irish bloodstock industry, and lists his hobbies as horseracing and GAA sports. Acreage not known. He is married with one son and one daughter.

MICHAEL MURPHY is reckoned to be one of the largest dairy farmers in this huge county and also in the country. He was educated at the Christian Brothers school in Cork and has an MBA from Cork University. Unusually he did not enter farming until he was 25 and served a stint in the Norwegian Merchant Navy before that. He is now thought to own over 1000 acres. He is married with two sons and two daughters.

RORY O'BRIEN, is a major pig-breeder at Killicane near Mitchelstown under the name Rory and Monica Pig Enterprises. In addition they own the Clonmel Arms Hotel, a feedstock company and a construction company. He is the chairman of the Industrial Committee of the Irish Farmers Association and lists his hobbies as hunting and racing.

LOIS, COUNTESS OF BANDON AND LADY JENNIFER JANE BERNARD. The Countess, who is Australian, still lives at the ancestral home of the Bernard family at Castle Bernard near Bandon with her daughter. The title became extinct when the 5th Earl died in 1979. He was Air Chief Marshall of the Royal Air Force, one of three Irishmen to hold that position since World War Two. He held the Distinguished Flying Cross of the USAF for his service in the Far East against the Japanese. His heir was his twin brother who predeceased him. The family still have some land in the area.

SIR RICHARD LA TOUCHE COLTHURST, the 9th Baronet, was born in 1928. The family still farm in the area and he began the highly successful Blarney Castle International Three Day Event in 1992. Educated at Harrow and Cambridge, his son and heir, Charles, is a solicitor in Cork.

Significant Institutional Landowners

1872: The Church of Ireland owned 1914 acres. Various Catholic orders of nuns owned 938 acres. The Railway Companies owned 3344 acres.
2001: Coillte owns 104,130 acres.

TOP 10 IN 1872

1	Earl of Bantry of Macroom Castle, East Ferry	69,500 acres	
2	Earl of Bandon of Castle Bernard, Bandon (Perpetual leases, of which Bandon had the freehold, not shown. Est 60,000 acres)	40,941 acres	
3	Duke of Devonshire (MP) of Chatsworth, Derbyshire	32,550 acres	with 166,022 elsewhere
4	Sir John St John Colthurst Bt of Blarney Castle	31,260 acres	
5	Countess of Kingston (Anna) of Mitchelstown Castle	24,421 acres	with 250 elsewhere
6	Earl of Kenmare (MP) Killarney House, Co Kerry	22,700 acres	with 95,906 elsewhere
7	Sir Henry Wrixon-Becher Bt of Castle Hyde, Fermoy	18,933 acres	with 358 elsewhere
8	Earl of Egmont (MP) of North House, Epsom, Surrey	16,776 acres	with 18,196 elsewhere
9	Viscount Doneraile of Doneraile Court	16,400 acres	with 12,300 elsewhere
10	Mr Robert Hedges Eyre White of Glengarriffe	16,175 acres	

DONEGAL

	1872	2001
Total acreage	1,172,526 acres	1,200,640 acres
Agricultural acreage	1,055,273 acres	519,147 acres
Non agricultural acreage	117,526 acres	681,493 acres
Population	217,992	128,117
Owners of nothing at all	215,818	66,329
Total Dwellings	40,800	35,757
Smallholdings: 1872 owners of less than one acre 2000 owners of 0–2ha (0–4.94 acres)	1171	34
Landowners over one acre (1872) Landowners over 2ha (2000)	1003	10,194
Landowners over 500 acres	98	3
Acreage (and percentage) of county owned by owners of over 500 acres	702,103 acres (59.8%)	

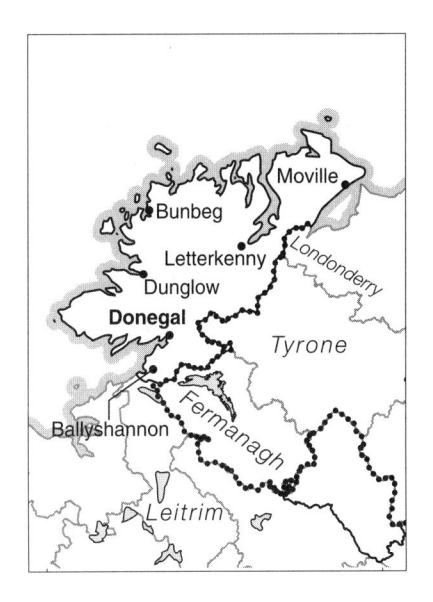

Top Landowners 2001

THE MCILHENNY FAMILY *22,000 acres*. The family bought the land and the house, which overlooks Lough Veagh in one of the most beautiful parts of Donegal, in 1938. In 1872 it belonged to John Adair, who had 16,000 acres which he had bought in 1857 from the Earl of Leitrim. It is the largest single personal landholding in the Irish Republic.

Where they are now:
THE MARQUESS OF CONYNGHAM. See Earl and Countess of Mount Charles, County Meath.

THE EARLDOM OF LEITRIM is long extinct.

SIR WILLIAM FREDERICK STYLE, the 13th Baronet born in 1945. Last heard of in the USA divorcing his first wife. *Debrett's* says that 'his name does not appear on the official roll of the Baronetage'.

SIR JOHN NORMAN LESLIE, 4th Baronet. See County Monaghan.

LORD HILL. See Marquess of Downshire, County Down.

Significant Institutional Landowners

1900: The Church of Ireland owned 21,489 acres.
2001: Coillte owns 76,465 acres.

TOP 10 IN 1872

1	Major General the Marquess of Conyngham of Bifrons, Canterbury, Kent	122,230 acres	with 44,410 elsewhere
2	Earl of Leitrim of 44 Grosvenor St, London	54,352 acres	with 2500 elsewhere
3	Mr Horatio Granville Murray-Stewart of Calley, Gatehouse, Scotland	50,818 acres	with 47,451 elsewhere
4	Sir William Henry Marsham Style Bt of Glenmore	39,564 acres	
5	Mr Alexander John Robert Stewart of Ards, Letterkenny	39,306 acres	
6	Sir John Leslie Bt MP of Glasslough, Monaghan	28,827 acres	with 15,654 elsewhere
7	Mr Robert Harvey of Fairfield House, Cheltenham, Glos	25,593 acres	
8	Lord George Augustus Hill of Ballyvar, Ramelton	24,189 acres	with 969 elsewhere
9	Mr James and Mr John Musgrave of Drumglass House, Belfast	23,693 acres	
10	Sir Samuel Hercules Hayes Bt of Drumboe Castle Stranorlar	22,825 acres	

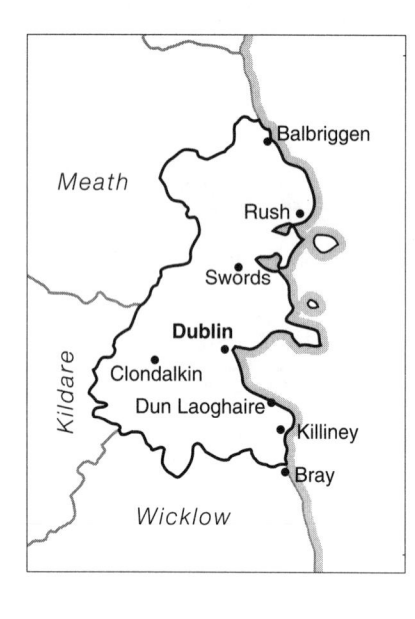

DUBLIN
(Excludes Dublin City)

	1872	2001
Total acreage	217,457 acres	285,440 acres
Agricultural acreage	195,713 acres	121,602 acres
Non agricultural acreage	21,745 acres	163,838 acres
Population	158,936	548,136
Owners of nothing at all	154,836	295,395
Total Dwellings	26,858	151,160
Smallholdings: 1872 owners of less than one acre	2526	
2000 owners of 0–2ha (0–4.94 acres)		62
Landowners over one acre (1872)	1574	
Landowners over 2ha (2000)		1448
Landowners over 500 acres	121	25
Acreage (and percentage) of county owned by owners of over 500 acres	163,078 acres (74.9%)	

Top Landowners 2001

THE COBBE FAMILY *900 acres*. The Cobbe family, descendants of Charles Cobbe, the Archbishop of Dublin in the mid 1700s, own the beautiful Newbridge House and still retain part of the 9000 acre estate of 1872 (no. 1 below). It is sited near Donabate.

PRINCE AND PRINCESS AZMAT GUIREY *300 acres*. The heart of the tiny estate at Swords is Rathbeal Hall, now restored. The Corbally family owned it from about 1810, selling it in 1958 and then buying it back again.

Dublin City in 2001. (The major known landowners in the modern city of Dublin are listed below. Most are developers with land in development company landbanks.)

MICHAEL BAILEY. He is the managing director and a key shareholder in Bovale Developments, Dublin's leading private builder. Insiders reckon that the company has around 1000 acres in its City landbank. He is married with five children.

MARK KAVANAGH. Ireland's *Who's Who* describes him as 'an urbane businessman in the international mode'. He was educated at top English Catholic public school Downsides and has long been the proprietor of Captain America's, a famous City restaurant. He heads and owns a large stake in Hardwicke, a leading Dublin developer and is also Chairman of the Customs House Dock's Development Company. Total landbank is reckoned to be between 500 and 1000 acres.

PATRICK DOHERTY. Born in Donegal, he worked his way up the UK property ladder with nothing but a national school education behind him. His company, Harcourt Developments, has a string of shopping centres across Ireland and some major Dublin development sites. He splits his life between London and Dublin. Estimated landbank in Dublin 400–800 acres.

KENNETH ROHAN. He is the MD and key shareholder in Rohan Group, a company he sold in 1987 and bought back in 1992, just as the Irish boom began. His landbank is said to be well in excess of 700 acres. He is married with two sons and a daughter.

Significant Institutional Landowners
1872: The Church of Ireland owned 615 acres.
2001: Coillte owns 4052 acres.

TOP 10 IN 1872

1	Mr Charles Cobbe of Newbridge House, Donabate	9948 acres	with 1419 elsewhere
2	Earl of Howth (MP) of Howth Castle, Dublin	7377 acres	with 2061 elsewhere
3	Sir Charles Compton Domville Bt of Santry House, Dublin	6262 acres	
4	Mr George Woods of Milverton Hall, Dublin	4141 acres	with 1433 elsewhere
5	Lord Annaly of Woodlands, Clonsilla	3954 acres	with 12,560 elsewhere
6	Lt Gen Sir Roger Palmer Bt of Keenagh, Crossmolina, Co Mayo	3991 acres	with 94,963 elsewhere
7	Lord Langford of Summerhill House, Co Meath	3659 acres	with 6068 elsewhere
8	Mr Ion Trant Hamilton MP of Abbotstown House, Dublin	3647 acres	with 3242 elsewhere
9	Mrs White of Kilakee, Whitechurch	3422 acres	
10	Mr WW Hackett of 36 Leeson Park, Dublin	3198 acres	

GALWAY

	1872	2001
Total acreage	1,483,367 acres	1,503,360 acres
Agricultural acreage	1,335,030 acres	791,883 acres
Non agricultural acreage	148,336 acres	711,477 acres
Population	248,458	180,304
Owners of nothing at all	246,691	94,848
Total Dwellings	45,564	49,916
Smallholdings: 1872 owners of less than one acre	741	
2000 owners of 0–2ha (0–4.94 acres)		40
Landowners over one acre (1872)	1026	
Landowners over 2ha (2000)		16,190
Landowners over 500 acres	111	39
Acreage (and percentage) of county owned by owners of over 500 acres	876,105 acres (59%)	

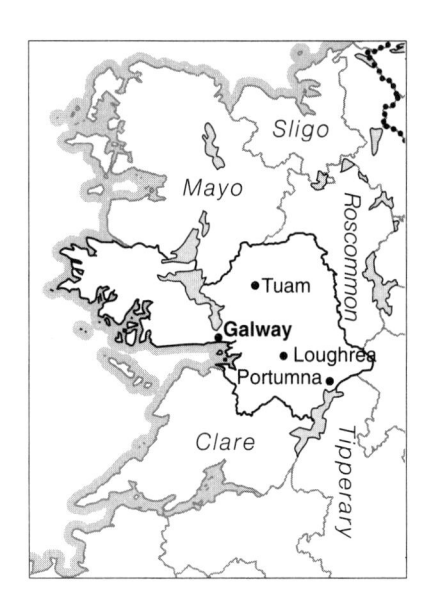

Top Landowners 2001

THE 4TH LORD BLYTHE AND THE BLYTHWOOD ESTATE *750 acres*. Anthony Audley Rupert Blythe, the 4th Baron, born in 1931, was one of the small number of hereditary peers who actually worked at the House of Lords prior to the Blair reforms. His heir is the Hon James Audley, born in 1970. The estate is a modern one, and was not in Bateman.

THE 5TH BARON HEMPHILL *700 acres*. Peter Martyn-Hemphill was born in 1928. He was educated at the English Catholic public school of Downsides, and at Oxford. His family were MPs and landowners in Tipperary in the 1800s with a total of about 1700 acres in that county and 600 in Dublin. The estate is at Kiltullen and he was a leading figure in the creation of the modern Irish bloodstock industry, as well as a huge influence on the creation of the modern Galway races. He was MFH of the Galway Blazers, one of the famous Irish hunts. His heir is the Hon. Charles, a banker with Morgan Grenfell in London.

Where they are now:

THE CLANRICARDE MARQUESSATE (*no. 2 in 1872*) is long extinct.

THE DUNSANDLE BARONY (*no. 3 in 1872*) is long extinct.

THE CLONBROCK BARONY (*no. 4 in 1872*) is long extinct.

THE ARDILAUN BARONY (*no. 6 in 1872*), was one of the earliest Guinness peerages, granted to Sir Arthur Guinness. It is now extinct.

THE 9TH BARONET, SIR STANLEY BURKE, born in 1956, lives in Switzerland. His heir, Martin Burke, was born in 1980.

THE 9TH EARL OF CLANCARTY, Nicholas le Poer Trench, who is also the Marquess of Heusden in Holland, was born in 1952. He sat as a Viscount in the House of Lords but lost his seat in 1999. He attended the House on 63 of the 79 sitting days in the last pre-Labour session (1996–97). He is an artist and film-maker and unmarried as of 2000.

Significant Institutional Landowners

1872: The Church of Ireland owned 2931 acres.
2001: Coillte owns 82,501 acres.

TOP 10 IN 1872

1	Mr Richard Berridge of Clifden Castle, Connemara	160,152 acres	with 10,365 elsewhere
2	Marquess of Clanricarde (MP) Portumna Castle, Galway	56,826 acres	
3	Lord Dunsandle and Clanconal of Dunsandle, Galway	33,543 acres	with 3514 elsewhere
4	Lord Clonbrock of Clonbrock, Ahascragh	29,550 acres	
5	Mr John Broom Pollok of Glasgow	29,366 acres	with 9770 elsewhere
6	Lord Ardilaun (MP) of St Ann's, Dublin (Sir Arthur Guinness)	27,111 acres	with 4231 elsewhere
7	Sir Henry George Burke Bt of Marble Hill	25,258 acres	with 2230 elsewhere
8	Earl of Clancarty of Garbally, Ballinasloe	23,896 acres	with 1614 elsewhere
9	Mr John Lloyd Neville Bagot of Ballymoe and Aughrane	19,303 acres	with 104 elsewhere
10	Mr Patrick Blake of Gortnamona	17,355 acres	

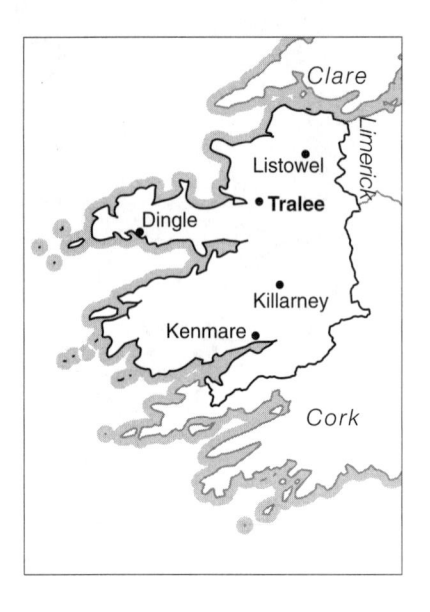

KERRY

	1872	2001
Total acreage	1,153,373 acres	1,161,600 acres
Agricultural acreage	1,038,035 acres	711,479 acres
Non agricultural acreage	115,337 acres	450,191 acres
Population	196,586	121,984
Owners of nothing at all	195,420	58,908
Total Dwellings	32,240	35,677
Smallholdings: 1872 owners of less than one acre	637	
2000 owners of 0–2ha (0–4.94 acres)		144
Landowners over one acre (1872)	529	
Landowners over 2ha (2000)		10,736
Landowners over 500 acres	99	66
Acreage (and percentage) of county owned by owners of over 500 acres	416,987 acres (36.1%)	

Top Landowners 2001

SIR GEORGE PETER MAURICE FITZGERALD MC, THE 5TH BARONET AND THE 23RD KNIGHT OF KERRY, was born in 1917. Educated at Harrow and the Royal Military College, he was awarded the Military Cross in World War Two and was officer commanding the 2nd Battalion the Irish Guards in 1946. He lives in Salisbury. His heir Adrian was born in 1940 and has a residence on Valentia Island, with a small acreage. He is also a member of the Kildare St Club in Dublin. His ancestor, Peter Fitzgerald, had 5372 acres of land at Glanleam, Valencia, in the 1872 Returns. The title of Knight of Kerry was conferred on the head of the family by the Lord of Decies and Desmond, John Fitz Thomas Fitzgerald.

SIR MAURICE MACCARTHY O'CONNELL, THE 7TH BARONET, was born in 1958 and educated at Ampleforth. He still lives at the family home of 1872, Lakeview House, Killarney. His is one of the greatest historic names in Ireland, being a descendant of the brother of Daniel O'Connell, the Liberator. He is also senior representative of the O'Connell sept or Clan. The family still have land but the acreage is unknown.

Where they are now:

ANDREW WESLEY DAUBENEY DE MOLEYNS, THE 8TH LORD VENTRY *(no. 1 in 1872)*, born in 1943, is married with one son and three daughters, one by a second marriage. He lives in Perth in Scotland.

THE EARLDOM OF KENMARE *(no. 2 in 1872)* is long extinct.

THE 6TH EARL OF LISTOWEL *(no. 4 in 1872)*, Francis Michael Hare, born in 1964, had a seat in the House of Lords as Baron Hare but did not attend once in the year before reform. He now lives in north London.

SIR ANTHONY DE WALTHAM DENNY, 8TH BARONET *(no. 8 in 1872)*, was born in 1925 and lives in Somerset. He is a hereditary freeman of Cork city and served in the RAF during World War Two. His heir is Piers de Waltham Denny, born in 1954. He lives in Devon.

Significant Institutional Landowners

1872: The Church of Ireland owned 1500 acres.
2001: Coillte owns 40,047 acres.

TOP 10 IN 1872

1	Lord Ventry of Burnham House, Dingle	93,629 acres	
2	Earl of Kenmare (MP) of Killarney House	91,080 acres	with 27,526 elsewhere
3	Mr Henry Arthur Herbert MP of Muckross Abbey	47,238 acres	
4	Earl of Listowel of Convamore, Mallow, Co Cork	30,000 acres	with 5541 elsewhere
5	Mr Robert Drummond of Palace Gate, London	29,780 acres	
6	Mr Richard Mahony of Dromore Castle, Kenmare	26,173 acres	
7	Mr Francis Bland of Derryquin Castle, Sneem	25,576 acres	
8	Sir Edward Denny Bt of West Brompton, London	21,479 acres	
9	Sir Maurice James O'Connell of Lakeview, Killarney	18,752 acres	
10	The McGilcuddy of the Reeks, Whitefield, Killarney	15,518 acres	

KILDARE

	1872	2001
Total acreage	412,490 acres	418,560 acres
Agricultural acreage	371,241 acres	303,841 acres
Non agricultural acreage	41,249 acres	114,719 acres
Population	83,614	122,656
Owners of nothing at all	81,848	65,561
Total Dwellings	14,166	32,589
Smallholdings: 1872 owners of less than one acre	920	
2000 owners of 0–2ha (0–4.94 acres)		41
Landowners over one acre (1872)	846	
Landowners over 2ha (2000)		3210
Landowners over 500 acres	63	46
Acreage (and percentage) of county owned by owners of over 500 acres	217,914 acres (52.8%)	

Top Landowners 2001

THE 7TH BARON CAREW *700 acres*. Patrick Thomas Connolly-Carew, born in 1938, was educated at Harrow and the Royal Military Academy, Sandhurst. A former captain in the Royal Horse Guards he was president of the ground jury for the Olympic Games in 1992 and 1996 and is a member of the Federation Equestre Internationale as well as president of the Irish Horse Trials Society 1998. Married, he has one son and three daughters. He lives at Naas in Co Kildare.

HIS HIGHNESS PRINCE KARIM AGA KHAN IV. Educated at Le Rosy Switzerland and Harvard. He is the leader of the Ismaeli tradition in Islam. He owns three key Kildare studs, totalling over 1000 acres in extent: Gilltown, Sallymount and Sheshoon.

CON COLLINS, educated at Newbridge College, a Dominican institution, obtained his trainer's licence in 1959 having joined his trainer father M.C. Collins after leaving school. Has had a series of winners in the UK including Goodwood in 1995 and 1997. His stud is Conyngham Lodge near the Curragh. Acreage over 400 acres.

Where they are now:
CARTON *(no. 1 in 1872)* is now in the hands of a high tech company. Gerald Fitzgerald, the 8th Duke, born in 1914, is the premier duke, marquess and earl of Ireland. Educated at Eton and Sandhurst, he lives in Oxfordshire. His heir, the Marquess of Kildare, also lives in Oxford. One son, the Earl of Offaly, was killed in a car accident in Ireland in 1997. His youngest son followed him to Sandhurst. He lost his seat in the House of Lords in 1999.

THE 12TH EARL OF DROGHEDA *(no. 2 in 1872)*, born in 1937 and educated at Eton and Cambridge, Henry Dermot Ponsonby Moore, is a photographer. He was an irregular attender at the House of Lords and lost his seat in 1999. His father was a prominent chairman of the Royal Opera House and of the *Financial Times*.

Significant Institutional Landowners

1872: The Church of Ireland owned 628 acres. The Grand Canal Company had 2182 acres.
2001: Coillte owns 8601 acres. The Irish Defence forces own significant parts of the Curragh, acreage unknown. There are many stud farms in Kildare, but acreages are not easy to establish.

TOP 10 IN 1872

1	Duke of Leinster (MP) of Carton, Maynooth	71,997 acres	with 1123 elsewhere
2	Marquess of Drogheda of Moore Abbey, Monastrevan (Perpetual leases would double this)	16,609 acres	with 2688 elsewhere
3	Sir Gerald George Aylmer Bt of the Castle, Donadea	15,396 acres	
4	Mr John La Touche of Harristown, Newbridge	11,282 acres	with 4029 elsewhere
5	Commander Richard Conway Dobbs MP of Castle Dobbs, Carrickfergus, Co Antrim	7971 acres	with 5060 elsewhere
6	Lord Cloncurry of Lyons, Hazlehatch	6121 acres	with 6366 elsewhere
7	Mr. Robert Higgison Borrowes of Gilltown, Newbridge	6089 acres	
8	Mr William Wilson of Coolcarrigan, Donadea	5432 acres	
9	Viscount Harberton of 60 Rutland Gate, London	5223 acres	
10	Mr Hugh Lynedoch Barton of Straffan House, Straffan	5044 acres	

KILKENNY

	1872	2001
Total acreage	505,309 acres	509,440 acres
Agricultural acreage	454,778 acres	414,636 acres
Non agricultural acreage	50,539 acres	94,804 acres
Population	96,669	73,613
Owners of nothing at all	95,518	38,140
Total Dwellings	18,287	20,294
Smallholdings: 1872 owners of less than one acre	323	
2000 owners of 0–2ha (0–4.94 acres)		47
Landowners over one acre (1872)	828	
Landowners over 2ha (2000)		4391
Landowners over 500 acres	101	21
Acreage (and percentage) of county owned by owners of over 500 acres	312,476 acres (61.8%)	

Top Landowners 2001

BARON AND BARONESS DE BREFFNY *500 acres*. Castletown, Piltown, is rated one of the most important eighteenth-century houses in Ireland, with a small estate not mentioned in Bateman or the 1872 Return.

JIM BOLGER, educated locally and at the College of Commerce in Rathmines, Dublin. He trained the largest number of winners ever in a flat season in Ireland – 125 in 1990. He has had his trainer's licence since 1976. Married with two daughters. The stud is at Coolcullen. Acreage unknown but estimated at over 500 acres.

FRANCES MAJELLA CROWLEY was educated at St Brigid's College, Callan and University College Dublin with a post-grad degree from the Veterinary College. She joined the family farm and stud at Eight Hills Stables near Pilltown after University and has been the champion amateur rider in 1996, 1997 and 1999, getting her trainer's licence in 1998. The stud has bred a number of international winners under her tutelage. Acreage unknown but in excess of 500 acres.

THE MOLONEY FAMILY stud farm at Warrington. This is the home of the Top Flight Equestrian Centre and the two sons of the family, Elie and his brother Richie are major European eventers and showjumpers. Acreage unknown, but over 500 acres.

JAMES 'JIM' BRETT, was educated locally and at University College Dublin, with a degree in agriculture. Started out as a producer at RTE, he took over the family agribusiness at Callan in 1989. The family owns farm land in the area. Acreage unknown.

Where they are now:
THE MARQUESS OF ORMONDE *(no. 6 in 1872)*. The Butler family, who changed their name from Fitzwalter, arrived in Ireland with Henry II in 1172 and later became one of the most influential families in the country for almost 700 years. The last Marquess, James Butler, born in 1914, was the hereditary Chief Butler of Ireland and served in the World War One as a lieutenant in the Rifle Corps. He died in 1997, in the USA, and the title is presumed extinct. However, the 17th Viscount Mountgarret, Richard Butler, a Yorkshire landowner with 2000 acres near Harrogate, is the heir presumptive to the Earldom of Ormonde and Ossory, titles also held by the late Marquess. Mountgarret did not survive the Blair cull of the Lords in 1999 but the title of Ormonde lives on with him.

Significant Institutional Landowners
1872: The Church of Ireland owned 2014 acres.
2001: Coillte owns 21,258 acres.

TOP 10 IN 1872

1	Viscount Clifden of Gowran Castle, Kilkenny	35,288 acres	with 13,789 elsewhere
2	Earl of Bessborough of Bessborough House, Piltown	23,967 acres	with 11,473 elsewhere
3	Mr Charles BC Wandesforde of Castlecomer (Not in Bateman)	22,232 acres	
4	Viscount Mountgarret of Ballyconra	14,073 acres	with 625 elsewhere
5	Mr Frederick Bunbury Tighe of The Priory, Christchurch, Hants	11,970 acres	with 9793 elsewhere
6	Marquess of Ormonde of The Castle, Kilkenny	11,960 acres	with 15,765 elsewhere
7	Viscount Ashbrook of The Castle, Durrow	9292 acres	with 13,758 elsewhere
8	Hon Mr George Leopold Bryan of Jenkinstown	8209 acres	with 4682 elsewhere
9	Earl of Desart of Desart Court, Kilkenny	8000 acres	with 932 elsewhere
10	Mr Arthur McMurragh Kavanagh of Borris House, Carlow	7341 acres	with 21,684 elsewhere

LAOIS
(Also known as Queen's County)

	1872	2001
Total acreage	423,828 acres	424,960 acres
Agricultural acreage	381,442 acres	298,958 acres
Non agricultural acreage	42,828 acres	126,002 acres
Population	79,771	52,325
Owners of nothing at all	78,722	26,891
Total Dwellings	15,519	14,130
Smallholdings:		
1872 owners of less than one acre	426	
2000 owners of 0–2ha (0–4.94 acres)		90
Landowners over one acre (1872)	623	
Landowners over 2ha (2000)		3830
Landowners over 500 acres	27	15
Acreage (and percentage) of county owned by owners of over 500 acres	197,800 (46.6%)	

Top Landowners 2001

THE 7TH VISCOUNT DE VESCI *1800 acres. (no. 3 in 1872)*. Thomas Eustace Vesey, born in 1955, is an old Etonian and an Oxford graduate. About 1800 acres of the estate remain in trust, but most of the lands and the house were sold in the 1990s. He is married to the daughter of the Maharaj of Burdwan. They live in London.

RICHARD BOOTH, was educated at Rockwell College and took over the family farm in 1981. He has a high national profile, having chaired the National Livestock Committee and the EU Meat Advisory Committee, as well as being a director of Bord Bia (The National Food Board). The farm is one of the largest in Laois, comprising tillage, commercial cattle and sheep farming around the Heath. Exact acreage unknown but locals suggest a figure over 1000 acres.

Where they are now:
THE COOTE FAMILY HOME AT BALLYFIN *(no. 1 in 1872)* is now a secondary school, set in beautiful grounds. The 5th Baronet, Sir Christopher Coote, is a coffee and tea merchant who lives in Wiltshire. His cousin, Nicola Harriette, is the Lady Clinton, married to the largest landowner in Devon, Lord Clinton and currently president elect of the Devon Agricultural Association.

THE 2ND BARON CASTLETOWN, BERNARD FITZPATRICK *(no. 2 in 1872)*, was still alive in the 1930s living at Granston Manor near Abbeyleix. Eton educated he was born in 1849 and was the Commanding Officer of the 4th Prince of Wales Leinster Regiment. As late as 1931 his *Who's Who* entry declared that he owned 20,000 acres. The title became extinct when he died later that decade, but a relative of his wife lived at Granston until the mid 1950s.

Significant Institutional Landowners
1872: The Church of Ireland owned 3738 acres. Trinity College Dublin owned 1265 acres.
2001: Coillte owns 34,230 acres. Bord Na Mona owns over 30,000 acres.

TOP 10 IN 1872

1	Sir Charles Henry Coote Bt of Ballyfin, Mountrath	47,451 acres	with 2235 elsewhere
2	Lord Castletown (MP) of Lisduff, Templemore	22,510 acres	with 633 elsewhere
3	Viscount De Vesci of Abbeyleix House, Abbeyleix	15,069 acres	with 1613 elsewhere
4	Earl of Portarlington of Emo Park	11,149 acres	with 8779 elsewhere
5	Mr Robert Ashworth Godolphin Cosby of Stradbally Hall, Stradbally	10,110 acres	
6	Mr John George Adair of Rathdaire, Ballybrittas	9655 acres	with 42,518 elsewhere
7	The Misses Dunne (three) of Brittas, Clonaslie	9215 acres	with 2127 elsewhere
8	Mr Robert Hamilton Stubber of Moyne, Durrow	7388 acres	
9	Mr Richard Warburton of Garryhinch, Portarlington	6285 acres	with 5841 elsewhere
10	Mr Thomas Kemmis of Shaen, Maryborough	5800 acres	

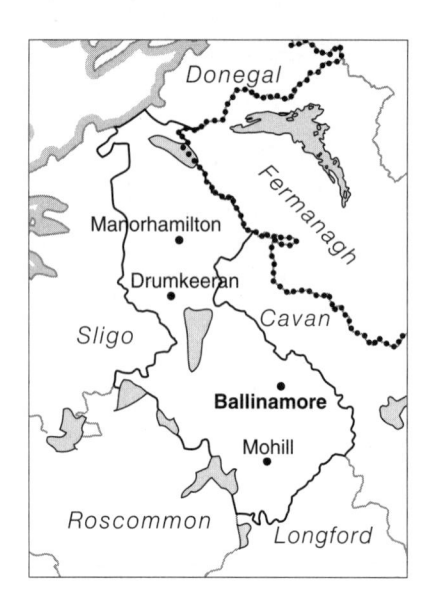

LEITRIM

	1872	2001
Total acreage	371,371 acres	392,960 acres
Agricultural acreage	334,233 acres	209,726 acres
Non agricultural acreage	37,371 acres	183,234 acres
Population	95,324	25,297
Owners of nothing at all	94,873	10,582
Total Dwellings	17,405	8112
Smallholdings: 1872 owners of less than one acre	124	
2000 owners of 0–2ha (0–4.94 acres)		8
Landowners over one acre (1872)	327	
Landowners over 2ha (2000)		4508
Landowners over 500 acres	46	2
Acreage (and percentage) of county owned by owners of over 500 acres	177,177 acres (47.7%)	

Top Landowners 2001

Where they are now:

THE 9TH BARON MASSEY, HUGH HAMON JOHN SOMERTSET MASSEY *(no. 1 in 1872)*, was born in 1921 and educated at Clongowes Wood school in Ireland. He served in World War Two as a private in the army.

GEORGE LANE FOX *(no. 2 in 1872)* was a relative of the family of the Earl of Ilchester, a title recently extinct.

ARTHUR LOFTUS TOTTENHAM *(no. 4 in 1872)* was a member of the family of the Earl of Ely. See Fermanagh.

THE 6TH LORD HARLACH, FRANCIS DAVID ORMSBY GORE *(no. 9 in 1872)*, was born in 1954. There is still a small estate in Shropshire and he succeeded his father, an eminent businessman and politician, who was killed in a car crash in 1985. He is divorced.

SIR HUGH DENIS CROFTON, THE 8TH BARONET *(no. 10 in 1872)*, was born in 1937 and succeeded his half-nephew, Patrick Crofton, in 1987 but does not use the title. He was educated at Eton, Oxford and Bristol University. His heir is his brother, Edward, educated at Eton, Sandhurst and retired as a Major in the Coldstream Guards. His brother's son Henry is the next generational heir.

Significant Institutional Landowners

1872: The Church of Ireland owned 11,950 acres.
2001: Coillte owns 27,213 acres.

TOP 10 IN 1872

1	Lord Massey of The Hermitage, Castle Connell	24,571 acres	with 8432 elsewhere
2	Mr George Lane Fox of Bramham Park, Tadcaster, Yorks	18,850 acres	with 20,219 elsewhere
3	Mr Owen Wynn of Hazlewood, Sligo	15,436 acres	
4	Mr Arthur Loftus Tottenham MP of Glenfarne, Enniskillen	14,561 acres	with 257 elsewhere
5	Mr William Johnston of Kinlough House, Kinlough	14,395 acres	with 1553 elsewhere
6	Colonel John Whyte of Glencar, Manor-Hamilton	10,989 acres	with 3133 elsewhere
7	Mr Hugh Lyons-Montgomery of Belavel	10,179 acres	
8	Miss Catherine Jones of Hayle Place, Maidstone, Kent	9839 acres	with 65 elsewhere
9	Lord Harlech (MP) of Derrycarne, Dromod	9634 acres	with 48,724 elsewhere
10	Sir Morgan George Crofton Bt of Mohill Castle, Mohill	9590 acres	with 1879 elsewhere

LIMERICK

	1872	2001
Total acreage	660,386 acres	680,960 acres
Agricultural acreage	594,347 acres	502,000 acres
Non agricultural acreage	66,386 acres	178,960 acres
Population	152,583	161,856
Owners of nothing at all	150,907	85,485
Total Dwellings	26,345	46,174
Smallholdings: 1872 owners of less than one acre 2000 owners of 0–2ha (0–4.94 acres)	670	173
Landowners over one acre (1872) Landowners over 2ha (2000)	1006	7214
Landowners over 500 acres	167	11
Acreage (and percentage) of county owned by owners of over 500 acres	278,100 (46.7%)	

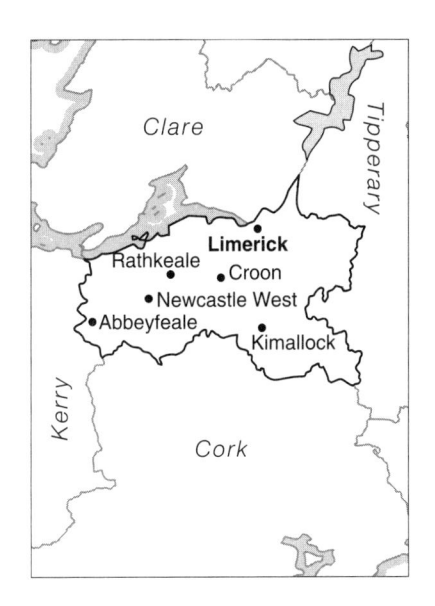

Top Landowners 2001

THE 11TH EARL HARRINGTON *stud farm and 900 acres*. Born in 1922, William Henry Leicester Stanhope was the heir to two great English fortunes, those of Harrington and Stanhope. A great fan of the turf, he liquidated or put in trust most of the English fortune and came to Ireland where he ran a very successful stud at Ballingarry. His son, Viscount Petersham, married Ginny Freeman Jackson, daughter of the late Captain Harry Freeman Jackson, a noted figure on the Irish racing scene. Now divorced, Ginny lives in Limerick, close to her ex father-in-law. Her daughter Serena is married to Viscount Linley, Princess Margaret's son.

THE 29TH KNIGHT OF GLIN, DESMOND JOHN VILLIERS FITZ-GERALD, born in 1937, is the owner of Glin Castle and estate. This small estate is over seven hundred years old and has survived, in the words of Desmond Guinness and William Ryan in their massive tome, *Irish Houses and Castles*, 'the usual series of massacres, attainders, and confiscations'. The title has defeated genealogists and historians but originated around 1261. The castle has been beautifully restored by the present owner and his Canadian wife. The acreage is much reduced from 1872 and is now thought to be less than 700 acres in extent.

J.P. McMANUS, is ranked as the 14th richest person in Ireland, worth £240 million, by the *Sunday Times* 2001 Rich List. He was the son of a plant hire operator who left school at 16 and then left his father's business to take up the profession of gambling. He is part-owner of the Sandy Lane Hotel in Barbados and runs his own highly successful racing stud from Martinstown near Kilmallock. In a county with just eleven landowners over 500 acres J.P. is reckoned one of those.

ALAN LILLINGSTON is an old Etonian who runs a very successful stud in Limerick, with a string of winners over the years. A European gold medal winner for three day eventing, he was also a director Bord Na gCoppal, the Irish Horse Board and a member of the Turf Club. Married with two sons and two daughters the acreage of the stud is unknown.

Significant Institutional Landowners

1872: The Church of Ireland owned 2202 acres. The convent of nuns at Mitchelstown owned 1202 acres.
2001: Coillte owns 26,242 acres. The Knight of Glin and Madam Fitzgerald own 300 acres. The name and estate are one of the oldest in Ireland. The castle was restored in the middle of the last century with the help of the Canadian H.R. Milner. In 1872 there were over 5000 acres at the castle.

TOP 10 IN 1872

1	Earl of Devon (MP) of Powderham Castle, Exeter, Devon	33,026 acres	with 20,049 elsewhere
2	Earl of Dunraven of Adare Manor, Limerick	14,298 acres	with 25,457 elsewhere
3	Lord Ashtown of Woodlawn, Co Galway	11,273 acres	with 35,370 elsewhere
4	Mrs Goold of Drumadda, Glin (Widow of Archdeacon of Limerick)	10,966 acres	
5	Lady Louisa Isabella Fitz-Gibbon of Mount Shannon, Lisnagry	10,316 acres	with 3178 elsewhere
6	Sir Croker Barrington Bt of Glenstal Abbey, Murroe	9485 acres	
7	Lord Massy of the Hermitage, Castle Connell	8432 acres	with 24,571 elsewhere
8	Rev Mr John Thomas Waller Castletown Manor, Pallaskenry	6996 acres	
9	Lord Monteagle of Mount Trenchard, Limerick	6445 acres	with 2310 elsewhere
10	Mr Desmond Fitzgerald. The Knight of Glin, of Glin Castle, Limerick	5697 acres	

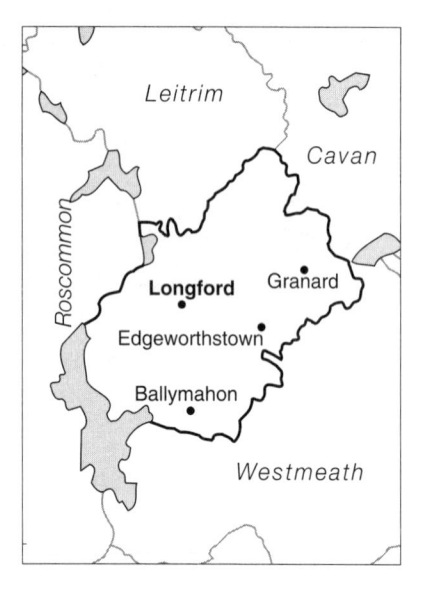

LONGFORD

	1872	2001
Total acreage	256,668 acres	257,920 acres
Agricultural acreage	231,001 acres	218,013 acres
Non agricultural acreage	25,666 acres	39,907 acres
Population	64,501	31,496
Owners of nothing at all	64,065	16,208
Total Dwellings	12,002	8827
Smallholdings: 1872 owners of less than one acre	64	
2000 owners of 0–2ha (0–4.94 acres)		9
Landowners over one acre (1872)	372	
Landowners over 2ha (2000)		3098
Landowners over 500 acres	62	3
Acreage (and percentage) of county owned by owners of over 500 acres	97,611 (38%)	

Top Landowners 2001

MICHAEL 'MIKE' MAGAN, was educated locally and at Warrenstown Agricultural College. He was Dairy Farmer of the Year in 1984 and 1985 and in 1994 he won the national award for best dairy breeder. He is a past President of the Irish Grassland Association and a former chairman of the European Dairy Farmers Irish Branch. He has extended a large farm over the years and is one of three in Longford who own or manage over 500 acres. He is married with three sons and three daughters and is a regular contributor to the *Irish Farmers Journal*.

Where they are now:
THE 10TH EARL OF GRANARD, PETER ARTHUR EDWARD HASTINGS FORBES *(no. 2 in 1872)*, was born in 1957 and educated at Eton. He is married to Nora Ann Mitchell from Portarlington, Co Laois. They have three sons and a daughter and live on the Isle of Man. His mother lives in Monaco.

LUKE RICHARD WHITE, THE 6TH BARON ANNALY, was born in 1954 and educated at Eton and the Royal Military Academy, Sandhurst. Married to the daughter of a Shropshire landowner, he farms in Oxford.

The Fetherstone baronetcy is long extinct.

Significant Institutional Landowners

1872: The Church of Ireland owned 1735 acres.
2001: Coillte owns 7252 acres.

TOP 10 IN 1872

1	Mr Edward Robert King-Harman MP of Rockingham, Boyle	28,779 acres	with 44,134 elsewhere
2	Earl of Granard of Castle Forbes, Longford	14,978 acres	with 6307 elsewhere
3	Lord Annaly of Woodlands, Clonsilla, Dublin	12,560 acres	with 3954 elsewhere
4	Mr George Maconchy of Corrinagh, Torquay, Devon (Estate at Rathmore)	10,319 acres	
5	Mr Algernon Bellingham Greville of 45 Sussex Gardens, London. (Estate at Granard)	8821 acres	
6	Rev Sir George Ralph Fetherston Bt of Chapmanslade, Westbury Wilts. (Estate at Ardagh House, Longford)	8711 acres	
7	Mr James Willoughby Bond of Farragh	6574 acres	with 2582 elsewhere
8	Rev Mr John Grey Porter of Lisnaskea, Fermanagh	5024 acres	with 16,636 elsewhere
9	Mr Thomas Cusack of 61 St Stephen's Green Dublin (Estate at Carraboola)	4980 acres	
10	Major Robert Blackall of Coolamber Manor, Lisryan	4643 acres	

LOUTH

	1872	2001
Total acreage	200,287 acres	203,520 acres
Agricultural acreage	180,258 acres	157,741 acres
Non agricultural acreage	20,287 acres	45,779 acres
Population	70,511	90,724
Owners of nothing at all	69,232	47,707
Total Dwellings	13,927	25,728
Smallholdings: 1872 owners of less than one acre	578	
2000 owners of 0–2ha (0–4.94 acres)		33
Landowners over one acre (1872)	701	
Landowners over 2ha (2000)		2247
Landowners over 500 acres	57	17
Acreage (and percentage) of county owned by owners of over 500 acres	111,103 acres (55.4%)	

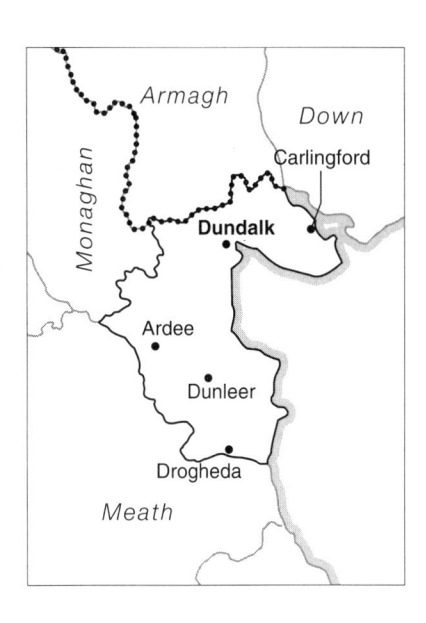

Top Landowners 2001

THE WADDINGTON FAMILY AT BEAULIEU DROGHEDA *750 acres*. The family had 1364 acres in the 1872 return. The family are prominent in Irish racing and came into the lands in the 1600s, from the Plunket family, which had held them since the twelfth century.

MR LARRY GOODMAN *1000 acres*. A prominent figure in the Irish meat and farming business, Mr Goodman has recently travelled with the Taoiseach (Prime Minister) to Russia to drum up business for Ireland. He is chairman of Anglo Irish Beef Processors which employs over 3500 people in Ireland and the UK and which had a turnover of over £700m in 1999. He is married with two sons.

JACK MARRY, educated at Mell Primary School and Warrenstown Agricultural College. He is one of Ireland's leading pig-breeders and producers, with units in both Louth and Meath. He bought and later sold the Oldbridge estate of the Coddington family, scene of the most fateful battle in Irish history, that of the Boyne in 1690 when the forces of Protestantism under William of Orange defeated the Catholic James I. He still has over 1200 acres along the banks of the Boyne and some of the best salmon fishing left in Europe west of Russia. He is married to Rosemary Gogarty, a nurse, and they have three sons and three daughters.

RAYMOND O'MALLEY is probably Ireland's leading beef producer and authority. Educated at De la Salle Brothers in Ardee and then Trinity College Dublin, he started out at the family farm straight from Trinity. He has extended his holdings considerably and is now reckoned to have over 1000 acres. His cattle have won the Supreme Champion at the Royal Dublin Society and, in the words of *Who's Who in Ireland*, 'have also won all major awards obtainable for cattle'. He is Chairman of the Irish Farmers Association National Livestock Commission and sits on many other bodies. He is married with one son and two daughters.

Significant Institutional Landowners

1872: The Church of Ireland owned 679 acres. Trinity College Dublin owned 1521 acres.
2001: The State owns 503 acres of the former Oldbridge Estate, scene of the Battle of the Boyne in 1690. Coillte owns 3355 acres.

TOP 10 IN 1872

1	Lord Cleremont MP of Ravensdale Park, Newry, Co Down	20,369 acres	with 758 elsewhere
2	Viscount Massereene and Ferrard of Oriel Temple	7193 acres	with 13,831 elsewhere
3	Mr James Hugh Smith-Barry of Foaty, Cobh, Co Cork	6273 acres	
4	Mr John Charles Fortescue of Stephenstown, Dundalk	5262 acres	
5	Rev Mr Henry Stobart of Warkton Rectory, England. (Estate at Mt Bagnal)	4249 acres	
6	Sir Alan Edward Bellingham Bt of Castle Bellingham	4186 acres	with 11,810 elsewhere
7	Earl of Roden of Hyde Hall, Sawbridgeworth, England. (Estate at Tullymore Park, Castlewellan, Co Down)	4151 acres	
8	Lord Bellew of Barmeath, Dunleer	4110 acres	with 204 elsewhere
9	Lord Louth of Louth Hall, Drogheda	3578 acres	with 521 elsewhere
10	Rev Sir Cavendish Hervey Foster Bt of Thoydon Garnon, Epping, Essex (Estate at Glyde Court, Louth)	3442 acres	with 64 elsewhere

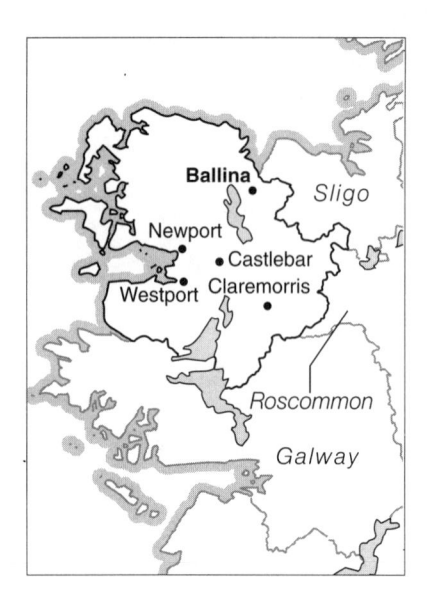

MAYO

	1872	2001
Total acreage	1,308,366 acres	1,381,760 acres
Agricultural acreage	1,177,529 acres	598,411 acres
Non agricultural acreage	130,836 acres	783,349 acres
Population	245,855	110,713
Owners of nothing at all	244,372	52,226
Total Dwellings	44,091	32,457
Smallholdings: 1872 owners of less than one acre	875	
2000 owners of 0–2ha (0–4.94 acres)		46
Landowners over one acre (1872)	608	
Landowners over 2ha (2000)		14,844
Landowners over 500 acres	109	13
Acreage (and percentage) of county owned by owners of over 500 acres	823,098 acres (62.9%)	

Top Landowners 2001

THE 11TH MARQUESS OF SLIGO *5000 acres. No. 1 in 1872.* Westport House is one of the best known tourist attractions in Ireland. It is owned by Jermy Ulick Browne, the 11th marquess who lives on the estate with his wife and five daughters. Born in 1939 he was educated at St Columbas's College in Ireland and the Royal Agricultural College, Cirencester.

Where they are now:
THE 22ND VISCOUNT DILLON'S ANCESTORS *(no. 2 in 1872)* were Presidents of Connaught and held Athlone against Cromwell. He was born in 1973 and lives in London. His grandmother, Irene, Viscountess Dillon, lives in Drogheda. His sister is an assistant private secretary to Princess Anne. Dytchley Park is an important government conference centre.

RICHARD BINGHAM, THE 7TH EARL OF LUCAN *(no. 4 in 1872)*, was born in 1934. Educated at Eton he was declared dead by the High Court in 1992, but remains entered as a living Earl in *Debrett's*. His declaration of death followed the murder of the family nanny in 1974, a crime for which he is wanted by the police but he has never been found. His son and heir, Lord Bingham, applied to the House of Lords for a writ of summons (to attend) which would confirm his assumption of the title and the residual ground rents in the county and in Galway. The Blair reforms ended the Lucan seat in the Lords and the fate of the application is not known.

THE 9TH EARL OF ARRAN (ORIGINALLY EARL OF THE ARRAN ISLANDS), ARTHUR GORE *(no. 7 in 1872)*, was born in 1938 and educated at Eton, Oxford and ended with a stint as a second lieutenant in the Grenadier Guards. He was a whip in the Thatcher Government and was a Northern Ireland minister in John Major's government 1992–1994. He saw out that administration as Under Secretary of State for the Environment. He is married to Eleanor, a daughter of the late Bernard van Cutsem and Lady Margaret Fortescue. He lives at the original Fortescue family home in Devon.

Significant Institutional Landowners

1872: The Church of Ireland owned 782 acres. The trustees of the Achill mission had 19,155 acres.
2001: Coillte owns 74,107 acres.

TOP 10 IN 1872

1	Marquess of Sligo of Westport House, Mayo	114,881 acres	
2	Viscount Dillon of Dytchley Park, Charlbury, England (The Estate was at Loughglyn House, Castlerea)	83,749 acres	with 11,015 elsewhere
3	Lieutenant General Sir Roger William Palmer Bt, of Keenagh, Crossmmolina	80,990 acres	with 17,964 elsewhere
4	General the Earl of Lucan of Laleham House, Chertsey, Surrey (Estate at Castlebar House, Castlebar)	60,570 acres	with 2366 elsewhere
5	Mr Henry Tilson Shaen Carter of Watling Park, Oxford	40,698 acres	with 1840 elsewhere
6	Colonel Edward Henry Clive of Perrystone Court, Ross, Hereford (The estate was at Calggan, Ballycroy)	35,000 acres	with 5389 elsewhere
7	Earl of Arran of Hans Place, London (Estate at Castle Gore, Mayo)	29,644 acres	with 6883 elsewhere
8	Mr Charles Howe Cuff Knox of Creagh, Ballinrobe	24,374 acres	with 446 elsewhere
9	Sir Robert Lynch-Blosse Bt of Athavallie, Balla	22,658 acres	
10	Sir Charles James Kox-Gore Bt of Beleek Manor, Ballina	22,023 acres	with 8569 elsewhere

MEATH

	1872	2001
Total acreage	577,893 acres	579,200 acres
Agricultural acreage	520,103 acres	473,577 acres
Non agricultural acreage	57,789 acres	105,623 acres
Population	95,558	105,370
Owners of nothing at all	94,234	53,841
Total Dwellings	18,814	28,596
Smallholdings: 1872 owners of less than one acre	278	
2000 owners of 0–2ha (0–4.94 acres)		77
Landowners over one acre (1872)	1046	
Landowners over 2ha (2000)		5571
Landowners over 500 acres	137	67
Acreage (and percentage) of county owned by owners of over 500 acres	401,104 acres (69.4%)	

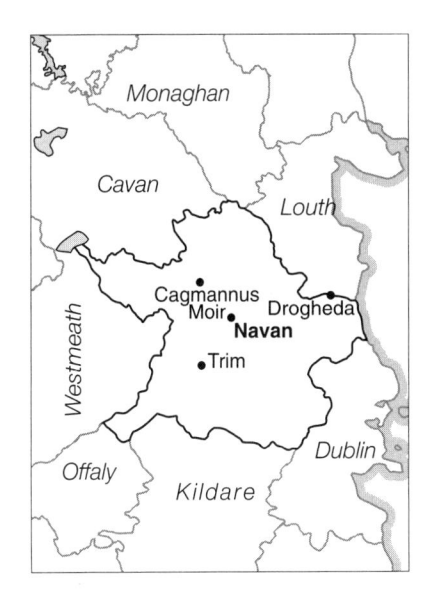

Top Landowners 2001

SIR JAMES HERCULES LANGRISHE, *8th Baronet 500 acres.* Sir James is the nephew of the 8th Viscount Powerscourt and was educated in England. There is no record of Langrishe lands in Meath in the 1872 Returns, but they are credited with 2615 acres in Kilkenny. The family name originates in Hampshire. He is married with a son and daughter.

THE 20TH BARON DUNSANY *900 acres.* Edward John Carlos Plunkett, born in 1939, inherited Dunsany Castle, one of the most beautiful restorations in modern Ireland. He is an art specialist and lives in London. His mother lives at the castle, whose history goes back to the Norman conquest.

THE EARL AND COUNTESS OF MOUNT CHARLES *1000 acres.* The Earl, Henry Vivian Pierpoint Conyngham, is the eldest son of the 7th Marquess of Conyngham, who lives on the Isle of Man. The earl is active in Irish public life and has a second seat at Beau Parc, near Navan. He divorced his first wife and is married to a daughter of the Earl of Verulam, Lady Iona Grimston.

Where they are now:

JOHN BRUTON, is probably the country's best-known farmer, having combined the family business with that of running the country from 1994 to 1997 as Taoiseach (Prime Minister). Educated at Clongowes Wood College and University College Dublin he is also a qualified barrister. He joined the party he led (Fine Gael) until 2000 at the age of 19 and remains a popular local TD (MP). He runs the family farm of about 300 acres in Meath and is married with one son and three daughters.

NOEL MEAD, who runs a stud farm of about 300 acres, started with a handful of horses on the family farm near Navan. He is one of the country's most prolific trainer of winners. He has clocked up 1600 since gaining his trainer's licence in 1975. Educated at St Pat's in Navan he lives with his partner Gillian O'Brien.

PATRICIA O'KELLY was educated at London University. According to *Who's Who in Ireland* she is considered one of the leading thoroughbred breeders world wide. She is a long time member of the Irish Thoroughbred Breeders Association. Her trophies include the 1000 Guineas, the Oaks and The Irish Derby. Her stud at Kilcarn was founded by her father Major E. O'Kelly in 1943. She is single and the stud runs to over 400 acres.

Significant Institutional Landowners

1872: The Church of Ireland had 2919 acres.
2001: Coillte owns 3674 acres.

TOP 10 IN 1872

1	Earl of Darnley of Cobham Hall, Gravesend, Kent (Estate at Clifton Lodge, Athaboy)	25,463 acres	with 9309 elsewhere
2	Mr James Lennox Naper of Loughcrew, Oldcastle	18,863 acres	with 176 elsewhere
3	Marquess of Lansdowne of Bowood Park, Calne, Wilts	12,995 acres	with 129,921 elsewhere
4	Lord Athlumney of Somerville House, Navan	10,213 acres	with 274 elsewhere
5	Viscount Gormanstown of Gormanstown Castle, Balbriggan	9657 acres	with 1300 elsewhere
6	Earl of Fingall of Kileen Castle, Dunshaughlin	9589 acres	with 5 elsewhere
7	Colonel The Rt Hon Thomas Taylor MP of Ardgillan Castle, Balbriggan	9000 acres	with 1261 elsewhere
8	Mr Robert Fowler of Rahinston, Enfield	8026 acres	
9	Mr Charles Nicholson of Balrath Bury, Kells	7693 acres	
10	Marquess of Headfort (MP) of Headfort House, Kells	7544 acres	with 35,210 elsewhere

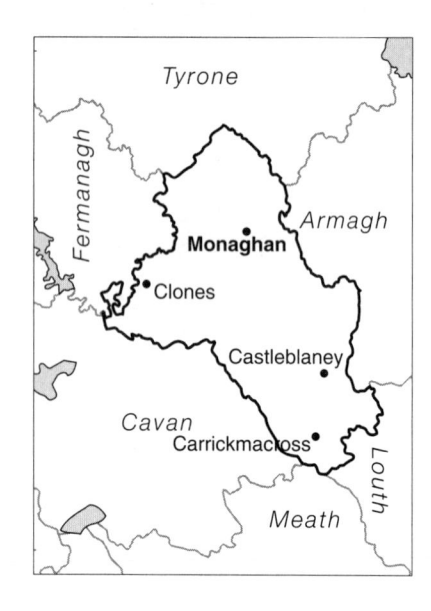

MONAGHAN

	1872	2001
Total acreage	311,439 acres	320,439 acres
Agricultural acreage	280,295 acres	218,745 acres
Non agricultural acreage	31,143 acres	101,694 acres
Population	112,785	58,494
Owners of nothing at all	111,315	32,547
Total Dwellings	21,821	14,512
Smallholdings: 1872 owners of less than one acre	833	
2000 owners of 0–2ha (0–4.94 acres)		116
Landowners over one acre (1872)	637	
Landowners over 2ha (2000)		5914
Landowners over 500 acres	73	1
Acreage (and percentage) of county owned by owners of over 500 acres	166,089 acres (53.3%)	

Top Landowners 2001

SIR JOHN NORMAN IDE LESLIE, 4TH BARONET, was born in 1916 and is the son of Sir Shane Leslie the writer, who died in 1971. Sir Shane's grandfather was MP for Monaghan and a noted painter. Although descended from a Protestant bishop, John Leslie, Bishop of the Isles, who was translated to Raphoe in 1633, the family are staunch Catholics. Sir John was educated at Downsides and his son and heir Desmond, the film producer and author, went to Ampleforth. Sir John holds two Catholic orders, being a Knight of Honour and Devotion of the Sovereign Military Order of Malta and a Knight Commander of the Order of St Gregory the Great. A Captain in the Irish Guards, he was a prisoner of war in World War Two. The family acquired Glasslough castle, where they live, in 1633 and there is still some land around the castle, believed to be about 700 acres in extent.

Where are they now:

THE 7TH MARQUESS OF BATH *(no. 2 in 1872)*. See Wiltshire (p.262).

THE EARL OF DARTRY *(no. 3 in 1872)*. Also held land in Waterford and Louth. The title became extinct in 1933 when Anthony Dawson, the 3rd Earl, died without a male heir. (He had three daughters.) The 3rd Earl was married to Baroness De Ros, the third oldest peerage in the House of Lords and that title was restored to her descendant Peter Maxwell, via her daughters. He sat as the 28th Baron De Ros and Premier Baron of England. He lost his seat in the Blair reforms in 1999 and lives in County Down in Northern Ireland.

THE 7TH BARON ROSSMORE *(no. 4 in 1872)*. William Warner Westenra was born in 1931 and educated at Eton and Cambridge. He now lives in Brighton. The family still own part of a small mountain in the county. He married Valerie Tobin from Riverstown in Birr, Co Offaly in 1982.

THE TEMPLETOWN VISCOUNTCY *(no. 6 in 1872)* became extinct in 1981 but the daughter of the 5th Viscount, Maureen Upton, lives in London

Significant Institutional Landowners

1872: The Church of Ireland owned 1519 acres.
2001: Coillte owns 6661 acres.

TOP 10 IN 1872

1	Mr Evelyn Shirley MP of Ettington Park, Stratford-on-Avon, Warwicks (Estate at Loughea, Carrickmacross)	26,386 acres	with 1374 elsewhere
2	Marquess of Bath of Longleat, Warminster, Wilts	22,762 acres	with 32,812 elsewhere
3	Earl of Dartrey of Dartry House, Coothill	17,732 acres	with 12,380 elsewhere
4	Lord Rossmore of Rossmore Park	14,839 acres	
5	Sir John Leslie Bt MP of Glasslough	13,674 acres	with 30,807 elsewhere
6	General the Viscount Templetown (MP) of Castle Upton, Templepatrick, Co Antrim (Estate at Templepatrick)	12,845 acres	with 11,924 elsewhere
7	Mrs Anne Adile Hope of Deepdene, Dorking Surrey (Estate at Castleblaney)	11,700 acres	with 10,073 elsewhere
8	Mr Edward Scudamore Lucas of Castle Shane	9955 acres	with 6510 elsewhere
9	Sir Thomas Barrett-Lennard Bt of Belhus, Romford, Essex	7920 acres	with 6492 elsewhere
10	Mr William Ancketill of Ancketill's Grove, Emyvale	7754 acres	

OFFALY
(Also known as King's County)

	1872	2001
Total acreage	491,629 acres	493,440 acres
Agricultural acreage	442,466 acres	297,839 acres
Non agricultural acreage	49,162 acres	195,601 acres
Population	75,900	58,494
Owners of nothing at all	74,762	30,453
Total Dwellings	14,799	15,951
Smallholdings:		
1872 owners of less than one acre	353	
2000 owners of 0–2ha (0–4.94 acres)		15
Landowners over one acre (1872)	785	
Landowners over 2ha (2000)		4085
Landowners over 500 acres	63	11
Acreage (and percentage) of county owned by owners of over 500 acres	216,700 acres (44%)	

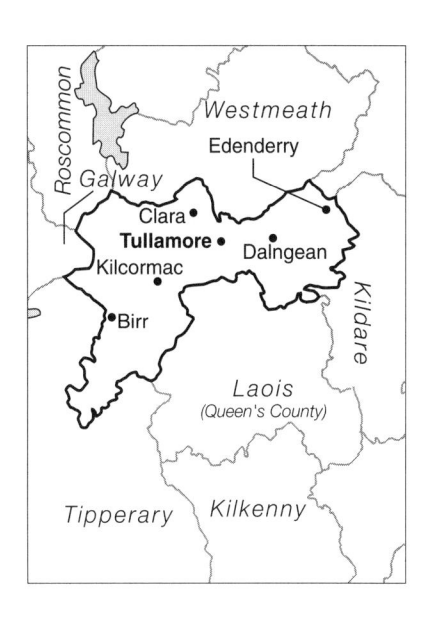

Top Landowners 2001

THE 7TH EARL OF ROSSE *5000 acres. No. 2 in 1872.* William Brendan Parsons, the 7th Earl, born in 1936, is one of the few Anglo-Irish aristocrats to bridge the egalitarianism created by independence and play a leading role in public life in the Republic. A former UN official, he is President of the Birr Scientific and Heritage Foundation, which looks after the scientific instruments accumulated by the family, including a huge telescope at Birr Castle. The 3rd Earl was President of the Royal Society and the family are connected to the engineering company Reyroll Parsons. Much of the estate went to the Land Commission but enough was retained, mostly woodlands, to maintain the Parsons as landowners in Offaly.

ROBERT ENRIGHT MOONEY OF THE DOONE *2300 acres.* The Mooney family were shown holding 4366 acres in the 1872 return. They are original Irish landed gentry, with a lineage that goes back to the Norman invasion and beyond. They still have the Norman castle, the mansion and, so it is rumoured, the ancestral cave on their lands.

TOM PARLON is President of the Irish Farmers Association, the strongest farmers group in Ireland, and was Offaly person of the year 1998. He is also a member of the board of the European Association of Farmers Unions. Described in *Who's Who in Ireland* as 'a very capable leader; one of the new breed of realists in today's agri business world'. Educated at Roscrea Christian Brothers and Gurteen Agricultural College he is married with two sons and three daughters. He farms about 500 acres of sheep and dairy cattle at Coolderry.

Where they are now:
THE 12TH BARON DIGBY, EDWARD KENELM DIGBY *(no. 1 in 1872)*, was born in 1924. Educated at Eton and Oxford he was a Captain in the Coldstream Guards. The family link with Offaly is ancient. His ancestor Robert Digby was appointed Governor of the County in 1620, in the aftermath of the Elizabethan plantations. The current peer still owns 15,000 acres in England and is the 180th largest landowner in the UK. His sister was the late Pamela Churchill Harriman, the US Ambassador to Paris during the Clinton presidency, and one time daughter-in-law of Sir Winston Churchill.

Significant Institutional Landowners

1872: The Grand Canal Company had 1706 acres. The Church of Ireland owned 7647 acres.
2001: One third of Offaly is classed as bog. Born Na Mona owns over 100,000 acres. Coillte owns 19,165 acres.

TOP 10 IN 1872

1	Lord Digby of Minterne House, Cerne, Dorset	29,722 acres	with 9783 elsewhere
2	Earl of Rosse of Birr Castle, Parsonstown	22,513 acres	with 3973 elsewhere
3	Countess of Charleville of Charleville Forest, Tullamore	20,032 acres	
4	Colonel Thomas Bernard of Castle Bernard, Kinnetty	14,629 acres	
5	Marquess of Downshire of Hillsborough Castle, Co Down	13,679 acres	with 106,510 elsewhere
6	Mr John Gilbert King MP of Ballylin, Ferbane	10,242 acres	with 954 elsewhere
7	Viscount Ashbrook of The Castle, Durrow, Co Kilkenny	7476 acres	with 15,304 elsewhere
8	Mrs Margaret Macneale of Cheltenham, Glos	6035 acres	
9	Mr Francis Bennnett of Thomastown House, Frankford	5480 acres	
10	Mr Jonathan Darby of Leap Castle, Roscrea Co Tipperary	4637 acres	

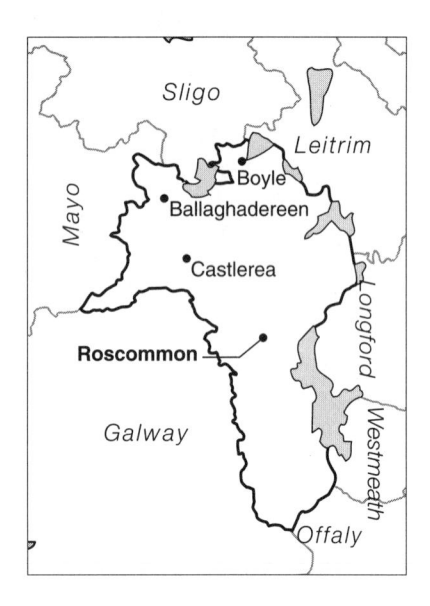

ROSCOMMON

	1872	2001
Total acreage	577,998 acres	629,760 acres
Agricultural acreage	520,198 acres	390,749 acres
Non agricultural acreage	57,799 acres	239,011 acres
Population	141,246	54,592
Owners of nothing at all	140,539	23,590
Total Dwellings	25,792	16,704
Smallholdings: 1872 owners of less than one acre 2000 owners of 0–2ha (0–4.94 acres)	132	21
Landowners over one acre (1872) Landowners over 2ha (2000)	575	7799
Landowners over 500 acres	99	1
Acreage (and percentage) of county owned by owners of over 500 acres	376,100 acres (65%)	

Top Landowners 2001

Where they are now:

FRANCIS ARTHUR FRENCH, THE 7TH BARON DE FREYNE *(no. 1 in 1872)*, born in 1927, is a knight of the sovereign order of Malta. He has given the House of Lords as his address for 20 years. A regular attender in the Conservative interest (57 days out of 75 in the last session before reform) he lost his seat in 1999. He is married to his second wife, Sheelki Deirdre Kane-O'Kelly of Co Wicklow.

THE 11TH EARL OF KINGSTON, BARCLAY EDWIN KING-TENISON *(no. 5 in 1872)*, was born in 1943. Educated at Winchester, he does not give an address in *Debrett's* and did not sit in the House of Lords, having no English peerage. He has been married three times and has one son and one daughter.

THE O'CONOR DON, DESMOND O'CONOR DON *(no. 8 in 1872)*, who succeeded to the title on the death of his father in July 2000, has a unique lineage. According to the *Irish Times* obituarist on 22 July 2000, he 'belongs to one of the oldest families in Europe . . . and would be the foremost claimant to the Irish throne, if one were proposed'. To find out quite how old a family, we have to go to *Burke's Landed Gentry* of Great Britain and Ireland of 1871, which begins the O'Conor Don lineage thus: 'Eochoid Morghmeodhin, son of Murdach Tireach, King of Ireland, died in AD 366.' This makes the present holder's title by far the oldest in this book. *BLG* says that the family have held land in the Cloonalis area of Roscommon since that period, a total of 1635 years. What *BLG* does not say, but what the Returns show, is that the O'Conor Don's were the fourth largest landowners in Roscommon in 1872, with 26,044 acres held by named members of the family. The family, though they remained Catholics over the centuries, were thoroughly anglicised. The incumbent in 1872 was an MP. The present holder's father, though he farmed in Wicklow for a while, was a major in the British army, educated at Downsides public school and Sandhurst. They are cousins of the earls of Belmore (see County Fermanagh). The family still own land in the area.

Significant Institutional Landowners

1872: The Trustees of Simpsons Hospital, Dublin owned 696 acres. The Church of Ireland owned 813 acres.
2001: Coillte owns 18,799 acres.

TOP 10 IN 1872

1	Lord De Freyne of French Park	34,400	acres	with 4388 elsewhere
2	Mr Robert King Harman MP	29,242	acres	with 43,671 elsewhere
3	Mr Henry Sandford Pakenham-Mahon of Strokestown House	26,980	acres	with 1143 elsewhere
4	Mr Thomas George Wills-Sandford of Castlerea House	24,410	acres	
5	Earl of Kingston of Kilronan Castle, Carrick-on-Shannon	17,726	acres	with 3581 elsewhere
6	Mr Edward Tenison of Kilronan Castle, Keadue (Not in Bateman)	16,915	acres	
7	Mrs French of Lough Erritt, Frenchpark	12,270	acres	with 1303 elsewhere
8	The O' Conor-Don MP of Belenegare, Frenchpark	11,466	acres	with 1184 elsewhere
9	Lord Crofton of Mote Park	11,053	acres	
10	Mr John Chidley Coote of Park Lane, London and Farmleigh, Castleknock, Dublin	10,348	acres	

SLIGO

	1872	2001
Total acreage	447,527 acres	453,760 acres
Agricultural acreage	402,774 acres	261,320 acres
Non agricultural acreage	44,752 acres	192,442 acres
Population	115,311	54,756
Owners of nothing at all	114,455	36,602
Total Dwellings	20,955	16,253
Smallholdings: 1872 owners of less than one acre 2000 owners of 0–2ha (0–4.94 acres)	451	10
Landowners over one acre (1872) Landowners over 2ha (2000)	405	5514
Landowners over 500 acres	145	9
Acreage (and percentage) of county owned by owners of over 500 acres	376,001 acres (84%)	

Top Landowners 2001

THE GORE BOOTH FAMILY. Although the head of the family now lives in England (see below), descendants of the owner of Lissadell in 1872 still live at the house, and still have an interest in the trust which owns the mansion and the estate. The Gore Booths were amongst the few good landlords of the famine period, mortgaging part of the estate to feed their stricken peasantry. A daughter of the house, Constance, the Countess Markiavitz, was sentenced to death for her part in the Rebellion of 1916 which eventually led to Irish independence. Reprieved, she refused the opportunity to become Britain's first woman MP in the 1918 election, becoming a member of the first Dail and a member of the first Irish Cabinet instead. W.B. Yeats wrote several poems in which the house is mentioned. The current acreage is unknown.

Where they are now:
SIR JOSSLYN HENRY GORE-BOOTH, THE 9TH BARONET *(no. 2 in 1872)*, born in 1950, was educated at Eton, Oxford and INSEAD. He is married to Jane Mary Hovell-Thurlow-Cummings-Bruce. They have one daughter and live in Co Durham. One of his cousins was recently British ambassador to Saudi Arabia.

THE O'CONOR DON. (See also Roscommon.) The family of the O'Conor Don, spelt O'Connor in the Returns for this county, held land here in Sligo. In 1872 the acreage was 1184 acres. Alongside this acreage is that of Peter O'Connor, almost certainly a relative of the O'Conor Don, with 4849 acres at Carmsfoot.

Significant Institutional Landowners

1872: The Church of Ireland owned 868 acres.
2001: Coillte owns 26,815 acres.

TOP 10 IN 1872

1	Mr Edward Henry Cooper MP of Markree Castle, Colloony	34,120 acres	with 1118 elsewhere
2	Sir Henry Gore-Booth Bt of Lissadell	31,774 acres	
3	Mr Charles William O'Hara MP of Cooper's Hill, Ballymote	21,070 acres	
4	Mr William Ormsby Gore of Derrycarne, Dromod (Not in Bateman)	21,019 acres	
5	Mr Owen Wynne of Hazlewood, Sligo	12,982 acres	with 15,436 elsewhere
6	Mr Edward Robert King Harman MP of Rockingham, Boyle, Roscommon	12,629 acres	with 60,284 elsewhere
7	Hon Mr Anthony Melbourne Ashley MP of Classybawn, Cliffany	12,436 acres	
8	Mr R.W. Orme of Owenmore, Sligo	11,771 acres	
9	Mr William Phibbs of Seafield, Sligo	10,507 acres	with 834 elsewhere
10	Lieutenant General Sir Roger Palmer Bt MP of Keenagh, Crossmolina, Mayo	9570 acres	with 89,384 elsewhere

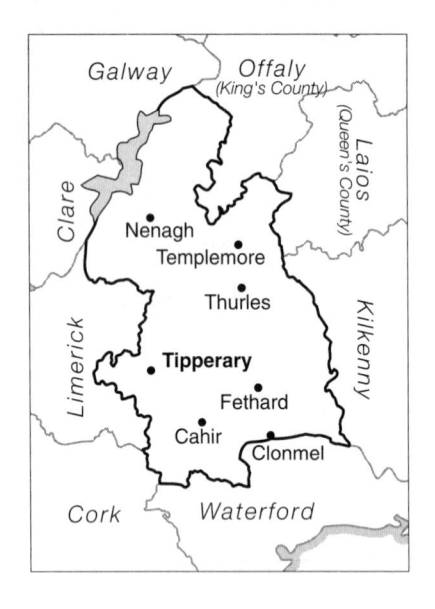

TIPPERARY

	1872	2001
Total acreage	1,042,457 acres	1,054,080 acres
Agricultural acreage	938,211 acres	778,352 acres
Non agricultural acreage	104,245 acres	275,728 acres
Population	216,713	132,747
Owners of nothing at all	214,341	67,630
Total Dwellings	38,544	38,036
Smallholdings: 1872 owners of less than one acre	666	
2000 owners of 0–2ha (0–4.94 acres)		82
Landowners over one acre (1872)	1706	
Landowners over 2ha (2000)		9406
Landowners over 500 acres	111	24
Acreage (and percentage) of county owned by owners of over 500 acres	376,987 acres (36.1%)	

Top Landowners 2001

THE HOLY GHOST FATHERS AT ROCKWELL COLLEGE. In the Returns the owners of what has become one of the most prominent secondary or public schools in Ireland, owned a mere 79 acres. With a catering college and agricultural school attached the farm is now over 500 acres, sited directly across the road from Vincent O'Brien's home stud (see below). The Holy Ghost Fathers later bought part of the estate of Francis Lowe at Kilshane, shown in the Returns at 4949 acres. The small surviving farm around the main house was about 200 acres in extent in the 1960s. The Lowe mansion was tucked well up an enfiladed drive, Cornish style, with gun ports in all the window shutters. Francis Lowe did not trust the natives much, nor they him.

THE COOLMORE STUD OF JOHN MAGNIER AND VINCENT O'BRIEN. This stud, in a county that always loved horse racing, even in the worst of times, is now said to be over 2000 acres in extent and is the heart of an international network of studs, in America, Australia and with plans for an extension to China in hand. Coolmore and its associated stables are described as 'the dominant force in Thoroughbred breeding world wide', by *Who's Who in Ireland*. John Magnier is the nephew of Clem Magnier, a well-known Irish trainer, and has been in the business since the early 1970s. Educated at Glenstal Abbey, the *Sunday Times* rates him worth £150 million in its year 2001 Rich List, and the 26th wealthiest person in Ireland. He is married to Susan O'Brien, daughter of his partner at Coolmore.

VINCENT O'BRIEN, born in 1917, is Ireland's most famous trainer, having obtained his trainer's licence in 1943 and won the Grand National three times, the Cheltenham Gold Cup four times and innumerable other races, usually more than once. A partner with his son-in-law John Magnier in the Coolmore Stud, his own stud, believed to be close to 1000 acres in size, is at Ballydoyle House, Cashel. He was educated at Mungret College and has two sons and three daughters.

Where they are now:
THE LISMORE PEERAGE *(no. 1 in 1872)* is long extinct.

CONNAN WYNDHAM LESLIE MAUDE, THE 9TH VISCOUNT HAWARDEN *(no. 8 in 1872)*, born in 1961, is a landowner near Canterbury in Kent. Having only an Irish peerage he could not sit in the House of Lords.

Significant Institutional Landowners

1872: Trinity College Dublin owned 893 acres. The Bluecoats School owned 994 acres. The Erasmus Smith schools owned 2903 acres. The Church of Ireland owned 2240 acres.
2001: Coillte owns 59,469 acres.

TOP 10 IN 1872

1	Viscount Lismore of Shanbally, Clogheen	34,945 acres	with 7261 elsewhere
2	Hon Mr Charles White of Cahercon (The estate was being sold at the time of the Returns)	23,957 acres	
3	Lord Dunalley of Kilboy, Nenagh	21,081 acres	
4	Mr George Staunton King Massey-Dawson of Ballynacourty	19,093 acres	with 165 elsewhere
5	Lady Margaret Charteris of The Lodge, Cahir	16,616 acres	with 13 elsewhere
6	Earl of Clonmell of Bishop's Court, Straffan, Co Kildare	16,187 acres	with 11,459 elsewhere
7	Marquess of Ormonde of the Castle, Kilkenny	15,765 acres	with 11,960 elsewhere
8	Viscount Hawarden of Dundrum, Cashel	15,272 acres	
9	Mr Nathaniel Buckley of Ryecroft, Ashton-under-Lyme, England (Estate at Galtee Castle, Mitchelstown)	13,260 acres	with 7638 elsewhere
10	Mr Arthur Moore MP of Moorsfort	10,199 acres	

WATERFORD

	1872	2001
Total acreage	455,435 acres	456,320 acres
Agricultural acreage	409,891 acres	318,044 acres
Non agricultural acreage	45,543 acres	138,276 acres
Population	123,310	91,624
Owners of nothing at all	122,117	48,255
Total Dwellings	21,252	26,607
Smallholdings: 1872 owners of less than one acre	532	
2000 owners of 0–2ha (0–4.94 acres)		35
Landowners over one acre (1872)	661	
Landowners over 2ha (2000)		3221
Landowners over 500 acres	88	35
Acreage (and percentage) of county owned by owners of over 500 acres	211,301 acres (46.3%)	

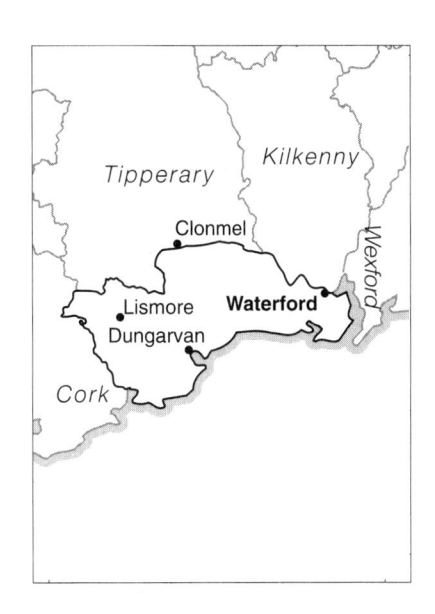

Top Landowners 2001

THE 8TH MARQUESS OF WATERFORD *10,000 acres with 900 in Wicklow. No. 1 in 1872.* John Hubert de la Poer Beresford, the 8th Marquess, was born in 1933. Educated at Eton, he was a lieutenant in the Royal Horse Guards. He is married to Lady Caroline Wyndham-Quin, a daughter of the 6th Earl of Dunraven and Mount-Earl. The family managed to retain a large acreage as bog and woodland which was excluded from the Land Commision distribution. He lives at Curraghmore and has a home in Wicklow. The Beresford family owned land all over Ireland at the time of the 1872 Return.

THE 11TH DUKE OF DEVONSHIRE *8000 acres, with 65,000 acres in England. No. 2 in 1872.* Lismore castle, the Irish home of the Devonshires, is a notable 'great house' and can now be rented from the family for special occasions. They were able to retain the large acreage because much of it is woodland, and revenues in the UK supported the house for many years. For further details see Derby (p.233).

SIR RICHARD MICHAEL KEANE, born in 1909 and educated at Sherborne and Oxford, was still living at the family seat, Cappoquin House, in 2000. His heir is John Keane, born in 1941 and educated at Eton and Oxford. There is no information on any landholdings still with the family.

Where they are now:
THE EARL OF DARTREY *(no. 8 in 1872)*, see County Monaghan.

LORD ASHTOWN *(no. 7 in 1872)*, see County Limerick.

SIR RICHARD JAMES MUSGRAVE, THE 7TH BARONET *(no. 10 in 1872)*, was born in 1922 and educated at Stowe. He later served in the Indian Army in World War Two and has two homes, one in County Meath and the other at Syros in Greece. His heir is Christopher Shane, born in 1959.

Significant Institutional Landowners

1872: Waterford College owned 1292 acres. The Trustees of the Leper Hospital owned 858 acres. The Church of Ireland owned 637 acres.
2001: Coillte owns 40,724 acres.

TOP 10 IN 1872

1	Marqess of Waterford (MP) of Curraghmore	39,883 acres	with 26,801 elsewhere
2	Mr Henry Villiers-Stuart MP of Dromana	30,882 acres	with 71 elsewhere
3	Duke of Devonshire (MP) of Chatsworth House, Derbyshire (Estate is at Lismore)	27,483 acres	with 171,098 elsewhere
4	Mr Henry Philip Chearnley of Salterbridge, Cappoquin	18,165 acres	
5	Count Edmond De La Poer MP of Gurteen la Poer, Kilsheelan	13,448 acres	with 12 elsewhere
6	Mr John Palliser of Comragh, Kilmacthomas	9825 acres	with 4021 elsewhere
7	Lord Ashtown of Woodlawn, Galway	9435 acres	with 34,208 elsewhere
8	Earl of Dartrey of Dartrey House, Coothill, Co Monaghan	8918 acres	with 21,194 elsewhere
9	Sir Richard Francis Keane Bt of Cappoquin House, Waterford	8909 acres	
10	Sir Richard John Musgrave Bt of Tourin, Cappoquin	8282 acres	with 124 elsewhere

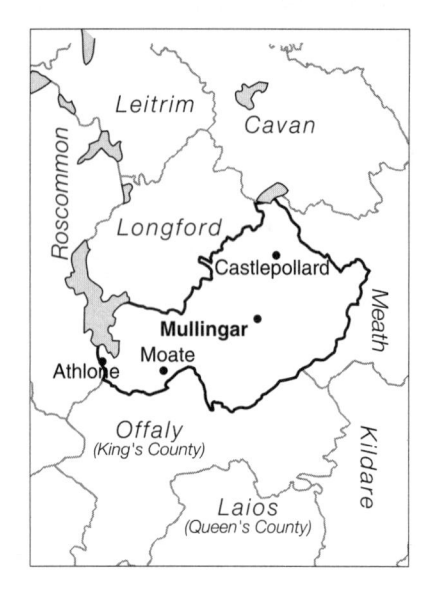

WESTMEATH

	1872	2001
Total acreage	430,003 acres	442,880 acres
Agricultural acreage	387,002 acres	293,821 acres
Non agricultural acreage	43,000 acres	149,059 acres
Population	78,432	61,182
Owners of nothing at all	77,764	30,598
Total Dwellings	15,152	17,477
Smallholdings: 1872 owners of less than one acre	111	
2000 owners of 0–2ha (0–4.94 acres)		13
Landowners over one acre (1872)	557	
Landowners over 2ha (2000)		16
Landowners over 500 acres	127	
Acreage (and percentage) of county owned by owners of over 500 acres	300,112 acres (69%)	

Top Landowners 2001

THE 7TH EARL OF LONGFORD *900 acres. No. 2 in 1872.* Tom Packenham, son and heir to the 7th Earl, was born in 1933 and educated at Ampleforth. He lives with his wife at the family home, Tullynally Castle, at Castle Pollard. His father, born in 1905, continues to attend the House of Lords daily, as he has a UK peerage from the first days of the Labour government in 1945, recreated in 1999 as a life peerage so he could remain as one of the upper house's longest serving members. The 7th Earl died in August 2001 and Tom Packenham is now the 8th Earl of Longford, but without a seat in the House of Lords.

THE BEAUMONT FAMILY *500 acres.* The family home of the Earls of Belvedere, who once owned the land around the Rugby club in Dublin, was left to Rex Beaumont by a relative of the Earls of Belvedere, a title long extinct. Most of the land, including the park, was redistributed by the Land Commission and the above may be an excessive estimate of what is left.

Where they are now:
SIR JOHN NUGENT, THE 7TH BARONET AND A COUNT OF THE AUSTRIAN EMPIRE, was born in 1933. The beautiful Ballinlough Castle at Clonmeellon was totally restored by his parents in 1939. He lives in Berkshire where he is a JP and was high sheriff in 1981. In the 1872 Return there are nine Nugents, all relatives, owning over 16,000 acres between them, but with no holding big enough to make the lists here. Members of the family still own land in the area.

THE 8TH BARON CASTLEMAINE, ROLAND HANDCOCK *(no. 4 in 1872),* was born in 1943 and is a major in the Army Air Corps. He lives in Wiltshire. Divorced and remarried, his son and heir is Ronan Handcock, born in 1989.

THE GREVILLE PEERAGE *(no. 5 in 1872)* is long extinct.

THE CHAPMAN AND ENNIS *(no. 8 in 1872)* baronetages are also long extinct.

Significant Institutional Landowners

1872: The Church of Ireland owned 1116 acres. The Midland Great Western Railway owned 695 acres. Wilson's Hospital in Dominick Street, Dublin, owned 4495 acres.
2001: Coillte owns 10,605 acres.

TOP 10 IN 1872

1	Mr George Augustus Rochfort-Boyd of Middleton Park, Castletown	16,397 acres	
2	General the Earl of Longford of Pakenham Hall, Castle Pollard	15,014 acres	with 4975 elsewhere
3	Mr John Malone of Baronstown, Ballinacargy, Mullingar	13,715 acres	
4	Lord Castlemaine of Moydrum Castle, Athlone	11,444 acres	with 597 elsewhere
5	Lord Greville (MP) of Clonyn Castle, Delvin	9783 acres	with 8825 elsewhere
6	Mr Thomas James Smyth of Ballynegall, Mullingar	9778 acres	with 1278 elsewhere
7	Mr Patrick Edward Murphy of Ballinacloon, Mullingar	9693 acres	
8	Sir Benjamin James Chapman Bt MP of Killua Castle, Clonmellon	9516 acres	with 3841 elsewhere
9	Mr Charles Brinsley Marlay of Belvedere, Mullingar	9059 acres	with 5226 elsewhere
10	Sir John James Ennis Bt of Ballinahown, Athlone	8774 acres	with 2161 elsewhere

WEXFORD

	1872	2001
Total acreage	573,051 acres	581,760 acres
Agricultural acreage	515,745 acres	483,893 acres
Non agricultural acreage	57,305 acres	97,867 acres
Population	132,666	102,045
Owners of nothing at all	130,909	54,727
Total Dwellings	24,982	28,099
Smallholdings: 1872 owners of less than one acre	581	
2000 owners of 0–2ha (0–4.94 acres)		52
Landowners over one acre (1872)	1176	
Landowners over 2ha (2000)		5645
Landowners over 500 acres	156	29
Acreage (and percentage) of county owned by owners of over 500 acres	199,301 acres (34.7%)	

Top Landowners 2001

BERT ALLEN, educated at Newtown School in Waterford, is reckoned to be one of the biggest farmers and livestock dealers in the county. He created a major food exporting business and has bought a series of hotels around Ireland and in Scotland. Local opinion suggests that his farms are close to or over 1000 acres in extent.

Where are they now:

THE 8TH MARQUESS OF ELY *(no. 4 in 1872)*. Charles John Tottenham, born in 1913, was a schoolmaster at Port Hope in Canada. His daughter, the Rt Rev Lady Ann Elizabeth Tottenham, has been the suffragan Bishop of Toronto since 1997. His family name is Tottenham, a name which crops up throughout the 1872 Return for Ireland.

THE 9TH EARL OF COURTOWN *(no. 3 in 1872)*. James Stopford, born in 1954 and educated at Eton and the Royal Agricultural College Cirencester, is descended from a family who were MPs in the area from the early 1700s. He farms in Gloucestershire. His heir is his son, James Stopford.

THE 7TH BARON CAREW *(no. 1 in 1872)*. See Kildare (p.337)

VISCOUNT POWERSCOURT *(no. 6 in 1872)*. See Wicklow.

LORD TEMPLEMORE *(no. 7 in 1872)*. Peerage is extinct.

THE TALBOT POWER *(no. 8 in 1872)* baronetcy is extinct.

Significant Institutional Landowners

1872: St Patrick's Hospital owned 2181 acres. The Church of Ireland owned 746 acres. The Midland Great Western Railway owned 695 acres. Wilson's Hospital in Dominick Street, Dublin, owned 4495 acres.
2001: Coillte owns 19,271 acres.

TOP 10 IN 1872

1	Lord Carew of Castleborough, Enniscorthy	17,830 acres	with 3136 elsewhere
2	Lord Fitzgerald of Johnstown Castle, Wexford (Land actually owned by his wife Lady Adelaide Forbes)	15,216 acres	with 15,216 elsewhere
3	Earl of Courtown of Courtown House, Gorey	14,426 acres	with 8888 elsewhere
4	Marquess of Ely of Ely Lodge, Enniskillen (Estate at Loftus Hall, Fethard)	14,023 acres	with 34,969 elsewhere
5	Mrs Anne Rossborough-Colclough of Tintern Abbey, New Ross	13,329 acres	
6	Viscount Powerscourt of Powerscourt, Enniskerry	11,729 acres	with 12,272 elsewhere
7	Lord Templemore of Preston House, Basigstoke, Hants (Estate at Dunbrody Park, Arthurstown)	11,327 acres	with 15,315 elsewhere
8	Sir John Talbot Power MP of Edermine House, Enniscorthy	10,205 acres	with 6 elsewhere
9	Mr William Orme Foster MP of Apley Park, Bridgenorth, England	9724 acres	with 11,338 elsewhere
10	Hon Mrs Deane Morgan of Ardcandrisk, Wexford (Not in Bateman)	9412 acres	

WICKLOW

	1872	2001
Total acreage	497,656 acres	500,480 acres
Agricultural acreage	447,890 acres	256,808 acres
Non agricultural acreage	49,765 acres	243,672 acres
Population	78,697	97,265
Owners of nothing at all	77,656	50,590
Total Dwellings	14,111	27,750
Smallholdings: 1872 owners of less than one acre	534	
2000 owners of 0–2ha (0–4.94 acres)		39
Landowners over one acre (1872)	507	
Landowners over 2ha (2000)		2751
Landowners over 500 acres	63	
Acreage (and percentage) of county owned by owners of over 500 acres	313,987 acres (63%)	

Top Landowners 2001

THE 8TH MARQUESS OF WATERFORD *900 acres* with 10,000 in Waterford. No. 3 in 1872. See Waterford (p.351).

THE 15TH EARL OF MEATH *800 acres.* No. 8 in 1872. John 'Jack' Anthony Brabazon, the 15th Earl of Meath, was born in 1941 and was educated at Harrow, followed by a stint in the Grenadier Guards as a lieutenant. A page of honour to the Queen in the 1950s, he later married Xenia Goudime, daughter of a Surrey landowner. In 2001 he sold his 4125 acre mountain sporting estate at Rathdrum in Wicklow for £10 million. He is moving down to his smaller 800 estate at Kilruddery near Bray. That estate is potentially worth between £400 million and £800 million if prices around Dublin hold. His heir is lord Ardee, born in 1977.

THE SLAZENGER FAMILY *800 acres.* The Slazenger family bought and restored the house and gardens of Powerscourt, one of the most attractive heritage sites in Ireland. For a period until 1974 their daughter was married to the current heir to the title. See entry for Viscount Powerscourt below.

THE GRIFFIN FAMILY AT MOUNT KENNEDY *300 acres.* The beautiful Mount Kennedy house and gardens command one of the finest views in Wicklow. The original estate was 64,000 acres, and is shown at just over 10,000 acres in 1872.

THE BEIT TRUST *700 acres.* There is a small estate of perhaps 700 acres surrounding Russborough at Blessington, an exquisite house which housed one of the most important private art collections in Ireland until robbed in the 1980s. Sir Alfred Beit, who died in 1994, was the last baronet but his wife still resides at the house, which can be viewed by appointment.

Where they are now:
MERVYN NIALL WINGFIELD, THE 10TH VISCOUNT POWERSCOURT *(no. 2 in 1872)*, was born in 1935 and was educated at Stowe followed by a spell in the Irish Guards. Married first to Wendy Anne Slazenger, they were divorced in 1974, the year the great house was destroyed in a fire. He divorced his second wife in 1995 and now lives in Thailand. His sister, Lady Langrishe, lives in Co Meath.

Significant Institutional Landowners

1872: Trinity College Dublin had 1287 acres. The Dublin, Wexford and Wicklow Railway Company had 721 acres.
2001: Coillte owns 66,296 acres.

TOP 10 IN 1872

1	The Earl Fitzwilliam (MP) of Wentworth House, Rotherham, Yorks (The estate was at Coolatin Park, Shillelagh)	89,981 acres	with 25,852 elsewhere
2	Viscount Powerscourt	40,986 acres	with 12,272 elsewhere
3	Marquess of Waterford (MP) of Curraghmore, Waterford	26,035 acres	with 40,649 elsewhere
4	Earl of Wicklow of Shelton Abbey, Arklow	22,103 acres	with 6610 elsewhere
5	Mr John Mandeville Hugo of Landscape (Not in Bateman)	17,937 acres	
6	Earl of Carysfort of Glenart Castle, Arklow	16,674 acres	with 9240 elsewhere
7	Marquess of Downshire of Hillsborough Castle, Co Down	15,766 acres	with 104,423 elsewhere
8	Earl of Meath (MP) of Kilruddery Castle, Bray	14,717 acres	with 731 elsewhere
9	Mr Cornwallis Robert Ducarel Gun-Cunninghame of Mount Kennedy	10,479 acres	
10	Mr William Kemmis of Ballinacor, Rathdrum	8041 acres	

PART III
The Land Lists

The Land Lists

The land lists which follow are the first to be published in the UK and Ireland since the sensational publication of the *Return of Owners of Land* in the 1870s. The lists reflect a perennial interest on the part of the public in such lists, an interest that is not merely prurient, but based on a legitimate instinct for sensing where secrecy plays against the public interest. The lists augment the work of Dr Philip Beresford at the *Sunday Times*, whose current Rich List (2001) had an extraordinary impact on the circulation of that paper on the day of publication, raising it by 16% in the United Kingdom and by 22% in Ireland. His rival at the *Mail on Sunday*, Rachel Oldroyd, proves the same point, with that paper also enjoying a significant circulation increase on the publication of its Rich List. The extension of the Register of Parliamentary interests to the House of Lords has come just too late to demonstrate the huge concentration of landowner interest that the House actually represented.

Introduction to the 1872 Lists

The 1872 lists are published because they still offer directly relevant history. They are the starting point for identifying the current landowners, and they remain the only way to fill the gap left by the defective English & Welsh Land Registry. They are drawn directly from the Returns and the corrections made to the top 3000 or so landowners by John Bateman between 1872 and 1883. It is important to note that, unlike the 2001 lists, at the time of their publication they were both accurate and verifiable. As such, they demonstrate the extent to which the country has moved from almost total enlightenment in matters of landownership to almost total ignorance. They show how the great landowners, the power behind the throne and politics, neutralised the spread of the franchise by progressively eliminating perhaps the most essential economic information that had ever been produced in the country.

A note on 1872 values

The 1872 Return indicated the rental income from (rather than the land value of) the acreage identified. As has been done previously in this book, the equivalent value of this in 2001 is calculated by using a factor of 70 (see Appendix I, Note on Comparative Values, p.395). A very approximate land value is calculated by multiplying the income stream by 25.

NB: London acreages were not included in the 1872 Return, and consequently are not included in the 1872 lists published here. For details of landowners in London see p.148.

Introduction to the 2001 Lists

Unlike the 1872 lists, these lists are based on estimates, estimates which cannot be checked in the Land Registry because the land is not registered and, where it is, is economically out of the reach of any normal research. These lists derive, initially, from the 1872 Return, and after that from information gleaned from press cuttings, especially obituaries in *The*

Times and the *Daily Telegraph*, the Rich Lists produced by Dr Philip Beresford at the *Sunday Times* and by Rachel Oldroyd at the *Mail on Sunday*, the pages of the *Estates Gazette*, old wills, Professor David Cannadine's masterly work on the *Decline of the British Aristocracy*, *Field and Country Life* magazine, *Debrett's*, *Burke's Landed Gentry*, *Whittaker's Baronetage & Peerage* and *Walford's County Families*. For Scotland, the lists are totally dependent on the work of the chroniclers John MacEwen and his successor Andy Wightman in their books *Who Owns Scotland*. Back issues of *BusinessAge* and *Eurobusiness* were consulted. The Land Registry staff in London and in Dublin gave what help they could. The British Library and the libraries at the House of Commons and the House of Lords were also used as was that of the Devon & Exeter Institution and of the West Country Studies library in Exeter.

A note on 2001 values

The source of land values for these lists is the prices stated in the Autumn 2000 Property Market Report from the Valuation Office of the UK Inland Revenue. For Ireland they are taken from the property and farm pages of the *Irish Times* over the period Jan–May 2001.

FARM LAND (PER ACRE)

England and Wales

	Untenanted	Tenanted
Arable	£3068	£1197
Dairy	£3135	£1256
Mixed	£2718	£1081
Hill	£1050	£470

Scotland

	Untenanted	Tenanted
Arable	£2243	£1117
Dairy	£2000	£1013
Mixed	£1442	£688
Hill	£145	£80

Northern Ireland

	Untenanted	Tenanted
Arable	£3875	Not available
Dairy	£6000	di
Mixed	£3333	di
Hill	£1675	di

Republic of Ireland

	Untenanted	Tenanted
Arable	£5000–7000	Not available
Dairy	£6000–9000	di
Mixed	£4000–6000	di
Hill	up to £2500	di

Residential building land (per acre)

England & Wales excluding London	£404,000–550,000
Inner London	£1,500,000–2,000,000
Outer London	£1,100,000–1,500,000
Scotland	£340,000–400,000
Northern Ireland	£300,000–350,000
Irish Republic excluding Dublin (IRL£)	£450,000–650,000
Dublin (IRL£)	£1,250,000–1,750,000

How these values are applied

All estates are assumed to have an untenanted home farm occupying an average of 10% of the estate.

All estates in England are assigned 1% of their acreage as potential house building land. In the home counties this is increased to 2%. For a number of estates, such as Braybrook, Raleigh, Norfolk, Iliffe, Whitbread and Northampton this is an underestimate. In the home counties of England, 'estates' are fetching a price out of line with the agricultural values in the Property Market Report, with a 2000-acre estate in Hampshire, part tenanted, offered for £10,000,000 in the *Financial Times* on 2 June 2001. Estates of 4000 acres are fetching between £15,000,000 and £20,000,000.

Scottish Estates close to Edinburgh and Glasgow are assigned 1% of their acreage as potential house building land.

Sporting estates with moor, scrub and hill land are assigned a figure of two times hill farm value in England and between two and three times hill land value in Scotland to reflect current sporting estate values. This is a conservative underestimate given that Scottish sporting estates are now a serious part of the international world of the wealth and remain one of the few places in Europe where such large tracts of land are available.

Estates close to Dublin are assigned a 50% value for potential building land.

List of Tables

1872:
1 – Top 100 landowners in UK & Ireland ranked by (a) acreage, and (b) land value
2 – Top 50 landowners in (a) England, (b) Wales, (c) Scotland, (d) Northern Ireland, (e) Republic of Ireland ranked by acreage
3 – Top 50 aristocratic landowners in the UK & Ireland ranked by acreage

2001:
4 – Top 100 landowners in the UK & Republic of Ireland ranked by (a) acreage, and (b) land value
5 – Top 100 landowners in the UK & Republic of Ireland ranked by wealth
6 – Top 100 aristocratic landowners in the UK & Republic of Ireland ranked by acreage

LAND LIST 1 (A)
1872
TOP 100 LANDOWNERS IN THE UK & IRELAND RANKED BY ACREAGE

	Title	Name of landowner	Home county	Total acreage 1872	Income value 1872	Equivalent income value 2001	Estimated land value of total acreage 1872	Equivalent estimated land value 2001
1	Duke of	Sutherland	Sutherland	1,358,545	£141,667	£9,916,690	£3,541,675	£247,917,250
2	Duke of	Buccleuch & Queensbury	Northants	460,108	£232,000	£16,240,000	£5,800,000	£406,000,000
3	Earl of	Breadalbane	Perth	438,358	£58,292	£4,080,440	£1,457,300	£102,011,000
4	Lady	Matheson	Ross	424,560	£20,346	£1,424,220	£508,650	£35,605,500
5	Sir	Charles Ross Bt	Ross	356,500	£17,264	£1,208,480	£431,600	£30,212,000
6	Earl of	Seafield	Inverness	305,930	£78,227	£5,475,890	£1,955,675	£136,897,250
7	Duke of	Richmond and Gordon	Sussex	286,411	£79,683	£5,577,810	£1,992,075	£139,445,250
8	Earl of	Fife	Banff	249,220	£72,563	£5,079,410	£1,814,075	£126,985,250
9	Sir	Alexander Matheson Bt	Ross	220,663	£3,238	£226,660	£80,950	£5,666,500
10	Duke of	Atholl	Perth	201,640	£42,030	£2,942,100	£1,050,750	£73,552,500
11	Duke of	Devonshire	Derby	198,572	£180,750	£12,652,500	£4,518,750	£316,312,500
12	Duke of	Northumberland	Northumbs	186,397	£176,048	£12,323,360	£4,401,200	£308,084,000
13	Duke of	Portland	Notts	183,199	£88,350	£6,184,500	£2,208,750	£154,612,500
14	Lord	Lovat	Inverness	181,791	£30,300	£2,121,000	£757,500	£53,025,000
15	Duke of	Argyll	Argyll	175,114	£50,842	£3,558,940	£1,271,050	£88,973,500
16	Mr	Richard Berridge	Galway	170,517	£9,503	£665,210	£237,575	£16,630,250
17	Marquess of	Conyngham	Kent	166,710	£50,076	£3,505,320	£1,251,900	£87,633,000
18	Sir	Kenneth Mackenzie Bt	Ross	164,680	£9,344	£654,080	£233,600	£16,352,000
19	Duke of	Hamilton and Brandon	Bute	157,368	£73,636	£5,154,520	£1,840,900	£128,863,000
20	Sir	John Ramsden Bt	Lincs	150,048	£181,294	£12,690,580	£4,532,350	£317,264,500
21	Sir	Watkin Williams-Wynn Bt	Denbigh	145,770	£54,575	£3,820,250	£1,364,375	£95,506,250
22	Marquess of	Lansdowne	Wilts	142,916	£62,025	£4,341,750	£1,550,625	£108,543,750
23	The	Macleod	Inverness	141,679	£8,464	£592,480	£211,600	£14,812,000
24	Earl of	Dalhousie	Forfar	138,021	£58,603	£4,102,210	£1,465,075	£102,555,250
25	Lord	Macdonald	Inverness	132,419	£16,613	£1,162,910	£415,325	£29,072,750
26	Baroness	Willoughby D'Eresby	Lincs	132,220	£74,006	£5,180,420	£1,850,150	£129,510,500

THE LAND LISTS 359

TOP 100 LANDOWNERS IN THE UK & IRELAND RANKED BY ACREAGE 1872 (CONT.)

	Title	Name of landowner	Home county	Total acreage 1872	Income value 1872	Equivalent income value 2001	Estimated land value of total acreage 1872	Equivalent estimated land value 2001
27	The	Mackintosh	Inverness	126,295	£29,011	£2,030,770	£725,275	£50,769,250
28	Mr	Donald Cameron	Inverness	126,008	£10,721	£750,470	£268,025	£18,761,750
29	Lady	Cathcart	Aberdeen	125,472	£38,188	£2,673,160	£954,700	£66,829,000
30	Sir	George Macpherson-Grant Bt	Banff	125,443	£11,546	£808,220	£288,650	£20,205,500
31	Marquess of	Downshire	Down	120,189	£96,961	£6,787,270	£2,424,025	£169,681,750
32	Earl of	Kenmare	Kerry	118,606	£34,473	£2,413,110	£861,825	£60,327,750
33	Marquess of	Bute	Bute	116,668	£151,135	£10,579,450	£3,778,375	£264,486,250
34	Earl of	Stair	Wigtown	116,370	£67,905	£4,753,350	£1,697,625	£118,833,750
35	Earl	Fitzwilliam	York	115,743	£138,801	£9,716,070	£3,470,025	£242,901,750
36	Marquess of	Sligo	Mayo	114,881	£19,000	£1,330,000	£475,000	£33,250,000
37	The	Chisholm (James Sutherland)	Inverness	113,256	£8,858	£620,060	£221,450	£15,501,500
38	Lord	Leconfield	Sussex	109,935	£88,112	£6,167,840	£2,202,800	£154,196,000
39	Mr	James Farquharson	Aberdeen	109,561	£12,974	£908,180	£324,350	£22,704,500
40	Earl of	Home	Lanark	106,550	£56,632	£3,964,240	£1,415,800	£99,106,000
41	Duke of	Cleveland	Durham	104,194	£97,398	£6,817,860	£2,434,950	£170,446,500
42	Duke of	Montrose	Stirling	103,447	£24,872	£1,741,040	£621,800	£43,526,000
43	Earl of	Cawdor	Pembroke	101,657	£44,662	£3,126,340	£1,116,550	£78,158,500
44	Lord	Middleton	Notts	100,002	£54,014	£3,780,980	£1,350,350	£94,524,500
45	Mrs	Edward Ellice	Inverness	99,559	£6,771	£473,970	£169,275	£11,849,250
46	Sir	Roger Palmer Bt	Mayo	98,954	£26,661	£1,866,270	£666,525	£46,656,750
47	Mr	Horatio Murray-Stewart	Donegal	98,269	£22,822	£1,597,540	£570,550	£39,938,500
48	Sir	Robert Menzies Bt	Perth	98,242	£11,467	£802,690	£286,675	£20,067,250
49	Viscount	Dillon	Oxford	94,764	£28,762	£2,013,340	£719,050	£50,333,500
50	Lord	Ventry	Kerry	93,629	£17,067	£1,194,690	£426,675	£29,867,250
51	Mr	Evan Baillie	Inverness	92,648	£11,881	£831,670	£297,025	£20,791,750
52	Mr	Arthur Balfour	Ross	87,196	£19,833	£1,388,310	£495,825	£34,707,750
53	Duke of	Bedford	Beds	86,335	£225,000	£15,750,000	£5,625,000	£393,750,000
54	Sir	John Campbell-Orde Bt	Inverness	85,745	£6,373	£446,110	£159,325	£11,152,750

TOP 100 LANDOWNERS IN THE UK & IRELAND RANKED BY ACREAGE 1872 (CONT.)

	Title	Name of landowner	Home county	Total acreage 1872	Income value 1872	Equivalent income value 2001	Estimated land value of total acreage 1872	Equivalent estimated land value 2001
55	Marquess of	Huntley	Aberdeen	85,711	£19,860	£1,390,200	£496,500	£34,755,000
56	Mr	John Malcolm	Argyll	85,661	£24,989	£1,749,230	£624,725	£43,730,750
57	Lord	Wimborne	Dorset	83,539	£46,856	£3,279,920	£1,171,400	£81,998,000
58	Mrs	Cameron-Campbell	Inverness	83,500	£5,658	£396,060	£141,450	£9,901,500
59	Earl of	Galloway	Wigtown	79,184	£32,197	£2,253,790	£804,925	£56,344,750
60	Duke of	Abercorn	Tyrone	78,662	£53,400	£3,738,000	£1,335,000	£93,450,000
61	Earl of	Dunmore	Inverness	78,620	£10,411	£728,770	£260,275	£18,219,250
62	Earl of	Carlisle	Cumbs	78,540	£49,601	£3,472,070	£1,240,025	£86,801,750
63	Colonel	George Walker	Inverness	78,439	£6,883	£481,810	£172,075	£12,045,250
64	Sir	John Sinclair Bt	Caithness	78,053	£12,833	£898,310	£320,825	£22,457,750
65	Earl of	Moray	Perth	77,612	£36,078	£2,525,460	£901,950	£63,136,500
66	Mr	Ian Grant	Inverness	77,567	£7,364	£515,480	£184,100	£12,887,000
67	Marquess of	Ailsa	Ayr	76,015	£35,825	£2,507,750	£895,625	£62,693,750
68	Mr	Charles Morrison	Berks	75,732	£31,434	£2,200,380	£785,850	£55,009,500
69	Mr	William Bankes	Ross	73,865	£18,572	£1,300,040	£464,300	£32,501,000
70	Duke of	Leinster	Kildare	73,100	£55,877	£3,911,390	£1,396,925	£97,784,750
71	Mr	Edward King-Harman	Longford	72,913	£40,105	£2,807,350	£1,002,625	£70,183,750
72	Mr	James Mackenzie	Aberdeen	72,729	£4,535	£317,450	£113,375	£7,936,250
73	Sir	Richard Wallace Bt	Suffolk	72,307	£85,737	£6,001,590	£2,143,425	£150,039,750
74	Duke of	Rutland	Leics	70,137	£97,486	£6,824,020	£2,437,150	£170,600,500
75	Earl of	Airlie	Forfar	69,875	£28,592	£2,001,440	£714,800	£50,036,000
76	Earl of	Bantry	Cork	69,500	£14,561	£1,019,270	£364,025	£25,481,750
77	Earl of	Derby	Lancs	68,942	£163,273	£11,429,110	£4,081,825	£285,727,750
78	Earl of	Zetland	York	68,170	£49,324	£3,452,680	£1,233,100	£86,317,000
79	Earl of	Lonsdale	Cumbs	68,095	£71,333	£4,993,310	£1,783,325	£124,832,750
80	Mr	John Baird	Inverness	68,000	£5,800	£406,000	£145,000	£10,150,000
81	Sir	James Colquhoun Bt	Dumbarton	67,041	£12,845	£899,150	£321,125	£22,478,750
82	Marqis of	Waterford	Waterford	66,684	£32,752	£2,292,640	£818,800	£57,316,000

THE LAND LISTS 361

TOP 100 LANDOWNERS IN THE UK & IRELAND RANKED BY ACREAGE 1872 (CONT.)

	Title	Name of landowner	Home county	Total acreage 1872	Income value 1872	Equivalent income value 2001	Estimated land value of total acreage 1872	Equivalent estimated land value 2001
83	Rev, Lord	O'Neill	Antrim	65,919	£44,000	£3,080,000	£1,100,000	£77,000,000
84	Mr	John Hope-Johnstone	Dumfries	65,366	£28,236	£1,976,520	£705,900	£49,413,000
85	Earl of	Morton	Midlothian	65,161	£22,288	£1,560,160	£557,200	£39,004,000
86	Mr	Hugh Mackenzie	Ross	64,335	£4,038	£282,660	£100,950	£7,066,500
87	Earl of	Lucan	Mayo	62,936	£17,423	£1,219,610	£435,575	£30,490,250
88	Earl of	Aberdeen	Aberdeen	62,444	£44,112	£3,087,840	£1,102,800	£77,196,000
89	Earl of	Wemyss and March	Haddington	62,028	£54,968	£3,847,760	£1,374,200	£96,194,000
90	Earl of	Powis	Montgomery	60,559	£57,024	£3,991,680	£1,425,600	£99,792,000
91	Duke of	Roxburghe	Roxburgh	60,418	£50,917	£3,564,190	£1,272,925	£89,104,750
92	Sir	Edward Scott Bt	Inverness	59,923	£5,752	£402,640	£143,800	£10,066,000
93	Lord	Harlech	Leitrim	58,358	£26,400	£1,848,000	£660,000	£46,200,000
94	Earl	Brownlow	Lincs	58,335	£86,426	£6,049,820	£2,160,650	£151,245,500
95	Mr	William Thomson-Sinclair	Caithness	57,757	£6,377	£446,390	£159,425	£11,159,750
96	Mr	John Dalgleish	Argyll	57,400	£7,445	£521,150	£186,125	£13,028,750
97	Earl of	Yarborough	Lincs	56,893	£84,649	£5,925,430	£2,116,225	£148,135,750
98	Earl of	Leitrim	Donegal	56,852	£11,006	£770,420	£275,150	£19,260,500
99	Marquess of	Clanricarde	Galway	56,826	£24,358	£1,705,060	£608,950	£42,626,500
100	Mr	William Forbes	Stirling	56,704	£25,442	£1,780,940	£636,050	£44,523,500

362   WHO OWNS BRITAIN

LAND LIST 1 (B)
1872
TOP 100 LANDOWNERS IN THE UK & IRELAND RANKED BY VALUE OF LAND

	Title	Name of landowner	Home county	Total acreage 1872	Income value 1872	Equivalent income value 2001	Estimated land value of total acreage 1872	Equivalent estimated land value 2001
1	Duke of	Westminster	Cheshire	19,749	£290,000	£20,300,000	£7,250,000	£507,500,000
2	Duke of	Buccleuch & Queensbury	Northants	460,108	£232,000	£16,240,000	£5,800,000	£406,000,000
3	Duke of	Bedford	Beds	86,335	£225,000	£15,750,000	£5,625,000	£393,750,000
4	Sir	John Ramsden Bt	Lincs	150,048	£181,294	£12,690,580	£4,532,350	£317,264,500
5	Duke of	Devonshire	Derby	198,572	£180,750	£12,652,500	£4,518,750	£316,312,500
6	Duke of	Northumberland	Northumbs	186,397	£176,048	£12,323,360	£4,401,200	£308,084,000
7	Earl of	Derby	Lancs	68,942	£163,273	£11,429,110	£4,081,825	£285,727,750
8	Marquess of	Bute	Bute	116,668	£151,135	£10,579,450	£3,778,375	£264,486,250
9	Duke of	Sutherland	Sutherland	1,358,545	£141,667	£9,916,690	£3,541,675	£247,917,250
10	Earl	Fitzwilliam	York	115,743	£138,801	£9,716,070	£3,470,025	£242,901,750
11	Earl of	Dudley	Salop	25,554	£123,176	£8,622,320	£3,079,400	£215,558,000
12	Lord	Calthorpe	Warwick	6,470	£122,628	£8,583,960	£3,065,700	£214,599,000
13	Marquess of	Anglesey	Staffs	29,737	£110,598	£7,741,860	£2,764,950	£193,546,500
14	Lord	Haldon	Devon	10,109	£109,275	£7,649,250	£2,731,875	£191,231,250
15	Marquess of	Londonderry	Durham	50,323	£100,118	£7,008,260	£2,502,950	£175,206,500
16	Duke of	Rutland	Leics	70,137	£97,486	£6,824,020	£2,437,150	£170,600,500
17	Duke of	Cleveland	Durham	104,194	£97,398	£6,817,860	£2,434,950	£170,446,500
18	Marquess of	Downshire	Down	120,189	£96,961	£6,787,270	£2,424,025	£169,681,750
19	Sir	John St Aubyn, Bt	Cornwall	6,555	£95,212	£6,664,840	£2,380,300	£166,621,000
20	Viscount	Boyne	Durham	30,205	£88,364	£6,185,480	£2,209,100	£154,637,000
21	Duke of	Portland	Notts	183,199	£88,350	£6,184,500	£2,208,750	£154,612,500
22	Lord	Leconfield	Sussex	109,935	£88,112	£6,167,840	£2,202,800	£154,196,000
23	Earl	Brownlow	Lincs	58,335	£86,426	£6,049,820	£2,160,650	£151,245,500
24	Sir	Richard Wallace Bt	Suffolk	72,307	£85,737	£6,001,590	£2,143,425	£150,039,750
25	Earl of	Yarborough	Lincs	56,893	£84,649	£5,925,430	£2,116,225	£148,135,750
26	Duke of	Richmond and Gordon	Sussex	286,411	£79,683	£5,577,810	£1,992,075	£139,445,250

THE LAND LISTS 363

TOP 100 LANDOWNERS IN THE UK & IRELAND RANKED BY VALUE OF LAND 1872 (CONT.)

	Title	Name of landowner	Home county	Total acreage 1872	Income value 1872	Equivalent income value 2001	Estimated land value of total acreage 1872	Equivalent estimated land value 2001
27	Earl of	Seafield	Inverness	305,930	£78,227	£5,475,890	£1,955,675	£136,897,250
28	Earl of	Pembroke	Wilts	44,806	£77,720	£5,440,400	£1,943,000	£136,010,000
29	Duke of	Norfolk	Sussex	49,866	£75,596	£5,291,720	£1,889,900	£132,293,000
30	Duke of	Newcastle	Notts	35,547	£74,547	£5,218,290	£1,863,675	£130,457,250
31	Baroness	Willoughby D'Eresby	Lincs	132,220	£74,006	£5,180,420	£1,850,150	£129,510,500
32	Duke of	Hamilton and Brandon	Bute	157,368	£73,636	£5,154,520	£1,840,900	£128,863,000
33	Earl of	Fife	Banff	249,220	£72,563	£5,079,410	£1,814,075	£126,985,250
34	Earl of	Durham	Durham	30,471	£71,671	£5,016,970	£1,791,775	£125,424,250
35	Earl of	Lonsdale	Cumbs	68,095	£71,333	£4,993,310	£1,783,325	£124,832,750
36	Earl of	Ellesmere	Lancs	13,222	£71,290	£4,990,300	£1,782,250	£124,757,500
37	Lord	Penrhyn	Caernarvon	49,548	£71,018	£4,971,260	£1,775,450	£124,281,500
38	Marquess of	Bath	Wilts	55,574	£68,015	£4,761,050	£1,700,375	£119,026,250
39	Earl of	Stair	Wigtown	116,370	£67,905	£4,753,350	£1,697,625	£118,833,750
40	Lord	Londesborough	York	52,655	£67,876	£4,751,320	£1,696,900	£118,783,000
41	Lord	Windsor	Salop	37,434	£63,778	£4,464,460	£1,594,450	£111,611,500
42	Earl of	Shrewsbury and Talbot	Stafford	35,729	£62,382	£4,366,740	£1,559,550	£109,168,500
43	Marquess of	Lansdowne	Wilts	142,916	£62,025	£4,341,750	£1,550,625	£108,543,750
44	Earl	Cowper	Herts	37,896	£60,392	£4,227,440	£1,509,800	£105,686,000
45	Lord	Tredegar	Mons	39,157	£60,000	£4,200,000	£1,500,000	£105,000,000
46	Mr	Thomas Weld-Blundell	Lancs	10,400	£60,000	£4,200,000	£1,500,000	£105,000,000
47	Marquess of	Ailesbury	Wilts	55,051	£59,716	£4,180,120	£1,492,900	£104,503,000
48	Earl of	Leicester	Norfolk	44,090	£59,578	£4,170,460	£1,489,450	£104,261,500
49	Earl of	Dartmouth	York	19,518	£58,657	£4,105,990	£1,466,425	£102,649,750
50	Earl of	Dalhousie	Forfar	138,021	£58,603	£4,102,210	£1,465,075	£102,555,250
51	Earl of	Stamford and Warrington	Leics	30,962	£58,393	£4,087,510	£1,459,825	£102,187,750
52	Earl of	Breadalbane	Perth	438,358	£58,292	£4,080,440	£1,457,300	£102,011,000
53	Lord	Overstone	Northants	30,849	£58,098	£4,066,860	£1,452,450	£101,671,500
54	Earl of	Powis	Montgomery	60,559	£57,024	£3,991,680	£1,425,600	£99,792,000

364 WHO OWNS BRITAIN

TOP 100 LANDOWNERS IN THE UK & IRELAND RANKED BY VALUE OF LAND 1872 (CONT.)

	Title	Name of landowner	Home county	Total acreage 1872	Income value 1872	Equivalent income value 2001	Estimated land value of total acreage 1872	Equivalent estimated land value 2001
55	Earl of	Home	Lanark	106,550	£56,632	£3,964,240	£1,415,800	£99,106,000
56	Duke of	Beaufort	Glos	51,085	£56,556	£3,958,920	£1,413,900	£98,973,000
57	Duke of	Leinster	Kildare	73,100	£55,877	£3,911,390	£1,396,925	£97,784,750
58	Earl of	Wemyss and March	Haddington	62,028	£54,968	£3,847,760	£1,374,200	£96,194,000
59	Sir	Watkin Williams-Wynn Bt	Denbigh	145,770	£54,575	£3,820,250	£1,364,375	£95,506,250
60	Lord	Middleton	Notts	100,002	£54,014	£3,780,980	£1,350,350	£94,524,500
61	Duke of	Abercorn	Tyrone	78,662	£53,400	£3,738,000	£1,335,000	£93,450,000
62	Mr	Andrew Montague	York	27,265	£53,034	£3,712,380	£1,325,850	£92,809,500
63	Mr	Augustus Savile	York	33,820	£52,213	£3,654,910	£1,305,325	£91,372,750
64	Earl	Manvers	Notts	38,036	£51,649	£3,615,430	£1,291,225	£90,385,750
65	Duke of	Roxburghe	Roxburgh	60,418	£50,917	£3,564,190	£1,272,925	£89,104,750
66	Duke of	Argyll	Argyll	175,114	£50,842	£3,558,940	£1,271,050	£88,973,500
67	Earl of	Wharncliffe	York	33,499	£50,823	£3,557,610	£1,270,575	£88,940,250
68	Marquess of	Conyngham	Kent	166,710	£50,076	£3,505,320	£1,251,900	£87,633,000
69	Earl of	Carlisle	Cumbs	78,540	£49,601	£3,472,070	£1,240,025	£86,801,750
70	Earl of	Zetland	York	68,170	£49,324	£3,452,680	£1,233,100	£86,317,000
71	Marquess of	Exeter	Lincs	28,271	£49,044	£3,433,080	£1,226,100	£85,827,000
72	Earl of	Normanton	Hants	42,961	£48,280	£3,379,600	£1,207,000	£84,490,000
73	Earl of	Longford	Westmeath	19,989	£47,198	£3,303,860	£1,179,950	£82,596,500
74	Hon Mr	Mark Rolle	Devon	55,592	£47,170	£3,301,900	£1,179,250	£82,547,500
75	Lord	Aveland	Lincs	31,275	£46,894	£3,282,580	£1,172,350	£82,064,500
76	Lord	Wimborne	Dorset	83,539	£46,856	£3,279,920	£1,171,400	£81,998,000
77	Earl	Spencer	Northants	27,185	£46,764	£3,273,480	£1,169,100	£81,837,000
78	Lord	Ashburton	Hants	36,772	£46,685	£3,267,950	£1,167,125	£81,698,750
79	Earl of	Haddington	Cheshire	34,046	£46,161	£3,231,270	£1,154,025	£80,781,750
80	Mr	George Wingfield-Digby	Dorset	26,883	£46,092	£3,226,440	£1,152,300	£80,661,000
81	Lord	Hothfield	Kent	39,276	£45,987	£3,219,090	£1,149,675	£80,477,250
82	Viscount	Portman	Somerset	33,891	£45,972	£3,218,040	£1,149,300	£80,451,000

TOP 100 LANDOWNERS IN THE UK & IRELAND RANKED BY VALUE OF LAND 1872 (CONT.)

	Title	Name of landowner	Home county	Total acreage 1872	Income value 1872	Equivalent income value 2001	Estimated land value of total acreage 1872	Equivalent estimated land value 2001
83	Duke of	Bedford	Devon	22,607	£45,907	£3,213,490	£1,147,675	£80,337,250
84	Earl of	Devon	Devon	53,075	£45,520	£3,186,400	£1,138,000	£79,660,000
85	Hon Mrs	Meynell-Ingram	York	25,205	£45,491	£3,184,370	£1,137,275	£79,609,250
86	Viscount	De Vesci	Queens	16,682	£45,214	£3,164,980	£1,130,350	£79,124,500
87	Marquess of	Lothian	Roxburgh	32,361	£45,203	£3,164,210	£1,130,075	£79,105,250
88	Mr	William Legh	Cheshire	13,800	£45,000	£3,150,000	£1,125,000	£78,750,000
89	Earl of	Cawdor	Pembroke	101,657	£44,662	£3,126,340	£1,116,550	£78,158,500
90	Earl of	Dysart	Lincs	27,190	£44,500	£3,115,000	£1,112,500	£77,875,000
91	Lord	Hastings	Norfolk	19,558	£44,452	£3,111,640	£1,111,300	£77,791,000
92	Earl of	Aberdeen	Aberdeen	62,444	£44,112	£3,087,840	£1,102,800	£77,196,000
93	Mr	Christopher Talbot	Glams	33,920	£44,057	£3,083,990	£1,101,425	£77,099,750
94	Rev, Lord	O'Neill	Antrim	65,919	£44,000	£3,080,000	£1,100,000	£77,000,000
95	Lord	Gerard	Lancs	7,107	£43,671	£3,056,970	£1,091,775	£76,424,250
96	Earl of	Ilchester	Dorset	32,849	£43,452	£3,041,640	£1,086,300	£76,041,000
97	Lord	Tollemache of Helmingham	Cheshire	35,726	£43,345	£3,034,150	£1,083,625	£75,853,750
98	Earl of	Sefton	Lancs	20,250	£43,000	£3,010,000	£1,075,000	£75,250,000
99	Earl of	Mansfield	Perth	49,074	£42,968	£3,007,760	£1,074,200	£75,194,000
100	Viscount	Falmouth	Cornwall	30,606	£42,904	£3,003,280	£1,072,600	£75,082,000

LAND LIST 2 (A)
1872
TOP 50 LANDOWNERS IN ENGLAND RANKED BY ACREAGE

	Title	Name of landowner	Home county	Total acreage 1872	Income value 1872	Equivalent income value 2001	Estimated land value of total acreage 1872	Equivalent estimated land value 2001
1	Duke of	Richmond and Gordon	Sussex	286,411	£79,683	£5,577,810	£1,992,075	£139,445,250
2	Duke of	Devonshire	Derby	198,572	£180,750	£12,652,500	£4,518,750	£316,312,500
3	Duke of	Northumberland	Northumbs	186,397	£176,048	£12,323,360	£4,401,200	£308,084,000
4	Duke of	Portland	Notts	183,199	£88,350	£6,184,500	£2,208,750	£154,612,500
5	Marquess of	Conyngham	Kent	166,710	£50,076	£3,505,320	£1,251,900	£87,633,000
6	Sir	Ramsden	Lincs	150,048	£181,294	£12,690,580	£4,532,350	£317,264,500
7	Marquess of	Lansdowne	Wilts	142,916	£62,025	£4,341,750	£1,550,625	£108,543,750
8	Baroness	Willoughby D'Eresby	Lincs	132,220	£74,006	£5,180,420	£1,850,150	£129,510,500
9	Earl	Fitzwilliam	York	115,743	£138,801	£9,716,070	£3,470,025	£242,901,750
10	Lord	Leconfield	Sussex	109,935	£88,112	£6,167,840	£2,202,800	£154,196,000
11	Duke of	Cleveland	Durham	104,194	£97,398	£6,817,860	£2,434,950	£170,446,500
12	Lord	Middleton	Notts	100,002	£54,014	£3,780,980	£1,350,350	£94,524,500
13	Viscount	Dillon	Oxford	94,764	£28,762	£2,013,340	£719,050	£50,333,500
14	Duke of	Bedford	Beds	86,335	£225,000	£15,750,000	£5,625,000	£393,750,000
15	Lord	Wimborne	Dorset	83,539	£46,856	£3,279,920	£1,171,400	£81,998,000
16	Earl of	Carlisle	Cumbs	78,540	£49,601	£3,472,070	£1,240,025	£86,801,750
17	Mr	Morrison	Berks	75,732	£31,434	£2,200,380	£785,850	£55,009,500
18	Sir	Wallace	Suffolk	72,307	£85,737	£6,001,590	£2,143,425	£150,039,750
19	Duke of	Rutland	Leics	70,137	£97,486	£6,824,020	£2,437,150	£170,600,500
20	Earl of	Derby	Lancs	68,942	£163,273	£11,429,110	£4,081,825	£285,727,750
21	Earl of	Zetland	York	68,170	£49,324	£3,452,680	£1,233,100	£86,317,000
22	Earl of	Lonsdale	Cumbs	68,095	£71,333	£4,993,310	£1,783,325	£124,832,750
23	Earl	Brownlow	Lincs	58,335	£86,426	£6,049,820	£2,160,650	£151,245,500
24	Earl of	Yarborough	Lincs	56,893	£84,649	£5,925,430	£2,116,225	£148,135,750
25	Hon Mr	Rolle, Mark George Kerr	Devon	55,592	£47,170	£3,301,900	£1,179,250	£82,547,500
26	Marquess of	Bath	Wilts	55,574	£68,015	£4,761,050	£1,700,375	£119,026,250

THE LAND LISTS 367

TOP 50 LANDOWNERS IN ENGLAND RANKED BY ACREAGE 1872 (CONT.)

	Title	Name of landowner	Home county	Total acreage 1872	Income value 1872	Equivalent income value 2001	Estimated land value of total acreage 1872	Equivalent estimated land value 2001
27	Marquess of	Ailesbury	Wilts	55,051	£59,716	£4,180,120	£1,492,900	£104,503,000
28	Earl of	Devon	Devon	53,075	£45,520	£3,186,400	£1,138,000	£79,660,000
29	Lord	Londesborough	York	52,655	£67,876	£4,751,320	£1,696,900	£118,783,000
30	Earl of	Kilmorey	Salop	52,412	£34,022	£2,381,540	£850,550	£59,538,500
31	Duke of	Beaufort	Glos	51,085	£56,556	£3,958,920	£1,413,900	£98,973,000
32	Marquess of	Londonderry	Durham	50,323	£100,118	£7,008,260	£2,502,950	£175,206,500
33	Duke of	Norfolk	Sussex	49,866	£75,596	£5,291,720	£1,889,900	£132,293,000
34	Earl of	Portsmouth	Hants	46,984	£36,271	£2,538,970	£906,775	£63,474,250
35	Earl of	Pembroke	Wilts	44,806	£77,720	£5,440,400	£1,943,000	£136,010,000
36	Earl of	Leicester	Norfolk	44,090	£59,578	£4,170,460	£1,489,450	£104,261,500
37	Mr	Bowes	York	43,200	£21,071	£1,474,970	£526,775	£36,874,250
38	Earl of	Normanton	Hants	42,961	£48,280	£3,379,600	£1,207,000	£84,490,000
39	Mr	Carter	Oxford	42,538	£4,153	£290,710	£103,825	£7,267,750
40	Colonel	Clive	Hereford	41,389	£6,250	£437,500	£156,250	£10,937,500
41	Sir	Acland, Thomas Dyke, Bt	Devon	39,896	£34,785	£2,434,950	£869,625	£60,873,750
42	Lord	Digby	Dorset	39,505	£15,968	£1,117,760	£399,200	£27,944,000
43	Earl of	Feversham	York	39,312	£34,328	£2,402,960	£858,200	£60,074,000
44	Lord	Hothfield	Kent	39,276	£45,987	£3,219,090	£1,149,675	£80,477,250
45	Lord	Tredegar	Mons	39,157	£60,000	£4,200,000	£1,500,000	£105,000,000
46	Mr	Lane-Fox	York	39,069	£26,000	£1,820,000	£650,000	£45,500,000
47	Earl of	Cork and Orrery	Somerset	38,313	£17,343	£1,214,010	£433,575	£30,350,250
48	Earl of	Manvers	Notts	38,036	£51,649	£3,615,430	£1,291,225	£90,385,750
49	Earl of	Cowper	Herts	37,896	£60,392	£4,227,440	£1,509,800	£105,686,000
50	Lord	Windsor	Salop	37,434	£63,778	£4,464,460	£1,594,450	£111,611,500

LAND LIST 2 (B)
1872
TOP 50 LANDOWNERS IN WALES RANKED BY ACREAGE

	Title	Name of landowner	Home county	Total acreage 1872	Income value 1872	Equivalent income value 2001	Estimated land value of total acreage 1872	Equivalent estimated land value 2001
1	Sir	Williams-Wynn	Denbigh	145,770	£54,575	£3,820,250	£1,364,375	£95,506,250
2	Earl of	Cawdor	Pembroke	101,657	£44,662	£3,126,340	£1,116,550	£78,158,500
3	Earl of	Powis	Montgomery	60,559	£57,024	£3,991,680	£1,425,600	£99,792,000
4	Lord	Penrhyn	Caernarvon	49,548	£71,018	£4,971,260	£1,775,450	£124,281,500
5	Earl of	Lisburne	Cardigan	42,716	£13,676	£957,320	£341,900	£23,933,000
6	Mr	Price	Merioneth	41,264	£11,091	£776,370	£277,275	£19,409,250
7	Mr	Duff-Assheaton-Smith	Caernarvon	34,482	£42,255	£2,957,850	£1,056,375	£73,946,250
8	Mr	Talbot	Glams	33,920	£44,057	£3,083,990	£1,101,425	£77,099,750
9	Mr	Powell	Cardigan	33,674	£9,597	£671,790	£239,925	£16,794,750
10	Sir	Pryse	Cardigan	32,357	£11,324	£792,680	£283,100	£19,817,000
11	Sir	Williams-Bulkeley	Anglesea	29,878	£21,138	£1,479,660	£528,450	£36,991,500
12	Lord	Newborough	Caernarvon	28,800	£22,756	£1,592,920	£568,900	£39,823,000
13	Sir	Bailey	Brecon	28,308	£25,559	£1,789,130	£638,975	£44,728,250
14	Lord	Ormathwaite	Radnor	26,261	£14,667	£1,026,690	£366,675	£25,667,250
15	Lord	Sudeley	Montgomery	23,953	£23,340	£1,633,800	£583,500	£40,845,000
16	Lord	Trevor	Denbigh	23,694	£17,700	£1,239,000	£442,500	£30,975,000
17	Lord	Philipps	Pembroke	23,105	£25,206	£1,764,420	£630,150	£44,110,500
18	Mr	Vaughan	Merioneth	16,588	£4,520	£316,400	£113,000	£7,910,000
19	Mr	Puxley	Carmarthen	16,373	£8,876	£621,320	£221,900	£15,533,000
20	Mr	Hughes	Denbigh	16,223	£23,097	£1,616,790	£577,425	£40,419,750
21	Mrs	Kirby	Merioneth	16,022	£4,988	£349,160	£124,700	£8,729,000
22	Mr	Vaughan-Lee	Glams	15,178	£21,993	£1,539,510	£549,825	£38,487,750
23	Mr	Wynne-Finch	Denbigh	15,158	£10,772	£754,040	£269,300	£18,851,000
24	Mr	Dillwyn-Llewelyn	Glams	14,867	£9,939	£695,730	£248,475	£17,393,250
25	Miss	Thomas	Brecon	14,256	£10,042	£702,940	£251,050	£17,573,500
26	Mr	Bailey	Monmouth	13,649	£12,888	£902,160	£322,200	£22,554,000

TOP 50 LANDOWNERS IN WALES RANKED BY ACREAGE 1872 (CONT.)

	Title	Name of landowner	Home county	Total acreage 1872	Income value 1872	Equivalent income value 2001	Estimated land value of total acreage 1872	Equivalent estimated land value 2001
27	Sir	Scourfield	Pembroke	13,439	£10,087	£706,090	£252,175	£17,652,250
28	Mr	Waddingham	Cardigan	13,334	£4,062	£284,340	£101,550	£7,108,500
29	Mr	Gwynne-Holford	Glams	12,726	£17,714	£1,239,980	£442,850	£30,999,500
30	Lord	Boston	Anglesea	12,474	£15,172	£1,062,040	£379,300	£26,551,000
31	Mr	Ellis-Nanney	Caernarvon	12,072	£5,814	£406,980	£145,350	£10,174,500
32	Mr	Jones	Carmarthern	12,071	£6,612	£462,840	£165,300	£11,571,000
33	Mr	Naylor	Montgomery	11,724	£12,840	£898,800	£321,000	£22,470,000
34	Sir	Buckley	Merioneth	11,286	£14,990	£1,049,300	£374,750	£26,232,500
35	Mr	Gibson-Watts	Radnor	11,036	£6,850	£479,500	£171,250	£11,987,500
36	Lord	Dynevor	Carmarthern	10,728	£12,562	£879,340	£314,050	£21,983,500
37	Mr	Mainwaring	Denbigh	10,685	£4,327	£302,890	£108,175	£7,572,250
38	Mr	Wynne	Merioneth	10,556	£6,229	£436,030	£155,725	£10,900,750
39	Mr, Hon	Wynn	Merioneth	10,504	£8,905	£623,350	£222,625	£15,583,750
40	Mr	Jones-Parry	Caernarvon	10,025	£5,750	£402,500	£143,750	£10,062,500
41	Rev, Sir	Lewis	Radnor	10,006	£7,005	£490,350	£175,125	£12,258,750
42	Mr	De Winton	Radnor	9,900	£15,642	£1,094,940	£391,050	£27,373,500
43	Sir	Cowell-Stepney	Carmarthen	9,847	£7,200	£504,000	£180,000	£12,600,000
44	Sir	Williams-Drummond	Carmarthern	9,763	£7,591	£531,370	£189,775	£13,284,250
45	Sir	Williams	Denbigh	9,371	£8,871	£620,970	£221,775	£15,524,250
46	Mrs	Colby	Pembroke	9,252	£5,147	£360,290	£128,675	£9,007,250
47	Mr	Edwards	Caernarvon	9,009	£6,915	£484,050	£172,875	£12,101,250
48	Mr	Wynne	Denbigh	9,000	£7,000	£490,000	£175,000	£12,250,000
49	Major	Rice-Watkins	Carmarthen	8,966	£4,897	£342,790	£122,425	£8,569,750
50	Mr	Jones	Carmarthern	8,832	£5,524	£386,680	£138,100	£9,667,000

WHO OWNS BRITAIN

LAND LIST 2 (C)
1872
TOP 50 LANDOWNERS IN SCOTLAND RANKED BY ACREAGE

	Title	Name of landowner	Home county	Total acreage 1872	Income value 1872	Equivalent income value 2001	Estimated land value of total acreage 1872	Equivalent estimated land value 2001
1	Duke of	Sutherland	Sutherland	1,358,545	£141,667	£9,916,690	£3,541,675	£247,917,250
2	Duke of	Buccleuch & Queensbury	Dumfries	460,108	£232,000	£16,240,000	£5,800,000	£406,000,000
3	Earl of	Breadalbane	Perth	438,358	£58,292	£4,080,440	£1,457,300	£102,011,000
4	Lady	Matheson	Ross	424,560	£20,346	£1,424,220	£508,650	£35,605,500
5	Sir	Ross	Ross	356,500	£17,264	£1,208,480	£431,600	£30,212,000
6	Earl of	Seafield	Inverness	305,930	£78,227	£5,475,890	£1,955,675	£136,897,250
7	Earl of	Fife	Banff	249,220	£72,563	£5,079,410	£1,814,075	£126,985,250
8	Sir	Matheson	Ross	220,663	£3,238	£226,660	£80,950	£5,666,500
9	Duke of	Atholl	Perth	201,640	£42,030	£2,942,100	£1,050,750	£73,552,500
10	Lord	Lovat	Inverness	181,791	£30,300	£2,121,000	£757,500	£53,025,000
11	Duke of	Argyll	Argyll	175,114	£50,842	£3,558,940	£1,271,050	£88,973,500
12	Sir	Mackenzie	Ross	164,680	£9,344	£654,080	£233,600	£16,352,000
13	Duke of	Hamilton and Brandon	Bute	157,368	£73,636	£5,154,520	£1,840,900	£128,863,000
14	Mr	Macleod (The Macleod)	Inverness	141,679	£8,464	£592,480	£211,600	£14,812,000
15	Earl of	Dalhousie	Forfar	138,021	£58,603	£4,102,210	£1,465,075	£102,555,250
16	Lord	Macdonald	Inverness	132,419	£16,613	£1,162,910	£415,325	£29,072,750
17	Mr	Mackintosh (The Mackintosh)	Inverness	126,295	£29,011	£2,030,770	£725,275	£50,769,250
18	Mr	Cameron	Inverness	126,008	£10,721	£750,470	£268,025	£18,761,750
19	Lady	Cathcart	Aberdeen	125,472	£38,188	£2,673,160	£954,700	£66,829,000
20	Sir	Macpherson-Grant	Banff	125,443	£11,546	£808,220	£288,650	£20,205,500
21	Marquess of	Bute	Bute	116,668	£151,135	£10,579,450	£3,778,375	£264,486,250
22	Earl of	Stair	Wigtown	116,370	£67,905	£4,753,350	£1,697,625	£118,833,750
23	The	Chisholm (James Sutherland)	Inverness	113,256	£8,858	£620,060	£221,450	£15,501,500
24	Mr	Farquharson	Aberdeen	109,561	£12,974	£908,180	£324,350	£22,704,500
25	Earl of	Home	Lanark	106,550	£56,632	£3,964,240	£1,415,800	£99,106,000
26	Duke of	Montrose	Stirling	103,447	£24,872	£1,741,040	£621,800	£43,526,000

TOP 50 LANDOWNERS IN SCOTLAND RANKED BY ACREAGE 1872 (CONT.)

	Title	Name of landowner	Home county	Total acreage 1872	Income value 1872	Equivalent income value 2001	Estimated land value of total acreage 1872	Equivalent estimated land value 2001
27	Mrs	Ellice	Inverness	99,559	£6,771	£473,970	£169,275	£11,849,250
28	Sir	Menzies	Perth	98,242	£11,467	£802,690	£286,675	£20,067,250
29	Mr	Baillie	Inverness	92,648	£11,881	£831,670	£297,025	£20,791,750
30	Mr	Balfour	Ross	87,196	£19,833	£1,388,310	£495,825	£34,707,750
31	Sir	Campbell-Orde	Inverness	85,745	£6,373	£446,110	£159,325	£11,152,750
32	Marquess of	Huntley	Aberdeen	85,711	£19,860	£1,390,200	£496,500	£34,755,000
33	Mr	Malcolm	Argyll	85,661	£24,989	£1,749,230	£624,725	£43,730,750
34	Mrs	Cameron-Campbell	Inverness	83,500	£5,658	£396,060	£141,450	£9,901,500
35	Earl of	Galloway	Wigtown	79,184	£32,197	£2,253,790	£804,925	£56,344,750
36	Earl of	Dunmore	Inverness	78,620	£10,411	£728,770	£260,275	£18,219,250
37	Colonel	Walker	Inverness	78,439	£6,883	£481,810	£172,075	£12,045,250
38	Sir	Sinclair	Caithness	78,053	£12,833	£898,310	£320,825	£22,457,750
39	Earl of	Moray	Perth	77,612	£36,078	£2,525,460	£901,950	£63,136,500
40	Mr	Grant	Inverness	77,567	£7,364	£515,480	£184,100	£12,887,000
41	Marquess of	Ailsa	Ayr	76,015	£35,825	£2,507,750	£895,625	£62,693,750
42	Mr	Bankes	Ross	73,865	£18,572	£1,300,040	£464,300	£32,501,000
43	Mr	Mackenzie	Aberdeen	72,729	£4,535	£317,450	£113,375	£7,936,250
44	Earl of	Airlie	Forfar	69,875	£28,592	£2,001,440	£714,800	£50,036,000
45	Mr	Baird	Inverness	68,000	£5,800	£406,000	£145,000	£10,150,000
46	Sir	Colquhoun	Dumbarton	67,041	£12,845	£899,150	£321,125	£22,478,750
47	Mr	Hope-Johnstone	Dumfries	65,366	£28,236	£1,976,520	£705,900	£49,413,000
48	Earl	Morton	Midlothian	65,161	£22,288	£1,560,160	£557,200	£39,004,000
49	Mr	Mackenzie	Ross	64,335	£4,038	£282,660	£100,950	£7,066,500
50	Earl of	Aberdeen	Aberdeen	62,444	£44,112	£3,087,840	£1,102,800	£77,196,000

372 WHO OWNS BRITAIN

LAND LIST 2 (D)
1872
TOP 50 LANDOWNERS IN NORTHERN IRELAND RANKED BY ACREAGE

	Title	Name of landowner	Home county	Total acreage 1872	Income value 1872	Equivalent income value 2001	Estimated land value of total acreage 1872	Equivalent estimated land value 2001
1	Marquess of	Downshire	Down	120,189	£96,961	£6,787,270	£2,424,025	£169,681,750
2	Duke of	Abercorn	Tyrone	78,662	£53,400	£3,738,000	£1,335,000	£93,450,000
3	Rev, Lord	O'Neill	Antrim	65,919	£44,000	£3,080,000	£1,100,000	£77,000,000
4	Marquess of	Ely	Fermanagh	48,992	£23,751	£1,662,570	£593,775	£41,564,250
5	Earl of	Erne	Fermanagh	40,365	£23,850	£1,669,500	£596,250	£41,737,500
6	Earl of	Castlestuart	Tyrone	34,875	£13,113	£917,910	£327,825	£22,947,750
7	Earl of	Antrim	Antrim	34,404	£20,910	£1,463,700	£522,750	£36,592,500
8	Earl of	Caledon	Tyrone	34,060	£22,321	£1,562,470	£558,025	£39,061,750
9	Mr	Archdale	Fermanagh	33,015	£16,991	£1,189,370	£424,775	£29,734,250
10	Earl of	Enniskillen	Fermanagh	30,204	£19,290	£1,350,300	£482,250	£33,757,500
11	Sir	Stewart	Tyrone	28,534	£6,752	£472,640	£168,800	£11,816,000
12	Sir	Brooke	Fermanangh	27,994	£15,288	£1,070,160	£382,200	£26,754,000
13	Earl of	Charlemont	Tyrone	26,820	£26,334	£1,843,380	£658,350	£46,084,500
14	General, Viscount	Templetown	Antrim	24,769	£19,217	£1,345,190	£480,425	£33,629,750
15	Sir	Verner	Armagh	24,257	£13,138	£919,660	£328,450	£22,991,500
16	Marquess of	Donegal	Antrim	22,996	£41,649	£2,915,430	£1,041,225	£72,885,750
17	Mr	Porter	Fermanagh	21,660	£10,512	£735,840	£262,800	£18,396,000
18	Sir	Bruce	Londonderry	21,514	£12,409	£868,630	£310,225	£21,715,750
19	Lord	Cleremont	Louth	21,127	£15,784	£1,104,880	£394,600	£27,622,000
20	Sir	McMahon	Tyrone	21,029	£5,302	£371,140	£132,550	£9,278,500
21	Mr	Ker	Down	20,544	£22,196	£1,553,720	£554,900	£38,843,000
22	Colonel	Forde	Down	20,106	£15,990	£1,119,300	£399,750	£27,982,500
23	Earl of	Belmore	Fermanagh	19,429	£11,015	£771,050	£275,375	£19,276,250
24	Earl of	Gosford	Armagh	18,594	£17,934	£1,255,380	£448,350	£31,384,500
25	Earl of	Dufferin (and Ava)	Down	18,238	£21,043	£1,473,010	£526,075	£36,825,250
26	Mr	Richardson	Londonderry	18,159	£7,424	£519,680	£185,600	£12,992,000

THE LAND LISTS 373

TOP 50 LANDOWNERS IN NORTHERN IRELAND RANKED BY ACREAGE 1872 (CONT.)

	Title	Name of landowner	Home county	Total acreage 1872	Income value 1872	Equivalent income value 2001	Estimated land value of total acreage 1872	Equivalent estimated land value 2001
27	Mr	McCausland	Londonderry	17,685	£9,168	£641,760	£229,200	£16,044,000
28	Sir	Bateson	Down	17,373	£14,888	£1,042,160	£372,200	£26,054,000
29	Major	Cole-Hamilton	Tyrone	16,811	£4,890	£342,300	£122,250	£8,557,500
30	Mr	Hope	Tyrone	16,691	£8,864	£620,480	£221,600	£15,512,000
31	Rev, Sir	Molyneux	Armagh	16,560	£10,000	£700,000	£250,000	£17,500,000
32	Lord	Garvagh	Londonderry	15,406	£8,752	£612,640	£218,800	£15,316,000
33	Lord	Lurgan	Armagh	15,276	£20,589	£1,441,230	£514,725	£36,030,750
34	Mr	Mulholland	Down	14,688	£19,424	£1,359,680	£485,600	£33,992,000
35	Rev	Pakenham	Antrim	14,629	£15,601	£1,092,070	£390,025	£27,301,750
36	Lord	Dorchester	Tyrone	14,521	£2,955	£206,850	£73,875	£5,171,250
37	Mr	Irvine	Fermanagh	14,114	£6,806	£476,420	£170,150	£11,910,500
38	Lord	Vane-Tempest	Antrim	13,781	£4,915	£344,050	£122,875	£8,601,250
39	Mr	Gordon	Down	13,574	£7,086	£496,020	£177,150	£12,400,500
40	Mr	Meade	Down	13,492	£13,719	£960,330	£342,975	£24,008,250
41	Mr	Macartney	Antrim	13,118	£6,783	£474,810	£169,575	£11,870,250
42	Mr	Dobbs	Antrim	13,031	£7,489	£524,230	£187,225	£13,105,750
43	Sir	Stronge	Armagh	12,954	£9,517	£666,190	£237,925	£16,654,750
44	Mr	Beresford	Londonderry	12,873	£4,482	£313,740	£112,050	£7,843,500
45	Mr	Close	Armagh	12,765	£13,441	£940,870	£336,025	£23,521,750
46	Mrs	De Bille	Tyrone	12,680	£2,503	£175,210	£62,575	£4,380,250
47	Mr	Montgomery	Tyrone	12,548	£4,925	£344,750	£123,125	£8,618,750
48	Mr	Perceval-Maxwell	Down	12,428	£12,132	£849,240	£303,300	£21,231,000
49	Mr	Batt	Down	12,010	£6,535	£457,450	£163,375	£11,436,250
50	Mr	Blacker-Douglas	Down	11,216	£5,976	£418,320	£149,400	£10,458,000

LAND LIST 2 (E)
1872
TOP 50 LANDOWNERS IN IRELAND RANKED BY ACREAGE (COUNTIES WHICH LATER FORMED THE REPUBLIC OF IRELAND)

	Title	Name of landowner	Home county	Total acreage 1872	Income value 1872	Equivalent income value 2001	Estimated land value of total acreage 1872	Equivalent estimated land value 2001
1	Mr	Richard Berridge	Galway	170,517	£9,503	£665,210	£237,575	£16,630,250
2	Earl of	Kenmare	Kerry	118,606	£34,473	£2,413,110	£861,825	£60,327,750
3	Marquess of	Sligo	Mayo	114,881	£19,000	£1,330,000	£475,000	£33,250,000
4	Sir	Roger Palmer Bt	Mayo	98,954	£26,661	£1,866,270	£666,525	£46,656,750
5	Mr	Horatio Murray-Stewart	Donegal	98,269	£22,822	£1,597,540	£570,550	£39,938,500
6	Lord	Ventry	Kerry	93,629	£17,067	£1,194,690	£426,675	£29,867,250
7	Duke of	Leinster	Kildare	73,100	£55,877	£3,911,390	£1,396,925	£97,784,750
8	Mr	Edward King-Harman	Longford	72,913	£40,105	£2,807,350	£1,002,625	£70,183,750
9	Earl of	Bantry	Cork	69,500	£14,561	£1,019,270	£364,025	£25,481,750
10	Marqis of	Waterford	Waterford	66,684	£32,752	£2,292,640	£818,800	£57,316,000
11	Earl of	Lucan	Mayo	62,936	£17,423	£1,219,610	£435,575	£30,490,250
12	Lord	Harlech	Leitrim	58,358	£26,400	£1,848,000	£660,000	£46,200,000
13	Earl of	Leitrim	Donegal	56,852	£11,006	£770,420	£275,150	£19,260,500
14	Marquess of	Clanricarde	Galway	56,826	£24,358	£1,705,060	£608,950	£42,626,500
15	Viscount	Powerscourt	Wicklow	53,258	£16,385	£1,146,950	£409,625	£28,673,750
16	Mr	John Adair	Queens	52,173	£4,822	£337,540	£120,550	£8,438,500
17	Earl of	Annesley	Down	51,060	£29,539	£2,067,730	£738,475	£51,693,250
18	Sir	Charles Coote Bt	Queens	49,686	£19,255	£1,347,850	£481,375	£33,696,250
19	Viscount	Clifden	Kilkenny	49,017	£38,915	£2,724,050	£972,875	£68,101,250
20	Mr	Henry Herbert	Kerry	47,238	£10,547	£738,290	£263,675	£18,457,250
21	Mr	Henry Clements	Cavan	45,504	£14,243	£997,010	£356,075	£24,925,250
22	Sir	John Leslie Bt	Monaghan	44,481	£16,579	£1,160,530	£414,475	£29,013,250
23	Mr	Alexander Stewart	Donegal	44,308	£15,655	£1,095,850	£391,375	£27,396,250
24	Lord	Ashtown	Galway	43,643	£34,689	£2,428,230	£867,225	£60,705,750
25	Marquess of	Headfort	Meath	42,754	£39,606	£2,772,420	£990,150	£69,310,500
26	Viscount	Lismore	Tipperary	42,206	£16,354	£1,144,780	£408,850	£28,619,500

THE LAND LISTS 375

TOP 50 LANDOWNERS IN IRELAND RANKED BY ACREAGE (COUNTIES WHICH LATER FORMED THE REPUBLIC OF IRELAND) 1872 (CONT.)

	Title	Name of landowner	Home county	Total acreage 1872	Income value 1872	Equivalent income value 2001	Estimated land value of total acreage 1872	Equivalent estimated land value 2001
27	Earl of	Bandon	Cork	40,941	£19,215	£1,345,050	£480,375	£33,626,250
28	Earl of	Dunraven	Limerick	39,755	£35,478	£2,483,460	£886,950	£62,086,500
29	Sir	William Style Bt	Donegal	39,564	£4,000	£280,000	£100,000	£7,000,000
30	Lord	De Freyne	Roscommon	38,788	£15,231	£1,066,170	£380,775	£26,654,250
31	Lord	Dunsandle and Clanconal	Galway	37,057	£17,193	£1,203,510	£429,825	£30,087,750
32	Earl of	Arran	Mayo	36,527	£10,112	£707,840	£252,800	£17,696,000
33	Earl of	Listowel	Kerry	35,541	£19,500	£1,365,000	£487,500	£34,125,000
34	Earl of	Bessborough	Kilkenny	35,440	£22,384	£1,566,880	£559,600	£39,172,000
35	Mr	Edward Cooper	Sligo	35,238	£12,735	£891,450	£318,375	£22,286,250
36	Lord	Massy	Limerick	33,003	£12,101	£847,070	£302,525	£21,176,750
37	Sir	Henry Gore-Booth Bt	Sligo	31,774	£17,346	£1,214,220	£433,650	£30,355,500
38	Lord	Ardilaun	Dublin	31,342	£6,573	£460,110	£164,325	£11,502,750
39	Sir	George Colthurst Bt	Cork	31,260	£9,664	£676,480	£241,600	£16,912,000
40	Mr	Henry Villiers-Stuart	Waterford	30,953	£11,573	£810,110	£289,325	£20,252,750
41	Sir	Charles Knox-Gore Bt	Mayo	30,592	£11,082	£775,740	£277,050	£19,393,500
42	Earl of	Dartrey	Monaghan	30,112	£21,699	£1,518,930	£542,475	£37,973,250
43	Mr	Robert Drummond	Kerry	29,780	£3,065	£214,550	£76,625	£5,363,750
44	Lord	Clonbrock	Galway	29,550	£11,873	£831,110	£296,825	£20,777,750
45	Mr	Arthur McMurrough Kavanagh	Carlow	29,025	£15,608	£1,092,560	£390,200	£27,314,000
46	Earl of	Wicklow	Wicklow	28,713	£15,717	£1,100,190	£392,925	£27,504,750
47	Viscount	Doneraile	Cork	28,700	£15,000	£1,050,000	£375,000	£26,250,000
48	Mr	Owen Wynne	Sligo	28,418	£14,091	£986,370	£352,275	£24,659,250
49	Mr	Henry Packenham-Mahon	Westmeath	28,123	£15,080	£1,055,600	£377,000	£26,390,000
50	Marquess of	Ormonde	Kilkenny	27,725	£15,431	£1,080,170	£385,775	£27,004,250

376   WHO OWNS BRITAIN

LAND LIST 3
1872
TOP 50 ARISTOCRATIC LANDOWNERS IN UK & IRELAND RANKED BY ACREAGE

	Title	Name of landowner	Home county	Total acreage 1872	Income value 1872	Equivalent income value 2001	Estimated land value of total acreage 1872	Equivalent estimated land value 2001
1	Duke of	Sutherland	Sutherland	1,358,545	£141,667	£9,916,690	£3,541,675	£247,917,250
2	Duke of	Buccleuch & Queensbury	Northants	460,108	£232,000	£16,240,000	£5,800,000	£406,000,000
3	Earl of	Breadalbane	Perth	438,358	£58,292	£4,080,440	£1,457,300	£102,011,000
4	Lady	Matheson	Ross	424,560	£20,346	£1,424,220	£508,650	£35,605,500
5	Sir	Charles Ross Bt	Ross	356,500	£17,264	£1,208,480	£431,600	£30,212,000
6	Earl of	Seafield	Inverness	305,930	£78,227	£5,475,890	£1,955,675	£136,897,250
7	Duke of	Richmond and Gordon	Sussex	286,411	£79,683	£5,577,810	£1,992,075	£139,445,250
8	Earl of	Fife	Banff	249,220	£72,563	£5,079,410	£1,814,075	£126,985,250
9	Sir	Alexander Matheson Bt	Ross	220,663	£3,238	£226,660	£80,950	£5,666,500
10	Duke of	Atholl	Perth	201,640	£42,030	£2,942,100	£1,050,750	£73,552,500
11	Duke of	Devonshire	Derby	198,572	£180,750	£12,652,500	£4,518,750	£316,312,500
12	Duke of	Northumberland	Northumbs	186,397	£176,048	£12,323,360	£4,401,200	£308,084,000
13	Duke of	Portland	Notts	183,199	£88,350	£6,184,500	£2,208,750	£154,612,500
14	Lord	Lovat	Inverness	181,791	£30,300	£2,121,000	£757,500	£53,025,000
15	Duke of	Argyll	Argyll	175,114	£50,842	£3,558,940	£1,271,050	£88,973,500
16	Marquess of	Conyngham	Kent	166,710	£50,076	£3,505,320	£1,251,900	£87,633,000
17	Sir	Kenneth Mackenzie Bt	Ross	164,680	£9,344	£654,080	£233,600	£16,352,000
18	Duke of	Hamilton and Brandon	Bute	157,368	£73,636	£5,154,520	£1,840,900	£128,863,000
19	Sir	John Ramsden Bt	Lincs	150,048	£181,294	£12,690,580	£4,532,350	£317,264,500
20	Sir	Watkin Williams-Wynn Bt	Denbigh	145,770	£54,575	£3,820,250	£1,364,375	£95,506,250
21	Marquess of	Lansdowne	Wilts	142,916	£62,025	£4,341,750	£1,550,625	£108,543,750
22	Earl of	Dalhousie	Forfar	138,021	£58,603	£4,102,210	£1,465,075	£102,555,250
23	Lord	Macdonald	Inverness	132,419	£16,613	£1,162,910	£415,325	£29,072,750
24	Baroness	Willoughby D'Eresby	Lincs	132,220	£74,006	£5,180,420	£1,850,150	£129,510,500
25	The	Mackintosh	Inverness	126,295	£29,011	£2,030,770	£725,275	£50,769,250
26	Lady	Cathcart	Aberdeen	125,472	£38,188	£2,673,160	£954,700	£66,829,000

THE LAND LISTS 377

TOP 50 ARISTOCRATIC LANDOWNERS IN UK & IRELAND RANKED BY ACREAGE 1872 (CONT.)

	Title	Name of landowner	Home county	Total acreage 1872	Income value 1872	Equivalent income value 2001	Estimated land value of total acreage 1872	Equivalent estimated land value 2001
27	Sir	George Macpherson-Grant Bt	Banff	125,443	£11,546	£808,220	£288,650	£20,205,500
28	Marquess of	Downshire	Down	120,189	£96,961	£6,787,270	£2,424,025	£169,681,750
29	Earl of	Kenmare	Kerry	118,606	£34,473	£2,413,110	£861,825	£60,327,750
30	Marquess of	Bute	Bute	116,668	£151,135	£10,579,450	£3,778,375	£264,486,250
31	Earl of	Stair	Wigtown	116,370	£67,905	£4,753,350	£1,697,625	£118,833,750
32	Earl	Fitzwilliam	York	115,743	£138,801	£9,716,070	£3,470,025	£242,901,750
33	Marquess of	Sligo	Mayo	114,881	£19,000	£1,330,000	£475,000	£33,250,000
34		Chisholm (James Sutherland)	Inverness	113,256	£8,858	£620,060	£221,450	£15,501,500
35	Lord	Leconfield	Sussex	109,935	£88,112	£6,167,840	£2,202,800	£154,196,000
36	Earl of	Home	Lanark	106,550	£56,632	£3,964,240	£1,415,800	£99,106,000
37	Duke of	Cleveland	Durham	104,194	£97,398	£6,817,860	£2,434,950	£170,446,500
38	Duke of	Montrose	Stirling	103,447	£24,872	£1,741,040	£621,800	£43,526,000
39	Earl of	Cawdor	Pembroke	101,657	£44,662	£3,126,340	£1,116,550	£78,158,500
40	Lord	Middleton	Notts	100,002	£54,014	£3,780,980	£1,350,350	£94,524,500
41	Sir	Roger Palmer Bt	Mayo	98,954	£26,661	£1,866,270	£666,525	£46,656,750
42	Sir	Robert Menzies Bt	Perth	98,242	£11,467	£802,690	£286,675	£20,067,250
43	Viscount	Dillon	Oxford	94,764	£28,762	£2,013,340	£719,050	£50,333,500
44	Lord	Ventry	Kerry	93,629	£17,067	£1,194,690	£426,675	£29,867,250
45	Duke of	Bedford	Bedford	86,335	£225,000	£15,750,000	£5,625,000	£393,750,000
46	Sir	John Campbell-Orde Bt	Inverness	85,745	£6,373	£446,110	£159,325	£11,152,750
47	Marquess of	Huntly	Aberdeen	85,711	£19,860	£1,390,200	£496,500	£34,755,000
48	Lord	Wimborne	Dorset	83,539	£46,856	£3,279,920	£1,171,400	£81,998,000
49	Earl of	Galloway	Wigtown	79,184	£32,197	£2,253,790	£804,925	£56,344,750
50	Duke of	Abercorn	Tyrone	79,184	£53,400	£3,738,000	£1,335,000	£93,450,000

LAND LIST 4 (A)

2001

TOP 100 LANDOWNERS IN THE UK & REPUBLIC OF IRELAND BY ACREAGE

	Title	Landowner	Home county	Overall acreage	Land value
1	Duke of	Buccleuch & Queensbury	Dumfries	270,700	£282,500,000
2	Dukedom of	Atholl (Trustees)	Perth	148,000	£430,000,000
3	Prince of	Wales	Cornwall	141,000	£1,250,000,000
4	Duke of	Northumberland	Northumberland	132,200	£800,000,000
5	Duke of	Westminster	Cheshire	129,300	£11,500,000,000
6	Captain	A.A. Farquharson	Aberdeen	106,500	£28,000,000
7	Earl of	Seafield	Banff	101,000	£104,000,000
8	Viscount	Cowdray	Aberdeen	93,600	£120,000,000
9	Mr	Robert Fleming	Argyll	88,900	£40,000,000
10	Mr	Edmund Vesty	Sutherland	86,300	£40,000,000
11	Countess of	Sutherland	Sutherland	83,239	£15,000,000
12	Mr	Paul Fentener van Vlissingen	Ross & Cromarty	81,000	£35,000,000
13	Baroness	Jane Willoughby d'Eresby	Perth	78,200	£121,000,000
14	Colonel Sir	Hamish Cameron of Lochiel	Inverness	76,000	£15,000,000
15	Duke of	Devonshire	Derbyshire	73,000	£435,000,000
16	Queen	HM Queen	Aberdeen	73,000	£3,000,000,000
17	Earl of	Lonsdale	Cumbria	70,000	£325,000,000
18	Mr	John Mackenzie	Ross & Cromarty	67,000	£12,500,000
19	Duke of	Roxburghe	Berwick	65,600	£150,000,000
20	Sheik	Mohammed bin Rashid al Maktoum	Ross & Cromarty	63,100	£30,000,000
21	Earl of	Granville	Inverness	62,200	£15,000,000
22	Lady	Anne Cavendish Bentinck	Caithness	62,000	£140,000,000
23	Captain	Fred Wills	Ross & Cromarty	62,000	£12,500,000
24	Duke of	Argyll	Argyll	60,800	£12,500,000
25	Earl of	Cawdor	Nairn	56,700	£25,000,000
26	Mr	Mohammed Al Fayed	Ross & Cromarty	55,000	£30,000,000
27	Mr	K.K. Christiensen	Ross & Cromarty	55,000	£30,000,000

THE LAND LISTS

TOP 100 LANDOWNERS IN THE UK & REPUBLIC OF IRELAND BY ACREAGE 2001 (CONT.)

	Title	Landowner	Home county	Overall acreage	Land value
28	Sir	William Gladstone Bt	Kincardine	54,700	£31,000,000
29	Baron	Margadale	Argyll	54,500	£55,000,000
30	Baron	Barnard	Durham	53,000	£190,000,000
31	Duke of	Beaufort	Gloucester	52,000	£310,000,000
32	Sir	Ivar Colquhoun of Luss	Dunbarton	50,000	£35,000,000
33	Mr & Lady	Jonathan & Marcia Bulmer	Inverness	49,900	£15,000,000
34	Marquess of	Bute	Ayr	49,700	£21,000,000
35	Mr & Ms	Joseph & Lisbet Koerner	Inverness	48,210	£22,000,000
36	Earl of	Dalhousie	Angus	47,200	£40,000,000
37	Mr	Stuart Murray Threipland	Caithness	46,900	£10,000,000
38	Mr	J.M. Colvin-Cayzer	Suffolk	46,200	£45,000,000
39	Duke of	Norfolk	Sussex	46,000	£210,000,000
40	Mr	Jonathan Bulmer	Ross & Cromarty	45,000	£9,000,000
41	Earl of	Stair	Wigtown	43,674	£25,000,000
42	Earl of	Wemyss and March	Fife	42,700	£30,000,000
43	Viscount	Falmouth	Cornwall	42,000	£245,000,000
44	Baron	Iliffe	Berks	41,853	£320,000,000
45	Mr	Christopher Moran	Banff	41,500	£40,000,000
46	Baron	Roborough	Devon	39,500	£35,000,000
47	Mr	Richard Kershaw	Ross & Cromarty	39,000	£10,000,000
48	Mr	P. Gordon Duff Pennington	Inverness	37,800	£8,500,000
49	Earl of	Airlie	Angus	37,300	£37,500,000
50	Mr	James Gutherie	Argyll	37,000	£24,000,000
51	Viscount	Thurso	Caithness	36,800	£24,000,000
52	Ms	Beverley Jane Malim	Perth	36,500	£15,000,000
53	Mr	Patrick Colvin	Ross & Cromarty	35,000	£12,000,000
54	Viscount	Leverhulme	Cheshire	34,700	£70,000,000
55	The	Raven family	Argyll	34,100	£23,000,000
56	Lady	Pauline Ogilvie Grant Nicholson	Inverness	34,000	£8,500,000

TOP 100 LANDOWNERS IN THE UK & REPUBLIC OF IRELAND BY ACREAGE 2001 (CONT.)

	Title	Landowner	Home county	Overall acreage	Land value
57	Earl of	Mansfield and Mansfield	Perth	33,800	£23,000,000
58	Messrs	Alan & N. Roger	Ross & Cromarty	33,600	£9,000,000
59	Baron	Vesty	Gloucester	32,900	£130,000,000
60	Messrs	D. Knowles, Leslie, Joicey	Sutherland	32,500	£9,000,000
61	Mr	Ewen Macpherson	Ross & Cromarty	32,000	£9,000,000
62	Mr	J.N. Oppenheim Eisken	Ross & Cromarty	32,000	£9,000,000
63	Duke of	Wellington	Hants	31,700	£50,000,000
64	Mr	John Macleod	Inverness	30,600	£9,000,000
65	Mr	Robert Miller	Yorks	30,000	£81,000,000
66	Mr	Patrick Wilson	Ross & Cromarty	30,000	£9,000,000
67	Marquess of	Northampton	Northants	30,000	£180,000,000
68	Earl of	Powis	Montgomery	30,000	£105,000,000
69	Earl of	Home	Lanark	30,000	£9,000,000
70	Mr	Michael A. Bruce	Aberdeen	29,150	£20,000,000
71	Hon Mr	Maurice Robson	Inverness	29,000	£7,500,000
72	Mr	Andrew Gordon	Inverness	28,100	£7,500,000
73	Earl of	Yarborough	Lincs	28,000	£170,000,000
74	Mr	R.M. Maclean of Ardgour	Argyll	27,900	£19,000,000
75	Mr	I. Hamish Melville	Ross & Cromarty	27,400	£7,000,000
76	Mr	James Clark	Sutherland	27,200	£10,000,000
77	Earl of	Derby	Lancs	27,000	£150,000,000
78	Mr	Urs Schwarzenbach	Inverness	27,000	£10,000,000
79	The	Lomas family	Ross & Cromarty	26,800	£7,500,000
80	Mrs	Macaire	Ross & Cromarty	26,600	£7,500,000
81	Mr	John B. Cameron	Perth	26,400	£18,000,000
82	Mr	Rodney Hitchcock	Inverness	26,400	£7,000,000
83	Earl of	Leicester	Norfolk	26,000	£160,000,000
84	Duke of	Rutland	Leics	26,000	£150,000,000
85	Baron	Clinton	Devon	26,000	£95,000,000

TOP 100 LANDOWNERS IN THE UK & REPUBLIC OF IRELAND BY ACREAGE 2001 (CONT.)

	Title	Landowner	Home county	Overall acreage	Land value
86	Mr	Charles R. Connell	Inverness	25,200	£7,000,000
87	Captain	A.A. Ramsay of Mar	Aberdeen	25,143	£17,500,000
88	Mr	Duncan Davidson	Northumberland	25,000	£155,000,000
89	Viscount	Mountgarrett	Yorks	25,000	£11,000,000
90	Earl of	Iveagh	Suffolk	25,000	£35,000,000
91	Mr	Stephen Gibbs	Bute	24,908	£6,500,000
92	Sir	William J. Lithgow	Argyll	24,700	£17,000,000
93	Sir	Andrew Buchanan-Jardine	Dumfries	24,500	£16,500,000
94	Viscount	Wimborne	Dorset	24,200	£18,000,000
95	Ms	Jean Balfour	Sutherland	24,000	£16,500,000
96	Count	Adam Knuth	Sutherland	24,000	£7,000,000
97	Mr	H. Roesner	Sutherland	24,000	£7,000,000
98	Mr	John Grant	Inverness	24,000	£7,000,000
99	Mr	Edward Humphrey	Aberdeen	23,800	£16,000,000
100	Messrs	Elliot	Sutherland	23,700	£6,800,000

LAND LIST 4 (B)
2001
TOP 100 LANDOWNERS IN THE UK & REPUBLIC OF IRELAND BY LAND VALUE

	Title	Landowner	Home county	Overall acreage	Land value
1	Duke of	Westminster	Cheshire	129,300	£11,500,000,000
2	Queen	HM Queen	Aberdeen	73,000	£3,000,000,000
3	Earl of	Cadogan	London	6,300	£3,000,000,000
4	Viscount	Portman	Hereford	9,100	£2,000,000,000
5	Mr	Paul Raymond	London	200	£1,900,000,000
6	The	Eyre family	London	190	£1,500,000,000
7	Sir	Euan Anstruther-Gough-Calthorpe	Warwicks	5,500	£1,500,000,000
8	Prince of	Wales	Cornwall	141,000	£1,250,000,000
9	Hon Mrs	Charlotte Townshend	Dorset	18,040	£910,000,000
10	Duke of	Northumberland	Northumberland	132,200	£800,000,000
11	Messrs	Mark, David & Trevor Pears	London	50	£750,000,000
12	Sir	Richard Sutton	Dorset	9,474	£720,000,000
13	Hon Mrs	Camilla Acloque	London	28	£500,000,000
14	Hon Mrs	Mary Czernin	London	28	£500,000,000
15	Hon Mrs	Blanche Buchan	London	28	£500,000,000
16	Hon Mrs	Jessica White	London	28	£500,000,000
17	Mr	Chris Lazari	London	45	£450,000,000
18	Duke of	Devonshire	Derby	73,000	£435,000,000
19	Dukedom of	Atholl (Trustees)	Perth	148,000	£430,000,000
20	Earl of	Meath	Wicklow	4,800	£400,000,000
21	Messrs	Bezion and Solomon Freshwater	London	35	£350,000,000
22	Duke of (Tavistock)	Bedford	Beds	23,020	£340,000,000
23	Earl of	Lonsdale	Cumbria	70,000	£325,000,000
24	Baron	Iliffe	Berks	41,853	£320,000,000
25	Duke of	Beaufort	Gloucester	52,000	£310,000,000
26	Mr	Samuel Whitbread	Beds	14,000	£295,000,000
27	Viscount	Petersham	London	29	£290,000,000

TOP 100 LANDOWNERS IN THE UK & REPUBLIC OF IRELAND BY LAND VALUE 2001 (CONT.)

	Title	Landowner	Home county	Overall acreage	Land value
28	Duke of	Buccleuch & Queensbury	Dumfries	270,700	£282,500,000
29	Duke of	Richmond & Go-don	Sussex	12,000	£260,000,000
30	Viscount	Falmouth	Cornwall	42,000	£245,000,000
31	Marquess of	Salisbury	Herts	7,020	£245,000,000
32	Duke of	Norfolk	Sussex	46,000	£210,000,000
33	Sir	Nicholas Bacon	Lincs	14,014	£210,000,000
34	Mr	Richard Walduck	London	620	£200,000,000
35	Baron	Barnard	Durham	53,000	£190,000,000
36	Marquess of	Northampton	Northants	30,000	£180,000,000
37	Earl of	Yarborough	Lincs	28,000	£170,000,000
38	Earl of	Leicester	Norfolk	26,000	£160,000,000
39	Mr	Duncan Davidson	Northumberland	25,000	£155,000,000
40	Earl of	Derby	Lancs	27,000	£150,000,000
41	Duke of	Roxburghe	Berwick	65,600	£150,000,000
42	Duke of	Rutland	Leics	26,000	£150,000,000
43	Lady	Anne Cavendish Bentinck	Caithness	62,000	£140,000,000
44	Baron	Vesty	Gloucester	32,900	£130,000,000
45	Baron	Brownlow	Lincs	22,000	£130,000,000
46	Viscount	Downe	Yorks	20,000	£125,000,000
47	Sir	William Benyon	Berks	19,650	£125,000,000
48	Baroness	Jane Willoughby d'Eresby	Perth	78,200	£121,000,000
49	Baron	Egremont	Sussex	22,000	£120,000,000
50	Viscount	Cowdray	Aberdeen	93,600	£120,000,000
51	Earl of	Powis	Montgomery	30,000	£105,000,000
52	Earl of	Seafield	Banff	101,000	£104,000,000
53	Marquess of	Normanby	Yorks	15,000	£95,000,000
54	Baron	Clinton	Devon	26,000	£95,000,000
55	Earl	Spencer	Northants	13,000	£95,000,000
56	Duke of	Abercorn	Tyrone	15,000	£95,000,000

TOP 100 LANDOWNERS IN THE UK & REPUBLIC OF IRELAND BY LAND VALUE 2001 (CONT.)

	Title	Landowner	Home county	Overall acreage	Land value
57	Baron	De Ramsey	Cambs	15,000	£95,000,000
58	Baron	Petre	Essex	15,000	£95,000,000
59	Mr & Ms	Henry & Mollie Dent Brocklehurst	Glos	15,000	£90,000,000
60	Earl of	Halifax	Yorks	15,000	£90,000,000
61	Earl of	Pembroke & Montgomery	Wilts	14,000	£85,000,000
62	Earl of	Rosebery	Peebles	20,900	£84,000,000
63	Mr	Robert Miller	Yorks	30,000	£81,000,000
64	Earl of	Portsmouth	Hants	3,000	£80,000,000
65	Sir	Christopher Tatton Sykes	Yorks	13,000	£80,000,000
66	Mr	Simon Howard	Cumbria	13,000	£79,000,000
67	Marquess of	Cholmondeley	Cheshire	11,500	£75,000,000
68	The	Williams family	Cornwall	20,000	£75,000,000
69	Baron	Derwent	Yorks	12,000	£72,000,000
70	Duke of	Sutherland	Suffolk	12,000	£72,000,000
71	Viscount	Leverhulme	Cheshire	34,700	£70,000,000
72	Sir	Anthony Bamford	Gloucester	6,500	£67,000,000
73	Sir	David Watkin Williams-Wynn	Denbigh	17,000	£65,000,000
74	Earl of	Radnor	Wilts	11,000	£65,000,000
75	Baron	O'Neill	Antrim	15,000	£65,000,000
76	Mr	Malcolm Healey	Yorks	11,000	£62,000,000
77	Baron	Rothschild	Bucks	12,000	£60,000,000
78	Marquess of	Bath	Wilts	10,000	£60,000,000
79	Earl of	Harewood	Yorks	10,000	£60,000,000
80	Sir	John Hall	Durham	4,500	£55,000,000
81	Earl of	Erne	Fermanagh	15,000	£55,000,000
82	Baron	Margadale	Argyll	54,500	£55,000,000
83	Baron	Digby	Dorset	15,000	£55,000,000
84	Sir	Richard Harry Rashleigh	Cornwall	15,000	£52,000,000
85	Sir	Hugh Stucley	Devon	15,000	£52,000,000

TOP 100 LANDOWNERS IN THE UK & REPUBLIC OF IRELAND BY LAND VALUE 2001 (CONT.)

	Title	Landowner	Home county	Overall acreage	Land value
86	Duke of	Wellington	Hants	31,700	£50,000,000
87	Mr	J.M. Colvin-Cayzer	Suffolk	46,200	£45,000,000
88	Messrs	Alan and Ronnie Bartlett	Cambridge	5,000	£40,000,000
89	Mr	Christopher Moran	Banff	41,500	£40,000,000
90	Earl of	Dalhousie	Angus	47,200	£40,000,000
91	Mr	Edmund Vesty	Sutherland	86,300	£40,000,000
92	Mr	Robert Fleming	Argyll	88,900	£40,000,000
93	Earl of	Airlie	Angus	37,300	£37,500,000
94	Viscount	Scarsdale	Derby	6,050	£36,000,000
95	Lady	Juliet de Chair	Kent	5,000	£35,000,000
96	Mr	Paul Fentener van Vlissingen	Ross & Cromarty	81,000	£35,000,000
97	Baron	Roborough	Devon	39,500	£35,000,000
98	Earl of	Iveagh	Suffolk	25,000	£35,000,000
99	Sir	Ivar Colquhoun of Luss	Dunbarton	50,000	£35,000,000
100	Sir	Christopher Wates	Kent	1,000	£32,000,000

LAND LIST 5
2001

TOP 100 LANDOWNERS IN THE UK & REPUBLIC OF IRELAND BY WEALTH

Key to sources of valuation:

ST 2001 = *Sunday Times* Rich List April 2001 by Dr Philip Beresford
STWR 97 = *Sunday Times* Wealth Register 1997 by Dr Philip Beresford
Mail on Sunday = *Mail on Sunday* Rich List 2001 by Rachel Oldroyd and Gaynor Pengelly
Eurobusiness 2000 = *Eurobusiness* 400 Richest Europeans Jan 2000 by Kevin Cahill
Forbes 2000 published by *Forbes* magazine in the USA
WOB 2001 = Author's calculated values for landowners not appearing elsewhere

	Title	Landowner	Home county	Overall acreage	Public wealth	Source of valuation
1	Sheik	Mohammed bin Rashid al Maktoum	Ross & Cromarty	63,100	£6,000,000,000	Forbes 2000
2	Mr	Hans Rausing	Sussex	800	£5,600,000,000	Mail on Sunday
3	Duke of	Westminster	Cheshire	129,300	£4,400,000,000	ST 2001
4	Queen	HM Queen	Aberdeen	73,000	£2,200,000,000	Eurobusiness 2000
5	The	Eyre family	London	190	£1,900,000,000	WOB 2001
6	Count	Bruno Schroeder	Argyll	16,500	£1,750,000,000	Mail on Sunday
7	Mr	Paul Raymond	London	200	£1,700,000,000	Eurobusiness 2000
8	Sir	Sir Adrian & Sir John Swire	Kent	4,000	£1,660,000,000	Mail on Sunday
9	Ms	Kirsten Rausing	Cambridge	1,400	£1,500,000,000	Mail on Sunday
10	Sir	Anthony Bamford	Gloucester	6,500	£1,300,000,000	Eurobusiness 2000
11	Viscount	Cowdray	Aberdeen	93,600	£1,300,000,000	ST 2001
12	Mr	Paul Fentener van Vlissingen	Ross & Cromarty	81,000	£1,300,000,000	Eurobusiness 2000
13	Mr	Robert Fleming	Argyll	88,900	£1,260,000,000	Mail on Sunday
14	Earl	Cadogan	London	6,300	£1,250,000,000	ST 2001
15	Mr	Robert Miller	Yorks	30,000	£1,000,000,000	Eurobusiness 2000
16	Mr	Mohamed Al Fayed	Ross & Cromarty	55,000	£750,000,000	ST 2001
17	Mr	Urs Schwarzenbach	Inverness	27,000	£750,000,000	ST 2001
18	Baron	Vesty	Gloucester	32,900	£750,000,000	Mail on Sunday
19	Mr	Edmund Vesty	Sutherland	86,300	£750,000,000	Mail on Sunday

THE LAND LISTS 387

TOP 100 LANDOWNERS IN THE UK & REPUBLIC OF IRELAND BY WEALTH 2001 (CONT.)

	Title	Landowner	Home county	Overall acreage	Public wealth	Source of valuation
20	Viscount	Portman	Hereford	9,100	£700,000,000	ST 2001
21	Mr & Ms	Joseph & Lisbet Koerner	Inverness	48,210	£696,000,000	Eurobusiness 2000
22	Earl of	Iveagh	Suffolk	25,000	£680,000,000	ST 2001
23	Prince of	Wales	Cornwall	141,000	£630,000,000	Eurobusiness 2000
24	Mr	Malcolm Healey	Yorks	11,000	£625,000,000	ST 2001
25	Messrs	Mark, David & Trevor Pears	London	50	£490,000,000	Mail on Sunday
26	Baron	Rothschild	Bucks	12,000	£460,000,000	ST 2001
27	Baron	Andrew Loyd Webber	Berks	1,200	£420,000,000	ST 2001
28	Sir	Cameron Mackintosh	Scotland	14,000	£400,000,000	ST 2001
29	Earl of	Meath	Wicklow	4,800	£400,000,000	WOB 2001
30	Sir	John Paul Getty	Gloucester	2,500	£350,000,000	ST 2001
31	Hon Mrs	Charlotte Townshend	Dorset	18,040	£350,000,000	ST 2001
32	Mr	J.M. Colvin-Cayzer	Suffolk	46,200	£347,000,000	Mail on Sunday
33	Messrs	Bezion and Solomon Freshwater	London	35	£316,000,000	Mail on Sunday
34	Rt. Hon. Baron	Michael Heseltine	Northants	800	£300,000,000	ST 2001
35	Duke of	Devonshire	Derby	73,000	£300,000,000	ST 2001
36	Mr	David Murray	Edinburgh – Midlothian	33	£260,000,000	Mail on Sunday
37	Duke of	Northumberland	Northumberland	132,200	£260,000,000	Mail on Sunday
38	Mr	Harry Hyams	Wilts	600	£256,000,000	Mail on Sunday
39	Marquess of	Salisbury	Herts	7,020	£250,000,000	ST 2001
40	Viscount	Falmouth	Cornwall	42,000	£245,000,000	WOB 2001
41	Mr	Chris Lazari	London	45	£235,000,000	Mail on Sunday
42	Sir	Timothy Landon	Hants	2,000	£200,000,000	Mail on Sunday
43	Senator	Edward Haughey	Cumbria	10,000	£200,000,000	Mail on Sunday
44	Earl of	Stockton	Devon	1,750	£190,000,000	Mail on Sunday
45	Hon Mrs	Camilla Acloque	London	28	£187,000,000	ST 2001
46	Hon Mrs	Jessica White	London	28	£187,000,000	ST 2001
47	Hon Mrs	Blanche Buchan	London	28	£187,000,000	ST 2001
48	Hon Mrs	Mary Czernin	London	28	£187,000,000	ST 2001
49	Mr	Tom Walkinshaw	Gloucester	2,000	£180,000,000	Mail on Sunday
50		McAlpine family	Bucks	4,000	£178,000,000	Mail on Sunday

TOP 100 LANDOWNERS IN THE UK & REPUBLIC OF IRELAND BY WEALTH 2001 (CONT.)

	Title	Landowner	Home county	Overall acreage	Public wealth	Source of valuation
51	Duke of (Tavistock)	Bedford	Beds	23,020	£170,000,000	ST 2001
52	Mr	Simon Keswick	Gloucester	4,000	£161,000,000	ST 2001
53	Sir	Euan Anstruther-Gough-Calthorpe	Warwicks	5,500	£150,000,000	ST 2001
54	Dukedom of	Atholl (Trustees)	Perth	148,000	£143,000,000	STWR 97
55	Duke of	Sutherland	Suffolk	12,000	£140,000,000	ST 2001
56	Marquess of	Normanby	Yorks	15,000	£140,000,000	ST 2001
57	Mr	Samuel Whitbread	Beds	14,000	£128,000,000	ST 2001
58	Mr	Michael Green	Wilts	200	£126,000,000	Mail on Sunday
59	Viscount	Downe	Yorks	20,000	£125,000,000	WOB 2001
60	Duke of	Norfolk	Sussex	46,000	£125,000,000	Mail on Sunday 2000
61	Sir	William Benyon	Berks	19,650	£125,000,000	WOB 2001
62	Mr	Richard Walduck	London	620	£123,000,000	Mail on Sunday
63	Marquess of	Northampton	Northants	30,000	£120,000,000	ST 2001
64	Baron	Iliffe	Berks	41,853	£120,000,000	ST 2001
65	Viscount	Petersham	London	29	£110,000,000	ST 2001
66	Sir	Richard Sutton	Dorset	9,474	£110,000,000	ST 2001
67	Marquess of	Bute	Ayr	49,700	£110,000,000	ST 2001
68	Earl of	Powis	Montgomery	30,000	£105,000,000	WOB 2001
69	Mr	Peter Kindersley	Berks	2,000	£101,000,000	Mail on Sunday
70	Mrs	Ann Gloag	Inverness	19,500	£101,000,000	Mail on Sunday
71	Duke of	Beaufort	Gloucester	52,000	£100,000,000	ST 2001
72	Lady	Anne Cavendish Bentinck	Caithness	62,000	£100,000,000	ST 2001
73	Earl	Spencer	Northants	13,000	£96,000,000	ST 2001
74	Baron	Petre	Essex	15,000	£95,000,000	WOB 2001
75	Baron	Clinton	Devon	26,000	£95,000,000	WOB 2001
76	Baron	De Ramsey	Cambs	15,000	£95,000,000	WOB 2001
77	Duke of	Abercorn	Tyrone	15,000	£95,000,000	WOB 2001
78	Mr	Nicholas Foreman Hardy	Nottingham	2,000	£93,000,000	ST 2001
79	Marquess of	Cholmondeley	Cheshire	11,500	£90,000,000	ST 2001
80	Mr	Michael Horton	Warwick	600	£88,000,000	ST 2001
81	Earl of	Inchcape	Ayr	13,000	£87,000,000	ST 2001

TOP 100 LANDOWNERS IN THE UK & REPUBLIC OF IRELAND BY WEALTH 2001 (CONT.)

	Title	Landowner	Home county	Overall acreage	Public wealth	Source of valuation
82	Baron	Daresbury	Cheshire	5,500	£85,000,000	ST 2001
83	Mr	Robert Sangster	Wilts	1,000	£80,000,000	ST 2001
84	Sir	John Hall	Durham	4,500	£80,000,000	ST 2001
85	Duke of	Rutland	Leics	26,000	£80,000,000	ST 2001
86	Earl of	Wemyss and March	Fife	42,700	£80,000,000	ST 2001
87	Earl of	Portsmouth	Hants	3,000	£78,000,000	ST 2001
88	Earl of	Pembroke & Montgomery	Wilts	14,000	£75,000,000	ST 2001
89	The	Williams family	Cornwall	20,000	£75,000,000	WOB 2001
90	Mr	Kevin McCabe	Yorks	3,000	£74,000,000	ST 2001
91	Mr	Noel Edmonds	Devon	840	£72,000,000	ST 2001
92	Messrs	Alan and Ronnie Bartlett	Cambridge	5,000	£72,000,000	WOB 2001
93	Baron	Derwent	Yorks	12,000	£72,000,000	ST 2001
94	Earl of	Yarborough	Lincs	28,000	£70,000,000	ST 2001
95	Earl of	Leicester	Norfolk	26,000	£70,000,000	ST 2001
96	Viscount	Leverhulme	Cheshire	34,700	£70,000,000	WOB 2001
97	Duke of	Roxburghe	Berwick	65,600	£70,000,000	ST 2001
98	Earl of	Rosebery	Peebles	20,900	£68,000,000	ST 2001
99	Baron	Brownlow	Lincs	22,000	£66,000,000	WOB 2001
100	Sir	Christopher Wates	Kent	1,000	£65,000,000	ST 2001

LAND LIST 6
2001
TOP 100 ARISTOCRATIC LANDOWNERS IN THE UK & REPUBLIC OF IRELAND BY ACREAGE

	Title	Landowner	Home county	Overall acreage	Land value
1	Duke of	Buccleuch & Queensbury	Dumfries	270,700	£282,500,000
2	Dukedom of	Atholl (Trustees)	Perth	148,000	£430,000,000
3	Prince of	Wales	Cornwall	141,000	£1,250,000,000
4	Duke of	Northumberland	Northumberland	132,200	£800,000,000
5	Duke of	Westminster	Cheshire	129,300	£11,500,000,000
6	Captain	A.A. Farquharson	Aberdeen	106,500	£28,000,000
7	Earl of	Seafield	Banff	101,000	£104,000,000
8	Viscount	Cowdray	Aberdeen	93,600	£120,000,000
9	Countess of	Sutherland	Sutherland	83,239	£15,000,000
10	Baroness	Jane Willoughby d'Eresby	Perth	78,200	£121,000,000
11	Colonel Sir	Hamish Cameron of Lochiel Bt	Inverness	76,000	£15,000,000
12	Duke of	Devonshire	Derby	73,000	£435,000,000
13	Queen	HM Queen	Aberdeen	73,000	£3,000,000,000
14	Earl of	Lonsdale	Cumbria	70,000	£325,000,000
15	Duke of	Roxburghe	Berwick	65,600	£150,000,000
16	Sheik	Mohammed bin Rashid al Maktoum	Ross & Cromarty	63,100	£30,000,000
17	Earl	Granville	Inverness	62,200	£15,000,000
18	Lady	Anne Cavendish Bentinck	Caithness	62,000	£140,000,000
19	Duke of	Argyll	Argyll	60,800	£12,500,000
20	Earl of	Cawdor	Nairn	56,700	£25,000,000
21	Sir	William Gladstone Bt	Kincardine	54,700	£31,000,000
22	Baron	Margadale	Argyll	54,500	£55,000,000
23	Baron	Barnard	Durham	53,000	£190,000,000
24	Duke of	Beaufort	Gloucester	52,000	£310,000,000
25	Sir	Ivar Colquhoun of Luss Bt	Dunbarton	50,000	£35,000,000
26	Mr & Lady	Jonathan & Lady Marcia Bulmer	Inverness	49,900	£15,000,000
27	Marquess of	Bute	Ayr	49,700	£21,000,000

THE LAND LISTS 391

TOP 100 ARISTOCRATIC LANDOWNERS IN THE UK & REPUBLIC OF IRELAND BY ACREAGE 2001 (CONT.)

	Title	Landowner	Home county	Overall acreage	Land value
28	Earl of	Dalhousie	Angus	47,200	£40,000,000
29	Duke of	Norfolk	Sussex	46,000	£210,000,000
30	Earl of	Stair	Wigtown	43,674	£25,000,000
31	Earl of	Wemyss and March	Fife	42,700	£30,000,000
32	Viscount	Falmouth	Cornwall	42,000	£245,000,000
33	Baron	Iliffe	Berks	41,853	£320,000,000
34	Baron	Roborough	Devon	39,500	£35,000,000
35	Earl of	Airlie	Angus	37,300	£37,500,000
36	Viscount	Thurso	Caithness	36,800	£24,000,000
37	Viscount	Leverhulme	Cheshire	34,700	£70,000,000
38	Lady	Pauline Ogilvie Grant Nicholson	Inverness	34,000	£8,500,000
39	Earl of	Mansfield and Mansfield	Perth	33,800	£23,000,000
40	Baron	Vesty	Gloucester	32,900	£130,000,000
41	Duke of	Wellington	Hants	31,700	£50,000,000
42	Marquess of	Northampton	Northants	30,000	£180,000,000
43	Earl of	Powis	Montgomery	30,000	£105,000,000
44	Earl of	Home	Lanark	30,000	£9,000,000
45	Hon Mr	Maurice Robson	Inverness	29,000	£7,500,000
46	Earl of	Yarborough	Lincs	28,000	£170,000,000
47	Earl of	Derby	Lancs	27,000	£150,000,000
48	Earl of	Leicester	Norfolk	26,000	£160,000,000
49	Duke of	Rutland	Leics	26,000	£150,000,000
50	Baron	Clinton	Devon	26,000	£95,000,000
51	Captain	A.A. Ramsay of Mar	Aberdeen	25,143	£17,500,000
52	Viscount	Mountgarrett	Yorks	25,000	£11,000,000
53	Earl of	Iveagh	Suffolk	25,000	£35,000,000
54	Sir	William J. Lithgow Bt	Argyll	24,700	£17,000,000
55	Sir	Andrew Buchanan-Jardine Bt	Dumfries	24,500	£16,500,000
56	Viscount	Wimborne	Dorset	24,200	£18,000,000

TOP 100 ARISTOCRATIC LANDOWNERS IN THE UK & REPUBLIC OF IRELAND BY ACREAGE 2001 (CONT.)

	Title	Landowner	Home county	Overall acreage	Land value
57	Count	Adam Knuth	Sutherland	24,000	£7,000,000
58	Hons Mrs & Mrs	D.C. Fleming & L.F. Schuster	Argyll	23,200	£16,000,000
59	Duke of (Tavistock)	Bedford	Beds	23,020	£340,000,000
60	Sir	Anthony Nutting	Sutherland	22,700	£6,500,000
61	Baron	Dulverton	Inverness	22,400	£6,000,000
62	Baron	Egremont	Sussex	22,000	£120,000,000
63	Baron	Brownlow	Lincs	22,000	£130,000,000
64	Baron	Newborough	Caernarvon	22,000	£12,000,000
65	Viscount	Astor	Oxford	21,500	£24,000,000
66	Earl of	Rosebery	Peebles	20,900	£84,000,000
67	Lt Cdr	Bryce McCosh of Huntsfield	Cumbria	20,000	£121,000,000
68	Baron	Gilmour	Fife	20,000	£15,000,000
69	Viscount	Boyd	Cornwall	20,000	£120,000,000
70	Vicomte	Adolphe de Speolbergh	Argyll	20,000	£15,000,000
71	Viscount	Downe	Yorks	20,000	£125,000,000
72	Marquess of (Trustees)	Bristol	Suffolk	20,000	£120,000,000
73	Viscount	Allendale	Northumbs	20,000	£105,000,000
74	Sir	William Benyon	Berks	19,650	£125,000,000
75	Marquess of	Linlithgow	Lanark	18,300	£15,000,000
76	Hon Mrs	Charlotte Townshend	Dorset	18,040	£910,000,000
77	Marquess of	Lothian	Roxburgh	18,000	£60,000,000
78	The	MacNeill of Barra	Inverness	17,500	£6,500,000
79	Baron	Bolton	Yorks	17,500	£107,000,000
80	Earl of	Strathmore	Angus	17,300	£12,000,000
81	Sir	David Watkin Williams-Wynn	Denbigh	17,000	£65,000,000
82	Viscount	Masserene & Ferrard	Argyll	16,600	£12,000,000
83	Earl of	Moray	Moray	16,500	£13,000,000
84	Count	Bruno Schroeder	Argyll	16,500	£7,177,500
85	Sir	William Gordon Cumming Bt	Moray	16,300	£12,000,000

TOP 100 ARISTOCRATIC LANDOWNERS IN THE UK & REPUBLIC OF IRELAND BY ACREAGE 2001 (CONT.)

	Title	Landowner	Home county	Overall acreage	Land value
86	Captain	Ian C. de Sales la Terriere	Perth	15,500	£6,750,000
87	Hon Mr	Philip Astor	Aberdeen	15,000	£11,000,000
88	Earl of	Halifax	Yorks	15,000	£90,000,000
89	Marquess of	Normanby	Yorks	15,000	£95,000,000
90	Baron	Petre	Essex	15,000	£95,000,000
91	Baron	Digby	Dorset	15,000	£55,000,000
92	Sir	Hugh Stucley	Devon	15,000	£52,000,000
93	Sir	Richard Harry Rashleigh	Cornwall	15,000	£52,000,000
94	Baron	De Ramsey	Cambs	15,000	£95,000,000
95	Duke of	Abercorn	Tyrone	15,000	£95,000,000
96	Earl of	Erne	Fermanagh	15,000	£55,000,000
97	Baron	O'Neill	Antrim	15,000	£65,000,000
98	Hon Mrs	A.G. Maclay	Ross & Cromarty	14,800	£6,500,000
99	Sir	John & Sandy Mactaggart	Argyll	14,300	£10,000,000
100	Sir	Nicholas Bacon Bt	Lincs	14,014	£210,000,000

Appendix 1

A Note on Comparative Values

Previous studies of wealth through history have used thee principal means of translating sterling values from their historic context into current values. These three are set out below, followed by the system adopted for this book.

1) The Bank of England

Information contained in report 'Equivalent Contemporary Value of the Pound: a Historical Series 1270 to 2000' (published by the Bank of England, 2000).

According to this report, 'The figures are derived from the Retail Prices Index, based on January 1987 = 100. There are no figures for individual years before 1800. The RPI is based on the combined cost of a number of specific goods and does not take into account other factors relevant to a comparison of values, for example the cost of real property or the level of wages. We know of no figures incorporating all possible factors.'

The following are some samples from the Bank of England list.

as at August 2000:
£1 in 1270 = £426.25
£1 in 1370 = £341.00
£1 in 1470 = £426.25
£1 in 1570 = £155.00
£1 in 1670 = £77.50
£1 in 1770 = £58.70
£1 in 1870 = £42.63
£1 in 1970 = £9.22
£1 in 2000 = £1.03

2) Professor William Rubenstein and the *Sunday Times*

On 26 March 2000 Dr Philip Beresford, the editor of the *Sunday Times* annual Rich List, together with Professor William Rubinstein, produced a list of the wealthiest 200 Britons for the ten centuries beginning with the Norman conquest in 1066. To obtain comparative values for wealth then and now, they used a figure known as Net National Income, an economic formula akin to Gross Domestic Product, or GDP. The wealth of those included in the list was calculated as a percentage of NNI. The baseline they used was NNI in 1999, which was £865 billion. They did not produce a running list of comparative values in the same way as the Bank of England, but a number of the key figures, who also occur in the land lists in this book, are given below.

Year	NNI	Name	Value	% of NNI	Year 2000 equivalent
1833	£362m	Duke of Sutherland	£7m	1.93%	£16.7bn
1842	£459m	Duke of Cleveland	£4.5m	0.98%	£8.5bn
1874	£1.075bn	Marquess of Downshire	£2.9m	0.26%	£2.2bn
1879	£1.075bn	Duke of Portland	£8.5m	0.79%	£6.8bn
1899	£1.591bn	Duke of Westminster	£14.0m	0.87%	£7.5bn

3) Philip Hall and *The Royal Fortune* (Bloomsbury 1992)

In a note on prices, Hall, who made a good habit of always giving contemporary values alongside historic values, states the following:

> 'It might be helpful for readers to know that this involves prices from 1850 to 1914 being multiplied by between 43 and 55, depending on the precise year; those from the 1920s and 1930s by between 20 and 34, and those from 1950 by about 15, from 1960 by about 10, from 1970 by about 7 and from 1980 by about 2.'

4) *Who Owns Britain*

Fundamentally, the Bank of England's method, and consequently Philip Hall's method which closely follows it, is based on too narrow a criterion, being primarily an index of consumed goods and services, many not available in the late 1800s. For the purposes of this book, the crucial comparison in land values is between 1872, the start date of the calculations for the *Return of Owners of Land*, and today. It makes sense to base the figure on land, land assets and land transactions, rather than consumed goods and services. An additional factor for most large landowners of the last century was the cost of labour, a major overhead in their big houses and on their huge acreages.

In the 1870s, when the *Return of Owners of Land* was produced, the best land was selling for a maximum of £60 an acre, and the poorest land at £20 an acre. In 1999, according to the Valuation Office, arable, dairy and mixed farmland was selling in the range of £3222 to £2729 an acre, an average of about £3000 an acre. Crudely put, £1 worth of land in 1872 would cost £75 in 1999.

Taking into account a much steeper rise in wages over a similar period, as well as the general change in prices tracked by the Bank of England, this book will use a figure of 70 to compare the values stated in the 1872 Return, with values in 2001.

Appendix 2

How land is owned in the UK and Ireland

A very brief history
Essentially dating back to Norman times, land ownership in the countries which make up the United Kingdom is based on the feudal system, as all occupants of the countries held their lands and premises as tenants of the King, who was deemed to hold the land from God. The original contract was the feudal one, whereby the tenants were bound not to pay something, but to do something, which was provide service to their feudal lord in gradations from the sub tenant, to tenant, to tenant in chief, to King. This gradually evolved into a financial agreement, whereby the tenants paid a fee, to avoid or substitute for service. Once a class of freemen existed, not bound by the feudal contract, the idea of holding land in the same way, i.e. without obligations other than those imposed by the law generally, took hold. Historically land tenure has developed differently within England and Wales, Scotland (where land reform is much more of a live issue at the beginning of the 21st century) and Northern Ireland, and what follows is a very broad outline.

Freehold
The bulk of private homes and estates in the UK are owned on a basis known generally as freehold. That is to say, the owner may do what he or she likes with his or her property, subject only to the public law and local bye laws. Owners pay no rent of any kind to any superior owner and have the absolute right of disposal to any party. A freehold may be owned by an individual, a group of individuals, or a corporation.

Leasehold
A lease is a contract to occupy a property for a specified period and usually involves an annual lease or ground rent payment to an owner, who may also be a leaseholder. A lease usually involves the leaseholder in the upkeep of the property and other restrictions as to use and disposal. At the end of a lease the property goes back to either the holder of the next lease in the chain, or to the freeholder. Much of London property is on leases of one kind or another, some as long as 999 years or more.

Feudal tenure in Scotland
Apart from the crown, nobody owns land absolutely, but each person holds a subsidiary title to land subject to certain conditions. These may include restrictions on use and, with increasing rarity, obligations to make (or receive) regular payments of feu duty or ground annual.

Common rights and interests
Particularly in urban situations, the law recognises the importance of a principle of commonality in relation to interests in land and buildings, and owners may be jointly entitled.

Tenancy or rental
A simple arrangement whereby an owner allows someone (the tenant) to occupy a premises or land, or to use it, for a fixed payment, usually on a short term basis, such as a month or a year and for which the owner as landlord retains responsibility for the upkeep and maintenance of the premises or land.

Registration of Title
The Land Registry (in Scotland, The Land Register) guarantees the title to, and records the ownership of, interests in registered land. However, about 2 million land titles, covering anything from 30% to 50% of the acreage of England and Wales, are not registered and the owners prove title from the actual deeds that they hold. In Scotland, where the concept of registration was enforced as far back as the thirteenth century, The Land Register is gradually superseding the General Register of Sasines as proof of interests in land ownership, use and occupancy.

Appendix 3

The inheritance of the Throne 1066–2001

The following brief chronology of the kings and queens of England following the arrival of the Normans, and with them the Plantagenets, is taken from *Burke's Peerage and Baronetage* of 1896 (and earlier versions). The sovereign lineage begins with William the Bastard and ignores the Anglo Saxon kings, upon whose claim to the throne William rested his. It does not give William's parentage or 'lineage'. However, in relation to the Scottish Crown, *Burke's* begins the lineage in 850 with Kenneth I. The latest *Debrett's* (2000) the successor to *Burke's* for many generations, no longer gives the kings and queens of Scotland or England, focusing instead on the descendants of Victoria I.

1. William I, known as the Conqueror — 1066 to 1087
2. William II (Rufus) (II son of William I) — 1087 to 1100 (killed while hunting)
3. Henry I (brother of William Rufus) — 1100 to 1135
4. Stephen (nephew of Henry I) — 1135 to 1154
5. Henry II. The first Plantagenet, son of the Holy Roman Empress, Maud, and of her second husband, Geoffrey Plantagenet, Count of Anjou. Maud or Matilda was the only surviving child of Henry I — 1154 to 1189
6. Richard I, the Lionheart (son of Henry II) — 1189 to 1199 (killed in battle)
7. John I, known as Lackland (brother of Richard I) — 1199 to 1216
8. Henry III (son of John I) — 1216 to 1272
9. Edward I (son of Henry III) — 1274 to 1307
10. Edward II (son of Edward I) — 1307 to 1327 (murdered)
11. Edward III (son of Edward II) — 1327 to 1377
12. Richard II (grandson of Edward III) — 1377 to 1399 (murdered)
13. Henry IV (cousin of Richard II) — 1399 to 1413
14. Henry V (son of Henry IV) — 1413 to 1422
15. Henry VI (son of Henry V) — 1429 to 1461 (deposed, and died in Tower of London 1471)
16. Edward IV (cousin of Henry VI) — 1461 to 1483
17. Edward V (son of Edward IV) — 1483 to 1483 (murdered)
18. Richard III (uncle of Edward V) — 1483 to 1485 (killed at Bosworth)

19. Henry VII (Tudor) (cousin of Richard III)   1485 to 1509

    Henry, a descendant of Edward III, married Princess Elizabeth Plantagenet in 1486. She was the eldest daughter and heiress to Edward IV. Their son was:

20. Henry VIII (son of Henry VII and Elizabeth Plantagenet)   1509 to 1547
21. Edward VI (son of Henry VIII and Jane Seymour)   1547 to 1553
22. Mary I (daughter of Henry VIII and Katherine of Aragon)   1553 to 1558
23. Elizabeth I (daughter of Henry VIII and Anne Boleyn)   1558 to 1603
24. James I (cousin of Elizabeth I and also King of Scotland)   1603 to 1625
25. Charles I (son of James I)   1625 to 1649 (executed)

    A Commonwealth and a Republic under the Lord Protector   1649 to 1661

26. Charles II (son of Charles I)   1661 to 1685
27. James II (brother of Charles II)   1685 to 1689
28. William of Orange and Mary (daughter of James II)   1689 to 1702 (Mary died in 1694)
29. Anne I (sister of Mary and daughter of James II)   1702 to 1714
30. George I (great grandson of James I)   1714 to 1727
31. George II (son of George I)   1727 to 1760
32. George III (grandson of George II)   1760 to 1820
33. George IV (son of George III)   1820 to 1830
34. William IV (brother of George IV)   1830 to 1837
35. Victoria I (niece of William IV)   1837 to 1901
36. Edward VII (son of Victoria)   1901 to 1910
37. George V (son of Edward VII)   1910 to 1936
38. Edward VIII (son of George V)   1936 to 1936 (abdicated)
39. George VI (son of George V)   1936 to 1952
40. Elizabeth II (daughter of George VI)   ascended 1952

Notes

Abbreviations used:

DETR – Department of Environment, Transport and the Regions
MAFF – Ministry of Agriculture, Fisheries and Food
SOAEFD – Scottish Office Agriculture, Environment and Fisheries Department
VO – Valuation Office

Preface
1 The Land Registry of England and Wales aims to 'complete' registration of titles by 2011, 86 years after the formal commencement of compulsory registration of basic transactions in land under Section 123 of the Land Registration Act 1925. (*Land Registry Annual Report 1996–7*, p.15.) Section 123 gave country-wide legal effect to an earlier Order in Council in 1898 when Lord Halsbury, the Lord Chancellor, commenced compulsory registration of transactions in parts of the old county of London. The legal effect of Section 123 was completed in 1990, when Section 120 of the same 1925 Act ended the piecemeal, rolling, adoption of registration and applied mandatory registration for sales of land throughout England and Wales. The last areas to have compulsory registration imposed by Section 120 were fourteen districts in Essex, Hereford, Worcester and Suffolk. The Land Registration Act of 1997 extended mandatory first registration for a number of earlier exemptions, such as deeds of gift and conveyances that do not constitute a formal sale. There is still no requirement in law to register land in which no transactions have taken place. In his annual report for 1996–7 Dr Stuart Hill, the Chief Land Registrar, identified local authorities as 'one of the largest groups of unregistered owners'. He makes no mention of the two million titles that are not local authority titles, and that are not included in the Land Registry goal for 2011. The extent of acreage represented by those two million titles is last referred to in his predecessor's annual report for 1992. The then Chief Land Registrar estimated that the unregistered titles might cover between 30% and 50% of the land area of England and Wales. (Land Registry Annual Reports 1990–9; *Completing the Land Register in England & Wales*, consultation paper, 1992; *HM Land Registry – An Historical Perspective*, Land Registry 1992.) The Quinquennial Review of the Land Registry written by Andrew Edwards and published by the Lord Chancellor in 2001 contains no proposal to address or remedy the situation of un-registered land.
2 Van der Weyer, Martin, *Falling Eagle: a History of Barclay's Bank* (Weidenfeld & Nicholson, London 2000), gives further details of Camoys.
3 *Historic Houses, Castles & Gardens* (Johansens Publications 1997 & 1999).
4 A figure of 70 times the 1872 figure for gross annual rental is used throughout this book to give the approximate equivalent value in 2001. See Appendix I on p.395.
5. Local valuers in each district of the UK provided an assessed rental value for acreages in their district. The actual rent obtained was a matter for the landlord.

6. Ministry of Agriculture Fisheries and Food (MAFF) Annual Report 1999. The total handed out, according to this report, is about £2.3 billion. But EU figures indicate that the total paid out in Common Agricultural Policy (CAP) grants to the 15 countries of the extended EU is over £65 billion for each year, 1997–9. This suggests that the total payout in the UK is closer to £4 billion, particularly as CAP does not include tax breaks through local country legislation or other grants made in the UK by the Department of Heritage or the Department of the Environment, Transport and the Regions.
7. Each parish of the Church of England and of the sister churches in Scotland, Wales and Ireland, were supported by tithes imposed on land from the mid 1500s. The parishes were each supposed to retain maps showing who owned land in the parish, in order that the tithe could be imposed. Tithes ceased to be a legal obligation in the late 1920s but the bulk of the Tithe Acts, seventeen in number dating from 1836, were only repealed in 1998, under the Statute Law (Repeals) Act 1998. Certain county record offices and some Dioscean registries still retain a number of tithe maps.

Chapter One
1 These figures are all taken from the Digest of Agricultural Statistics, 1997 edition, published by the Government statistical service. EU figures are taken from the European Commission statistical database (Europe, Agricultural Enterprises 1997).
2 All values are from the Valuation Office Property Market Report for autumn 2000, distributed and marketed by *Estates Gazette*..
3 *Burke's Landed Gentry* listed those county families with the right to bear arms but normally without a title. First published in 1836, 18 editions followed, the last appearing in three volumes between 1965 and 1972. Those listed obtained their place in the book by dint of lineage, rather than acreage. Typical entrants are families like the Fursdons at Cadbury in Devon with 700 acres, Francis Fulford, from Fulford in Devon, with 1800 acres and William Benyon of Englefield Green in Surrey with 14,250 acres.
4 See Van der Weyer, Martin, *Falling Eagle*: a *History of Barclay's Bank* (Weidenfeld & Nicholson, London 2000).
5 Quoted in Shoard, Marion *This Land is Our Land* (Paladin, London 1987).
6 See 'Final Acts of the Irish Land Commission' a report by the Irish Ministry of Agriculture, 1999.
7 *Financial Times*, 20 March 1998.
8 MAFF Annual Report 1999.
9 DETR Press Office June 2000
10 Figures taken from the Department of the Environment's *Urbanisation in England*, Projections 1991–2016, as updated by the DETR in 2000. Also Sinclair, C *The Lost Land: Land Use Changes in England 1945–1990* (Council for the Protection of Rural England 1990).
11 DETR figures. These figures exclude most of the empty dwellings in the UK, which number between 780,000 (Shelter 1999) and 1,000,000 (an estimate by the Housebuilders Association 2000). The figure we allow for this is 2.5% and through this book a housing breakdown of 65% privately owned and 35% publicly owned or empty is used.
12 *Residential Property Report* April–June 2000 (HM Land Registry).
13 Council of Mortgage Lenders 'Mortgage arrears and possessions' (July 2000), Table 1.

14 Figures from House Builders Federation (England & Wales) Press Department, June 2000.
15 Other speakers at the same conference spoke of specific difficulties in establishing ownership of unregistered land, though this was mainly addressed to local authority land.
16 *Sunday Times*, 7 November 1999.
17 *Urbanisation in England*, Projections.
18 Valuation Office Property Market Report, Autumn 2000.
19 Sampson, Anthony *Anatomy of Britain* (Hodder & Stoughton 1962), ch. 2.
20 Sources for these figures: Bateman, *The Great Landowners of Great Britain and Ireland*; The Forestry Commission annual report 1997/1998; The National Trust annual report and accounts 1999; The Ministry of Defence, Report to Parliament 1999; The Church Commissioners, Report and Accounts 1997. Scottish figures are from Wightman, *Who Owns Scotland*. Other figures are from the *Sunday Times* Rich List, compiled by Dr Philip Beresford.
21 A freeholder has no superior landlord or owner, and owns his or her property outright. Figures from *Royal Finances*, Buckingham Palace (1995).

Chapter Two

1 Quoted by Professor Mancur Olsen in an Occasional paper 1978, published in the LSE Quarterley of Winter 1989.
2 De Juvenel, Bertrand *On Power* (Greenwood Press (and Beacon Press) New York 1981).
3 St Augstine, *City of God* Book IV, ch. IV.
4 See Hallam, Elizabeth *Domesday Book* (Thames & Hudson 1986), pp.36–7.
5 Hallam, *Domesday Book*
6 Richardson, H.G and Sayles, G.O. *The Governance of Medieval England*. Quoted in Hallam, *Domesday Book*.
7 Goldwin Smith, *Legal and Constitutional History of England* (Dorset Press NY 1990), p.132.
8 Madge was an academic who compiled a *Domesday of Crown Lands During the Cromwellian Commonwealth* for the London School of Economics Series of Studies in Economic and Social History which was compiled between 1920 and 1938 and published in the latter year. He was also the secretary and editor of the British Record Society.
9 Abolition of Feudal Tenure Act, 2000.
10 D'Auvergne, M. Nelson *Tarnished Coronets* (2nd edition, Werner Laurie 1937).
11 Madge, Sidney *The Domesday of Crown Lands* (Routledge, London 1938).
12 Madge, *Domesday of Crown Lands*.
13 Bateman, John *The Great Landowners of Great Britain & Ireland* (4th Edition Harrison & Sons 1883).
14 See Cannadine, David *The Decline and Fall of the British Aristocracy* (Yale University Press 1990)., Appendices, especially B.
15 There are a number of good books on the enclosures, in particular Thompson, F.M.L. *English Landed Society in the 19th Century* (Routledge & Kegan Paul, London 1963); Mingay, G.E. *Land and Society in England 1750–1980* (Longmans, London 1994); and Scott, John *The Upper Classes: Property and Privilege in Britain* (Macmillan, London 1982).
16 See Cannadine, *Decline and Fall of the British Aristocracy.*

Chapter Three

1. There are innumerable books on the land agitations in Wales, Scotland and Ireland, where those seeking reform were substantially boosted in their arguments by the 1872 Return. Professor Cannadine in *The Decline and Fall of the British Aristocracy* gives a useful and readable summary in pages 54 and following. He points out that demands for fair rents, fixity of tenure and free sale, were as strong in Scotland and Wales as they were in Ireland. Only the Irish agitation, which had the ultimate objective of removing landlords altogether, fully succeeded in its aims. The Scottish agitation, especially in Skye and Ross, despite media support, was the least successful.
2. Ruoff, T.B.F. *HM Land Registry 1862–1962: A Centenary History* (Land Registry 1962).
3. The approximate total number of titles found by the Clerks of the Union as they compiled the Return.
4. A detail picked up by Professor David Spring in his introduction to the Leicester University edition of Bateman's *Great Landowners*.
5. As previous note.
6. Bright had argued that 'Fewer than 150 men own half the land of England'.
7. See Cannadine, *The Decline and Fall of the British Aristocracy*, p.55.
8. *The Return of Owners of Land*, Introduction
9. Bateman, John *The Great Landowners of Great Britain & Ireland* (4th Edition, Harrison & Sons 1883).
10. Mingay, G.E. *Land and Society in England 1750–1980* (Longmans, London 1994), p.42.
11. *Agricultural History Review*, Vol XXXV.1 of 1987.
12. Professor David Spring's introduction to Bateman *The Great Landowners*.
13. Cannadine, *The Decline and Fall of the British Aristocracy*, p.59. Cannadine surveys in just a page both the links and the extent of the influence of Irish land agitation on attempts at land reform in Wales and Scotland. These are connections not often referred to nowadays anymore than is the fact that the London government was sending both gunboats and marines to Skye, Tiree and Ross in the 1880s during the Crofters War. Despite the fact that Davitt, the Irish Land League leader, toured the Highlands in 1882 and 1887, educating the crofters in the techniques the Irish were using, and despite the fact that branches of the HLRA, later renamed the Highland Land League, appeared in almost every town in Scotland, the campaign never broke the back of the Scottish landlord system, which persists to this day (see Chapter 13).
14. See also Chapter 1, note 3. The first BLG in 1833 contained only 400 families. By 1906 it was 1891 pages long and contained over 5000 families, each of whom had to possess more than 2000 acres of land, and have some kind of family tree, preferably with endorsement by the College of Heralds. The second requirement was not as difficult as it sounds. Burke's *General Armory*, a companion volume, had more than 60,000 families listed with a right to a family shield and crest.
15. See Hinde, Thomas (ed.) *The Domesday Book: England's heritage then and now* (Guild Publishing for the English Tourist Board, London 1985), and Hallam, Elizabeth *Domesday Book* (Thames & Hudson 1986), as well as others.
16. The University of Leicester reprint incorrectly gives the date of the Census as 1871.
17. The first edition of Bateman's work, called the *Acreocracy of England*, published by Harrison of Pall Mall in 1876.
18. See Bibliography including Cannadine, Thompson, Shoard, Brodrick, Sampson,

Paxman, Clemenson, Scott, Beard and others.
19. Professor Spring notes that Bateman was 'an agricultural improver, an experimenter in forestry and tobacco growing who had firm ideas about proper ensilage. He was kindly to his dependants, to Nonconformists no less than to Anglicans.' Introduction to 1971 edition of Bateman *The Great Landowners*.
20. *Financial Times*, February 1999, from an advertisement for an estate of this size.
21. Average growth in the Republic is just under 10%, as against 2.5% in the UK, according to government figures in 1999.
22. Hinde, Thomas (ed.) *The Domesday Book: England's heritage then and now* (Guild Publishing for the English Tourist Board, London 1985).
23. George, Henry *Progress and Poverty* (1st edition 1879; Centenary Edition 1979 published by Hogarth Press, London 1979).
24. Cannadine, *The Decline and Fall of the British Aristocracy*, pp. 47–9.
25. Mingay *Land and Society in England 1750–1980*, p.54.
26. The *FT* has a worldwide circulation of 450,000 daily, up 19% on the previous year. The UK circulation has also risen significantly in recent years, up 10% from 169,000 in August 1999 to 186,000 in August 2000. Source: Audit Bureau Of Circulation.
27. See Chapter 1, note 10
28. MAFF *Agricultural Statistics* 1997.
29. HMSO abstracts detailed in *Whittaker's Almanac 2001*.

Chapter Four
1. Author's database of landowners based on 1872 Return and Bateman's *Great Landowners*. Part II of this book draws on this database to draw up lists of the top 100 landowners in 1872.
2. Bateman, John *The Great Landowners of Great Britain & Ireland* (Leicester University Press. Leicester 1970).
3. Hall, Philip *Royal Fortune* (Bloomsbury, London 1992), pp. 14–16.
4. Crown Private Estates Act 1862
5. *Business Age*, November 1992.
6. Buckingham Palace, *Royal Finances* 1993 and 1995.
7. The Crown Estate Office, Annual reports and accounts 1990–2000.
8. The Crown Estate Office, Annual reports and accounts 1990–2000.
9. Buckingham Palace, *Royal Finances* 1995 p.33.
10. Wightman, Andy *Who Owns Scotland* (Canongate Books, Edinburgh 1996).
11. Wightman, *Who Owns Scotland*.
12. Whitlock, Ralph *Royal Farmers* (Michael Joseph, London 1980).
13. Whitlock, *Royal Farmers*.
14. Whitlock, *Royal Farmers*.
15. Whitlock, *Royal Farmers*.
16. Whitlock, *Royal Farmers*.
17. Wightman, *Who Owns Scotland*.
18. Sampson, Anthony *Anatomy of Britain* (Hodder & Stoughton, London 1962 and subsequent editions).
19. Olson, Mancur *The Logic Of Collective Action* (Harvard University Press 1990).
20. Olson, *The Logic Of Collective Action*.
21. In the Quarterly Journal of The London School of Economics, Winter 1989, Olson

notes Sir Samuel Brittan, the *Financial Times* Economics correspondent, pointing out as early as 1978 that despite government in Britain taking less resources as a percentage of GDP than Holland, Sweden, Norway and West Germany, Britain had a poorer economic performance than any of those countries in the 1970s. Olson points out that Brittan had traced the beginning of Britain's decline to the last two decades of the nineteenth century.
22 Scott, John *The Upper Classes: Property and Privilege in Britain* (Macmillan Press, London 1982).
23 Olson, *The Logic Of Collective Action*.
24 As covered by Michael Prowse in the *Financial Times* 'Weekend', 21 October 2000.

Chapter Five
1 Madge, Sidney *The Domesday of Crown Lands* (Routledge, London 1938).
2 Madge, *The Domesday of Crown Lands*.
3 £1.2 million in 1760 would be worth about £70 million today, according to the Bank of England, or £140 million, by the formula used in this book to convert land values. See Appendix I.
4 Hall, Philip *Royal Fortune* (Bloomsbury, London 1992).
5 The Crown Estate Office, Annual reports and accounts 1990–2000.
6 Buckingham Palace, *Royal Finances* 1993 and 1995, p. 7.
7 The Crown Estate Office, Annual reports and accounts 1990–2000.
8 Buckingham Palace, *Royal Finances* 1993 and 1995.
9 This system is used by the Stock Exchange, along with most forms of probate in relation to shares in private companies.
10 National Asset Register (HM Treasury 1997 & 2001). The list has not so far included the Crown Estate and the Duchy of Lancaster.
11 Income of the duchies of Cornwall, Lancaster, plus the Crown Estates on a 10 year multiple.
12 Hall, *Royal Fortune*, pp. 74–79.
13 McEwen, John *Who Owns Scotland* (2nd edition, Polygon, Edinburgh 1981).
14 Wightman, Andy *Who Owns Scotland* (Canongate Books, Edinburgh 1996).
15 By the author.
16 Keswick, Hon. Tessa Informal Paper On Crown Estate Privatisation, Institute For Policy Studies, 1996.
17 *BusinessAge*, September 1995.
18 *Financial Times* Mining conference 1997. Information supplied to author by delegates.
19 *Financial Times* assessment of privatisation results, March 1999.
20 The Crown Estate Office, Annual reports and accounts 1990–2000.
21 The Crown Estate Office, Annual reports and accounts 1990–2000.

Chapter Six
1 Duchy of Cornwall Act 1982.
2 As opposed to the original constitutional convention which was that the Crown should be dependent on Parliament for its finances.
3 Much of the recovery was due to Albert, husband of Queen Victoria. See Hall, Philip *Royal Fortune* (Bloomsbury, London 1992), pages 52 onwards.

4 There are a number of good books on the matter but the critical issue of Edward's loyalty has surfaced again as more wartime records become available. See Allen, Martin *Hidden Agenda: How the Duke of Windsor Betrayed the Allies* (Macmillan, London 2000).
5 The exercise of persistent semantic deceit in the public accounts given of the Duchy revenues and how they were distributed and taxed, or not taxed, is covered in Hall, *Royal Fortune*, pages 56 onwards, especially page 58, re Willie Hamilton MP.
6 In relation to comments elsewhere in this book about the overall nature of the UK statute book and the influence of the landowning elite on legislation, an analysis of the provisions made for the Crown, and for landowners, is long overdue. In this case the provisions in question are those which exempted the Duchy from tax.
7 See Picknett, Lynn; Prince, Clive; and Prior, Stephen *Double Standards* (Littlebrown, London 2001).
8 Hall, *Royal Fortune*.
9 The accounts of the Duchy were not published in the ordinary sense until 1982. Prior to that, as Hall points out, one copy was sent to the House of Commons Library and one to the House of Lords Records Office. While legally amounting to publication, it rendered the actual accounts all but inaccessible.
10 Duchy accounts 1988.
11 Various Duchy accounts as indicated in later text.
12 40 acres at £10 million per acre.
13 The share portfolio would have paid for the Prudential purchase in full, if used for that purpose. The accounts for the purchase are not yet available.
14 The point Hall makes in *Royal Fortune* about the 50% 'donation' is that it was voluntary and it was a lot less than the rate of tax paid by other taxpayers, which rose to 80% or more as their income rose above £40,000.

Chapter Seven
1 Accounts of the Duchy of Lancaster, March 2000.
2 The latest available.
3 This estate is essentially a Plantagenet inheritance. See Chapter Nine.
4 Hall, Philip *Royal Fortune* (Bloomsbury, London 1992).
5 Crown Land Act 1702.
6 Hall, *Royal Fortune*.
7 Accounts of the Duchy of Lancaster March 2000.

Chapter Eight
1 Private conversation with author, House of Lords, 1996.
2 In the unreformed House of Lords more than 60% of the hereditaries had been to school at Eton.
3 Smith, Goldwyn *A Constitutional and Legal History of England* (Dorset Press 1990).
4 Cannadine, David *The Decline and Fall of the British Aristocracy* (Yale University Press 1990), p. 2.
5 Cannadine, *The Decline and Fall of the British Aristocracy*, chapter 2.
6 House of Lords Information, March 2001.
7 Figures are from House of Lords Information cross-referred to the relevant *Vacher's*

Parliamentary Companion, 1998 and 2000.
8 As at March 2001.
9 Weber, Max *Essays in Sociology* 1958. The methodology is used by Professor Cannadine in *The Decline and Fall of the British Aristocracy*, see p. 8.
10 McEwen, John *Who Owns Scotland* (2nd edition, Polygon, Edinburgh 1981).
11 Wightman, Andy *Who Owns Scotland* (Canongate Books, Edinburgh 1996).
12 Devonshire, Duchess of *The Estate: A view from Chatsworth* (Macmillan London 1990).
13 Cannadine, *The Decline and Fall of the British Aristocracy*.
14 Cannadine, *The Decline and Fall of the British Aristocracy*.
15 Beresford, Dr Philip *The Sunday Times Book of the Rich* (Weidenfeld & Nicholson, London 1990).
16 Cannadine, David *Aspects of Aristocracy* (Viking Penguin, London 1998).

Chapter Nine

1 List of all electoral registers in the UK 2001. From I-CD Publishing Ltd, Dame Court, Dublin.
2 Rootsweb.com
3 See Appendix 3.
4 Turton, Lt. Colonel *The Plantagenet Ancestry: 7000 descendants of Princess Elisabeth Plantagenet* (Genealogical Publishing Co. Baltimore USA 1928).
5 Mingay, G.E. *Land and Society in England 1750–1980* (Longmans, London 1994). 'Enclosure . . . proceeded in three ways; first by piecemeal creation of closes from the land taken out of common fields by its owners, a process which by 1750 had already halved the size of common fields in some villages; secondly by private agreements between proprietors, leading to the enclosure of whole parishes; and thirdly by private acts of Parliament which authorised the enclosure by nominated commissioners of the remaining common fields and commons and often also of the waste lands within a parish.' Mingay says that the first two affected some hundreds of thousands of acres. But the Parliamentary-led enclosures, he notes, affected 8.4 million acres of England and Wales, 24% of the total acreage. This, then, was an early form of privatisation, that in effect amounted to a fourth land grab, and one that was as fundamentally unjust and unlawful as its predecessors.
6 See table 9/2 for a snapshot of the Plantagenet bloc in 1872.
7 Mingay, *Land and Society in England*
8 For the purposes of this book the core Plantagenet lineage is as it is defined and listed in *Burke's Peerage & Baronetage*, 1896 and previous, which *Burke's* defined as having a family shield which the College of Arms allowed to carry the Plantagenet arms in one of its quarters. There are two exceptions to this. The dukedoms of Somerset and Beaufort, which claim direct descent from the Plantagenet kings and queens, are also included. Although much fun has been poked at the 'descents from Adam and Eve,' created for the *nouveau riche* from the sixteenth century onwards sometimes with the help of the College of Arms incumbents, the Plantagenet descent in particular was deadly serious. It was about land and wealth on an inconceivable scale, and about keeping the land and the wealth in the family. There was no way an interloper could get the Plantagenet arms illegitimately onto his shield. By 1896, it was impossible to be in *Burke's* without being properly registered at the College. So how reliable was

the College? In most cases, very, despite various scandals. But an outsider needs to know one vital fact about the hereditary principle aligned with male primogeniture in the wider sense. Its overriding purpose was to prevent the break-up of landed estates. In this the principle was hugely successful, in so far as its workings can be checked without a complete land registry. About 70% of England, and to a slightly lesser extent Scotland, are still in the hands of descendants of those who owned the country in 1872 and for long before that. Where the male line has failed, estates have often been transferred to cousins, sometimes very distant cousins, as was the case between the 10th and 11th dukes of Beaufort. Peerages long extinct have been revived on the same basis. The earldom of Devon, for instance, became dormant when Edward, recreated Earl in 1553, died, unmarried and heirless in Padua in 1556. The earldom was not revived until 1831, when the then 3rd Viscount Courtney established the right to the title. The study of the Plantagenet descent within the wider nobility, the landed gentry, is perhaps for another book. Indeed, the modern bible of the Peerage and Baronetage, *Debrett's*, no longer always carries a full summary of the origins of a particular family. To compile our list it has been necessary to go back to the nineteenth century, to a range of books including *Burke's*, *Shirley's* and other references of the period.

9 *Sunday Times* Richest of the Rich, the British Rich from 1066 to 2000, edited by Dr Philip Beresford and Professor W.D. Rubinstein.
10 Rootsweb.com
11 *Burke's Peerage and Baronetage* 1896 and previous.
12 Cannadine, David *The Decline and Fall of the British Aristocracy* (Yale University Press 1990).
13 See Chapter 8, note 9.
14 The Inland Revenue estimate that in 2001 there are over 153,800 people in the UK with a net worth of over £1 million and the *Sunday Times* listed 5000 of those millionaires in its Wealth Register published in 1997.

Chapter Ten

1 Marion Shoard in her book *This Land is Our Land* says on page 489 that no individual in Denmark may own a farm of over 180 acres without special permission, something the Danish embassy says no longer applies.
2 The Land registry – annual report 1992 and later, reckons that there are two million unregistered titles, mostly those of the big estates.
3 The author's attempts to establish how many acres were privatised with just the big water utilities, were frustrated and derailed by the water utilities in 1995.
4 Even while Sampson was writing his ground-breaking book a former Scottish forester, John McEwen, was compiling the first new list of landowners anywhere in the UK, subsequent to the Returns, or Bateman, the latter of which he used. This was eventually published in Scotland in 1977 as *Who Owns Scotland*, fifteen years after Sampson's book was first published.
5 The figures reproduced here and which follow are taken from the annual Reports and Accounts of the Forestry Commission, mostly up to 1997. They were all but opaque, and were the least informative of all public account documents produced in that era. There has been a significant improvement since 1998, but the Forestry Commission remains reluctant to divulge key facts about all its present transactions or the historic purchases that created it. In the 1920s it was much derided, and McEewen repeats the derision, as

a scheme of outdoor relief for impoverished landowners, especially in Scotland.
6 See Madge, Sidney *The Domesday of Crown Lands* (Routledge, London 1938). It is not unfair to say that the part of Britain which paid the highest price for Empire was its woodlands, denuded to build ships of war.
7 Norton-Taylor, Richard *Whose Land is it Anyway?* (Turnstone Press, Wellingborough 1982).
8 Wightman, Andy *Who Owns Scotland* (Canongate Books, Edinburgh 1996).
9 Wightman, *Who Owns Scotland.*
10 Norton-Taylor, *Whose Land is it Anyway?*
11 Hobson, Dominic *The National Wealth* (HarperCollins, London 1999).
12 *Defence Lands*, Report of the Defence Lands Committee 1971–1973 (The Nugent Report) HMSO 1973, Chapter 1.
13 DETR Urbanisation in England, Projections 1991–2016.
14 There were a number of UK participants in the Nomura consortium.
15 UK Defence Estimates 2000.

Chapter Eleven
1 *The Times*, 21 April 2001.
2 *Evening Standard*, 18 February 2000.
3 *Burke's Peerage and Baronetage* (1896).
4 *Sunday Times* Richest of the Rich, the British Rich from 1066 to 2000, edited by Dr Philip Beresford and Professor W.D. Rubinstein.
5 This potted history of the Grosvenors is mainly taken from two enchanting volumes called *Mary Davies and the Manor of Ebury*, written by Charles Gatty and published by Cassells in London in 1921. There is additional material in *The Selling of Mary Davies and other Writings* by Simon Jenkins (London 1993).
6 See Leslie Field's book, *Bendor, the Golden Duke of Westminster* (Weidenfeld & Nicholson, London 1983).
7 Green, Shirley *Who Owns London?* (Weidenfeld & Nicholson, London 1986).
8 *Sunday Times* Richest of the Rich.
9 'Who Owned Victorian England?' *Agricultural History*, Vol. 61, No. 4 (Fall 1987) pp. 25–51.
10 For anyone seriously interested in the evolution of London as a whole, and for details of its various landowners over the centuries there are few better places to go than Peter Thorold's book *The London Rich* (Viking, London 1999) and its extensive list of sources. Lloyd's map of the London owners is also reproduced in Thorold's book.

Chapter Twelve
1 Sampson, Anthony, *Anatomy of Britain*, Hodder & Stoughton, London 1962.
2 The tables were compiled from the Returns themselves, by the simple process of examining the clerical landholding for each of the 13,662 parishes of England, including those in Monmouthshire, then an English county. The technique used was to add up the glebe and parsonage acreage of each parish in the counties of Devon and Cornwall, to provide an exact total for church landholdings for each of the two counties. The total number of parishes involved was 697. This provided a full scale reference and monitor for the remaining 40 counties, which were sampled by adding up about 20%

to 30% of the parish landholdings and averaging the outcome for the total number of parishes in each county. Holdings over 1000 acres were excluded as a number of these were almost certainly personal landholdings. It is quite possible that most, if not all, of the holdings over 1000 acres, with the exception of the 74 landowners identified in Bateman's *Great Landowners of Great Britain and Ireland* as landowners who were also clerics, were actually Church possessions. This would move the total acreage closer to the figure of two million acres which represents the amount of land transferred to the Church of England from the Roman Catholic church in the time of Henry VIII and Elizabeth I.

3 Endowments & Glebe Measures Act 1976.
4 *Sunday Times* Richest of the Rich, the British Rich from 1066 to 2000, edited by Dr Philip Beresford and Professor W.D. Rubinstein.
5 Sampson, *Anatomy of Britain*.
6 Over 2000 'livings' remain in private or non-Church hands in 2001.
7 Bateman, John *The Great Landowners of Great Britain & Ireland* (Leicester University Press, Leicester 1970).
8 Sampson, *Anatomy of Britain*.
9 Shoard, Marion *This Land is Our Land* (Paladin, London 1987).
10 Norton-Taylor, Richard *Whose Land is it Anyway?* (Turnstone Press, Wellingborough 1982).
11 Hobson, Dominic *The National Wealth* (HarperCollins, London 1999).
12 The incumbent was known in 'head office' in London as a 'corporate soul'.
13 Anthony Sampson notes that Archbishop Temple, when he took the see of Canterbury at the beginning of the twentieth century, sold the country estate of the archbishopric, 'believing it wrong for the Primate of All England to be associated with landed wealth'. Sampson, *Anatomy of Britain*, p.163.
14 Hobson, *The National Wealth*.
15 Lovell, Terry *Number One Millbank: The Financial Downfall of the Church of England* (HarperCollins, London 1997).
16 Until the late twentieth century a significant number of the Church of England's bishops and archbishops attended public school. According to Anthony Sampson in the first edition of *Anatomy of Britain* in 1962 more than three quarters of the bishops went to public schools, with one an old Etonian.
17 Telephone conversation with author, 8 November 2000.
18 Graham, Ysenda Maxtone *The Church Hesitant* (Hodder & Stoughton, London 1993).
19 Between 1970 and 1997 more than 1500 parish churches, out of a total of about 11,000, were closed. Church House Spokesman to the author, Nov. 2000.
20 Annual Report and Accounts for the Church Commissioners to 31 Dec. 1999.
21 The Church Commissioners pay most of the pension cost of approximately 11,000 retired clergy, and about 21% of the salary costs of working clergy. The Commissioners also pay a substantial proportion of the costs of the Church of England's bishops. Source: Annual Accounts of the Church Commissioners 31st December 1999.
22 Hobson, *The National Wealth*.
23 Bedarida, Francois *A Social History of England 1851–1990* (London 1991).
24 Quoted in Gill, Robin *The Myth of the Empty Church* (SPCK, London 1993), p.278.
25 Gill, *The Myth of the Empty Church*, p.203.
26 Annual Report And Accounts For The Church Commissioners to 31 Dec. 1999.
27 Cahill, Kevin. *BusinessAge*, May 1993.

Chapter Thirteen

1. Wightman, Andy *Land Reform: Politics, Power and the Public Interest* (Friends of John McEwen, Edinburgh 1999 – The 1999 McEwen Lecture on Land Tenure in Scotland).
2. McEwen, John *Who Owns Scotland* (2nd edition, Polygon, Edinburgh 1981).
3. Wightman, Andy *Who Owns Scotland* (Canongate Books, Edinburgh 1996).
4. The average value of good arable acre in the UK is £3000 (Inland Revenue figures). In Ireland it is £5000 to £6000 (*Irish Times*).
5. The actual EU grants to Ireland were often less than 3% of GDP but the impact of what might be called 'marginal money' was simply staggering. This is an area in urgent need of study and analysis, so that all underdeveloped areas can benefit in the same way from EU funds.
6. Callander, Robin *How Scotland is Owned* (Canongate, Edinburgh 1998), chapter 4 pp. 45–48.

Chapter Fourteen

1. Quoted in Woodham-Smith, Cecil *The Great Hunger: Ireland 1845–1849* (Penguin Books, London 1991). Woodham-Smith argues that Lalor's thesis that land ownership was more important than politics was ultimately far more important than the various revolutionary movements which Lalor himself supported and joined.
2. The statistics were supplied by the Irish Government Statistics service and by the Irish Ministry of Agriculture. The non agricultural area seems very large but is consistent with the same figure in the UK. See also Part II.
3. Emigration, the curse of Ireland for 150 years, has reversed. Ireland now has an immigrant problem, and with it the unpleasant discovery of racism in its midst. The official unemployment figure from the Government is 3.5%.
4. See tables, Chapter One
5. At average agricultural values of £3000 (before the outbreak of Foot & Mouth disease in early 2001).
6. Said to be falling to 140,000 by the end of 2001 by the Irish Agriculture Minister who also told the Dail on 2 May 2001 that Irish farms received an average of £11,000 each in direct subsidies in the year 2000. *Irish Times*, 3 May 2001.
7. 32 million acres at £3000 per acre and shared amongst 56 million people, with 3.5 million Irish sharing 17.2 million at, say, £3000 per acre.
8. Woodham-Smith, *The Great Hunger*.
9. George, Henry *Progress and Poverty* (1st edition 1879; Centenary Edition 1979 published by Hogarth Press, London 1979).
10. Quoted in Woodham-Smith, *The Great Hunger*.
11. Quoted in Woodham-Smith, *The Great Hunger*.
12. Quoted in Woodham-Smith, *The Great Hunger*.
13. Quoted in Woodham-Smith, *The Great Hunger*.
14. Beckett, J.C. *Ireland* (Faber & Faber 1966 and 1969).
15. Expected to fall to 140,000. See note 6 above.
16. Lord Rees Mogg, writing in *The Times*, 11 Oct 1998.

Chapter Fifteen
1. Bateman, John *The Great Landowners of Great Britain & Ireland* (Leicester University Press, Leicester 1970).
2. Cannadine, David *The Decline and Fall of the British Aristocracy* (Yale University Press 1990).
3. Hobhouse, Henry *The Seeds of Change: Five plants that transformed mankind* (HarperTrade, London 1997).

Chapter Sixteen
1. Cannadine, David *The Decline and Fall of the British Aristocracy* (Yale University Press 1990).
2. Moore, Barrington *Social Origins of Dictatorship and Democracy: Lord and Peasant in the Making of the Modern World* (Penguin Books. London 1966).
3. OECD Economic Surveys, Ireland 1997. HM Treasury Report Dec 2000. Irish Dept of Finance Economic Indicators Dec 2000.
4. MAFF Agricultural Statistics 1999 – See tables accompanying Chapter 1.
5. NFU Press Release, Feb 2000.
6. De Juvenel, Bertrand *On Power* (Greenwood Press (and Beacon Press) New York 1981), p.95.
7. Buildings Societies Association figures 1990–1997.
8. Hobson, Dominic *The National Wealth* (HarperCollins, London 1999). Hobson cites £5bn as the Ministry of Agriculture's Budget and £4.2bn as the subsidy handout in 1996/1997. As recounted elsewhere, this author had intense difficulty in pinning down the Ministry of Agriculture on the actual subsidy paid out, but concluded that Hobson's figure is about right when all subsidies, direct and indirect, but not Capital Gains Tax relief, is taken into account.
9. *Debrett's Peerage and Baronetage* (Macmillan, London 2000), edited by Charles Kidd and David Williamson.
10. Soros, George *Soros on Soros: Staying Ahead of the Curve* (John Wiley & Sons, Chichester & NY, 1995), pages 37 onwards.
11. *Sunday Times* Richest of the Rich, the British Rich from 1066 to 2000, edited by Dr Philip Beresford and Professor W.D. Rubinstein.
12. *Times* 21 June 2001, 'The New Whitehall'.

Bibliography

There are a small number of books which a lay reader may find directly useful in pursuing matters raised in this book. They are given here, separately from the general bibliography.

Main references on landownership
The Return of Owners of Land (HMSO London 1873–1876). Available in most county libraries' special reference sections or 'cages'.
Bateman, John *The Great Landowners of Great Britain & Ireland* (Leicester University Press, Leicester 1970). Earlier editions were published in 1876, 1878, 1879 and 1883, by Harrison, the Queen's bookseller.
McEwen, John *Who Owns Scotland* (2nd edition, Polygon, Edinburgh 1981).
Wightman, Andy *Who Owns Scotland* (Canongate Books, Edinburgh 1996).

Land and landownership
Mingay, G.E. *Land and Society in England 1750–1980* (Longmans, London 1994).
Norton-Taylor, Richard *Whose Land is it Anyway?* (Turnstone Press, Wellingborough 1982).
Shoard, Marion *This Land is Our Land* (Paladin, London 1987).
Thompson, F.M.L. *English Landed Society in the 19th Century* (Routledge & Kegan Paul, London 1963).

Modern Politics
Hall, Philip *Royal Fortune* (Bloomsbury, London 1992).
Hutton, Will *The State We're In* (Vintage, London 1996).
Paxman, Jeremy *Friends in High Places* (Michael Joseph, London 1990).
Paxman, Jeremy *The English* (Penguin, London 1999).

The Aristocracy
Debrett's Peerage and Baronetage (Macmillan, London 2000 and previous editions – it is published every 5 years).

Politics
De Juvenel, Bertrand *On Power* (Greenwood Press (and Beacon Press) New York 1981).
Olson, Professor Mancur *The Rise and Decline of Nations* (Yale University Press 1986).

General bibliography

Acland, Anne *A Devon Family* (Phillimore, London and Chichester 1981).
Angel, Heather *The Natural History of Britain & Ireland* (Peerage Books 1986).
Aslet, Clive and Moore, Derry *Inside the House of Lords* (HarperCollins, London 1998).
Astaire, Leslie, Martine, Roddy and Von Schulenburg, Fritz *Living in Scotland* (Thames & Hudson, London 1987).
Ball, Michael *Housing Policy and Economic Power* (Methuen, London 1983).
Banks, F. R. *English Villages* (BT Batsford Ltd, London 1963).
Beard, Madeleine *English Landed Society in the 20th Century* (Routledge, London 1989).
Beckett, J.C. *Ireland* (Faber & Faber 1966 and 1969).
Bedarida, Francois *A Social History of England 1851–1990* (London 1991).
Beresford, Dr Philip *The Sunday Times Book of the Rich* (Weidenfeld & Nicholson, London 1990).
Bonham-Carter, Victor *The English Village* (Pelican, London 1952).
Brodrick, George C. *English Land and English Landlords* (Augustus M. Kelley Inc. New York 1968).
Bryant, Arthur *English Saga* (William Collins and Co, London). Also published as *The Story of England* (various editions 1963–77).
Bryant, Arthur *Years of Victory* (William Collins and Co, London 1963).
Caird, James *English Agriculture in 1850–1851* (Longmans, London 1852).
Callander, Robin *How Scotland is Owned* (Canongate, Edinburgh 1998).
Cannadine, David *Lords and Landlords: The Aristocracy & the Towns 1774–1967* (Leicester University Press, Leicester 1980).
Cannadine, David *Aspects of Aristocracy* (Viking Penguin, London 1998).
Carter, Harold *The Study of Urban Geography* (4th edition, Arnold 1995).
Cave-Brown, Anthony *'C:' biography of Sir Stewart Menzies, wartime head of M16* (MacMillan, London 1987).
Clemenson, Heather *English Country Houses and Landed Estates* (Croom Helm, New York 1982).
Corti, Count *The Rise of the House of Rothschild* (Victor Gollancz, London 1928).
Cramb, Auslan *Who Owns Scotland Now?* (Mainstream Publishing, Edinburgh 1996).
D'Auvergne, M. Nelson *Tarnished Coronets* (2nd edition, Werner Laurie 1937).
Davis, William *Rich* (Sidgwick & Jackson, London 1983).
De Smith, *Constitutional and Administrative Law*, edited by Harry Street and Rodney Brazier (Penguin Books, London 1971).
De Tocqueville, Alexis *Journeys to England & Ireland* (Faber & Faber, London 1957).
Delderfield, Eric *West Country Historic Houses and their Families* (David & Charles, Newton Abbot 1973).
Dempster, Nigel *Nigel Dempster's Address Book* (Weidenfeld & Nicholson, London 1990).
Devonshire, Duchess of *The Estate: A view from Chatsworth* (Macmillan London 1990).
Dorrill, Stephen *The Silent Conspiracy* (William Heinemann Ltd, London 1993).
Drucker, Peter *The Age of Discontinuity* (Harper & Row, New York 1968).
Evans, Harold *Good Times, Bad Times* (Atheneum, London 1984).
Fergueson, Niall *The House of Rothschild*, 2 vols (Penguin Books, London 2000).
Field, Leslie *Bendor: The Golden Duke of Westminster* (Weidenfeld & Nicholson, London 1983).
Gatty, Charles *Mary Davies and the Manor of Ebury*, 2 vols. (Cassell, London 1921).

George, Henry *Progress and Poverty* (1st edition 1879; Centenary Edition 1979 published by Hogarth Press, London 1979).
Gill, Robin *The Myth of the Empty Church* (SPCK, London 1993).
Girouard, Mark *Life in the English Country House* (Yale University Press, 9th printing 1984).
Girouard, Mark *The Victorian Country House* (Book Club Associates, London 1979).
Goddard, Nicholas *Harvest of Change The Royal Agricultural Society of England 1838–1988* (Quiller Press, London 1988).
Graham, Ysenda Maxtone *The Church Hesitant* (Hodder & Stoughton, London 1993).
Graves, Charles *Leather Armchairs: The Chivas Regal Book of London Clubs* (Cassel, London 1963).
Green, Shirley *Who Owns London?* (Weidenfeld & Nicholson, London 1986).
Guinness, Desmond and Ryan, William *Irish Houses and Castles* (Thames & Hudson, London 1971).
Guinness, Michele *The Guinness Legend* (Hodder & Stoughton, London 1990).
Guttesman, W.L. (ed) *The English Ruling Class* (Weidenfeld & Nicholson, London 1969).
Hallam, Elizabeth *Domesday Book* (Thames & Hudson 1986).
Hennessy, Peter *Whitehall* (Fontana Press, London 1990).
Hobhouse, Henry *The Seeds of Change: Five plants that transformed mankind* (HarperTrade, London 1997).
Hobson, Dominic *The National Wealth* (HarperCollins. London 1999).
Hoey, Brian *The Princess Anne: A Biography* (Country Life Books, London 1984).
Holden, Anthony *The Tarnished Crown* (Transworld Publishers, London 1993).
Hone, N.J. *The Manor and the Manorial Record* (Dutton, London 1906).
Inwood, Stephen *A History of London* (Macmillan London 1998).
James, Gerald *In the Public Interest* (Little Brown & Company, London 1995).
Kennedy, Paul *Preparing for the 21st Century* (HarperCollins, London 1993).
Lacey, Robert *Aristocrats* (Hutchinson, London 1983).
Lee, J.J. *Ireland 1912–1985* (Cambridge University Press 1989).
Livingstone, Ken *If Voting Changed Anything, They'd Abolish It* (Fontana/Collins, London 1987).
Lovell, Terry *Number One Millbank: The Financial Downfall of the Church of England* (HarperCollins, London 1997).
Lundberg, Ferdinand *The Rich and the Super Rich* (Lyle Stuart Inc, New York 1968).
Macdonald, Stuart *Information for Innovation* (Oxford University Press, Oxford 1998).
Macdonald, Stuart *The Role of the Individual in agricultural change; the example of George Culley of Fenton* (Northumberland Institute of British Geographers, London 1979). See also Macdonald's PhD thesis on aspects of Agriculture in Northumberland (Newcastle University 1974).
Madge, Sidney *The Domesday of Crown Lands* (Routledge, London 1938).
Manthorpe, John *Ten Chief Land Registrars* (The Land Registry, London 1997).
Marx, Samuel *Queen of the Ritz* (Bobbs-Merrill Company Inc, New York 1978).
McEwen, John *A Life in Forestry*, edited by Doris Hatvany (Perth & Kinross Libraries, Perth 1998).
Montgomery, Maureen E. *Gilded Prostitution: Status, money and transatlantic marriages 1870–1914* (Routledge, London 1989).
Moody, T.W. and Martin F.X. *The Course of Irish History* (Radio Telefis Eireann, Dublin 1978).

Moore, Barrington *Social Origins of Dictatorship and Democracy: Lord and Peasant in the Making of the Modern World* (Penguin Books, London, 1966).

Morris, Jan *The Matter of Wales: Epic Views of a Small Country* (Oxford University Press, Oxford 1984).

Mortimer, Penelope *Queen Elizabeth: A Life of the Queen Mother* (Viking, London 1986).

Morton, Fredric *The Rothschilds* (Seker & Warburg, London 1962).

Moule, Thomas *The County Maps of Old England* (Studio Editions, London 1990).

Mountbatten: Eighty Years in Pictures (Macmillan, London 1979).

Newman, Peter *The Canadian Establishment* (McClelland and Stewart Ltd, Toronto 1975).

Olson, Mancur *Power and Prosperity* (Basic Books 2000).

Olson, Mancur *The Logic of Collective Action* (Harvard University Press 1990).

Peel, J. H. B. *Peel's England* (David & Charles, Newton Abbot 1977).

Perkins, Benjamin *A Secret Landscape Diary of Lapwing Meadows* (Cantury, London 1986).

Perry, Bliss (ed.) *Selections from Burke* (Henry Holt & Co, New York 1896).

Picknett, Lynn; Prince, Clive; and Prior, Stephen *Double Standards* (Littlebrown, London 2001).

Pixley, Francis *The History of the Baronetage* (Duckworth, London 1900).

Rawnsley, S. and Singleton, F. B. *A History of Yorkshire* (Phillimore, Chichester 1986).

Richardson, Rosamond *Swanbrook Down: A Century of Change in an English Village* (Macdonald, London 1990).

Rollinson, William (ed.) *A History of Cumberland and Westmorland* (Phillimore, Chichester 1978).

Rossmore, Lord *Things I Can Tell: Recollections of an Irish Landowner* (Eveleigh Nash, London 1912).

Roth, Cecil *The Magnificent Rothschilds* (Robert Hale Ltd, London 1939).

Ruoff, T.B.F. *HM Land Registry 1862–1962: A Centenary History* (Land Registry 1962).

Sampson, Anthony *Anatomy of Britain* (Hodder & Stoughton, London 1962 and subsequent editions).

Sayce, Roger *The History of the Royal Agricultural College, Cirencester* (Alan Sutton Publishing Ltd, Stroud 1992).

Scott, John *The Upper Classes: Property and Privilege in Britain* (Macmillan, London 1982).

Sinclair, C *The Lost Land: Land Use Changes in England 1945–1990* (Council for the Protection of Rural England 1990).

Smith, Goldwyn *A Constitutional and Legal History of England* (Dorset Press 1990).

Soros, George *Soros on Soros: Staying Ahead of the Curve* (John Wiley & Sons, Chichester & NY 1995).

Stephenson, Tom *Forbidden Land: The struggle for access to mountain and moorland*, edited by Ann Holt (Manchester University Press, Manchester 1988).

Summers, Judith *Soho: A history of London's most colourful neighbourhood* (Bloomsbury London 1989).

Thorold, Peter *The London Rich* (Viking, London 1999).

Van der Weyer, Martin, *Falling Eagle: a History of Barclay's Bank* (Weidenfeld & Nicholson, London 2000).

Whitlock, Ralph *Royal Farmers* (Michael Joseph, London 1980).

Wightman, Andy *Land Reform: Politics, Power and the Public Interest* (Friends of John McEwen, Edinburgh 1999 – The 1999 McEwen Lecture on Land Tenure in Scotland).

Wilkinson, Roderick *The Trout and Sea Trout Rivers of Scotland* (Swan Hill Press, Shrewsbury 1990).
Williamson, Tom and Bellamy, Liz *Property and Lanscape* (George Philip, London 1987).
Woodham-Smith, Cecil *The Great Hunger: Ireland 1845–1849* (Penguin Books, London 1991).
Wormell, Peter *Anatomy of Agriculture* (Harrap, London 1978).
Wright-Mills, C. *The Power Elite* (Oxford University Press, New York 1956).
Yardley, Michael *Sandhurst: A Documentary* (Harrap, London 1987).
Young, Hugo *One of Us* (Macmillan, London 1989, 1990).
Ziegler, Anthony *The Sixth Great Power* (William Collins, 1988).

Other specific reference works

The AA Book of British Villages (Drive Publications Ltd, published by the Automobile Association, Basingstoke 1980).
The Ancestor, Quarterly Review of Family History, Heraldry and Antiquities, published by Archibald Constable & Co. London, vols I–X.
Andrews, Allen (ed.) *Kings & Queens of England & Scotland* (Marshall Cavendish 1994).
Burke, Sir Bernard *Burke's Colonial Gentry* (1891–95 and Clearfield edition 1997).
Burke's Landed Gentry (1871, 1906, 1921, 1952 and 1965–1972). Burke's Landed Gentry in this form is no longer published.
Burke's Peerage and Baronetage (1896, 1906. *Burke's* has reappeared in 2000).
Cairnduff, Maureen (ed.) *Who's Who in Ireland: The Influential 1000* (Checkout Publications/Kevin Kelly, Dublin 1999).
Debrett's Peerage and Baronetage. Specific editions consulted for this book: 1985, 1990, 1995 and 2000. *Debrett's Peerage* is published every five years by Macmillan, London.
Papers from the *Financial Times* Corporate Property Conference, 6–7 July 1998, published by the *Financial Times*, London 1998.
Foss, Arthur *Country House Treasures of Britain* (The National Trust with Weidenfeld & Nicholson, London 1980).
Hinde, Thomas (ed.) *The Domesday Book: England's heritage then and now* (Guild Publishing for the English Tourist Board, London 1985).
Historic Houses, Castles & Gardens (Johansens Publications 1997 & 1999).
Humphrey-Smith, Cecil (ed.) *Index of Parish Registers* (Phillimore, Chichester 1995).
Jackson-Stops, Gervais (ed.) *The Treasure Houses of Great Britain* (Yale University Press, Newhaven and London 1985).
Johnson, Paul *British Castles* (The National Trust with Weidenfeld & Nicholson, London 1978).
Kelly, Kevin *Europe's Elite 1000* (Cadogan Publications, London 1998/1999).
Lejune, Anthony *The Gentlemen's Clubs of London* (Bracken Books, London 1984).
Montgomery-Massingberd, Hugh (ed.) *Great British Families* (Debrett's Webb & Bowyer, London 1988).
Roth, Andrew *Parliamentary Profiles* (Parliamentary Profiles Ltd, London 1988).
Sykes, Christopher Simon (ed.) *Country House Album* (The National Trust with Little Brown, London 1989).
Twelve Great Country Houses, a tour with Arthur Negus (Peerage Books, London 1985).
Vacher Parliamentary Companion, published each quarter by Vacher DOD Publishing.

The Valuation Office Property Market Report, published by Estates Gazette in four editions 1999–2000.

Walford, Edward (ed.) *Old and New London* (Cassell & Co, London circa 1900).

Walford's County Families of the United Kingdom (1900).

Directory of Westminster & Whitehall 1998/99 (Carlton Publishing, London 1998).

Whitaker's Almanack, published annually by J. Whitaker and Sons, London.

Who's Who. Specific editions consulted for this book: 1907, 1912, 1920, 1931, 1947, 1955, 1964, 1976, 1981, 1992, 1997, 1998, 1999, 2000. *Who Was Who 1987–1915*. *Who's Who* is published annually by A & C Black, London.

Periodicals, yearbooks, newspapers and special editions

BusinessAge Richest 250 Women in the UK 1992, edited by Kevin Cahill.

BusinessAge Richest 500 individuals on the UK Stock Exchange 1993, edited by Kevin Cahill.

BusinessAge Richest 500 people in the UK 1993, 1994, edited by Tom Rubython.

BusinessAge (VNU) Richest 500 people in the UK 1995, edited by Kevin Cahill.

Estates Gazette. The journal of the estate and land business profession, published fortnightly in London. This is an indispensable source, together with the Valuation Office Property Market Report, to land values, past and present.

Eurobusiness Richest 400 Europeans 1999, edited by Kevin Cahill.

Eurobusiness Richest 200 Women in the World June 2000, edited by Kevin Cahill.

Forbes Magazine (USA) The Billionaires, annually 1995–2001.

Fulford, Francis 'Keeping it in the Family. The families who have kept their lands for over 500 years.' *The Field*, February 1994.

Gardens of England & Wales Open for Charity (National Gardens Scheme, Guildford 1997 onwards).

Gardens of Scotland Open for Charity (Scotland's Gardens Scheme, Edinburgh 1997 onwards).

Land & Liberty, published monthly by The Georgist Society.

Mail on Sunday Rich Report 2000 and 2001, edited by Rachel Oldroyd and Rodney Gilchrist.

Monastic Britain (The Ordnance Survey, Southampton 1978).

Montgomery-Massingberd, Hugh *Country Houses and their Owners: The Field Book of Family Seats of the British Isles* (Webb & Bower, London 1988).

National Asset Register (HM Treasury 1997 & 2001).

The National Trust Handbook, published annually by the National Trust.

Observer Young Rich 1999 and 2000.

OECD Economic Surveys, published by Organisation for Economic Co-operation and Development, Paris. Surveys consulted: Ireland 1997; United Kingdom 1998.

The Ordnance Survey Atlas of Great Britain (Book Club Associates, London 1982).

Platt, Colin *Medieval Britain from the Air* (Guild Publishing, London 1984).

Properties of the National Trust (The National Trust). Vols consulted 1973, 1978, 1983, 1988, 1997.

Sunday Times Rich Lists 1989–2001, edited and written by Dr Philip Beresford.

Sunday Times Richest of the Rich, the British Rich from 1066 to 2000, edited by Dr Philip Beresford and Professor W.D. Rubinstein.

Government sources

Agricultural Land, Report of the Committee of Inquiry into the Acquisition and Occupancy of Agricultural Land (The Northfield Report) HMSO 1979.

Buckingham Palace, *Royal Finances* 1993 and 1995. (These pamphlets have not been updated by the Palace.)

The Cabinet Office, The Duchy of Lancaster annual reports.

Common Land, Royal Commission on Common Land, HMSO 1958, 2 vols.

The Crown Estate Office, Annual reports and accounts 1990–2000.

Defence Lands, Report of the Defence Lands Committee 1971–1973 (The Nugent Report) HMSO 1973.

Department of the Environment, Transport & the Regions *Urbanisation in England* and other publications.

The Duchy of Cornwall, Annual reports and accounts 1990–2000.

Duchy of Cornwall, The Parliamentary Survey of the Duchy of Cornwall of 1650, edited by Norman J.G. Pounds (Devon & Cornwall Records Society, Exeter 1982).

Government Information Office Dublin, Irish housing statistics 1995–2000

The Land Registry of England & Wales, Annual Reports and Housing Price Reports from 1990.

The Land Registry of Ireland, Centenary publication, annual reports.

Ministry of Agriculture Fisheries & Food, *Agricultural Statistics* 1990 onwards and currently on the Web.

Ministry of Works and Planning, *Public Control of Land*, Expert Committee on Compensation and Betterment (HMSO 1942).

The Northern Ireland Office, *Urbanisation and Housing in Northern Ireland*.

The Northern Ireland Public Records Office, *Landowners in Northern Ireland* and other web-sourced publications, especially *Townlands by Major Estates*, page created 18 April 1998. The list of estates is incomplete – see Part II of this book for a more complete list.

The Public Records Office, Kew (Lloyd George Survey 1910–1915).

The Scottish Executive and the Scottish Office, Scottish agricultural and housing statistics.

The Welsh Office, Welsh urban and housing statistics.

Index

Notes

1. **Emboldened** page numbers indicate major discussions and those in *italics* indicate tables or maps and their captions.
2. Places in the *tables* for the counties (pages 217–354) are omitted if only mentioned once.
3. Where names of people and places are identical, people are listed first e.g. Windsor family before Windsor estate

Abbey House 237
Abbeystead estate 244
Abbots Ripton Hall 229
Abdy, Sir William Neville, Baronet 36
Aberconway, Charles 310
Aberconway, Charles Melville McLaren, 3rd Baron 212, 310
Abercorn, Dukes of 110
   acreage and value of land *107, 203, 325*
   Debrett's entry 212
   James Hamilton, 5th Duke of (later Marquess of Abercorn) 105, 113, 325
   in Land Lists (1872) *361, 365, 373, 378*
   in Land Lists (2001) *384, 389, 394*
Abercromby, Sir Robert John *274, 278*
Aberdare, Baron 212
Aberdeen, Earls of *362, 270, 366, 372*
Aberdeen, Marquess of *161, 162*
Aberdeen and Temair, Marquess of 212
Aberdeenshire 180, *206*, **270**
   Balmoral 19, **61–4**, *61, 65*, 270
Abergavenny, Marquesses of 212, *259*
   5th Marquess 68
Abergavenny, Mary Patricia Harrison, Marchioness of 68
Abergeldie 62
Abingdon, Earls of 130, *227, 252*
Abinger, Baron 212
Abolition of Feudal Tenure Act (2000) 403
Aboyne Castle *242*, 270
Acland family 307
Acland, Rt Hon Sir Thomas Dyke, Baronet 141, *234*, 255, *368*
Acland timber committee 140
Aclands estate 25
Acloque, Hon Mrs Camilla 153, 161n, *383, 388*
acreage and value of land (including agricultural acreage)
   big acreages 15
   breakdown by size *17*
   bulk of returns shown *see Return of Owners of Land*

Church of England *18*, 138, 139, *147*, 169
England *see under* England
Forestry Commission *18*, 138, *139*, 140, 143, *147*
and House of Lords 107
housing 9, 56–7, *357*
Ireland *see under* Ireland
local authorities *139*, 147, *158*, 180
London *158*, **160–2**
map of *7*
Ministry of Defence *18*, *139*, 145, *147*
Northern Ireland 7, 11, 13, 15, *17, 357*
Plantagenets 124, *131–3*
ranking in Land Lists
   of 1872 *359–62, 367–78*
   of 2001 *379–82, 391–4*
royalty and royal land *18*, 19, *158*
   Crown Estate *18*, 73, 74, 80–1, 138, *139, 147*
   Duchy of Cornwall *18*, 84, *88, 147*, 160, *162*
   Duchy of Lancaster 93, *147*
Scotland *see under* Scotland
tenure 15
total 9, *11*
utilities *18*, *139*, *147*, *158*, 409
Wales 7, 11, 13, 15, *17*
see also agricultural holdings and acreage
Act of Succession 76
Act of Union (1707) 176, 183
Acton, Baron 212
Acton Reynold estate 254
acts of Parliament *see* legislation
Adair, John George 333, 339, *375*
Adam, Rt Hon William 286
Adare Manor *312, 341*
Addington, Baron 212
Addison, Viscount 212
Adeane, Charles 229
Affeton Castle 234
Aga Khan IV, His Highness Prince Karim 115, 337
Agar family *159*

Shaun James Christian Welbore Ellis, 6th Earl of Normanton 239
Agnelli family 115
Agnew, Sir Andrew, Baronet *303*
agricultural holdings *see* acreage and value; subsidies and grants
Ailsa, Marquesses of
   acreage *273*
   Archibald Angus Charles Kennedy, 8th Marquess of 273
   in Land Lists (1872) *361, 364, 372*
Airlie, Earls of
   acreage and value of land *271*
   David George Coke Patrick Ogilvy, 13th Earl of 66, 67, 68, 78, 212, 271
   in Land Lists (1872) *361, 372*
   in Land Lists (2001) *380, 386, 392*
Airlie, Virginia Fortune (neé Ryan) 67, 68
Airlie Castle 271
Albany and Clarence, Dukes of 105
Albemarle, 1st Earl of 155
Albemarle estate 155, *159*
Albert, Prince Consort 40n, 58, 59, 61, 62, 64
Albury estate 258
Albyns 36
Alcan Highland Estates *18*, *147*
Aldenham, Baron 69
Alderley Edge, Baron, Timothy Irby Stanley, 10th Baron Boston 305
Aldershot 146–7
Aldwych 157
Alexander family *159*
Alexander, Viscount 321
Alexander, Granville Henry Jackson 321
Alexander, Lady Jane 320
Alexander, Nicholas James, 7th Earl of Caledon 321, 325
Alexandra, Princess 68, 99
Alexandra of Denmark, Princess (later Queen) 64
Alfred of Marlborough 240
Alington, Lord *160*, 235
Allathan estates 180
Allen, Bert 353

INDEX   421

Allen, Martin 407
Allendale, Wentworth Hubert Charles Beaumont, 3rd Viscount 250, *393*
Allenheads Hall 250
Alnwick and Alnwick Castle 125, 250
Alsaud, Prince al Waleed 155, *161, 162*
Althorp, Viscount 249
Althorp Park 249, *249*
American Embassy on Grosvenor Square 149
Amhuinnsuidhe 249
Ampleforth School 67, 78, 91, 115, 127, 128, *131–3*
Ancaster, Dukes of 202
Ancketill, William *346*
Ancram, Michael, Earl of 297
Anderton, Henry 299
Andrew, Prince 104, 271
Angevin, Geoffrey (Count of Anjou) 122
Anglesey **305**
Anglesey, Marquesses of *256*
Anglesey, Marquesses of
  2nd Marquess 36
  George Henry Victor Paget, 7th Marquess 305, *305*
  in Land Lists (1872) *363*
Angus (formerly Forfarshire) 180, **271**
Anjou, Geoffrey, Count of 122
Annaly, Barons of *334*, *342*
  Luke Richard White, 6th Baron 342
Annandale and Hartfell, Patrick Anthony Wentworth Hope-Johnston, 11th Earl of 280
Anne Boleyn 23, 126
Anne, Princess 65
Anne, Queen 72, 95, 229, 344, 400
Annesley, Earls of *322*, *330*, *375*
  10th Earl 330
Anson, Thomas Patrick John, 4th Earl of Lichfield 256
Anstruther family 277, 283, 288
Anstruther, Sir Robert, Baronet 277
Anstruther, Sir Windham Charles James, Baronet 288
Anstruther-Gough-Calthorpe, Euan *383*, *389*
Anstruther-Thomson, John 283
Anti-Corn Law Association 29–30
Antrim **320**
Antrim, Earls of *320*, *373*
  Alexander Randal Mark McDonnell, 9th Earl of 320
Apsley, Lord 238
Apsley House 239
Aran, Earls of 234, *344*
  8th Earl of 111
  Arthur Gore, 9th Earl of 234, 344
  in Land Lists (1872) *376*
Arbuthnott, Captain the Viscount *285*
Archdale, William Humphrys *323*, *373*
Ardee, Lord 354
Ardgour, R.M. Maclean of *381*
Ardgowan 295
Ardilaun, Lord 335, *335*, *376*
Argyll, Dukes of 40, 56
  acreage and value of land *107*, *204*, *272*, *281*

Ian Campbell, 10th Duke of 272
  11th Duke of 272
Ian Campbell, 12th Duke of 111, 113
Ian Torquil Campbell, 13th Duke of 111, 272
  in Land Lists (1872) *359*, *365*, *371*, *377*
  in Land Lists (2001) *379*, *391*
Argyll, Iona, Duchess of 281
Argyllshire 62, 68, **272**
Arkwright family of Kinsham Court 317
Arkwright, John Hungerford 240
Armagh **321**
Arnold, Lord 87
Arrallas estate 88
Arran, Earls of 276
Arundel and Surrey, Earls of 116, 127, 259
Arundel Castle 116, 127, 259, 265
Ashbrook, Viscount *347*, *338*
Ashburnham, Earls of 259
Ashburton, Lord 239, 240, *365*
Ashdown Park 227, 260
Ashley, Hon Anthony Melbourne 349
Ashtown, Lord *341*, *351*, *351*, *375*
Aske Hall 278, 292, 299
Askew, John Marjoriebanks 108
Askham Hall 232
Asquay Group 79
Asquith, Herbert Henry, 1st Earl of Oxford and Asquith 25, 27, 53, 140
Astor, Hon Philip *394*
Astor, William Waldorf, 4th Viscount of 252, *393*
Athlumney, Lord *345*
Atholl, Dukes of 16, 18, 40, 63, 266
  acreage and value of land *18*, *107*, *204*, *294*
  Blair Trust 16, 18, 110
  George Ian Murray, 10th Duke of 110, 294
  John Murray, 11th Duke 294
  in Land Lists (1872) *359*, *371*, *377*
  in Land Lists (2001) *379*, *383*, *389*, *391*
  as Plantagenets 124, *131*, 134, 135, *136*
Attenborough, Sir David 276
Attlee, Clement Richard, 1st Earl Attlee 25
Attorney General 172
  of Duchy of Cornwall 86
  of Duchy of Lancaster 100
Aubigny, Louise de Keroualle, Duchess of 109
Aubyn, Sir John St John, Baronet *363*
Auchmar 300
Auditor General 144
Audley, Hon James 335
Audley End 237
Augustine, Saint 20–1, 22–3, 403
Aveland, Lord 246, 253, *365*
Avington Manor 227
Awdeley, Hugh 150–1
Aylesbury, Marquesses of 265
  Debrett's entry 212
  in Land Lists (1872) *364*, *368*
  Michael Sydney Cedric

Brudenell-Bruce, 8th Marquess of 262
Aylesford, Earls of 260
Aylmer, Sir Gerald George, Baronet *337*
Ayrshire **273**
Azmat Guirey, Prince and Princess 334

Bacon, Mrs *321*
Bacon, Sir Nicholas, Baronet 160, *162*, *384*, *394*
Badminton 238, *314*
Bagot, Barons of *335*
  6th Baron 256
  Heneage Charles Bagot, 9th Baron 256, 310, *310*
Bagot, John Lloyd Neville *335*
Bagot, Hon Shaun 310
Baikie of Tankerness, Robert 292
Bailey family *360*, *369*
Bailey, Sir Joseph Russell, Baronet 306
Bailiwick of St James *see* St James
Baillie, Michael Evan Victor, Baron Burton 256, 334
Baillie, Sir William, Baronet 302
Baillie-Hamilton, John George, Earl of Haddington 275, 282
Baird family 273, 285
Baird, Alexander 285
Baird, John *361*, *372*
Baker, William 241
Balcarres *see* Crawford and Balcarres
Baldwin, Stanley, 1st Earl Baldwin of Bewdley 60, 86
Balfour, Earls of 283
Balfour, Andrew 283
Balfour, Arthur 282, 296, *360*, *372*
Balfour, David 292
Balfour, Jean *382*
Balfour, Lords of 283
Balfour of Balbirne, Jean 283
Balfour of Balbirne, John 283
Balgonie, Lord 291
Ballindalloch Castle 274, *284*, *290*
Ballinlough Castle 352
Ballydoyle House 350
Ballyfin 339
Balmoral 19, *61*, **61–4**, 65, 270
Balnagown Castle 296, *301*
Balneil, Lord Anthony Robert Lindsay 283
Bamford, Sir Anthony *385*, *387*
Bandon, Earls of *332*, *376*
  5th Earl of 332
Bandon, Lois, Countess of 332
Bangor, William Maxwell David Ward, 8th Viscount of 322
Bank of England *395*, *396*
Bankes family of Kingston Lacey 311
Bankes family of Soughton Hall 311
Bankes, Robert Wynn amd John 311
Bankes, Walter 235
Bankes, William 296, *361*, *372*
Banks, B. 39
banks *see* financial institutions
Bantry, Earls of 192, 332, *332*, *361*, *375*
Barbour, Rosemund 307
Baring, Francis Anthony 69
Baring, Nicholas and Peter 69

Baring, Lady Rose 69
Barings (Northbrook) estate 157, *158*
Barnard, 11th Baron of *380*, *384*, *391*
Baron de Ros 128
Baron Hill 305, *307*
Barons' War 94, 97
Barrett-Lennard, Sir Thomas, Baronet 346
Barrington, Sir Croker, Baronet *341*
Barrington Park *226*, 312
Barron, Sir *158*
Barrow-in-Furness 96
Bartlett, Alan and Ronnie *386*, *390*
Barton, Hugh Lynedoch *337*
Basildon Park 227
Baskerville *see* Mynors Baskerville
Basset, Gustavus *231*
Bastard family 255
Bateman, Agnes Mary 44
Bateman, James 43
Bateman, John 16, 25, 27, 139, 404, 405, 409
   on Church of England 163, 168, 171, 411
   on Duchy of Cornwall 85
   errors remedied 37
   family and land owned 42–4, 47–8
   on House of Lords 106
   interpretation of 41–8
   as Irish landowner 47–8
   and Land Lists 356
   on Plantagenets 128, 129, *131–3*
   as racist 48
   on Lord Raglan 314
   and *Return of 1872* 36, 39, 48, 49, 56
      illustration of imaginary landowner 46–7
      summary of landowning for Brodrick's book 44–5, *45*, *50*, *51*, *57*
   on Shetland landowners 299
   top ten from tables 200
   obituary 42, 43
Bateman, Katherine, Rowland, Robert and John 43
Bateman, Lord 240
Bateson, Sir *374*
Bath, Marquesses of 255
Bath, Marquesses of
   7th Marquess 115, 255, 262, 346
   acreage and value of land *346*
   in Land Lists *364*, *367*, *385*
Bath, Henrietta Laura Poultney, Countess of 154
Bath, Sir William Poultney, 1st Earl of 154
Bath 87, 90
Bathurst, Henry Allen John, 8th Earl of *238*
Batson Trustees *160*
Batt, Robert Narcissus *322*, *374*
Beaford 141
Beau Parc *345*
Beauchamp, Baron 126
Beauchamp, Earls of 68, *263*
Beaudesert Park 36, *256*, *305*
Beaufort, Duchess of 115
Beaufort, Dukes of 314, 408
   8th Duke of 115

   10th Duke of 115, 130, *238*, 409
   acreage and value of land *107*, *314*
   David Robert Somerset, 11th Duke of 115, *238*, 409
   in Land Lists (1872) *365*, *368*
   in Land Lists (2001) *380*, *383*, *389*, *391*
   as Plantagenets 124, *131*, *136*
Beaulieu Drogheda *343*
Beaumont family 352
Beaumont, Lord 128
Beaumont, Rex 352
Beaumont, Wentworth Hubert Charles, 3rd Viscount Allendale 250, *393*
Beaumont, Hon Wentworth Peter Ismay 250
Beaverbrook, Lord 157
Beckett, J.C. 194, 412
Bective, Earls of *330*
Bedarida, François 173, 411
Bedford, Dukes of 134, 135, *159*, 229
   11th Duke of 154
   acreage and value of land *107*, *158*, *162*
   John Robert Russell, 13th Duke 112–13, 226, *234*
   pro-appeasement 87
   in Land Lists (1872) *360*, *363*, *366*, *367*, *378*
   in Land Lists (2001) *383*, *389*, *393*
   in London 154, *158*, *159*, *162*
   as Plantagenets 124, *131*, *136*
Bedford Corporation *159*
Bedfordshire 75, *164*, 170, **226**
Bedgebury estate 75
Beerbohm, Max 109
Beevor, Stuart 14
Beit, Sir Alfred and Beit Trust 354
Bekker-Dundas, Mrs 288
Belgravia 18, 118, 149, 150, 152
Bell, George 293
Bellamy-Gordon, Hon Louisa 287
Bellew, Lord *343*
Bellingham, Sir Alan Edward, Baronet *343*
Bellingham Greville, Algernon *342*
Belmore, Earls of *325*, *348*, *373*
   John Armar Lowrey-Corry, 8th Earl of 323
Belper, Alexander Ronald George Strutt, 4th Baron 251
Belton House *241*, *246*, *254*
Belvedere, Earls of 352
Belvoir Castle 114, *229*, *233*, *245*
Benchmark 80
Benn, Tony Wedgewood, Viscount Stansgate 105
Bennett, Francis *347*
Bentinck, Lady Anne Cavendish 111, 152, 202, 251, 277, *379*, *384*, *389*, *391*
Bentinck, Baron 251
Benyon, Richard 227
Benyon, Sir William 227, *384*, *389*, *393*, 402
Benzion Freshwater, Mr *161*
Beresford, Lord Charles *324*, *330*
Beresford, John Barre *324*, *374*
Beresford, John Hubert de la Poer,

   8th Marquess of Waterford *132*, 351, 354
Beresford, Philip 408, 410
   see also Sunday Times Rich Lists
Berkeley family *159*
Berkeley, Baroness 155
Berkeley, Barons of 128, *132*, 150
Berkeley, Robert *263*
Berkeley estate 155, *159*
Berkshire 36, 75, *164*, **227**
   see also Suffolk and Berkshire
Bernard, Lady Jennifer Jane 332
Bernard, Colonel Thomas *347*
Berners, Baroness *133*
Berners, Baron of *160*
Berney family 248
Berridge, Richard 191, *203*, *335*, *359*, *375*
Bertram, William 288
Berwickshire 201, **275**
Bessborough, Earls of *329*, *338*, *376*
   11th Earl of 329
Bessborough House *329*, *338*
Bethell, William 265
Bewes, Rev Thomas 171
Biddick Hall 236
Biddulph Grange 43
Bifrons 202, *243*, *331*, 333
Bill of Rights (1688) 59
Bille, Louisa Elizabeth de *325*, *374*
Billingsborough estate 75
Bills, David 143
Bingham, Baron 192
Bingham, Lord *344*
Bingham, Richard, 7th Earl of Lucan 192, *344*
Bingham estate 75
Binning, Lord George Edmund Baldred Baillie-Hamilton 275, 282
Birkhall 62
Birmingham 165
Birr Castle *347*
'Black' Prince *see* Woodstock
Black Rod 103
Blackall, Major Robert *342*
Blackburn 165
Blackburn Trustees *160*
Blacker-Douglas, Mr *374*
Blackett, Sir Edward, Baronet 250
Blackett-Ord, Mrs 250
Blackie, Professor 40
Blackmount estate 272
Blackwood family of Clandeboye 322
Blackwood, Perdita Maureen 322
Blackwood, Dowager Marchioness Serena Belinda 322
Blackwood Ker, Richard William 322
Blagdon 250
Blair, Tony 29, 104, 105, 115, 204, 230
   evictions from House of Lords 27, 59, 120, 121, 134, 136, 173, 199–200, 211, 240
Blair Castle 110
Blair Charitable Trust (Dukedom of Atholl) 16, 18, 110
Blake, Patrick *335*
Blake, William 26, 28
Bland, Francis *336*
Blandford, Marquess of 117, 252

INDEX   423

Blandy-Jenkins, Mrs John 312
Blantyre, Lord 281, 295
Blarney Castle 332
Blenheim Palace 252
Bletso, Lord Anthony St John of 226
Bletso, Baron Beauchamp of 226
Blithfield Hall 256, 310
Bloom, Bridget 141, 142
Bloomsbury 154, 157, *159*, 226
Blunt, Sir Anthony 86
Blythe, Lords of 102
    Anthony Audley Rupert, 4th Lord 335
Blythwood estate 335
Board of Trade 29
Boconnoc 231
Bodnant 310
Bodrhyddan 311
Boleyn, Anne 23, 126
Bolger, Jim 338
Bolingbroke, Henry *see* Henry VII
Bolton, Lord 265
Bolton, Richard William Algar Orde Powlett, 7th Baron 239, 264, 265, 393
Bona Vacantia 22, 99
Booth, Richard 339
Bootle-Wilbraham, Hon Jessie Caroline 43
Borland, Mrs O. 299
Boroughbridge estate 75
Borris House 329, 338
Borrowes, Robert Higgison 337
Borthwick, John Hugh, 25th Lord 289, *289*
Borthwick, Malcolm and John 289
Borthwick, Sir William 289
Bosanquet, Anthony 143
Boscawen, Evelyn 231
Boscawen, George Hugh, 9th Viscount of Falmouth 90, 231
Boston, Barons of 370
    Timothy Irby Stanley, 10th Baron of 305
    Timothy Stanley, 8th Baron of 305
Bothal Castle 251
Botreux, Barons of 130
Bottio, Horatio 126
Boughton House 109, 249
Boulton, Matthew Piers Watt 252
Bourdett-Coutts 160
Bourn, Sir John 144
Bouverie-Pusey, Sidney 227
Bowes, Mr 368
Bowes, John 236, *265*
Bowes Lyon, Lady Elizabeth *see* Elizabeth, Queen Mother
Bowes Lyon, Lady Mary Frances 69
Bowes Lyon, Michael Fergus, 18th Earl of Strathmore and Kinghorn 271, *393*
Bowhill 109
Bowmont and Cessford, Marquess of 114
Bowood Park and House 202, 262, 286, 345
Boyd, Viscount 393
Boyle family *see* Burlington
Boyne, Viscounts of 236

Gustavus Michael Stucley Hamilton-Russell, 11th Viscount 230
    in Land Lists (1872) 363, 364
Brabazon, John Anthony, 15th Earl of Meath 354, *383*, 388
Bradford, Richard Thomas Orlando, 7th Earl of Bradford *131*, 135, 254
Bradford 166
Bradlaugh, Charles 173
Brahan estate 179
Bramham Park 265, 340
Bramston, Colonel Thomas 237
Branthwayt, Robert 42–3
Braybrooke, Barons of 8, 358
    Robin Henry Charles Neville, 10th Baron *131*, 237
Braybrooke, Caroline 237
Breadalbane, Duke of 16
Breadalbane, Earls of 16, 63, 179
    acreage and value of land *204* 272, 294
    in Land Lists (1872) 359, 364, 371, 377
Brechin Castle 271
Brecknock 304, **306**
Breffny, Baron and Baroness de 338
Brett, James 338
Bridges Court 115
Bright, John 29, 30–1, 39, 40, 42, 49, 404
Brightlingsea Hall 43
Bristol, Marquesses of 246, 257
    7th Marquess of 257
    Frederick William Augustus Hervey, 8th Marquess of 246, 257
    in Land Lists (2001) 393
Bristol 165
British Association for Advancement of Science, Statistical Section 31
British Coal 180
British Empire 24, 124, 140, 176
    'inner' *see* Ireland; Scotland; Wales
British Land 80
British Museum site 154
British Rail 139, *178*
Brittan, Sir Samuel 406
Brittany, Count Brian of 84
Brocket, Lord 105
Brodick Castle 276
Brodie, Ewen John, 16th Laird of Lethen 291, *291*
Brodie, Hugh 290
Brodie, James Campbell *291*
Brodie Castle 290, *291*
Brodrick, Hon George: criticism of *Return of 1872* 49–53, 168
    Bateman's summary for 44–5, *45*, 50, 51, 57
Bromley-Davenport, William 230
Bronydd Mawyr estate 75
Brooke, Lord 237
Brooke, Sir Victor, Baronet 323, 373
Broughton, Sir Henry Delves, Baronet 230
Brown, Charles Edward Peter Neil, 3rd Earl of Halifax 264
Browne, Jeremy Ulick Browne, 11th Marquess of Sligo 191, 344

Brownlow, Earls of 241, 254, 362, 363, 367
Brownlow, Edward John Peregrine Cust, 7th Baron 132, 246, 384, 390, *393*
Bruce, Sir 373
Bruce, Charles Lennox Cummings 290
Bruce, Sir Henry Hervey, Baronet 324
Bruce, John 299
Bruce, Michael A. 381
Bruce, Stewart C. 324
Bruce, William 299
Brudenell-Bruce, Michael Sydney Cedric, 8th Marquess of Aylesbury 262, 265
Bruen, Rt Hon Henry 329
Bruton, John 345
Bryan, Hon George Leopold 338
Bryanston estate 75, 155
Buccleuch and Queensbury, Dukes of 6, 16, 18, *40*, 52, 63, 200, 226, 249
    7th Duke of 69
    acreage and value of land 18, 85, 107, 147, *204*, 280, 297, 298
    in Land Lists (1872) 359, 363, 371, *377*
    in Land Lists (2001) 379, 384, *391*
    Walter John Francis Douglas Montague-Scott, 9th Duke of 6, 16, 18, 69, 85, 108–9, 249, 280, 297, 298
    pro-appeasement 87
Buchan, Hon Mrs Blanche 153, 161n, *383*, 388
Buchanan Castle 281, 294, 300
Buchanan-Jardine, Sir Andrew Rupert John, 4th Baronet 280, *382*, *392*
Buckhurst, Lord 259
Buckhurst Park 259
Buckingham and Chandos, Dukes of 107, 152, 228, 310
Buckingham Palace 59
Buckinghamshire 228
    Camoys land in 4
    Church of England land in *164*, 228
Buckley, Sir E. 313, 370
Buckley, Nathaniel 350
Buckminster Park 245, 246
buildings 170
    residential *see* housing/domestic dwellings
Bulkeley Hughes, William 305
Bulmer, Jonathan and Lady Marcia 380, *391*
Bunbury, Sir Michael 100
Bunbury Tighe, Frederick 338
Burdett, Colonel Sir Francis, Baronet 227, 233
Burford, Marquess of 104
Burghley House 249, 253
Burke, Charles Granby 43
Burke, Sir Henry George, Baronet 335
Burke, Sir Stanley, 9th Baronet 335
Burke's Peerage/Burke's Landed Gentry (1826–1972) 4, 6, 41, 399, 402
    and Land Lists 357
    and London 150, 153, 410
    and Plantagenets 123, 129, *131–3*, 408

Burleigh, Lord 278
Burlington, Earls of 155, *159*
Burn, Sir Clive 86
Burnett, Sir Robert, Baronet 285
Burns, John William 281
Burns-Lindow, Jonas 232
Burroughs, General Traill 292
Burrowes, Robert James 330
Burton, Michael Evan Victor Baillie, 3rd Baron 256
Bury, Lindsay 252
Business Age and Rich List (1995) 60, 79
Bute (including Arran) **276**
Bute, Marquess of 273, 276, 312
   acreage and value of land *273, 276, 303, 312*
   in Land Lists (1872) *360, 363, 371, 378*
   in Land Lists (2001) *380, 389, 391*
Butler family (once Fitzwalter) 338
Butler, Misses Anna, Sophia and Henrietta *331*
Butler, James, Marquess of Ormonde 338
Butler, Richard, 17th Viscount Mountgarret 329, 338
Butler, Sir Thomas, Baronet 329
Byram 202
Bywell Hall 250

Cabinet 25, 34
Cadbury 402
Cadogan, Baron 153
Cadogan, Dukes of 18, *159*
Cadogan, Earls of 18, 69, 103
   Charles Gerald John Cadogan, 8th Earl of 153, 294
   in Land Lists (2001) *383, 387*
Cadogan, Edward 153
Cadogan estate 149, 153, *159*
   acreage and value *158, 162*
Cadogan Group 153
Cadrodd Hardd 310
Caernarvonshire **307**
Cagwgn, Thomas 153
Cahill, Kevin 411
Cahill, Stella 221
Cairns, Earl of 91
Caithness 76, 266, **277**
   Earls of 277
Caledon, Earls of 320, 325, 373
   Nicholas James Alexander, 7th Earl of 321, 325
Caledon Castle and House 321
Calke Abbey *233*, 256
Callaghan, James, Baron 105
Callander, George Frederick 272
Callander, Henry 289
Callander, Robin 183–5, 412
Callendar House 287, *300*
Calthorpe, Lord *363*
Cambridge University *158*, 173, 229
Cambridgeshire 75, 88, *164*, **229**
Camden, Marquess of *160*, 243
Cameron, Donald *360*
Cameron, John B. *381*
Cameron, Mr *371*
Cameron of Lochiel, Colonel Sir Hamish 284, *284, 379, 391*

Cameron-Campbell, Mrs *361, 372*
Camoys, Lady 3, 5, 8
Camoys, Lords of 4, 66, 212
   Ralph Thomas Campion George Sherman Stonor, 7th Baron 3, 5, 8, 66, 252
Campbell, Arthur 276
Campbell, Colin 278, 281
Campbell, Colin Robert Vaughan, Earl of Cawdor 291, 309
Campbell, Ian, 12th Duke of Argyll 111, 113
Campbell, Ian Torquil, 13th Duke of Argyll 111, 272
Campbell, James 272
Campbell, Lady 281
Campbell-Orde, Sir John William, Baronet 284, *360, 372, 378*
Campden, Viscount 253
Camperdown, Earls of 271
Camscadden estate 281
Cannadine, David 26, 28, 56, 177, 242, 403, 404, 405, 409, 413
   on Abercorn 113
   buyers of land not recorded by 206
   on Churchill 118
   on Grafton 116–17
   on House of Lords 104, 407–8
   on Ireland's lost acreage 200, 201, 413
   and Land Lists 357
Canterbury 165, 411
   Archbishops of 105, 171, 175
CAP (Common Agricultural Policy) 29, 402
capital gains tax avoided 90, 92, 99, 413
Cappoquin House 351
Cardigan, Earls of 50, 262
Cardigan, Countess of 249
Cardiganshire 35, 76, 308, **308**
Cardross, Lord 302
Carew, Patrick Thomas Connolly-Carew, 7th Baron 336, 353
Carew Wallop, Quentin Gerard, 10th Earl of 239
Carlingford, Lord 255
Carlinghill 42–3
Carlisle, Earls of 128, *131*, 232
   George William Beaumont Howard, 13th Earl of 232
   in Land Lists (1872) *361, 365, 367*
Carlow *193*, **329**
Carmarthenshire **309**
Carnarvon, Earls of 227, *255*
   Henry George Herbert, 7th Earl of 227
Carnegie, James George Alexander Bannerman, 3rd Duke of 110
Carrington, Lord 228
Carter, Mr 368
Carter, Henry Tilson Shaen 344
Carton, Gerald Fitzgerald, 8th Duke of 337
Carysfort, Earls of 242, *354*
Cashman, Liam 332
Cassilis House 273
Casteja, Marquis de 244
Castle Ashby 249, *286*
Castle Bernard 332, *347*

Castle Coole 323
Castle Dobbs 320, *337*
Castle Grant 274, 284, 290
Castle Hill 234, *308*
Castle Howard 232
Castle Milk 280
Castle Stewart, Earls of *373*
   Arthur Patrick Avondale Stuart, 8th Earl of 255, 325
Castle Upton 320, *346*
Castle Ward 322
Castlemaine, Roland Handcock, 8th Baron 352
Castlestuart, Earls of 325
Castletown 338
   Bernard Fitzpatrick, 2nd Baron 339
Cater, Frederick 247
Cathcart, Jean 287
Cathcart, Lady 270, *360, 371, 377*
cathedrals 170
Catherine of Aragon 22
Catholicism
   and House of Lords 104, 115
   in Ireland 22–3
   and London 151
   monasteries dissolved and land taken 22–3, 166–8, 182, 411
   and Plantagenets 127, 128
   school *see* Ampleforth
   survival 174
   see also monasteries
Cator, acreage and value of London land *158*
Catterson, Louisa 288
Cavan *192*, *193*, **330**
Cavendish, Andrew, 11th Duke of Devonshire 233, 234, 244, 265 110–11, 351
Cawdor, Earls of
   acreage and value of land *203*, 291, 309, 316
   Colin Robert Vaughan Campbell, 7th Earl of 291, 309
   in Land Lists (1872) *360, 366, 369, 378*
   in Land Lists (2001) *379, 391*
Cayzer family 290
   see also Colvin-Cayzer
Cayzer, Elizabeth 257
Cayzer, Sir James Arthur, Baronet 257
Cayzer, Lord 257
Cayzer, Nicola 257
Cecil *see* Gascoyne-Cecil
Cecil, Henry 67
Cefntilla Park 314
Census returns (1861) and *Return of Owners of Land* 30, 31, 32, 33, 41, 50
Chair, Lady Juliet de 202, *386*
Chamberlayne, Tankerville 239
Chancellor of Duchy of Lancaster 49, 93, 95, 99, 100
Chancellor of Exchequer 53–4, 172, 190
   and Crown Estate 77, 78, 81
Chaplin, Henry 246
Chapman baronetage 352
Chapman, Sir Benjamin James 352
Chapman, Helen 82

INDEX   425

Chapman, John 37
Charing Cross 97, 157
charities
　Charity Commissioners 172
　land in London 157, *158*
Charlemont, Earls of *321, 373*
　now 14th Viscount 321
Charles I 24, 25, 154, 400
Charles II 58, 67, 72, 109, 116, 119, 154, 248, 305, 400
Charles, Prince of Wales 19, 20, 78, 184
　and Balmoral 270
　and Church of England 174
　on Crown Estate 76
　and Duchy of Cornwall 65, 84, **88–91**
　and House of Lords 104
　in Land Lists (2001) *379, 383, 388, 391*
　and royal land 59, 61, 63, 64, 65
Charleville, Countess of *347*
Charlton, William Oswald *250*
Charteris, David, 12th Earl of Wemyss and March 283, 298
Charteris, Lady Margaret *350*
Charteris Trustees *158*
Chatelberault, Dukes of 113
Chatsworth House 110–11, 233, *244, 265, 332, 351*
Cheape, George Clerk *283*
Chearnley, Henry Philip *351*
Chelsea, Viscount 153
Chelsea 151, 153, 172, 294
Cheltenham, Plantagenet name in 121
Chesham, Lord *242*
Cheshire 18, *75*, 96, 150, 151, *164*, 192, **230**
Chesment-Severn, John Percy *317*
Chester, Hugh Lupus Earl of 150
Chesterfield, Philip Dormer, Earl of 155
Chetwode, Mrs *228*
Chewton Mendip *255*
Chichester family 320
Chichester, Earls of *259*
Chichester, Giles 25, 27
Chichester *165*
Chicksands estate *75*
Chidley Coote, John *348*
Chief Butler of Ireland 338
Chief Clerk of Duchy of Lancaster 99
Chief Secretary of Ireland 194
Childers, John Walbanke *229*
Chisholm, The *284, 360, 371, 378*
Cholmondeley, Marquesses of *248*
　David, 7th Marquess of 202, *230, 246, 248, 385, 389*
Cholmondeley, Thomas and Francis 151
Cholmondeley Castle *230, 248*
Chrichton-Maitland, Mark A. *294*
Christie, John *178*
Christiensen, K.K. *379*
Chudleigh, Clifford of *132*
Church Commissioners *163*, 166, 168, 169, 170, 172
　role of 171–4, 411
Church of England 88, **163–75**, 403, 410–11

acreage and value of land *18*, 138, 139, *147*
dioceses *165–6, 174*, 411
as failure 175
glebeland and parsonage land 163–4, *163, 164–5,* 166, 169, 172
history 16, 24
and legislation 163–4, 169, 411
London land *158*, 169, 172
missing land *164, 165–6*
mission 170–1, 175, 411
numbers on rolls 174
parishes 167–8, 170, 174
　maps 4, 22, 402
　tithe maps 4, 22, 402
and Plantagenets 134
power, access to 172
and royal family 19
and state 166–8
survival and landholdings 174–5
tax (tithes) 4, 22, 167, 169, 172, 402
see also Church Commissioners; tithe maps
Church of Ireland 402
Church of Scotland 266, 402
Church of Wales 402
Churchill Harriman, Pamela *235, 347*
Churchill, Sir Winston Leonard Spencer 25, 77, 87, 115, 118, 204, 235, 347
City of London 148
Civil List 19, 58, 60, 73
　and Duchy of Lancaster 95, 99
　and George III 73, 76, 77
Civil Service 73
Civil War (1642–6) 24, 123, 150
Clackmannanshire **278**
Clancarty, Nicholas le Poer Trench, 9th Earl of *335, 335*
Clandeboyne 322
Clanricarde, Marquesses of 192, *335, 335, 362, 375*
Clanwilliam, 6th Earl of *323*
Clare *193*, 202, **331**
Clarence, Dukes of
　George, Duke of 122
　Lionel, Duke of and daughter, Phillipa 122
Clarendon, Earls of 43
　George William Frederick Villiers, 4th Earl of 43, 190
Clark, James *381*
Clarke, Kenneth 78, 95
Clarke, Sir Symon 150
Clayton, Sir William, Baronet *258*
Clearances 137, 176
Clearwell estate *75*
Clements, Henry *375*
Cleremont, Lord *343, 373*
Clerk, Sir George Douglas, Baronet *289*
Clerk of the Council of Duchy of Lancaster 99, 100
Clerkenwell 152, 154, 157, 158, *159*
Cleveland, Duchess of (Ann Fortune) 117
Cleveland, Duchess of (Barbara Villiers) 67, 115, 247, 248

Cleveland, Dukes of *236, 254, 360, 363, 367, 378*
　acreage and value of land *107*
　Net National Income *396*
Clifden, Viscount *338, 375*
Clifden Castle 191, *335*
Clifford, Baron *244*
Clifford, Baroness *155*
Clifford-Constable, Sir Frederick Augustus Talbot, Baronet *265*
Clifton, John Talbot *244*
Clinton, Bill *235*
Clinton, Gerard Nevile Mark Fane Trefusis, 22nd Baron 141, *234, 381, 384, 389, 392*
Clinton, Lord *339*
Clinton, Lady Nicola Harriett *234, 339*
Clive, Colonel Edward Henry *344, 368*
Clive, Charles Meysey Bolton *240*
Clive, Lindsay Claude Neils Bury, Viscount Windsor *254, 263*
Clive of Plassey, Robert, Baron 315
Clive, Robert, Viscount 315
Clive, Robert Ivor Windsor, 3rd Earl of Plymouth *254*
Clonbrock, Lord *335, 335, 376*
Cloncurry, Lord *337*
Clonmell, Earls of *350*
Close, Mr *374*
Close, Maxwell Charles *321*
coastal land *see* marine estate
Cobbe family 334
Cobbe, Archbishop Charles *334, 334*
Cobbold, David Anthony Fromanteel Lytton, 2nd Baron *241*
Cobden, Richard 29, 30
Cobden Club 49
Cobham, Viscount *132*
Cobham Hall *243, 345*
Cockermouth Castle 203, 331
Cockfosters 97
Coddington family *343*
Coke, Edward Douglas, 7th Earl of Leicester 248
Coke, Viscount *248*
Colborn Hall 44
Colby, Mrs *316, 370*
Cold War 145
Cole, Andrew John Galbraith, 7th Earl of *323*
Colebrooke, Sir Thomas Edward, Baronet *288*
Cole-Hamilton, Major Arthur William *325, 374*
College of Arms 408–9
College of Heralds 404
Collins, Con *337*
Collins, M.C. *337*
Colquhoun, Sir Ivar, 8th Baronet 111, *281, 281, 380, 391*
Colquhoun, Sir James, Baronet *361, 372*
Colquhoun, Robert *281*
Colquhoun, Sir Robert *281*
Colthurst, Sir George *376*
Colthurst, Sir John St John, Baronet *332*
Colthurst, Sir Richard la Touche, 9th Baronet *332*

Coltman, Mary 293
Colvin, James Cayzer 257, *380*
Colvin, Michael 257, 290
Colvin, Nicola 290
Colvin, Patrick 257, *380*
Colvin-Cayzer, J.M. *386*, *388*
Commissions and Commissioners
    Charity 172
    Countryside 89
    of Crown Estate 78, 80, 81–2, 91
    European 402
    of Inland Revenue 101
    Irish Land 182, 191, 195, 318, 326, 402
    of Public Works 194
    see also Church Commissioners; Forestry Commission
Common Agricultural Policy 29, 402
common land and waste 397
    acreage 9
    in Crown Estate 76
    and Forestry Commission 140
    and Ministry of Defence 145–6
    in *Return of Owners of Land* 37–8, 45, 51
    see also enclosures
Commons *see* House of Commons
Commonwealth *see under* Cromwell
comparative values *209*, 395–6
compensation for confiscation of property 77
Compton, Earls of 249
Compton, Spencer Douglas David, 7th Marquess of Northampton 249, 258, 260
Compton Verney 260
Compton Wynyates 249
Conant, Guy 253
Conant, Simon Edward 253
Confiscation Act (1640) 24
Connaught/Connacht 191, *192*, *193*
Connell, Charles R. *382*
Conservative Party 5, 200, 211
    and Forestry Commission 140, 141
    in House of Lords 105
    need to reinvent 27
    and royalty 70
        Crown Estate 77, 78, 81, 82
    and Scotland 182, 185
Conspiracy Bill (1865) 31
Constable-Maxwell, Alfred Peter 287
Conyngham, Marquesses of *243*
    acreage and value of land *200*, *203*, 204, *331*, *333*
    Frederick William Henry Francis, 7th Marquess of 202, 243, 331, 345
    in Land Lists (1872) *359*, *365*, *367*, *377*
    see also Mount Charles
Conyngham Lodge Stud 337
Cooke, T.B.D. *311*
Coolcullen Stud 338
Coolmore Stud 359
Cooper, Anthony Ashley, 10th Earl of Shaftesbury 235
Cooper, Edward *349*, *376*
Cooper, William 226
Co-operative farms 16, *18*, 147

Coote, Sir Charles Henry, Baronet *339*, *375*
Coote, Sir Christopher, 5th Baronet 339
Coote, Nicola Harriett 234, 339
Coote, Richard 330
Coothill 330
Cope, Francis Robert *321*
Corbally family 334
Corbet, Athelstan J.G. *313*
Corbet, Henry Reginald 254
Corbet, Sir John Vincent 254
Corbett family 254
Corbett-Corbett-Winder, Major *315*
Cork 191, 192, *193*, **332**
Cork and Orrery, Earls of *368*
Corn Laws (1815 & 1828), opposition to 29–30
Cornewall, Rev Sir George Henry, Baronet *240*
Cornwall, Charles Windsor, 24th Duke of *see* Charles, Prince
Cornwall 164, **231**, 410
    see also Duchy of Cornwall
Coronation Act 183
corporation tax avoided 47, 90, 91, 99
Corse-Scott, Mrs *298*
Cortachy Castle 271
Cosby, Robert Ashworth Godolphin *339*
Costessy Park 256
Council of Mortgage Lenders 402
council tax 5, 12, 207, 213
counties 217–354
    of England **222–65**
        listed 222–3
        maps of *224–5*
    of Ireland, Republic of **326–54**
        listed 326–7
        maps of *328*
    of Northern Ireland **318–25**
        listed 318
        maps of *319*, *328*
    of Scotland **266–303**
        listed 267
        maps of *268–9*
    of Wales **304–17**
        listed 304
Country Landowners Association 28, 82, 210–11
Countryside Alliance 27–8, 214
Countryside Commission 89
County Farms *147*
Courtfield 240
Courtney, 3rd Viscount 81, 409
Courtney family *see* Devon, Earls of
Courtown, Earls of *329*, *353*
    James Stopford 9th Earl of 329, 353
Covent Garden 154
Coventry 165
    Earls of *263*
Cowan, Charles *289*
Cowan, William *302*
Cowdray, Viscounts of 180, 259, 285
    in Land Lists (2001) *379*, *384*, *387*, *391*
    Michael Oralndo Weetman Pearson, 4th Viscount 270
Cowell-Stepney, Sir Arthur Keppel, Baronet *309*, *370*

Cowper, Charles Spencer 64
Cowper, Earls of *226*, *241*, *364*, *368*
Cox, Edward 221
Craiglaw estate 303
Cranbourne, Viscount 241
Cranfield, Sir Lionel *150*
Crauford Priory *273*, *276*, 295
Craven, Earls of *227*, *260*
Crawford, 6th Lord 130
Crawford and Balcarres, Earls of
    27th Earl 66
    29th Earl and 12th Earl of Balcarres, Robert Lindsay 66, 283
Crawley, John 226
Credit Lyonnais Securities Europe 14
Crewe, Sir John, Baronet 233
Crewe, Lord 230
Crewe Survey of Duchy of Lancaster 96–7, 98
Crichton-Maitland, Mark A. *295*
Crighton, Henry George Victor John, 6th Earl of Erne 323
Crofters War (1880s) 404
Crofton, Baronetcy *348*
    Sir Hugh Denis, 8th Baronet 340
    Sir Morgan George, Baronet 340
    Patrick, 7th Baronet 340
Crofton, Edward and Henry 340
Crom Castle 323
Cromarty (now Ross & Cromarty) *279*
Cromer, 3rd and 4th Earls of 69
Cromwell, Oliver: Republic 22, 24–6, 41, 72, 128, 182, 245, 305
    Commonwealth and Parliament (1648) 24, 85, 95, 168
Cromwell, Thomas 167
Cross Bench members of House of Lords 105
Crossley, Savile William Francis, 3rd Baron Somerleyton 67
Crowley, Frances Majella 338
Crown Estate 58–9, 70, **72–83**, 208, 406
    acreage and value of land *18*, 73, 74, 80–1, 138, *139*, *147*
    Commission and Commissioners 78, 80, 81–2, 91
    and Forestry Commission 73, 141
    future of 82–3
    history 16, 22, 24, 25, 72–3
    in London 80–1, 148–9, 154–5
    as neo-monopoly 74
    ownership 76–7
    revenues 73
        surrendered in return for stipend *see* Civil List
    in Scotland 74, 76, 78–9, 81, 183–4
    in twentieth century 74–83
        acquisitions 75–6
        ownership 76–7
        privatisation plans 77–8, 154
        value of 78–81
    urban estate 79–80, *79*, 82
    value 60–1, 61, 73, 78–81, *79*
    see also royalty and royal land
Crown jewels 59
Crown Land Act (1702) 407
Croxton 76

INDEX   427

Cubbitt, Rt Hon George 258
Culmony House 291
Cumberland and Teviotdale, Dukes of 105
Cumbria 202, **232**
    Church of England land in *164*, 232
    Crown Estate land in *75*, 232
Cumming, Sir William Gordon, Baronet *393*
Cunliffe-Lister, Samuel 265
Cunninghame, John Charles *303*
Curraghmore 351
Curwen, Henry 232
Curzon, Major General Frederick, 7th Earl of Howe 228, 245, 251
Cusack, Thomas *342*
Cust, Ernest Richard 246
Cutsem, Bernard van 234, *344*
Cutsem, Eleanor 344
Czernin, Count 153
Czernin, Hon Mrs Mary 153, 161n, *383*, *388*

Dacre, Lord 241
Daglinworth estate 88
Dalgleish, John 272, *362*
Dalgleish, Lawrence 283
Dalhousie, Countess of 67
Dalhousie, Earls of
    16th Earl of 271
    acreage *271*
    James Hubert Ramsay, 17th Earl of 78, 271
    in Land Lists (1872) *359*, *364*, *371*, *377*
    in Land Lists (2001) *380*, *386*, *392*
Dalhousie Castle 271
Dalitz, Maurice 'Mo' 67
Dalkeith, Richard Walter John Montague Douglas Scott, Earl of 109
Dalkeith Palace 249, 280, 297, 298
Dalmeny Park and House 289, 293, 302
Dalrymple, Charles 276
Dalrymple, John David James, 14th Earl of Stair 273, *303*
Dancey, Sir Claude 67–8
Darby, Jonathan *347*
Daresbury, Peter Gilbert Greenall, 4th Baron 230, *390*
Darnaway Castle 290
Darnley, Earls of *243*, *345*
Dartmoor 86, 146
    National Park and Preservation Society 89, 146
Dartmouth, Earls of *364*, *158*, *351*
Dartrey, Earls of *346*, *351*, *376*
    Anthony Dawson, 3rd Earl of 346
Dartrey House *346*, *351*
Dashwood, Sir Henry William, Baronet 252
D'Aumale, HRH le Duc 263
D'Auvergne, M. Nelson 23, 25, *403*
David II, King of Scotland 284
Davidson, Duncan *382*, *384*
Davidson, Hugh 291
Davies, David 35
Davies, Mary 119, 150–1, 230
Davies, Colonel Nicholas 100

Davies, Rev Ven Archdeacon *306*
Davies, Robert *305*
Davitt, Michael 404
Dawnay, John Christian George, 11th Viscount Downe 264, *384*, *389*, *393*
Dawson, Antony, 3rd Earl of Dartrey 346
de Crespigny, Sir *160*
De Gray family 248
De Juvenal, Bertrand 20, 22, 26, 28, *403*, *413*
de Percy *see* Percy
de Ramsey *see* Ramsey
De Ros, Baroness 346
De Ros, Peter Maxwell, 28th Baron 346
de Vere Beauclerk, Murray, 14th Duke of St Albans 119
Deane, Francis 247
Debenham family 148
Debrett's Baronetage and Peerage 49, 211, *399*, *413*
    example *212*
    and Land Lists 357
    and London 149, 153
    Norfolk dukedom in 116
    on Plantagenets 126, *409*
    Westminster dukedom in 119
Decies, Lord of 336
Defence Lands Committee (Nugent Report, 1973) 410
DEFRA (Department of Environment, Food, Rural Affairs and Agriculture, earlier MAFF) 15, 187
Delamere estate 75
Delcour, Captain John 244
Delnadamph 19, 63
Delpierre, Lady 247
Dempster, Nigel 67
Denbigh, Earls of *311*
Denbighshire 202, **310**
Denny, Sir Edward, Baronet 336
Dent Brocklehurst, Henry and Mollie *385*
Departments, government *see* Ministries and government Departments
Deputy Prime Minister 102
Derby, Earls of 97, *132*, 230, 237, 244
    14th Earl of 31, 44
    15th Earl of 8, 30, 31–2, 33, 39, 41, 44, 49
    19th Earl of 8
    in Land Lists (1872) *361*, *363*, *367*
    in Land Lists (2001) *381*, *384*, *392*
    Robert Ferrers 94, 97
Derbyshire 36, **233**
    Church of England land in *164*, 166
    Duchy of Lancaster land in 96
    and House of Lords 110–11, 114
    Ministry of Defence land in 146
Dering, Sir Edward Cholmeley, Baronet 243
Derry (Londonderry) **324**
Derwent, Baron *385*, *390*
Derwent estate 75
Desart, Earls of *338*
Desmond, Dermot 201
DETR (Department of Environment, Transport and Regions) 9, 12, 402

development land, windfall gains on 27
Devizes estate 75
Devon, Earls of 128–9, *132*, *409*
    6th Earl of 129
    acreage and value of land *341*
    in Land Lists (1872) *366*, *368*
Devonshire **234**
    Church of England land in *164*, 171, 234, *410*
    Crown Estate land in *75*, 234
    Duchy of Cornwall land in 84, 86, 87, *88*, 89
    earls of *see* Courtney
    and Forestry Commission 141
    and Galway compared 188
    Plantagenet land in 129
    population (2001) 26
    population and landownership in 1872 206
Devonshire, Duchess of 111, *408*
Devonshire, Dukes of 40, 68, 233, 244, 265
    4th Duke of 155
    11th Duke of 201
    acreage and value of land *107*, *200*, *201*, *332*, *351*
    Andrew Cavendish, 11th Duke of 233, 234, 244, 265 110–11, 351
    in Land Lists (1872) *359*, *363*, *367*, *377*
    in Land Lists (2001) *379*, *383*, *388*, *391*
Diana, Princess of Wales 89, 127, 249, 271
Digby, Barons of *347*
    Edward Henry Kenlem, 12th Baron 235, *347*, *368*, *385*, *394*
Digby, Henry Noel 235
Digby, Robert 347
Digest of Agricultural Statistics 402
Dillon, Viscount 252, *344*, *360*, *367*, *378*
    22nd Viscount 344
Dillon, Viscountess Irene 344
Dillwyn-Llewelyn, John *312*, *369*
Dingestow estate 143
Diocese of Church of England *see* Church of England
dissolution of monasteries *see under* Henry VIII
D'Lisle, Ambrose Charles Phillips de 245
D'Lisle, Hon Philip 243
D'Lisle, Philip John Algernon Sidney, 2nd Viscount 243
D'Maule, Duc de 106
Dobbs family 320
Dobbs, Mr *374*
Dobbs, Commander Richard Conway 337
Dobbs, Richard Francis 320
Dogherty, Patrick 334
Domesday Book (1086) 21–2, 38, 41, 51, 52–3, 150
    Inland Revenue 54
    second *see Return of Owners of Land*
    as William's swag list 21
domestic dwellings *see* housing

Domville, Sir Charles Compton, Baronet *334*
Donegal, Marquess of *373*
Donegal *192*, *193*, *202*, *320*, *326*, **333**
Doneraile, Viscounts of *332*, *376*
Doone, The *347*
Dorchester, Lord *325*, *374*
Dorrien Smith family *90*
Dorset *36*, **235**
    Church of England land in *164*, *235*
    Crown Estate land in *75*, *235*
    Duchy of Cornwall land in *88*
    and London landowners *148*, *153*, *154*
Douglas and Clydesdale, Marquess of
Douglas, Miss E.J.M. *296*
Douglas-Hamilton, Angus Alan, 15th Duke of Hamilton and Brandon *112*, *282*
Douglas-Home *see* Home
Douglas-Montague-Scott-Spottiswood, Lady John *275*
Doune Lodge *283*, *294*
Doune, Lord *290*
Doune Park *290*
Down **322**
Downe, Dowager Duchess of *265*
Downe, Viscounts of *265*
    John Christian George Dawnay, 11th Viscount *264*, *384*, *389*, *393*
Downshire, Marquesses of *227*, *360*, *363*, *373*, *378*
    acreage and value of land *203*, *322*, *347*, *354*
    Arthur Robin Hill, 8th Marquess of *322*, *333*
    Net National Income *396*
Drogheda, Henry Dermot Ponsonby Moore, 12th Earl of *337*, *337*
Drumlanrig Castle *109*
Drummond Castle *246*
Drummond, Robert *336*, *376*
Drummuir Castle *274*
du Maurier, Daphne *231*
Du Pre, Caledon *228*
Duberly, William *242*
Dublin (city) *199*, *334*, *358*
Dublin (county) *10*, *191*, *192*, *193*, *202*, **334**
Duchy of Cornwall *18*, *59*, *70*, *82*, **84–92**, *208*, *406–7*
    accounts inaccessible *407*
    acreage and value *18*, *84*, *88*, *147*, *160*, *162*
    Act (1982) *406*
    and Charles, Prince of Wales *65*, *84*, **88–91**
    and Dartmoor *86*, *146*
    Duchy Council *86*, *91–2*
    and Edward (VIII), 23rd Duke of *85–7*
    and George VI *87–8*
    history of *16*, *19*, *25*, *84–8*
    as neo-monopoly *74*
    privatisation suggested *92*
    Prudential Insurance land bought by *88*, *89*, *90*
    urban estate *85*, *88*, *89*, *90*
    value *89*, *98*

Duchy of Lancaster *59*, *70*, **93–101**, *208*, *407*
    acreage and value of land *93*, *147*
    government of *93*, *99–101*
    history of *18–19*, *25*, *94–6*
    lands of *96–7*
    and *Return of Owners of Land* *35*
    revenue *76–7*, *98–9*
    urban estate *97*
    value *61*, *97–8*
Ducie, Earls of *69*, *238*, *252*
Duckett, William *329*
Dudley, Earls of *68*, *131*, *263*, *363*
Dudley, John, Earl of Warwick *126*
Duff, Robert William *285*
Duff House *270*, *274*, *290*
Duff Penington, P. Gordon *380*
Duff-Assheaton-Smith, Mr *307*, *369*
Duff-Dunbar, Garden *277*
Dufferin and Ava
    5th Marquess of *322*
    Marquesses of *322*, *322*
Dufferin and Ava, Earls of *56*, *373*
Dugdale, Sir John, Baronet *68*
Dugdale, Lady *68*
Duke of Windsor *see* Edward VIII
Duleep Singh, Maharaja, His Highness *257*
Duloe estate *88*
Dulverton, Baron *393*
Dumbartonshire *111*, **281**
Dumfries & Galloway *76*
    see also Dumfriesshire; Kirkcudbrightshire; Wigtownshire
Dumfries, Johnny *see* Bute, Marquess of
Dumfriesshire *109*, **280**
Dunalley, Lord *350*
Dunbar, Baronets of *303*
Duncombe, Charles Anthony Peter, 6th Baron Feversham *265*
Duncombe, Jason Orlando *265*
Duncombe, Walter *242*
Dundas, James *302*
Dundas, Lawrence Mark, 4th Marquess of Zetland *264*
Dundas, Robert *289*
Dunearn Lodge *291*
Dunecht estate *180*
Dunmore, Earls of *132*, *361*, *372*
Dunn, Lady Mary *276*
Dunne, Misses *339*
Dunraven and Mount-Earl, Earls of *341*, *376*
    6th Earl of *351*
    Thady Windham Thomas Wyndham-Quin, 7th Earl of *312*, *312*
Dunrobin Castle *254*, *256*, *296*, *301*
Dunsandle and Clanconal, Lord *335*, *335*, *376*
Dunsany, Edward John Carlos Plunkett, 20th Baron *345*
Dunsany Castle *345*
Dunster estate and Castle *75*, *255*
Duntreath *300*
Duoro, Marquess of *25*, *110*, *239*
Durham, Earls of *236*
    Anthony Lambton, 6th Earl of *236*

    in Land Lists (1872) *364*
Durham, Hon Edward Richard, Baron *236*
Durham *125*, **164**, **236**
Durrow Castle *338*, *347*
dwellings *see* housing
Dyfed *see* Merionethshire; Montgomeryshire
Dyke, Rt Hon Sir William Hart, Baronet *243*
Dyke, Sir Acland Thomas
Dyneley *244*
Dynevor, Richard Charles Uryan Rhys, 9th Baron *309*, *309*, *370*
Dysart, Earls of *245*, *246*, *366*
Dytchley Park *252*, *344*

Earl Marshal of England, hereditary *see* Norfolk, Duke of
East Lothian (earlier Haddington) **282**
East Riding *see* Yorkshire
Easter Rebellion *195*
Eaton Hall *87*, *151*, **230**
Ebury, Manor of *150*, *410*
    see also Mayfair; Victoria
Ecclesiastical Commissioners *see* Church Commissioners
Ecclesiastical Leasing Acts (1571 & 1880) *163*, *169*
Eden, Sir William, Baronet *236*
Edenhall *231*, *261*
Edgar the Peaceful *122*
Edinburgh *33*
    Duke of *see* Philip, Prince
Edmonds, John *141*, *142*
Edmonds, Noel *390*
Edmonstone, Vice Admiral Sir William, Baronet *300*
Edmonstone, Sir Archibald Bruce Charles, 7th Baronet *300*
Edmonstone, Mary *300*
Edmund Ironside *122*
Edmund of Woodstock *127*, *128*
Edward I *127*, *153*, *201*, *246*, *399*
Edward II *94*, *399*
Edward III *85*, *94*, *122*, *126*, *399*
Edward IV *94*, *122*, *129*, *399*
Edward V *399*
Edward VI *126*, *400*
Edward VII *43*, *110*, *232*, *400*
    as 23rd Duke of Cornwall *85–7*
    as Prince of Wales *61*, *62*, *64*
Edward VIII *64*, *74*, *78*, *400*
    as Duke of Windsor *86*, *87*, *407*
Edward, Prince *104*
Edwards, Mr *370*
Edwards, Francis William Lloyd *307*
Edwards, Victoria *143*
Effingham, Earls of *128*, *133*
Egerton, John Sutherland, 6th Duke of Sutherland *108*, *134*, *135*, *230*
Eglinton and Winton, Earls of *273*, *276*
Egmont, Earls of *259*, *332*
Egremont, Baron *203*, *384*, *393*
Eia, Manor of *150*
Eight Hills Stables *338*
Eldon, Earls of *236*, *238*
Eleanor, Queen *94*
electricity *see* utilities

INDEX   429

Elgin (later Moray) 76, **290**
Eliott, Sir William Francis Augustus, Baronet 297
Elizabeth I 24, 26, 95, 122, 123, *150*, 241, 400
    and Church of England 171, 411
Elizabeth II 19, 20–1, 135, 248, 265, 400
    acreage and value of London land 162
    and Balmoral 270
    and Church of England 171, 172
    and Crown Estate 74, 76–8, 81, *159*, 183
    and Duchy of Cornwall 84, 86, 88
    and Duchy of Lancaster 93, 95, 98–9, 101
    and House of Lords 105, 113
    in Land Lists (2001) 379, *383*, 387, 391
    as Princess 69
    and royal land 58, 59, 63, 65–6, 67, 69–70
    wealth 58, 59–61, 71, 74
Elizabeth, Queen Mother 62, 66, 67, 69, 87, 109, 234, 265
    and Scotland 180, 271
Ellesmere, Earls of 244, 364
Ellice, Edward 284
Ellice, Mrs 360, 372
Elliot, Edward 284
Elliot, Messrs 382
Ellis, Sir Henry 52, 53
Ellis-Nanney, Hugh John 307, 370
Elphinstone, 16th and 17th Lords 69
Elphinstone, Rev the Hon A.C.V. 69
Elphinstone, Jean Francis 69
Elsick 61
Eltham, John of 85
Elton, 2nd Lord 68–9
Elton, Lady Richenda 68
Elveden 257
Ely 151, 165
Ely, Earls of 340
Ely, Marquesses of 323, 353, 373
    Charles John Tottenham, 8th Marquess of 323, 353
Ely Court (Wales) 255, 323
enclosures 25, 26, 137, 211, 215
    Enclosure Acts 37, 72
    and Plantagenets 124, 125, 408
    and *Return of Owners of Land* 37
Encumbered Estates Act (1849) 194
Endowment & Glebe Measures Act (1976) 411
Enfield Chase 97
England **222–65**
    acreage and value of land (including agricultural acreage) 7, *11*, *13*, *15*, *17*, 187
    compulsory registration (1990) 401
    counties *see under* counties
    Crown Estate land in 74, 75, 78–9
    dukes in House of Lords 109, 110–11, 112–13, 114, 115–19
    English Tourist Board 52
    estates over 1000 acres 75
    Forestry Commission in 141–2, 143
    housing/domestic dwellings 7, *11*, *13*
    institutional landowners 147
    and Ireland, comparison with 186–9, 196–7
    in Land Lists 371–2
    land use structure, basic 9
    Parliament *see* House of Commons; House of Lords
    Plantagenet land in *see* Plantagenets
    population 7, *11*, 206
    top landowners in 177, 200–1, 367–8
    see also Church of England; Duchy of Cornwall; history; House of Lords; London; *Return of Owners of Land*
England and Inner Empire **199–205**, 413
    English landowners with land in Scotland, Wales and Ireland 200–3, *200–1*, 204–5
    Irish landowners with land in England 203
    Scottish landowners with land in England 204
    Welsh landowners with land in England 203
Englefield Green 402
Englefield House 227
Ennis, Sir John James, Baronet 352
Enniskillen, Earls of 323, 373
    Andrew John Galbraith Cole, 7th Earl of 323
Enville Hall 245, 256
environmentalists 27–8, 144, 214
    Environment Agency 82
    see also National Trust
Eochoid Morghmeodhin 348
Eresby, Baroness Willoughby de
Erne, Earls of 323, 373, 385, 394
    Henry George Victor John Crighton, 6th Earl of 323
Erskine-Wemyss, James Hay 283
escheat 85
Essex 36, 43, 47, 75, 146, 156, 164, 222, **237**, 401
    Earls of 241
Eton family 159
Eton College estate 157
Eton as significant school 3, 50
    accents changed 28
    and Church of England 411
    and Crown Estate 78
    and Duchy of Cornwall 91
    and Duchy of Lancaster 100, 101
    and House of Lords 103, 108–15 *passim*, 117, 119, 407
    and institutional landowners 141
    and Ireland 191
    and London landowners 156
    and Plantagenets 131–3, 134, 135
    and Royal Household 63, 66, 67, 68, 69–70
European Commission 402
European Community *see* European Union
European Convention on Human Rights
    adopted as law (2000) 21
    compensation for confiscation of property 77
    and Crown Estate 77, 81
    and Duchy of Cornwall 84
    and Duchy of Lancaster 94
    and Plantagenets 136
    and Scotland 182, 185
    and Westminster dukedom 118
European Union/European Community
    Common Agricultural Policy 29, 402
    European Court of Human Rights 118
    European Parliament 25
    and Ireland 181, 187–8, 195–6, 205, 207, 412
    law 137
    royal family as greatest landowners in 69–71
    and Scotland 181
    subsidies 12, 181, 187–8, 195–6, 402, 412
Euston, Earls of 117, 248
Euston Hall 67, 116–17, 248, *249*, 257
Evans, Thomas 233
Evans-Lombe, Henry 248
Evelyn, Mr 158
Evelyn, W.J. 258
Evening Standard 148, 410
Ewerby estate 75
Ewing, Jane T 281
Exeter, Marquesses of 129, 130, *132*, 135, *249*, 253
    in Land Lists (1872) 365
Exeter 166
Exton Park 253
Eyre family 18, 156, *159*, *383*, 387
Eyre, Alethea Fanny 4
Eyre, Charles 227
Eyre, Charles George Samuel 156
Eyre, Dorothy Sybil Wilkins 156
Eyre, Edwin Rufus 156
Eyre, Frederick Charles 156
Eyre, Henry Samuel Robert 155, 156
Eyre, John Stephen Giles 156
Eyre, Mary Francis Elizabeth 4
Eyre, Michael Robert 156
Eyre, Rosemary Irene Margaret 156
Eyre, Ruth Evelyn 156
Eyre, Sheila 156
Eyre, Walpole 156
Eyre, Commander Walpole John 156
Eyre estate 155–6, *159*
    acreage and value 158, 162
    'tenants for life' 156
    see also St John's Wood

Fabian Society 179
Fairholme, George 289
Falkland, Viscount *132*
Falmouth, Viscounts of 231
    George Hugh Boscawen, 9th Viscount 90, 231
    in Land Lists 366, 380, 384, 388, 392
famine *see under* Ireland
Farleigh House 239
Farnham, Lady Diana Marion (neé Gunnis) 68

Farnham, Lords of 330
   Barry Owen Somerset Maxwell, 12th Lord 68, 330
Farquharson, James 379
Farquharson, Colonel James Ross 270
Farquharson, Mr 371
Farquharson of Invercauld, Captain A.A.C., 16th Farquharson 270, 379, 391
Farringdon's fly sheet diary 106
Al Fayed, Mohammed 379, 387
Fellenberg, Montgomery Hugh de 323
Fellowes, Edward 242
Fellowes, John, 4th Lord de Ramsey 82, 229, 242, 385, 389, 394
Fellows, F.P. 31
Fenton-Boughey, Sir Thomas Fletcher 256
Fenwick, Edward 151
Fenwick, Montague 245
Ferguson, Lt Colonel George 274
Ferguson, Rt Hon Sir James, Baronet 273
Ferguson, Colonel Robert Munro 283
Fermanagh 118, 323
Fermor-Hesketh, Sir Thomas George 244
Ferrers, Robert, Earl of Derby 94, 97
Fetherston, Rev Sir George Ralph 342
Fetherstonhaugh, Harry 142
feudal system 53, 56
   in Scotland 22, 184–5, 397
      abolished 403
Feversham, Earls of 33, 368
Feversham, Charles Anthony Peter Duncombe, 6th Baron 265
Fforde, Charles J.G. 276
Fforde, Lady Jean 276
Field Books (Inland Revenue) 54
Field, Leslie 151, 410
Field, The 179, 357
Fife 283
Fife, Dukes and Earls of 40, 61, 63
   1st Duke of 110
      acreage and value of land 204, 270, 274, 290
   James George Alexander Bannerman Carnegie, 3rd Duke of 110
   in Land Lists (1872) 359, 364, 371, 377
Filmer, Sir Edmund, Baronet 243
Finance Act (1867) 35
Finance Act (1909, 'People's Budget') 53–4
Finance Act (1920) 54
financial institutions 14, 16, 118, 211–12, 213–14, 395, 396, 402
   and royal land 69, 82, 86
   see also Stock Exchange
Financial Times 55, 148, 405
Finch, George Henry 253
Fingall, Earls of 345
First Lord of Treasury *see* Prime Minister
Fisher, D. 281
Fitzclarence-Hunloke, Hon Mrs 233
Fitzgerald, Adrian 336
Fitzgerald, Sir Augustine, Baronet 331

Fitzgerald, Desmond John Fitz Thomas 336
Fitz-Gerald, Desmond John Villiers, 29th Knight of Glin 236, 341
Fitzgerald, Sir George Peter Maurice, 5th Baronet, 23rd Knight of Kerry 336
Fitzgerald, Gerald, 8th Duke of Leinster 113–14, 192
Fitzgerald, Lord John 114
Fitzgerald, Lord 353
Fitzgerald, Peter 336
Fitz-Gibbon, Lady Louisa Isabella 341
Fitz-Hardinge, Lord 238
Fitzhardinge (Berkeley), Baroness 160
Fitzherbert, Hon Benjamin John 256
Fitzherbert, Francis Melford William, 15th Baron Stafford 256
Fitz-Herbert, Sir William, Baronet 251
Fitzherberts of Swynnerton 256
Fitzpatrick, Bernard, 2nd Baron Castletown 339
Fitzroy family 159
Fitzroy, Fortune 248
Fitzroy, Henry John, Marquess of Worcester 115, 238
FitzRoy, Hugh Denis Charles, 11th Duke of Grafton 116–17, 159, 248, 249, 257
Fitzwilliam, Earls of 265, 354, 360, 363, 367, 378
   8th Duke of 202
      acreage and value of land 200, 202, 204
Fitzwilliam, George 242
Fitz-William Burton, William 329
Fleetwood Hesketh, Edward 244
Fleetwood Hesketh, Roger 244
Fleetwood Hesketh, Sir Thomas Fermor 244
Fleming, Hon Cornwallis 281
Fleming, Diana Rosemund 303
Fleming, Hon Mrs D.C. 393
Fleming, Robert 272, 379, 386, 387
Fleming, Stanley Hughes le 261
Fletcher, Angus 38
Fletcher, James 279
Fletcher, P.L. 311
Fletcher-Campbell, Captain Henry 300
Flintham estate 251
Flintshire 311
Floors Castle 114, 282, 297
Florence Court 323
Fochabers estate 76
Foley, Lady Emily 240
Foljambe, Francis John Savile 251
Fonthill House 68, 272
Forbes, Sir Charles John, Baronet 270
Forbes, Peter Arthur Edward Hastings, 10th Earl of Granard 342
Forbes, William 287, 300, 362
Forbes, Captain William Frederick Eustace 300
Forbes, William Nathaniel 285
Forde, Colonel 373
Forde, Colonel William Brownlow 322
Fordyce, Alexander Dingwall 270
Forest of Dean 73, 141, 142
Forester, Barons of
   7th Baron 322

George Cecil Brooke Weld-Forester, 8th Baron 254
Forester, General the Lord 254
Forester, John 254
Forestier-Walker, L. 141
Forestry Commission 16, **140–5**, 208, 403, 409–10
   accounts 142–3, 144
   acreage and value of land 18, 138, 139, 140, 143, 147
   Commissioners, board of 141, 143–4
   creation (1919) 140
   Crown Estate woodland transferred to 73, 141
   and environmentalism 144
   Forest Enterprise Ltd. 142–3
   future, suggestions for 144–5
   and privatisation 140–1, 144, 145
   purchases 143
   sales to private interests 140, 141, 143
   in Scotland 141–2, 143, 178, 180
   secrecy of 140, 141–2, 144
Forfarshire (now Angus) 180, **271**
Fort Belvedere 86
Fortescue, Earls of 90, 234
Fortescue, Cyril 231
Fortescue, Edward 231
Fortescue, Eleanor 234
Fortescue, John Charles 343
Fortescue, Lady Margaret 234, 344
Fortune, Ann, Duchess of Cleveland 117
Fortune, Sir Richard 66
Fortune, Virginia 66
Foster, Rev Sir Cavendish Hervey 343
Foster, Michael 14
Foster, William 244
Foster, William Orme 254, 353
Fotheringham, Captain T.S.F. 271
Foundling charity 157, 159
Fowler, John 296
Fowler, Robert 345
Fox, George Lane 340, 340
Fox-Pitt-Rivers, Major-General 235
France-Hayhurst, Rev Thomas 230
Francis, Arthur 331
Francis, Hon Henry 236
Fraser, Hon Teresa (Keswick) 20, 78, 406
Frazer, Hugh 279
freehold explained 397
Freeman Jackson, Ginny 341
Freeman Jackson, Captain Harry 341
Freeman Jackson, Serena 341
Freeman-Mitford, Deborah 111
French, Francis Arthur, 7th Baron Freyne 348
French, Mrs of Lough Erritt 348
Freshwater, Benzion 162, 383, 388
Freshwater, Solomon 383, 388
Freuchie, Sir John Grant of 291
Freyne, Lord de 348, 376
Freyne, Francis Arthur French, 7th Baron 348
Friends of the Earth 214
Frischman, Dr 281
Friskney estate 75

Fulford, Francis 257, 305, 306, 311, 402
Fullerton Bowden, Jane A. 276
Fullerton-Acland-Hood, Sir Alexander Bateman, Baronet 255
Fursdon family 402
future 82–3, 144–5

Gage, Viscount 131, 259
Gainsborough, Anthony Gerard Edward Noel, 5th Earl of 253
Galloway, Earls of 287, 287, *303*, 361, *372*, 378
Galloway House 287, *303*
Galsworth, Michael 91
Galway 188, 191, 192, *193*, **335**
Galway, 9th Viscount 148, 235
game laws 125, 176, 190
Garden-Campbell, Francis William 274
Gardham estate 75
Gardner, John Dunn 229
Garrowby estate 264
Garton On the Wolds estate 75
Garvagh, Lord 374
Garvagh, Dowager Lady Charlotte 324
Gascoyne-Cecil, Robert Arthur Talbot, Marquess of Salisbury 25, 33
Gascoyne-Cecil, Robert Edward Peter, Marquess of Salisbury 241
Gatcombe 65
Gatty, Charles 410
George I 400
George II 165, 400
George III 73, 76, 77, 95, 400
George IV 400
George V 66, 85, 87, 400
George VI 64, 65, 84, 86, 265, 400
  as Duke of York 62
  and Duchy of Cornwall 87–8
George, Charles St 67
George, Edward Gerald Patrick St 67
George, Henry 53, 190, 192
Geraldine family 191
Gerard, Lord 366
Getty, John Paul 388
Gibbs, Jewan Francis 69
Gibbs, Stephen 276, 382
Gibbs, Captain the Hon Vicary Paul 69
Gibson-Carmichael, Rev Sir William, Baronet 293
Gibson-Watts, Mr 370
Gibson-Watts, James 317
Giffard, Walter Thomas Courtenay 256
Gifford, Thomas 299
Gilbert Le Grosvenour 150
Gilchrist, Douglas 301
Gill, Alan 148
Gill, Robin 411
Gilltown Stud 337
Gilmour, Allan 295
Gilmour, Baron 393
Ginge Manor 252
Gladstone, Andrew 303
Gladstone, Sir Hugh 303
Gladstone, John 303
Gladstone, Sir Thomas 285
Gladstone, Sir William, Baronet 285, 380, *391*

Gladstone, Rt Hon William Ewart 25, 29, 44, 49, 56, 134, 285, *311*
Glamis Castle 271
Glamis of Glamis 271
Glamorganshire 206, **312**
Glasgow, Earls of 273, 276, 295
Glasslough Castle 346
glebeland see under Church of England
Glen Etive estate 272
Glenapp, Viscount 273
Glenarm Castle 320
Glenart Castle 242, 354
Glencarse & Harvieston estate 278
Glenferness House 291
Glenkinglass estate 272
Glenlivet estate 76
Glin, Desmond John Villiers Fitz-Gerald, 29th Knight of 236, *341*
Gloag, Ann 389
Glodrydd, Elystan, Prince of Fferlys 153
Glorious Revolution (1688) 59
Gloucester, Duchess of 66
Gloucester, Dukes of 66, 99, 104
Gloucestershire 65, 75, 88, 164, **238**
Goatland Moor 96
Godwin-Austin, Robert Cloyne 258
Gogarty, Rosemary 343
Golet, Mary 116
Golspie estate 301
Goodman, Larry 343
Goodwood estate 259, 270, 274
Goold, Mr of Drumadda *341*
Gopsal Hall (Warwickshire) 245, 251
Gopsall Park (Leicestershire) 76
Gordon family 63
Gordon, Mr 374
Gordon, Andrew 381
Gordon, John 291
Gordon, Mavis 283
Gordon, Sir Robert 61
Gordon Duff, Major Lachlan Duff 274, 274
Gordon Duff, L.A. and P.M. 274
Gordon Lennox, Charles Henry see under Richmond and Gordon
Gordon Lennox family 109
Gordon-Cummings, Sir William Gordon, Baronet 290, 291
Gore, Arthur, 9th Earl of Arran 234, 344
Gore, John R.O. 307
Gore, W.O. 313
Gore-Booth family 349
Gore-Booth, Sir Henry, Baronet 349, 376
Gore-Booth, Sir Josslyn Henry, 9th Baronet 349
Gorhamury 75
Goring, Rev John 259
Gormanstown, Viscounts of 345
Gosford, Earls of 321, 373
  Charles Acheson Sparrow, 7th Earl of 321
Gosford Castle 321
Gosford House 283
Goswell Road 157, *159*
Gotto 161
Goudime, Xenia 354
government/state
  and Church of England 166–8

sources 420
  see also Ministries and Departments; Parliament
Gower, Granville see Granville
Graeme, Alexander Sutherland 292
Grafton, Ann Fortune, Duchess of 67
Grafton, Dukes of *107*, 249
  Hugh Denis Charles FitzRoy, 11th Duke 116–17, *159*, 248, 257
Graham, Sir Frederick 232
Graham, James, Marquess of 112
Graham, James, 8th Duke of Montrose 105, 112, 300
Graham, Patrick 112
Graham, Ysenda Maxtone 172, 411
Graham-Bontine, William 300
Granard, Earls of 342
  Peter Arthur Edward Hastings Forbes, 10th Earl of 342
Granby, Marquess of 114, 245
Grandison, Viscount 247
Grange, The (Alresford) 239, 240
Granston Manor 339
Grant, Sir George Macpherson 274
Grant, Henry Alexander 290
Grant, Ian 82, *361*, 372
Grant, Sir John 290
Grant, John 382
Grantchester Holdings 79
Grant-Kinloch, Colonel 274
grants see subsidies
Granville, Granville George Fergus Leveson Gower, 6th Earl of 284, *379*, *391*
Great Chamberlain of England 202
Great Easton Manor 245
Great Stucley Hall 245
Green, Michael 389
Green, Shirley 154, 410
Green Park 154
'green and pleasant land' myth 26–7
greenhouse gas emission quotas 144
Green-Price, Sir Richard, Baronet 317
Greig, Thomas 295
Gren, Werner 87
Greville peerage 352
Grey, Earls of 250
Grey, Lady Jane 126
Grey, Lady Katherine 126
Grey-Egerton, Sir Philip, Baronet 230
Grierson, Andrew 299
Griffin family 354
Griffiths, D.E.G. 82
Grimsthorpe, Lord 67
Grimsthorpe Castle 246, *294*
Grimston, Lady Iona 345
Grimston, Viscount 241
Gros Veneur, Hugh le 119
Grosmount, Henry, Earl of Lancaster 94
Grosmount, Maude and Blanche 94
Grosvenor family 150–2, *159*, 410
Grosvenor, Bendor, 2nd Duke of Westminster 86, 87, 151
Grosvenor, Brigadier Gerald see under Westminster
Grosvenor, Lady Jane 114, 275
Grosvenor, Lady Leonora 255
Grosvenor, Baron and Earl, Sir Richard 149–50, 151

Grosvenor, Sir Richard, Knight (later Baron then Earl of Westminster) 149–50, 151
Grosvenor, Sir Thomas 119, 150–1
Grosvenor/Ely family 323
Grosvenor estate 148, **149–52**, *159*
    acreage and value of land *158, 162*
    Grosvenor Estate Holdings 118, 148
    land overseas 151–2
    and royal family 19
        Crown Estate 80, 82
    see also Belgravia; Mayfair; Westminster
Guest, Ivor Mervyn Vigors, 4th Viscount Wimborne 235, 294
Guildford 165
    Earls of *243*
Guinness, Arthur Edward Rory *see* Iveagh
Guinness, Desmond 341
Gulston, Alan James *309*
Gun-Cunninghame, Cornwallis Robert Ducarel *354*
Gunnersbury Park 152, 228
Gunnerside estate 264
Gunnis, Diana Marion, Lady Farnham 68
Gunter family *158, 159, 162*
Gutherie, James *380*
Gutherie, John *290*
Guthrie, C.S. *277*
Gwent *see* Monmouthshire
Gwyn, Nell 119
Gwynedd *see* Caernarvonshire; Merionethshire; Montgomeryshire
Gwynne-Holford, Mr *370*
Gyarmarthy, Anna Gael 262

Hackett, W.W. *334*
Hackwood Park 239, *265*
Haddington, Earls of
    acreage *275*
    John George Baillie-Hamilton, 13th Earl of 275, 282
    in Land Lists (1872) *365*
Haddington (East Lothian) **282**
Haddon Hall 114, 245
Hadley Wood 97
Hadwen, Sidney *301*
Hagloe estate *75*
Haig, James 286
Haldane, Richard Burdon, Viscount of Cloan 53
Haldon, Lord *363*
Hale, Charles Cholmeley *241*
Halifax, Sir Charles Wood, Viscount 32, 33, 34
Halifax, Earls of
    Charles Edward Peter Neil Brown, 3rd Earl of *264*
    Edward Frederick Lindley Wood, 1st Earl of 87
    in Land Lists (2001) *385, 394*
Hall, Sir Basil *275*
Hall, Dare *329*
Hall, Sir John *385, 390*
Hall, Phillip 58, 71, 94–5, 99, 396, 405, 406, 407
Hall, Richard *323*

Hall, William *229*
Hallam, Elizabeth *403*
Hallett, Robert 30
Halsbury, Lord *401*
Halys, Alice *127*
Hamborough, D.A. *247*
Hambro, Captain Angus Vladimar 69
Hambro, Charlotte 91
Hamilton, Alexandra Anastasia 113
Hamilton, Grace *281*
Hamilton, Ion Trant *334*
Hamilton, James, 5th Duke and later Marquess Abercorn 105, 113, 325
Hamilton, Rt Hon Lord James Douglas, Earl of Selkirk 112, *287, 302*
Hamilton, Marquess of 113, 325
Hamilton, William Charles Stewart 303
Hamilton, Willie *407*
Hamilton and Brandon, Dukes of *40*
    12th Duke of 113
    acreage and value of land *107, 276, 288, 302*
    Angus Alan Douglas-Hamilton, 15th Duke of 112, 282
    in Land Lists (1872) *359, 364, 371, 377*
Hamilton Palace *276, 288, 302*
Hamilton-Russell, Frederick Gustavus 236
Hamilton-Russell, Gustavus Michael Stucley, Viscount of Boyne 23
Hampshire, earlier Southampton county 146–7, *164*, 170, **239**, *358*
Hampton, Lord *263*
Hanay, Colonel Frederick Rainsford *287*
Hanbury, John Capel *314*
Hanbury Tenison, Richard *314*
Hanbury-Kincaid-Lennox, Hon Charles Spencer *300*
Handcock, Roland, 8th Baron Castlemaine *352*
Handcock, Ronan *352*
Handley, John *253*
Hanmer, Sir Wyndham Edward, Baronet *311*
Hanover, Prince Ernst August of 105
Harberton, Viscount *337*
Harcourt, 2nd Viscount *252*
Harcourt, Edward William *252*
Harcourt, Hon Elizabeth Ann Gascoigne *252*
Hardwicke, Earls of *229*
Hardy, Nicholas Foreman *389*
Hare, Colonel *302*
Hare, Francis Michael, 6th Earl of Listowel *336*
Hare, Sir George Ralph Leigh, Baronet *248*
Harewood, George Henry Hubert Lascelles, 7th Earl of *265, 385*
Harewood House 265
Harlech, Lords *340, 362, 375*
    Francis David Ormsby Gore, 6th Lord *340*
Harley family *159*
Harley, Robert Daker *240*
Harman, Edward Robert King *349*

Harmsworth, Alfred Charles, 1st Viscount Northcliffe 71
Harmsworth, Harold Sidney, 1st Viscount Rothermere 69
Harper Crewe, Sir John *256*
Harries, George *316*
Harriman, Avril 235
Harrington, Earls of 152, *159*
    William Henry Leicester Stanhope, 11th Earl of 155, 291, 341
Harris, John Morgan *306*
Harrison, Mary Patricia, Marchioness of Abergavenny 68
Harrison-Broadley, William Henry *265*
Harrogate 96
Hartington, Marquess of 111, 201, 233
Hartopp, Edward Bourchier *245*
Harvey, Robert *333*
Haslam, Graham 85, 86, 87
Hastings, Lord *248, 366*
Hatfield House 241
Hatherton, Lord *256*
Haughey, Senator Edward *388*
Hawarden Castle 285, *311*
Hawarden, Viscounts of *350*
    Connan Wyndham Leslie Maude, 9th Viscount *350*
Hawkins, Christopher *231*
Hay, Rear Admiral Sir John, Baronet *303*
Hay, R.J.A. *302*
Hay, Sir Robert, Baronet *293*
Hayes, Sir Samuel Hercules, Baronet *333*
Haynes Park 226, *231*
Hazelrigg, 2nd Baron and 14th Baronet *245*
Headfort, Marquesses of *261, 330, 345*
    in Land Lists (1872) *375*
    Thomas Geoffrey Charles Taylour, 6th Marquess of *330*
Headfort House *261, 330, 345*
Headley, Baron *156*
Healey, Malcolm *385, 388*
Hean Castle *316*
Heanton Satchville 234
Heathcote, John Moyer *242*
Heathcote Perceval, Sir William *239*
Heathcote-Drummond-Willoughby, Nancy Jane Marie, 27th Baroness Willoughby de Eresby 202, 228, 246
Hebden, Robert *292*
Heddle, John *292*
Helmington, Lord Tollemache of *230, 366*
Hemphill, Hon Charles *335*
Hemphill, Peter Martin-Hemphill, 5th Baron *335*
Henderskelf, Lord Howard of 128, 232
Henderson, Sir Denys 81, 82
Henham Hall *257*
Henniker, Lord *257*
Henrietta Maria 154, 155
Henry I *122, 399*
Henry II *122, 338, 399*
Henry III 94, 97, *399*
Henry IV *128, 399*

INDEX   433

Henry V 399
Henry VI 156, 399
Henry VII 94, 95, 122, 125, 129, 226, 229, 305, 399
Henry VIII 24–5, 26, 28, 41, 104, 113, 117, 400
  and Church of England 173
  and counties 226, 229, 237, 254
  dissolution of monasteries and land grab 22–3, 150, 153, 154, 166–8, 182, 411
  and Duchy of Lancaster 95
  and Plantagenets 122, 123, 126, 129
Henry de Percy, Earl of Northumberland 125–6
Henry Plantagenet, 1st Duke of Lancaster 94
Herbert, Lt Colonel George Edward 315
Herbert, Henry 375
Herbert, Henry Arthur 336
Herbert, Henry George, 7th Earl of Carnarvon 227
Herbert, Henry George Charles Alexander, 17th Earl of Pembroke and Montgomery 262
Herbert, John 314
Herbert, John George, 8th Earl of Powis 315
Herbert, Lord 262
Herbert, William 314
Hereditary Chief Butler of Ireland 338
Hereditary Marshall of England 115
Hereditary Great Chamberlain of England, Joint 202
Hereditary Keeper of Palace of Holyroodhouse 112, 282
Hereditary Earl Marshal of England *see* Norfolk, Duke of
Hereditary Master of Queen's Household 272
Hereford, Viscount *133*
Hereford, Earls of 126
Herefordshire 75, *164*, **240**, 401
  Hereford 165
Hereward Wac 249
heritage, natural *see* environmentalists
Hermitage (Castle Connell) *340, 341*
Heron-Maxwell, Captain Sir John, Baronet *280*
Heron-Maxwell, John Maxwell *287*
Herries, Lady of Terreagles, 16th 128, *132*
Herriot-Maitland family 286
Hertford, Marquess of *260*
Hertfordshire 33, 69, *164*, **241**
Hervey, Frederick William Augustus, 8th Marquess of Bristol 246, *257*
Heseltine, Michael, Baron *388*
Hesketh, Sir Thomas Fermor
Hess, Rudolf Walter Richard 87
Heusden, Marquess of *335*
Hicks-Beach, Rt Hon Sir Michael, Baronet *238*
High Sheriffs 43, 101, 127
Higham Ferrers estate 97
Highclere Castle 227, *255*
Highgrove estate 65, 88
Highlands 182

Clearances 137, 176
Crown Estate land in 76
Highland & Island Enterprises *180*
Highland Land League (earlier Highland Land Reform Association) 40, 404
Hildyard, Myles Thoroton 251
Hildyard, Captain Robert Maxwell D'Arcy 44
Hill, Arthur Robin, 8th Marquess of Downshire 322, 333
Hill, Lord George Augustus *333*
Hill, Stuart 401
Hill, Viscount *254*
Hillsborough, Earl of 322
Hillsborough Castle 227, 322, *347*, 354
Hinde, Thomas 52, 53, 404, 405
Hirsel 288, 297
history **20–8**, 403
  Church of England 16, 24
  Crown Estate 16, 22, 24, 25, 72–3
  dissolution of monasteries *see under* Henry VIII
  Duchy of Cornwall 16, 19, 25, 84–8
  Duchy of Lancaster 18–19, 25, 94–6
  House of Lords 25, 63, 103–4
  lingering bonds 28
  Norman Conquest 20–2
  Parliament 23, 24, 25, 27, 28, 85
  power of land 26–8
  Republic 22, 24–6, 85
  Republic *see* Cromwell, Oliver
  royalty and royal land 19, 25
Hitchcock, Rodney *381*
Hitler, Adolf 87, 141
Hobhouse, Henry 204, 413
Hobson, Dominic 144, 145, 169–70, 410, 411, 413
Hoghton, Sir Richard Bernard Cuthbert de, 14th Baronet 244
Hoghton Tower 244
Holford, Robert Stayner *238*
Holkham Hall 248
Holland family *159*
Holland Park 148
Holland/Ilchester estate 18, 148, 157, 235
  acreage and value *160, 162*
Holmesdale, Viscount *243*
Holmewood estate 75
Holy Ghost Fathers 359
Holyroodhouse, Palace of, Hereditary keeper of 112, 282
Home, Earls of 199
  acreage *288*
  Alec Douglas Home, 14th Earl of 288
  David Alexander Cospatrick Douglas-Home, 15th Earl of 288
  in Land Lists (1872) *360, 365, 371, 378*
  in Land Lists (2001) *381, 392*
Home, Countess of *297*
Home Office, Secretary of State for 172
Home Rule for Ireland 49
Home-Drummond-Moray, Charles Stirling *294*

homes and homeownership *see* housing/domestic dwellings
Home-Speirs, Sir George, Baronet *300*
Honywood, Mrs *237*
Hood, Nicholas 91
Hope, Anne Adile *258*, *346*
Hope, Captain Henry Walter *282*
Hope, Rev R.M. 170
Hope, Thomas Arthur *325*, *374*
Hope-Johnston, Patrick Anthony Wentworth, 11th Earl of Annandale and Hartfell 280
Hope-Johnstone, John 280, *362*, *372*
Hopetoun, Earl of *282*, 288, 302, *302*
Hopetoun House *282*, 288, *302*
Hope-Vere, James *288*
Hopkinson, Rev R.S. 170
Hopton Wafers Manor House 308
Horn, John *286*
Horton, Michael *389*
Hotham, Lord *265*
Hothfield, Lord *243*, *365*, *368*
Hotspur, Harry 250
Houblon, John *237*
House Builders Federation 403
House of Commons 23, 24, 172, 199
  and Ireland 191
  landowners in 25, 63, 104, 124
    Plantagenets 124, 130, *131–3*, 135
  and *Return of Owners of Land* 29
  and Scotland 176
  Select Committees
    on Civil List 95
    on Defence 145, 147
  see also Conservative; Labour
House of Lords 4, **102–20**, 211, 407–8
  and Church of England 171, 173
  composition of 104–6
  dukes and their land (list of 25) 106–25, *107*
  eviction of hereditaries from (1999) 27, 59, 120, 121, 134, 136, 173, 199–200, 211, 240
  history of 25, 63, 103–4
  non-landowners in 107
  and Plantagenets 124, 126–7, 130, *131–3*
  and *Return of Owners of Land* 29, **31–4**, 35, 40–1, 53–4
  and Scotland 176
  see also peers
Housebuilders Association 402
Household, Royal *see under* royalty
Housing Associations 189
housing/domestic dwellings 12–16, 402–3
  acreage and value of land 9, 56–7, *357*
  empty 402
  homeownership 10, *11*, 13, 209, 210
  in Ireland 186, 187, 188–9, *193*, 197
  and Land Lists 358
  Land Registry entries compulsory 5
  map (1972 & 2001) 7
  prices inflated 148
  reducing land costs 213
  rented *11*
Houston, Colonel Alexander *282*

Hovell-Thurlow-Cummings-Bruce, Jane Mary 349
Howard family 43, 127–9, 130, 152, 227
   as Plantagenets *133*
Howard, George William Beaumont, 13th Earl of Carlisle 232
Howard, Henry *232*
Howard, Katharine 23, 25
Howard, Lord Mark Fitzalan 127
Howard, Lord Martin Fitzalan 127
Howard, Lord Michael Fitzalan 127
Howard, Major General Miles Francis Stapleton Fitzalan, 7th Duke of Norfolk 105, 115, 128, 155, *233*, *259*, 265
Howard, Sir Robert 128
Howard, Simon 232, *385*
Howard de Walden, Lords of 18, 161n, 227
   4th, 6th, 7th and 9th Lords 152
   8th Lord 153
   Baron 128, *131*
Howard de Walden estate 152–3, *159*, *160*, *162*
Howard of Glossop *see* Howard, Major General Miles
Howard of Henderskelf, Lord 128, 232
Howe, Earls of *160*, 228, *245*, 251
   Major General Frederick Curzon, 7th Earl of 228, *245*, 251
Howes, Christopher 82, 91, 100
Howland, Lord 135, 226
Howth, Earls of *334*
Huddart, George Augustus *307*
Hughes, Hugh Robert *310*
Hughes, John William Gwynne *309*
Hughes, Mr *369*
Hugo, John Mandeville *354*
Hull, Rev Richard 170
Hulme, Lords of 150
Hulton, Sir Edward 112
Hulton, Jillian 112
human rights
   Bill of Rights (1688) 59
   stolen 182–3
   see also European Convention
Hume-Campbell, Sir Hugh 275
Humphrey, Edward *382*
Humphreys-Owen, Arthur Charles *315*
Hunter, Richard *282*
Hunter-Blair, Sir Edward, Baronet *303*
Huntingdon, Earls of *132*
Huntingdonshire *164*, **242**
Huntingfield, Lord *257*
Huntly, Marquesses of 180, *242*
   acreage *270*
   in Land Lists (1872) *361*, *372*, *378*
Hurstborne Park *234*, *239*
Hussey, Lord Marmaduke 68
Hussey, Lady Susan 68
Hutchinson, Sir Peter 141, 143
Hyams, Harry *388*
Hyde Park 150, 172
Hyde Parker, Sir William Stephen, Baronet 3, 66
Hylton, Lord *258*

Ickworth Park *246*, 257
Ievers family *331*

Ilchester *see* Holland/Ilchester estate
Ilchester, Earls of *235*, *255*, 340, *366*
   7th Earl of 148
Iliffe, Robert Peter Richard 3rd Baron 227, 358, *380*, *383*, 389, *392*
importance of land **6–19**, 401–2
Inchcape, Kenneth Peter Lyle Mackay, 4th Earl of 273, *389*
Inchquin, Lords of *331*
   Conor O'Brien, 18th Baron 331
industrial revolution 25
inflation of prices 148, 358
Ingatestone Hall 237
inheritance tax 65
Inland Revenue 53, 412
   Commission of 101
   on development land 14
   Domesday Books 54
   Field Books 54
   on millionaires 409
   Property Market Report *13*, 358
   and *Return of Owners of Land* 38
   see also Valuation Office
Inner Royal Household *see under* royalty
Innes, Alexander *285*
Innes-Ker, Guy David, 10th Duke of Roxburghe 114, 116, 275, 297
Insole, James Harvey *255*
institutional landowners, big **137–47**, 409–10
   lists of (1962 and 2001) *139*, *147*
   see also Defence *under* Ministries; Forestry Commission; top landowners
insurance companies *see* financial institutions
Inverary Castle 111, 272, *281*
Invercauld and Torlisk Trusts *18*, *147*
Inverness-shire 141, 202, **284**
Ireland (generally) and Republic of Ireland 155, **186–98**, **326–54**, 412
   acreage and value of land (including agricultural acreage) 7, *11*, *13*, *15*, 181, 184–5, 186, 187, 194–5, 198, *357*
   see also land agitations *below*
   conquest (1172) 22, 24
   counties *see under* counties
   dukes in House of Lords 113–14
   and England and Wales, comparison with 186–9, 196–7
   English landowners with land in 200–3, *200–1*, 204–5
   EU subsidies to 181, 187–8, 195–6, 205, 207, 412
   famine, potato blight and extermination of peasantry 137, 186, **189–92**, 194, 198, 200, 204, 205, 211, 215, 326
   Home Rule 49
   homeownership 186, 187, 188–9, *193*, 197
   and House of Lords 105, 118
   housing/domestic dwellings 7, *11*, *13*
   land agitations and reform 10, 30, 130, 181, *192*, 194–6, 197, 404
   see also agricultural *above*
   in Land Lists 375–6

land reform and redistribution 10, 30, 130, 181, 207, 404
landowners with land in England 203
legislation 130, 186, 194
'miracle' and relaxed planning consents 12
Plantagenet land in 27, 124, 129, 130
population 7, *11*, 205, 326
   and landownership 206
   migration to and from 186, 196, 204, 412
and Scotland, comparison with 176, 181, 183, 197
top landowners in *177*, 187, 190, 192, 200, *203*, *375–6*
see also Northern Ireland; *Return of Owners of Land*
Irish Free State (1922–49) 195, 326
Irish Land Commission 182, 191, 195, 318, 326, 402
Irish Land League 404
Irish Times 357
Irvine, Mr *374*
Irvine, John Gerard *323*
Irwin, Lord 264
Isabelle of France 85
Ismay, Wentworth Peter
Iveagh, Arthur Edward Rory Guinness, 4th Earl of 86, 257, *382*, *386*, *388*, *392*

Jackson, Sir Henry Mather, Baronet *314*
Jackson's Trustees *160*
James I and VI 42, 95, 245, 343, 400
James II 58, 400
James II of Scotland 112
James, Sir Jimmy 91
James, Sir John 82
Janson, Charles Noel 108
Janson, Mrs *see* Sutherland, Elizabeth
Janson, Noel 301
Jardine, Andrew *280*
Jardine, James 297
Jenkins, Mr *160*
Jenkins, Simon 410
Jermyn family *159*
Jersey, Earls of *247*, *252*
   George Francis William Child Villiers, 10th Earl of *131*, *247*, *312*, *312*
John of Gaunt, Duke of Lancaster 94
John, King 21, 23, *399*
Johnston, William 340
Johnstone, Frederick John, Baronet *280*
Johnstone, George *283*
Johnstone, James 278, *298*
Joicey, Edward 236
Joint Hereditary Great Chamberlain of England 202
Jones, Miss Catherine *340*
Jones, General Sir Edward 103
Jones, Frederick Arthur *309*
Jones, John 35
Jones, Miss *308*
Jones, Morgan *309*
Jones, Mr *370*

INDEX   435

Jones, Tom Bruce 142, 144
Jones-Parry, Thomas Love Duncombe 307, 370

Kane-O'Kelly, Sheelki Deirdre 348
Kavanagh, Arthur McMurrough 376
Kavanagh, Mark 334
Kay-Shuttleworth, Lord Charles Geoffrey Nicholas 101
Kay-Shuttleworth, Mary 101
Keane, John 351
Keane, Sir Richard Francis, Baronet 351
Keane, Sir Richard Michael 351
Kedleston 233
Keeper of the Privy Purse 95, 99
Keeper of the Records of Duchy of Lancaster 99, 100
Keirnan, Buddy 330
Kemeys-Tynte, Colonel 314
Kemmis, Thomas 339
Kemmis, William 354
Kenlis, Baron 330
Kenmare, Earls of 191, 336, 360, 375, 378
    acreage and value of land 203, 332, 336
Kennedy, Archibald Angus Charles, 8th Marquess of Ailsa 273
Kennedy of Blairquahan 287
Kennedy, Calcraft 253
Kenneth I, King of Scotland 399
Kennington 85, 88, 89
Kensington, Lord 158, 316
Kensington (London) 157
Kent 45, 75, 86, 164, 191, 202, **243**
    Dukes of 99, 104
Kentchurch 240
Kenyon, Lord 311
Ker, Mr 373
Keroualle, Louise de 109
Kerr, Lady Elisabeth 109
Kerr, Peter Francis Walter, 12th Marquess of Lothian 67, 109, 297
Kerry 191, 193, 202, **336**
Kershaw, Richard 380
Kesteven, Baroness Thatcher of see Thatcher, Margaret
Keswick, Henry 78, 287
Keswick, Simon 78, 287, 389
Keswick, Hon Tessa 20, 78, 406
Kilcarn Stud 345
Kildare 191, 193, **337**
    Maurice Fitzgerald, Marquess of 114, 337
Kilkenny 193, **338**
    Castle 338, 350
Killarney House 332, 336
Killerton 234, 255
Killian estate 296
Kilmorey, Earls of 322, 368
    Rt Hon Sir Richard Needham, 6th Earl of 322
Kilruddery estate and Castle 354
Kilshane estate 359
Kiltullen estate 335
Kimball, June Mary 245
Kimball, Marcus Richard, 1st Baron 245
Kimberley, Earls of 248

Kimbolton Castle 116, 242
Kinbrace estate 230
Kincardineshire 61, **285**
Kindersley, Peter 389
King, John Gilbert 347
King Massey-Dawson, George Staunton 350
King-Harman, Edward Robert 203, 342, 348, 361, 375
King's County see Offaly
King's Lynn estate 75
Kingston, Countess of 332
Kingston, Earls of 348
    Barclay Edwin King-Tenison, 11th Earl of 348
Kingston Lacy 235, 311
King-Tenison, Barclay Edwin see Kingston, Earls of
Kinloss, Lady 132
Kinross, Barons of 283
Kinross House 286
Kinross-shire **286**
Kinsham Court 317
Kintore, Earls of 285
Kirby, Mrs 313, 369
Kircudbrightshire **287**
Knaresborough and Castle 96, 128
Knebworth Park 241
Knightley, Sir Rainald, Baronet 249
Knights of the Garter 117
Knole 243
Knowles, D., Leslie and Joicey 381
Knowsley 8, 230, 244
Knox, Charles Howe Cuff 344
Knox-Gore, Sir Charles James 344, 376
Knuth, Count Adam 382, 393
Knypersley Hall 43
Koerner, Joseph and Lisbet 380, 388

Labour Party and governments 8, 30
    and Crown Estate 77–8
    and Duchy of Cornwall 88
    and House of Lords 105
    Blair's expulsions from 27, 59, 120, 121, 134, 136, 173, 199–200, 211
    and institutional landowners 138
    Forestry Commission 140, 143
    New Labour see Blair
    and Scotland 31, 185
Ladbroke family 159
Ladies of the Bedchamber 66, 67–8, 330
Lakeview House 336
Lalor, James Fintan 186, 189, 412
Lambert, John 34–5, 36, 37, 38
Lambton, Anthony, 6th Earl of Durham 236
Lambton, Hon Edward Richard, Baron Durham 236
Lamington, Lord 288
Lamport, Stephen 91
Lanarkshire **288**
Lancashire 43, **244**
    Church of England land in 164, 244
    as county Palatine (1351) 94, 99
    and Duchy of Lancaster 94, 99, 101
    Survey 96, 98

Lord Lieutenant of 100
    Westminster land in 18, 244
Lancaster, Dukes of 94
Lancaster, Earls of
    Edmund Plantagenet, 1st Earl of 97, 99
    Edward Plantagenet 94
    Henry Grosmount 94
    Thomas Plantagenet 94
land
    importance of **6–19**, 401–2
    major topics see acreage; Church of England; history; House of Commons; House of Lords; housing; institutional landowners; Land Lists; land reform; Land Registry; Plantagenet; *Return of Owners of Land*; royalty; tenure; top landowners
    places see counties; England; Ireland; Northern Ireland; Scotland; Wales
    without heirs, reversion to Crown 22, 99
Land Commission (Ireland) 182, 191, 195, 318, 326, 402
Land League (Ireland) 40
Land Lists **355–94**
    in 1872 356, 359–78
        ranking by acreage 359–62, 367–78
        ranking by value of land 363–6
    in 2001 356–8, 379–94
        ranking by acreage 379–82, 391–4
        ranking by value of land 383–6
        ranking by wealth 387–90
    in England 367–8
    in Ireland and Republic of Ireland 375–6
    in Northern Ireland 373–4
    in Scotland 371–2
    in UK and Ireland generally 359–66, 377–94
    in Wales 369–70
Land Purchase Acts (Ireland, 1880s) 25
land reform and redistribution
    in Ireland 10, 30, 130, 181, 207, 404
    non-existent 207
    in Scotland 40, 180–2
Land Registration Act (1862) 30
Land Registration Act (1925) 53, 401
    see also Land Registry
Land Registration Act (1997) 401
Land Registry 398, 404, 409
    begun 25, 30
    domestic dwellings recorded 5
    incomplete 4, 8, 14, 16, 19, 25, 121, 139, 164, 222, 304, 318
    access difficult 54–5
    delays registering 49
    intention to complete records 401
    logic of including all land in 28
    reform needed 214, 215
    in Ireland 54, 326
    and Land Lists 356

in Northern Ireland 54
in Scotland (Sasines/Land Register) 54, 178, 398
Land Securities 80
land use structure, basic 9
Landlord and Tenant Acts (1876 & 1881-9) 194
Landon, Timothy 388
Lane-Fox, George 265
Lane-Fox, Mr 368
Langford, Colonel Geoffrey Alexander Rowley-Conwy, 9th Baron 311
Langford, Lord 334
Langham, Sir James Hay 249
Langrishe, Lady 354
Langrishe, Sir James Hercules Langrishe, 8th Baronet 345
Langwell 251
Lansdowne, Dowager Marchioness of 286
Lansdowne, Marquesses of 131, 262
   acreage and value of land 200, 202, 204, 345
   George Nairne Petty-Fitzmaurice, 8th Marquess of 91, 202
   in Land Lists (1872) 359, 364, 367, 377
Laois (Queens County) 186, 193, 202, 206, 326, **339**
largest landowners see top landowners
Lascelles, Viscount 265
Latham, Alex 14
Lathom, Earl of, 2nd Lord Skelmersdale 43
Lauderdale, Earls of 275
law see legislation
Lawson, Sir Wilfred, Baronet 232
Laxton estate 75
Lazari, Chris 161, 162, 383, 388
Le Heyr see Eyre
Le Strange family 248
Leader, Mr 158
leasehold explained 397
Leask, Joseph 299
Leconfield, Barons of
   2nd Baron 203, 331
   Henry Scawen Wyndham, 7th Baron 331
Leconfield, Lord 232, 259, 265, 360, 363, 367, 378
   acreage and value of land 200, 202-3, 204, 331
Leeds 166
   Dukes of 107, 130, 265
Lee-Harvey, Henry 295
Leeson, Nick 69
Legh, William 366
legislation 25, 207, 209, 402
   and Church of England 163-4, 169, 411
   and confiscation of land 24
   Corn Laws and opposition to 29-30
   enclosure 37, 72
   EU 137
      see also European Convention on Human Rights
   and feudalism 403
   and finance/budgets 35, 53-4
   and Forestry Commission 140

game and penal laws 124, 125, 176, 190
in Industrial Revolution to control dispossessed masses 26
and Ireland 130, 186, 194
and Plantagenets 124, 125, 408
reform (parliamentary) 29, 55
registration of land 30, 53, 401
and royalty 76, 183, 406, 407
   Duchy of Cornwall 84, 85, 407
   Duchy of Lancaster 94, 407
   revoking bar on land ownership 59
   sale of Crown and royal land prevented 72, 95, 98
and Scotland, union with 176, 183
Lehmann, Rosamond 306
Leicester, Earls of 243
   Edward Douglas Coke, 7th Earl of 248
   in Land Lists (1872) 364, 368
   in Land Lists (2001) 381, 384, 390, 392
   Simon de Montfort 94, 103
Leicestershire 4, 75, 96, 164, **245**
   Leicester 166
Leigh, Hon Christopher 260
Leigh, John Piers Leigh, 5th Baron 260
Leigh, Mrs 226
Leinster, Dukes of 237
   7th Duke of 191-2
   acreage and value of land 107, 203, 337
   Gerald Fitzgerald, 8th Duke of (Viscount Leinster) 113-14, 192
   in Land Lists (1872) 361, 365, 375
Leinster 191, 192, 193
Leitrim 192, 193, 333, **340**
   Earls of 192, 362, 375
Lennox see Gordon Lennox
Lennox Naper, James 345
Lennoxlove 276
Leslie, Desmond 346
Leslie, Bishop John 346
Leslie, Sir John Ide, 4th Baronet 333, 333, 346, 346, 375
Leslie, Sir Shane 346
Letterewe estate 179, 226, 296
Lettes Trustees 160
Leven and Melville, Earls of 291
Leverhulme, Viscounts of
   in Land Lists (2001) 380, 385, 390, 392
   Philip William Bryce Lever, 3rd Viscount 230
Leveson-Gower, Granville William Gresham 258
Lewes, Earls of 68
Lewis, Charles Edward 314
Lewis, Rev Sir Gilbert Frankland, Baronet Rev. Sir 370, 317
Lewis, Mrs M.A. 308
Leyland, Thomas 250
Liberal Democratic Party 66, 105, 185
Liberal Party 130
   and Return of Owners of Land 39-40, 53, 56
Lichfield 166
   Thomas Patrick John Anson, 4th Earl of 256

life peers 105
Lilford, Lord 249
Lillingston, Alan 341
Limerick 191, 193, **341**
Lincolnshire 75, 88, 114, 164, **246**
   Lincoln 166
Lindert, Peter 157-8, 158, 160-2
Lindsay, Anthony Robert, Lord Balneil 283
Lindsay, Robert, Earl, 29th Earl of Crawford 66, 283
Lindsay, Sir Robert Lloyd, Baronet 227
Lindsay, Sir Thomas Coutts, Baronet 283
Linley, Viscount 341
Linlithgow, Adrian John Charles Hope, 4th Marquess of 288, 302, 393
Linlithgow (West Lothian) **302**
Lisburne, Earls of 369, 203
   John David Malet Vaughan, 8th Earls of 308, 308
Lisgar, Lady 330
Liskeard 90
Lismore, Viscount 350, 375
Lismore Castle 201, 351
Lissadell 349
Listowel, Earls of 336, 376
   Francis Michael Hare, 6th Earl of 336
Litchfield, Leon G. 290
Lithgow, Sir William J., Baronet 382, 392
Livanos, Stavros 117
Liverpool 166
Livery companies omitted from Lloyd map 157, 158
Llanover, Lady 314
Llanstephan House 306
Lloyd George of Dwyfor, 3rd Earl of 316
Lloyd George of Dwyfor, David, 1st Earl of 8, 25, 53, 54, 140, 316
Lloyd, John: map of London 158, 159
   estates described 152-7
   lost fortunes 155-6
   outwith centre 155-6, 159
Lloyd, T.E. 308
Lloyd-Baker estate 157, 159
Lloyd-Mostyn, Llewelyn Nevill Vaughan 311
Llywelyn the Great, William ap Griffith of Cochwillan 305
local authorities 139, 147, 158, 180, 401
Local Government Board see Return of Owners of Land
Lochaber 143
Lochinch Castle 303
Lochmaben Castle 280
Lochwood Castle 280
Lomas family 381
Lomas, Florence Beatrix 156
Lomas, Giles John 156
Lomas, Hugh Eyre 156
Lomas, Margaret Florence 156
Londesborough, Lord 265, 364, 368
London 18, **148-62**, 410
   acreages and values 158, 160-2
   Commercial Research Agency 149

INDEX   437

cost per acre 14
Crown Estate land in 80–1, 148–9, 154–5
Duchy of Cornwall land in 85, 88, 89
Duchy of Lancaster land in 94, 96, 97
and dukes 111
estates outwith centre 155–6, 159
Grafton land in 117
great estates, *see also* Grosvenor estates
list of land owners (1890–2001) 157–8, *158*, 160–2
lost fortunes 155–6
map *see* Lloyd, John
Lord Mayor of 172
not included in *Return of Owners of Land* 35, 51
Plantagenet land in 128, 135
top landowners *162*
in wartime 64
Westminster family land in 118–19
London, Bishop of 159
Londonderry 324
 Marquess of 87, *236*, *315*, *322*, *363*, 368
Long, Viscount 68
Long, Walter 262
Longford, Earls of
 7th Earl of 352
 General 352
 in Land Lists (1872) 365
 Tom Packenham, 8th Earl of 352
Longford *193*, **342**
Longleat *255*, 262, *346*
Longnor estate 254
Lonsdale, Earls of *232*, *261*
 5th Earl of 232
 James Lowther, 7th Earl of 232
 in Land Lists (1872) *361*, *364*, *367*
 in Land Lists (2001) *379*, *383*, *391*
Looe 90
Lopes, Henry Massey, 3rd Baron Roborough *234*, *380*, *386*, *392*
Lord Chamberlain 3, 43, *66*, 67, 78, 191, 283
Lord Chancellors 166–7, 401
Lord Chief Justice 153, 172
Lord Deputy in Ireland 202
Lord Justice of Common Pleas 156
Lord Justice in Ireland 202
Lord Lieutenants and Deputies 67, 68, 100, 117, 134, 192
Lord of Manor 167
Lord Mayor of London 172
Lord Mayor of York 172
Lord President of Council (Leader of House of Commons) 172
Lord Privy Seal 32, 34, 135
Lord Steward 67
Lord Warden of the Stannaries 91
Lords *see* House of Lords
Lorne, Marquess of, 13th Duke of Argyll 111, 272
Lothian, Marquesses of
 acreage and value of land *289*, *297*
 in Land Lists *366*, *393*
 Peter Francis Walter Kerr, 12th Marquess of 67, 109, *297*

Loudoun, Countess of *132*
Loudoun, Earls of 130, *273*
Louis XIV 109
Louise, Princess 61, 110
Louth, Lord 343
Louth estate (Lincolnshire) 75, 76
Louth (Ireland) *193*, **343**
Lovat, Lords 63, 141, 179, 266
 14th Lord 78
 acreage and value of land *204*, *284*
 in Land Lists (1872) *359*, *371*, *377*
Lovelace, Earls of *132*, 134, *258*
Lovell, Terry 170, 411
Lowe brothers 281
Lowe, Francis 350
Lowndes family *159*
Lowrey-Corry, John Armar, 8th Earl of Belmore 323
Lowther, James, 7th Earl of Lonsdale 232
Lowther Castle *232*, *261*
Loxdale, J. 308
Lucan, Earls of *344*, *362*, *375*
 8th 192
 Richard Bingham, 7th Earl of 192, 344
Lucas, Richard 253
Lucas Scudamore, John Edward 240
Lucas Scudamore, Lt Cdr John Harford 240
Luce, Rt Hon Lord Richard 66
Luce, Sir William 66
Lucy, Henry Spencer 260
Lumley, Lady Elisabeth 67
Lurgan, Lord 374
Luss, Sir Ivar Colquhoun of 111, 272
Luton Lye 262
Luttrell, Colonel Sir Geoffrey Walter Fownes 255
Lymington, Viscount 239
Lynch-Blosse, Sir Robert, Baronet 344
Lyoness *see* Scilly Isles
Lyons-Montgomery, Hugh 340
Lyttleton, Lord 263
Lytton, 2nd Earl of 241

Macadam, Frederick 273
Macaire, Mrs *381*
McAlpine family 388
Macartney, Carthenac George 320, *374*
McCabe, Kevin 390
McCausland, Mr 374
McCausland, Connoly Thomas 324
Macclesfield, Earls of 252
McCombe, Richard 100
McCosh of Huntsfield, Lt Cdr Bryce 393
Macdonald, Calum 142
MacDonald Lockhart, A.M. 288
MacDonald Lords of Tradeston *see* Tradeston
Macdonald-Lockhart, Sir Simon, Baronet 288, *288*
McDonnell, Alexander Randal Mark, 9th Earl Antrim 320
Macdougal, Rev Robert 279
MacDougal, James 303
McEwen, John: on Scotland 107, 138, 142, **177–81**, 184, 185, 357, 406, 408, 409, 412

counties of 266, 276, 278, 283, 287, 292, 299, 303
Macgeogh, Robert John *321*
McGilcuddy of the Reeks, The 336
MacGillivary, Neil John *291*
McIntosh, Bob 143
MacKay, Elizabeth *276*
Mackenzie, Colin Lyon *279*
Mackenzie, Hugh *296*, *362*, *372*
Mackenzie, James *270*, *271*, *361*, *372*
Mackenzie, John A. Shaw *279*, *379*
Mackenzie, Sir Kenneth, Baronet *296*, *359*, *371*, *377*
Mackenzie, William Ord *279*
Mackintosh, Sir Cameron *388*
Mackintosh, The *284*, *360*, *371*, *377*
MacKirdy, John *276*
McKissack, Robert *290*
Maclay, Hon Mrs A.G. *394*
Macleod, Gordon *301*
Macleod, John *381*
Macleod, Norman Macleod, The *284*, *359*, *371*
McMahon, Sir William Samuel, Baronet *325*, *373*
McManus, J.P. *341*
Macmillan, Harold, Earl of Stockton 105
McMurragh, Arthur *329*, *338*
Macnamara, Arthur *226*
Macnamara, Henry Valentine *331*
Macneale, Margaret *347*
McNee, Roy *302*
MacNeil of Barra, The *393*
Maconchy, George *342*
Macpherson, Ewen *381*
Macpherson-Grant, Sir George *274*, *284*, *290*, *360*, *371*, *378*
Mactaggart, John and Sandy *394*
Madden, John *323*
Maddock, Rev W.H. 170
Madge, Sidney 22, 24, 26, 28, 72, 403, 406, 410
MAFF (Ministry of Agriculture Fisheries and Food, now DEFRA) 15, 139, 210, 214–15, 413
 subsidies 4, 12, 140, 187, 402
Magan, Michael 342
Magna Carta 21, 53, 59
Magnier, John and Clem 350
Mahathir bin Mohamad 60
Mahony, Richard 336
Maiden Bradley 117, 126
Mail on Sunday Rich Report (Rachel Oldroyd) 116, *135*, *136*, *356*, *357*
Mainwaring, Townshend 310, *370*
Major, John 19, 20, 68, 112, 188, 228, 252, 344
al-Maktoum, Sheik Mohammed bin Rashid *296*, *379*, *387*, *391*
Malcolm, John *272*, *361*, *372*
Malcolm-Douglas, Miss *297*
Malim, Beverley Jane *294*, *380*
Malone, John 352
Manchester, Dukes of 105, 242
 acreage and value of land *107*, *321*
 Angus George Drogo Montague, 12th Duke of 116
 as Plantagenets 124, *132*, *136*
Manchester, Greater 99, 100

Manners, Baron *133*
Manners, David Robert Charles, 11th Duke of Rutland 114, 233, 244
Mansfield, Earls of
   7th Earl of 290
   8th Earl of 290, 294
   acreage and value of land *158, 278, 280, 294*
   in Land Lists *366, 381, 392*
   William David Mungo James Murray, 8th Earl of *78, 81*
Manvers, Earls of *251, 365, 368*
Mao Zedong, Chairman People's Republic of China 10
maps
   acreage, dwellings and population (1872 & 2001) *7*
   of counties (1872 & 2001) *224–5, 268–9, 319, 328*
   of London *see* Lloyd, John
   parish *see* tithe maps
Mar, Captain A.A. Ramsay of *382, 392*
Mar and Kellie, Earls of *278*
Mar, Margaret, Countess of 108, 301
March and Kinrara, Earls of *259*
March, Mortimer, Roger, Earl of 122
Margadale, Baron *380, 385, 391*
Margadale, Lord 68, 262
   James Ian Morrison, 2nd Lord 272
Margaret, Princess 69
Margaret, Princess of France 127
marine estate of Crown Estate 60, 78–80, *79, 80, 81*
Marjoriebanks, Lady *275*
Markiavitz, Countess Constance 349
Marlay, Charles Brinsley *352*
Marlborough, Alfred of 240
Marlborough, Duchess of 117
Marlborough, Dukes of *107*
   John George Vanderbilt Henry Spencer-Churchill, 11th Duke of 117–18, 252
Marry, Jack 343
Martinstown Stud 341
Mary I 126, 400
Mary II 400
Marylebone 152, 153
Maryon Wilson family *159*
Maryon Wilson, Rev Canon Sir George 156
Maryon Wilson, Sir Hubert Guy 156
Maryon Wilson, Spencer *158*
Maryon Wilson estate 156, *158, 159, 160, 162*
Masserene and Ferrard, Viscount *320, 343, 393*
Massey, Haworth Peel *308*
Massey, Hugh Hamon John Somerset Massey, 9th Baron 340
Massy, Lord *340, 341* 376
Master of Common Pleas 43
Master of the Horse 67, 115, 116, 135, 151
Master of Queen's Household 272
Master of the Rolls 172
Master, Thomas William *238*
Matheson, Lady 63, *204, 296, 359, 371, 377*

Matheson, Sir Alexander, Baronet *296, 371, 377*
Matheson, Lady James *301*
Matilda, Empress 122
Maud, Princess 110
Maule, Hon Mrs Elizabeth *271*
Maxwell, Barry Owen Somerset, 12th Lord Farnham 68, 330
Maxwell, Sir Herbert Eustace, Baronet *303*
Maxwell, Sir John Stirling 141
Maxwell, Peter, 28th Baron De Ros 346
Maxwell, Robert 71
Maxwell, Sir William Stirling *295*
Mayfair 18, 118, 119, 148, 149, 152, 172, 192
Mayo 47, 191, 192, *193*, 326, **344**
Mead, Noel 345
Meade, Hon Robert Henry *322, 374*
Meath, Earls of *354*
   John 'Jack' Anthony Brabazon, 15th Earl of *383*, 354, *388*
Meath 191, *193*, 202, **345**
media
   censorship 86
   and Crown Estate 74
   suppression of *Return of Owners of Land* not noticed 55–6
   see also press
Meikleour 202
Melbury estate 148
Melford Hall 66
Mellerstain 275
Melville, I. Hamish *381*
Menabilly 90, 231
Menzies, Sir Robert, Baronet *294, 360, 372, 378*
Menzies, Sir Stuart 68, 115
Meols 244
Merionethshire **313**
Merseyside 99, 100, 101
Merthyr, Trevor Oswin Lewis, 4th Baron 316
Meux, Sir Henry, Baronet 262
Mey, Castle of 271
Meynell-Ingram, Hon Mrs *366*
Mgilhenny family 333
Middlesex *164*, 191, 192, **247**
Middleton, 7th Viscount 49
Middleton, Lord *251*, 265
   acreage 296
   in Land Lists (1872) *360, 365, 367, 378*
Middleton Park *247, 252, 312, 352*
Midlothian 76, 289, **289**
Milford, Hugo John Lawrence Phillips, 3rd Baron 306
Milford, Wogan Phillips, 2nd Baron
Miller, J. *278*
Miller, Jane 111
Miller, John *293*
Miller, M.C. 285
Miller, Robert 264, *381, 385, 387*
Millichope estate 254
Millman, John 299
Mills, Mr and Mrs Brian 330
Mills, Sir Charles, Baronet 247
Milne-Home, David *275*
Mingay, G.E. 37, 403, 404, 405, 408

Ministries and government Departments
   of Agriculture, Environment and Fisheries 180
   of Agriculture Fisheries and Food *see* DEFRA; MAFF
   of Agriculture, Irish 195, 197, 402, 412
   of Agriculture, Scottish *147*, 178
   of Culture, Media and Sport, Secretary of State for 170, 172
   of Defence 16, 86, 89, 139–40, **145–7**, 208, 403
      acreage and value of land *18, 139, 145, 147*
      housing sold 145, 212
      in Scotland *178, 180*
   of Environment 82
   of Environment, Food, Rural Affairs and Agriculure *see* DEFRA
   of Environment, Transport and Regions 9, 12, 402
   of Heritage 402
   of Trade and Industry 172
   see also Ministry of Defence
Minterne House 235, *347*
Minto, Earls of *297*
Mistress of the Robes 67, 117
Mitchell, Alexander, heirs of *289*
Mitchell, Nora Ann 342
Mochrum Park 303
Moir, John *278*
Molesworth 90
Moleyns, Barons of 130
   Andrew Wesley Daubeney de, 8th Lord Ventry 191, 336
Moloney family 338
Moloney, Elie and Richie 338
Moloney, Major William Wills *331*
Molyens, Andrew Wesley Daubeney de, 8th Lord Ventry 191, 336
Molyneux, Rev. Sir *374*
Monaghan 192, *193*, **346**
monarchy *see* royalty
monasteries 22, 154
   dissolved and land taken 22–3, 166–8, 182, 411
   see also Catholicism
Monckton, Edward, Viscount *253*
Moncton, Sir Walter 86
Monmouthshire 75, 143, *164*, 222, **314**, 410
Monson, John, 11th Baron 246
Monson, Sir Thomas 246
Montague, Andrew 265, *365*
Montague, Angus George Drogo, 12th Duke of Manchester 116
Montague, Lord Henry Pole 123
Montague-Scott, Walter John Francis Douglas *see under* Buccleuch and Queensbury
Monteagle *see* Browne, Jeremy
Montfort, Simon de 94, 103
Montgomery, Sir David, Baronet 286
Montgomery, Sir Graham, Baronet 286, *293*
Montgomery, Mr *374*
Montgomeryshire 304, **315**
Montrose, 1st Earl of 112

INDEX   439

Montrose, 5th Earl of 300
Montrose, Dukes of *40*
  6th Duke of 276
  acreage and value of land *107*, *281*, *294*, *300*
  James Graham, 8th Duke of 105, 112, 300
  in Land Lists (1872) *360*, *371*, *378*
Montrose, Marquesses of 112
Mooney of the Doone, Robert Enright 347
Moore, Arthur *350*
Moore, Barrington 413
Moran, Christopher *161*, *380*, *386*
  acreage and value of London land *161*, *162*
Moray, Earls of
  acreage and value of land *290*, *294*
  Douglas John Moray Stuart, 20th Earl of 290
  in Land Lists (1872) *283*, *290*, *361*, *372*
  in Land Lists (2001) *393*
Moray, William of 301
Moray (Elgin in 1872) *76*, **290**
Moreton Corbet 254
Morgan, Hon Mrs Deane *353*
Morris, Charles John *315*
Morrison, Charles *227*, *272*, *361*
Morrison, James 68
Morrison, James Ian, 2nd Lord Margadale 272
Morrison, Hon Mary 68
Morrison, Mr *367*
Morrison, Sir Peter 68
Morrison, Walter *265*
Morrison-Townshend, Hon Charlotte 18
Mortain, Count Robert of 84
Mortlock, E.J. *229*
Morton, Earls of *272*, *289*, *362*, *372*
Mosley, Sir Oswald 111
Mostyn, Llewellyn Roger 311
Mostyn, Sir Pyres William, Baronet 311
Mostyn, Roger Edward Lloyd Lloyd, 5th Baron 311
Mouat Cameron, Major Thomas *299*
Mount Charles, Earls of 202, 243
  Henry Vivian Pierpoint Conyngham *333*, *345*
Mount Ievers Court 331
Mount Kennedy 354
Mount Stuart *273*, *276*, *312*
Mount-Edgcumbe, Earls of *231*
Mountgarret, Viscounts of *338*, *382*, *392*
  Richard Butler, 17th Viscount 338
Mowbray, 6th Lord 128
Mowbray and Stoughton, Baron *133*
Muchland and Torver, Manor of *75*
Mulholland, John *322*, *374*
Mullins, William and Pat 329
Municipal Reform League 152, 157
  see also Lloyd, John
Munro, George *279*
Munster 191, *192*, *193*
Murdach Tireach, King of Ireland 348
Murdoch, John 40

Murdoch, Rupert 60, 71
Mure, Colonel William *295*
Murphy, Michael 332
Murphy, Patrick Edward *352*
Murray, David *388*
Murray, Rev D.H. 170
Murray, George Ian Murray, 10th Duke of Atholl 110, 294
Murray, John 110
Murray, Lt Colonel John *300*
Murray, John, 11th Duke of Atholl 294
Murray, Sir John, Baronet *298*
Murray, John, of Touchadam and Polmaise 244
Murray, Lady Malvina Dorothea 290
Murray, William David Mungo James, Earl of Mansfield 78, 81
Murray-Dunlop, Eliza Esther *287*
Murray-Stewart, Horatio Granvile *203*, *287*, *333*, *360*, *375*
Musgrave, Christopher Shane 351
Musgrave, James and John *333*
Musgrave, Sir Richard, Baronet *232*, *261*
Musgrave, Sir Richard James, 7th Baronet 351
Musgrave, Sir Richard John, 7th Baronet 351
Musters, John Chaworth *251*
Myddleton-Biddulph, Richard *310*
Myerscough estate 96
Mynors Baskerville, Robert *317*
Mynors Baskerville, Water Thomas *317*

Naesmyth, Sir James, Baronet *293*
Nairnshire **291**
Napier and Ettrick, Lord *298*
Napoleon III 113
National Asset Register 406
National Coal Board *139*, *178*
National Farmers Union 82, 207
National Parks 89, 97, 146
National River Authority 82
National Trust 16, *18*, *139*, *147*, 203, 215, 403
nationalisation of land, threat of 77, 181
Navestock *255*
Naworth Castle 232
Naylor, John *315*, *370*
Neal, Mr *161*
Neats Court estate *75*
Neave, Sir Thomas Lewis Arundel, Baronet *305*
Needham, Rt Hon Sir Richard, 6th Earl of Kilmorey 322
Needwood estate and forest 97
Neeld, Sir John, Baronet *262*
Neeld, Mr *160*
Neidpath, Lord *283*
Neil, Andrew 60
Nesbitt, Alexander *330*
Nesbitt, Catherine Downing *324*
Net National Income *395*, *396*
Nevill, Cicely 122
Nevill, Isabel 122
Nevill, Ralph, Earl of Westmoreland 122

Nevill, Richard, Earl of Westmoreland 122
Neville, Caroline 237
Neville, Robin Henry Charles, 10th Baron Braybrooke *131*, 237
New Forest 73, 141
New River estate 157, *159*
Newbattle Abbey *289*, *297*
Newborough, Lords *307*, *310*, *369*, *393*
  7th and 8th Barons 307
Newbridge House 334
Newcastle, Dukes of *107*, 130, *251*, *364*
Newdegate, Charles *247*
Newport, Viscount *254*
Newquay 90
Newry and Mourne, Robert Needham, Viscount 322
Newton, George *229*
Newton, Philip Jocelyn *329*
Newton Park estate 87
Niall the Great, King of Ireland Prince of Tir Owen 320
Nicholson, Charles *345*
Nicholson, Emma, Baroness 66
Nicholson, Sir Godfrey 66
Nicholson, Pauline Ogilvie Grant *380*, *392*
Nicolson, James *285*
Nisbet-Hamilton, Lady Mary *282*
NNI (Net National Income) *395*, *396*
Noble, Hugh *279*
Nomura Corporation 145, 212
non-landowners
  in House of Lords 107
  and *Return of Owners of Land* 206–7, *206*
    omitted 44–5
Norfolk (county) 67, *75*, 116–17, 146, *164*, **248**
  Sandringham 16, *61*, 64–5
Norfolk, Dukes of 23, 43, *131*, *136*, 157, *159*, 199, 227, *259*, *265*, *287*
  1st and 3rd Dukes of 127
  2nd Duke of 128
  4th Duke of 127, 128, 152
  13th Duke of 116
  acreage and value of land *107*, *160*, *162*
  in Land Lists (187?) *358*, *364*, *368*
  in Land Lists (2001) *380*, *384*, *389*, *392*
  Major General Miles Francis Stapleton Fitzalan Howard, 17th Duke of 105, 115, 128, 155, *259*, 265
  as Plantagenets 124
Norman Conquest 20–2
Normanby, Constantine Edmund Walker Phipps, 5th Marquess of *264*, *384*, *389*, *394*
Normanton, Earls of *239*
  in Land Lists (1872) *365*, *368*
  Shaun James Christian Welbore Ellis Agar, 6th Earl of 239
Normanton Park *246*, *253*
Norris, John 82
North, Hon William *229*
North Yorkshire *see* Yorkshire

Northampton, Earls of 97, *159*
Northampton, Marquesses of
    acreage and value of London land *160, 162*
    in Land Lists 358, *381, 384, 389, 392*
    Spencer Douglas David Compton, 7th Marquess of 249, 258, 260
    Vice Admiral *249, 286*
Northamptonshire 97, *164*, **249**
Northbrook (Barings) estate 157, *158*
Northcliffe, Alfred Charles Harmsworth, 1st Viscount 71
Northern Ireland 102, 139, 151, **318–25**
    agricultural holdings and acreage 7, *11, 13, 15*
        breakdown by size *17*
        rental rare *15*
    church in 174
    counties *see under* counties
    housing/domestic dwellings 7, *11, 13*
    in Land Lists *373–4*
    land use structure, basic *9*
    Ministry of Defence in 145
    population 7, *11*
    top landowners in *373–4*
    total acreage *357*
    'uninhabitable' *16*
Northumberland 146, *164*, 207, **250**
Northumberland, Duchess of 106
Northumberland, Dukes of 18, *40*, 135, 202
    11th Duke of 111, 250
    12th Duke *see* Percy, Ralph George
    acreage and value of land *18, 107, 200, 201*
    in Land Lists (1872) *359, 363, 367, 377*
    in Land Lists (2001) *379, 383, 388, 391*
    as Plantagenets 124, *125, 131, 135, 136*
Northumberland, Earls of
    6th Earl *126*
    Henry de Percy, Earl of 125–6
    Sir Hugh Smithson (later Percy) *126*
    Percy, Earl of 23
    Thomas de Percy *126*
Northwick, Lord *247, 253*
Northwick Park *247, 253*
Norton-Taylor, Richard 410, 411
Noseley Hall 245
Notting Hill 148
Nottingham, De Mowbray, 1st Earl of 128
Nottinghamshire *75, 85, 165*, **251**
Nugent, Sir John, 7th Baronet, Count of Austrian Empire 145, 146, 352
Nutting, Sir Anthony *393*

Oakeley, William Edward *313*
Oakly Park (Shropshire) 254, *263, 312*
O'Brien, Conor, 18th Baron Inchquin *331*
O'Brien, Gillian *345*
O'Brien, Horace Stafford *331*
O'Brien, Rory *332*

O'Brien, Susan *350*
O'Brien, Vincent *350*
O'Brien, William Smith 192
Ochtery, John, 6th Cameron chief *284*
O'Connell, Daniel *336*
O'Connell, Sir Maurice James *336*
O'Connell, Sir Maurice MacCarthy, 7th Baronet *336*
O'Connor, Peter *349*
O'Conor Don, Desmond O'Conor Don, The 348
O'Conor Don, The *348*, *349*
Octavia Hill 172
Offaly (King's County) 193, 326, **347**
    Earl of *337*
Ogilby, Robert Alexander *324*
Ogilvie-Grant, Ian Derek Francis, 13th Earl of Seafield 85, 141, 274, *284, 284*
Ogilvie-Grant Nicholson, Pauline *380, 392*
Ogilvy, Sir Angus 68
Ogilvy, David George Coke Patrick, 13th Earl of Airlie 66, 67, 68, *78, 212, 271*
Ogilvy, Donald *271*
Ogilvy, Sir James *271*
Ogilvy, Sarah *271*
Ogmore 97
O'Hagan, Lord 25
O'Hara, Charles William *349*
Okehampton 89
O'Kelly, Major E. *345*
O'Kelly, Patricia *345*
Old Cullen *274*
Oldbridge estate *343*
Oldroyd, Rachel *see Mail on Sunday*
Oliphant, Captain Lawrence *286*
Oliver-Rutherfurd, William *297*
Olney 97
Olsen, Fred *287*
Olson, Mancur 20, 22, 70, 71, *403, 405, 406*
O'Malley, Raymond *343*
Onassis, Aristotle 117
O'Neill, Domhnel Oge *320*
O'Neill, Hug-Boy, Yellow *320*
O'Neill, Hugh, Prince of Tir Owen *320*
O'Neill, Hugh Dubh, King of Ulster *320*
O'Neill, Raymond Arthur Clanaboy, 4th Baron *320*, *385*, *394*
O'Neill, Rev. Lord *320, 362, 366, 373*
O'Neill, Shane *320*
O'Neill of the Maine *320*
Onslow, Michael William Coplestone Dillon Onslow, 7th Earl of 258
Open Access Bill 9
Oppenheim Eisken, J.N. *381*
Orde, Sir John *284*
Order in Council (1898) *401*
O'Reilly, Sir Tony *201*
Orford, Earls of *248*
Orkney **292**
Ormathwaite, Lord *369, 317*
Orme, R.W. *349*
Ormonde, Marquesses of *338, 350, 376*
    James Butler *338*

Ormonde and Ossory, Earls of *338*
Ormsby Gore, Francis David, 6th Lord Harlech *340*
Ormsby Gore, William *349*
Ormskirk 244
Orr, James *278*
Orr-Ewing, Archibald *300*
Ossory, Bishop of *329*
Osterley Park 247
Oswald, Richard Alexander *287*
Otterburn 146
Overstone, Lord *228*, 249, *364*
Overstone Park *228*, 249
Oxenfoord Castle *273*, *303*
Oxford Street and New Oxford Street 149, 153
Oxford University and Colleges 49, 53, 67, *158*, 173
Oxfordshire 4, *75*, 127, *165*, **252**
Oxshott estate *75*

Pack-Beresford, Denis Robert *329*
Packenham, Tom, 8th Earl of Longford *352*
Packenham-Mahon, Henry *376*
Padstow 90
Paget, George Henry Victor, 7th Marquess of Anglesey 256, *305, 305*
Paisley, Rev Ian 174
Pakenham, Rev. Arthur Hercules *320, 374*
Pakenham, Hon E.M. *261*
Pakenham-Mahon, Henry Sandford *348*
Palatine county, Lancashire as *see* Duchy of Lancaster
Palliser, John *351*
Palmer, Major Sir Anthony Frederick Mark 69
Palmer, Sir Richard *203*
Palmer, Lieutenant General Sir Roger William, Baronet 191, *334, 344, 349, 360, 375, 378*
Palmerston, Henry John Temple, 3rd Viscount 31
Panshanger *226, 241*
parishes *see under* Church of England
Parker, Harriett *330*
Parker, Hon Sir Jonathan Frederick 100
Parker-Jervis, Hon Edward Swynfen 256
Parliament 27–8
    Act (1911) 54
    acts of *see* legislation
    and Duchy of Lancaster 95
    European 25
    history of 23, 24, 25, 27, 28, 85
    and Plantagenets 124–5, 126, 128
    see also Commonwealth; House of Commons; House of Lords; Scottish Parliament
Parlon, Tom *347*
Parnell, Charles Stewart 30
Parsons, William Brendan, 7th Earl of Rosse *347*
Paterson, William and Jean *286*
Patshull estate *75*
Paul, Leslie 174
Pawton estate 87

INDEX   441

Peacock, Sir Edward 86
Peacock House 148
Peak District National Park 146
Pears, David and Trevor *383*, *388*
Pears, Mark *161*, *162*, *383*, *388*
Pearson of Rannoch, Lord 294
Peat, Michael 100
Peeblesshire **293**
Peel, 3rd Earl of 91
Peel, Edmund *311*
peers
   life 105
   ranks explained 129–30
   see also House of Lords
Pembroke and Montgomery, Earls of 227
   Henry George Charles Alexander Herbert, 17th Earl of 262
   in Land Lists *364*, *368*, *385*, *390*
Pembrokeshire 146, **316**
Pencalenick estate 88
Penn House 228
Penrhyn, 6th Baron 307
Penrhyn, Lord *203*, *307*, *364*, *369*
Penrhyn Castle 307
Penrith, Lord Howard of 128
Penshurst Place 243
pension funds 18
   see also Ropemaker
Penton estate and family 157, *159*
'People's Budget'(1909) 53–4
Perceval-Maxwell, Mr *374*
Percy, Barons of 125, 202
   Henry de, 3rd Baron (later Earl of Northumberland) 125
   William de, 1st Baron 125
Percy, Earls of 23, 111, 126, 250
   Henry de Percy, Earl of Northumberland 125–6
Percy, Elizabeth (Smithson) 126
Percy, Sir Hugh (Smithson), 7th Duke of Somerset 126
Percy, Ralph George Algernon, 12th Duke of Northumberland 18, 108, 111, 201, 246, 247, 250, 258, 275
Percy, Thomas de, Earl of Northumberland 126
Perry-Herrick, Mrs *245*
Perthshire 62, 179, 191, 202, **294**
Peterborough *160*, *166*
Petersham, Viscount *383*, *160*, *162*, *341*, *389*
Petre, Hon Dominic William 237
Petre, John Patrick Lionel Peter, 18th Baron *132*, *237*, *385*, *389*, *394*
Petre, Lord *237*
Petty-Fitzmaurice, George Nairne, 8th Marquess of Lansdowne 91, 202
Petworth House *203*, *232*, *259*, *265*, *331*
Phibbs, William *349*
Philip IV of France 85
Philip the Hardy of France 127
Philip, Prince, Duke of Edinburgh 63, 65, 88, 104, 120
Philipshaugh 298
Phillips, Charles Edward Gregg *316*, *369*
Phillips, John Frederick Lort *316*
Phillips, Wogan 306

Phipps, Constantine Edmund Walker
   see Normanby
Piccadilly 152
Picknett, Lynn *407*
Pimlico 118, 152
planning restrictions 12
Plantagenet, Edmund, Earl of Lancaster 97, 99
Plantagenet, Edward, Earl of Lancaster 94
Plantagenet, Princess Elizabeth 122
Plantagenet, Hamelin 125
Plantagenet, Henry, 1st Duke of Lancaster 94
Plantagenet, Lady Mary 125
Plantagenet, Richard 85
Plantagenet, Thomas, Earl of Lancaster 94
Plantagenet inheritance **121–36**, 211, 399, 408–9
   in 1872 and today 27, 129–35, 202, 314
      extinct since 1872 *133*
      survivors, list of *131–3*
   acreages 124, *131–3*
   families 125–9
      largest group *see* Howard
   and House of Lords 124, 126–7, 130, *131–3*
   kings 121–3
   power after throne 123–5
   War of Roses 95, 122
   wealth *136*
   see also Northumberland, Duke of
Plas Meigan 305
Plas Newydd 305
Plunket family *343*
Plymouth, Robert Ivor Windsor Clive, 3rd Earl of 254
Plynlimon estate 76
Pochin, William Ann *245*
Poer, Count Edmond de la *351*
Pollock, John Broom *295*, *335*
Polmaise Castle *300*
Poltimore, Lord *234*
Pontefract Castle 94
Pontypool Park 314
population 11, 26, 206
   map of (1872 & 2001) 7
   see also under Ireland
Porritt, 1st Baron 214
Porritt, Sir Jonathan, Baronet 214
Portal, Melville 239
Portarlington, Earls of *339*
Porter, Mr *373*
Porter, Rev John Grey *323*, *342*
Porter, Dame Shirley 277
Portland, Dukes of 111, *159*, 200–1, *233*, *251*
   4th Duke of 152
   7th Duke of 202, 251
   9th Duke of 202
   acreage and value of land *18*, *107*, *160*, *200*, 201–2, *273*, *277*
   in Land Lists (1872) *359*, *363*, *367*, *377*
   Net National Income *396*
Portland/Howard de Walden estate 152–3, *159*, *160*, *162*
Portman, Lord Chief Justice 153

Portman, Viscounts of 18, *159*, *255*
   1st Viscount 153
   7th and 9th Viscounts 240
   10th Viscount 153, 240, 255
   in Land Lists *365*, *383*, *388*
Portman estate 153, *158*, *159*, *162*
Portman Settled Estates Ltd 153
Portsmouth, Earls of *234*, *239*
   in Land Lists *368*, *385*, *390*
   Quentin Gerard Carew Wallop, 10th Earl of 239
Portsmouth, Louise de Keroualle, Duchess of 109
Pott, George *298*
Poulett, Earls of *255*
Poulteney, Sir John 154
Poulteney, Sir William 154
Powderham Castle 91, 129, *234*, *341*
Powell, G. *203*, *369*
Powell, George Ernest John *308*
Powell, W.E *306*
power of land 26–8, 208–10
Powerscourt, Viscounts of 353, *353*, *354*
   8th Viscount *345*
   in Land Lists (1872) *375*
   Mervyn Niall Wingfield, 10th Viscount 354
Powis, Earls of *254*
   4th Earl of 315
   acreage *203*
   John George Herbert, 8th Earl of 315
   in Land Lists (1872) *362*, *364*, *369*
   in Land Lists (2001) *381*, *384*, *389*, *392*
Powis Castle *254*, 315
Powlett, Richard *see* Bolton
Powys 75
   see also Brecknock; Merionethshire; Montgomeryshire; Radnorshire
Powys-Keck, Harry Leycester *245*
Poynder, Sir *160*
Poynings estate 75
Pratt, Mervyn *330*
press 55, 148, 180, 196, 357, 419
   censorship 86
   and House of Lords 104, 106, 116
   major papers *see Financial Times*; *Sunday Times*
   and royalty and royal land 39–40, 49, 55, 71, 86
Preusen, Princess Antonia von 119
Price, Richard John Lloyd *203*, *313*, *369*
Price-Lloyd, T. *313*
prices
   price-earnings ratio 79, 88–9
   see also value
Prickard, Mrs M.M. *317*
Prime Minister 31, 105, 288
   and Church of England 171
   former, peerage offered to 105–6
   and Ireland 190
   Lloyd George 8, 25, 53, 54, 140, 316
   major *see* Blair; Major; Thatcher, Margaret

see also Gladstone, Rt Hon
  William Ewart; Rosebery
primogeniture, male 409
Prince, Clive 407
Prince of Wales Trust 82
Princes of Wales 19
  Edward VII as 61, 62, 64
  Edward of Woodstock 85, 122
  see also Charles, Prince
Pringle, Lady E. 275
Pringle, James 298
Pringle Pattison, Ann 298
Prior, Stephen 407
Private Woodland Owners Woodland
  Grant Scheme 142
privatisation
  acreage *139*
  Forestry Commission 140–1, 144,
    145
  secrecy about 138–9, 140–1
  suggestions about royal land 77–8,
    92, 154
  of utilities 143
Privy Council 105, 156, 174, 209
Property Investment Forum 14
Property Market Report *13*, 358
Prowse, Michael 406
Prudential Insurance land bought 88,
  89, 90
Pryse, Sir Pryse, Baronet *308*, 369
Public Records Office 54
Pugh, David *309*
Pugh, L.P. *308*
Pugsley, John 91
Purdy, Frederick 39
Putteridge estate 75
Puxley, Mr 369

Queen Anne's Bounty 169
Queens *see* Anne, Queen; Elizabeth II;
  Elizabeth, Queen Mother; Victoria
  and under royalty
Queens County *see* Laois
Queensbury, Marquesses of *280*
Quinn, Geoffrey *see* Raymond, Paul

Raby Castle 236, 254
Radicals *see* Bright
Radnorshire 304, **317**
  Earls of Radnor *161, 162,* 262,
    385
Raglan, Fitzroy John Somerset, 5th
  Lord 314
railways *see* utilities
Rainsford-Hannay, R.W. 287
Raleigh estate 222, 358
Ramsay, James Hubert, 17th Earl of
  Dalhousie 78, 271
Ramsay, John 272
Ramsay, Robert Balfour Wardlaw 278
Ramsay-Gibson-Maitland, Sir James,
  Baronet, *300*
Ramsbury Manor 227, *233*
Ramsden, Sir John, Baronet *359, 363,
  367, 377*
  acreage *200,* 202
Ramsey, Archbishop Arthur Michael
  171, 175
Ramsey, John Fellowes, 4th Baron de
  82, 229, 242, *385, 389, 394*

Rannoch, Lord Pearson of 294
Rashleigh, Jonathan *231*
Rashleigh, Sir Richard Harry, 6th
  Baronet 90, 231, *385*
Rashleigh estate 90
Rathbarry Stud 332
Rathbeal Hall 334
Rathdrum estate 354
Rausing, Hans and Kirsten *387*
Raven, Andrew 143
Raven family *380*
Rayleigh, John Gerald Strutt, 6th
  Baron 237
Raymond, Debbie 157
Raymond, Paul *383,* 387
  Soho estate 157, *159, 160, 162*
Reade, Sir Chandos Stanhope
  Hoskyns, Baronet *305*
Reade, Sir Kenneth Ray, 13th Baronet
  305
Reay, Lord 78
Receiver General 91, 100
Red Hill 305
Redesdale, 2nd Baron 111
Redesdale, Earls of *250*
Redlynch 235, *255*
Redmond, Lynette 321
Rees Mogg, Lord 412
Reform Act (1832) 55
Reform Act (1867) 29, 55
reform of land ownership system *see*
  land reform
Regent Street 80–1, 148–9
Regent's Park 149
registration of title *see* Land Registry
Registry of Deeds (Ireland) 326
religion *see* Catholicism; Church of
  England
Rendlesham, Lord 257
Renfrewshire **295**
rental/tenancy 398
  agricultural land *15,* 188, 190,
    207–8
  housing 11
Republic *see* Cromwell, Oliver; Ireland
residential land *see* housing/domestic
  dwellings
Residential Property Report 402
Restoration (1660) 24, 25
Retail Prices Index 395
Return of Owners of Land (1872)
  3–4, 6, **29–57,** 204, 396, 404–5
  accuracy, errors and omissions 25,
    34–5, 45, 50
    90–95% accurate 55
    double counting 51–2
  Bateman on *see under* Bateman,
    John
  Brodrick's criticisms of 49–53, 168
  buried *see* suppressed *below*
  and Church of England 163,
    165–6, 168, 169, 170–1
  compilation of 34–8
  creation of 30–4
    recommended 8
  disappearance *see* suppressed
    below
  and Duchy of Cornwall 85
  and House of Lords 104, 105
  and institutional landowners 138

interpretation 41–8
  see also under Bateman
Land Lists 359–78
legacy of 54–7
and London 152
map of acreage, dwellings and
  population 7
non-landownership 206–7, *206*
and Plantagenets 130, *131–3*
publication of 38–41
reasons for 8
rental income, calculation of 35–7
and royalty 58
and Scotland 179, 180–2, 184
suppressed 5, 10, 19, 26, 48–54,
  139, 209–10
  never republished 22
waste and common land 37–8, 45,
  51
see also counties; Land Lists (1872)
Return of Owners of Land for Ireland
  (1876) 191, 194
Revelstoke, Lord 69
Rhodes, Cecil 110
Rhodes, Hon Margaret 69
Rice-Watkins, Major 370
Rich Lists 19
  *see also Mail on Sunday; Sunday
    Times* Rich List; top landowners
Richard I 155–6, 399
Richard II 94, 399
Richard III 122, 399
Richardson, H.G. 403
Richardson, Thomas *324,* 373
richest people
  ever in England 125
  two (2001, Sainsbury *and*
    Westminster) 103, 135, 199
  see also top landowners; wealth
Richmond, Dukes of 16, 32–3, 40,
  124, *131,* 135
Richmond and Gordon, Dukes of 259
  acreage and value of land *107,*
    200, 201, 270, 274, 290
  Charles Henry Gordon Lennox,
    10th Duke of 109, *136,* 201, 259
  in Land Lists (1872) *359, 363,
    367, 377*
  in Land Lists (2001) *384*
Riddell, Sir Thomas Miles, Baronet
  272
Ridley, George 151
Ridley, Matthew White, 4th Viscount
  67, *250*
Ridley, Michael Kershaw 100
Ridley, Nicholas (later Lord Ridley) 67
rights *see* human rights
Ripon 50, *166*
  Marquess of *265*
Riverdale, Barons of 283
roads, acreage of 9
Robartes, Lord *231*
Robert de Stafford 256, 310
Robert III, King of Scotland 295, 300
Robertson, Barbara 299
Roborough, Henry Massey Lopes, 3rd
  Baron 234, *380, 386, 392*
Robson, Hon Maurice *381*
Roch, William Francis 316
Rochfort-Boyd, George Augustus 352

Rockwell College 359
Roden, Earls of *343*
Roesner, H. *382*
Roger, Alan and N. *381*
Roger de Hesilrige 245
Roger de Mowbray 128
Roger of Wendover 21, 23
Rogers, Charles Coltman *317*
Rogerson, James Alexander *280*
Rohan, Kenneth 334
Roland de Sutton 235
Rolle, Hon Mark George Kerr *234*, *365*, *367*
Rolls, John Allan *314*
Romanoff family 113
Romney Marsh estate 75
Romsey 27
Ropemaker (BP-Amoco pension fund) 148, 149, 153
Roper family 229
Roscommon *193*, **348**
Rose, Rev Hugh *291*
Rose, Major James *291*
Roseberry, Neil Archibald Primrose, 7th Earl of 289, *289*, 293, 302
    in Land Lists (2001) *385*, *390*, *393*
Rosebery of Dalmeny, Earl of *302*
Ross & Cromarty 226, 266, 404
    Ross-shire *179*, **296**
Ross, Sir Charles William Augustus, Baronet 63, *204*, *296*, *301*, *359*, *371*, *377*
Ross, Colonel George *279*
Ross, Robert 91
Rossborough-Colclough, Anne *353*
Rosse, Earls of *347*
    3rd Earl of *347*
    William Brendan Parsons, 7th Earl of *347*
Rossmore, Lord *346*
Rossmore, William Warner Westenra, 7th Baron *346*
Ross-shire *see under* Ross & Cromarty
Rothermere, Viscounts of
    Harold Sidney Harmsworth, 1st Viscount 69
    2nd Viscount 69
    4th Viscount 69, 71, 87
Rothes estate 290
Rothschild family 152, 161n
Rothschild, Baron *385*, *388*
    acreage and value of London land *161*, *162*
Rothschild, Sir Evelyn de 228
Rothschild, Lionel de 173
Rothschild, Nathan 228
Rothschild, Sir Nathaniel, Baronet 228
Rothschild, 4th Lord 228
Rous, Robert Keith, 4th Earl of Stradbroke 257
Rouse-Boughton-Knight, Andrew Johnes *240*
Rowley family 235
Rowley-Conwy, Captain Conwn Grenville Hercules *311*
Rowley-Conwy, Peter Alexander *311*
Roxburghe, Dukes of
    acreage and value of land *107*, *282*, *297*

Guy David Innes-Ker, 10th Duke of 114, 116, 275, *297*
    in Land Lists (1872) *362*, *365*
    in Land Lists (2001) *379*, *384*, *390*, *391*
Roxburghshire **297**
Royal Agricultural Society 64
Royal Chartered Institute of Housing (2001) 7
Royal Ordnance 139
Royal Scottish Forestry Society 178
Royal Society for Protection of Birds 18, *147*, 292
royalty and royal land **58–71**, 209, 403, 405–6
    acreage and value of land *18*, *19*
    and Church of England (head of) 167, 172
    continuance doubted 78
    as greatest landowners in Europe 69–71
    history of 19, 25
    Inner Royal Household 65–9
        Mistress of the Robes 67
        Lord Steward 67
        see also Ladies of the Bedchamber; Lord Chamberlain; Master of the Horse; Women of the Bedchamber
    monarchs list of 399–400
        see also Elizabeth II; Henry VIII; Victoria; William I; William III
    Queen's personal land holdings 61–5
        Balmoral 19, 61–4, *61*, 65, 270
        Delnadamph 19, 63
        Sandringham 16, *61*, 64–5
    Queen's wealth 58, 59–61, 71, 74
    and *Return of Owners of Land* 49
    see also Crown Estate; Duchy of Cornwall; Duchy of Lancaster
RSPB (Royal Society for Protection of Birds) 18, *147*, 292
Rubenstein, William D. 395–6, 410, 411, 413
Rubython, Tom 60
Rufford Abbey *251*, 265
Rug *307*, *313*
Rugby estates 80
Rugby family *139*
Runnymede *see* Magna Carta
Ruoff, T.B.F. 404
Rushcliffe, Lord 87
Russel, Rev George *279*
Russell, Bertrand 113
Russell, Henry Robin, Marquess of Tavistock 113, 134, 135, 226
Russell, John 154
Russell, Lord John 190
Russell, John Robert *see under* Bedford, Dukes of
Rust, William 306
Rutland, Dukes of *229*, *233*
    acreage and value of land *107*
    David Robert Charles Manners, 11th Duke of 114, 233, 244
    in Land Lists (1872) *361*, *363*, *367*

in Land Lists (2001) *381*, *384*, *390*, *392*
    as Plantagenets *124*, *131*, *136*
Rutland *165*, **253**
Rutzen, Baron de *316*
Ryan, Barry Fortune 67
Ryan, Virginia Fortune (Airlie) 67, 68
Ryan, William 341

Sackville, Lionel Bertrand
Sackville-West, 6th Baron 243
Sackville, William Herbrand de la, 11th Earl of Warr 259
Sainsbury, David 103, 135
St Albans 166
St Albans, Dukes of 104, *107*
    Murray de Vere Beauclerk, 14th Duke of 119
St Albans, Henry Jermyn, Lord 155, *159*
St Germans, Earls of *131*, *157*, *158*
St Giles 235
St James 18, 150, 152, 154, 156
    Park 157
St John's Wood 4, 18, 155–6, *159*
    see also Eyre
St Quentin 158
Salisbury, Margaret, Countess of 122, 123
Salisbury, Marquesses of *157*, *159*, *241*
    acreage and value of London land *160*, *162*
    in Land Lists (2001) *384*, *388*
    Robert Arthur Talbot Gascoyne-Cecil, 3rd Marquess of 25, 33
    Robert Edward Peter Gascoyne-Cecil, 6th Marquess of 241
Salisbury 156, *166*
Salisbury Plain 146
Sallymount Stud 337
Salwick estate 96
Samoens Plantagenet 122
Sampson, Anthony 16, 67, 138–9, 403, 405, 409, 410
    on Church of England 167, 169, 411
Sandringham 16, *61*, 64–5
Sangster, Robert *390*
Sasines 178, 398
Saunderson, Edward *330*
Saurin, Mark Anthony *316*
'Save the Countryside' lobby 214
Savernake estate and Forest 75, 262, 265
Savile, Augustus William *251*, 265, *365*
Savoy, manor of 94, 96, 97
Sawbridge-Erle-Drax, John 235
Saxe-Coburg and Gotha, Prince Hubertus of 105
Sayles, G.O. 403
Scarborough, 11th and 12th Earls of 67
Scarsdale, Rev Lord 233
Scarsdale, Francis John Nathaniel Curzon, 3rd Viscount *132*, 233, *386*
schools *see* Ampleforth; Eton

Schroeder, Count Bruno *387*, *393*
Schuster, Hon Mrs L.F. *393*
Schwarzenbach, Urs *381*, *387*
Scilly Isles 85, *88*, 90
Sclater, John Richard 100
Scone Castle and Palace 78, *278*, *280*, *294*
Scotland **176–85**, **266–303**, 412
    acreage and value of land (including agricultural acreage) 7, *11*, *13*, *15*, *17*, *18*, *85*, *107*, *147*
    chroniclers 178–83
        see also Callander; McEwen; Wightman
    clearances 137
    counties see under counties
    Crown Estate in 74, 76, 78–9, 81, 183–4
    Duchy of Cornwall not allowed land in 89
    English landowners with land in 201, 202
    estates over 1000 acres 76
    history of 22, 25
    and House of Lords 108
        dukes in 108–9, 110, 111–12, 114, 118
    housing/domestic dwellings 7, *11*, *13*
    institutional landowners *147*, 409
        Forestry Commission 141–2, 143, *178*, *180*
    and Ireland, comparison with 176, 181, 183, 197
    in Land Lists 371–2
    land use structure, basic 9
    landowners with land in England *204*
    National Trust for 18
    and Plantagenets 27, 129, 409
    population 7, *11*, 206
    royal property in see in particular Balmoral
    self-government 22, 63, 176, 185, 199
    tenure
        redistribution 40, 180–2
        see also under feudal system
    top landowners in *40*, *41*, 62–3, *177*, *179*, 200, *204*, *371–2*
    total acreage *357*
    'uninhabitable' 16
    Westminster land in 18
    see also Return of Owners of Land
Scott, Sir Edward, Baronet *362*
Scott, Hugh *298*
Scott, John 70, *403*, *406*
Scott, John and Wendy *299*
Scott, Sir Richard 68
Scott, Richard Walter John Montague Douglas, Earl of Dalkeith 109
Scott, Robert *299*
Scott, Sir Walter, Baronet 112
Scott, Walter Francis John Montague Douglas 109
Scott-Douglas, Sir Henry George, Baronet *297*
Scottish Landowners Federation 178–9
Scottish Nationalists 185
Scottish Natural Heritage *180*

Scottish Office 139
Scottish Parliament 22, 63, 176, 185
Scourfield, Sir Owen Henry Phillips *316*, *370*
Scropes family 150
Scudamore Lucas, Edward *346*
seabed see marine estate
Seafield, Earls of 18, 63
    acreage and value of land *18*, *204*, *274*, *290*
    Ian Derek Francis Olgivie-Grant, 13th Earl of 85, 141, 274, 284, *284*
    in Land Lists (1872) *359*, *364*, *371*, *377*
    in Land Lists (2001) *379*, *384*, *391*
Seaham Hall *236*, *315*
Sefton, Earls of *244*, *366*
Selby, Walter Charles *250*
Selby-Lowndes, William *228*
Selkirk, Rt Hon Lord James Douglas Hamilton, Earl of 112, *287*, *302*
Selkirkshire 109, *298*
Senior, Nassau William 190
'Seven Hundred 39–40
Seymour, Sir Edward, 1st Duke of Somerset 126
Seymour, Jane 117, 126
Seymour, Lord 117
Sforza, Duchess 106
Shaftesbury, Anthony Ashley Cooper, 10th Earl of *235*
Shakespeare, William 94
Shane Castle 310, *346*
Shaw Stewart, Major Sir Houston Mark, Baronet *295*
Shaw Stewart, H. *295*
Shaw Stewart, Sir William, Baronet *295*
Sheffield, Timothy Stanley 8th Baron Boston 305
Shelbourne, Earls of 91, *294*
Shelbourne, Lady Nicolson of *299*
Shelswell-White family *332*
Shelter 402
Sherborne, Earls of *238*
Sheridan, Richard Brinsley *235*
Sheshoon Stud *337*
Shetland (earlier Zetland) **299**
Shirley, Evelyn *346*
Shoard, Marion 169, 402, 409, 411
Shoeburyness 146
shoreline and foreshore 96
    and Duchy of Cornwall see marine estate
Shrewsbury and Talbot, Earls of *364*
Shropshire 68, *75*, *96*, *165*, *254*
Shugborough Park and Hall 256
Shuttleworth, Charles Geoffrey Nicholas Kay-Shuttleworth, 5th Lord 101
Simpson, Mrs Wallis 86, 87
Sinclair, C. 402
Sinclair, John Archibald, 3rd Viscount *277*
Sinclair, Sir John George Tollemache, Baronet 185, *277*, *361*, *372*
Sinclair, Sir Robert Charles, Baronet *277*
Sion House 247

Sites of Special Scientific Interest 146
Skelmersdale, 2nd Lord (later Earl of Lathom) 43
Skelmersdale, 7th Lord 43
Slane Castle 202
Slazenger family 354
Slazenger, Wendy Anne 354
Sligo, Marquesses of 191, *341*, *344*, *360*, *375*, *378*
    acreage *203*
    Jeremy Ulick Browne, 11th Marquess of 191, 344
Sligo 191, *193*, 326, *349*
Sloane, Elizabeth 153
Sloane, Sir Hans 153
Slough estates 80
Small, James *271*
Smith, Abel *241*
Smith, Lady Abel 69
Smith, Brigadier Sir Alexander Abel 69
Smith, Cecil Woodham 189–90
Smith, D.A. *203*
Smith, Captain (Evan Cadogan) Eric 67
Smith, Goldwin 103
Smith, Goldwyn A. *403*, *407*
Smith-Barry, James Hugh *343*
Smith's Trustees *159*
Smithson, Elizabeth (Elizabeth Percy) 126
Smithson, Sir Hugh (later Percy), 7th Duke of Somerset and Earl of Northumberland 126
Smurfit, Michael 201
Smyth, Sir John Henry Greville, Baronet *255*
Smyth, Thomas James *352*
Soames, Lord 91
Sodor & Man 166
Soho see Raymond
Solicitor General 172
Somerley *239*
Somerleyton, Savile William Francis Crossley, 3rd Baron 67
Somerleyton Hall 67
Somers, Earls of *159*, *240*, *263*
    Somers charity 157, *159*
Somerset, Dukes of 135, 408
    acreage and value of land *107*
    Sir Edward Seymour, 1st Duke of 126
    4th Duke of 126
    Sir Hugh Smithson (later Percy) 7th Duke of 126
    8th Duke of 126
    16th Duke of 126
    as Plantagenets 124, *131*, *136*
Somerset, David Robert, 11th Duke of Beaufort 115, 238, 409
Somerset, Hon Geoffrey 314
Somerset *75*, *88*, *90*, *141*, *153*, *165*, *255*
Somerton, Viscount *239*
Somerville, Sir Robert 94–5
Sondes, Earls of *243*
Soros, George 213, 413
Soughton Hall 311
South Carlton estate 246
South Survey of Duchy of Lancaster 97, 98

INDEX   445

South Uist estates *18*, *147*
South Yorkshire *see* Yorkshire
Southesk, Earls of 110, *271*
Southill Park 226
Sparrow, Charles Acheson, 7th Earl of Gosford 321
Spartlingus, Dean of Whalley 244
Speaker of House of Commons 172
Spectator 39–40, 49
Speirs, Alexander Archibald *295*
Spencer, Earls of 249
 Charles Edward Maurice Spencer, 9th Earl of *131*, 249
 in Land Lists *365*, *384*, *389*
Spencer-Churchill, John George Vanderbilt Henry, 11th Duke of Marlborough 117–18, 252
Spencer-Churchill, Tina, Duchess of Marlborough 117
Speolbergh, Vicompte Adolphe de *393*
Spring, David 31, 39, 41, 42, 44, 49, 404, 405
Sprot, Lt Colonel *293*
Stafford, Earls of *324*
Stafford, Barons 128, 129, *131*
 Francis Melford William Fitzherbert, 15th Baron 256
Staffordshire 4, *36*, 43, *75*, *165*, 170, **256**
Stair, Earls of
 acreage and value of land *273*, *303*
 John David James Dalrymple, 14th Earl *273*, *303*
 in Land Lists (1872) *360*, *364*, *371*, *378*
 in Land Lists (2001) *380*, *392*
Stamford 146
Stamford and Warrington, Earls of *245*, *256*, *364*
Stanhope, Earls of 152, *157*, *159*, *160*
Stanhope, Viscount Petersham *160*, *162*, *341*, *383*, *389*
Stanhope, William Henry Leicester, 11th Earl of Harrington 155, 291, 341
Stanley, Lyulph 39, 49
Stanley, Sir Oliver 122
Stanley, Timothy, 8th Baron of Boston 305
Stanley, Timothy Irby, 10th Baron of Boston 305
Stanley, William Owen *305*
Stansgate, Tony Wedgewood Benn, Viscount 105
Stanton Harcourt 252
Stapleford Abbots estate *75*
Stationery Office 38
Statute Law (Repeals) Act (1998) *402*
Steel, Sir Fiennes Michael Strang 141, 142, 144, 298
Stephen, King 244, *399*
Steuart, Andrew *274*
Steuart-Menzies, William George *294*
Steven, Alasdair 179
Stewart, Sir *373*
Stewart, Alexander John Robert *333*, *375*
Stewart, Lady Arabella 126
Stewart, Sir Archibald, Baronet *294*
Stewart, James *292*

Stewart, John Marcus *325*
Stewart-Beatle, Mary *280*
Stirling, Mary Wedderburn Morries *278*
Stirlingshire *76*, 112, **300**
Stobart, Rev Henry *343*
Stobo Castle *286*, *293*
Stock Exchange/stocks and shares 28, 55, *209*
 and Crown Estate 79–81
 and Duchy of Cornwall 88–9, 90
 and Duchy of Lancaster 93
Stockdale, Lady Louisa 63
Stocks, Major Michael *277*
Stockton, Earls of *388*
 Harold Macmillan, Earl of 105
Stoke Climsland 88
Stoneleigh Abbey 260
Stonor, Ralph Thomas Campion George Sherman, 7th Baron Camoys 3, 5, 8, 66, 252
Stonor Park 3–4, 5, 6, 8
Stopford, James, 9th Earl of Courtown 329, 353
Stopford-Blair, Edward James *303*
Stormont, Viscount *294*
Stourton, Alfred Joseph 128
Stourton, Charles Edward 128
Stowe Gardens and school 228
Stowell Park 238
Stradbroke, Robert Keith Rous, 4th Earl of *257*
Strafford, Earls of *247*
Strand 97
Strange, Barons of 128
Stratfield Saye 239
Strathmore estate 180, *277*
Strathmore and Kinghorn, Earls of 62
 Michael Fergus Bowes Lyon, 18th Earl of *271*, *393*
Strathnaver, Lord Alistair 108
Streatlam Castle *236*, *265*
Strickland, Sir Charles William, Baronet *265*
Stronge, Sir *374*
Strutt, Alexander Ronald George *see* Belper
Strutt, Hon Richard Henry 251
Stuart, Arthur Patrick Avondale, 8th Earl of Castle Stewart *255*, *325*
Stuart, Douglas John Moray, 20th Earl of Moray 290
Stuart, Hon Mrs Flora *303*
Stuart, Viscount *255*, *325*
Stuart Hall *325*
Stubber, Robert Hamilton *339*
Stucley, Sir Hugh George Coplestone Bampfylde, 6th Baronet *234*, *385*, *394*
Style, Sir William Francis, 13th Baronet *333*, *376*
Style, Sir William Henry Marsham, Baronet *333*
subsidies and grants (mainly agricultural) 4, 140, 207, 208, 209, 210, 413
 and Corn Laws 29–30
 and Duchy of Cornwall 85
 EU 12, 181, 187–8, 195–6, *402*, 412

 and Forestry Commission 142
 to Ireland 181, 187–8, 195–6, 205, 207, 412
 and MAFF 4, 12, 140, 187, *402*
 possible termination of 120
 and *Return of Owners of Land* 38, 56, *402*
Sudeley, Lord *238*, 314, *315*, *369*
Sudeley Castle 314
Suffield, Lord *248*
Suffolk 66, 67, 108, *165*, **257**, 401
Suffolk and Berkshire, Earls of 128, *131*, *262*
Sun Alliance 82, 118, 212
Sunday Times: on property developers 14, 403
Sunday Times Rich Lists (1989–2000, Philip Beresford) 8, 21, 49, 213, 403, 413
 biggest landholding *see* Buccleuch
 and Church of England 167, 411
 and England and Inner Empire 201
 and House of Lords 103, *106*, 107
  dukes 109, 111, 114–15, 117, 118, 166
 and institutional landowners 410
 and Land Lists 356, 357
 and London 148, 152, 153
 Net National Income used in 395, 396
 and Plantagenets 27, 121, 125, 127, 128, 129, 134–5, *136*, 409
 and Queen's wealth 59–60, 71, 74
 see also richest people; top landowners
Sunk Island estate *75*
Surrey *36*, *45*, *75*, 127, 128, *165*, 192, **258**
Surrey, Earls of 125
Surtees, Henry *236*
Susi, Count *324*
Sussex *75*, *109*, 127, 128, *165*, 201, **259**
Sutherland, Duchess of *296*
Sutherland, Dukes of 16, *40*, 176, 200, *254*, 256
 1st and 5th Dukes of 301
 4th Duke of 108
 acreage and value of land 107, *204*, *301*
 John Sutherland Egerton, 6th Duke 108, 134, 135, 230
 in Land Lists (1872) *359*, *363*, *371*, *377*
 in Land Lists (2001) *385*, *389*
 Net National Income *396*
 as Plantagenets 124, *131*, *136*
 and royal land 58, 62–3
Sutherland, Elizabeth Millicent, 24th Countess of 108, 130, *131*, 135, 301, *379*, *391*
Sutherland, James *see* Chisholm
Sutherland (county) 63, 266, **301**
Sutherland-Leveson-Gower, Lord Alistair St Clair 108
Sutherland-Walker, Evan *301*
Suttie, Sir George Grant, Baronet *282*
Sutton family 159
Sutton, Sir Richard, Baronet 152, 154, 157, 235, *383*, *389*

Sutton estate 18, 154, *160*, *162*
Swinburne, Commander Sir John, Baronet 250
Swine estate *75*
Swire, Sir Adrian and Sir John *387*
Sykes, Sir Christopher Tatton *385*
Sykes, Sir Tatton Mark Sykes, 8th Baronet 265
Syme, David *286*
Symons, Mrs *240*
Synnot, Mark Seton *321*
Syon Park 111

Al-Tajir family *294*
Talbot, Christopher *203*, *312*, *366*
Talbot, Lady Mary 126
Talbot, Mr *369*
Talbot Power, Sir John *353*
Talbot Power, The *353*
Tankerville, Earls of *132*, 135, *250*
Taunton estate *75*, 90
Tavistock, Henry Robin Russell, Marquess of 113, 134, 135, 226
Tavistock Abbey 154
tax
   Church of England tithes 4, 22, 167, 169, 172, 402
   council 5, 12, 207, 213
   see also tax avoidance; Treasury
tax avoidance 56, 138, 208
   capital gains 90, 92, 99, 413
   corporation tax 47, 90, 91, 99
   royal family exemptions 19, 65, 138
      Crown Estate 77
      Duchy of Cornwall 84, 86, 88, 90, 407
      Duchy of Lancaster 93, 99
      secret deal 60
Taylor, Richard Norton 142, 143, 145, 169
Taylor, Colonel the Rt Hon Thomas *345*
Taylour, Thomas Geoffrey Charles, 6th Marquess of Headfort *330*
Taymouth Castle 62, *272*, *294*
Temple, Archbishop William *411*
Temple 152
Templemore, Lord *353*, *353*
Templetown, Viscounts of *346*
     General, the Viscount *320*, *346*, *373*
tenancy *see* rental
Tenison, Edward *348*
Tennant, Robert *301*
tenure of land 15, 397–8
   common rights and interests *see* common land
   freehold 397
   leasehold 397
   ownership *see* institutional landowners; royalty; top landowners
   registration of title *see* Land Registration; Land Registry
   see also feudal system; rental *and under* Scotland
Terling Place *237*
Terreagles, 16th Lady Herries of 128, *132*

Terriere, Captain Ian C. de Sales la *394*
'territorialists' *see* top landowners
Teynham, Baron *132*
Thatcher, Sir Dennis, Baronet 105–6
Thatcher, Margaret Hilda 25, 27, 28, 246
   and economy 188, 189, 214
   and House of Lords 102–3, 105–6
   and royal land 43, 67
Thatcher, Mark 106
Theobald: *London Rich, The* 159
Thirty Nine Articles 173
Thom, Robert *276*
Thomas, Miss *369*
Thomas, Miss Clara *306*
Thomas, E. *306*
Thomas of Brotherton 127
Thompson, F.M.L. 177
Thompson, Mrs *261*
Thompson, Roy Herbert, 1st Baron Thomson of Fleet 71
Thompson-Sinclair, William Sinclair *277*, *362*
Thornhill estate *160*, *280*
Thornton Hough estate 230
Thorold, Peter *410*
Thoroton, Colonel *251*
Threipland, Stuart Murray *277*, *380*
Throckmorton, Sir Nicholas William *260*
Throne *see* royalty and royal land
Thurso, Viscounts of
   2nd Viscount *277*
   John Archibald Sinclair, 3rd Viscount *277*
   in Land Lists (2001) *380*, *392*
Thynne, Francis 226, *231*
Tiarks, Henrietta 113
Tickwood Hall 68
Tillcoultry estate *278*
timber *see* Forestry Commission
Times 357
   on DEFRA 215
   on Ireland 194
   obituary of Bateman 42, 43
   on *Return of Owners of Land* 39
Timmins, Colonel John Bradford 101
Tintern Abbey and estate *75*, *353*
Tipperary 193, **350**
Tiree *404*
tithes 4, 22, 167, 169, 172
   Tithe Acts repealed (1998) 402
Tobin, Valarie Baroness *346*
Tollemache of Helmingham, Lord *366*, *230*
Toller, Angela *234*
Tomline, Colonel George *257*
Tonbridge family 157, *159*
top landowners 13, 16, 18–19
   in 1872 39–40, *40*, 41, 62–3, 359–78
   in 2001 356–8, **379–94**
   in England 177, 200–1, 367–8
   in Europe, royal family as 69–71
   in Ireland 177, 187, 190, 192, 200, *203*, 375–6
   in London 162
   in Northern Ireland 373–4

   in Scotland *40*, 41, 62–3, *177*, 179, 200, *204*, 371–2
   top two *see* Defence *under* Ministries; Forestry Commission
   typical 3–5
   in Wales 177, 200, *203*, 369–70
   see also institutional landowners; Land Lists; richest people; top fifty; top hundred; wealth
Torlisk *see* Invercauld and Torlisk
Tortworth Court *238*, *252*
Tottenham family *323*
Tottenham, Rt Rev Lady Ann Elizabeth *353*
Tottenham, Arthur Loftus *340*, *340*
Tottenham, Charles John, 8th Marquess of Ely *323*, *353*
Touchadam and Polmaise, John Murray of *244*
Touche, John la *337*
Towneley, Colonel John *244*
Towneley, Lucy, Mabel, Mary and Theresa *244*, *265*
Towneley, Sir Simon 100, 101, *244*
Townshend, Hon Mrs Charlotte 148, 235, *383*, *388*, *393*
Townshend, James Reginald 235
Townshend, Marquess of 134, *248*
Tradeston, Lords MacDonald of 100, *284*, *359*, *371*, *377*
Traill, George *292*
Traill, James Christie *277*
Traill, Thomas *292*
Traquair, Earls of *293*, *298*
Treasury 10, 12, 210
   and Crown Estate 78, 406
   and Duchy of Cornwall 88
   and Duchy of Lancaster 99
   First Lord of *see* Prime Minister
   and Ireland 190
   see also tax
Tredegar, Barons of *161*, *203*, *312*
   6th Baron and wife 314
   in Land lists *364*, *368*
Tredegar Park *306*, *312*, 314
Trefusis, Gerard Nevile Mark Fane, 22nd Baron Clinton 141, *234*, *381*, *384*, *389*, *392*
Tregothnan *231*
Tremayne, Colonel Arthur *231*
Trenchard, Viscount 68
Tresco 90
Trevelyan, Charles 73, 190, 198
Trevor, Lord *369*
Tring Park 228, *228*
Trotter, Lt Colonel *275*
Troughton, Sarah *294*
Truro *166*
Tudors 126, 399–400
   Henry VII 122, 125
   and Plantagenets 122–3, 125, 126
   see also Elizabeth I; Henry VIII
Tufnell, John Joliffe *237*
Tufnell Trustees *160*
Tulcahn estate *290*
Tullynally Castle *352*
Turnor, Christopher *246*
Turton, Lt Colonel *408*
Turville, Sir Francis *330*
Tutbury, Honour of 97

Tweedale, Marquess of 275, 282
Tweedie, James 293
Tyndall-Bruce, Lt Colonel W.H. 283
Tyninghame, LOrd 275
Tyrone 325
Tyrwhitt-Drake, Thomas 228
Tyrwhitt-Wilson, Hon Harry 245

Ulster (Irish Republic) 191, 193
  see also Cavan; Donegal; Monaghan
Ulster (Northern Ireland) see Northern Ireland
underwater property see marine estate
United Nations 181, 185
Upton, Gen the Hon Arthur 261
urban areas and estates 145, 180, 187, 188–9
  of Crown Estate 79–80, 79, 82
  of Duchy of Cornwall 85, 88, 89, 90
  of Duchy of Lancaster 97
  see also London
utilities (water, electricity, railways) 16
  acreage and value 18, 139, 147, 158, 409
  privatisation 143
Uxbridge, Earl of 305

Vale Royal 151
Valuation Office (Inland Revenue) 13, 54, 357, 396, 402
value of land 412
  comparative 209, 395–6
  in Land Lists 357–8
    ranking by (1872) 363–6
    ranking by (2001) 383–6
  underestimated 148–9
  see also acreage and value
Van der Weyer, Martin 401, 402
Vandeleur, Colonel Hector Stewart 331
Vane family 236
Vane, Sir Henry, Baronet 232
Vane-Tempest, Lord Herbert Lionel 320, 374
Vaughan, Cardinal 240
Vaughan, David 308
Vaughan, John 313
Vaughan, Mr 369
Vaughan, Patrick Charles More 240
Vaughan-Lee, Hanning 312, 369
Vaux of H, Baron 132
Ventry, Lords 191, 203, 336
  Andrew Wesley Daubeney de Moleyns, 8th Lord 191, 336
  in Land Lists 360, 375, 378
Verner, Sir 373
Verney, Captain E.H. 305
Verney, Harry, Baronet 228
Verney, Leopold David, Baron Willoughby de Broke 260
Vernon, Harry Foley 263
Vernon, Lord 233
Verulam, John Duncan Grimston, 7th Earl of 241, 345
Vesci, Thomas Eustace Vesey, Viscount de 339, 339, 366
Vesty, Edmund 238, 301, 379, 384, 386, 387

Vesty, Samuel George Armstrong, 3rd Baron 238, 381, 387, 392
Vesty, Hon William Guy 238
Vice Chancellor of Duchy of Lancaster 100
Viceroy of Ireland 190
Victoria, Queen 43, 53, 400
  and counties 229, 246, 251, 255
  and House of Lords 117, 119
  and Ireland 190, 191
  and London 151, 152, 158
  and royal land 58–9, 61–3, 64, 65, 66, 70
    Balmoral 270
    Crown Estate 72, 154
    Duchy of Cornwall 84
    Duchy of Lancaster 95–6
Villiers, Barbara (later Duchess of Cleveland) 67, 115, 247, 248
Villiers, Frederick Ernest 280
Villiers, George William Frederick, 4th Earl of Clarendon 43, 190
Villiers-Stuart, Henry 351, 376
Viner, Henry Frederick Clare 246
Vlissingen, Paul Fentener van 179, 296, 379, 386, 387
VO see Valuation Office
Vychan, Ednyfed 305
Vyvyan, Rev Sir Vyell 231

Waddesdon Manor House and estate 228
Waddingham, John 308, 370
Waddington family 343
Wake, Major Sir Hereward, 14th Baronet 249
Wakefield, William Henry 261
Wakefield 166
Waldegrave, Earls of
  12th Earl of 68
  John Sherbrooke Waldegrave, 13th Earl of 255
Waldegrave, William 68, 255
Walden see Howard de Walden
Walduck, Mr 161, 162
Walduck, Richard 384, 389
al-Waleed Alsaud, Prince 155, 161, 162
Wales 304–17
  agricultural holdings and acreage 7, 11, 13, 15, 357
    breakdown by size 17
  compulsory registration (1990) 401
  counties see under counties
  English landowners with land in 201
  estates over 1000 acres 75–6
  history of 25
  housing/domestic dwellings 7, 11, 13
  institutional landowners 147
    Forestry Commission in 141–2, 143
    Ministry of Defence 145, 146
  and Ireland, comparison with 186–9, 196–7
  in Land Lists 369–70
  land use structure, basic 9
  landowners with land in England 203

and London landowners 153
and Plantagenets 27, 129
population 7, 11, 206
royal land in 35
  Crown Estate 74, 75–6, 78–9
  Duchy of Lancaster 97
top landowners in 177, 200, 203, 369–70
see also Princes of Wales; Return of Owners of Land
Walford's County Families 357
Walker, Colonel George 361, 372
Walker, James 286
Walker, Thomas 260
Walkinshaw, Tom 388
Wall, Commander and Mrs Michael E. St Q. 69
Wallace, Sir Richard, Baronet 257, 320, 361, 363, 367
Waller, Rev John Thomas 341
Walpole family 248
Walpole, Sir Robert 156
Walsham-le-Willows 257
Walsingham, Lord 248
Waltham Denny, Sir Anthony de, 8th Baronet 336
Waltham Denny, Piers de 336
Walton, James 315
Wandesforde, Charles B.C. 338
War Office 10, 145
  see also Defence under Ministries
Warburton, Maria-Sybella Egerton 43
Warburton, Richard 339
Ward, Tracey
Ward, William George 239
Wardell, Gareth 143
Warenne, Earls of 125
Warenne, Isabel de 125
Warenne, William of 125
Warr, William Herbrand Sackville de la, 11th Earl of 259
wars 94, 404
  Barons' 94, 97
  Civil (1642–6) 24, 123, 150
  War of Roses 95, 122
  see also Defence under Ministries; World War One; World War Two
Warwick and Brooke, Earls of 260
Warwick, Earls of
  Edward, Earl of 122, 123, 129
  John Dudley, Earl of 126
Warwickshire 4, 165, 260
waste land see common land and waste
water 9
  see also utilities
Waterford, Marchioness of 312, 193, 201, 351
Waterford, Marquesses of
  acreage and value of land 351, 354
  John Hubert de la Poer Beresford, 8th Marquess of 132, 351, 354
  in Land Lists (1872) 361, 375
Waterworth, Alan William 101
Wates, Sir Christopher 161, 162, 386, 390
Watson-Taylor, Simon 262
Waveney, Lord 257

wealth
  concentration of *see* House of Lords
  of Elizabeth II 58, 59–61, 71, 74
  Plantagenet 136
  ranking by in Land Lists (2001) 387–90
  see also Rich Lists; top landowners
Webb, William 251
Webber, Andrew Lloyd 388
Weber, Max 106, 129, 408
Welbeck Abbey 233, 251, 273, 277
Welbeck Woodhouse 251
Weld, Reginald 235
Weld-Blundell, Thomas 244, 364
Weld-Forester, George Cecil Brooke, 8th Baron Forester 254
Weld-Forester, Juliet 322
Wellesley *see under* Wellington
Wellington, Dukes of 25, *107*, 239
  Brigadier General Arthur Valerian Wellesley, 8th Duke 119, 239
  Arthur Wellesley, 1st (Iron) Duke 119
  in Land Lists (2001) 381, 386, 392
Wells, William 242
Wemyss and March, Earls of 282, 293, 303, *362*, 365
  11th Earl of 283
  acreage and value of land 282, 293
  David Charteris, 12th Earl of 283, 298
  in Land Lists (2001) 380, 390, 392
Wenlock, Lord 265
Wentworth Woodhouse 202
West, William Cornwallis 310
West Lothian (formerly Linlithgow) **302**
West Yorkshire *see* Yorkshire
Westenra, William Warner, 7th Baron Rossmore 346
Wester Ross 179
Western, Sir Thomas 237
Westmeath 193, **352**
Westminster, Dean of *159*
Westminster, Duchess of 113
  Dowager 323
Westminster, Dukes of 16, 18, 148, 150, 151, 230, 256
  acreage and value of land 18, 85, *107*
  Bendor, 2nd Duke of 86, 87, 151
  3rd and 4th Dukes of 151
  5th Duke of 114, 151
  Brigadier Gerald Grosvenor, 6th Duke of 85, 103, 118–19, 199, 212, 230, 244, 301
  and London 149–52, 157
  see also Grosvenor
  in Land Lists (1872) 363
  in Land Lists (2001) 379, 383, 387, 391
  Net National Income 396
  see also Grosvenor
Westminster, Marquess of (later Duke) 41, 62
Westminster Abbey 150
Westmoreland 42, *165*, **261**
  Earls of 122
Weston Park 254

Westport House 191, 344
Wexford 193, **353**
Weyer, Martin van der 401, 402
Weymouth, Viscount 262
Whaplode estate 75
Wharncliffe, Earls of 265, *365*
Wharton, 9th Baron 314
Wheeler-Bennet, Sir John 64
Whitbread family 358
Whitbread, Samuel 226, *383*, *389*
White, Hon Charles 350
White, Hon Mrs Jessica 153, 161n, *383*, *388*
White, Luke Richard, 6th Baron of Annaly 342
White, Miss 293
White, Mrs 334
White, Robert Hedges Eyre 332
White, Robin Grove 141
Whitehill estate 76
Whitelaw, Willie, Viscount 102
Whitewell estate 96
Whitlock, Ralph 62, 63, 64, 65, 405
Whittaker's 7, 156, 357
Who Was Who 49
Who's Who 95, 100, 156
Whyte, Colonel John 340
Wicklow, Earl of 376
Wicklow 193, *354*, **354**
Wightman, Andy: on Scotland 10, 107, 142, *176–80*, 184, 185, 191, 403, 405, 408, 410, 412
  counties of 266, 276, 278, 283, 287–8, 290, 292, 299, 302–3, 357
  farmland 281
Wigsell, Mrs 258
Wigtownshire **303**
Wilkinson, Anthony 236
Willey Park 254
William I, the Bastard (Conqueror) 20–1, 22, 23, 24, 28, 41, 52, 53, 72, 99, 399
  and English counties 240, 245, 255
  and London 150
  and Plantagenets 121–2, 123, 125
  and Scotland 182, 310
William II (Rufus) 122, 399
William III (of Orange) 58, 155, 251, 343, 400
William IV 400
William, Prince 84
Williams family 231, *385*, *390*
Williams, Penry 306
Williams, Sir 370
Williams, Susan 306
Williams-Bulkeley, Sir Richard Mostyn, 14th Baronet 305 *369*, *305*, 307
Williams-Drummond, Sir James Hamlyn 309, 370
Williamson, Rev David 301
Williams-Vaughan, John 306
Williams-Wynn, Sir, 1st Baronet 310
Williams-Wynn, Sir David Watkin, 11th Baronet 203, 310
  acreage and value of land 310, 313, 315
  in Land Lists (1872) 359, 365, 369
  in Land Lists (2001) 385, 393

Willings, Fred 14
Willis-Fleming, John Edward Arthur 239
Willoughby, Roger 246
Willoughby Bond, James 342
Willoughby de Broke, Barons of 128
  Leopold David Verney, 21st Baron 260
Willoughby de Eresby, Baronesses 246, 294
  acreage and value of land 200, 202, 294, 307
  in Land Lists (1872) *359*, *364*, 367, 377
  in Land Lists (2001) 379, 384, 391
  Nancy Jane Marie Heathcote-Drummond-Willoughby, 27th Baroness 202, 228, 246
Wills family 139
Wills, Sir Edward, Baronet 294
Wills, Captain Fred 296, *379*
Wills, Hon Jean Constance 69
Wills-Sandford, Thomas George 348
Wilson, Christopher Wyndham 261
Wilson, Edward Hugh 261
Wilson, Sir (James) Harold, Baron 25, 105
Wilson, Patrick *381*
Wilson, Sir Spencer Pocklington Maryon 156
Wilson, Thomas 156
Wilson, William *337*
Wilton Park and House 228, 262
Wiltshire 117, 126, 146, *165*, 202, **262**, 272, 273
  royal land in 68, *75*, 87, *88*, 90, 91, 262
Wimborne, Viscounts of
  Ivor Mervyn Vigors Guest, 4th Viscount 235, 294
  in Land Lists (1872) *361*, *365*, 367, 378
  in Land Lists (2001) 382, 392
Wimpole Hall 229
Winchester 164, *166*
windfall gains on development land 27
Windsor family 59
  see also Charles, Prince of Wales; Edward VII; Edward VIII; Elizabeth II; George V; George VI
Windsor, Duchess of (Mrs Wallis Simpson) 86, 87
Windsor, Lindsay Claude Neils Bury Clive, Viscount 254, 263
Windsor, Lord 254, 312, *364*, 368
Windsor estate 70, *75*, 76
Wingfield, Edward Rhys 226, 312
Wingfield, John Maurice 253
Wingfield, Mervyn Niall, 10th Viscount of Powerscourt 354
Wingfield-Baker, Digby Hanmer 237
Wingfield-Digby, George 235, *365*
Wingfield-Digby, John 260
Winmarleigh estate 96
Winterton, Earl 160
Winton, Mr de 370
Winton, Walter de 317
Wise, Lord 102
Woburn Abbey 112–13, 154, 226, 229, 234

Wollaton Hall *251*, *265*, *296*
Wolsey, Cardinal 166–7
Women of the Bedchamber 68–9
Wood, Charles 190
Wood, Edward Frederick Lindley, 1st Earl of Halifax 87
Wood, John D. (estate agent) 148
Wood, Thomas *247*
Woodham-Smith, Cecil 192
woodland *see* Forestry Commission
Woodroffe, Jean Francis 69
Woodroffe, Lieutenant Colonel J.W.R. 69
Woods, George *334*
Woodstock, Edward of, 'Black' Prince of Wales 85, 122
Woolcombe, Rev Archdeacon 171
Worcester, Marchioness of 115
Worcester, Marquess of 115, 238
Worcestershire *165*, **263**, *401*
World War One 8, 25, 54, 73, 86
    dukes 'deprived' for fighting against king 105
    and Ireland 195
    and timber needs 140
World War Two 8, 25, 145
    pro-appeasement group 87
    and royal family 64, 66, 68, 86–7
    and timber needs 140–1
Wormell, Peter 220

Woude, Hon Mrs van der 69
Wrey, Rev Sir Henry 171
Writtle Park 237
Wrixon-Becher, Sir Henry, Baronet *332*
Wroughton, Philip *227*
Wryeside estate 96
Wyatt, Lord Woodrow 264
Wychwood estate *75*
Wyndham, Henry Scawen, 7th Baron Leconfield 331
Wyndham-Quin, Lady Caroline 351
Wyndham-Quin, Thady Windham Thomas, 7th Earl of Dunraven and Mount-Earl 312, *312*
Wynn, Hon Charles Henry *313*, *370*
Wynne, Brownlow 310
Wynne, John Lloyd 310
Wynne, Mr (Denbigh) *370*
Wynne, Mr (Merioneth) *370*
Wynne, Owen *340*, *349*, *376*
Wynne-Finch, Charles Arthur *310*, *369*
Wynnstay 310
Wytham Abbey *227*, *252*

Yarborough, Earls of *246*
    in Land Lists (1872) *362*, *363*, *367*
    in Land Lists (2001) *381*, *384*, *390*, *392*
Yattendon 156
Yeats, W.B. 349

Yeoman of the Guard 43
Yester House *275*, *282*
York, Bruce 314
York, Dukes of 104
    Richard, Protector of England 122
York House 64
Yorke, John *265*
Yorkshire 202, 222, **264–5**
    Church of England land in *165*
    Crown Estate land in *75*
    Plantagenet land in 127, 128
    Survey of Duchy of Lancaster 96, 98
    York, archbishop of 105
    York, Lord Mayor of 172
Young, Harry *286*
Young Ireland Movement 186
Young, James *285*

Zetland, Marquesses of
    acreage *278*
    in Land Lists (1872) *361*, *365*, *367*
    Lawrence Mark Dundas, 4th Marquess of 264
Zetland, Earl of 292, 299, *299*
Zetland (Shetland) *299*
Zhu Rongji, Premier of China 10
Zimmerman, Helen 116